BLUE GUIDE

SOUTHERN ITALY

Paul Blanchard

Somerset Books • London
WW Norton • New York

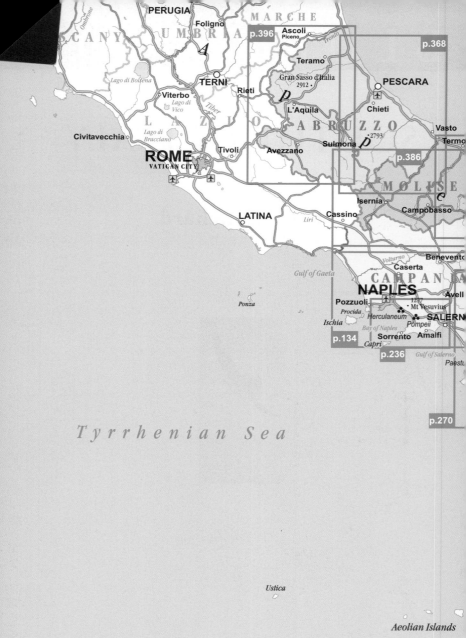

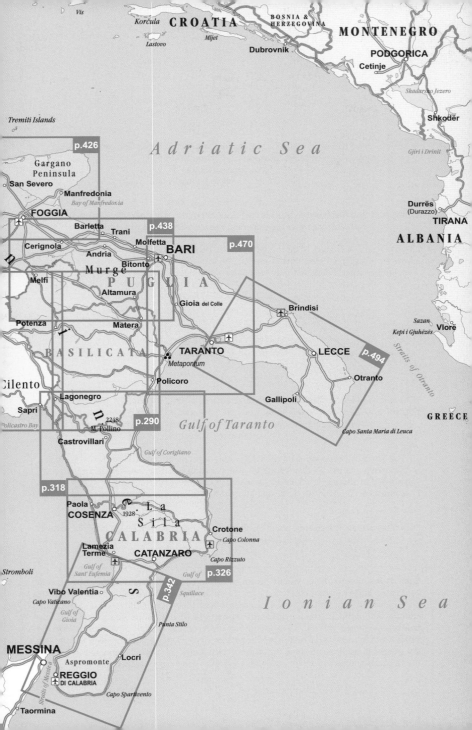

Eleventh edition 2007

Published by Blue Guides Limited, a Somerset Books Company
49–51 Causton St, London SW1P 4AT
www.blueguides.com
'Blue Guide' is a registered trademark.

ISBN 978–1–905131–18–1

A CIP catalogue record of this book is available from the British Library.

Published in the United States of America by
WW Norton and Company, Inc
500 Fifth Avenue, New York, NY 10110
USA ISBN 978–0–393–33006–9

The author and the publishers have made reasonable efforts to ensure the accuracy of all the
information in *Blue Guide Southern Italy*; however, they can accept no responsibility for any loss,
injury or inconvenience sustained by any traveller as a result of information
or advice contained in the guide.

The first Blue Guide—*London and its Environs*—was published in 1918 by two Scottish
brothers, James and Findlay Muirhead. The first edition of *Blue Guide Southern Italy* was
compiled by them in 1925. Subsequent editions were revised, compiled or written by the
Muirhead brothers (1930); L. Russell Muirhead (1959); and Paul Blanchard (1982, 1984,
1986, 1990, 1996, 2000, 2004).

All other acknowledgements, photo credits and copyright information are given on p. 584,
which forms part of this copyright page.

Your views on this book would be much appreciated. We welcome not only specific
comments, suggestions or corrections, but any more general views you may have: how this
book enhanced your holiday, how it could have been more helpful. Blue Guides authors and
editorial and production team work hard to bring you what we hope are the best-researched
and best-presented cultural, historical and academic guide books in the English language.
Please write to us by email (editorial@blueguides.com), via the comments page on our website (www.blueguides.com) or at the address given above. We will be happy to acknowledge
useful contributions in the next edition, and to offer a free copy of one of our titles.

CONTENTS

Historical sketch 9

THE GUIDE

Naples	29
Campania	135
The Phlegraean fields	135
The Capuan plain	149
Caserta	154
Mount Vesuvius	160
Pompeii	168
Herculaneum	196
The Vesuvian shore	210
Capri, Ischia and Procida	214
The Amalfi coast	237
Salerno and Benevento	259
Paestum and the Cilento	271
Basilicata	291
Melfi and environs	292
Matera	299
Southern Basilicata	306
Ancient Lucania	309
Calabria	319
The Tyrrhenian coast to Paola	320
The Coscile and Crati valleys	323
Crotone	327
Cosenza and environs	331
La Sila	333
Vibo Valentia	343
Tropea and environs	344
Palmi and the Aspromonte foothills	349
Reggio Calabria	353
Aspromonte	357
The southern Ionian coast	359

Abruzzo & Molise	369
Pescara	371
Chieti	373
Lanciano and environs	377
Termoli and Larino	387
Southern Molise	388
Western Molise	390
Parco Nazionale d'Abruzzo	397
Sulmona	398
Celano	401
L'Aquila	406
The Gran Sasso d'Italia	414
Teramo and environs	417
Puglia	427
Foggia and the Gargano	427
The Tremiti islands	434
Terra di Bari	439
Bari	451
South of Bari	461
Massafra	473
The Murge	475
Taranto	480
The Adriatic coast to Ostuni	484
Brindisi	495
Lecce	501
Manduria and environs	509
The Salentine peninsula	511
Gallipoli and environs	518

Practical information	527
Food and drink	536
Glossary of special terms	552

Rulers of Naples	561
Index	564

MAPS & PLANS

Regional maps
Campania
Naples, Salerno and Benevento 134
The Amalfi Coast 236
Eastern Campania 270
Basilicata
Melfi and the north 270
Central Basilicata 290
Southern Basilicata 318
Calabria
Northern Calabria 318
Central Calabria 326
Reggio and the far south 342
Abruzzo & Molise
The Adriatic coast 368
Molise and eastern Abruzzo 386
The western highlands 396
Puglia
Foggia and the Gargano 426
Terra di Bari 438
Bari, Taranto and the Ionian
coast 470
Brindisi, Lecce and the
Salentine peninsula 494

Island maps
Capri 218–19
Ischia 231

Town plans
L'Aquila 407
Bari (Città Vecchia) 454
Brindisi 497
Lecce 503
Naples general 50–51
Naples centre 52–53
Pozzuoli 139
Sorrento 241
Taranto 481

Site plans
Alba Fucens 403
Herculaneum 200–01
Ancient Locri 361
Metapontum 311
Paestum 275
Pompeii 176–77
A Pompeian house 172
Villa Jovis (Capri) 220

The author
Paul Blanchard was born in Amsterdam, New York. He studied art history in Florence and has lived in Italy since 1975. He has taught at the Italian study centres of several American universities, has shown his own artwork (which includes a large body of landscape photographs) in Europe and the US, and has lectured on college campuses throughout the US. He has published widely in North America, Great Britain, France and Italy, and has contributed to European and American art magazines.

HISTORICAL SKETCH

by Michael Pratt

'The Neapolitans are like their own Vesuvius, which after appearing to have slumbered for many years, bursts forth suddenly, more terribly than ever, and causes the whole land to tremble'. Thus an adventurous British traveller, Craufurd Tait Ramage, described southern Italy and its volatile people in the early 19th century. The South is above all a land of contrasts, where wildly beautiful countryside clashes with urban decay, and where the legacy of many great civilizations combines with illiteracy and destitution. It has a confused and rather sad history, ruled by a succession of foreigners: Greeks and Romans, barbarian invaders, Normans and Hohenstaufens, Angevins and Aragonese, Habsburgs and Bourbons. All this makes for a rich and fascinating country, often difficult to understand, always impossible to categorise.

Prehistory

There is little evidence for early human settlement in Italy. Man first appeared here some 200,000 years ago, but nothing has yet been found older than some Neanderthal skulls from c. 50,000 BC—the Middle Palaeolithic Age. As soon as the civilizations of the Near East had learned the skills of seafaring, however, southern Italy began to be influenced by their cultures. It is then that its history truly begins.

The south of the Italian peninsula was settled from the eastern Mediterranean, although there were occasional northern influences, such as the Villanovan culture from the Danube basin during the Iron Age after 800 BC. During the whole Neolithic period from c. 5,000 BC agricultural settlers, principally from the Levant, and Anatolia, slowly replaced the nomadic hunter-gatherers, the original inhabitants of southern Italy. They brought many skills with them: the ability to create settled communities with domesticated animals, seed for crops, and the development of rudimentary architecture. Worked metals began to appear (although the north produced objects of higher quality), and painted vases, the so-called Molfetta style, supposedly introduced from the Balkans.

The far south of Italy, modern Calabria, had been first settled by Italic tribes speaking a language known as Oscan, a cousin of that used by the related Latin tribes who lived around Rome. Two of these tribes were the 'Oenotri', or vine-cultivators, and the 'Itali', who were to give their name to the entire peninsula. Further north in Apulia (modern Puglia) they were joined by Illyrian settlers from the Balkans, while in neighbouring Lucania (modern Basilicata), another tribe from across the Adriatic, the Lucanians, invaded the country, pushing the earlier inhabitants into the interior.

Another important external influence already existed. During the Bronze Age (post-1700 BC) the Greeks make their first appearance in southern Italy. Definite trading links were formed, both with the Mycenaeans from mainland Greece and with

Minoan Crete. Mycenaean objects have been found at Taranto and a growing body of evidence suggests they traded as far north as the borders of Etruria. Thus a pattern of exploration, commerce and perhaps colonisation from the Aegean can dimly be traced to this early period. Yet the decline of first the Minoan and then the Mycenaean civilizations by about 1200 BC meant that contacts with the eastern Mediterranean became far more intermittent, a state of affairs that was to last for some four centuries.

Magna Graecia

The first great formative period of southern Italian history began soon after 800 BC. The establishment of a number of purely Greek colonies in the peninsula had two underlying causes. The arrival of hostile, non-Greek immigrants in the Aegean impelled many indigenous Greeks to move westwards, and on the Greek mainland there was overpopulation and economic crisis. The attraction of founding new settlements overseas was obvious; after all, the Greek word for a colony, *apoikia*, means 'a home away from home'.

Early Greek colonies were established in a steady stream, both on the Italian mainland and in Sicily. Chalcis and Corinth led the way, with their settlements of Naxos and Syracuse respectively. It does, however, seem likely that Cumae in Campania, with nearby Pithecusae (the modern Ischia) may antedate them by some 20 years, to c. 750 BC.

Cumae and Pithecusae were founded by Chalcis, probably to promote the flourishing trade in copper. Soon they began to spawn further colonies: Dikaearchia (the modern Pozzuoli), and Parthenope, which merged with the later adjacent settlement of Neapolis to form the great city of Naples. Expansion further north was blocked by the Etruscans and later by the rising power of Rome, so these colonies round the Bay of Naples formed the outer edge of Magna Graecia.

Many other new settlements were formed in this brief era of less than a century, to 670 BC. On the Ionian coast, well situated between the heel and toe of the Italian peninsula, the Achaeans founded Sybaris and Croton. Not far distant northwards the Spartans founded Taras (the modern Taranto). For a time Taras became the hub of Magna Graecia, rich from its wool, wine, figs and salt, as well as from the precious purple dye extracted from the murex mollusc. Metapontum, founded by Peloponnesians from Pylos, although perfectly successful in its own way, served mainly as a buffer between these competing communities. Finally Rhegion (the modern Reggio Calabria) was founded by the Chalcidians right at the tip of Italy, to ensure (with her sister settlements of Messina and Milazzo in Sicily) a lasting command of the Straits of Messina.

For all its wealth and dynamism, Magna Graecia remained a collection of small city states forming leagues and alliances among themselves and frequently at war with one another. The will to coalesce and form a more significant political entity was entirely lacking. Thus Metapontum's growth was definitely restricted by the incessant squabbling between its more powerful neighbours. Even colonies founded by the same Greek forebears could turn on one another, as happened with Croton and Sybaris.

The latter, a byword for luxury and corruption, was eventually incapable of putting up any effective resistance, and in 510 was destroyed by its rival, by the flooding of the city with the waters of the Crathis river, on the banks of which it stood. So thorough was the devastation that the exact site of Sybaris remains uncertain to this day.

Sometimes these petty quarrels descended into farce. When Locri, a small city state, was threatened by its aggressive neighbour Croton, with an army ten times the size, its citizens took suitable precautions. They sacrificed in the temple of the Dioscuri (Castor and Pollux) at Sparta, to ensure the gods would fight on their side. Then having heard that Croton had appealed to Apollo at Delphi, offering one tenth of the spoils of war, they offered one ninth from the spoils of their much richer adversary. Apollo changed sides, and when battle was joined the well-trained Locrian army, 10,000 strong, trounced over 100,000 soldiers fielded by Croton.

Many distinguished figures, such as Xenophon the historian, and Pythagoras the mathematical genius, were attracted from mainland Greece, and some major native talents appeared in Magna Graecia too: Empedocles, Zeno and Stesichorus, to name but three. The arts flourished: splendid figured pottery, charming terracotta statuettes, magnificent armour and sophisticated silver coinage all attest to an age of stability and well-being. Little Greek architecture has survived in southern Italy by comparison with Sicily, yet the superb Doric temples at Paestum (the ancient Poseidonia, a trading entrepôt founded by Sybaris) demonstrate the local building skills.

A major threat to the continuing prosperity of Magna Graecia was posed by the Etruscans, who were under pressure from Celtic invaders from the north, and who wished to expand southwards. They both traded with the Greeks, as great admirers of Hellenic pottery, and fought with them, capturing several minor colonies. A decisive Greek victory at Cumae in 525 managed to halt their expansion, and 16 years later the fledgling Roman Republic expelled its Etruscan kings. Henceforward Rome was to form an effective barrier between the two powers.

During the 5th century BC the incessant in-fighting and the Greek colonists' disastrous involvement in the Peloponnesian Wars, which ruined Athens and exposed Sicily to the rising power of Carthage, left Magna Graecia weakened. The inability of the cities to unite enabled the Samnites and Sabines to conquer much of the area. These hill tribes had the good sense to respect the superior civilizations which they vanquished, and Greek culture and custom were not entirely overthrown. Nevertheless, for the colonies of Magna Graecia, once the glory of southern Italy, and which had created more settlements in their own image in Gaul and even in distant Spain, this represented a sad decline. There was, however, one solution in prospect. This lay in alliance with the Roman Republic, which had the same mutual foes in Etruscans, Samnites and Carthaginians, and which had already learned the art of setting up individual alliances with neighbouring states in such a way as to ensure Roman supremacy. Allies were protected, untaxed and still autonomous. In return they were expected to provide troops for the Republic's armies, while taking an oath of fealty to it. As long-standing admirers of Hellenic culture, the Romans would seem to be the Greeks' natural allies.

MAGNA GRAECIA

The term Magna Graecia, 'Greater Greece', used to describe the Greek colonies of southern Italy, has a long history. At first the Greek form, *Megale Hellas*, was used by the Greeks to describe all Greek settlements outside Greece itself, but by the 4th century BC the term was being used of Italy alone. In effect, it referred to the wealthy Greek cities of the coastal areas of southern Italy. The Roman writers of the 1st century AD used the term specifically to describe the region between Locri, or in some accounts Cumae, and Tarantum. Strabo extended the term to include Sicily, but the narrower definition seems to have been the most widely used.

The first settlements of Magna Graecia took place in the 8th century after a toe-hold was established by Greek and Phoenician traders at Pithecusae on the island of Ischia. The land was much more fertile than that of mainland Greece, and the best sites were soon occupied by colonists from a number of Greek cities. Settlers from Pithecusae moved onto the mainland at Cumae about 750 BC, and these in turn founded Neapolis (Naples) ten miles to the south. Archaeological evidence suggests that of the 22 major Greek settlements, 18 were founded before 600 BC.

The long-term success of a settlement depended on two major factors: having access to land on the plains, so that an economy based on commerce and agriculture could mature, and establishing peaceful relations with the native population. Tarantum was the most successful foundation, exploiting its harbour, defensive site and hinterland, so that by the middle of the 4th century BC it boasted a population of some 300,000 within its ten-mile circuit of walls. The local Iapygian settlements, which had been flourishing in the 8th century, disappear abruptly suggesting that they were destroyed by the new arrivals.

The colonists had to contend with a variety of native Italians. The names of Ausonians, Oenotrians, Chones, Opici, Messapians and Iapygians survive from Greek sources, but it has proved difficult to assign specific cultures to each one. The Iapygians in Apulia are the most distinct. Their settlements close to Tarantum may have been destroyed, but further inland they survived and were even able to mount an attack on Tarantum in the 5th century. The Messapians appear to have been part of a wider cultural group which extended across the Adriatic into Dalmatia. Most of these peoples lived in large village settlements, some on plains, others on more defensive sites on high ground, and even before the Greeks arrived there appears to have been extensive trade between them and with Etruscans and Phoenicians.

The interactions between the Greek and native populations were varied. Some native settlements were wiped out, others survived under Greek cultural domination. In some areas new settlements in the hills suggest that the Italic peoples retreated inland beyond the grasp of the Greeks (who always clung to the coast). There are even cases such as Pompeii, Herculaneum and Puteoli, originally Greek, which appear to have fallen under the control of native tribes. In other cases, when two Greek cities squabbled with each other, they might each align themselves to a native tribe in order to strengthen themselves. From the 6th century onwards cities such as Cumae found themselves in constant conflict with the Etruscans as they spread southwards into Campania. A major naval battle off Cumae between the Etruscans and the forces of Cumae and Syracuse in 474 BC saw the defeat, isolation and then decline of the Etruscan presence in Campania. Rome, still a small city confined to the plain of Latium, had already expelled its Etruscan rulers in 509 BC.

There is no evidence that the inhabitants of the cities of southern Italy saw themselves as having a common identity other than through their shared Greekness. Disputes between the cities were common. The city of Siris was destroyed by an alliance of rivals in the mid-6th century, and Sybaris fell to its nearest neighbour Croton in 510 BC. In the next century, Athens began expanding its own interest in the area, founding the colony of Thurii on the deserted site of Sybaris in 444/3, but the devastating defeat of her naval expedition to Sicily in 413 brought her influence to an end. In the 390s Dionysius I, the dictator of Syracuse, the most powerful of the Greek cities of Sicily, ruled over several cities of the mainland.

Meanwhile in Campania, the void left by the decline of the Etruscans allowed the aggressive Sabelli (of whom the Samnites were a subgroup) to move south. Here they adopted the Oscan language, and began to attack the Greek cities. Capua fell to the invaders in 423 BC, Cumae in 421 and Paestum (originally Poseidonia) in 410. Oscan speakers spread further south and appear as the Lucanians in Lucania (modern Basilicata) by the 4th century, where they controlled the the whole region outside the Greek areas. In the Calabrian peninsula they displaced the Oenotrians and Chones and emerged as the distinct group of the Bruttii (the name means 'breakaway' in Oscan). The Bruttii too began attacking Greek cities.

When Rome began expanding in the late 4th century BC, therefore, the Greek cities were already under pressure. The term Magna Graecia had important connotations for the Romans. It carried the resonance of Greek culture, which educated Romans revered; yet the actual cities of Magna Graecia were denigrated by Romans for having become decadent as a result of their luxurious lifestyles (the word 'sybaritic' is derived directly from Sybaris). There were few inhibitions about absorbing Magna Graecia, especially when some of the cities challenged Roman expansion. By 270 BC the whole of the region was under Roman control. Under the Empire many of the ancient Greek cities, such as Naples, Paestum and Cumae flourished, others collapsed. Greek styles of pottery, statuary and metalwork disappeared, but civic institutions derived from Greece, such as magistracies and the age-grouping of citizens, usually survived. In some cities traditional Greek festivals were sustained or revived by the Roman elite, who enjoyed the association with a culture much more ancient than their own. Gradually, however, economic life shifted from the cities to the villa estates, as it did in much of the Western Empire, and by AD 200 inscriptions in Greek disappear from even the oldest Greek foundations.

C.F.

The Roman Empire

A formal treaty of alliance in 326 BC bound Rome to Greek Naples. Within 50 years their mutual local enemies had all been vanquished. Some of the more distant city-states chafed at the increasing authoritarianism of the Republic and its willingness to interfere more and more in their internal affairs. Nevertheless, few were prepared to take matters to an open breach.

An exception was Taras, which expelled the Roman emissaries and summoned to its aid the ambitious Pyrrhus, King of Epirus in northwestern Greece. With an army over 20,000 strong, he defeated the Roman troops at Heracleia, and then again at Asculum (modern Ascoli Satriano, in Puglia) in 280. This second battle was so narrowly won, and at such cost to his own solders, that the expression 'Pyrrhic victory' (won at too great a cost) was born. Within five years Pyrrhus had lost two-thirds of his force and was finally defeated at Benevento. Discomfited, he retired to Greece, to be remembered most for his use of elephants in battle, a new and initially terrifying weapon. Taras, reborn as the Latin Tarentum, opened its gates again to the Republic.

Within a few years Roman domination stretched through southern Italy as far as Rhegion and the Straits of Messina. To consolidate their position, the Via Appia was extended from Capua to Brundusium (Brindisi) on the Adriatic coast. For the first time Rome could draw upon the maritime skills of its southern allies to challenge the naval power of Carthage. This Phoenician state in North Africa aspired to dominate Sicily, and also founded settlements along the Gallo-Iberian coast, stepping-stones in its eventual aim of controlling the sea routes of the Mediterranean. Now that Rome had subjugated its foes on the Italian peninsula, it had to contend with its major rival overseas.

The struggle was to last for over a century, during which time Rome regained control of Sicily, while leaving Syracuse independent. Sardinia was seized as enemy territory, a move countered by the Carthaginians' creation of a new empire in Spain. The Second Punic War saw the invasion of Italy by that remarkable general, Hannibal. With his army of 40,000, he gained three successive victories and control over the northern half of the peninsula. Unable to lay siege to the city of Rome itself, he marched into Apulia and Calabria, hoping to encourage the Greek cities to revolt against their overlord.

At Cannae, near modern Barletta, Hannibal inflicted the most devastating defeat in their history upon a larger Roman army, which left nearly 50,000 dead upon the field. After this epic victory some southern cities did indeed desert the Roman cause: Capua and Tarentum especially, although Naples remained loyal. When Hannibal, still unable to gain the decisive victory, had eventually to withdraw from Italy, these cities were to pay a terrible price for their treachery. The citizens of Capua were butchered *en masse*, while those of Tarentum were sold into slavery. Only in 202 BC was Hannibal finally defeated by Scipio Africanus at Zama; yet even then the struggle continued. It was to take a third Punic War, some 50 years later, to complete the total destruction of Carthage.

At last southern Italy seemed at peace, under a strong, unified government. Yet much discontent persisted, for many in the South resented the alien exploitation of the land and the native people's exclusion, as non-Roman citizens, from political rights. The unrest could indeed become violent, as with Spartacus' revolt at Capua (*see p.153*) and the so-called Social War in Samnite territory. The Social War began as a revolt by Italic allies of Rome angered by Rome's failure to grant them citizenship. They formed their own independent capital at Corfinium (later Pentima, renamed Corfinium again by Mussolini) and held out in a number of battles for almost ten years. The war was finally brought to an end by Sulla in 88 BC, with a Roman victory in the field, though Rome in fact made many concessions to the Italic rebels. Wise government of this kind was slowly to allay much discontent, so that Roman Italy became more of a nation and less a loose federation of city states.

As Republic turned into Empire, southern Italy remained stable, seldom troubled by the convulsions in the capital. By the 1st century AD Campania had become a haven of wealthy and gracious living. Imperial and patrician villas littered the coast from Cumae to Salerno, as well as the islands of Ischia and Capri, home to Tiberius' infamous palace. Mount Vesuvius did admittedly cast a shadow over the Bay of Naples. Long quiescent, the volcano erupted in AD 79 to terrible effect. The seaside towns of Pompeii and Herculaneum were buried under continuous showers of pumice, then a burning cloud of hot gas, followed by the pyroclastic flow of hot liquefied rock which destroyed the buildings and rolled on to the sea. Although this catastrophe exposed the instability of the area, many prominent people continued to build and retire around Naples, even if choosing a site somewhat further south.

Despite a few exceptions, such as the Arch of Trajan at Benevento, there are not many striking memorials from the Roman world in the rest of southern Italy. Much of the land was already concentrated in a few hands, and those were frequently absentee—the beginnings perhaps of the tradition of the *latifondi*. Greek and Roman settlers had gradually assimilated, but even by the 3rd century, to cite one example known as the *Album of Canusium* (modern Canosa in Puglia), which recorded the names of the town's governing classes, there still existed families of decidedly Greek, and others of decidedly Roman, origins.

Within a hundred years this was to matter less and less. The emperor Diocletian, finding his dominions too unwieldy, split the imperial power into four. Rome soon became a backwater, for none of his tetrarchs would have dreamed of living there. His great successor, Constantine, had within a generation re-established control of the Empire under his rule alone, and decided to move the capital to Byzantium, a Greek settlement between the Aegean and Black seas. His reasoning was sound, for the whole focus of civilization had shifted eastwards; there was renewed vigour in Hellenic intellect and culture, with the great libraries of Pergamon, Antioch and Alexandria better than anything in the West. Italian agricultural wealth had dwindled with falling populations and the spread of malaria, while much land in the East could still be developed. Last, but hardly least, the ancient pagan traditions in Italy co-existed with the newly spreading beliefs of Christianity. Southern Italy provided a good instance of this. A Pope, or Bishop of Rome, was now in existence, but his authority was limited. Constantine, a belated convert to the faith, hoped that a new capital, imbued with the new religion, might reignite the vigour and strength of his subjects, many of whom still considered themselves as belonging to a Roman Empire. Unfortunately his legacy, particularly in the West, of an orderly, united dominion was to prove short-lived.

The Dark Ages

Not only had the Roman Empire split apart; for the first time in centuries the Italian peninsula lay open to barbarian invasion. Rome was sacked several times during the calamitous 5th century, by the Goths, by the Vandals from North Africa, and—but for quasi-divine intervention—would have suffered a similar fate from the Huns. The last Western Emperor, Romulus Augustulus, was formally deposed in AD 476. The barbarians who had ousted him were in turn removed by Theodoric the Ostrogoth who, acting in the name of the Eastern Emperor, Zeno, managed to reunite Italy more or less for a further 35 years. Yet by now it had become a curious mixture of Italians and Germans, of Catholic and schismatic Arian Christians.

Southern Italy suffered under the prevailing anarchy. The maritime cities largely managed to repel barbarian attacks, except for Naples, which the Goths took and occupied. So when a counter-blow came from Constantinople, it received a ready welcome. Emperor Justinian sent his remarkable and ambitious general, Belisarius, with quite a small army, half composed of barbarian mercenaries (mostly Huns), to the peninsula in 535. He had already achieved a meteoric conquest of the Vandals in North Africa, and the initial collapse of Ostrogothic Italy was surprisingly sudden. Sicily fell with hardly a struggle, and in spring 536 Belisarius crossed to the mainland. Most of southern Italy hailed the Byzantine army as redeemers and threw open their town gates—except for Naples, where the Goths had already put down roots, and which mounted a stiff resistance. Thus when the city eventually fell, it was so thoroughly sacked by the Byzantine mercenaries as to discredit the emperor's good name, although the pope hastened to offer his submission.

War with the Goths was to continue for years. The apparent triumph of Belisarius, who by 540 could offer his sovereign the entire Italian peninsula, was soon undone. The Goths reconquered Rome and Ravenna, the general was ordered home in undeserved disgrace, and on his return could regain little ground. It took his successor, the septuagenarian eunuch Narses, to inflict two decisive defeats on the Goths, thus persuading them to leave Italy for good.

Justinian's reconquest proved transient. In less than a decade yet more northern barbarian invaders, the Lombards, arrived. Rapidly subduing the north Italian plain, they proceeded to venture ever further south. They founded the duchies of Spoleto and Benevento, while the Byzantines maintained a tenuous control over the Exarchate of Ravenna and of the territories of the deeper South, including Sicily.

So many upheavals inevitably led to political fragmentation. Even more communities disengaged themselves from their nominal allegiance to Byzantium. By 769 Naples was effectively independent; enlightened dukes, like John IV, maintained libraries with copies sent from Constantinople, keeping learning alive in the South and thereby sowing the seeds of the Renaissance. A clutch of maritime states emerged nearby: Gaeta, Sorrento and above all, Amalfi. Perhaps the first of Italy's great trading entrepôts, it was governed by its own 'doge', while its ships opened up ever more trade routes. The population was to rise to over 70,000. Indeed it retained its independence for the next two centuries, only beginning to decline after two sacks by the Pisans in the late 12th century.

The fall of Ravenna to the Lombards in 751 marked the end of the Byzantine Exarchate. Meanwhile the popes, increasingly isolated against the Lombard threat, appealed to the new power from the West, the Franks. King Pepin the Short, sensing a chance to establish his own legitimacy, sent an army which defeated the Lombards and created a swathe of papal territory across central Italy, largely based on the forged Donation of Constantine. The Franks found stronger resistance in the South, where the Lombard duchies of Benevento, Capua and Salerno survived, and where Greek was still studied and spoken in a deep-seated Hellenic tradition. Even the coronation of Pepin's son, Charlemagne, at Rome in 800, which created the Holy Roman Empire, seemed a distant, northern irrelevance.

A deadlier adversary was about to attack southern Italy. In 827 a Saracen army landed at Mazara in Sicily, soon conquering the whole island. The mainland followed rapidly: Brindisi, Taranto, Bari. Then in 846 the Saracens sacked Rome itself. Only by summoning the combined navies of his maritime neighbour did Pope Leo IV, in personal command, defeat them off Ostia. Thereafter the threat subsided: in Sicily Christians gradually acquired greater religious and social equality. On the mainland Bari was retaken and formed the capital of the revived Byzantine catapanate for the next two centuries. The catapanate comprised all territory south of an imaginary line from the Gargano peninsula in Apulia to the Gulf of Salerno, with the important cities of Naples and Amalfi also owing allegiance to Constantinople.

A patchwork of competing, independent principalities, dukedoms and Byzantine territory now covered the South. It was to remain substantially unchanged for some time. The efforts of the Holy Roman Emperors (the Saxon Ottonians) to gain sway met with scant success beyond Rome, but the differing rates of development between the northern cities, with their trade reviving and organised industries, and their southern counterparts, was all too evident. It was to be further accentuated when a political earthquake turned the South into one united country.

The Normans

This earthquake was to be produced by a group of footloose adventurers from northwestern France. The Normans, Viking by origin but Gallicised after a century of settlement there, were a remarkable people. Eager for land, fame and fortune, they were prepared to try their luck anywhere. Indeed their cousins were soon to conquer England.

Their first glimpse of southern Italy came when 40 pilgrims made the journey to Monte Gargano in northern Apulia in 1015. Within a few years, sensing the opportunities, a group had returned as mercenaries, prepared to fight indiscriminately for the highest bidder. They were employed by many of the petty princedoms in the South, such as the Duchy of Naples, which used them to such good effect against rival Capua that their leader, Rainulf, was invested with the County of Aversa. Realising that they could use their military might against, as well as for, their paymasters, the Normans began to exact land from those they served as well. By 1050 they controlled so much of southern Italy that the pope, feeling himself threatened, raised an army to defeat them.

Despite vastly inferior numbers, it was the Normans who conquered, at Civitate, taking the pope himself (Leo IX) prisoner. His astute successor realised that a change of policy was necessary, and that with Norman support southern Italy could be cleared of both Byzantines and Saracens. By now the leader of the Normans was Robert de Hauteville, one of the twelve formidable sons of an obscure and penniless knight. Ruthless in thought and execution, he was aptly nicknamed 'Guiscard' (or 'the Crafty'), and in 1059 was invested with the dukedoms of Apulia, Calabria and Sicily. The fact that the two former were largely in Greek hands, and the latter in those of the Saracens, merely presented a challenge, to which he was well able to rise. The Byzantines were very soon driven from the land: Bari fell in 1071, signalling the end of Eastern power in the peninsula. The Normans then began on their immense programme of church building, the legacy of which is still to be admired today in the magnificent creations of the style known as the Apulian Romanesque (*see p. 455*). Led by Guiscard's brother Roger, the Normans also crossed into Sicily. Palermo was soon captured and by slow degrees the entire island taken.

This elimination of Byzantine and Saracen power was of the greatest significance: it meant that thereafter all Italy would become a part of western Christendom, speaking a Romance language derived from Latin, rather than Greek, and identifying itself with the primacy of the Roman Church. Many areas in southern Apulia and Calabria had been ruled for some five centuries by the Eastern Empire. Their consequent cultural orientation, emphasised by scholastic tradition and the spread of orthodox monasticism, was obvious. Only now were such ties to be slowly broken.

Such developments were not, however, immediately apparent. The Normans established a magnificent and cosmopolitan court at Palermo, imbued with the ethos of its former Saracenic masters. In this semi-oriental atmosphere Roger II, son of Guiscard's brother, born of an Italian mother and raised in Sicily, where he learned to tolerate all creeds and races, ruled as a benevolent autocrat, on the firm foundations established by his brilliant father. In 1127 he inherited all the Norman mainland from a cousin, bringing the whole of southern Italy once more under a single sovereign. Pope Honorius II, reluctant at first, finally gratified his wish for a crown, and Roger's coronation as King of Sicily, Apulia and Calabria, took place in 1130.

Norman energy had managed to weld the South, after a prolonged state of virtual anarchy, into a stricter feudalism than anything northern Italy had ever known. As time passed, the contrasts between the southern cities of the so-called *Regno* and their northern counterparts became yet more marked. The government suppressed all communal stirrings, while enforcing a regime of high taxation to pay for an expensive administrative machine. This worked, despite numerous minor local rebellions, so long as central government remained as strong and competent as during Roger's reign. Alas, this was not long to be the case.

Neither of Roger's successors—William I, nicknamed 'the Bad', nor his son William II, nicknamed 'the Good'—really deserved their epithets. When problems occurred, they showed that their dynasty could still rise invincibly to the occasion: Byzantine attempts to reconquer Apulia were crushingly defeated in the 1150s and the city of Bari destroyed, as an example to future traitors. The papacy was again humiliated and the Holy Roman Emperor, Frederick Barbarossa, successfully kept at bay. The superb machine of government created by the Normans continued to function, but it was staffed by professional and frequently foreign bureaucrats. Neither monarch was a ruler in Roger's great mould.

In 1189 the Hauteville line died out with William II. He left no children, and was succeeded by his aunt, Constance, Roger's posthumous daughter, who was married to Henry VI of Hohenstaufen, son of Frederick Barbarossa. Though the southern barons preferred the claims of an illegitimate cousin, Tancred, they lacked powerful allies, and after Tancred's death the Hohenstaufen claim was accepted and Henry crowned in 1194. Although he would only survive another three years, a new chapter in the history of southern Italy was about to open.

The Hohenstaufen era

The dynasty of Hohenstaufen provides perhaps the most glamorous episode in south Italian history. By 1270 it was extinct, but its foremost member, Emperor Frederick II, had become the most controversial and brilliant monarch of his age. Nicknamed *Stupor Mundi*, he was a man of extraordinary accomplishments in so many fields, yet he failed to leave an enduring legacy to his heirs.

Orphaned in his infancy, Frederick had theoretically been the ward of the pope. In fact he had been left free to run wild in the exotic world of Palermo, where the tenor of life remained semi-oriental. A lonely child, surrounded by potential enemies, he developed a passion for nature and the countryside, which culminated in the scholarly treatise on falconry he was to write. Fluent in six languages, he was fascinated by science and architecture and would become a generous patron of the arts. He also carried with him an unshakable faith in his personal destiny and an iron will to attain his ends.

Recognised as being of age in 1208, at fourteen, Frederick was offered and occupied the imperial throne of Germany four years later. He was, however, to spend most of his life in Italy. In 1220 he was crowned Holy Roman Emperor in Rome. Sicily, which had been in a state of near anarchy, was quickly pacified and the entire Saracen community was removed to Lucera in Apulia. There, granted total freedom of worship and in their mode of life, they provided Frederick with a faithful praetorian guard. In 1224 the University of Naples was founded, reinvigorating what had become a provincial backwater and recruiting many eminent scholars for its faculties.

In 1215 Frederick had promised to lead a crusade. With reluctance, he fulfilled this vow in 1228 (though delays to his voyage caused Pope Gregory IX to accuse him of temporising and to excommunicate him). The crusade, when it finally took place, was astonishingly successful. A treaty was concluded with the Sultan of Egypt whereby Christians regained access to the shrines in Jerusalem, while other holy places,

Nazareth and Bethlehem, were handed back. Without a drop of blood spilled, Frederick returned triumphant. Pope Gregory had to lift his excommunication, and Frederick reasserted his imperial authority, fortifying a chain of castles throughout southern Italy. There he was undisputed master.

Perhaps Apulia was Frederick's favourite province, where stands his enduring monument: the magnificent Castel del Monte. From the former Hauteville stronghold of Melfi he produced the first medieval legal code. The constitution of 1231 (*see p. 292*) divided the realm into nine provinces, set the currency on a sound footing, abolished internal tolls while increasing import-export duties, and overhauled the state tax machinery. Citing the absolute equality of everyone before the law, Frederick assumed control of criminal justice. The privileges of the barons, Church and towns, were curtailed, but all were afforded representative bodies in a gesture hitherto unprecedented.

The *Regno* (the Kingdom of Sicily and the South; *see p. 25 below*) was certainly the most stable part of Frederick's dominions, a fact which he instinctively understood. The 1230s marked his apogee; thereafter a new, aggressive pope, with the perennially fractious northern cities, especially Milan, wore him down. His later life saw virtually incessant warfare; indeed Pope Innocent IV formally deposed him in 1243. Frederick was to die suddenly in 1250, leaving an uncertain succession. Despite his brilliance, his vision of international empire was incompatible with a papacy that wielded temporal power. But his cultural interests foreshadowed the Renaissance (*see pp. 294–95*), and Dante was right to call him the father of Italian poetry.

The Hohenstaufen heirs did not long survive him. His son, Conrad, was dead within four years, but his favourite bastard, Manfred, recreated much of the court, and the *Regno* flourished under his rule. This the pope found intolerable. Declaring the Sicilian throne vacant, he sought a suitable candidate. One was found in the ruthless Charles of Anjou, brother of the French king, who agreed to lead a 'crusade'. In 1266 the French invaded in force, vanquished and slew Manfred. Two years later, Frederick's grandson, Conradin, was similarly defeated and executed. The Hohenstaufen dynasty had ceased to exist, while the division of Italy between the Ghibellines, imperial supporters who resisted the Church's intervention in imperial affairs, and the Guelphs, who disliked control by a central monarchy and thus supported the Church, was absolute.

The House of Anjou

The Angevin age cannot be described as a happy one in southern Italy. Charles had to reward his French followers generously, which occasioned widespread resentment. A 40,000 florin annuity was owed to the papacy, while Florentine and Genoese merchants, granted a virtual monopoly of southern markets, drained money from the countryside.

Charles was rich, thanks to his marriage with the heiress of Provence, and was possessed of an overweening ego. Italian power was not enough for him; he dreamed of an expedition to Tunis, which ended in complete disaster. Undeterred, he cajoled a new French pope to organise a campaign against Byzantium to depose the schismatic emperor. For unexpected reasons, this was never to happen.

Nemesis had struck. At Easter 1282, in Palermo, where Angevin rule was loathed both for is exactions and its arrogance, revolt broke out almost spontaneously. The Sicilian Vespers was an uprising which killed 2,000 Frenchmen on the first day and had cleared them from the island within a month. It was well orchestrated by a veteran Hohenstaufen supporter, John of Procida, who encouraged Peter III of Aragon, husband of Manfred's daughter, Constance, to assert his claim. Peter duly crossed to Sicily and was crowned king. The ensuing struggle lasted 20 years, until the exhausted Angevins ceded their rights over Sicily. The battle-lines for an enduring Franco-Hispanic conflict to control the central Mediterranean were now clearly drawn.

Naples, to which Charles had immediately transferred his capital, was to enjoy a happier period. Guelph by sympathy, it benefited from the sophisticated and cosmopolitan court established there under Angevin rule. Both Charles's successors, Charles II and Robert the Wise, continued the royal patronage of learning, so that Naples University, along with Salerno Medical School, 500 years older, became two of Europe's centres of academic excellence. Dante disparaged Robert the Wise, calling him 'the King of Talk'. Yet Petrarch counted him a personal friend and wished he might one day rule Italy. Boccaccio, Petrarch's cleverest disciple, came to Naples in 1327. Son of a partner in the Florentine Bardi Bank, he was soon appointed royal counsellor and chamberlain, worthily celebrating the city's opulence and the sensuous luxury of the gulf resort in the beautiful descriptions of his early works (*see p. 35*).

Alas, most of the *Regno* was not in such flourishing condition. By 1302 the Angevins abandoned Sicily to Aragon, though never losing hope of regaining it. The long wars had vastly increased baronial power; castles, once solely a royal prerogative, had proliferated. Heavy taxation blighted prospects of an economic revival, though by his death Robert had managed to reduce both royal debt and papal interference in his affairs.

The succession of his daughter, Joan, in 1343, led to a flurry of coups, as rival Angevin factions battled for the throne. Instability became endemic, while the nobility grew ever more obstreperous and irresponsible. Only when Alfonso 'the Magnanimous' of Aragon seized Naples in 1435 did a measure of peace return. A brilliant court was re-established, state control of the provinces reasserted. Sadly it did not last, for by 1458 Alfonso was dead, his realm again split into two halves.

His Aragonese successors proved capable, if grasping. Yet the inherent problems of a mediaeval monarchy remained: feudal principles still prevailed and the entrepreneurial spirit of the northern cities scarcely existed. The population, perpetually overtaxed, tried to ignore central government. Moreover, Angevin claims to the *Regno* persisted, for this was the excuse of Charles VIII of France ('the young and licentious hunchback of doubtful sanity'), who invaded Italy with a great army in 1494.

Welcomed initially in Naples, Charles aroused opposition from the emperor, the papacy and Spain; soon he had to fight his way home. France and Spain were left locked in a straight fight for dominion. After various vicissitudes, Spain prevailed, though having once fled, the Aragonese kings never really returned. Sicily and Naples were separated into two viceroyalties, the outstanding general Gonzalo de Córdoba being the first to fulfil that role in Naples from 1503.

The preceding two and a half centuries had done terrible damage to southern Italy. Constant instability and warfare had strangled economic development, leaving the country as merely the provider of food and raw materials for the trading cities of the north. A sustained period of peace and wise government was badly needed to restore the proper balance. Could a long Spanish domination accomplish this?

Spanish rule

'A country whose manners and habits are so little congenial with those of other nations of Europe' is how the great Duke of Wellington memorably described Spain. Yet its influence is everywhere apparent in southern Italy today, in many of its buildings, in the mentality of its people, even in their preoccupation with the more macabre sides of religion and death. The foundations for this lie in the two centuries when southern Italy was a viceroyalty of Imperial Spain.

King Charles V of Spain inherited through his mother a country recently reunited by his grandparents in the *Reconquista*, and enriched by bullion wealth from its American possessions. Through his Habsburg father he inherited the Netherlands and much else, and would become Holy Roman Emperor as well. Southern Italy was a small part of his vast empire, but of vital strategic importance to Spain in its long-running battle with France for control of the peninsula. In 1525 Charles won a dramatic victory at Pavia, capturing the French king, Francis I—although this solved nothing permanent. Three years later, a French army was besieging Naples, albeit unsuccessfully.

Thanks to its greatest viceroy, Don Pedro de Toledo, who was appointed in 1532 and remained over 20 years, southern Italy became a safer place to live. Bound by the necessity of 'preserving the state to his master', Toledo's aim was to divide and rule. He managed successfully to separate the interests of the nobility from those of the populace, thereby weakening both sides. From the Middle Ages Naples had had five *seggi*, or sessions, four noble and one popular. As the membership never expanded, they became hereditary, closed corporations, seldom able to agree on anything. Toledo treated the nobles with severity, forbidding duelling or carrying arms at night, even beheading two of them for harbouring criminals. He tempered this severity with a judicious use of titles or favours when co-operation was needed. Only once, in 1547, did his policy fail, when attempts to introduce the Inquisition aroused such universal outrage that they had to be abandoned. Toledo drove the long, straight avenue which bears his name—still the city's main thoroughfare—through Naples' fetid alleys, making it a more elegant and safer city. A skilled *torero* himself, he even introduced bullfighting, though without lasting results. And by encouraging the emperor Charles V to pay visits, he re-established a glamorous and brilliant court.

Charles's successor was a much narrower and less cosmopolitan monarch. Philip II lacked his father's interest in Italy, seeing it merely as a source of money and troops. The nobles abandoned their estates in search of lucrative sinecures and amusement at the viceregal court, which was to have lasting repercussions in the abandoned provinces. But though taxation rocketed, southern Italy at least remained peaceful; the main threat to security came from the Barbary Corsairs, who regularly pillaged the coasts. Indeed

Kheir-ed Din Barbarossa, the greatest of them all, who had created a navy for the Ottoman sultan, even stormed Capri and landed in Naples. But the resounding victory of Lepanto in 1571 destroyed the Ottoman navy and much restricted the pirate threat.

Open revolt finally broke out in Naples in 1647. The viceroy, the Duke of Arcos, had demanded an extra million ducats in gold, to be paid for by a tax on fruit, a staple of the Southern diet. A veteran agitator, one Genovino, fanned the discontent, and a handsome, 27-year-old fisherman from Amalfi, Masaniello, was acclaimed the revolution's leader. Quarrels with the tax collectors quickly arose and riots followed. Arcos' failure to produce the charter of Charles V, which granted tax exemption on basic goods, led to demands for the abolition of recently imposed duties and an equality of popular and noble representation.

For a week Masaniello controlled Naples, raising a militia and dispensing justice. Then, deceived by Arcos' promise to obtain ratification of all the demands from Madrid, he let his men disarm. Increasingly irrational, he alienated many supporters, and the viceroy's assassins soon murdered him. Revolt spread to the provinces, a republic was briefly declared and the French Duke of Guise took advantage of the confusion to reassert Angevin claims to the throne. Making a few concessions, Spanish authority was gradually re-established, and the nobility's co-operation bought by recognition of their feudal claims and the granting of increased influence on government.

The later 17th century was uneventful. Peace returned, but Spanish power had declined, while the cumbrous tax system did not foster prosperity. The extinction of the Spanish Habsburgs in 1700 was followed by the War of the Spanish Succession, in which rival French (Bourbon) and Austrian (Habsburg) princes claimed the crown.

The Bourbon era in the South

The Bourbon claimant to the Spanish throne was recognised as King Philip V by the Treaty of Utrecht in 1713. As part compensation, the Austrian Habsburgs received the former Spanish territories in Italy. They were, however, too preoccupied with problems nearer home to take an active interest in distant Naples. Like the Spanish before them, the Austrians also maintained a viceregal system. But they were deeply unpopular, regarded as both alien and arrogant.

Thus it was that when a Spanish army invaded southern Italy in 1734, and took control of Naples, they received a warm welcome. The leader of that army, Philip V's son Charles, was a politic prince who was to prove a conscientious and skilful ruler, as Charles III of Bourbon. He was possessed of a love of justice, and was content to leave the *minutiae* of administration to his capable minister, Tanucci. This clever, pedantic lawyer was to remain Chief Minister for over 40 years.

Firmly supported by his master, Tanucci set about the abolition of many noble and clerical privileges, curtailing the legal rights of landowners within their fiefs. He similarly restricted ecclesiastical jurisdiction and the immunity granted by asylum, taxing the property of the Church, then reputed to own almost a third of the land. The security of travel in the provinces improved after the endemic brigandage was controlled. With the overhaul of taxation he even brought back some order into public finances.

In 1759 Charles succeeded to the Spanish throne. In his 25-year reign he might fairly claim a place among southern Italy's outstanding rulers. His son, Ferdinand, was very different. Even more of a passionate sportsman than his father, he was a crack shot and skilful fisherman, who could outrow any boatman in the Bay of Naples. Idle and boorish, he was also easy-going and beloved by the *lazzaroni*, the Neapolitan underclass. It was the arrival of his Austrian Habsburg queen, the intelligent, wilful and imperious Maria Carolina, which shook up his relaxed regime. Tanucci's dismissal was soon engineered, for opposing the new queen's Austrophile policies. Yet Maria Carolina did not object to all reform, the further eradication of the nobility's feudal rights being one notable example. And for all her irritation with her wayward husband, she was a dutiful wife, bearing him 18 children.

Tanucci's successor as Chief Minister was Sir John Acton, an expatriate member of an English Catholic family. His priority was to reform the kingdom's armed forces. The logic of this became apparent as the threat posed by the French Revolution loomed ever larger. After 1789 society was increasingly polarised between liberals and royalists. The queen, meanwhile, obsessed by the fate of her sister, Marie Antoinette, became fanatically Francophobe. In 1793 Naples joined the First Coalition, and despite the 'good omen' of a spectacular eruption of Vesuvius, was humiliatingly crushed. When the French occupied Rome in 1798, Ferdinand nevertheless sent an army to evict them. Instead his troops fled without a shot fired, while the French counter-attack on Naples was so rapid that the entire court had to be evacuated to Sicily on British warships.

The 'Parthenopean Republic' was declared. Composed of idealists and impractical radicals, it relied on French bayonets from the start. A royalist insurgence followed. Within six months Cardinal Ruffo's 'Army of the Faith' had marched up from Calabria and recaptured Naples. However, the lack of mercy shown by the victorious royalists sowed seeds of republicanism, while Ferdinand, returning for barely a month to his capital, and again only after the Treaty of Amiens in 1802, forfeited much respect. When hostilities resumed, Napoleon, enraged by what he saw as intransigent Neapolitan opposition, occupied parts of the kingdom. Finding the government still in secret negotiations with Austria, he declared Ferdinand deposed, fuming that the Bourbon presence was 'incompatible with the honour my crown'. Nepotistic to the end, he awarded Naples to his brother Joseph. Ferdinand retreated to Sicily once more.

Joseph proved a mild ruler, and took important steps towards abolishing feudalism. Taxes for the French garrison remained high, however, while royalist resistance continued in the countryside. Given the throne of Spain in 1808, Joseph was replaced by Napoleon's brother-in-law, Joachim Murat, a dashing cavalry general of notable charm. He sustained the policy of abolishing all feudal laws, stamped out lawlessness for a time and endeared himself to many by respecting local traditions. He was unable to do much, however. Until the Emperor's disasters began after 1812, he chafed under his domineering wife, Caroline, and under Napoleon's tutelage. Then, after trying to steer an independent course and invoking Italian nationalism, he supported the Bonapartist Hundred Days, was defeated, captured and shot. In 1815 Ferdinand at last returned to his capital, as Ferdinand I of the Two Sicilies.

TWO SICILIES: THE REGNO

The Kingdom of Sicily forged in the 11th century by the Norman Hauteville knights, and which Charles of Anjou seized from the house of Hohenstaufen in 1266, comprised the island of Sicily itself and the mainland territory of Naples and southern Italy. After the uprising known as the Sicilian Vespers in 1282, a popular revolt which broke out following rumours that a French soldier had raped a Sicilian woman, Charles lost the Sicilian half of his realm to Peter of Aragon. After that two 'kingdoms of Sicily' were in existence: the southern Italian peninsula, which the Angevins persisted in referring to as Sicily, to indicate that they had not renounced their claim over the island; and Sicily proper. The kingdoms were fleetingly reunited during the brief and brilliant reign of Alfonso of Aragon (1443–58). After his death, they split again, and it was only in 1735, when Charles of Bourbon ousted the Austrian Habsburg viceroys from Naples, that the two halves of the kingdom came back under a single crown. Formal union came after the Congress of Vienna in 1815, when Ferdinand IV of Bourbon, Charles' son, reclaimed his kingdom from Napoleon and dubbed himself Ferdinand I of the Two Sicilies.

Maria Carolina had died in 1814, and Ferdinand was rapidly married again, morganatically, to his longtime mistress, the Duchess of Floridia. After the return of peace, international society flocked back to the Bay of Naples and court festivities resumed. But life could never really be the same again. The king, once so at ease with his subjects, was now terrified of popular discontent, yet still determined to rule as an absolute monarch. Changes made by the Bonapartist regime were nullified. The countryside, full of discharged soldiers, became more lawless than ever. The so-called *Carbonari* liberal secret societies, often in league with the Freemasons, attracted wide support.

When the news broke in 1820 that Spain had granted a constitution, insurrection broke out in the army, and under General Pepe's leadership the insurgence swelled to a formidable size. Left with no choice, Ferdinand conceded a constitution of his own, duly swearing to uphold it, while a new parliament was elected. But the king had no intention of keeping his word, and appealed to the Holy Alliance to restore order. Within a few months an Austrian army had captured Naples and a garrison was stationed in the kingdom for several years.

Ferdinand died suddenly in 1825. His successor, Francis, was weak and foolish, on several occasions refusing an alliance with Piedmont which could have arranged the division of Italy. His five-year reign left a troubled legacy to his son, Ferdinand II. An abler and more forceful character, the new king lived in near bourgeois simplicity at Caserta. Popular with the army, he denounced his father's repression and for some years, while the Holy Alliance maintained the monarchical order established by the Congress of Vienna, the situation could be contained.

In 1848, the Year of Revolution, everything changed. Sicily witnessed a violent revolt which expelled the Bourbons, and Ferdinand, already frightened by demonstrations in Naples, panicked. Granting all liberal demands, he even joined an anti-Austrian alliance, but within a few months reneged on his promises and staged a counter-revolution. Revolt was crushed on the mainland and the royal army crossed into Sicily, behaving so brutally that Ferdinand was nicknamed 'King Bomba'. In its last decade Bourbon rule was hated throughout liberal Europe.

An unwilling bystander, Ferdinand could only watch as the great Piedmontese statesman Cavour, backed by France, undermined Austrian dominion in Lombardy and the Veneto and succeeded in clearing northern Italy of foreign rule in 1859. The same year the king died, leaving a young and indecisive heir. Sicily revolted once more, calling on the national folk hero, Garibaldi, for support. In May 1860, with Cavour's tacit approval, the General landed in Sicily. A half-hearted resistance was shown by Bourbon troops, who then evacuated *en masse*. Garibaldi quickly followed them to the mainland, and amid popular enthusiasm, made a lightning advance up the peninsula. In September he entered Naples, while the hapless Francis II fled to Gaeta. Although the king's still-loyal troops were soon defeated, Garibaldi was not left as dictator of Naples for long. Cavour, determined to keep control of events, persuaded his king to march the Piedmontese army south. The symbolic meeting of Garibaldi with Vittorio Emanuele, and their triumphant entry into Naples, signified the extinction of the Bourbon kingdom.

United Italy

Enthusiasm for union with the north proved short-lived. To amalgamate two very different regions, to win over a hostile Church and steer a middle path between Republicanism and the old Bourbon order, was far from easy. Cavour's death in 1861 removed the presiding genius behind the Risorgimento, and soon the Piedmontese regime was worse hated than its predecessors.

In the early 1860s violent lawlessness ravaged the countryside. Traditional loathing of the foreign invader was fuelled by many priests and by loyal supporters of the Bourbons. Brigands could find both arms and shelter within the borders of the Papal States. The Piedmontese reaction was equally violent; a full-scale military campaign killed hundreds of soldiers and thousands of malcontents, while many more were imprisoned. The tradition of *omertà* (the conspiracy of silence) made law enforcement all the harder, as much of the population sympathised with the recalcitrants.

To produce a united Italy, even on paper, took a further decade. Napoleon III of France blew hot and cold over his protection of the papacy. Only in 1870, facing defeat by the Prussian armies, did he finally abandon the papal cause. Piedmontese troops entered Rome and Pius IX retired behind the walls of the Vatican.

Any subsequent history of southern Italy then merges into the whole country's story, although the South retained its very separate development. Discontent remained, for Garibaldi's subsequent government promises to redistribute land proved worthless. The imbalance between the 'real nation', in other words the whole population, where the peasantry remained illiterate and thus had no right to vote (indeed in some areas the literacy vote was reckoned at 5%), and the 'legal nation', constituted by the nobility and middle classes, which enjoyed the franchise, persisted. Successive parliamentary commissions of enquiry failed to resolve matters. Agricultural development was stifled by the prevailing system of large estates with absentee proprietors, and by an uneducated workforce using primitive methods of cultivation.

One check on overpopulation lay in emigration. Beginning in the late 19th century, hundreds of thousands of southern Italians sought a new life overseas, mainly in the Americas. Around 1900, about 70 per cent of all Italian emigrants came from the South, and their remittances formed a vital part of peasant incomes. The countryside remained at the mercy of the *gabellotti*, middlemen, who collected landowners' rents for a huge cut. In the towns criminal organisations, such as the Camorra in Naples, or the N'Drangheta in Calabria, flourished. Taxes remained high, and when government money was pumped into such improvements as roads, railways and public buildings, a heavy toll was exacted by corrupt local bureaucrats. The South has remained notable for its numerous lawyers and officials, and the number of recruits supplied to the armed forces.

The First World War affected southern Italy only slightly, as all the fighting was far away to the north. But the consequent depression and inflation, coupled with the frustration of Italian territorial claims, rocked the whole country. It paved the way for autocracy and Mussolini's March on Rome, which led to the establishment of a one-party state. Fascist financial policy did at first bring some stability and a little prosperity to the countryside, while the firm suppression of organised crime certainly made the governmental machine appear more efficient and less corrupt.

The Second World War brought far worse devastation: fighting in Campania and the destruction of Naples' port, and civil strife in the countryside between the supporters and opponents of Fascism. After 1945 the South represented a fertile constituency for right-wing politicians, frequently allied to associates of dubious legality. Land reform legislation was introduced, applied with variable justice but good results. Continued economic underdevelopment led to further mass emigration to northern Europe or the industrialised north of Italy.

Although in recent years the gaps in wealth, education and growth have narrowed, southern Italy remains a country apart within a united nation. It has never enjoyed real independence for very long, nor has it been properly integrated into a united Italy. Its character is elusive; its charm unique. Goethe, who was fascinated by it, wrote: 'Just as it is asserted that a man who has seen a ghost is never afterwards seen to smile, so it may in the opposite sense be affirmed that a man can never be utterly miserable who retains the recollections of Naples and the South'.

NAPLES

During the 18th century the warm climate, the beauty of the setting, and the sophisticated social life of Naples drew thousands of visitors from Europe and North America—aristocrats, but also intellectuals, such as the British novelist Laurence Sterne and the American artist John Singleton Copley. Most waxed enthusiastic over the city, like the German poet, playwright and philosopher Goethe, who declared (in the *Italian Journey*, 1786–88), 'Naples proclaims herself from the first as gay, free and alive. A numberless host is running hither and thither in all directions, the King is away hunting, the Queen is pregnant and all is right with the world'. But some viewed it with reservation. In *A Tour through Sicily and Malta* (1773), Goethe's British contemporary Patrick Brydone underscored the sometimes striking contrasts which, even today, are the city's hallmark: 'It is hard to say, whether the view is more pleasing from the singularity of many of the objects, or from the incredible variety of the whole. You see an amazing mixture of the antient and modern; some rising to fame, and some sinking to ruin. Palaces reared over the tops of other palaces, and antient magnificence trampled under foot … Mountains and islands that were celebrated for their fertility, changed into barren wastes, and barren wastes into fertile fields and rich vineyards.'

Nevertheless the appeal of the city lasted well into the 19th century. In 1817 the French novelist Stendhal wrote that it was 'the only capital of Italy', and the British *Gentleman's Magazine* reported that 'the emigration of our countrymen to Italy is so extensive, that 400 English families now reside at Naples alone'.

By the middle of the century, however, generations of misrule and a general awakening of social conscience on the part of its visitors had severely tarnished the appeal of Naples. Even the least sensitive foreigner noticed the contrast between the abject misery of the *lazzaroni*, the city's disenfranchised poor, formerly seen as picturesque, and the spectacular luxury of the Neapolitan court. 'What would I give that you should see the *lazzaroni* as they really are,' wrote Charles Dickens in a letter of 1845, 'mere squalid, abject, miserable animals for vermin to batten on; slouching, slinking, ugly, shabby, scavenging scarecrows! And oh the raffish counts and more than doubtful countesses, the noodles and the blacklegs, the good society! And oh the miles of miserable streets, and wretched occupants.' By 1890 Karl Baedeker observed in his *Guide to Southern Italy*, that 'In Naples the insolence of the mercenary fraternity has attained to such an unexampled pitch that the traveller is often tempted to doubt whether such a thing as honesty is known'. This portrait of Naples, reiterated by many subsequent guides, still survives to the present day. But it is a grossly unfair image, especially in the light of developments over the past few years.

Today Naples is one of the most densely populated cities in Europe (pop. 1,300,000) and the intellectual and commercial centre of the South. Under the guidance of mayors Antonio Bassolino and Rosa Rossi Jervolino, it has become a much safer place in recent years, and dozens of new developments have made it an attractive destination for visitors. A vast urban renovation programme has enhanced the beauty of the city centre, buildings have been restored and repainted, and a considerable area of the waterfront, as well as several of the elegant shopping streets further inland, have become pedestrian zones. In the derelict industrial district flanking the rail yards, a whole new city, the Centro Direzionale, has been built to designs by the Japanese architect Kenzo Tange.

The world-famous Museo di Capodimonte has been granted administrative autonomy, the galleries have been renovated and the collection augmented. A special section devoted to contemporary art has been added on the top floor, and the Farnese Collections, which Naples inherited 'by marriage' from Parma, and which contain many masterpieces by Italian and foreign artists, have been installed in specially designed new quarters. The works commissioned from prominent Neapolitan painters by the wealthy Carthusian community of San Martino have returned to the monastery; and the immense collection of figured vases, formerly in storage at the Museo Archeologico Nazionale, is once again on public display. Naples has become an attractive centre for cutting-edge art as well, hosting Italy's second most intense concentration (after Milan) of world-class commercial galleries.

One of the special things about Naples is that you can walk from the city centre to its garland of hills in just a couple of hours—or even less, if you hop on one of the famous *funicolari* (cable cars). In the description that follows you can explore the heart of the city, ascend to the magnificent museums of Capodimonte and San Martino, and wander the lush paths of the Posillipo headland.

NEAPOLITAN HISTORY

To tell the story of Naples is to tell the story of Europe, for ever since the first inhabitants of the Old Continent came to its shores nearly six millennia ago, Naples and its bay have figured prominently in European history. All the great powers—from the Greeks and Romans to the British, French and Austrians—have aspired to control it; several of the continent's most powerful rulers made it their capital. To understand contemporary Naples it is essential to know something of its complex history.

The early years
The area around Naples was inhabited as early as the Stone Age (before 3500 BC). Human remains and stone tools have been found on the island of Capri, as well as along the coast and in the hills and valleys of the Neapolitan hinterland. Artefacts dating from the Bronze Age (after 3500 BC) and the Iron Age (after 1100 BC) are also common. Many of these early inhabitants came to Italy by sea from the eastern Mediterranean: traces of the Bronze Age cultures of Crete and Mycenae, for instance, are visible in burial artefacts from around the 15th century BC onwards.

References to the Naples area may be glimpsed in the myths and legends of ancient Greece. On the northern shore of the crescent-shaped gulf stands Cumae, home of the ancient prophetess, the Sibyl; Olympian gods defeated the Giants and buried them beneath the Phlegraean Fields (Campi Flegrei), which tremble in the earthquakes characteristic of the region whenever the imprisoned monsters try to break free. To the south lie the Isole Sirenuse, the rocks into which the Sirens were metamorphosed after they had enticed Odysseus to land.

The earliest Greek colonies in the Naples area were Cumae and Pithecusae (Ischia), thought to have been founded by Chalcis in the 8th century BC. These were soon followed by the neighbouring centres of Dikaearchia (Pozzuoli), Parthenope (Naples), and a little further to the south, Poseidonia (Paestum). The Gulf of Naples marked the outer edge of what came to be called Magna Graecia (Greater Greece). Sybaris, Croton, Taranto and Naples on the mainland, and Messina and Syracuse on the island of Sicily, became the chief centres of a flourishing Hellenic civilization that attracted distinguished visitors from the homeland and gave rise to a splendid local culture.

Naples, and all of southern Italy, may have continued to flourish under Greek domination had it not been for the powerful Etruscans, who lived primarily in the area now known as Tuscany and Umbria. Attracted by the mild climate and lucrative trade, they established their first colonies in the south-central part of the peninsula in the 9th century. Later, as their northern homeland was invaded by the Celts, they migrated to the region in large numbers. The Etruscans, like the Greeks, had reached a high degree of political, social and artistic development, though they were more warlike than the Greeks and perhaps more actively colonialist. As the years passed, they gradually consolidated their foothold in the south, conquering one Greek city after another. At one point their influence was so strong that new houses in southern towns were built almost exclusively in the Etruscan manner.

The tide finally turned against the Etruscans, however, as a consequence of two Greek victories at Cumae, in 525 and 474 BC. The resulting decline in their power was so rapid that between these dates the Etruscan kings were also chased out of Rome. Eventually, the expanding Roman Republic interposed itself between the Etruscan homeland to the north and its extension around Naples; deprived of a land connection, the southern settlements dwindled.

The expulsion of the Etruscans and the involvement of the Greek colonies in the fratricidal Peloponnesian Wars created a power vacuum in Magna Graecia. This was filled when the indigenous Samnites (a simple people who lived in the hills north and east of Naples) rose up and conquered the region, with relative ease, c. 420 BC. The Samnites were so keenly aware of the inferiority of their own civilization with respect to those they had conquered, that instead of governing the occupied territory according to Samnite law and custom, they created a federation of city-states, each governed by its own magistrate and faithful to its own traditions. In this way, they managed to maintain their hold over the area although they were themselves gradually being conquered by the Romans in a series of conflicts known as the Samnite Wars (343–290 BC).

Campania felix

Naples and its environs prospered once again under the Romans, who occupied the area after the Social War (*see p. 15*) in 88 BC. The region became known as the *Campania felix* ('Blissful Country') on account of its beauty and fertility. The alluvial plains and fertile hills produced the finest grains, vegetables, olives and vines. The slopes of Mount Vesuvius produced highly prized wines, as well as the more common *vinum vesuvium*. The forests yielded wood in abundance, the mountains provided numerous varieties of building stone, and the sea supplied fish from which the ancient peoples made the sauces *garum*, *liquamen* and *muria*, which Pliny says were a special treat.

In the 1st century AD the area developed its character as a rich man's playground. It became a place where Romans went to escape the tensions of the capital—to retire, or simply for a holiday. The coast along the Bay of Naples was adorned with towns, summer homes and plantations, which spread out in unbroken succession, presenting the appearance of a single city.

Parthenope and Neapolis

Naples proper is the modern successor of two ancient towns that had merged to form a single metropolis even before Roman times. The colony of Parthenope was founded by Rhodian navigators in the 9th century BC. It stood on Mount Echia, the volcanic hill now occupied by the Pizzofalcone quarter. This site was chosen because it was easy to defend—it was surrounded by the sea on three sides, with steep cliffs, and was separated from the hinterland by a deep valley, today Via Chiaia.

After the Greek victory over the Etruscans the population of Parthenope grew rapidly, and it soon became clear that the city would have to be enlarged. This posed problems: the lie of the land, which made Parthenope impregnable, also made urban development virtually impossible. So a decision was made to build a new town, Neapolis (from which the modern Napoli is derived), on a hillside on the other side of the harbour. Neapolis soon surpassed the older city in importance, its population swelled by the arrival c. 450 BC of Greek colonists from Chalcis, Pithecusae and Athens. Both towns were conquered by the Samnites in c. 400 BC and by the Romans in 326 BC.

The population of Neapolis expanded under the Romans, but the town held on more tenaciously than any other city in Magna Graecia to its Greek customs, culture and institutions. Every five years the Neapolitans held Greek games, in which musical competitions alternated with gymnastic events, and Greek was preserved as the official language. The emperor Nero was particularly fond of Naples' Hellenic culture, and he sang in the city several times.

A place of learning

Because of its Hellenic character, Naples was regarded as a city of learning. Roman youth flocked here to cultivate the arts of rhetoric, poetry and music. Although the city lacked an amphitheatre, it did have a famous odeon, and the Neapolitan actors were renowned throughout the Roman world. Plutarch, the Greek biographer and moralist, recounts that Brutus came personally to Naples to beg one of these actors, Canutius, to recite in Rome. The theatres of Naples offered plays in Latin and in Greek; among the latter that written by Claudius to honour his brother Germanicus. The great masters included the orator Polemon, one of whose pupils was the Roman emperor and Stoic philosopher Marcus Aurelius.

Virgil, not yet famous, came to Naples in search of the atmosphere that his spirit demanded and that the hustle and bustle of the capital denied him. He wrote his exquisite *Georgics* here, and when he died at an early age in Brindisi, his wish to be buried in Naples was fulfilled on Augustus' orders. According to Dante, his tomb is on the hill of Posillipo.

For the Romans, Naples and its splendid surroundings—the slopes of Vesuvius, the Capodimonte hill, the Phlegraean Fields, the harbours of Pozzuoli, Baiae, Pompeii, Stabiae and Herculaneum—afforded an extraordinary oasis of peace. Horace, the famous poet and satirist, wrote of 'restful Naples', and Ovid claimed that 'Parthenope was born in idleness'.

The Medieval and Renaissance city

Three centuries of resistance against barbarian invasion took their toll on the Roman empire, economically, politically and psychologically. The eastern provinces were successful in defending their borders and preserving imperial institutions of law and government, but the provinces of the west were overrun one by one by the Germanic peoples who, driven from their homelands by other invaders, sought a safe refuge on Roman soil. These historical events found concrete expression in the art and architecture of southern Italy. The early Christian churches and catacombs that appeared in Naples and its environs in the late Roman period reflect both classical and medieval values, setting the spiritual tone for much of the art produced in later centuries. The finest of these works—the 5th-century mosaics in Naples (in the Baptistery of San Giovanni in Fonte and in the Catacomb of San Gennaro) and at San Prisco, near Santa Maria Capua Vetere (in the chapel of Santa Matrona, attached to the parish church)— are distinguished by an explicit naturalism that is rarely seen outside Rome.

During the 5th century Campania fell prey to the Goths, and for the next five centuries the region lacked both the financial resources and the political stability necessary for major civil or cultural undertakings. In 535 the Byzantine general Belisarius, acting for the emperor Justinian, conquered the area but Totila, another Gothic leader, drove them out again in 547; ten years later, it reverted to Byzantine rule. Towards the end of the 6th century, the already weak hold of the eastern emperors relaxed still further under pressure from the Lombards, who gained control of the important provinces of Capua, Benevento, Nola, Acerra and Nocera, reaching the sea at Salerno in 646.

While the Lombards ruled over the interior of Campania, the part of the province remaining under the Byzantine Empire gave its allegiance to the Duke of Naples, who was originally a Greek envoy. In 763, however, Duke Stephen II, while ostensibly maintaining his loyalty to Byzantium, secured the privilege of hereditary power for his family and gradually detached Naples from the direct domination of the empire. His allies in Sorrento, Amalfi and Gaeta soon followed suit. Their dukes, likewise separated by distance and political interest from their nominal allegiance to Byzantium, disengaged themselves from the Eastern Empire in 768, 786 and 899 respectively. During the age of the Independent Duchy (763–1139), Latin replaced Greek as the official language in Naples, and the Roman image of St Januarius (San Gennaro) replaced the Greek effigy of the emperor on municipal seals and coins.

Naples developed one of the strongest fleets in Europe, and in the 9th century it joined forces with other Campanian cities—Gaeta, Sorrento and Amalfi—to rid the Tyrrhenian Sea of the marauding Saracens, who terrorised the coasts and interfered with vital maritime trade.

The Normans and the Hohenstaufen

The Norman conquest (1030–1130) restored political unity to southern Italy. The Norman adventurers who first came to the area in 1016 to seek their fortunes in Apulia (Puglia) and Calabria seem to have had no political ambitions. Lacking organisation and experienced leadership, they were prepared to live as mercenaries in the service of the Byzantines or the Lombards.

It was not until 1030 that Sergius of Naples, by awarding the Norman leader Rainulf the County of Aversa in payment for services rendered, gave them the opportunity to begin an organised conquest of the land. In the years that followed, Norman knights, led by the sons of Tancred de Hauteville, intervened in local conflicts and by so doing gradually gained control of Capua (1062), Salerno (1076) and Amalfi (1137). Naples was the last to fall: it maintained its independence until 1139, its citizens resisting even after the submission of its duke.

By the middle of the 12th century, Campania had been overpowered by the conquerors, whose dominion extended over all southern Italy and Sicily. This vast territory became the Norman Kingdom of Sicily, with its capital at Palermo. It was administered efficiently and with great tolerance of the region's Arab, Jewish, Greek and Roman traditions. Naples, in this scheme of things, was reduced to the status of a provincial town.

In 1194 Henry VI of Hohenstaufen claimed the crown of the Holy Roman Empire in the name of his wife, Constance (daughter of the Norman king, Roger II). He was succeeded as emperor and as King of Sicily by his son Frederick II (1197–1250), whose splendid court at Palermo drew on Islamic and Jewish, as well as Christian cultures. Frederick's belief in the principles of just government is reflected in the famous code of laws known as the *Constitutiones augustales* (*see p. 292*). His interest in rational science and love of Classical sculpture foreshadow the Renaissance.

Naples initially challenged Frederick's sovereignty and suffered a humiliating defeat at the hands of an imperial army. In a gesture of calculated magnanimity, Frederick regained the favour of the Neapolitans by making their city, and not Palermo, the intellectual capital of his kingdom.

Frederick's son Conrad was nominated to succeed him. He spent his brief life locked in a bitter struggle with the implacably anti-Hohenstaufen pope, Urban IV. When Conrad died in 1254 Pope Urban at once set about finding an alternative candidate for the Sicilian throne. He chose Charles of Anjou, the younger brother of St Louis of France. Charles was victorious, killing Frederick II's illegitimate son Manfred at Benevento in 1266. At Tagliacozzo in 1268 he defeated the last of the Hohenstaufen, the 16-year-old Conradin, whom he executed in the market square at

Naples, thus establishing himself as the first French king of Naples and Sicily. To mark the sharp contrast between his monarchy and that of his predecessors, he transferred his capital from Palermo to Naples, which naturally grew in importance.

The Angevins

The Angevin court (the court of Anjou) at Naples was sophisticated and cosmopolitan. As allies of the pope, the French kings employed Florentine bankers and patronised Florentine intellectuals, many of whom, like the poet Boccaccio, became quite fond of their adopted home.

BOCCACCIO IN NAPLES

The Florentine writer Giovanni Boccaccio (1313–75) is best known as the author of the *Decameron,* a collection of tales recounting medieval life, brilliantly adapted to the screen by Italy's most controversial film-maker, Pier Paolo Pasolini, in 1971.

Boccaccio came to Naples as a young man, around 1327, to gain practice as a merchant and banker. He served a long (but fruitless) apprenticeship at the Bardi bank in the lively Portanova neighbourhood, an experience that brought him into daily contact with clients from all areas of the Mediterranean. Boccaccio's life could not have been that of an ordinary apprentice-clerk, for he was the son of a partner of the Bardi who in 1328 became a 'counsellor and chamberlain' of King Robert. The refined, reposeful life of the Neapolitan upper classes, divided between the aristocratic opulence of the city and the carefree, voluptuous idleness of the gulf-shore resorts (particularly Baia), is delightfully portrayed in his early works. In his *Rhymes,* for instance, he voices a curious lament.

If I fear the sky and sea of Baia,
the ground and waves and lakes and fountains,
the wild and the domestic places,
no one should be surprised.
Here one spends all one's time celebrating
with music and song, and with vain words
seducing wandering minds
or telling of love's victories.

Against this background he chose to set his great romantic novel, *Elegia a Madonna Fiammetta.*

The gaiety of the Angevin court unfortunately did not extend to the rest of the kingdom. Indeed, the political life of these years was as turbulent as its social life was exuberant. Charles initially enjoyed the favour of his subjects, but his political ambitions, which necessitated oppressive taxation, led to resentment. Revolt broke out in Palermo on Easter Tuesday, 1282, in the uprising known as the Sicilian Vespers. The French garrisons on the island were either expelled or massacred, and the Sicilian nobles summoned the Catalan Peter of Aragon to be their king.

Charles of Anjou died in 1286, succeeded by his eldest son, Charles II, who in turn was succeeded by his second son Robert (the Wise), who proved a capable ruler and patron of the arts (it was he who financed Boccaccio's literary endeavours), but whose authority was limited by a restive and rebellious baronage. His death (1343) was followed by a whirlwind of coups and counter-coups. He was succeeded by his granddaughter Joan I, whose husband, Andrew of Hungary, crown prince of Naples, was assassinated in 1345, probably with the queen's complicity. Joan nominated Louis of Anjou her heir, and he was recognised by the antipope Clement VII. Pope Urban VI, however, named Charles of Durazzo, great-grandson of Charles II, king of Naples. Charles conquered the kingdom, took Joan prisoner in 1381 and had her murdered the following year. Louis of Anjou died in exile three years later. The anarchic reigns of Charles III and his son Ladislas were followed (1414) by the dissolute rule of Joan II, which was torn by the rival inheritance claims of Louis III of Anjou and of Alfonso of Aragon. Alfonso seized Naples on Joan's death in 1435, and in 1443 assumed the title King of the Two Sicilies (that is to say, of Sicily and Naples; *see p. 25*).

Fifteenth-century Naples

During the brief reign of Alfonso of Aragon, called 'the Magnanimous', Naples was again united with Sicily. The kingdom enjoyed a period of renewed splendour, for Alfonso was at once a brilliant ruler, a scholar and a patron of the arts. When he died (1458) his brother John II succeeded to the throne of Sicily, while Naples adopted his illegitimate son Ferdinand I (Ferrante) as king. Like his father, Ferrante surrounded himself with artists and humanists—and was in this respect a typical Renaissance prince, though often perverse and cruel (it was his policy, so rumour has it, to imprison his enemies in the Castel Nuovo until they died; they would then be mummified and exhibited to his guests, dressed in the clothes they had worn when living).

Ferrante was succeeded by Alfonso II, who in September 1495 surrendered the kingdom to Charles VIII of France. Many months later Alfonso's son Ferdinand II (Ferrandino), with the help of Spain, returned to his capital, where he died in 1496. During the reign of his successor, Frederick, the country was torn by civil war and brigandage, as both the French and the Spanish continued to press their claims. A series of victories by Spanish forces under Gonzalo de Córdoba secured the kingdom for Spain in 1503. Naples was not reunited with Sicily, but governed by a separate viceroy, Gonzalo being the first.

The Spanish viceregal city

During the period of the Spanish viceroys, Naples was oppressed by excessive taxation and delegated rule. Brigands terrorised the countryside and pirates roamed the seas, discouraging trade and endangering travellers. The scarce attention that the

Spanish governors paid to the provinces brought increasing numbers of immigrants to the capital, causing severe overcrowding—at the end of the century, Naples had 240,000 inhabitants; 300,000 counting the suburbs. Several viceroys, especially Don Pedro de Toledo (1532–53), tried to alleviate the problem by constructing new roads and buildings, but they were outpaced until the terrible plague of 1656 killed or dispersed half the population.

In the provinces, as in the capital, life was dominated by the burden of high taxes. Despite reduced profits, country dwellers devoted themselves as always to the cultivation of fields and orchards, and the sale of agricultural products remained their principal source of income. In the cities an educated and ambitious middle class climbed steadily to wealth and political power, the successful buying titles and estates (it is estimated that 17th-century Naples had at least 119 princes, 156 dukes, 173 marquises and several hundred counts). In contrast to these, and to the virtual army of clergy (which came to represent one fortieth of the population), stood the hordes of ragged beggars known as *lazzaroni*. On one hand, they were considered as thieving, treacherous, seditious, lazy and corrupt ('There is not such another race of rogues as the common people of Naples', Henry Swinburne commented); but on the other their 'way of being satisfied with so little, of living on the air of time', was idealised, especially by northern Europeans like Goethe, who attributed to them a peculiarly Mediterranean sense of freedom.

The French never fully accepted the idea that they had lost the Kingdom of Naples to the Spanish (a French army under Odet de Foix, Viscount of Lautrec, laid siege to the capital in 1528), and the Neapolitans themselves considered the foreigners tyrants whose unjust rule was to be cast off at the earliest possible opportunity. When Viceroy Pedro de Toledo levied a new round of taxes in 1535, the people appealed in vain to Spanish king and Holy Roman Emperor Charles V.

Naples is nevertheless deeply indebted to this energetic viceroy, for he undertook the most ambitious (and successful) urban development programme in the city's history. He curbed ecclesiastical building (a sticky political problem throughout the viceregal period) by acquiring property in the city centre so that tenement houses would not be torn down and convents built in their place. He alleviated day-to-day commuter traffic by moving administrative offices out of the city centre (by his order the law courts were moved to their present seat at the Castel Capuano). Most importantly, he doubled the area available for building within the city walls by constructing a new set of fortifications that ran from the Castel Capuano, on the east side of town, to the Castel Sant'Elmo (rebuilt in the form of a six-pointed star) on the Vomero hill, and from the latter to the Castel dell'Ovo, on the sea to the west. In place of the now obsolete Aragonese walls, he built the great thoroughfare known in his honour as Via Toledo (now also Via Roma).

To the west of this road he constructed a whole new quarter to house the Spanish garrison at Naples (the labyrinthine lanes and steep staircases that characterise this quarter have changed little since then and repay a visit). Via Toledo became the fashionable residential street of the aristocracy. At its southern end, Don Pedro erected a new viceregal palace. It became known as the Palazzo Vecchio at the beginning of the following century, when Viceroy Ferrante de Castro commissioned Domenico Fontana to build the magnificent Palazzo Reale, in anticipation of a never-fulfilled visit by King Philip III.

The Bourbons

The last years of Spanish rule were undistinguished. Burdensome taxation roused the Neapolitans to insurrection (1647) under Masaniello, an Amalfi fisherman who was used as a figurehead by liberal reformers seeking to undermine the power of the nobility. The ensuing 'Parthenopean Republic' lasted only a few months. After the War of the Spanish Succession, the throne of Spain passed to the Bourbon French, and that of Austria to the Holy Roman Emperor, the Spanish Habsburg Charles VI, who also inherited Naples, though he did not rule it personally; the viceregal system was continued. In 1734, however, the Infante Charles of Bourbon (Charles VII, known as Charles III, his regnal number in Spain) seized Sicily and subsequently Naples and in 1744 defeated the Austrians at Velletri, near Rome, thus founding the Neapolitan Bourbon dynasty.

Charles (reigned 1734–59) was the first of the Bourbon kings, who ruled Naples until the Unification of Italy in the 19th century. Although not without his faults, he was certainly the most generous and enlightened member of this controversial dynasty. He restored order to public finance, curtailed ecclesiastical jurisdiction and immunities and taxed ecclesiastical property, then about one third of the whole kingdom. He modernised the university and gave it a new home in the Palazzo degli Studi (now the Museo Archeologico). He also began the excavations at Pompeii and Herculaneum and published the finds in nine splendidly illustrated volumes.

Charles was uncommonly generous as a patron of the arts. His ambition to make Naples the most brilliant centre of musical culture in Italy (a position it would maintain throughout the 18th century) culminated in the construction of the famous Teatro San Carlo, so named because it was inaugurated on his saint's day, 4th November, 1738. These and many other improvements made in public and private life bear witness to this sovereign's acute mental vision, especially if one considers the brevity of his reign (25 years, compared to Frederick the Great's 46 and Louis XV's 59), and to the sound political and economic position in which he left the kingdom at the end of it.

Charles's son and heir Ferdinand IV (1759–1825) unfortunately possessed few of his father's virtues. He reigned with the enthusiastic approval of the Neapolitan mob, which fondly called him '*Nasone*' on account of his bulbous nose. To his peers he was known as the Lazzarone King, 'beloved by the vulgar Neapolitans ... from his having been born amongst them,' and inclined 'rather to seek the company of menial servants and people of the very lowest class than those of a better education' (this and the following quotations are drawn from Sir Harold Acton's brilliant study, *The Bourbons of Naples*). Ferdinand was famous for his indolent bonhomie, his love of hunting, his inclination for crude practical jokes and his indifference to anything not directly related to his physical well-being.

THE FIRST OF THE BOURBONS

The first of the Neapolitan Bourbons, Charles, and his son and heir, Ferdinand, were as different as night and day.

Sir James Gray, British resident at Naples, had this to say of Charles: 'The King of Naples is of a very reserved temper, a great master of dissimulation, and has an habitual smile on his face, contracted by a constant attention to conceal his thoughts; has a good understanding and a surprising memory, as his father had, is unread and unlearned, but retains an exact knowledge of all that has passed within his own observation, and is capable of entering into the most minute detail. He is in many things his own Minister, passing several hours every day alone in his cabinet'. Let there be no doubt: Charles was an absolute ruler. 'He has too good an opinion of his own judgement, and is so positive and obstinate, that he is seldom induced to alter his resolutions,' said Gray. 'He has very high notions of his prerogative and his independency, and thinks himself the most absolute monarch in Europe.' Yet the king chose his servants wisely. Beginning with Bernardo Tanucci, the Tuscan law professor whom he made his prime minister, and the architect Vanvitelli, who designed the magnificent palace and gardens of Caserta, he appointed to high office men of competence and unquestioned personal integrity.

Sir William Hamilton, who succeeded Gray as resident English minister in 1764, found Charles's successor insensitive, choleric and obstinate, commenting that at the end of his regency 'the young King ... seems to have been more desirous of becoming his own master to follow his caprices, than to govern his kingdoms'. When Ferdinand married Maria Carolina of Austria (daughter of Maria Theresa and sister of Marie Antoinette), Sir William described the young husband as follows: 'On the morning after his nuptials, which took place in the beginning of May 1768, when the weather was very warm, he rose at an early hour and went out as usual to the chase, leaving his young wife in bed. Those courtiers who accompanied him, having inquired of his majesty and how he liked her: "Dorme come un'ammazzata," replied he, "e suda come un porco" [she sleeps as if she had been killed, and sweats like a pig]. Such an answer would be esteemed, anywhere except at Naples, most indecorous; but here we are familiarized to far greater violations of propriety and decency.... When the king has made a hearty meal and feels an inclination to retire, he commonly communicates that intention to the noblemen around him in waiting, to the favoured individuals, whom, as a mark of predilection, he chooses shall attend him. "Sono ben pranzato," says he, laying his hand on his belly, "adesso bisogna una buona panciata" [I've eaten well, now I need to move my bowels]. The persons thus preferred then accompany his majesty, stand respectfully round him, and amuse him by their conversation during the performance.'

War with France

At the outbreak of the French Revolution (1789) Ferdinand was not at first hostile to the new movement; but in the months that followed he was compelled to take action against republicanism at home and abroad. Every tremor that emanated from Paris was registered with particular anxiety in Naples, where the opposing forces had polarised more sharply than elsewhere in Italy. Rightly or wrongly, the Neapolitan liberals believed that they had suffered more under the Bourbons than the inhabitants of other regions of Italy had under their sovereigns; and they saw in the cause of revolutionary France the glimmer of hope for a free and united Italy.

The royalists, on the other hand, rallied in defence not only of their beloved *Nasone*, but also of their queen, the sister of the martyred Marie Antoinette. Sir John Acton, the French-born English baronet who became Ferdinand's prime minister, counselled prudence; but Queen Maria Carolina, who exercised considerable influence over the king, maintained that the best defence was a strong offence. In 1793 Naples joined the First Coalition against republican France, severely persecuting all those who were even remotely suspected of French sympathies. The eruption of Vesuvius in May 1794, widely regarded as an expression of divine wrath over the execution of Louis XVI and Marie Antoinette, won popular approval for the initiative.

In 1798, during Napoleon's absence in Egypt and after Nelson's destruction of the French fleet at the Nile, Maria Carolina persuaded Ferdinand to go to war with France. The king promptly sent an army against French-held Rome, which fell without resistance. For a few ecstatic days that December, the Neapolitans occupied the Eternal City; but the French under Championnet quickly counter-attacked, recaptured Rome and entered Naples so swiftly that the royal family had to be evacuated by Nelson himself, with the aid of Emma Hamilton, the lovely young bride of Sir William, who had her servants carry the crown jewels of Naples aboard the British flagship before it set sail for Sicily.

On 23rd January 1799 the second Parthenopean Republic was proclaimed, but like its predecessor (*see p. 38 above*), it was short-lived. Governed by local liberals and precariously supported by the French army, it claimed dominion over the peninsular portion of the former kingdom, while Ferdinand and Maria Carolina ruled Sicily from Palermo, protected by the British navy patrolling the Straits of Messina.

Although the republicans had noble aims, they were doctrinaire and unpractical, and they knew very little about the ordinary people in their own country. A violent anti-French feeling in southern Italy coincided with French defeats by Austro-Russian forces in the north. The following year the king and queen, with the aid of Nelson and Cardinal Ruffo, who swept up from Calabria with a band of peasants, brigands, convicts and a few soldiers, managed to reconquer the mainland provinces of the kingdom. The French and their republican allies found themselves confined to Naples proper, and before long surrendered on the promise of an amnesty. The foreigners were allowed to leave with the implicit blessing of St Januarius, the liquefaction of whose blood was supposedly helped along in that year by the President of the Parthenopean Republic (who held the archbishop at gunpoint during the ceremony).

Had the miracle not taken place, the French might well have been seized and lynched by the angry mob, whose sympathies were, as always, with their king.

A period of severe repression followed. Nelson, prompted by Emma Hamilton (now his mistress) and Maria Carolina, set out to eradicate all traces of the Parthenopean Republic, while the two husbands gave him *carte blanche*. Sir William was too busy lamenting the loss of much of his precious collection of antiquities, which had gone down with the ship that was transporting them to England; and Ferdinand had grown so fond of his Sicilian hunting grounds that he could barely be persuaded to return to the throne in Naples.

While the *lazzaroni* plundered the republicans' property to cries of *Chi tien pan' e vino ha da esser giaccobino* (He who has bread and wine is surely a Jacobin), Nelson unabashedly violated the terms of surrender, summarily executing the liberal leaders—among them Admiral Francesco Caracciolo, the philosopher Mario Pagano, the scientist Domenico Cirillo, and other prominent Neapolitan intellectuals.

Bonaparte and Murat

After Napoleon's successful second Italian campaign, Ferdinand was forced to grant another amnesty to the surviving republicans, to close all the ports of his kingdom to the British fleet and to allow a French garrison to be stationed deep within his territory, at Taranto. Even so, the Neapolitans could consider themselves lucky, for Napoleon had treated them more leniently than he had his other, more powerful enemies. Only when he found out that they had been negotiating with Austria with a view to joining the Third Coalition, did Napoleon's patience give out: after the Austerlitz campaign (1805), he issued the famous proclamation, 'the Bourbon dynasty has ceased to reign', and sent his brother Joseph to dethrone Ferdinand, who again fled to Sicily under the protection of a British fleet.

Joseph Bonaparte, though certainly no genius, was a cultivated and well-meaning man. He abolished the privileges of the nobility and the clergy and introduced several important reforms. But his taxes and forced contributions were resented, and royalist risings undermined his authority in much of the kingdom. In 1808 Napoleon gave Joseph the crown of Spain and appointed his colourful and flamboyant brother-in-law, Joachim Murat, King of Naples. Murat continued Joseph's reforms, quashed the Bourbon guerrilla bands in the provinces and instituted a programme of public works that included new roads to Posillipo and Capodimonte.

Meanwhile, in Sicily, where King Ferdinand's extravagance and methods of police espionage rendered the royal presence a burden instead of a blessing, a bitter conflict broke out between the court and parliament. In 1812 Sir William Bentinck, the British minister, obliged Ferdinand to grant a liberal constitution. But the wind changed as a result of Napoleon's defeat at Waterloo, and the king dissolved parliament in May 1815, having concluded a treaty with Austria for the recovery of his mainland dominions.

A month later Ferdinand re-entered Naples, amid some discontent, while Murat fled to Corsica. At first the king abstained from persecution and received many of the usurper's officers into his own army. Murat, believing he still had a strong following

in the kingdom, landed with a few companions at Pizzo in Calabria, but was immediately captured, court-martialled and shot.

The struggle for a constitution

Ferdinand proclaimed himself King Ferdinand I of the Two Sicilies at the Congress of
Vienna, incorporating Naples and Sicily into one state and abolishing the Sicilian constitution of 1812. In 1818 he signed a Concordat with the Church, reinstating ecclesiastical jurisdiction over education and censorship. But ideas of national unity and personal freedom continued to make progress. In 1820 a spontaneous insurrection, which
began in the army at Nola, quickly took fire under the leadership of General Guglielmo
Pepe. The mutineers demanded a new constitution, while assuring the king of their continued loyalty. Ferdinand, helpless to resist, agreed to their demands. These events seriously alarmed the powers responsible for the preservation of the peace in Europe, who
at the Congress of Troppau (October 1820) issued the famous protocol affirming the
right of collective 'Europe' to interfere to crush dangerous internal revolutions.

The following year Ferdinand abandoned his agreement with the rebels, and the
powers authorised Austria to march an army into Naples and restore the autocracy of
the monarchy. General Pepe was sent to the frontier at the head of 8,000 men, but was
defeated by the Austrians at Rieti on 7th March 1821. A period of severe repression
ensued, the inevitable state trials resulting in the usual harvest of executions and
imprisonments.

The conditions of the country continued to worsen under Ferdinand's successors,
Francis I (1825–30) and Ferdinand II (1830–59). Francis I refused several opportunities to strike an alliance with Vittorio Emanuele, King of Piedmont and Sardinia, for the
division of Italy. But the desire for a constitution became ever more fervent. Revolution
broke out in Sicily on 12th January 1848, under the leadership of Ruggero Settimo,
while demonstrations also shook Naples. On 28th January 1848, King Ferdinand II
granted the constitution; but the following spring he refused to open parliament, and
sent an army under Carlo Filangieri against the revolutionary government of Palermo,
which fell on 14th April 1848. Open despotism followed, during which liberal sympathisers were condemned to gaol or the galleys for life. Thousands of citizens were
thrown into prison, including Luigi Settembrini, Carlo Poerio and Silvio Spavento.

Enter Garibaldi

On 5th May 1860 the Piedmontese general Giuseppe Garibaldi embarked at Quarto,
near Genoa, with 1,000 handpicked followers on board two steamers, and sailed for
Sicily. On 11th May the expedition reached Marsala and landed without opposition.
The astonished population received Garibaldi coldly, but he set forth at once for
Salemi, where he issued a proclamation assuming the dictatorship of Sicily in the
name of Vittorio Emanuele, with Francesco Crispi as Secretary of State. On 15th May
he attacked and defeated 3,000 Bourbon loyalists under General Landi, at Calatafimi.
The news of this brilliant victory revived revolutionary agitation throughout the
island. By a clever ruse, Garibaldi avoided General Colonna's forces, which were

expecting him on the Monreale road, and entered Palermo from Misilmeri, receiving an enthusiastic welcome.

After three days' street fighting the Bourbon commander, General Lanza, not knowing that the *Garibaldini* had scarcely a cartridge left, asked for and obtained a 24-hour armistice (3rd June). Garibaldi went on board the British flagship to confer with the Neapolitan generals Letizia and Chrétien; then he informed the citizens by means of a proclamation of what he had done, and declared that he would renew hostilities on the expiration of the armistice. Lanza became so alarmed that he asked for an unconditional extension of the armistice, which Garibaldi granted, and 15,000 Bourbon troops embarked for Naples on 7th June, leaving the revolutionaries masters of the situation.

The news of Garibaldi's astonishing successes entirely changed the situation in the capital, and on 25th June 1860 the king again granted a constitution. He appealed to Great Britain and France to prevent Garibaldi crossing the Straits of Messina and only just failed. On 19th August Garibaldi crossed with 4,500 men and took Reggio by storm. He was soon joined by the rest of his troops—15,000 in all. The Neapolitan army collapsed before Garibaldi's advance. As the Piedmontese entered Naples, Francis II retired to Gaeta, where he capitulated in October 1860 after a last, desperate stand on the Volturno.

Modern Naples

In 1884 a terrible cholera epidemic swept Naples, taking many lives, particularly in the crowded alleys and tall tenements of the medieval city centre. As a result special laws were passed to hasten urban renewal. Wide thoroughfares were driven through the slums, the waters of the Serino river were brought into the city, and complete new quarters were built. Naples lost much of its picturesque quality without gaining in improved health, as the population evicted from the condemned buildings was housed in neighbouring blocks, increasing density even further.

The greatest achievement of the *Risanamento*, as the urban renewal programme was called, was the construction of the Corso Umberto I (popularly the Rettifilo) from Piazza Garibaldi and the railway station to the Piazza del Municipio, the centre of local government. Other 'improvements' included the rebuilding of the quarter of Santa Lucia, the founding of a new residential district on the Vomero hill and the establishment of the first industries in the Vasto Arenaccia area, the most easterly link in the chain of industrial suburbs that encircles Naples today, presenting a serious obstacle to the successful expansion of the city.

Quite independently of the *Risanamento*, wealthier Neapolitans began to build their luxurious villas on the hillside above the Riviera di Chiaia around the turn of the century (Piazza Amedeo, Parco Margherita). Many of these elegant dwellings, which continued to be built up until the eve of the First World War, are in a curious local variant of the Art Nouveau style.

The period between the wars witnessed a revival of building without any precise guidelines. During the Fascist period both urban expansion and rebuilding activity in the city centre were important. The suburban quarters grew rapidly, particularly at

Fuorigrotta, where development was stimulated by the construction of the Mostra d'Oltremare fairground and of the tunnel under Posillipo hill.

In central Naples the most striking changes took place in the Carità quarter, between Via Toledo, Via Monteoliveto and Via Medina. Here the central post office, the provincial office building and the police headquarters were erected, concentrating administrative services even more in an already overburdened area. Finally, in 1939, the need for an organic design stimulated the drafting of a general town plan, which was not, however, applied until many years after the war.

The events of the Second World War nullified many earlier improvements. Naples was heavily bombed on 4th August 1943 by the advancing Allies, then attacked and captured by the Germans after the armistice of 8th September. A Neapolitan uprising (*Le Quattro Giornate*, 28th September–1st October) drove out the Germans, who before retreating destroyed the port, utilities and public archives. A typhus epidemic followed by a bad winter added to the distress and aggravated the age-old problem of the *scugnizzi*, deprived children who managed to survive only by resorting to crime.

The contemporary city

Commercial and industrial development radically changed the city's appearance in the post-war years. The coastline from Pozzuoli to Castellammare di Stabia and the inland suburbs now hosts an array of industrial plants (including ironworks, food processing plants, an oil refinery, cement works, aircraft and automobile assembly plants), and residential building has expanded over the surrounding hills and to the eastern plains. This apparent burgeoning of wealth and activity is illusory, however, and does not reflect the true economic condition of the city, which, notwithstanding costly and elaborate plans for development, remains substantially poorer than its northern counterparts.

Naples has the highest population density of any European city and is severely lacking in social services. Despite the efforts of the local authorities to provide adequate housing, many Neapolitans still live in *bassi*—street-level, single-room dwellings in which light and air are admitted by a double door alone. At the same time, illegal building activity has altered the appearance of the town beyond recognition. A special investigatory committee of the Ministry of Public Works revealed in 1971 that almost everything built in Naples since 1945 was in violation of the law. Judiciary action in 1975 resulted in the incrimination of a former mayor, the demolition of 22 buildings erected on lands destined for parks, schools, and other public facilities, and the arrest of several contractors. In spite of intimidatory actions brought by the profiteers and their sympathisers, the effort to restore Naples to her former elegance continues.

The task is not an easy one, for even the force of nature must be taken into account. The violent earthquake that rocked Campania and the neighbouring region of Basilicata on 22nd November 1980 claimed over 3,000 victims and caused incalculable damage. In Naples 200,000 people were left homeless. An effort is now being made to make all new buildings part of an overall design. Particularly in recent years, countless monuments have been cleaned, renovated, or restored; attempts have been made to extend restricted traffic zones, and major renovation programmes have been launched.

NEAPOLITAN ART & ARCHITECTURE

Ancient Naples

There are few ancient ruins in Naples to speak of. Most of Naples' ancient treasures lie buried beneath the modern city. The few remains that can be seen have been camouflaged by time. Incorporated into later structures, they crop up in unexpected places.

Via dei Tribunali follows the course of the ancient *decumanus maximus*, the main street of Graeco-Roman Naples, and several buildings on this and neighbouring streets—mainly churches, but residential buildings, too—incorporate vestiges of the very distant past. Greek and Roman remains have been brought to light beneath the church of San Lorenzo Maggiore, and tours are given of Naples' fabulous underground aqueduct, which in this area has been patiently restored and eloquently lighted.

Via dell'Anticaglia (*map p. 53, 3*) corresponds to the *decumanus maximus* of Roman Neapolis. The street is crossed by two massive brick arches—the only existing remains of the walls that joined the baths, which were located on the far side of the street, with the ancient theatre. The theatre was built to accommodate 11,000 spectators. It was here that Claudius had the play he wrote in honour of his brother Germanicus performed, and here that Nero sang to an enthusiastic audience. More Graeco-Roman remains, including fragments of a mosaic pavement, can be seen beneath the cathedral.

Early Christian and medieval art

Legend says that St Peter visited Naples on his way to Rome, breaking his journey to establish a diocese and to name St Asprenus as its first bishop; numerous chronicles describe the martyrdom, near Pozzuoli, of Bishop Januarius (San Gennaro); and unsubstantiated tales attribute the foundation of the city's first Christian churches to the time of Constantine (AD 306–77). But recent studies show that St Peter did not visit Naples—the birth date of the Neapolitan episcopate is still uncertain—and although there is evidence that followers of the new religion existed in the city shortly after the time of Christ, it is now known that Naples' first Christian churches were erected only at the end of the 4th century. The Catacomb of San Gennaro (*map p. 50, 2*) dates from the 2nd century AD and seems to have developed around the family tomb of an early Christian.

The Norman influence is most clearly seen in the environs of Naples, rather than the city itself. It reaches its highest expressions in the maritime cities, which prospered through trade with Sicily and the Orient and were the chief channels through which the Norman court of Palermo administered its holdings on the mainland. Siculo-Norman artists, or local artists trained in the Norman schools of Sicily, were active at Salerno, Ravello, Sessa Aurunca, Gaeta and elsewhere in this area throughout the 11th and 12th centuries. They left an extraordinary series of sculptures—mainly decorated episcopal thrones, pulpits, paschal candelabra and altar screens, incorporating coloured glass inlay and marble intarsia work inspired by Saracenic art. The Normans were also responsible for introducing French architectural forms and styles.

The rebuilding of the Benedictine abbey of Monte Cassino, under the enlightened direction of the 11th-century abbot Desiderius, stimulated artistic activity in the area.

From Monte Cassino, Desiderius masterminded a real revolution of the arts. He brought in architects from Lombardy and artists from Constantinople and trained his monks in their methods, giving rise to a new artistic sensibility that combined the splendour of Oriental mosaic and allied crafts with revived early Christian narrative methods. A reflection of this 11th-century blend of styles may be seen in the marvellous series of contemporary frescoes in the basilica at Sant'Angelo in Formis, near Capua.

Further contacts between Eastern and Western artistic cultures are evident in the bronze doors that appeared on Campanian cathedrals in the 11th and 12th centuries. The first of these were installed at Amalfi in 1065. They had been commissioned in Constantinople by the wealthy Amalfitan merchant, Pantaleon, who had business interests in the Byzantine capital and must have seen bronze doors on churches there. Desiderius of Monte Cassino was so impressed by these doors when he visited Amalfi that he ordered a pair for his abbey. The fashion spread from there to Salerno, Atrani, Ravello, Benevento and other southern Italian cities.

Angevin and Renaissance art in Naples

During the 13th and early 14th centuries the artistic impetus in Naples, which came through the Angevin dynasty, was understandably foreign. The Angevins generally imported their architects from France, but they chose their artists from among the representative masters of the major Italian schools: Pietro Cavallini from Rome, Giotto from Florence, Simone Martini and Tino da Camaino from Siena. In so doing they established a pattern of patronage (favouring foreign artists or artists from further north over local masters) that would continue, with rare exceptions, until the 17th century. One of the most talented local artists who studied under Giotto and incorporated elements of his style was Roberto d'Oderisio.

While Renaissance painters in Florence, Rome, and Venice produced works of art that are known the world over, very little of note was done in 15th-century Naples. Like the Angevins, the Aragonese entrusted their most important commissions to the famous names of the north (notably the Florentines Donatello, Michelozzo, Antonio Rossellino and Benedetto da Maiano). The major Neapolitan painter of the 15th century is Colantonio, whose style shows a debt to Flemish painting. Andrea da Salerno, too, has left many fine works throughout Campania. Despite the fine sculptured works by northern Italian artists in the major churches of Naples, there was no local school of any merit. The most successful architects were Tommaso Malvito and his son Giovanni Tommaso Malvito, and Giovanni Francesco Mormanno.

Art and architecture in 16th–18th-century Naples

By the end of the 16th century, Naples bristled with churches and convents: there were at least 400 of the former, not counting private chapels, and about 200 of the latter. At the beginning of the 18th century, a petition was sent to the viceroy, urging him to prevent the clergy from acquiring more property.

Yet the construction of churches and convents led to the great artistic flowering of the 17th and 18th centuries, characterised by the presence of architects, sculptors, and painters who were famous throughout Europe—Cosimo Fanzago, Caravaggio, Jusepe de Ribera, Domenichino, Giovanni Lanfranco, Batistello Caracciolo, Massimo Stanzione, Bernardo Cavallino, Salvatore Rosa, Mattia Preti, Luca Giordano and others. In the words of a contemporary observer, 'That which seemed to us most extraordinary at Naples was the number and magnificence of the churches. It may be justly said, that in this respect it surpasses imagination... If you would look upon rare pictures, sculptures, and the rarity of vessels of gold and silver, you need but go to the churches: the roofs, the wainscots, the walls are all covered with pieces of precious marble, most artificially laid together, or with compartments of *basso rilievo*, or of joiner's work gilded, and enriched with the works of the most famous painters. There is nothing to be seen but jasper, porphyry, mosaic of all fashions, all masterpieces of art.'

Another connoisseur of the Neapolitan Baroque, the eminent British art historian Anthony Blunt, warned that 'the architecture of Naples is like its inhabitants: lively, colourful, and with a tendency not to keep the rules,' adding that 'if you go to Naples expecting its architecture to behave like that of Rome, you will be as surprised as if you expected its traffic to behave like Roman traffic, though you will be in less physical danger.' Many of the architects who worked in Naples at this time were not natives of the city—Cosimo Fanzago, the most imaginative architect and sculptor of the period, came from Bergamo—yet they all seem to have become acclimatised. They either ignored or, in some cases, anticipated the accomplishments of their contemporaries in Rome and elsewhere in Europe to a remarkable degree.

In ecclesiastical architecture, the most characteristic examples of the Neapolitan Baroque style are those that combine simple ground plans with rich, varied decoration; for Neapolitan architects were accomplished at carrying out elaborate decorative schemes without bringing confusion to the overall form of their buildings. Consequently, the great churches of 16th- and 17th-century Naples show a lack of interest in new spatial forms that distinguishes them from the ecclesiastical architecture in Rome during the same period. It was not until the 18th century and the Rococo creations of Domenico Antonio Vaccaro and Ferdinando Sanfelice that Neapolitan church architects displayed inventiveness in planning.

In domestic architecture, the pressure of overcrowding caused Neapolitans to build higher than their counterparts in other Italian cities. This permitted them to move the *piano nobile*, the most sumptuous level of lordly palaces, from the first to the second floor and to introduce the vast, monumental doorways or *portes cochères* which, together with the magnificent external staircases, are the most striking and individual features of Neapolitan palaces.

In painting, the 17th century was dominated by the dark, dramatic styles of the Spaniard Jusepe Ribera (José de Ribera or Giuseppe Ribera) and of Caravaggio. The latter, exiled from Rome where he had killed a man in a moment of rage, and from Malta, where he had insulted the Grand Master of the Order of St John, took refuge in Naples until his involvement in a brawl in a waterfront tavern got him expelled from this city too. Ribera and another foreigner, Belisario Corenzio, born to a Greek family near Lecce, joined forces with the native Caracciolo in the 'Cabal of Naples' to prevent competition from the north. Using methods of intimidation characteristic of the *Mezzogiorno*—sabotage and the hired assassin—they hounded Annibale Carracci, the Cavaliere d'Arpino and Guido Reni from Naples, and Domenichino to his death (1641). After Caracciolo's death in the same year, and Ribera's in 1652, the soul of Naples found its most perfect expression in the exuberant compositions of Luca Giordano (*see p. 67*).

The first school of sculpture in Naples was founded in the 16th century with Girolamo Santacroce and Giovanni da Nola and their pupils, alongside whom worked the Florentines Michelangelo Naccherino and Pietro Bernini (the father of the great Gian Lorenzo). In the 17th century the fanciful Fanzago was prominent, followed in the 18th century by the disciples of Gian Lorenzo Bernini and the technicians of the Cappella Sansevero.

The Bourbons and the arts

The building projects undertaken during the reigns of Charles III and his successors changed the face of Naples. The architects who were most involved in these initiatives (which to a large extent gave the city the appearance that it has today) were Ferdinando Sanfelice, Domenico Antonio Vaccaro, Ferdinando Fuga and Luigi Vanvitelli.

Other art forms also played a major role in making Naples a truly European capital. Francesco Solimena (*see p. 126*) was the last and perhaps the greatest of the Neapolitan Baroque painters; Giuseppe Sammartino made hundreds of statuettes for the *presepi* that filled the churches and palaces of the city; and the Capodimonte Porcelain Works produced some of the finest porcelain in Europe.

EXPLORING NAPLES

This visit starts in the heart of the city, at the great Castel Nuovo on the waterfront. From here you cross the Piazza del Municipio and follow the broad, modern Via Medina and Via Monteoliveto, busy with traffic, to the former convent of Monteoliveto. The Calata Trinità Maggiore then curves up to the old city centre, which is entered from Piazza del Gesù. From here you proceed along the street popularly known as the Spaccanapoli (the *decumanus inferior* of Neapolis), which changes its modern name several times during its length, but never its straight and narrow course, crossing Via del Duomo (another modern thoroughfare) just south of the cathedral. This dark, crowded quarter gives you a feeling for medieval Naples. Here, in fact, are the major monuments of the Middle Ages: the great conventual complexes of Santa Chiara, San Domenico and San Gregorio Armeno, on the west side of the city centre; the Porta Capuana, the churches of San Giovanni a Carbonara and Santa Maria Donnaregina, and the cathedral, on the east. Many of the churches will be closed, but do not be discouraged: there are also many opportunities to look into doorways along the way to discover the magnificent interior courtyards and open staircases of Neopolitan patrician homes.

CASTEL NUOVO & THE ROUTE NORTH

Map p. 51, 11.

Above Naples harbour rises the royal residence of the Angevin kings, the Castel Nuovo, commonly—but less correctly—called the Maschio Angioino ('Angevin fortress'). Built for Charles I by Pierre de Chaulnes (1279–82), it was largely reconstructed under Alfonso of Aragon and rearranged by Ferdinand IV for use as the royal and viceregal residence. Now beautifully restored, it houses the offices and library of the Società Napoletana di Storia Patria, the Biblioteca Comunale Cuomo, and the meeting rooms of the city and regional councils, as well as a fine museum.

Among the events that have taken place here are the abdication of Pope Celestine V (*see p. 409*) and the mock marriage of Ferdinand I's grand-daughter to a son of Count Sarno, at which the king arrested Sarno and other barons who were conspiring against him. It was this same Ferdinand who is said to have exhibited the mummified bodies of his murdered opponents here at Castel Nuovo. Emperor Charles V stayed at the castle on his return from Tunis, and the republican revolt of Masaniello (*see p. 23*) was formally ended here in the pacts signed by the viceroy and the Prince of Massa Lubrense.

Detail from the mid-15th-century *Triumph of Alfonso* relief on the triumphal arch of Castel Nuovo.

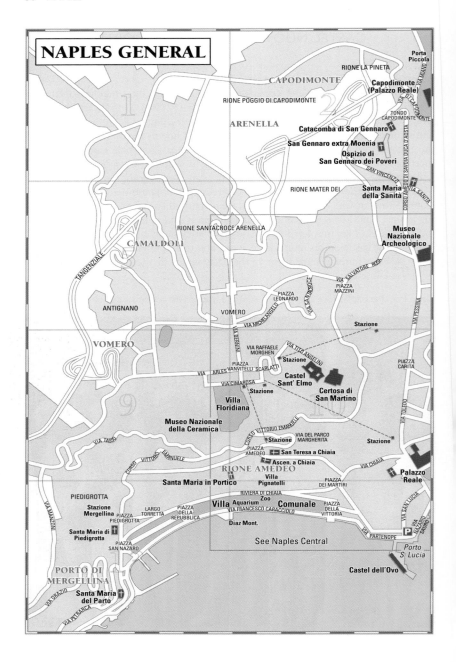

NAPLES GENERAL

Porta
Piccola

RIONE LA PINETA

CAPODIMONTE

**Capodimonte
(Palazzo Reale)**

RIONE POGGIO DI CAPODIMONTE

TONDO
CAPODIMONTE

ARENELLA

Catacomba di San Gennaro

San Gennaro extra Moenia

**Ospizio di
San Gennaro dei Poveri**

SAN VINCENZO

RIONE MATER DEI

**Santa Maria
della Sanità**

RIONE SANTACROCE ARENELLA

CAMALDOLI

**Museo
Nazionale
Archeologico**

TANGENZIALE

VIA SALVATORE ROSA

PIAZZA
MAZZINI

ANTIGNANO

PIAZZA
LEONARDO

VIA SANTACROCE

VIA PESSINA

VOMERO

VIA MICHELANGELO

Stazione

VOMERO

VIA BERNINI

VIA RAFFAELE
MORGHEN

VIA TITO ANGELINI

Stazione

PIAZZA
CARITA

PIAZZA
VANVITELLI SCARLATTI

**Castel
Sant' Elmo**

VIA ARLES

VIA CIMAROSA

Stazione

**Certosa di
San Martino**

Stazione

**Villa
Floridiana**

**Museo Nazionale
della Ceramica**

VIA TASSO

CORSO VITTORIO EMANUELE

VIA TOLEDO

VIA DEL PARCO
MARGHERITA

Stazione

CORSO VITTORIO EMANUELE

Stazione

PIAZZA
AMEDEO

San Teresa a Chiaia

Ascen. a Chiaia

RIONE AMEDEO

Santa Maria in Portico

**Villa
Pignatelli**

VIA CHIAIA

**Palazzo
Reale**

PIAZZA
DEI MARTIRI

PIEDIGROTTA

RIVIERA DI CHIAIA

Zoo

Villa Aquarium

Comunale

PIAZZA
DELLA
VITTORIA

**Stazione
Mergellina**

LARGO
TORRETTA

PIAZZA
PIEDIGROTTA

PIAZZA
DELLA
REPUBBLICA

VIA FRANCESCO CARACCIOLO

Diaz Mont.

VIA MARZIO

**Santa Maria di
Piedigrotta**

PIAZZA
SAN NAZARO

VIA PARTENOPE

VIA SAN LUCIA

See Naples Central

Porto
S. Lucia

PORTO DI
MERGELLINA

Castel dell'Ovo

VIA ORAZIO

**Santa Maria
del Parto**

VIA PETRARCA

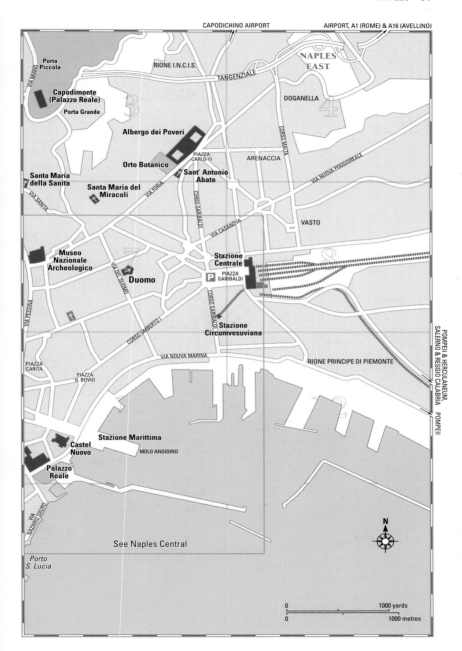

CAPODICHINO AIRPORT

AIRPORT, A1 (ROME) & A16 (AVELLINO)

NAPLES EAST

RIONE I.N.C.I.S.

TANGENZIALE

DOGANELLA

Porta Piccola

VIA MIANO

Capodimonte (Palazzo Reale)

Porta Grande

Albergo dei Poveri

PIAZZA CARLO III

ARENACCIA

CORSO MALTA

VIA NUOVA POGGIOREALE

Orto Botanico

Sant' Antonio Abate

Santa Maria della Sanita

VIA SANTA

Santa Maria del Miracoli

VIA FORIA

CORSO GARIBALDI

VIA CASANOVA

VASTO

Museo Nazionale Archeologico

VIA PESSINA

VIA DEL DUOMO

Duomo

Stazione Centrale

P PIAZZA GARIBALDI

CORSO GARIBALDI

Stazione Circumvesuviana

CORSO UMBERTO I

VIA NOUVA MARINA

RIONE PRINCIPE DI PIEMONTE

PIAZZA CARITA

PIAZZA G. BOVIO

Stazione Marittima

MOLO ANGIOINO

Castel Nuovo

Palazzo Reale

VIA NAZARIO SAURO

See Naples Central

Porto S. Lucia

POMPEII & HERCULANEUM,
SALERNO & REGGIO CALABRIA
POMPEII

N

0		1000 yards
0		1000 metres

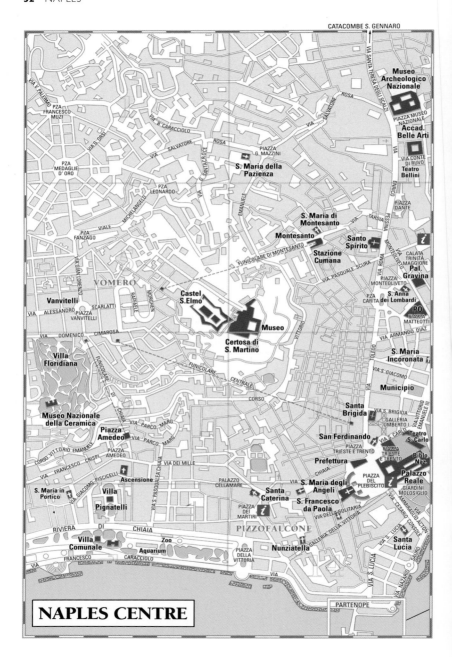

CATACOMBE S. GENNARO

Museo Archeologico Nazionale

Accad. Belle Arti

Teatro Bellini

S. Maria della Pazienza

PIAZZA MUSEO NAZIONALE

VIA CONTE DI RUVO

PIAZZA G. MAZZINI

PIAZZA DANTE

S. Maria di Montesanto

Montesanto

Santo Spirito

Stazione Cumana

CALATA TRINITA MAGGIORE

Pal. Gravina

S. Anna dei Lombardi

PZA CARITA

PO

PIAZZA MONTEOLIVETO

PZA MEDAGLIE D'ORO

PZA FRANCESCO MUZI

PZA LEONARDO

PZA FANZAGO

VOMERO

Vanvitelli

PIAZZA VANVITELLI

Castel S.Elmo

Museo

Certosa di S. Martino

S. Maria Incoronata

Municipio

Villa Floridiana

Santa Brigida

GALLERIA UMBERTO I

San Ferdinando

Teatro S. Carlo

Museo Nazionale della Ceramica

Piazza Amedeo

PIAZZA AMEDEO

Prefettura

Biblo. Naz.

Palazzo Reale

GIARDINI MOLOSIGLIO

Ascensione

S. Maria in Portico

Villa Pignatelli

PALAZZO CELLAMARE

Santa Caterina

S. Maria degli Angeli

S. Francesco da Paola

PIAZZA DEL PLEBISCITO

RIVIERA DI CHIAIA

PIAZZA DEI MARTIRI

PIZZOFALCONE

Santa Lucia

Villa Comunale

Zoo

Aquarium

PIAZZA DELLA VITTORIA

Nunziatella

PARTENOPE

NAPLES CENTRE

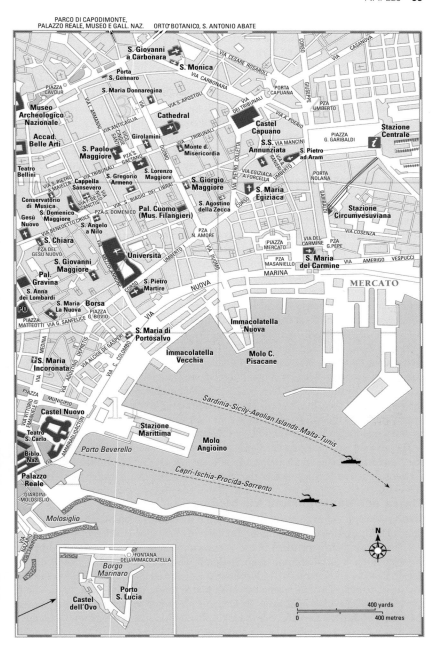

PARCO DI CAPODIMONTE,
PALAZZO REALE, MUSEO E GALL. NAZ.   ORTO BOTANICO, S. ANTONIO ABATE

S. Giovanni
a Carbonara

S. Monica

Porta
S. Gennaro

VIA CESARE ROSAROLL

VIA CARBONARA

CORSO

VIA CASANOVA

VIA

S. Maria Donnaregina

PIAZZA
CAVOUR

Museo
Archeologico
Nazionale

Accad.
Belle Arti

S. Paolo
Maggiore

Teatro
Bellini

Cappella
Sansevero

Conservatorio
di Musica

Gesù
Nuovo

S. Domenico
Maggiore

S. Angelo
a Nilo

S. Chiara

PZA DEL
GESÙ NUOVO

S. Giovanni
Maggiore

Pal.
Gravina

S. Anna
dei Lombardi

P.O.

PIAZZA
MATTEOTTI

VIA ANTICAGLIA

Cathedral

Girolamini

DUOMO

VIA A.POSTOLI

VIA DEI TRIBUNALI

TRIBUNALI

Monte d.
Misericordia

S. Lorenzo
Maggiore

S. Gregorio
Armeno

VIA DEI TRIBUNALI

VIA S. PIETRO
A MAIELLA

VIA S. GREGORIO

VIA DE SANCTIS

PZA S. GAETANO

VIA S. BIAGIO DEI LIBRAI

PZA S. DOMENICO

VIA BENEDETTO CROCE

Pal. Cuomo
(Mus. Filangieri)

S. Giorgio
Maggiore

S. Agostino
della Zecca

PZA
N. AMORE

Castel
Capuano

PORTA
CAPUANA

S.S.
Annunziata

VIA MANCINI

S. Pietro
ad Aram

S. Maria
Egiziaca

GIUSEPPE

PZA
UMBERTO

VIA A. POERIO

PIAZZA
G. GARIBALDI

PORTA
NOLANA

GARIBALDI

CORSO

VIA EGIZIACA
A FORCELLA

UMBERTO

VIA PIETRO COLLETTA

Stazione
Centrale

i

Stazione
Circumvesuviana

VIA COSENZA

PIAZZA
MERCATO

PZA
MASANIELLO

MARINA

VIA DEL
CARMINE

PZA
G.PEPE

S. Maria
del Carmine

VIA AMERIGO VESPUCCI

MERCATO

Università

S. Pietro
Martire

UMBERTO

VIA DUOMO

NUOVA

VIA

MEZZOCANNONE

CORSO

Borsa

S. Maria
La Nuova

PIAZZA
G. BOVIO

VIA G. SANFELICE

S. Maria di
Portosalvo

Immacolatella
Nuova

Immacolatella
Vecchia

Molo C.
Pisacane

S. Maria
Incoronata

VIA ALCIDE DE GASPERI

VIA AGOSTINO DEPRETIS

VIA C. COLOMBO

PIAZZA
MUNICIPIO

MEDINA

Castel Nuovo

Teatro
S. Carlo

Biblio.
Naz.

Palazzo
Reale

GIARDINI
MOLOSIGLIO

VIA VITTORIO
EMANUELE III

VIA

VIA AMMIRAGLIACOTON

Stazione
Marittima

Porto Beverello

Molo
Angioino

Sardinia-Sicily-Aeolian Islands-Malta-Tunis

Capri-Ischia-Procida-Sorrento

Molosiglio

VIA NAZARIO

FONTANA
DELL'IMMACOLATELLA

Borgo
Marinaro

Porto
S. Lucia

Castel
dell'Ovo

N

| 0 | | 400 yards |
| 0 | | 400 metres |

Fronting the square across the dry moat is the long north wall between two massive 15th-century towers, the Torre del Beverello at the seaward end and the Torre di San Giorgio. Beyond this is the impressive main façade, which you enter between two further towers, under the famous triumphal arch, erected between 1454 and 1467 to commemorate the entry of Alfonso I into Naples (1443). This masterpiece of the Italian Renaissance was probably inspired by the celebrated Porta Capuana of Frederick II (*see p. 71 below*). However, it differs in that it is not free-standing, but adapted to serve as the entrance to the castle. In this sense it is unique among the architectural inventions of its day, having no parallel in Tuscany or Lombardy. Many prominent sculptors, including Domenico Gagini, Isaia da Pisa and Francesco Laurana, were brought to Naples to assist in its decoration. The large bas-relief shows the *Triumph of Alfonso*. Above the second arch stand the four Cardinal Virtues (Prudence, Justice, Temperance and Fortitude), followed by two large river gods and, topping the whole, St Michael.

The focal point of the **Museo Civico di Castel Nuovo** (*open Mon–Sat 9–7; May and Dec also Sun 9–7; T: 081 795 5877*) is the Cappella Palatina or Church of Santa Barbara, the only interior to survive intact from the Angevin period. It has a delicate Renaissance door surmounted by a *Madonna* by Francesco Laurana. The interior holds 14th- and 15th-century sculptures, some by Domenico Gagini and Francesco Laurana from the triumphal arch of Alfonso I; detached frescoes by the Florentine painter Niccolò di Tommaso, and others from the destroyed castle of Casaluce. There is also an extensive collection of 15th–19th-century painting (including undistinguished works by Battistello Caracciolo and Francesco Solimena), and silver and bronze objects. The chapel is lit by a large rose window of Catalan (Aragonese) design and by tall Gothic windows, the splays of which contain frescoes attributed to Maso di Banco. The adjacent Sala dei Baroni, a large (26m by 28m) hall damaged by fire in 1919, is now the meeting place of the City Council. The door next to the entrance leads to the viceregal apartments, which occupy the north side of the castle; on the wall opposite there is a monumental fireplace and choir lofts of Catalan workmanship.

The seaward side of the castle affords an impressive view of the huge bastions, with the Torre del Beverello on the right and the Torre dell' Oro set back to the left; between them rises the restored east end of the chapel, flanked by two polygonal turrets.

Piazza del Municipio and Via Medina

The long Piazza del Municipio, with a central monument commemorating Vittorio Emanuele II, overlooks the harbour. On the west side stands Palazzo San Giacomo (1819–25), the Bourbon Palace of the Ministers and now the town hall, incorporating the church of **San Giacomo degli Spagnoli**. The latter, founded by Don Pedro de Toledo in 1514 and rebuilt in 1741, follows a Latin-cross plan. The first chapel in the south aisle contains a *Madonna and Child* by Marco Pino. Above the altar in the south transept is a *Martyrdom of St James* by Domenico Antonio Vaccaro, who also painted the *Dead Christ* in the frontal above the main altar. In the apse the tomb of the founder can be seen, executed in his lifetime by Giovanni da Nola.

Via Medina leads north past (left) the Gothic doorway of **Santa Maria Incoronata**, a church built and named by Joan I (1352) to commemorate her coronation of 1351 and embodying the chapel of the old Vicaria, where she had married Louis of Taranto, her second husband, in 1345. The interior has kept its original form. In the vault are remarkable frescoes of the seven sacraments and the *Triumph of the Church* by the Neapolitan pupil of Giotto, Roberto d'Oderisio (c. 1370); the Cappella del Crocifisso contains other frescoes of similar date. The street rises gently between huge new buildings to an important crossroads: Via Sanfelice leads right to Piazza Bovio; Via Diaz, realigned since 1945, leads left, opening almost at once into Piazza Matteotti, the focal point of Naples' business district. Its north side is dominated by the Post Office, a vast but handsome edifice in marble and glass (1936).

Via Monteoliveto

The church of **Santa Maria la Nova** (*map p. 53, 7*), built by Charles I for Franciscans expelled from the site of Castel Nuovo (1279), was redesigned by Agnolo Franco in the 16th century. The façade is a fine Renaissance work. The aisleless nave has a richly painted ceiling incorporating works by Fabrizio Santafede, Francesco Curia and others. The first chapel on the south side contains a *St Michael* by Marco Pino. The angels on the dome are by Battistello Caracciolo. The second chapel on the north side (dedicated to St James of the Marches) was built by the first Spanish viceroy, Gonzalo de Córdoba, in 1504. It contains the tomb of Marshal Lautrec (who died of the plague in 1528 while besieging Naples; *see p. 37*) by Annibale Caccavello, and statues by Giovanni Domenico d'Auria. In the transept is a wooden *Crucifixion* by Giovanni da Nola. The high altar, which combines complex and unusual architectural members with fine floral inlay, is one of the most important works of the Baroque master Cosimo Fanzago, whose vibrantly imaginative works are scattered across Naples. The two cloisters contain 15th-century tombs and later frescoes.

Behind the post office, in Via Monteoliveto, is the **cloister of Monteoliveto** (*the church is described below*). The double order of arcades, built to compensate for the sloping land (monks entering the cloister from the church emerged on the upper level), opens directly onto the street, a reminder that the convent was once surrounded by gardens. In 1588 the poet Torquato Tasso took refuge from the (real or imagined) persecution of Alfonso d'Este in the former Olivetan monastery. On the opposite side of the street, a bit further on, is Palazzo Gravina, a beautiful Renaissance building in the purest Tuscan style, by Gabriele d'Agnolo and Giovanni Francesco Mormanno (1513–49), spoilt by the addition of a storey in 1839. It now houses the university's Faculty of Architecture.

The **church of Sant'Anna dei Lombardi**, known also as Monteoliveto (*map p. 53, 7*), stands in the piazza of that name, fronted by a Baroque fountain. Begun in 1411, the church contains a wealth of Renaissance sculpture, mostly undamaged in spite of a direct bomb hit in March 1944. It is an excellent place to see the work of Naples' 16th-century school of sculpture, which flourished under Giovanni da Nola and Girolamo Santacroce. The façade, shorn of its 18th-century additions, has been reconstructed in its original style. The vestibule contains the tomb (1627) of Domenico Fontana, architect to Pope Sixtus V. Inside, on either side of the entrance, are marble altars, by Giovanni da Nola (right) and Girolamo Santacroce. On the south side, the first chapel (Cappella Mastrogiudice) contains an *Annunciation* and other sculptures by Benedetto da Maiano (1489) and the tomb of Marino Curiale (1490), in a similar style. The third chapel has an altar attributed to Giovanni da Nola. Beyond the fifth chapel a passage leads to the Chapel of the Holy Sepulchre, with a terracotta *Pietà* by Guido Mazzoni (1492); the eight life-size figures are said to be portraits of the artist's contemporaries. A corridor on the right leads to the Old Sacristy, which is frescoed by Giorgio Vasari and contains fine intarsia stalls by Giovanni da Verona (1510).

The apse contains 16th-century stalls and the tombs of Alfonso II (d. 1495), by Giovanni da Nola, and of Guerello Origlia, founder of the church. The sixth chapel on the north side was designed by Giuliano da Maiano; it also contains some repainted 16th-century frescoes. In the fifth chapel are a *St John the Baptist* by Giovanni da Nola and a *Pietà* by Girolamo Santacroce. The third chapel has a *Flagellation* (1576) in marble relief, and the first chapel an *Ascension* (on wood) by Riccardo Quartararo (c. 1492). From here entrance is gained to the Piccolomini Chapel, with a charming *Nativity* (c. 1475) by Antonio Rossellino, one of the several celebrated Florentine sculptors who worked for the Angevins of Naples. The beautiful tomb of Mary of Aragon (d. 1470), daughter of Ferdinand I, was begun by Rossellino and finished by Benedetto da Maiano.

The Gesù Nuovo

Map p. 53, 7.

Calata Trinità Maggiore climbs to the right, past the Baroque church and square of the Gesù Nuovo. In the centre of the square stands the Guglia dell' Immacolata, a fanciful Baroque column (1747–50) typical of Neapolitan taste. *Guglie* are neighbourhood ex-votos: this one was erected for deliverance from an epidemic. Its ornateness is emphasised by the severe west front of the church of the Gesù Nuovo (also called Trinità Maggiore), built between 1584 and 1601. This church is a conversion of a Renaissance palace (by Novello da San Lucano, 1470), purchased by the Jesuits from Roberto Sanseverino, Duke of Salerno. The aggressively diamond-rusticated stone façade, once a wall of the palazzo, is pierced by three sculptured doorways. Those on the sides date from the 16th century, the central doorway from 1685.

The rich interior (1601–31), ornate with coloured marbles, has frescoes by the Baroque painters Corenzio, Stanzione and Ribera. That of *Heliodorus Driven from the Temple*, above the entrance, is by Francesco Solimena (1725). The original design of the interior, by Giuseppe Valeriano, one of the distinguished architects working in Naples at the end of the 16th century, was much more severe, featuring white plaster walls and a discreet use of coloured marble and black *piperno*. A highly original design, it differs considerably from the Gesù in Rome, which served as the model for many Jesuit churches of the day. Its centralised plan and the flat, continuous wall surface, which defines the space with maximum clarity, are still visible beneath the beautiful decoration of inlaid coloured marbles. Cosimo Fanzago, the inventor of the decoration,

Diamond rustication on the façade of the palazzo-turned-church of the Gesù Nuovo, formerly a residence of the Sanseverino family.

seems to have gone to great lengths to respect the intrinsic qualities of the spatial plan. The original dome was damaged by an earthquake in 1688 and replaced by the present structure in 1744. Another casualty of the earthquake was the tomb of the musician and murdered Carlo Gesualdo (d. 1613); he is commemorated by a plaque.

Santa Chiara

Map p. 53, 7.

At the far end of Piazza Gesù Nuovo is the great church and Franciscan convent of Santa Chiara, built in 1310–28 for Queen Sancha, second wife of Robert the Wise, who died here a nun. The church was completely burnt out by incendiary bombs on 4th August 1943, when the magnificent Baroque interior of 1742–57 was destroyed and most of the large monuments wrecked. The reconstruction has preserved the original Provençal-Gothic austerity, a quality so foreign to Naples as to be all the more striking. The Gothic west porch was undamaged.

The aisleless interior, the largest in Naples, has an open roof 45m high and tasteful modern glass in the lancet windows. Of the glorious series of Angevin royal monuments, the principal survivals are the lower portions of the tombs of Robert the Wise (d. 1343), the work of the Florentine brothers Giovanni and Pacio Bertini (behind the high altar) and of his son Charles, Duke of Calabria (father of Joan I), by Tino da Camaino and his followers (to the right). Also undamaged is the beautiful monument (1399) to Charles' youngest daughter, Mary (to the left). Every chapel has some tomb or Gothic sculpture that merits a glance. It was in this church that Joan I was crowned, and here that her remains lie buried (*see box overleaf*).

Joan I of Anjou, Queen of Naples (1326–82)

This most unfortunate sovereign should have been the subject of a Shakespearean tragedy. Joan was the daughter of Charles, Duke of Calabria, son and heir of Robert the Wise, and his wife Marie de Valois. Following the early death of her father, she inherited the Kingdom of Naples and the County of Provence, succeeding her grandfather in 1343. Two years previously she had married her cousin Andrew, younger brother of King Louis the Great of Hungary. The union, planned since Joan was seven (and Andrew six), had been the wish of Andrew's father, Charles Robert, Angevin King of Hungary, as a way of uniting the Hungarian and Neapolitan branches of the Anjou family. The power axis that an alliance between both Angevin houses would create held little appeal for either pope or Holy Roman Emperor. And the assertiveness of the Hungarians who followed Andrew to Naples (particularly that of Andrew's mother, Elisabeth of Poland, a domineering woman who ruled the lives of all her sons, and who worked ceaselessly to wrest power from her daughter-in-law) antagonised Queen Joan. It had after all been specified in her late grandfather's will that she would be sole sovereign of the kingdom. When Andrew was murdered following a hunting party at Aversa castle on 28th August 1345, suspicion

at once fell on Joan. She had been present in the room when Andrew was dragged from his bed and strangled. Though she had apparently done nothing to prevent the killing, there was no firm evidence against her, and she was able to appease her accusers by executing the servant who had actually done the deed, and by imprisoning the ringleaders of the conspiracy in the Castel dell'Ovo.

After enjoying a love affair with Robert of Taranto, another cousin, in 1347, she married his younger brother Louis, an arrogant, violent man who humiliated and probably beat her (he was detested by Petrarch and Boccaccio). In the years that followed, the new king of Hungary, Louis the Great, invaded the kingdom twice to avenge Andrew's assassination

Queen Joan in her Angevin fleur-de-lys gown, depicted as a donor. Church of the Certosa di San Giacomo, Capri.

and seize the throne of Naples in his name, but Joan fled to Provence, where she agreed to sell the city of Avignon to the papacy on the condition that she be acquitted of Andrew's murder. Armed with a formal certificate of innocence and the blessing of Pope Innocent VI, in 1352 Joan made peace with King Louis and returned permanently to Naples.

Louis of Taranto died in 1362 and his brothers, Robert and Philip, fearing Joan might marry their arch enemy, Louis of Durazzo (the brother of her sister's husband Charles), had the Duke of Durazzo poisoned; his five-year old son, Charles, was spared only thanks to the intervention of Queen Joan, who nursed a lifelong passion for the youth, a love that was never to be requited.

In 1363 the queen, now thirty-seven, married James III of Majorca, a madman who had spent the previous twelve years in an iron cage as a prisoner of Peter IV of Aragon. Perhaps fearing for his life after failing to give Joan the heir she needed (the queen delivered a still-born child in the summer of 1365), he abandoned Naples in 1366, remaining outside the kingdom until his death in 1375. Meanwhile, with the consent of Pope Gregory XI, Joan settled an age-old dispute between the Angevins and the Aragonese by acknowledging Frederick III of Aragon (to whom she had betrothed a niece) as legitimate king of Sicily.

Widowed again in 1375, she married the military adventurer Otto of Brunswick-Grubenhagen and later recognised as her heir to the throne Louis, Duke of Anjou, brother of the French king Charles V. However, Charles of Durazzo, whom Joan had previously recognised as her heir, with the aid of Pope Urban VI (who crowned him King Charles III of Naples in Rome in 1381 in retaliation for Joan's recognition of the antipope Clement VII at Avignon) checked her move by invading the kingdom in June 1381. Joan overestimated the ability of her husband, Otto, to keep Charles' army at bay while Louis of Anjou brought reinforcements from France. Otto was defeated and captured on 25th August 1381; the queen surrendered the next day and was taken prisoner, first to Castel dell'Ovo, then to Nocera and finally to the remote castle of Muro Lucano, in Basilicata.

When Louis of Anjou finally set out from the Languedoc to take back his new kingdom (13th June 1382), Charles, fearing that Joan might be freed, had the woman who had saved his life twenty years earlier suffocated between two pillows. He then ordered that her body be brought to Naples and laid in state in Santa Chiara, by the tomb of her grandfather Robert, to give the impression of a natural death. The schismatic queen was denied a Christian burial; today her remains lie, unmarked, in an ossuary beneath the church floor. Charles himself, an unpopular successor to the Hungarian throne in 1385, was murdered in Visegrád the following year, victim of a plot by supporters of his rival claimant, the daughter of Louis the Great, and thus the niece of Prince Andrew, unjustly murdered all those years before.

The conventual buildings of Santa Chiara (*open Mon–Sat 9.30–5.30 or 6.30, Sun and holidays 9.30–1.30; T: 081 797 1256*) are reached by walking between the north side of the church and the detached campanile (not finished until 1647), passing through the first court and turning right. The parts seen include a particularly fine 18th-century Nativity crib and the huge 14th-century cloister, transformed in 1742 by Domenico Antonio Vaccaro into a rustic garden adorned with majolica tiles and terracottas. The austere friars' refectory, with a charming fountain in the centre, lies off the east side. The Museo dell'Opera di Santa Chiara traces the history of the complex.

SAN DOMENICO MAGGIORE & ITS NEIGHBOURHOOD

Map p. 53, 7.

Via Benedetto Croce marks the beginning of the **Spaccanapoli**, the street that 'splits Naples', whose decayed medieval and Renaissance palaces make it the most characteristic of old Neapolitan streets. Beyond the house (plaque) where the eminent philosopher Benedetto Croce (*see p. 398*) spent his last years, is Piazza San Domenico, with the Baroque Guglia di San Domenico (1737), enclosed by 16th-century mansions. **San Domenico Maggiore**, a noble Gothic church built in 1289–1324, rebuilt after earthquake and fire damage (1465 and 1506) and much altered since, is reached by a staircase on the left. This was the church of the Aragonese nobility. Its Renaissance sculpture and monuments, commissioned by the Spanish dynasty from leading artists of the day, include some of the finest expressions of the Tuscan manner in Naples.

The interior, with aisles and transepts, is 76m long. Walk the length of the nave, to the main (west) door. In the south aisle, on the right of the entrance, is the Cappella Saluzzo, with decorated Renaissance arches (1512–16) and the monument to Galeotto Carafa (1507–15), all the work of Romolo di Antonio da Settignano. The tomb of Archbishop Brancaccio (d. 1341) in the second chapel is by a Tuscan follower of Tino da Camaino. The next chapel on this side has frescoes attributed to Pietro Cavallini, the 14th-century Roman artist, in a style resembling that of Giotto. The seventh chapel leads to the Cappellone del Crocifisso. Here is the little painting of the *Crucifixion* that is said to have spoken to St Thomas Aquinas when he was living in the adjacent monastery in 1273. The event was the saint's greatest revelation. After the voice had spoken, he brought his theological writings to an end and began to prepare himself for the reward that the icon had promised: union with his Maker. He died five months afterwards. To the left stands the fine tomb of Francesco Carafa (d. 1470), by Tommaso Malvito, and behind is a side-chapel (1511) with other family tombs and frescoes by Bramantino. From the eighth chapel you enter the sacristy, the ceiling of which hosts a brightly coloured fresco by Francesco Solimena. Above the presses are the coffins of ten princes of Aragon and 35 other illustrious persons, including the Marquis of Pescara (d. 1525), leader of the forces of Holy Roman Emperor Charles V against the French king Francis I at the Battle of Pavia.

The south transept contains the tomb of Galeazzo Pandone (1514), a fine work probably by a Tuscan artist; above this is the tomb slab of John of Durazzo (d. 1335), youngest son of Charles II and brother of Robert the Wise, by Tino da Camaino. Perhaps the best of the tombs in the *chiesa antica* (Sant'Angelo a Morfisa) is that of Tommaso Brancaccio by Jacopo della Pila (1492); note also that of Porzia, wife of Bernardino Rota, by Annibale Caccavello and Giovanni Domenico d'Auria (1559), in the vestibule. The beautiful altar and recessed seats at either side of the choir are adorned with inlaid marbles by Cosimo Fanzago (1646); the paschal candlestick (1585) is supported by nine sculptured figures from a tomb by Tino da Camaino.

The first chapel in the north transept contains a contemporary copy, by Andrea Vaccaro, of the *Flagellation* by Caravaggio (1607); the original, formerly on the opposite wall, is now at Capodimonte. The second chapel houses the Spinelli monument (1546) by Bernardo del Moro. The north aisle chapels have many good 15th–17th-century tombs, including that of the poet G.B. Marino (d. 1625) in the eighth, where there is a lovely sculptural group by Giovanni da Nola. A *St John the Baptist* by the same artist and two paintings by Mattia Preti (above) hang in the fourth chapel. A *Crowning of St Joseph* by Luca Giordano adorns the end chapel.

Cappella Sansevero

The neighbourhood is dominated by the palaces of the Sangro family, one of the most ancient Neapolitan patrician dynasties. In Piazza San Domenico Maggiore, at no. 3, is the Palazzo del Balzo, built in the early 15th century and renovated after the earthquake of 1688; the marble doorway and the courtyard belong to the original building. The low arches of the courtyard, as well as its elegant first-floor portico, are elements typical of the Catalan architectural style that was brought to Naples by the Aragonese rulers.

To the right, at no. 17, is an 18th-century palace of the Sangro family designed by Mario Gioffredo and remodelled by Luigi Vanvitelli. The impressive portico is carried by ancient Greek columns unearthed during the construction of the building.

Number 9 is the Neapolitan residence of the main line of the family, dukes of Torremaggiore and princes of Sansevero. It was here, in 1590, that Carlo Gesualdo, the great composer of madrigals, brutally murdered his wife and her lover, and his own infant son. The palace was built in the early 16th century and later enlarged. The magnificent portal was made by Vitale Finelli, to a design by Bartolomeo Picchiatti (1621). The stucco bas-reliefs of the entry foyer were executed by Giuseppe Sammartino, when the palace belonged to Raimondo di Sangro, Prince of Sansevero (1710–71), soldier, amateur chemist, engineer and inventor of a number of wonders, including a prototype colour printer and a type of waterproof cloth. It was Raimondo di Sangro who transformed the Cappella Sansevero into its present form.

The **Cappella Sansevero** (Cappella di Santa Maria della Pietà dei Sangro, 1590), the tomb-chapel of the princes of Sangro di Sansevero (*open as a museum, daily except Tues, 10–2.40, Sun and holidays 10–1.10; T: 081 551 8470*), stands in Via de Sanctis. It is remarkable for its 18th-century interior decoration, a profusion of frescoes, marbles and statuary (*see box overleaf*).

THE CAPPELLA SANSEVERO

The impression made on the visitor by the interior of this inconspicuous chapel is hard to forget. Its rich decoration comprises an extraordinary mixture of Masonic symbolism; one of the most arresting groups of virtuoso sculpture in Italy; and some bizarre alchemical memorabilia of the family's most eccentric scion, Raimondo di Sangro. Built in the late 16th century as a votive chapel enshrining a miraculous fresco (now above the altar) and dedicated to Santa Maria della Pietà, it was soon adopted as a private memorial chapel by the Sangro family, princes of Sansevero, whose origins go back allegedly to 10th-century France. What the visitor sees today is mostly the mid-18th-century transformation of the chapel by Raimondo di Sangro (1710–71), who wished to leave in the building an unforgettable memorial not only to his own immediate family but also to the esoteric learning which he had accumulated during his lifetime. Orphaned of a mother who died prematurely and of an eccentric father who subsequently retreated into monastic life in atonement for the lassitude of his early years, Raimondo grew up with his grandfather and devoted his privileged existence and wealth to the pursuit of science and esoteric knowledge— something which brought him more than once into conflict with the Church authorities, culminating in an excommunication by Pope Benedict XIV in 1751. Raimondo was at the time Grand Master of the Masonic Lodge of Naples.

Of the chapel's dense and allusive decoration, a number of sculptures and features stand out in particular. Above the entrance door is the remarkable monument to Don Francesco ('Cecco') di Sangro, who is seen (following the tale of a legendary episode of his military life) climbing purposefully out of a sarcophagus, with one leg swung over its side, and his whole body in a position which has been interpreted by some as tracing the form of the Masonic symbol for lead. This is the work of Francesco Celebrano (1766). To either side of the main altar are two works commissioned by Raimondo di Sangro: first (on the left side), the statue of *Veiled Modesty* (1751) by Antonio Corradini is in memory of his mother, Cecilia Gaetani d'Arragona, who died at the age of 23 (hence the broken stone tablet at her side); the second (right side) is in memory of his father, Antonio di Sangro, and is an allegory of the *Liberation from Illusion* (1752) by Francesco Queirolo, in which a nude male figure is seen breaking free from a heavy rope net, aided by a winged youth symbolising intelligence. The human figures and their poses are not in themselves remarkable, but the subtlety with which the diaphanous veil clinging to the female figure, and the dense netting covering the male figure, are achieved in the intractable medium of marble is astonishing. Most dramatic in its technical virtuosity is the centrepiece of the whole ensemble: the supine figure of the *Dead Christ* by Giuseppe Sammartino (1753), once intended to be placed in the crypt below, but now in the centre of the chapel. The sculptor was in his early 30s when he received the commission for this *tour de force* of his career: the piece was later intently admired and coveted by Antonio Canova. The effect of the damp shroud delicately covering and yet revealing every detail of the Saviour's body (even down to the impressions of the stigmata) has few parallels for technical bravura in the history of sculpture: it acquires further depth when seen (as was originally intended) by low, raking lantern light. Masonic symbolism plays much on what is 'veiled' and what is 'revealed', and the piece in this respect is cognate with Corradini's *Veiled Modesty*.

Dead Christ by Giuseppe Sammartino (1753).

Although the *Dead Christ* was probably achieved through minute observation of a model and was facilitated by the use of an unusually soft alabastrine marble, some accounts fancifully maintain that the artist prepared a marble sculpture of the body alone; this was then covered with a sheet of natural tissue which Raimondo di Sangro petrified by an obscure alchemical process known only to himself. Further evidence of these occult processes may also be found in the chapel's crypt, where two shocking human cadavers can be seen, illustrating perfectly the complete vascular, renal and digestive systems of the human body. By some little understood process, Raimondo appears to have embalmed or 'petrified' these human *interiora*—down to the minutest capillary—in a perfect absence of any remains of bodily flesh or bone. It is not known whether this process was achieved before or after the death of the subjects.   N.McG.

San Pietro a Maiella and the Conservatorio

Map p. 53, 7.

The church of San Pietro a Maiella was built in 1313–16. It contains a magnificent series of paintings by Mattia Preti (1656–61) depicting the life of Celestine V and the legend of St Catherine of Alexandria. Adjoining the church, in the former convent of San Pietro, is the Conservatorio di Musica San Pietro a Maiella. The oldest music school in existence, it was founded in 1537 and moved here in 1826. The Conservatorio evolved from the gradual merging of four institutions established in the 16th and 17th centuries as homes for foundlings. Catechism and singing were taught in all four. Later on, when the private donations that were their only source of income dwindled or ceased altogether, the young musicians began to offer their services in churches, theatres and private *palazzi*. In time, the Conservatorio produced singers, instrumentalists, virtuosi and composers, the demand for which was insatiable. Domenico Cimarosa, Nicola Antonio Porpora, Giovanni Paisiello, Domenico and Alessandro Scarlatti, and Giovanni Battista Pergolesi all graduated from the Conservatorio di Musica San Pietro a Maiella and its illustrious predecessors. The library has an extraordinary collection of autograph manuscripts, and the museum has portraits of eminent musicians and memorabilia such as Martucci's piano and Rossini's desk. Both are opened on request.

Via San Pietro a Maiella passes under Port'Alba to Piazza Dante just west of the Conservatorio. The difference in atmosphere is remarkable as you leave the narrow, dark lanes of the medieval centre and enter the wide, luminous avenues of the Bourbon city.

Sant'Angelo a Nilo

East of San Domenico Maggiore the Spaccanapoli changes its name to Via San Biagio ai Librai. The little church of **Sant'Angelo a Nilo**, on the southeast corner of the street, has a fine Renaissance doorway. It contains the tomb of Cardinal Rinaldo Brancaccio, the first Renaissance sculpture to be brought to Naples (in 1428). The tomb was executed in Pisa and sent by ship. The architectural framework, the Classical detail of which represents a clean break with Angevin Gothic style, is designed by Michelozzo; the relief of the *Assumption* is by Donatello.

Keeping straight on, you pass (left) an antique statue of the Nile. Also in this street are the former Palazzo Carafa, birthplace of Pope Paul IV, and (right; no. 121) the Palazzo Santangelo (1466), an elegant town house in the Tuscan style.

San Gregorio Armeno

A little to the north lies San Gregorio Armeno, a Benedictine convent, whose charming cloister, an oasis of tranquillity in contrast with the noise of the streets outside, is over-looked by the 17th-century campanile and a tiled cupola. At the centre of the garden is a Baroque glorification of the Well of Samaria, carved by Matteo Bottiglieri in 1730, with figures of Jesus and the Samaritan woman which from a distance appear to be walking among the orange trees. The church has a fine gilded ceiling of 1582, a gilded bronze *comunichino* (1610), and frescoes by Luca Giordano of the life of St Gregory.

The nuns here were traditionally the daughters of noble families, accustomed to a life of luxury that they could hardly be expected to renounce. An 18th-century English traveller provides an account of a royal visit to the convent, and of the somewhat unusual conventual cuisine:

'The company was surprised, on being led into a large parlour, to find a table covered, and every appearance of a most plentiful cold repast, consisting of several joints of meat, hams, fowl, fish and various other dishes. It seemed rather ill-judged to have prepared a feast of such a solid nature immediately after dinner; for those royal visits were made in the afternoon. The Lady Abbess, however, earnestly pressed their Majesties to sit down; with which they complied ... The nuns stood behind, to serve their royal guests. The Queen chose a slice of cold turkey, which, on being cut up, turned out [to be] a large piece of lemon ice, of the shape and appearance of a roasted turkey. All the other dishes were ices of various kinds, disguised under the forms of joints of meat, fish, and fowl, as above mentioned. The gaiety and good humour of the King, the affable and engaging behaviour of the royal sisters (Queen Maria Carolina and the Princess of Saxe-Teschen), and the satisfaction which beamed from the plump countenance of the Lady Abbess, threw an air of cheerfulness on this scene; which was interrupted, however, by gleams of melancholy reflection, which failed not to dart to mind, at the sight of so many victims to the pride of family, to avarice and superstition. Many of those victims were in the full bloom of health and youth, and some of them were remarkably handsome'.

Via San Gregorio is famous for its craftsmen, called *pastorari*, who make the figures for Neapolitan Nativity scenes, or *presepi*. Several shops also specialise in making elaborate bouquets of silk flowers, a tradition that dates back to the 18th century.

SAN LORENZO MAGGIORE & DISTRICT

Map p. 53, 3.

The Franciscan church of San Lorenzo Maggiore is one of Naples' most important religious buildings, built over the Roman basilica of Neapolis; its form corresponds almost perfectly to that of the ancient apsidal hall. Its builders used the massive walls of the existing edifice as the foundation for their own building—a common practice in the Middle Ages. The great medieval church that stands today was begun by Charles I of Anjou to commemorate the victory over Manfred of Hohenstaufen at Benevento in 1266, and completed by his son, Charles II. Here, on Easter Eve, 1334, Boccaccio first saw Maria, natural daughter of Robert the Wise, whom he immortalised as Fiammetta in his *Elegia a Madonna Fiammetta*. There is a fine doorway of 1325 in the 18th-century façade.

Inside, the nave has been patiently restored to its original Gothic simplicity, which is echoed in the transepts and the apse, designed by an unknown French architect of the late 13th century. The apse has nine radiating chapels; the high altar is by Giovanni da Nola. There are two chapels of inlaid coloured marbles by Cosimo Fanzago—the third chapel on the right, the Cappella Cacace (1643–55), and the magnificent, bold Cappellone di Sant'Antonio (c. 1638), in the left transept—and a number of good medieval tombs, notably that of Catherine of Austria (d. 1323), first wife of Charles, Duke of Calabria, possibly by Tino da Camaino. In the chapels are two large canvases by Mattia Preti: a *Crucifixion with St Francis and Franciscan Saints*, and a *Madonna and Child with St Clare and Franciscan Saints*. A 15th-century doorway to the left of the campanile (1507) leads to the cloister, where Petrarch experienced a storm in 1345. The chapter house is supported on Roman columns. Archaeological excavations beneath the cloisters (*open Mon–Sat 9–5, Sun and holidays 10–1.30; T: 081 211 0860*) have unearthed traces of Greek, Roman and early medieval buildings. Especially interesting are the remains of a Roman street flanked by shops.

San Paolo Maggiore

This 16th-century church stands on the site of a Roman temple dedicated to the Dioscuri—Zeus' twin sons Castor and Pollux, who were reunited after Castor's death by Zeus' decree that they live in the upper and lower worlds on alternate days. The front of the temple originally included six fluted Corinthian columns. It was used as the façade of the church until 1688, when it was destroyed in an earthquake. Today all that remains of the ancient edifice are two tall columns with their architrave, the bases of two more columns in front of the church, another column along the right side, and, beneath the statues of St Peter and St Paul, some weathered sculptures of the Dioscuri. The Chiostro di San Paolo incorporates 22 ancient granite columns. These did not apparently belong to the Temple of the Dioscuri.

The church was rebuilt by Francesco Grimaldi in 1603. The spacious interior has alternating large and small bays in the nave arcade that create an unprecedented sense of movement. The transept and apse are less ingenious. The church is decorated with frescoes by Massimo Stanzione (1644), and (in the sacristy) by Francesco Solimena. There are also two interesting Baroque chapels: the first chapel left of the high altar, the Cappella Firrao (1641) by Dionisio Lazzari, decorated with inlaid coloured marbles and mother of pearl; and the fourth south chapel, the Cappella della Purità (1681) by Giovanni Domenico Vinaccia, again with inlaid coloured marbles and paintings by Massimo Stanzione.

The Girolamini

The narrow Via dei Tribunali, *decumanus maximus* of ancient Naples, broadens before the Girolamini (or San Filippo Neri), built in 1592–1619 by Giovanni Antonio Dosio and Dionisio di Bartolomeo, with a façade by Ferdinando Fuga (c. 1780). The main entrance is now blocked up, so enter from the side facing the cathedral.

The richly decorated interior has 12 monolithic granite columns; the fine wooden ceiling was damaged in 1943. Over the main entrance is a masterly fresco by Luca Giordano of *Christ Driving the Moneylenders from the Temple*. Near the last column on the left is the tomb of Giovanni Battista Vico (1668–1744), pioneer of the philosophy of history. The apse contains paintings by Corenzio; and the chapel of St Philip Neri (left) is decorated with frescoes by Solimena. In the convent, a small pinacoteca (*open Mon–Sat 9.30–1; T: 081 449139; entrance opposite the cathedral at Via Duomo 142*) has paintings by Andrea da Salerno, Guido Reni, Massimo Stanzione and others. The Girolamini's library, which occupies a fine room by Marcello Guglielmelli (1727–36), is also interesting.

Luca Giordano (1634–1705)

Known to his contemporaries as Luca Fa-Presto ('Speedy Luca') on account of his legendary facility of execution, Luca Giordano is perhaps the greatest exponent of Neapolitan painting in its grand heyday of the 17th century. Far from being a negative factor, his prodigious speed of production permitted him to impart a fluency, vivacity and coherence to his often large and complex tableaux. It is this quality of improvisation that makes his work great. Some say that it was achieved with the aid of half-nude models who would pose on the scaffolding for him, as he painted the walls or ceilings of a building. Late in his career, when he had become internationally famous, Luca was also master of an extensive workshop, and was able to sustain the momentum of his production with the aid of numerous talented students.

He was an artist who responded easily and unaffectedly throughout his life to the influence of others, and his success depended on his ability to adapt his style exactly to the tastes of his patrons. He trained early in the circle of Jusepe Ribera in Naples, at first adopting the master's dramatic and powerful naturalism; this was reinforced by an exposure to Caravaggio's works on his first visit to Rome in 1652. But their darker style did not come naturally to his more open temperament, and his contact with the work of Rubens in the Chiesa Nuova in Rome definitively lightened the tone of his palette and brought out the natural exuberance in his imagination. In 1665 he travelled to Florence and then to Venice, where in the works of Titian and Veronese he at last discovered the colours and tones which he truly sought, and which he was to take back with him and to pass on to subsequent Neapolitan painting. After a period working for the Medici court in Florence again, he was appointed Court Painter in 1692 to Charles II of Spain, where he stayed for nearly ten years, absorbing there some of the characteristics—in particular the dissolved contours—which he admired in Velázquez.

This hugely mobile and international career meant that Luca left works—secular and religious—in many places in Europe. In Naples, however, his innate dynamism and magnificence of composition can be best appreciated in the superb fresco of *Christ Driving the Moneylenders from the Temple* (1684) in the Girolamini church (*map p. 53, 3*). Here, the sense of contrast which he first imbibed from Ribera, the dynamism and brilliant lighting he took from Rubens, the lessons of design he learned from Pietro da Cortona, and the sense of drama he absorbed from the great Venetian painters, all come together in a style which he has made his own and which is uniquely Neapolitan.   N.McG.

THE CATHEDRAL OF SAN GENNARO

Map p. 53, 3.

The cathedral was founded in the 4th century on the site of a Greek sanctuary dedicated to Apollo. The present building was begun in the French Gothic style by Charles I in 1294 and finished by Robert the Wise in 1323. The façade, shattered by an earthquake, was rebuilt by Antonio Baboccio in 1407; only his portal remains, however, the rest being mainly from a Gothic Revival design by Enrico Alvino (1877–1905). The remainder of the church was rebuilt after the earthquake of 1456.

The interior

The nave has an elaborate painted ceiling by Fabrizio Santafede (1621), supported on 16 piers incorporating over 100 antique columns of Oriental and African granite. On the walls above the arches are 46 saints, painted by Luca Giordano and his pupils. The chief monuments of the church are as follows:

1 Angevin tombs: Over the central doorway are (left to right) the tombs of Charles I of Anjou (d. 1285); of Clementina of Habsburg and her husband Charles Martel, the eldest son of Charles II, whose early death (1296) prevented him from succeeding to the Neapolitan throne. His son Charles Robert (or Carobert) became King of Hungary (*see below*). All the tombs here were moved from the choir in 1599, when the monuments were executed by Domenico Fontana.

2 Chapel of St Januarius: This chapel, also the treasury, was built by Francesco Grimaldi in 1608–37 in fulfilment of a vow made by the citizens during the plague of 1526–29. It is closed by an immense grille of gilded bronze, based on a design by Cosimo Fanzago (1668). The luminous interior, faced with marble, has seven ornate altars, four of which have paintings by Domenichino, who began the frescoes; these were completed by Lanfranco after Domenichino had been hounded from the city (*see p. 48*). Above the altar on the right side is a large oil painting by Jusepe de Ribera. The balustrade of the main altar is by Cosimo Fanzago, with small doors by Onofrio d'Alessio. The sumptuous silver altar-front is by Francesco Solimena. In a tabernacle behind the altar are preserved the head of St Januarius (Gennaro; martyred at Pozzuoli), in a silver-gilt reliquary bust (1305), and two phials of his congealed blood, which, according to tradition, first liquefied in the hands of the sainted Bishop Severus, when the saint's body was translated from Pozzuoli to Naples. The miracle has been documented since 1389 and is reported to occur three times a year: on the first Saturday in May at Santa Chiara, and in the cathedral on 19th September and 16th December. The prosperity of the city is believed to depend on the speed of the liquefaction. The ceremony attracts an enormous crowd, and travellers who wish to be present should secure a place near the altar in advance by applying to the sacristan.

CATHEDRAL OF SAN GENNARO

1 Angevin tombs
2 Chapel of St Januarius
3 Tomb of Cardinal Carbone
4 Cappella Minutolo
5 Cappella Tocco and Crypt
6 North transept
7 Basilica of Santa Restituta
8 Baptistery
9 Side chapels

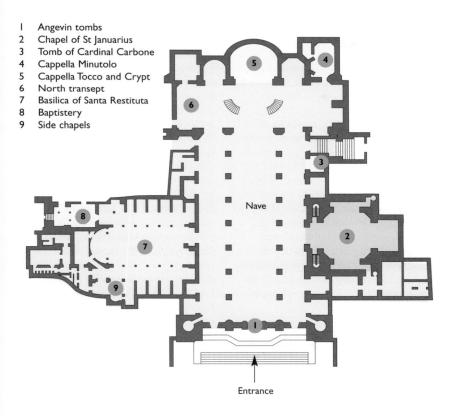

Nave

Entrance

3 Tomb of Cardinal Carbone: The tomb of the cardinal (d. 1504) lies under a Gothic canopy.

4 Cappella Minutolo: Paved with majolica, this contains the tomb of Cardinal Arrigo Minutolo, crafted by Roman marble-workers who came to Naples with Baboccio (1402–05). Here also are other tombs by a follower of Arnolfo di Cambio, and repainted 14th-

century frescoes. The polyptych on the side altar is by Paolo di Giovanni Fei.

5 Cappella Tocco: Also Gothic, with frescoes (1312; restored). Below the high altar is the **Crypt of St Januarius** or Cappella Carafa (*apply to the sacristan if closed*), by Tommaso Malvito (1497–1506), perhaps the masterpiece of Renaissance art in Naples. Entrance is gained through two fine bronze doors. Within, note the delicate ornamental carving; likewise the statue of the founder, Cardinal Oliviero Carafa, near the altar which covers the remains of the patron saint.

6 **North transept:** The tomb of Innocent IV (d. 1254), who spent much of his reign attempting to curb the imperial powers of Frederick II of Hohenstaufen, is a Cosmatesque work of 1315, partially reconstructed in the 16th century. Here also is the tomb of Andrew of Hungary, wife of Joan I, whose marriage was brokered by his father Charles Robert, with the aim of uniting the Angevin houses of Hungary and Naples. His murder in 1345 by strangling (the method was chosen because a ring given him by his mother was believed to protect him against poisoning and stabwounds) is thought to have occurred with the complicity of his wife.

7 **Basilica of Santa Restituta:** Founded in the 4th century on the site of a temple of Apollo, this was rebuilt in the 14th century and again after an earthquake in 1688. This is the city's oldest surviving church. Recent restorations have revealed the bases of various columns and fragments of the early Christian mosaic floor. The 27 columns may be relics of the old temple. The ceiling painting, showing the *Arrival of Santa Restituta at Ischia*, is by Luca Giordano. Beneath the chapel is an

archaeological area (*open 9–12 & 4.30–7, Sun and holidays 9–12*) with Graeco-Roman remains, including fragments of a mosaic pavement.

8 **Baptistery:** The chapel of San Giovanni in Fonte is square in plan, with a small dome, and is believed to be the earliest (5th century) example of this form of building in Italy. It preserves fragmentary 5th-century mosaics. In the centre of the dome is a gold Cross on a blue background with white and gold stars, flanked by the Greek letters Alpha and Omega and surmounted by the hand of God holding a gold crown. Around this runs a band of flowers, fruit and birds, including a phoenix with a halo, symbol of the Resurrection. Eight radial bands containing flowers, fruit, festoons and birds divide the cupola into eight wedges, four of which are well preserved. The mosaics depict a turquoise drapery with gilded detail, a vase with two birds, the *Women at the Sepulchre* (largely ruined), *Christ Saving Peter from the Waters*, the *Miracle of the Fish*, the *Traditio Legis* (haloed Christ giving the book of laws to St Peter), and *St Paul* (ruined).

9 **Side chapels:** The fifth and seventh chapels on the left contain beautiful 13th-century bas-reliefs in marble; in the sixth is a fine mosaic (1322) of the Virgin enthroned, by Lello da Roma, showing Byzantine influence.

Monte della Misericordia

This charitable institution was founded in 1601. In its octagonal church (1658–78; entrance in Via dei Tribunali) is a huge **painting by Caravaggio** of the *Seven Acts of Mercy* (1607). These acts are: the Burial of the Dead, Visiting the Incarcerated,

Feeding the Hungry, Clothing the Naked; Sheltering Pilgrims; Giving Drink to the Thirsty and Tending the Sick. The recently reordered pinacoteca has paintings by Fabrizio Santafede, Francesco de Mura, Luca Giordano and others (*church and pinacoteca open daily 8.30–2; T: 081 446944*).

San Giorgio Maggiore

The church of San Giorgio Maggiore was founded by St Severus in the late 4th century, destroyed by fire in 1640 and rebuilt by the Baroque architect Cosimo Fanzago, who reversed its orientation. Just inside the entrance are the extensive remains of the apse of the early Christian basilica. These include a half-dome resting on three arches that spring from two columns. The Corinthian capitals were taken from ancient Roman buildings. The walls are made of alternating courses of brick and tufa, in the Roman manner.

CASTEL CAPUANO & PORTA CAPUANA

Map p. 53, 4.

The **Castel Capuano**, also called La Vicaria, was begun by William I and finished by Frederick II. It was the residence of the Hohenstaufen and of some of the Angevin kings. Sergianni Caracciolo, Joan II's lover, was murdered here in 1432. Much altered, the castle has been used as the Court of Justice since 1540.

Across the square to the northeast, near the little Renaissance church of Santa Caterina a Formiello, rises the beautiful **Porta Capuana**, between two mighty Aragonese towers. The extant exterior decoration of this former city gate was begun by Giuliano da Maiano and completed, after his death in 1490, by Luca Fancelli. Smaller and more delicate than Alfonso of Aragon's triumphal arch at the Castel Nuovo, it is a rare and particularly fine application of late 15th-century Florentine sculptural style to a town gate. The only other project of this kind undertaken during the Renaissance was Agostino di Duccio's gate at Perugia, dating from around 1475. The open space in front of the gate is used as a market-place and is always animated and colourful.

San Giovanni a Carbonara

San Giovanni a Carbonara was built in 1343 and enlarged by King Ladislas at the beginning of the 15th century. Inside, facing the entrance, is the Cappella Maroballo, a richly decorated Renaissance monument with 15th-century statues. The tomb of King Ladislas (d. 1414), a masterpiece by Marco and Andrea da Firenze, towers behind the high altar. Beneath this three-storeyed composition of trefoil arches, statues and pinnacles, is the door to the Cappella Caracciolo del Sole (1427). Here you can see Andrea da Firenze's unfinished tomb of Sergianni Caracciolo, steward and lover of Joan II, stabbed at the Castel Capuano in 1432. On the walls are 15th-century frescoes of the life of the Virgin and scenes of eremitic life by Leonardo da Besozzo and Perrinetto da Benevento. The scenes of friars and angels playing musical

Fragment of a 15th-century *Annunciation*, by Leonardo da Besozzo, in San Giovanni a Carbonara.

instruments have led scholars to conclude that the chapel was once used as a choir. The tiled floor dates from 1440. To the north of the sanctuary is the marble-lined Cappella Caracciolo di Vico (1517), attributed to Tommaso Malvito; one of the most remarkable early 16th-century designs in Naples, this contains tombs and statues by Giovanni da Nola. In the sacristy is the tomb of Scipione Somma (d. 1553).

Santa Maria Donnaregina

Dating originally from the 8th century, this convent was reconstructed by Mary of Hungary, Charles II of Anjou's queen, following an earthquake of 1293. A second church, in the Baroque style, was added when the nuns were incorporated in the

Theatine Order. The 14th-century church is reached from the Vico Donnaregina. The presbytery, stripped in 1928–36 of later additions, ends in a plain polygonal apse. To the right is the Cappella Loffredo, to the left the tomb of Queen Mary by Tino da Camaino and Gagliardo Primario (1326). In the nuns' choir, a rectangular gallery built over the west end of the church, are the celebrated **frescoes by Pietro Cavallini** and his pupils (begun 1308) representing the *Passion*, the *Legends of Saints Elizabeth of Hungary, Catherine and Agnes*, and the *Last Judgement*. Another Cavallini fresco may be seen above the choir roof. The 17th-century church, elaborate but in good taste, has coloured marbles, majolica pavements and paintings by Luca Giordano.

PIZZOFALCONE

Map p. 52, 14.
This tour leads through the historic area south and west of the Castel Nuovo. The first part takes in some of the city's most notable public buildings, which grew up as the Spanish viceroys and their Austrian successors, anxious to mark the distinction between their rule and that of the Aragonese, moved the civic centre of Naples from the Castel Nuovo to the area immediately to the southwest. Highlights in this area include the Palazzo Reale, the centre of viceregal government, and the monumental church of San Francesco da Paola with its square, today called Piazza del Plebiscito. The latter is now closed to traffic, allowing you to imagine the extraordinary visual and symbolic impact that such an immense open space had, when first built, on the inhabitants of this crowded city.

The second part of the itinerary explores the city's finest old residential quarter, Pizzofalcone, which stands on a hill (the site of the ancient Parthenope) between the gulf shore and Via Chiaia, Naples' main shopping street. Here some truly spectacular examples of Neapolitan palace architecture (as well as one or two small churches supported by aristocratic families) can be seen. Finally, the walk ends on the busy Via Partenope, a scenic boulevard carved out of the slums when the old fishing port of Santa Lucia was 'improved' in the late 19th century, and now home to many of the city's luxury hotels.

TEATRO SAN CARLO

Map p. 53, 11. Open by appointment except on performance days, T: 081 797 2331.
Via Vittorio Emanuele II leads southwest from the Castel Nuovo, to Via San Carlo, which branches right. On the left, at the entrance to the Giardino Reale and the Biblioteca Nazionale, are groups of *Horse Trainers*, by the 19th-century sculptor Baron Clodt, presented by Czar Nicholas I, whose favourite sculptor Clodt was. The library was founded in 1734 and is the most important in southern Italy.

Further along on the left lies the Teatro San Carlo. This is the largest opera house in Italy. It was built for Charles of Bourbon by the contactor and impresario Angelo Carasale, on a plan by court architect Giovanni Antonio Medrano. Begun in March

1737, it was finished in the following October and opened to the public on 4th November, the king's saint's day in the Roman Catholic calendar.

KING CHARLES & MUSIC IN NAPLES

The Teatro San Carlo was built at a time when Italy was the centre of European musical culture and Naples was the centre of music in Italy, thanks to Charles III's generous patronage of composers and performers. Rousseau, in his famous essay on genius, advised aspiring musicians to go to Naples to study; his eminent contemporary Delalande declared that music could be discerned in the gestures, the inflection of the voice and even the cadence of everyday conversation in Naples. 'Music is the triumph of the Neapolitans,' he wrote. 'Everything there expresses and exhales music.'

In the light of these considerations it is hardly surprising that Charles should have desired to provide his capital with a large, splendid opera house, even though he had no personal passion for this particular art form. Indeed, as one observer noted, the king often talked during one half of the performances and slept during the other—a habit that scandalised his foreign guests. The 18th-century English traveller Samuel Sharp has left a description of the original appearance of the theatre (which today is lost), as well as an amusing account of the Neapolitan manner of enjoying a performance.

The King's Theatre, upon the first view, is, perhaps, almost as remarkable an object as any man sees in his travels. The amazing extent of the stage, with the prodigious circumference of the boxes and the height of the ceiling, produce a marvellous effect on the mind ... Notwithstanding the amazing noisiness of the audience during the whole performance of the opera, the moment the dances begin there is a universal dead silence, which continues so long as the dances continue. Witty people, therefore, never fail to tell me, the Neapolitans go to see not to hear an opera ... It must be confessed that their scenery is extremely fine; their dresses are new and rich; and the music is well adapted, but, above all, the stage is so large and noble, as to set off the performance to an inexpressible advantage... It is customary for gentlemen to run about from box to box between the acts, and even in the midst of the performance; but the ladies, after they are seated, never quit their box the whole evening. It is the fashion to make appointments for such and such nights. A lady receives visitors in her box one night, and they remain with her the whole opera; another night she returns the visit in the same manner. In the intervals between the acts, principally between the first and second, the proprietor of the box regales her company with iced fruits and sweetmeats. (Acton, cit.)

The original theatre has been remodelled a number of times, notably in 1762 by Giovanni Maria Bibiena, in 1768 by Ferdinando Fuga, in 1797 by Domenico Chelli, and in 1812 by Antonio Niccolini (who added the courtyard and loggia). Destroyed by a fire on the night of 12th February 1816, the old theatre was rebuilt in its present form by Niccolini (who, it is said, inserted hundreds of clay pitchers in the walls in order to improve the acoustics). The foyer on the garden side was added in 1938.

The concert hall, seating 3,000, is famous for its perfect acoustics. The 185 boxes are arranged in six tiers; above the centrally located Royal Box, the fifth and sixth tiers open up in the manner of an amphitheatre. Throughout the theatre red upholstery and gold trim combine to create an opulent, festive atmosphere. The ceiling is adorned with a painting of *Apollo Introducing the Greek, Latin and Italian Poets to Minerva*, by Giuseppe Cammarano, and the curtain bears a representation of *Homer and the Muses with Poets and Musicians*, the work of Giuseppe Mancinelli. The premières of Rossini's *Lady of the Lake* and *Moses*, Bellini's *Sonnambula* and Donizetti's *Lucia di Lammermoor* were all performed on this stage.

Opposite the Teatro San Carlo is the main entrance to the cross-shaped **Galleria Umberto I** (1887–90, rebuilt since 1945), a shopping arcade. The dome is 56m high and is one of the first major iron-and-glass constructions in Italy. The street ends in the busy Piazza Trieste e Trento, still generally known as Piazza San Ferdinando, with the beautiful Gambrinus coffee house. The square lies at the junction of several important streets: to the north runs Via Toledo; to the west, Via Chiaia.

PIAZZA DEL PLEBISCITO

Map p. 52, 10.
Piazza del Plebiscito is a wide hemicycle with a Doric colonnade and frigid equestrian statues of Charles III and Ferdinand IV, by Antonio Canova and Antonio Calì. Here rises the **church of San Francesco da Paola**, founded by Ferdinand IV to celebrate the restoration of the Bourbon dynasty after the Napoleonic interlude, and designed by Pietro Bianchi (1817–32) in obvious imitation of the Pantheon in Rome. The north and south ends of the piazza are occupied respectively by the Prefecture and the Palazzo Salerno, residence of the military commandant.

Palazzo Reale
Map p. 52, 10. Open daily except Wed 9–7; T: 081 400547.
The east side of Piazza del Plebiscito is entirely taken up by the façade of the Palazzo Reale, a 167m medley of architecture and sculpture. Built by Domenico Fontana in 1600–02, in anticipation of a visit by Philip III of Spain, this majestic building was intended to be the residence of Naples' rulers. It was in fact occupied only by viceroys, as the Bourbons resided at Capodimonte (*see p. 97 below*). The statues in the ground-floor niches represent the eight dynasties of Naples: Roger de Hauteville, Frederick II of Hohenstaufen, Charles I of Anjou, Alfonso of Aragon, Charles V of Habsburg, Charles III of Bourbon, the Bonapartist Joachim Murat, and Vittorio Emanuele II of Savoy.

Restored in 1838–42 after a fire, and again after damage in the Second World War, the palace interior is now the Museo dell'Appartamento Storico del Palazzo Reale—a complex of fine halls with period furniture, tapestries, paintings (the ceilings are by Belisario Corenzio and Francesco de Mura) and porcelain. Highlights include the Cappella Palatina, attributed to Cosimo Fanzago (1668), at the foot of a grand staircase (1651, restored 1837) and, at the top of the stairs, the small Teatro di Corte, built by Ferdinando Fuga in 1768 for Maria Carolina of Habsburg's wedding to Ferdinand IV, and restored after war damage in 1950. Here also are the original bronze doors of the Castel Nuovo, by Guillaume le Moine and Pietro di Martino (1462–68), on which six reliefs depict Ferdinand of Aragon's struggle with the barons. The cannon-ball lodged in the lower relief on the left door is a relic from the naval battle between the French and the Genoese; the doors and other booty en route to France from Naples were recovered and returned to the city.

Pizzofalcone

From the northwest corner of Piazza del Plebiscito the steep quarter of Pizzofalcone is reached by Piazza Carolina and Via Serra. These lead to the piazza and church of **Santa Maria degli Angeli** (*map p. 52, 14*), the masterpiece of the priest and architect Francesco Grimaldi. Begun in 1600, the church is built to one of the most daring designs of its day. Grimaldi's clear, decisive treatment of solids and voids and his handling of architectural ornament are well ahead of contemporary developments in Naples or even in Rome. The third south chapel contains a *Holy Family* by Luca Giordano; the second on the north an *Immacolata* by Massimo Stanzione.

Via Monte di Dio ascends to the left from the piazza. In the Middle Ages this street was lined with convents, but in the 18th century it became the centre of a fashionable residential area. Today it is known for its aristocratic palaces, the most noteworthy of which is **Palazzo Serra a Cassano** (nos 14–15), built in the early 18th century to plans by Ferdinando Sanfelice, and recently restored. With two courtyards and a scenographic double staircase, it is perhaps the most impressive of all Neapolitan palaces.

Via Parisi leads west to the former convent of the **Nunziatella**, now a military college, with an 18th-century church begun by Ferdinando Sanfelice at the request of the Jesuits. Returning by Via Parisi, and continuing along the north side of Palazzo Serra a Cassano, you turn left into Via Egiziaca a Pizzofalcone to reach the Baroque church of **Santa Maria Egiziaca a Pizzofalcone**. Attributed to Cosimo Fanzago, this little church is sumptuously adorned with marble; a painting of the titular saint by Andrea Vaccaro hangs over the high altar. Just beyond the church, Via della Solitaria descends to the Istituto d'Arte, with a small museum of applied arts (*open by appointment; T: 081 764 7471*). From here, steps go back down to Piazza del Plebiscito.

Castel dell'Ovo and Santa Lucia

Map p, 52, 14: Metro 2 to Piazza Amedeo.

The Borgo Marinaro, the ancient island of *Megaris*, was once the site of a villa belonging to the Roman patrician Lucullus. It was later joined by a pier to the shore to form the little Porto di Santa Lucia. Restaurants line the quay. On the island is the **Castel dell'Ovo**, a fortress dating from 1154. The name (literally 'Castle of the Egg') is a corruption of *Löwe* (German for 'lion'), the emblem of Frederick II, whose troops were garrisoned here. After Frederick's death in 1250, the castle became the prison of the luckless Conradin and of Beatrice, daughter of Manfred, the last of the Hohenstaufen. It is now used for meetings, lectures and exhibitions. The Museo di Etnopreistoria, operated by the Club Alpino Italiano, is open by appointment (*T: 081 764 5343*).

At the end of Via Partenope stands the huge Baroque **Fontana dell'Immacolatella** (1601), with statues by Pietro Bernini and caryatids by Naccherino. The **Santa Lucia quarter** is reached by any of the streets leading inland. Once highly characteristic, with fishermen's houses and the old shellfish market, it is now quite ordinary.

THE ROAD TO CAPODIMONTE

Via Toledo

Map p. 52, 10.

Via Toledo, so called after Don Pedro de Toledo, the Spanish viceroy who had it built, begins on the north side of Piazza Trieste e Trento. This is Naples' high street. Although closed to traffic, it is filled by a noisy and lively throng all day, especially in the late afternoon. Numerous streets and alleys diverge from it: those on the right are broad and modern up to the south side of Piazza della Carità, descending through the business district of Carità towards the harbour, while those on the left are narrow and ancient, ascending steeply, sometimes in steps, towards Corso Vittorio Emanuele.

On the corner facing Piazza Trieste e Trento is **San Ferdinando**, a Jesuit church. Begun by Giovanni Giacomo Conforto and altered by Cosimo Fanzago, it was again modified and renamed, after the expulsion of the order in 1767, in honour of Ferdinand I, whose morganatic second wife, Lucia Migliaccio (d. 1826) is buried within. Beyond the Galleria Umberto I, on the right, is the church of **Santa Brigida**, built in 1612 in honour of St Brigid of Sweden. Here Luca Giordano (*see box on p. 67*) is buried; his ingenious perspective paintings add apparent height to the dome. Luca was known to his contemporaries as 'Fast Hand Luke' (Luca Fa-Presto) because of his ability to turn out works like these with amazing speed. The painting of *St Francis Receiving the Stigmata*, in the transept, is by Massimo Stanzione.

Via Roma

Map p. 52, 6.

North of Piazza della Carità Via Toledo changes its name to Via Roma. At the intersection with Via Benedetto Croce stands the Baroque Palazzo Maddaloni (right), an ancient building redesigned by Cosimo Fanzago. A bit further up, on the opposite side of the street, is the church of **Santo Spirito**. Altered between 1757 and 1774 by Mario Gioffredo, it rivals Vanvitelli's Annunziata as the most masterful expression of the new Classical taste that grew up in Naples under Charles III. Within, Gioffredo's main order of powerful columns almost swamps the earlier interior. But the architect remains faithful to the Neapolitan tradition in such devices as the choir gallery above the main altar, the design of the altar itself and the overall proportions of the building. At the sides of the entrance are the tombs of Ambrogio Salvio and Paolo Spinelli, by Michelangelo Naccherino. In the south transept is a *Madonna and Saints* by Fedele Fischetti; in the apse, *Pentecost*, by Francesco de Mura. The first north chapel has a *Purification*, *Conversion of St Paul*, and *Fall of Simon Magus* by Fischetti; the fourth chapel a *Madonna del Soccorso* by Fabrizio Santafede. The tomb on the left is also by Naccherino. In the fifth chapel is a *Baptism of Christ* by Santafede. The façade, which is much less advanced than the interior, adheres to the contemporary Roman type.

Opposite Santo Spirito is the **Palazzo d'Angri**, by Luigi and Carlo Vanvitelli (1755), where Garibaldi stayed in 1860. Continuing up Via Roma you pass (left) Via Tarsia, which leads to the beautifully renovated Montesanto Station and Montesanto Funicular. Alessandro Scarlatti is buried in the church of **Santa Maria di Montesanto**, opposite. Via Roma ends in Piazza Dante, enclosed on the east side by Luigi Vanvitelli's hemicycle and the 17th-century Port'Alba.

MUSEO ARCHEOLOGICO NAZIONALE

Map p. 52, 2: Metro 1 to Piazza Dante then bus 24, or Metro 3 to Museo-Dante. Piazza Museo 18; T: 081 440166, www.archeona.arti.beniculturali.it. The museum is open daily except Tues 9–7.30 (last entry 6).

This is one of the most varied and interesting museums of antiquities in the world. It is of prime importance for the study of Greek and Roman sculpture, but is more widely known for its display of magnificent finds from Pompeii, Herculaneum and Stabiae. A visit to the museum is an essential part of the exploration of the great sites of the Bay of Naples; the one cannot be fully understood without the other. Although it is tempting to lament that many of the beautiful and evocative decorations and objects are not able to be seen in their original setting in the Roman houses where they were found, it should be recalled that the museum came into existence principally to give them a safe home away from the danger of further eruptions of Mount Vesuvius.

The building

The grandiose building of the museum (itself constructed near the site of an ancient Greek cemetery) was originally designed in 1582 to house the Royal Riding School. When the site was later found to have an insufficient supply of water, it was given over in 1599 to the Royal University. This in turn was moved in 1787, after which the building slowly began to fulfil its new role as a repository for the ever-increasing number of objects coming from the excavations in Pompeii and Herculaneum. In the same period, the antiquities in the possession of the Farnese family (inherited by King Charles of Bourbon through his mother, Elisabetta Farnese, daughter of the duke of Parma, who had married Philip V of Spain) were moved to Naples and housed here, creating together a composite collection of scarcely equalled scope and grandeur.

The plan of the building is simple and symmetrical, evolving around two open courts separated by a central hall which culminates in an exedra with grand double staircase leading up to the Salone della Meridiana. This upper hall takes its name from a working sundial added in 1790, which utilises a ray of light entering the room through a hole in the upper southwest corner. It is read along a diagonal axis across the floor of the room. The hall has traditionally contained the Hellenistic statue known as the *Farnese Atlas*, which includes a detailed ancient representation of the Zodiac. The sculpture may have been made in Alexandria, a centre of astronomic science in Antiquity; it is thought that it once adorned the libraries at the edge of Trajan's Forum in Rome.

The collections

At the time of writing, the museum is undergoing a complete rearrangement of the exhibits. The sculpture galleries will continue to occupy the ground floor, and the finds from Pompeii and the other Vesuvian sites will mostly remain on the upper floor; but their organisation and display is scheduled to change substantially. The description below is divided thematically into three principal sections, which it is hoped will be reflected by the new arrangement: 1) The Greek and Roman sculpture collections (ground floor); II) Artefacts from Pompeii, Herculaneum, Stabiae and the other Vesuvian sites (upper floor); III) Specialised collections: gems, coins, epigraphs, and the Egyptian, prehistoric and early Campanian collections (probably to be distributed between the basement and mezzanine floors).

The Greek and Roman sculpture collections

The Farnese sculptures

A majority of the greatest works here belonged to the Farnese Collection, begun by Alessandro Farnese, who reigned from 1534 to 1549 as Pope Paul III. Farnese was a man of considerable taste; he employed Michelangelo, Raphael, Titian and the most celebrated artists of his day. He built what is undoubtedly the greatest of all Roman residential palaces, and adorned the gardens, courtyards and rooms of his properties with the magnificent sculptures seen here, many of which were excavated in Rome at his request. A number of the statues came from the Baths of Caracalla, some from Nero's Domus Aurea, others from Hadrian's Villa at Tivoli. It is important to imagine these works in their original settings, first in surroundings of appropriate size and grandeur in ancient Rome, and then later in Farnese's majestic residences. Anyone familiar with the countless copies of these works to be seen in gardens and state rooms at Blenheim Palace, Syon House, Stourhead or Chatsworth in England; in Vienna; in St Petersburg or in Paris, can appreciate the extraordinary hold they had on the imagination of many early visitors to Naples.

The *Farnese Bull*: The collection is dominated by the *Farnese Bull*, one of the largest known free-standing works of antique sculpture. It is purportedly the work of 2nd-century BC Greek sculptors from the island of Rhodes, identified by

Pliny the Elder (*Nat. Hist. 36. 33–34*) as the brothers Apollonius and Tauriscus of Tralles—although he may be referring to a smaller original, of which this is a later and much larger Roman copy. (The fact that Pliny goes on to assert that the sculpture to which he was referring was made from a single block of marble could be seen as lending support to this view.)

Discovered in 1545 in the Baths of Caracalla, it was moved the same year into the second courtyard of Palazzo Farnese by Paul III. It was later shipped to Naples in 1788, where it arrived escorted by a warship, and was placed in the garden of the Royal Palace at Capodimonte as the central ornament of a fountain; it was brought here to this building in 1826. The immense size of the present work was proportionate to the vast domed spaces of the Baths of Caracalla (probably the palaestra), of which the *Bull* was the fitting centre-piece: the walls in the background would have been highly decorated, enhancing the monochrome purity of the sculptural group. Today it amazes by the display of different textures achieved in marble (the ropes, the basket, the fur of the dog, the stones, the drapery etc), and by its ingenious and brilliant carving. Its pyramidal design is complex, without being exaggeratedly contrived. It tells a story somewhat typical of the gruesome history of Thebes. The two young men (the twin brothers Amphion and Zethus, who later ruled and forti-fied the city of Thebes) are tying their evil stepmother, Dirce, to a bull in revenge for her maltreatment and sup-planting of their natural mother, Antiope. The bull subsequently drags Dirce to her death over the rocks.

Antiope, standing to one side, looks on passively, together with a young seated boy who personifies Mount Kithairon.

The *Farnese Hercules*: Found in the same area in 1546, and of comparable size, is the *Farnese Hercules*, originally displayed in the first courtyard of Palazzo Farnese, where the statement it made to anyone entering the grand resi-dence was obvious. It bears the signature (on the rock under the cudgel) of Glycon of Athens, and is a marble copy, execut-ed at the beginning of the 3rd century AD, of a lost bronze statue of the 4th cen-tury BC attributed to the Greek sculptor Lysippus. At 3.2m in height, the copy is probably much larger than the original, and would have been created, once again, in proportion to its grand setting in the Baths of Caracalla. It represents a departure from traditional depictions of Hercules as a strong, active hero, by showing him absorbed in thought after the last of his labours—the procuring of the Golden Apples of the Hesperides, one of which, in an ingenious stroke of design that leads the viewer around the work, Hercules holds in his hand behind his back. The statue was originally found without its legs; at the recommendation of Michelangelo, the sculptor Guglielmo della Porta was chosen to complete the piece. The original legs were found soon after, but they aroused considerable debate because they were deemed less elegant than della Porta's tapering limbs: the Farnese family even refused to have them substituted. They were not replaced with the originals until 1787.

The *Tyrannicides*: The two figures of Harmodius and Aristogeiton, who stride forward threateningly into the viewer's space, constitute the most important and most problematic sculptural group in the collection. Known as '**The Tyrannicides**', they were among the first images of real people, as opposed to legendary heroes, to find expression in a publicly commissioned sculpture in ancient Greece. In an access of rage arising from a personal quarrel, the two men had killed Hipparchus, tyrant of Athens, in 514 BC, and paid for the deed with their own lives. When the tyranny fell only a few years later, the pair were hailed as icons of democracy, and sculptures created in their honour were erected in the Athenian Agora, as a visible admonition to all future aspiring tyrants. The original bronze monument (510 BC) by Antenor disappeared when Xerxes sacked Athens in 480 BC; three years later, the Athenian sculptors Critios and Nesiotes created (from memory presumably) a 'copy' of Antenor's work, now also lost; and the present version is a marble copy of that, executed in Rome in the 2nd century AD. Much intensity and accuracy is inevitably lost when copies are made of copies of a partially-remembered work: when the material is changed furthermore from bronze, with its natural receptivity to fine detail, into stone, yet more is lost. Marble also requires cumbersome and ungainly supports (such as the tree stumps here), which bronzes, as hollow metal sculptures, can do without. What we are looking at is therefore so far from the original that we might as well consider it a different piece: we cannot know what the original arrangement was, nor where the epigram by Simonides praising freedom, which evidently accompanied the figures, was inscribed.

The head of the bearded Aristogeiton (in different material) is probably closer to the original than anything: it is made from a cast, apparently taken from Critios' original bronze statue. The cast was excavated from a copyist's workshop in Baiae, and is now in the Museum of the Campi Flegrei at Baia. The undoubtedly fine abdominal definition of the figures owes more to Roman than to Archaic Greek art. It is ironic that this powerful image to democratic freedom should have been excavated and found at Hadrian's Villa near Rome—the retreat of one of history's greatest autocrats. It shows how far the Roman mind had gone in seeing such works in purely aesthetic terms, devoid of the political message they originally possessed for their Greek creators.

The *Venus Callipyge*: This work (the epithet means 'of the beautiful buttocks') came to the Farnese collection from Nero's Domus Aurea in Rome. Extensively restored by the 18th-century sculptor Albacini (he supplied the head, arms and one leg), it is a Roman copy of a Hellenistic original of the late 3rd century BC, and appears to belong to the large corpus of artistic variations on the theme of Venus at, or emerging from, her bath. She must be imagined standing in a pool of still water, which would reflect her turning gaze, thereby completing and giving sense to her pose. Some have linked the Hellenistic original of this piece to a delightful story told by Athenaios of Syracuse, about two sisters who sought to settle a dispute as to which one of them had the more shapely bottom, by asking a stranger to be the impartial judge. The

Pan teaching the shepherd Daphnis to play the pipes. Copy of an original of the 2nd century BC.

sister chosen was to be the stranger's reward in marriage. His brother, also hearing of the contest, preferred, and therefore won, the other sister. On the strength of this happy outcome they dedicated a temple to Callipygean Aphrodite in Syracuse, complete with a cult statue—perhaps the forerunner of this—which was seen by many early travellers, among them Edward Gibbon.

The Artemis of Ephesus: This alabaster Artemis, with (restored) bronze face, hands and feet, was one of the most famous and widespread images of the ancient Greek world's eastern frontier, copied many times and reproduced on coins minted in Ephesus. The image was believed to possess miraculous powers not dissimilar to those of the Black Madonnas, many of whose characteristics she shares. A veritable bestiary of animals and insects, real and mythological, cling to her arms and tightly clad legs; signs of the zodiac and symbols of the seasons adorn her neck; her head has both a turreted, earthly crown, and a divine nimbus or halo. On her front hang what were for long considered to be a multitude of breasts; they possess no teats, however, and are in fact the scrota of sacrificed bulls, an image of fertility. Of the many copies of this famous statue from the ancient Temple of Artemis in Ephesus, this one in the Farnese Collection, executed in the 2nd century AD, is one of the finest. Few works give a more immediate sense of the latent animism of cultic imagery on Greece's oriental, Asian border.

Works from the Carracci Gallery: One sub-group of the Farnese antiquities are those that were displayed in the Carracci Gallery in Palazzo Farnese in Rome, beneath walls and ceilings extravagantly painted in 1597 by the Bolognese artist Annibale Carracci. These include the *Antinoüs*, Hadrian's favourite, deified by the emperor after his death and depicted thereafter in sculptures, gems and coins as a model of youthful beauty, often seen as here in thoughtful, almost elegiac, pose; *Pan and Daphnis*, a celebrated copy of an original sculpture, probably in bronze, by the 2nd century BC sculptor Heliodorus of Rhodes, in which the ambiguity of the relationship between the divine, but bestial, Pan and the reticent innocence of the shepherd Daphnis is marvellously evoked; and the *Farnese Caracalla*, a 3rd-century AD portrait bust, famous in the 17th and 18th centuries for its brooding evocation of the Roman emperor's notorious temper—something which led Winckelmann, nor-mally a champion of Greek over Roman art, to concede that Lysippus himself could not have made a better portrait.

Portrait sculpture: In the Farnese Collection are a number of other famous (imaginary) likenesses of poets and philosophers, which are Roman works based on Greek originals of the Hellenistic age: for example the *Euripides*, a *Homer* and the **herm of Socrates**. Socrates' unattractive appearance was known from ancient descriptions: Xenophon referred to his protruding eyes, bulbous nose with wide nostrils, and full lips (*Symposium, V, 5–7*), and Plato, in his *Symposium* (*215–17*), makes Alcibiades compare the philosopher to Silenus and to Marsyas, both in their way gifted and wise despite their unprepossessing looks.

Sculpture from Pompeii, Herculaneum and other sites

The *Doryphorus*: From the Samnite Palaestra in Pompeii, this is the most complete of many copies of the famous spear-bearer of Polyclitus (c. 440 BC), which was considered the perfect model, or 'canon', of proportions for the male body. The work illustrated a book (called the *Kanon*) in which the artist set down ideal mathematical proportions for the parts of the human body and proposed for sculpture of the human figure a dynamic counterbalance—between the relaxed and tensed body parts and between the directions in which the parts move. Italian Renaissance artists would call this twisting of the human body's vertical axis *contrapposto*. In Greece the concept was called *symmetria*, and Polyclitus' statues of young ath-letes—balanced, rhythmical, and finely detailed—were considered the best demonstrations of the principle.

The Artemis of Pompeii: This is a late Republican Roman copy of an Archaic Greek original, perhaps the Diana of Segesta mentioned by Cicero. It reveals the Roman passion for antiquarianism, and the copying of antique works: but although it faithfully mimics its Greek prototype in the rhythmic treatment of drapery and in the Archaic smile, it inexplicably lacks that natural, inner vitality which is characteristic of true Archaic art.

The Aphrodite of Capua: This, by contrast, was copied in Hadrianic times from a famous Greek model of the late

Classical period. It represents the goddess of beauty and love looking at her reflection in the shield of her lover Ares, god of war: the Classical idiom was closer and more familiar to Roman sensibility, and the copy therefore is much more successful. She originally decorated the portico of the upper seating area of the amphitheatre at Capua.

The *Aphrodite Sosandra*: A very different image of the same goddess is glimpsed in the *Aphrodite Sosandra*. Completely wrapped in a heavy *himation* (cloak), head covered and wearing sandals, she is here all modesty, and a little unapproachable. There is a severity to the style which accords with the attribution of the original of this work to the early 5th-century sculptor Kalamis, a great Athenian artist in whom Cicero noted a certain 'hardness of style'. The original would have been created in bronze, around 470 BC, and may have been the one that Pausanias refers to on his visit to the Acropolis of Athens (*Description of Greece, I. 23. 2*), and which he says was dedicated by Callias, a rich Athenian citizen, and the brother in law of Cimon, the political leader of Athens. Some have argued that the fact that Callias saved the reputation of Cimon's family by his munificence at one crucial moment may have given the statue the epithet which it bears today: '*Sosandra*', meaning 'saver of men'. The present piece was found in a Roman copyist's studio in Baiae, and dates from the 1st century AD. In order to imitate the much more expressive effects of bronze, the copyist has had to work with great technical skill, drilling and undercutting the deep spaces between the cheeks and the

cloak where it covers the head. The effect of this shadow is beautiful, as is the contrast of the heavy *himation* with the deeply pleated *chiton* beneath. The statue was famous enough in Antiquity that the 2nd-century AD humorist Lucian, when imagining an image of the perfectly beautiful woman, chooses particularly memorable qualities of the greatest statues to combine in her: from the *Aphrodite Sosandra*, he selected her 'modesty … her holy and inscrutable smile… and the simplicity and orderliness of her dress' (*Imagines 6*).

Equestrian statues of Marcus Nonius Balbus and Balbus the Younger: These come from the area of the Basilica of Herculaneum, and at the time of their excavation in the 1740s were the most highly regarded sculptures from the site. They represent an unusual departure from the long-standing prohibition in Republican Rome of monuments or statues in which the subject wore military dress. These partially armed figures reflect the considerable transformations that Roman society was undergoing in the 1st century AD. The Balbus family was prominent in Herculaneum—the younger Marcus Nonius was proconsul for the Province of Crete and Cyrenaica—and the two generations are portrayed here with some of the self-promoting idealisation associated with statues of Renaissance *condottieri*. The '*Elder Balbus*' has been extensively restored, and the head of the '*Younger Balbus*' has been replaced after the original was destroyed by a stray cannon ball in 1799.

Smaller portraits: There are a number of smaller portraits of excellent quality: a bronze head of the actor Norbanus Sorex, and another of **Caecilius Iucundus**, whose protruding ears and wart on the left cheek express the late Republican taste for naturalistic detail. Caecilius was a prominent banker and businessman, and a large archive of wax tablets was found in his house in Pompeii.

Two neglected masterpieces: Often overlooked, but of great quality, is the **Venus of Sinuessa**, a Greek original of the 3rd century BC in Parian marble, once depicting the goddess with arms raised to tie back her hair. Her fragmentary remains display a remarkably beautiful contrast between the pure, nude form and the deeply undercut drapery. A different kind of technical skill, no less developed, can be seen in the densely carved figures on the **Sarcophagus of the Myth of Prometheus**. This is a late Roman work of considerable virtuosity; it is one of the unsung treasures of the museum. The crowded scene depicts almost the whole cosmos packed into a rectangle: the elements, light and dark, life and death, winds, waters, sun and moon, Mercury, Pluto, Cupid, Vulcan, Juno, Neptune; and at its centre, Prometheus sits, bemused, with a clay model of Man resting on his knees.

Finds from the Villa of the Papyri: The Villa of the Papyri at Herculaneum is the single most important residence to have come to light from the area of the Vesuvian excavations. It was first excavated between 1750 and 1761, and much of it is still unexplored, buried under the modern town of Ercolano: a debate is still alive as to how far excavations could, or should, proceed. The celebrated finds—nearly 50 marble sculptures, more than 20 bronzes and an extraordinary collection of papyri with Greek and Latin texts on Epicurean philosophy—suggest that the villa belonged to an important and highly cultured individual, possibly Lucius Calpurnius Piso, Julius Caesar's father-in-law, or Appius Claudius Pulcher, the brother-in-law of Lucullus. A good sense of the size, beauty and layout of this villa is given by the other 'Villa Papyri' constructed by J. Paul Getty in Malibu Beach, California.

The greatest treasures on show here are the magnificent Hellenistic and Roman bronzes, a wonderful and varied group of sculptures which adorned the villa's peristyles and pools: the delightful *Drunken Silenus*, precariously balanced on his rock; the *Sleeping Satyr*, with delicately relaxed limbs; and the perfectly realised *Hermes Resting*, naked but for his winged sandals. All are probably copies by skilled Roman craftsmen, working from Classical and Hellenistic originals: the *Hermes* is based on a work of the 4th century BC by Lysippus. The naturalism of all these figures was enhanced in Antiquity by the fact that the bronze was made to maintain its natural metallic tone, similar to deeply tanned skin.

Art and artefacts from Pompeii, Herculaneum and the other Vesuvian sites

The objects and decorations which come from the Vesuvian excavations have immeasurably enhanced our understanding of ancient Roman life, in a way that even the plentiful literature which we possess could never have done. What astonishes the visitor is both the extraordinary quality and the seeming familiarity of so many of the items. But when looking at this wealth of art, it should always be borne in mind that Pompeii and Herculaneum were small and relatively insignificant provincial towns, and that the quality of the finds made here must be little more than a shadow of the refinement and sophistication we might expect to have found in Rome itself. The painters of the walls of these houses were largely itinerant decorators, often executing by rote copies of famous works by celebrated Greek painters that were familiar to their patrons. They were paid by the day or by the area they covered; they were not 'artists' with vocations, as we might understand the concept today. No ancient Greek painting has survived into modernity, and the closest we can get to imagining its masterpieces are these distant copies made by the Roman decorators. Yet they transmit no better sense of the true qualities of great Greek painting than a souvenir copy of scenes from the Sistine ceiling can give any inkling of the true greatness of Michelangelo's masterpiece.

It should also be noted that there were usually two kinds of craftsman at work in both the paintings and the mosaics: there was the decorator, who covered the large areas of background wall-space or floor-space with abstract or architectural designs; and there was the artist, who would be responsible for the *emblemata*. An *emblema* (which simply means 'a thing to be looked at') is the far more intricate panel, often with a detailed figurative scene, which is set into the centre of the mosaic floor or plastered wall. It represents a very different quality of craftsmanship, and was the work of a different rank of artisan. *Emblemata* panels were frequently changed—cut out and replaced with new ones, without disturbing the background—just as today we might wish to change the pictures on our walls, or the rugs on our floors. The border, where the incision has been made in order to move or set them, can often be seen. It is helpful to distinguish these different levels of craftsmanship and to understand the limitations of the provincial environment in which the craftsmen were working. Taking all this into consideration, however, the quality of these unpretentious works still astounds.

Mosaics

The origins of this remarkable and durable art-form are probably to be sought in the East, where examples from ancient Egypt have survived. The Greek world, too, presents many examples, among the best known being those in the courtyards of houses on the island of Delos. But it was the Romans who really perfected this art in its many forms. Both Pliny the Elder and Vitruvius write in detail about it, and they distinguish three different kinds of mosaic art, all of which are represented in this collection. *Opus sectile* (or *intarsio*) refers to the creation of images from thin plaques of coloured stone and marble, cut into varying sizes and shapes and laid on a soft cement so as to compose a picture. *Opus tessellatum* (or 'tessellated') is composed of uniformly small square or rectangular tesserae in a limited number of colours (mostly black and white); this was used principally for large areas of floor and background designs. The last, *opus vermiculatum* (or 'vermiculated'), refers to the intricate, often minute, work done in many different colours, occasionally with differently shaped or carefully fashioned tesserae so as to adapt better to the ('vermicular' or 'worm-like') flow of a complex figurative design. This technique was reserved for the *emblemata*, and was considered almost a branch of painting. Its wide range of brilliant colours was sometimes provided by semi-precious stones, such as malachite or lapis lazuli. The preparatory base (*suspensura*) was built up from many layers of increasingly fine plaster and cement; the design was etched into the upper surface, and areas of that design were then covered with a final layer of cement, small enough for the artist (the *tessellarius*) to complete in one day's work. These processes may lie behind the origins of medieval and Renaissance fresco method. Mosaic was an expensive and labour-intensive technique by comparison with wall painting: but it was incomparably more durable, and was a desirable expression of wealth and luxury.

Mosaics from the House of the Faun:
A number of the finest examples anywhere of the art of mosaic come from the House of the Faun in Pompeii, one of the richest residences in the town, and the property of a merchant who may have used the high quality of the art in his house to impress his clients. On the fateful night of 24th August 79 AD, having already set off once to evacuate his family, it appears that he returned home again in order to collect his strong-box, and was overcome and died in the entrance of his own house. The mosaics from here are all *emblemata* of magnificent quality, nearly all executed in *opus vermiculatum*; they adorned different rooms in the house: the *Festoon of Flowers and Fruit* was from the threshold between the entrance vestibule and the Tuscan atrium; the *Cat Capturing a Partridge*, and *Nile Ducks with Lotus Flowers*, from a room next to the atrium; the *Satyr and Nymph*, from one of the bedrooms. Appropriate for its setting in the centre of the dining couches of the triclinium is a collage of *Crustacea and Marine Creatures*, featuring over 20 species, all of remarkable zoological accuracy. This should be imagined sunk into the floor below a layer of water,

which would make the colours—and the creatures—seem yet more alive. The most impressive work of all was the large rectangular mosaic of **Alexander and Darius at the Battle of Issus**, in the inner tablinum of the house: beautiful in its decorative quality and technical refinement as a mosaic, and supremely important in what it tells us about Hellenistic painting, on which it is based. The brilliant foreshortening of the bolting horse in the middle foreground, the subtle highlighting of every detail, and the evocation of solidity and three-dimensionality in the modelling of animal and human alike—achievements that we associate with the European Renaissance of 1,500 years later—show that the mosaic was based upon a tradition of painting of the greatest sophistication, which was moving towards a fuller understanding of the principles of perspective. All this is achieved in *opus vermiculatum*, availing itself of tesserae in basically no more than four different shades. It is generally believed to be the work of mosaic artists from Alexandria, and to be based upon a painting by Philoxenos of Eretria (late 4th century BC), which was latterly displayed in the Temple of Concord in Rome, and was

Alexander and Darius at the Battle of Issus. Mosaic from the House of the Faun at Pompeii.

much admired by Pliny (*Nat. Hist.* 35.110). The mosaic depicts the Battle of Issus (333 BC), often considered the decisive moment for the fortunes of Alexander in his campaign against the Persian king; it depicts the pivotal moment in the battle, in which Darius (centre right, with Persian cap on his head) first senses that the turning tide of battle is unstoppable in the face of the onslaught of Alexander (left).

Other mosaics: Other highlights of this collection include: the *Academy at Athens*, seven figures (Plato in the centre) with the Acropolis of Athens in the background; the *Comic Actors* (sometimes described as street musicians), from the so-called 'Villa of Cicero', representing two women, a man and a dwarf, all masked and playing musical instruments; and *Consulting the Sorceress*, a typical scene from Roman comedy. These last two mosaics are both signed, 'Dioscorides of Samos', and are more likely to be faithful and complete copies of signed paintings by Dioscorides, than mosaics executed and signed by him. There are columns, encrusted in mosaic work, an exquisitely decorated wall-niche for a statuette, fountains and even naturalistic portraits.

The paintings

Pompeian interiors were dark; the town houses had no windows and the only light entered from the doorway. The brilliant, deep colours and surfaces of these paintings, which were polished to a shine with warm beeswax, must be seen in this context: they maximised a minimal light and virtually glowed in the shadow. They are not frescoes (*see box on p. 186*) painted in the way a Renaissance fresco was painted, i.e. with a water-soluble pigment bound into the wall by the drying of fresh plaster. Here, the detail was all painted with a saponified wax and pigment, once the coloured plaster surface was dry. This gives them an enamel-like quality (especially in the highlights), which was further enhanced by regular wax-polishing. The highlights stand up on the surface, and help increase the delicate modelling which gives the flesh substance and solidity. The painters appear to feel their way towards a grasp of perspective in some of the landscape and townscapes—a perspective that is not perfect, but which reveals a keen sense of the potential of opening the surface up as if it were a window looking onto an imaginary space. These are characteristics which vanish from the pictorial imagination after the 4th century AD, and do not recur until the 15th century in

Europe. And if such characteristics are not perfect here, it should be remembered that these artists were mostly no more than copyists and decorators.

THE FOUR STYLES OF POMPEIAN PAINTING

The so-called 'four styles' of Pompeian painting are a conventional definition used since the late 19th century. Like any system, they are not ideal, but since the habit of categorisation dies hard, they are summarised here:

The **first style** was common throughout the Mediterranean world during the 2nd century BC. It consisted in covering the wall with plaster, painted and shaped to look like coloured marble, which it substituted. This was a common form of interior decoration for those who could not afford the considerable expense of real polychrome marble revetments, and is therefore widely used except in the very richest residences of the capital. The best examples are the House of Sallust and the House of the Faun at Pompeii, or the Samnite House at Herculaneum.

The **second style** was an original Roman creation, fashionable from about 80 BC to the end of the 1st century BC, in which the plane of the wall is illusionistically opened up and made to recede in space with perspective architecture, landscapes or figure scenes. The Villa of Poppaea at Oplontis has very fine examples of this. The preferred themes of the figured paintings seem to be mythological or religious narratives, of which there are magnificent examples in the Villa of the Mysteries, outside Pompeii.

The **third style** has a greater decorative emphasis, and a play of light, atmosphere and fantasy, to which some have applied the term 'baroque'. It developed from about 20 BC to AD 45. Walls are divided into brilliant monochrome panels, decorated with a delicate ornamentation of various motifs, garlands, swags, small-scale architectural features and light-hearted figures: this can be seen, for example, in the House of Marcus Lucretius Fronto in Pompeii. It was this style that inspired the craze for 'Pompeian interiors' in 18th- and 19th-century European decoration.

The **fourth style** developed after AD 62, when Pompeii was shaken by an earthquake and many houses needed redecorating. For this reason it is the most commonly found in the Vesuvian area. In essence, it is a mixture of everything—or more precisely, an eclectic synthesis of the illusionism of the second style and the flatter elegance of the third style, which combine to frame prominent figurative and narrative panels. The clearest example of this style is the decoration in the House of the Vettii in Pompeii.

Pigments in Pompeian painting were, with the notable exception of Egyptian Blue (a chemically prepared silicate of copper and calcium), naturally occurring earth or mineral pigments: different tones of ferrous oxides (soft reds and greens, browns and yellows) and copper carbonates (strong blues and greens). Vegetable and animal pigments were also used: charred vine-wood for black, bleached, ground chicken-bones for white, and dragon's blood—the resin of the *Calamus Draco* tree—for orange. The most celebrated of all Pompeian colours is the cinnabar red, a naturally occurring mercuric sulphide which Pliny says was almost exclusively extracted in Spain, at the Almadén mines (c. 250km southwest of Madrid). Some of the surface veins were so difficult of access that military lancers were employed to dislodge the mineral-bearing rock with javelins.

Highlights of the Pompeian painting collection

Many of the figurative panels, or *emblemata*, worthy of note are copies or variations of ancient Greek masterpieces. The picture of **Perseus and Andromeda** is considered to be a faithful copy of a painting by Nikias, the 4th-century BC Athenian painter. His contemporary, the great sculptor Praxiteles, once said that it was only to Nikias that he would ever entrust his statues for their colouring. **Hercules Finding his Son Telephus in Arcadia**, from the Basilica at Herculaneum, is based on a famous work by Apelles, which Pliny says adorned the Temple of Diana on the Aventine Hill in Rome. It represents the Greek hero watching a doe suckle his child Telephus before a seated personification of Arcadia flanked by the eagle of Zeus, the Nemean lion, and a basket of fruit (the area's fertility). Of note is the masterful modelling and highlighting of the naked body of Hercules. A contemporary Roman would not have missed the connection between this scene and the story of Romulus and Remus, who were nurtured by a she-wolf. The legend of Hercules' son also inspired the neo-Attic *Relief of Telephus*, from the house of the same name at Herculaneum.

One *emblema*, the **Theseus and the Minotaur**, has an unexpected similarity to an early Renaissance depiction of a scene from the life of a saint. The central figure of Theseus stands beside the dead body of the Minotaur, while a grateful and somewhat reflective group of citizens crowd forward to kiss his feet and hands in gratitude.

Four tiny, and much reproduced, paintings of women—**Medea**, **Leda and the Swan**, **Diana**, and a girl gathering flowers (the so-called **Flora** or *Spring*)—all set against a single-coloured background, reveal a sensitivity to delicate drapery and an effortless naturalism of pose: these beautiful pieces were no more than minor elements in a background wall at the Villa of Ariadne at Stabiae.

Amongst other miscellaneous works is the interesting depiction of a **Brawl in the Amphitheatre at Pompeii** between citizens of Pompeii and Nuceria. This records an ugly event that took place in AD 59, and whose seriousness prompted the temporary closure of the amphitheatre by Nero, a fact commented on by Tacitus (*Annals XIV. 17*). The image clearly shows the *velarium*, or awning, partly drawn over the seating area, and the presence of drinks-stalls in the square before the entrance.

The so-called **Girls Playing with Knuckle-bones** (or the *Astragal Players*) represents a rather different and unusual technique. It is an image of remarkable elegance and bears the signature of a certain Alexander of Athens. It is executed in an encaustic (wax and pigment) monochrome on marble. The scene represents an early moment in the evolving vengeance of Leto on Niobe (narrated by Ovid in *Metamorphoses VI*), which culminates in the tragic death of Niobe's twelve children.

There are a number of portraits among these paintings, but few as arresting as that of ***Paquius Proculus and his Wife***, a double portrait of a young local official and his wife, probably the owners of the bakery attached to the house in Pompeii where the painting was found. The large eyes and frontal gaze are reminiscent of the style of the Fayum portraits from Roman Egypt, although the quality here is not so high. The liveliness of these portraits makes it all the more uncomfortable to contemplate the ignorance that these two confident individuals had of the imminent destruction of their city only a few years later—and of the demise of their civilization within a few generations.

Both Pompeii and Herculaneum had large communities of devotees of the goddess Isis, whose popular cult had wide appeal on account of its promised hope of salvation in the afterlife: for this reason, it presented a severe obstacle to the progress of a nascent Christianity. By chance, almost the entire **pictorial decoration of the Temple of Isis from Pompeii** is preserved, and the paintings are displayed in an attempt to recreate their installation *in situ*. The reconstruction is based on original documents surrounding the building's discovery, which was in the early years of the Bourbon excavations (1764–66). It is instructive to think of this series in relation to a painted church interior of later centuries. The paintings have a quality of delicacy and fantasy, consonant with the gentler tenets of the cult. The Nilotic landscapes of almost impressionistic beauty in blues and greens with symbolic animals, delicately suggested figures, and a natural sense of space, reveal yet another remarkable facet of the versatility of Roman painting.

The Gabinetto Segreto: erotica

This small collection contains paintings, mosaics, statuettes and reliefs of erotic subjects. Its segregation, and its original subjection to rules limiting access, reflect the social awkwardness felt at of some of the discoveries made at Pompeii and Herculaneum during the Bourbon excavations. Documents of the time compared Pompeii to Sodom and recorded over a hundred objects that were deemed 'infamous monuments of heathen licentiousness'. Ancient Romans had a generally easy and uncomplicated relation to matters of sex and eroticism, and the objects exhibited in this group can be both amusing and instructive of changing fashions and unchanging obsessions. The marble group of *Pan and a Goat*, from the Villa of the Papyri at Herculaneum, is a work of succinct design and great energy.

Decorative arts and furnishings from Herculaneum, Stabiae and Pompeii

This fascinating and wide-ranging collection of household furnishings and personal effects shows how complete the Hellenisation of Roman lifestyles had been by the 1st century AD. Pliny, Seneca and many Roman thinkers lamented Rome's increasing dependence and expenditure on unnecessary imports from the East: they witnessed what they considered the advent of Oriental *luxuria* into the once austere homes of Republican Rome. The simple, functional household items of early times were replaced by highly refined and often precious objects that the well-to-do displayed and recognised as signs of social and economic status. As Roman domestic life acquired style and sophistication, antiques were increasingly sought-after, and the ornamental sculptures of homes and gardens were copied from Classical and Hellenistic prototypes. As is explained below, the technology behind many of these beautiful objects was also of Eastern origin.

The section has a wealth of objects that contribute to a living vision of ancient Roman life: ivory boxes with make-up items, vanity mirrors, ceiling and table lamps, water-heaters, room-heaters, food-scales, jewellery, gladiatorial helmets, cooking utensils, games, toys and ornaments both banal and beautiful. So much has survived and so well, because it was sealed from the atmosphere by the volcanic dust and ash that filled and surrounded the objects: the first rains that came after the eruption had the effect of turning that packed ash into a hard-setting case of cement. The organic material was mostly purged; but the inorganic was marvellously preserved for posterity.

Silver, bronze and other metalwork

The single most impressive display in this section—comparable with the Boscoreale treasure now in the Louvre—is the assortment of **tableware in silver from the House of Menander**. The service was found—packed and carefully wrapped in cloth for protection—in a deposit underneath the house in Pompeii, together with the family jewels and a hoard of gold and silver coins, all of it stowed away during building works which were under way in the house to repair damage after the earthquake of AD 62. The owner of the home is thought to have been Quintus Poppaeo, a well-known entrepreneur and a relative of Poppaea, Nero's second wife, who was probably the owner of the grand villa at Oplontis (*see p. 210*). Many of the items, such as jugs, wine-strainers and cutlery, seem surprisingly modern and familiar in design. The exquisite drinking cups, with mythological scenes intricately depicted in embossed repoussé work, enhanced with etching and chiselling, were probably imported from Hellenistic workshops in the East, though some scholars suggest they may be locally made copies. Note how they possess a second, smooth interior shell in silver: in this way, rather like a primitive thermos flask, they preserved for longer the hot or cool temperature of the contents. Amongst the bronze items are a well-preserved variety of cooking implements, pans and skillets. The cooking moulds in the form of different animals give a rich visual sense of the Roman dinner table, laden with moulded pâtés of hare, and cold salad of pork, fruit and nuts, shaped in the form of a suckling-pig.

Glassware

Because of their perfection of the technology of glass-blowing (a skill whose rudiments were first developed in 1st-century BC Syria), Roman artists hugely expanded the possibilities and the beauty of their glassware, creating objects of brilliant chromatic appeal, and of thinner and lighter body. They possess a sense of colour and abstract design which naturally appeals to modern taste.

Deservedly the centerpiece of the collection is the 1st-century **blue cameo glass vase with Dionysiac scenes,** discovered in December 1837 in the Via dei Sepolcri Necropolis in Pompeii, and comparable in technique and design with the Portland Vase in the British Museum. Both are executed in cameo, which involves the intricate cutting away and engraving of an outer casing of white glass, to create a design against a darker glass background. Such vases as these involved a complex and difficult method of manufacture (known as 'casing'), in which a molten lump of blue glass was inserted inside a still very hot, cup-shaped blank of white glass, and the two were inflated together, with frequent re-heatings, until they obtained the shape and thickness required. This example, so exquisitely embellished with birds, vine foliage and scenes of the grape-harvest, is a cinerary urn which contained the ashes of an unknown citizen of Pompeii. The idea of the grape-bunch and its treading and maceration as a symbol of the decay of the body and the release of its spirit was already an ancient image in pagan art by the time it was adopted in Christian iconography. It is hard to conceive of a more beautiful receptacle in which to pass eternity.

Specialised collections

The Farnese Gems
Gems were among the first antiquities to become collectibles, entering the possession of kings and high prelates first as charms, then as devotional objects, thanks to a transferral of Christian themes to pagan iconography. Poseidon and Athena became Adam and Eve; Perseus and Medusa, David and Goliath; and Leda and the Swan—of all things—the Annunciation. In the Renaissance, gems were among the most fashionable objects one could possess. This collection, one of the most important of its kind in the world, was begun by Ranuccio and Alessandro Farnese, the heirs to Pope Paul III. Later, the collection of Fulvio Orsini, a humanist scholar who worked as librarian to the Farnese family, was added to the original core, together with several pieces belonging to the Medici family that were brought as dowry by Margaret of Austria, mother of Alessandro Farnese, the future Duke of Parma and hero of the Battle of Lepanto. By the beginning of the 17th century there were over 500 gems in the collection.

There are fundamentally two kinds of work represented here: intaglio work, which is incised to make seals in largely monochrome material such as chalcedony, jasper or cornelian (or else clearer, harder materials such as amethyst, topaz or ruby); and cameo work, which uses a naturally stratified material such as onyx or sardonyx in which the figurative decoration is chiselled away in relief.

Centrepiece of the collection—and perhaps the most extraordinary example of its kind—is the celebrated *Tazza Farnese*, a cameo dish made from a veined and layered sardonyx. This work presupposes two very rare things: first, a naturally occurring piece of sardonyx with a perfect and regular superimposition of two unblemished layers, one opaque and light, the other transparent and dark; and second, an artist capable of cutting the stone along exactly the right axis, and then carving it to the precise depth required, but no further, so as to leave his intricate design clearly on one stratum against the background of the contrasting stratum, and circumscribed exactly by the interior form of the dish. Those two requirements came together in 3rd-century BC Alexandria (a centre for fine stone-crafting which had no equal in the ancient world). There has been much time-consuming debate about what exactly the design shows; and the different suggestions are laboriously explained by the museum's label. It is, in short, a complicated allegory of the origins and mechanisms of the fertility of Egypt, personified by the divinity of the Nile, seated to the left. Irrespective of what it signifies, however, the object itself embodies an apex—and a supreme love—of craftsmanship.

Egyptian collection
This section displays hieroglyphics, mummies, sculptures of sacred animals and funerary statuettes (ushabti). Noteworthy for its intrinsic beauty and excellent state of preservation is a mummy case of the 22nd Dynasty, dating from the 9th century BC. A specific section is dedicated to Egyptian artefacts discovered in the cities of Campania. These document the relationship that existed between Campania and Egypt, which began in the Ptolemaic period through Phoenician trade with Greek colonists, and lasted throughout the 2nd century BC, when the worship of Isis reached Italy. The taste for things Egyptian spread throughout the Roman world after the victory of Octavian over Antony and Cleopatra at the Battle of Actium in 31 BC.

Epigraphic collection
This is a recent addition to the museum and comprises inscriptions acquired from private collections by the Bourbons, and discoveries made throughout southern Italy. The first part of the collection is dedicated to inscriptions brought from Greece; the second, to Greek-language inscriptions from Naples. There are also pre-Roman epigraphs of the Italic peoples of central and southern Italy. Lastly, there is a selection of the numerous inscriptions found in Campanian cities, including wax tablets recording loans, which formed part of the ledger of L. Caecilius Iucundus, the Pompeian banker (*see p. 85 above*). Perhaps the most intriguing piece is the tiny Orphic gold lamina from Thurii (4th century BC), bearing an inscription initiating a soul to eternal bliss at the end of its cycle of transmigrations.

Numismatic collection
The museum has a superb collection of over 200,000 coins and medals (of which a selection is on view at any one time), mostly assembled for the Farnese family by the humanist librarian Fulvio Orsini, or from excavations in Campanian cities carried out under the Bourbons. The collection ranges from fine examples of 6th-century BC Greek silver *staters*, through Roman Republican and Imperial coins, Byzantine and mediaeval *solidi*, to gold ducats and 19th-century coins of the Kingdom of the Two Sicilies.

Women performing a funeral dance, from a 4th-century BC tomb found at Ruvo.

Prehistoric Campania

Included in this section are archaeological finds which trace the development of Campanian cultures from prehistory to the Greek colonisation; exhibits reconstructing the history and material culture of the non-Greek cities of ancient Campania populated by Etruscans, Samnites and Campanians; and material from sites throughout the Bay of Naples and Magna Graecia.

The **Vivenzio Hydria** is named after its excavators, the brothers Vivenzio, who supplied the collections of 18th-century Europe with finds from Nola. Their sack of the city's necropolis yielded numerous examples of Attic ceramics, including this beautiful water vessel (unearthed in 1791), decorated by the Cleophrades Painter with scenes from the final moments of Troy. Used as a cinerary urn, the vase was found inside a large jar together with several alabaster *unguentaria* and a gem engraved with the eagle of Zeus. Its condition is superb for a vase of this date (early 5th century BC).

The **murals from the Tomb of the Warrior** are an example of ancient vernacular art from Campania. The tomb dates from c. 350 BC, and was also found at Nola. The scene is of the bestowal of public and private honours on the warrior who returns from battle enriched with spoils: on the longer panels a female figure offers a *skyphos* to an armoured horseman accompanied by two foot-soldiers and an equerry; on the shorter sides the horseman bears a trophy and a table holds vessels for water and wine. The scenes are created in simple earth pigments against a pale background, and framed by running borders with 'Greek key' and wave motifs, of clearly Hellenic influence. Another superb example of funerary decoration is the **painting from a chamber tomb from Ruvo** (4th century BC) showing women, their hair modestly covered, dancing a line dance, their arms linked across each other's chests.

Catacomba di San Gennaro

Map p. 50, 2: Bus B24 from Piazza Trieste e Trento or Metro 1 to Piazza Dante, then Bus

B24. *Entrance in Via Capodimonte; open daily for guided tours, 9.30, 10.15, 11, 11.45.*
The Catacomb of San Gennaro, located beneath the church of San Gennaro extra
Moenia, dates from the 2nd century AD and seems to have developed around the family tomb of an early member of the Christian community. It probably became the official cemetery of Christian Naples after the burial here, in the 3rd century, of the bishop-saint Agrippinus, over whose tomb a basilica was built. Later, when St Januarius,
the 5th-century martyr and patron saint of the city, was entombed here, the catacomb
became a place of pilgrimage. The first dukes of Naples, notably Stephen I (d. AD 800)
and Stephen III (d. 832), are also buried here. In 831 Sicone, prince of Benevento,
carried the relics of San Gennaro off to his city; and around the mid-9th century the
bishop-saint John IV transferred the remains of his illustrious predecessors to the
cathedral. But he, like his successor St Athanasius (d. 877), was nevertheless buried
here, and the catacomb remained in use throughout the 10th and probably the 11th
century. The catacomb contains burial cells and fragmentary frescoes and mosaics, but
is interesting above all for its extent and overall ambience.

A second early Christian burial ground lies beneath the church of Santa Maria della
Sanità. Once quite extensive, only a small part remains. Known as the Catacomb of
San Gaudioso, it was named after the African bishop-saint Gaudiosus who, according
to a very old legend, was deposed by the Vandal king Genseric, and set adrift in a
small boat. After many vicissitudes, he landed at Naples, where he founded a
monastery. Gaudiosus died in 451 or 452 and was venerated as a saint. An extensive
cemetery grew up around his tomb, of which only a small part remains today.

MUSEO E GALLERIE NAZIONALI DI CAPODIMONTE

PALAZZO REALE DI CAPODIMONTE

Map p. 51, 3. Museum open daily except Weds 8.30–7.30; T: 081 749 9111. Entrance
through the most northerly of the building's three courtyards. Café. Gabinetto Stampe e
Disegni (print and drawing room) open by appointment. The palace is 4km from Piazza del
Municipio and 3.5km from Piazza Garibaldi (Stazione Centrale). Regular bus services run
from the city centre to the museum: no. 24 from Piazza Vittoria via Piazza Dante stops at
the Porta Grande, the entrance to the magnificent park (open 9–dusk; free). Kilns from the
famous porcelain works founded by Charles of Bourbon in 1739 may be seen inside.

The Palazzo Reale di Capodimonte is magnificently situated in a fine park, enjoying a wide view of Naples and Campania. In May 1957 it was opened as the new seat of the Museo e Gallerie Nazionali di Capodimonte, comprising the National Gallery of Naples, and important exhibitions of tapestries, furniture, armour, porcelain and ivories from the royal collections. The first floor holds the Farnese Collections and the Royal Apartments, both of which merit close attention. A large section on the arts in Naples from the 13th–18th centuries, and an exhibit of drawings, have opened on the second floor. The former store-rooms and restoration laboratories on the third floor now house a good collection of 19th-century Italian paintings, previously in the Accademia di Belle Arti, and a selection of photographs and contemporary art.

Intended by Charles III of Bourbon to be the most important summer hunting-lodge in Europe, the palace was begun in 1738 by Giovanni Antonio Medrano, and the park was designed by Ferdinando Sanfelice. The construction by Joachim Murat of the Sanità bridge and of a new approach road stimulated further enlargements, which were completed by Antonio Niccolini for Ferdinand II in 1838. After the decline of the Bourbons, the palace became a favourite haunt of Vittorio Emanuele II, and in 1906–47 of the Dukes of Aosta.

First floor

The Farnese Collections
The fabulous Farnese Collections, which constitute the core of the museum's holdings, have been brought together in the monumental rooms on the main floor. The arrangement highlights the museum's oldest and most important collection of master paintings and drawings, inherited by Charles of Bourbon from his mother, Elisabetta Farnese. The rooms are reached by the grand staircase designed by Tommaso Giordano. At the bottom, introducing the richness of the collection, is the impressive *Jupiter Shooting Arrows at the Titans*, a group in biscuit porcelain by Filippo Tagliolini, chief modeller at the Capodimonte porcelain manufactory (*see p. 119*).

The original collection has been augmented by later purchases. In the description of highlights below, works which were not part of the Farnese holdings are indicated.

Room 2. Works celebrating Pope Paul III and the Farnese family: Here are some famous portraits by Titian including *Paul III* (1545), painted for Odoardo Farnese and bequeathed to the family's humanist scholar and librarian, Fulvio Orsini; *Paul III with his Grandsons Alessandro and Ottavio Farnese* (1545–46), a painting of great psychological insight in which the young men are shown as continuing the family's ecclesiastical and secular traditions; and *Cardinal Alessandro Farnese* (1545–46), famous for the detail of his gloves, which suggests that Alessandro (cardinal at the age of fourteen) was something of a dandy. Also in this room is a portrait of the future Pope Paul III (1509–11) while still a cardinal (as Cardinal Alessandro Farnese, he is not to be confused with his grandson of the same name). The work is attributed to Raphael and was painted on the occasion of Alessandro's election as Bishop of Parma, the first step in his climb to power. Though much younger, he is recognisably the same man as is shown in the Titian portrait, with his canny eyes, and the head thrust forward on the neck. Here too are Giorgio Vasari's *Allegory of Justice, Truth and Vice;* a fine Medici tapestry showing the *Sacrifice of Alexander*, after a cartoon by Francesco Salviati (after 1542); and Andrea del Sarto's *Leo X with Two Cardinals* (1525) showing the pope with his cardinal-nephews Giulio de' Medici (the future Pope Clement VII) and Luigi de' Rossi. This is a copy of the famous work by Raphael, secretly commissioned by Ottaviano de' Medici and sent in guile to Federico Gonzaga instead of the original, which Federico had demanded as a gift from Clement VII. The composition is meant to express approval of the transfer of ecclesiastical power along blood lines.

Portrait (1545–46) by Titian of Cardinal Alessandro Farnese, grandson of Pope Paul III.

Room 3: The highlight here is a *Crucifixion* by Masaccio, from a polyptych painted in 1426 for the private chapel of Giuliano da San Giusto, a wealthy notary, in the Carmine in Pisa. The polyptych is now dismembered, its parts on display in London (main panel: the enthroned Madonna holding the Christ Child, eating grapes as a prefiguration of the Passion); the Getty Museum in Malibu (*St Andrew*); Pisa (*St Paul*) and Berlin (the three predella panels and four side panels with saints). This work was purchased for the collection in 1901.

Room 4. Cartoons from the private collection of Fulvio Orsini: Orsini was librarian and artistic adviser to Paul III's grandsons Ranuccio and Alessandro Farnese. Works include Michelangelo's group of soldiers (c. 1546), a cartoon for the fresco of the *Crucifixion of St Peter* in the Vatican; copies after Michelangelo attributed to Pontormo and Hendrik van der Broecke; Giovanni Francesco Penni, *Madonna of Divine Love;* Raphael, *Moses Before the Burning Bush* (c. 1514), a cartoon for another Vatican fresco, in which the scale and sculptural quality of the figure recall Michelangelo's ceiling in the Sistine Chapel (unveiled in 1512).

THE FARNESE

The origins of the Farnese family may date as far back as the 10th century. The name derives from a modest fief, Castrum Farneti, near Lake Bolsena in northern Lazio. The first family members to be admitted to the Roman aristocracy were Ranuccio the Elder, who commanded the papal army in the early 15th century, and his son Pier Luigi, who married Giovannella Caetani of the ducal family of Sermoneta. Pier Luigi had two children, both of whom distinguished themselves at an early age: Giulia became the mistress of Rodrigo Borgia, continuing her relation with the prince after his election as Pope Alexander VI. Alessandro became a cardinal at the age of twenty-five, then pope (as Paul III) in 1534.

Alessandro's papacy marked the high point of the family's fortunes—not only because of the prestige of the office, but also because of the way he managed power. He detached Parma and Piacenza from the Papal States and made them into independent duchies, which he gave to his son Pier Luigi. The latter's second son and heir (after 1547), Ottavio, was married to Margaret of Austria, natural daughter of Emperor Charles V. Ottavio's brothers, Alessandro (Bishop of Parma, Avignon and Tours; *pictured on previous page*) and Ranuccio (Bishop of Bologna and Archbishop of Naples) were both made cardinals, Alessandro when just fourteen.

Paul III's great-grandson, also named Alessandro, succeeded Ottavio in 1586. The third Duke of Parma and Piacenza was educated at the court of Madrid. Like his ancestors, he followed a career of arms. After his father's death, he continued in command of the Spanish forces in Flanders because Philip II of Spain would not permit him to return to Italy. Five other dukes—Ranuccio I, Odoardo I, Ranuccio II, Francesco and Antonio—succeeded Alessandro before the dynasty finally died out in 1731. When Antonio's niece Elisabetta, a woman of acute intelligence and brilliant character, married Philip V of Spain and secured the succession for her son Charles (he would become Charles III of Spain), the blood line of the Dukes of Parma merged with that of the Spanish sovereigns.

The Farnese also distinguished themselves as patrons of the arts. They financed the church of the Gesù in Rome, Villa Farnese at Caprarola, and the royal palace ('La Pilotta') and theatre in Parma; they supported important archaeological excavations in and around the Eternal City; and they commissioned original paintings from artists such as Raphael and Titian. In 1731 Elisabetta Farnese bequeathed the family art collections to her son Charles of Bourbon, who built the Royal Palace of Capodimonte in Naples expressly to hold them. Later joined by archaeological treasures unearthed at Pompeii, Herculaneum, Cumae and Stabiae; major antiquities (such as the *Farnese Hercules* and *Farnese Bull*) brought from Rome; and various acquisitions, they were moved to the present Museo Archeologico in 1818. In 1954 the paintings, prints and drawings were brought back to Capodimonte, where they now form the core of one of the world's great public collections.

Room 5: The *Assumption of the Virgin* and *Foundation of the Basilica of Santa Maria Maggiore* (c. 1428) by Masolino are two panels of a triptych commissioned by Pope Martin V from Masolino and Masaccio (the latter died before they were completed) for Santa Maria Maggiore in Rome. In the *Foundation of Santa Maria Maggiore* the artists' research into single-point perspective is evident in the architecture of the middle ground, which recedes toward a central vanishing point. The overriding atmosphere, given by the miraculous snowfall which according to the legend traced the ground plan of the new church, is magical.

Room 6. Early Renaissance in Tuscany and Umbria: Sandro Botticelli's *Madonna and Child with Two Angels* (1468–69), painted when the young artist was still under the influence of his masters Filippino Lippi (the influence seen, for example, in the Virgin's diaphanous veil) and Verrocchio (in the modelling of the figures); Perugino (or after), *Madonna and Child* (1496–98); and a tondo by Sebastiano Mainardi depicting the *Madonna and Child with Angels*, belong to the Farnese Collection. Luca Signorelli's *Adoration of the Child* (1493–98); Lorenzo di Credi's *Adoration of the Child* (1523); and fragments of an early altarpiece by Raphael painted with an assistant for the church of Sant'Agostino at Città di Castello (1501), come from other Bourbon collections, as do the small *Christ Carrying the Cross* by the Emilian painter Francesco Zaganelli, showing the influence of Dürer, and Filippino Lippi's *Annunciation with Saints* (1483), with the city of Florence clearly depicted in the background.

Room 7. Objets d'art and paintings from the eclectic collection of Cardinal Stefano Borgia: This room affords a brief respite from the Farnese Collection. It holds items from the collection of the cardinal who co-ordinated Catholic missions throughout the world in the last quarter of the 18th century, acquired from his heirs by Ferdinand I in 1817. Here are masterpieces of European art, such as Bernardo Daddi's, *Madonna and Child;* a beautiful triptych by Taddeo Gaddi (1336); Andrea Mantegna, *St Euphemia* (1454), the saint shown with one arm in the jaws of a lion, an allusion to her martryrdom (she was allegedly thrown to the wild beasts for refusing to worship the pagan gods). The collection also contains objects of historical and ethnographic interest from Egypt, Asia and Central America (*Second Incarnation of Vishnu*, a watercolour showing the Hindu god seated on a mountain—the Earth—carried by a turtle, while Brahma and Shiva fight off demons and the serpent Vasughi, representing Evil), and scientific instruments (an Arabic sky chart, and an astrolabe from Moorish Spain, c. 1476).

Room 8. 15th- and 16th-century Venetian art: Giovanni Bellini's *Transfiguration* (1478–79) is perhaps the artist's masterpiece, showing perfect command of light and atmosphere, with perfectly rendered wintry colours, a gentle pastoral background, and an extraordinary humanisation of Christ. Other works include Lorenzo Lotto's *Madonna and Child with St Peter Martyr* (1503), the artist's earliest known work, commissioned by Bishop Bernardo de' Rossi as a votive offering for having

CAPODIMONTE
(FIRST FLOOR)

2–30	Farnese Collections
31–60	Royal Apartments
46–50	Armoury
52	Porcelain Salottino

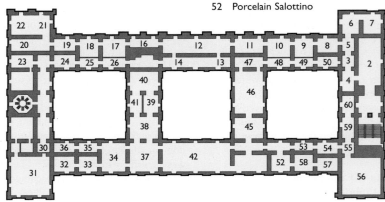

escaped a murder plot; and a portrait of the patron himself, Bernardo de' Rossi, Bishop of Treviso (1505), a work of unmitigated realism, perfectly rendering the sitter's freckled complexion, red hair and pale green eyes; also Andrea Mantegna's *Francesco Gonzaga* (1406–62), cardinal at seventeen, later portrayed by the artist in the *Camera degli Sposi* in Mantua. The memorable portrait of the Franciscan mathematician Luca Pacioli is attributed to Jacopo de' Barbari (1495); the young student is thought to be Guidubaldo da Montefeltro, to whom Pacioli dedicated his best-known treatise, the *Summa de Arithmetica, Geometria, Proportione*. The work was purchased in 1903.

Room 9. Painting in Rome in the first half of the 16th century: Giulio Romano's *Madonna della Gatta* (c. 1523) is clearly indebted to Raphael in its compositional scheme. St Joseph appears in the remote shadows of the 16th-century patrician interior, whereas the cat that gives the painting its name looks balefully out from the extreme foreground. The room also holds two paintings by the school of Raphael, the *Madonna of Divine Love* by Giovanni Francesco Penni, and *Holy Family* ('*Madonna of the Veil*') by Sebastiano del Piombo, (1533–35), drawing also on the style of Michelangelo. Also by Sebastiano are two wonderful portraits of Clement VII (one showing the pope seated, his red robe against a green background; the other, a small-scale profile of the head only, painted in very dark colours, interesting for that age). Marcello Venusti's copy after Michelangelo's *Last Judgement* was executed before Daniele da Volterra overpainted the fresco to cover the nakedness of the figures.

Room 10. Painting in Florence in the first quarter of the 16th century: The highlights here are Pontormo's *Scene of Sacrifice* (c. 1540), a mysterious exercise in anti-Classicism executed in grisaille, with two sheep (one with sinisterly carnivorous teeth) burning on an altar; Francesco Salviati's *Gentleman* (c. 1545), a work of singular psychological intensity, possibly the artist's self-portrait; Rosso Fiorentino, *Young Man* (c. 1527), thought to represent Parmigianino; Agnolo Bronzino (attributed), *Lady;* copy after Bronzino, *Madonna and Child with St Anne and the Infant St John.*

Room 11. 16th-century Venetian painting: El Greco, *Portrait of Giulio Clovio* (1571–72), the famous Dalmatian illuminator, holding his *Book of Hours* (now in the Pierpont Morgan Library in New York). The freedom of the brushwork suggests the influence of Titian, under whom El Greco worked on his arrival in Venice in 1567; *Young Man Lighting a Taper with a Glowing Coal* ('*El soplón*', c. 1575), in which the artist brings Venetian colourism to bear on a subject celebrated by Pliny in the *Naturalis Historia;* Titian, *Danaë* (1544–46), painted for the private rooms of Cardinal Alessandro Farnese and representing the story, from Ovid's *Metamorphoses*, of a young princess seduced by Zeus in the form of a shower of gold; the provocative sensuality of the figure contributes to the ambiguity of the scene, which some scholars believe depicts Alessandro's mistress; *Young Lady* (1545–46), thought by some to represent the artist's daughter, Lavinia Vecellio, and by others,

Titian: *Danaë* (1544–46), painted for the private apartments of Cardinal Alessandro Farnese.

Alessandro's young lover, subject of the Danäe; *Mary Magdalene* (c. 1560), with the artist's trademark 'Titian red' hair.

Room 12. 16th-century Emilian painting: Correggio's *St Anthony Abbot*; *St Joseph and a Donor*; *Madonna and Child* ('*La Zingarella*') and *Mystic Marriage of St Catherine* (c. 1520) all belonged to Barbara Sanseverino Sanvitale, a prominent aristocrat of Parma, until the discovery of her involvement in a plot against Ranuccio I Farnese, Duke of Parma and Piacenza, a man of great culture and great cruelty. When the plot against him was discovered (1612), Barbara Sanseverino Sanvitale's assets were confiscated.

There are also works by Girolamo Mazzola Bedoli: *Portrait of a Tailor* (c. 1545), a smiling old man with a bolt of gold damask; *Annunciation* (c. 1560), a magnificent scene showing the young Virgin at her sewing basket suddenly disturbed by the apparition of a beautiful angel, his naked torso bathed in light, the Holy Spirit above his head, and shadowy putti in every corner of the small room; and Parmigianino: *Galeazzo Sanvitale* (1524), showing the spatial ambiguity and disquieting effects of light and shadow on which the artist built his reputation; *Holy Family* (c. 1527); *Young Woman* (1530–35), richly attired with a fur tippett, identified with a court lady named Antea, possibly the artist's mistress during his years in Rome; and Dosso Dossi, including a very attractive *Sacra Conversazione*, an early work, skilfully composed and with bold use of colour (though the draughtsmanship of the hands and arms is unsuccessful).

Rooms 13–14: These rooms make up a sort of *Wunderkammer*, or room of marvels, displaying a wealth of precious and rare objects. On the entrance walls between Rooms 12 and 13 are a portrait miniature of *Settimia Iacobacci* by Giulio Clovio and an amber plaquette of the *Holy Family with the Infant St John*. The paintings in Room 13 reflect the artistic climate of the Farnese court at Parma: Girolamo Mirola, *Intervention of the Sabine Women in the Battle between the Romans and Sabines*; Jacopo Zanguidi ('Bertoja'), *Madonna and Child*; Jan Sons, *Tabula Cebetis Thebani*; *Baptism of Christ*; *St Cecilia and the Vision of St John*; *Loves of the Gods* (ceiling). Renaissance bronze statuettes are displayed here and in the adjoining room, Room 14: Giambologna, *Rape of the Sabines* (1578), a small bronze prototype of the marble group in Florence, commissioned by Duke Ottavio for his study; *Mercury*; Giacomo della Porta, *Cupid*; Francesco di Giorgio Martini, *David* (1475–85), combining iconographic traditions of the Middle Ages (David as elderly prophet) and the Renaissance (as young hero); L'Antico, *Venus*; Baccio Bandinelli, *Cleopatra*; Niccolò Roccatagliata, *Minerva*; bronzes by Il Riccio (Andrea Briosco); and a female figure by Alessandro Vittoria. Also in Room 14 are the *Farnese Casket* (1548–61), a box in gilt silver, lapis lazuli, enamel and carved crystal made for Cardinal Alessandro Farnese; as well as the crystal Farnese bread-tray incised with a drunken Silenus from a design by Annibale Carracci. The display cases contain Renaissance medals (Pisanello, among others), plaquettes, incised crystals, ambers, ivories, goldsmiths' work (centrepiece of *Diana the Huntress*, 1610, by Jacob Miller the Elder), and the majolica Farnese dining service, made for Cardinal Alessandro in the Castelli manufactory.

Room 16. 15th- and 16th-century Lombard painting: Bernardino Luini, *Madonna and Child* (1510–20), showing a strong Leonardesque influence, notably in the Virgin's features.

Room 17. Flemish and German painting: Pieter Brueghel the Elder, *The Misanthrope* (1568), showing the world as a common cutpurse. The Flemish proverb at the bottom reads, 'As the world is so untrustworthy, I am in mourning'; *The Blind Leading the Blind* (1568), illustrating the well-known New Testament parable ('if the blind lead the blind, both shall fall into the ditch', *Matthew 15, v. 14*); both paintings were confiscated from Cosimo Masi, an agent of Alessandro Farnese in Flanders who fell from favour after taking part in the conspiracy hatched in Parma against the iron rule of Duke Ranuccio I (1612). There are also a number of landscapes by Herri met de Bles ('Civetta'), and, by the workshop of Konrad Witz, a striking *Sacra Conversazione*, with the holy group shown inside a large church.

Room 18: Sixteenth-century genre scenes by Joachim Beuckelaer: *Street Market*; *Country Market*; *Vendor of Exotic Animals*; *Game Vendor*; *Butcher's Shop*; *Fish Market*.

Room 19: This room is almost entirely dedicated to the art of the Bolognese brothers Annibale and Agostino Carracci and their cousin Ludovico. Founders at Bologna of the 'Accademia degli

Incamminati', they called for a return to the Classical and balanced art of Raphael, avoiding the contrived and intellectual style of late Mannerism. In 1595 Annibale was called to Rome by Cardinal Odoardo Farnese in order to decorate the gallery in the family palace with the Loves of the Gods. His art proved to be extremely influential on the first generation of Baroque painters working in Rome in the early 17th century, many of whom followed their master from Bologna. Particularly noteworthy are: Agostino Carracci, *Lute Player* (?Orazio Bassani); *Arrigo Peloso*, *Pietro Matto and Amon Nano* (c. 1598), representing three characters from the Roman court of Cardinal Odoardo Farnese: Pietro the buffoon, Rodomonte the dwarf, and Arrigo Gonzalez, the 'wild man of the Canary Islands'; Annibale Carracci, *Marriage of St Catherine* (c. 1585), a masterpiece of Classicism commissioned by Ranuccio Farnese as a gift to his brother, Cardinal Odoardo; *Musician* (Claudio Merulo); workshop of Annibale Carracci, *Annunciation* (recto); *Madonna and Child with St Francis* (verso); Ludovico Carracci, *Rinaldo and Armida* (1593), a literary subject drawn from Tasso's *Gerusalemme Liberata*. The scene shows the Crusader knight Rinaldo in thrall to the beauty of Armida, and neglecting the war he has come to fight.

Room 20: The paintings here show the influence of Bolognese art in Rome in the late 16th and early 17th centuries. Sisto Badalocchio, *Deposition;* Agostino Carracci, *St Jerome; Holy Family with St Margaret;* Annibale Carracci, *Satyr* (perhaps directed against Caravaggio; the smiling head in the corner is a portrait of the artist); *Bacchus; River Allegory; Hercules at the Crossroads* (1596), executed for Cardinal Odoardo Farnese and showing the choice between the 'easy way' of earthly pleasure, indicated by Voluptuousness, and the rocky path to glory, pointed out by Virtue; *Pietà* (1599–1600), a painterly homage to Michelangelo's sculpture in St Peter's. Notable by Giovanni Lanfranco is the extraordinary *Assumption of Mary Magdalene* (c. 1605), where the saint ascends to heaven above a pastoral landscape bathed in silvery light, her nakedness covered only by her hair. Two figures point in wonder at the scene.

Room 21: This room is dedicated to the art of the Emilian painter Bartolomeo Schedoni (1578–1615), who worked almost exclusively for the Farnese court at Parma. Noteworthy for their absolute realism are: *Announcement of the Massacre of the Innocents; Cupid; Charity; St Sebastian healed by the Pious Women; Portrait of Vincenzo Grassi* (shoemaker of Ranuccio I Farnese).

Room 22. 17th-century Emilian painting: The focus of this room is on Guido Reni and Giovanni Lanfranco as key exponents of two opposite trends: a return to Classicism on the one hand, and early Baroque solutions on the other. Guido Reni, *Atalanta and Hippomenes* (1620–25): the painting is based on Ovid's *Metamorphoses* and shows the nymph Atalanta, who challenged her suitor Hippomenes to a race, stopping to pick one of the golden apples that he intentionally threw to the ground as he ran in order to distract her attention and so win the competition (and her hand). By Lanfranco, *Madonna and Child with Sts Charles Borromeo and Bartholomew; Madonna and Child with Sts Mary of Egypt and Margaret.*

Room 23: The bedroom of Francis I of the Two Sicilies and his second wife Isabella of Spain, decorated *alla Pompeiana* by Antonio Niccolini (1830), is a cosy prelude to the Royal Apartments.

Royal Apartments

The Royal Apartments are entered from Room 30, and are a rich showcase of European decorative arts from the 18th and the first half of the 19th centuries. The rooms also hold some major paintings.

Room 31 (Sala della Culla): So named ('Rome of the Cradle') because it was here that royal births took place, the room has an elliptical floor from Tiberius' villa at Capri (extensively restored); two 19th-century history paintings by Vincenzo Camuccini, two landscapes by Alexandre Hyacinthe Dunoy and Jean Joseph Xavier Bidauld. There are also Neapolitan clocks and

furniture, and a model of the Temple of Isis at Pompeii (*see p. 92*).

Room 32: Giovanni Paolo Panini, *Charles of Bourbon Visiting Pope Benedict XIV in the Coffee House of the Quirinal Palace; Charles of Bourbon Visiting St Peter's in Rome* (both 1745); Antonio Sebastiani, *Charles of Bourbon in Hunting Costume;* English black lacquer furniture (first quarter of the 18th century) with chinoiseries; an English clock by Joseph Martineau (second half of the 18th century).

Room 33: Wonderful landscapes by Antonio Joli, *Departure of Charles III Viewed from the Sea*; *Departure of Charles III Viewed from the Dock*, both painted in 1759 when Charles, upon the death of Ferdinand VI, left Naples to became King of Spain; *Ferdinand IV with his Court on Horseback*; Claude-Joseph Vernet, *Charles of Bourbon Hunting Ducks at Lake Licona*; Anton Raphael Mengs, *Ferdinand IV as a Child*, painted in 1759 when he became King of Naples at the age of eight. English red lacquer furniture (first half of the 18th century) with chinoiseries; two Neapolitan sedan chairs (second half of the 18th century).

Room 34: An important portrait collection of royal couples, including Goya's *King Charles IV of Spain and Queen Maria Luisa*; Neapolitan furniture of the first quarter of the 19th century.

Rooms 35–36: An outstanding collection of porcelain, including the fabulous *Servizio dell'Oca* from Capodimonte (1739–95). The service takes its name from the putto strangling a goose (after a Roman figure group in the Capitoline museums), which decorates the lids. It should actually be called the 'Neapolitan View' service, as it is decorated with a series of views, probably inspired by prints or paintings by Antonio Joli and Jakob Philipp Hackert. The miniatures on the pieces were executed by various artists, first amongst them Giacomo Milani. The set, comprising some 300

pieces, was commissioned by Ferdinand IV from the royal manufactory at Capodimonte in 1793–95. Notable among the other pieces are a series of biscuit figurines executed by Filippo Tagliolini; an altar set comprising a porcelain Crucifix and six candelabra by Giuseppe Gricci; a déjeuner set from the Royal Manufactory of Naples, decorated with Etruscan subjects taken from a series of prints by Tischbein and d'Hancarville; a déjeuner set sent from Vienna by Queen Maria Carolina to her husband Ferdinand IV in 1800–01 (remarkable quality); and four Meissen white figure groups.

Room 37 (Sala da Pranzo): At the two ends of this former dining room are two large-scale family portraits: Angelika Kauffmann, *Family of Ferdinand IV*; and Giuseppe Cammarano, *Family of Francis I* (son and successor of Ferdinand IV).

Rooms 38–41: The Raccolta de Ciccio, a collection of 1,300 objets d'art. *Closed at the time of writing.*

Room 42 (Salone delle Feste): This is the ballroom, adorned in pale blue, pastels and gold by Salvatore Giusti (1835–38); the wall paintings, curtains and furnishings have recently been restored to their original splendour. The room also has three large crystal chandeliers and a collection of musical instruments. The adjoining rooms contain an elaborate *Aurora* in Capodimonte biscuit, by Filippo Tagliolini (c. 1807), paintings of Vesuvius by Pierre Jacques Volaire, landscapes by Jakob Philipp Hackert (1737–1807) and a beautiful, anonymous *presepio* (Nativity scene).

Room 45: Tapestries depicting stories of Henry VI of Hohenstaufen, and a display of precious objects in cases.

Rooms 46–50 (Farnese armoury): Notable for its fine examples of 15th–17th-century ceremonial armour.

Room 52 (Salottino di Porcellana): A delightful little room covered with chinoiseries entirely executed in Capodimonte porcelain (*see p. 119*), in opulent Rococo style, in 1757–59. It was originally intended for the Palace of Portici and was moved here in 1866.

Rooms 53–55: Portraits of young royals by Elisabeth Vigée-Lebrun; portraits of Napoleon and Murat; and a plaster replica of Canova's *Letitia Bonaparte*, c. 1808 (the original in marble is at Chatsworth House, Derbyshire).

Rooms 56–57: Paintings by Vincenzo Camuccini, and Neoclassical sculptures including a relief with the personification of *Night* by Bertel Thorvaldsen; a round Neoclassical table designed by Antonio Niccolini and inlaid with a late antique mosaic; landscapes of Neoclassical and Romantic taste as well as some remarkable examples of Empire furniture.

Rooms 58–60: Paintings and furniture of the early 19th century. Highlights are the Mechanical Table 'in the Herculaneum style' and the Jardinière Table with miniatures depicting views of Naples and market scenes, and a Ciborium in coloured marbles and precious stones by Cosimo Fanzago. This fine example of miniature architecture was completed in 1624 and cost the enormous sum of 5,000 ducats.

Second floor

Painting in Naples from 1200–1700

This vast section (44 rooms) illustrates the development of painting in Naples at the hands of local artists and of foreigners working in the city. The core of the collection was formed during the 19th century when many paintings entered the Royal Museum following Napoleon's suppressions of monasteries. Many others were donated, acquired, or relocated, for reasons of conservation, from Neapolitan churches.

Room 62: Here are the splendid *Arazzi d'Avalos*, a set of seven tapestries illustrating the famous Battle of Pavia (1525) fought between Charles V of Spain and Francis I of France for supremacy on Italian soil and ending with the imprisonment of the French king. The tapestries were executed in Brussels, in the workshop of Bernaert van Orley, and were donated by the city's administration to Charles V. In 1571 they passed into the hands of Francesco Ferdinando d'Avalos, the commander who had orchestrated the emperor's victory, and in 1862 were donated by his descendants to the Italian state.

Room 63. Works of the 13th century including Giovanni da Taranto, *St Dominic*; and a panel with a Madonna (c. 1290) by an unknown Campanian

CAPODIMONTE
(SECOND FLOOR)

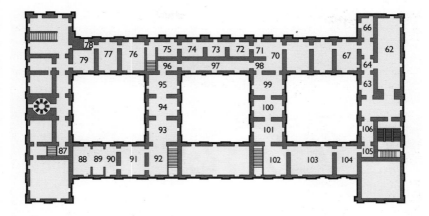

painter working in a Byzantine style. In the next three rooms are works produced under the Angevin kings. They reflect the refined taste of the French court that brought to Naples figures such as Giotto and Simone Martini, as well as other Tuscan artists.

Room 64: Lippo Vanni, *Christ the Redeemer*; Andrea Vanni, *St Jacob*; two works by the Neapolitan Roberto d'Oderisio, who studied under Giotto: *Crucifixion* and *Madonna of Humility*, from the church of San Domenico Maggiore.

Room 66: Here is the stunning *St Louis of Toulouse Crowning Robert of Anjou*, by the great Sienese painter Simone Martini (signed and dated 1317), painted for the church of San Lorenzo Maggiore. Louis, Robert's elder brother, was heir to the throne before entering

the Franciscan Order, leaving the throne vacant for his brother. The painting was made to commemorate Louis' canonisation in 1317. The darkened room and theatrical lighting exalt the painting's gold ground but make it hard to distinguish detail, especially in the predella.

Room 67: Important works by Colantonio (who was Antonello da Messina's teacher), including *St Jerome in his Study* (from San Lorenzo Maggiore, c. 1445), with a magnificent lion; *Polyptych of St Vincent Ferrer* (from the church of St Peter Martyr) and *Deposition* (1455–60) from San Domenico Maggiore. The latter shows a strong influence of Rogier van der Weyden, whose work was known to Colantonio through a set of Flemish tapestries acquired in 1455 by Alfonso of Aragon.

Caravaggio: *Flagellation* (1607 and 1609–10).

Room 70: Andrea da Salerno, *Deposition* (c. 1520), showing a clear debt to Rosso Fiorentino's 1506 painting of the same subject in the museum of Volterra.

Rooms 71–77: Here are 16th-century sculpture, Mannerist works inspired by Polidoro da Caravaggio, and examples of Tuscan Mannerism, including Giorgio Vasari, *Presentation at the Temple*; Sodoma, *Resurrection*; Marco Pino, *Adoration of the Magi*; as well as Titian's *Annunciation* (c. 1557) and Fabrizio Santafede's *Adoration of the Shepherds*.

Rooms 78–79: Here (Room 78) is the fabulous *Flagellation* by Caravaggio

(1607, 1609–10). This dark, disturbing painting comes from the de Franchis Chapel in the church of San Domenico Maggiore, where you can still see a 17th-century copy by Andrea Vaccaro. It was commissioned in May 1607, but completed only in 1609–10, during the painter's second period in Naples. Caravaggio was known to work in a darkened studio using point-source lighting to increase the contrast, hence the dramatic effect of his images. The technique was taken up and exploited to the hilt by the Caravaggeschi (Battistello Caracciolo, among others) displayed in Room 79.

The Golden Age of Neapolitan Art

A considerable part of the second floor is dedicated to Baroque painting in Naples, especially that made during the 17th century, when the reputation of Neapolitan artists spread throughout Europe.

Room 87: This room opens the extensive section with the famous *Judith and Holofernes* by Artemisia Gentileschi (1612–13). The Old Testament narrates the episode of the Hebrew heroine Judith, who saved her city of Bethulia from the siege of Holofernes, general of the Assyrian king Nebuchadnezzar, by killing him after a banquet, beheading him and bringing his head to her fellow citizens. Gentileschi's rendering of the episode is dramatic, even gory: modelling her composition on Caravaggio's famous painting of 1598–99 (Palazzo Barberini, Rome), she enlivens the action with realism and powerful female figures.

    Other highlights from this section are Simon Vouet's *Circumcision*; Jusepe Ribera's *St Jerome and the Angel of*

Judgement and *Drunken Silenus;* Pietro Novelli's version of *Judith and Holofernes*; works by the second generation of 17th-century Neapolitan painters (in which Caravaggio's inspiration is still recognisable, but is mediated by the classical achievements of the Bolognese school and French masters such as Poussin and Vouet), notably Andrea Vaccaro, *Triumph of David*; *Adoration of the Golden Calf*; Francesco de Rosa, *Susanna and the Elders*; Francesco Guarino, *St Agatha*; *St Cecilia*. There is also a large collection of still lifes by Neapolitan and European artists.

Rooms 103–104: Paintings by Luca Giordano, perhaps the most important and certainly the most prolific

Neapolitan artist of the second half of the 17th century (*see p. 67*), introduce (Room 104) the 18th-century painting of Francesco Solimena (*Aeneas and Dido*, 1739–41), Paolo de Matteis and the eclectic Domenico Antonio Vaccaro (painter, sculptor and architect). Francesco de Mura, pupil of Solimena, takes to the extreme his master's work using an exuberant style that announces the Rococo.

Third floor

19th-century art
The third-floor gallery offers a selection of 19th-century art ranging from the history paintings of Domenico Morelli (*Sicilian Vespers*; *Iconoclasts*) to the Naturalism of Filippo Palizzi. Well represented also are the Realist painters, in particular Gioacchino Toma, Francesco Paolo Michetti and Michele Cammarano. Some rooms are dedicated to the Impressionist-influenced paintings of Giovanni Boldini, Antonio Mancini and Giuseppe de Nittis. Also exhibited are sculptures by Vincenzo Gemito and paintings by Francesco Saverio Altamura and Giuseppe Pellizza da Volpedo. Interesting is the presence of a portrait, *The Carelli Family*, by Giacomo Balla, painted in 1901 before the artist became an adherent of the Futurist movement.

Contemporary art
Capodimonte is the only gallery of Old Masters in Italy that shows and acquires works by living artists. The paintings, sculptures and installations exhibited in the contemporary section document this unusual tradition, and include Italian masters such as Alberto Burri, Carlo Alfano, Mario Merz, Michelangelo Pistoletto, Luciano Fabro, Eliseo Mattiacci, Mimmo Paladino and Guido Tatafiore; as well as international artists such as Hermann Nitsch, Andy Warhol, Joseph Kosuth, Sigmar Polke, Jannis Kounellis, and Sol LeWitt. An interesting exhibition of photographic portraits of artists in the collection, by the brilliant and sensitive Neapolitan photographer Mimmo Jodice, concludes the contemporary section.

The **Osservatorio Astronomico di Capodimonte** has a small museum (*Salita Moiariello 16; open by appointment, T: 081 293266*) featuring astronomical instruments in use from the establishment of the observatory by Ferdinand I in 1819, until the early 20th century. The collection is displayed, in part, on the original premises.

CASTEL SANT'ELMO, SAN MARTINO & VILLA FLORIDIANA

Castel Sant'Elmo, a former fortress now used for temporary exhibitions; the Certosa di San Martino, with displays on the history of the Carthusian Order and of Naples; and Villa Floridiana, a beautiful mansion housing a museum of ceramics, all are set in splendid surroundings on the slopes of the Vomero hill. The best way to see the museums is to take a funicular to the top of the hill (bus connections are too complicated), then walk down.

Take the Montesanto funicular from Piazza Montesanto (*map p. 52, 6*) to Via Alessandro Scarlatti, just behind the museums of Castel Sant'Elmo and San Martino. Alternatively, take the Centrale from Via Toledo (*map p. 52, 10*) or the Chiaia from Via Parco Margherita (*map p. 52, 9*) to Via Cimarosa (*map p. 52, 9*) 5mins from Via Scarlatti by Via Raffaele Morghen. From the upper station of the Montesanto funicular in Via Scarlatti, follow Via Morghen right to Via d'Auria, Via d'Auria right to Via Angelini, and Via Angelini right to Castel Sant'Elmo and the Certosa di San Martino.

Castel Sant'Elmo

Map p. 52, 5. Open daily except Weds 8.30–7.30.
The Castel Sant'Elmo, built in 1329–43 and altered to its present star-shaped form in the 16th century by Pier Luigi Scrivà of Valencia, was originally intended to discourage popular insurrection. Long used for political prisoners, it has recently been restored and reopened to the public as an exhibition space. It hosts many of the city's larger temporary exhibitions and commands an extensive, magnificent view of Naples and its bay.

THE MONASTERY OF SAN MARTINO

Map p. 52, 5. Open daily except Weds 8.30–7.30; T: 081 578 1769.
Adjoining Castel Sant'Elmo is the Carthusian monastery of San Martino, founded in the 14th century but transformed in the late 16th and early 17th centuries by Giovanni Antonio Dosio (active at San Martino 1589–1609) and Cosimo Fanzago (director of works 1623–56). Architecturally beautiful in themselves, the conventual buildings now also provide an admirable setting for the treasures of the Museo Nazionale di San Martino. The extensive museum illustrates the history, life and art of Naples.

The church

From the outer gate you enter the Cortile Monumentale and the church, one of the few instances where Baroque decoration has been satisfactorily applied to a Gothic building (the original ribs of the 14th-century vault are still visible), and certainly the most cogent expression of the Baroque aesthetic in Naples. The church originally had three aisles, which were unified into a single space with side chapels.

The first plans to change the medieval structure were produced by Giovanni Antonio Dosio (1580), although the interior decoration, with its extraordinary wealth of inlaid marble, was executed much later under Cosimo Fanzago. The marble floor is the work of Fra' Bonaventura Presti (1664–67). At the sides of the entrance are two statues by Fanzago, *St John the Baptist* and *St Jerome* (finished by Alessandro Rondone), and two impressive paintings, *Moses* and *Elijah*, by Jusepe Ribera (1638); two frescoes, of the same subject, by Cavaliere d'Arpino (master of Caravaggio), have been dis-

Jusepe Ribera: *Moses* (1638).

covered beneath. Interestingly, Ribera's *Moses* is represented with two rays of light emanating from his forehead, and not with the two horns which a mediaeval mistranslation of the Hebrew word for radiance gave him in earlier art—most famously in Michelangelo's *Moses* in Rome. Over the door is the *Deposition*, Massimo Stanzione's masterpiece of 1638. In the spandrels above the chapels more prophets by Jusepe Ribera complete the series (1638–46). The remarkable ceiling fresco, by Giovanni Lanfranco, represents the *Ascension of Christ* (1637–40).

The side chapels contain many notable works of art. The first chapel on the right (not visible from the nave and entered from the second chapel) is decorated with fine stucco work, paintings and a marble floor by the versatile Domenico Antonio Vaccaro. The latter, together with his father Lorenzo, is responsible for the greater part of the sculptural work in the first three chapels on either side of the nave (c. 1700). The fourth chapel on the right and its pendant on the left were furnished in the mid-18th century by Nicola Tagliacozzi Canale and Giuseppe Sammartino, who made the fine statues of *Fortitude* and *Charity*. The fourth chapel on the left also contains three canvases by Francesco de Mura (*Assumption of the Virgin*, *Annunciation*, *Visitation*), and magnificent frescoes with stories of Mary by Battistello Caracciolo (1623–26). More frescoes by the same artist are in the second chapel on the left. The two central chapels, with frescoes by Massimo Stanzione, were begun by Fanzago in 1656 and completed in the 18th century.

The **presbytery** is divided from the rest of the church by a balustrade of coloured marbles designed by Nicola Tagliacozzi Canale. Beyond is the high altar, actually a gilded wooden model by Francesco Solimena for a final design that was to have been executed in *pietre dure*. The monks' choir was commissioned from Orazio de Orio in 1629. The ceiling above is decorated with scenes from the Old and New Testaments

MONASTERY OF SAN MARTINO

Gardens

Gardens

Prior's Apartment

Orilia Beques

Carrozze e Stemme

Orilia Bequest

South wing (Museo dell'Opera)

Pharmacy

East wing

Great

Chiostrino dei Procuratori

Refectory

Chiostrino Fanzago

Cloister

Church

Cortile Monumentale

North wing

N

by Cavaliere d'Arpino. At the back are statues of the *Contemplative Life* by G.B. Caccini (on the left) and the *Active Life* by Pietro Bernini (on the right). On the back wall is a *Nativity* by Guido Reni (1642) and, in the lunette above, a *Crucifixion* by Lanfranco (1638). On the wall to the left are *Institution of the Eucharist* by Ribera and *Washing of the Disciples' Feet* by Caracciolo; on the wall to the right, *Last Supper* by Stanzione and *Institution of the Eucharist* by a son and pupils of Paolo Veronese.

Leading off the choir is the **sacristy**, with ceiling frescoes by Cavaliere d'Arpino (1596–97) and walnut wardrobes decorated with late 16th-century intarsia of biblical stories. Over the entrance is a canvas of the *Crucifix* by Cavaliere d'Arpino (1589–91) flanked by perspectives by Viviano Codazzi. By the same artist is the double staircase painted in the lunette over the exit, whereas the figurative composition showing an *Ecce Homo* is by Massimo Stanzione. From the sacristy, passing through an antechamber with ceiling frescoes by Stanzione (1644) and two paintings by Luca Giordano (*Calling of the Apostles*), you enter the treasury. Here, above the altar, is Ribera's masterpiece, the *Deposition*. The fresco on the vault showing the *Triumph of Judith* is Luca Giordano's last work (1704).

Returning to the presbytery, by a door on the right, you enter the **Coro dei Conversi** with frescoes by Domenico Gargiulo (called Micco Spadaro), executed around 1640, and beautiful intarsia stalls (1510–20), depicting saints and views, including two representations of the Gothic monastery. From here a passageway leads to the **Cappella della Maddalena** with early 18th-century frescoes by Giovan Battista Natali and an altarpiece by Andrea Vaccaro (1636). Returning to the monks' choir, a door on the right leads to the chapter house, richly decorated with wooden stalls, 17th-century frescoes (the vault is by Belisario Corenzio) and a number of paintings, including Simon Vouet's *St Bruno Receiving the Rule of the Order*. The adjoining parlour gives access to the Great Cloister.

Gardens and prior's apartment

Returning to the Cortile Monumentale, proceed to the Chiostrino dei Procuratori, built by Giovanni Antonio Dosio in the late 16th century, and cross the courtyard to the Salone delle Carrozze e Stemme (carriages and coats of arms). From here you may enter the pharmacy with frescoes by Paolo de Matteis (1699), and the beautiful **convent gardens**, arranged on three levels, with extraordinary views over the city and the bay. The topmost level was once the herbarium of the pharmacy. The prior's vegetable garden, with an 18th-century pergola, was on the intermediate level. Below were the monks' vineyards: visitors can still take part in the grape harvest, at the end of September. The other rooms in this part house the Maria Teresa Orilia bequest of porcelain, Castelli majolica, furniture, fans, walking sticks and other *objets d'art;* as well as 15th- and 16th-century polychrome wood sculpture from Neapolitan churches.

From the Salone delle Carrozze e Stemme you can also descend to the **prior's apartment** (the Quarto del Priore), with ceiling frescoes by Micco Spadaro. Here an outstanding series of artworks, representing four centuries of Carthusian patronage in Naples, is displayed. The works range from an important triptych by Jean Bourdichon (*Virgin and Child*, 1494) to the art of the major figures of the 17th and 18th centuries (Pietro Bernini, Caracciolo, Corenzio, Guarino, de Rosa, Vaccaro and others). Pietro Bernini's statue of the *Virgin and Child*, in 8, shows both the influence of Michelangelo and the development of Mannerism. Spadaro's frescoes in 14 and 15, begun in 1642, represent landscapes with hermit saints. They show the influence of northern European landscape painters such as Herman Swanevelt and Gaspard Dughet, active in Rome at about the same time. Although retouched, the central landscape decorating the ceiling of 15 is particularly interesting. It shows a view of Naples and the still-bare hill of San Martino, on which the Certosa would later be erected. A model of the monastery is held by Charles of Anjou (son of Robert of Anjou), who ordered its construction in 1325.

Battistello Caracciolo: *Adoration of the Magi.*

The **library**, decorated in 1741 with frescoes by Crescenzo della Gamba, depicting the *Triumph of Faith*, *St Martin in Glory* and *St Bruno Receiving the Rule of the Order*, bordered with the Rococo chinoiseries typical of the age, adjoins the Quarto del Priore, in 32–33. The lower frescoes in 32 show the monogram CAR SM (standing for the Carthusian Order of St Martin). The floor of 33 is decorated with astrological symbols and a meridian (by Leonardo Chiaiese, 1771). The decorative scheme of the two rooms is linked by a common iconographical programme, which is both a summary and a celebration of the bases of the Carthusian order.

Close by is the ***sezione presepiale***, with a renowned collection of *presepi* (Nativity scenes), some by prominent Neapolitan sculptors. One, the *Presepe Cuciniello*, includes 180 shepherds, 10 horses, 8 dogs and 309 objects. In front of the *sezione presepiale*, across a corridor, is the **refectory**, built in the 18th century by Nicola Tagliacozzi Canale and adorned with a big painting of the *Wedding at Cana* by Nicola Malinconico (1724). Adjoining the refectory is a pretty inner courtyard called the Chiostrino Fanzago, although it was rebuilt by Nicola Tagliacozzi Canale in the 18th century.

The Great Cloister

The Great Cloister (Chiostro Grande), with its white and grey marble ornamentation and beautifully-kept gardens, is undoubtedly one of the most striking achievements of Italian Baroque architecture. The original plan is by Giovanni Antonio Dosio (16th century), but its present character results largely from the sculptural and architectural programme developed by Cosimo Fanzago in 1623. His design is strongly conditioned by the style of the Florentine Bernardo Buontalenti (note especially the curved and twisted framework of the niches above the doors), introduced to Naples in the first quarter of the century by Michelangelo Naccherino, Michelangelo Buonarroti and other Florentine artists. Five of the seven busts (*St Martin of Tours, Bishop Nicola Albergati, St Bruno, St Hugh* and *St Dionysius*) are by Fanzago's hand, whereas the last two (*St Januarius* and *St Martin*) are early works of Domenico Antonio Vaccaro. Fanzago is also either partly or wholly responsible for the eight statues at the corners and centre of the arcade (that of the *Resurrected Christ* was begun by Naccherino).

The **Museo dell'Opera**, in the south wing of the cloister, displays works that reconstruct the history of the complex. It includes portraits of the various priors and images of the founder saints; plans, views and a model of the Certosa; decorative marbles and architectural elements by Cosimo Fanzago as well as a self-portrait; paintings by Giacinto Gigante, Frans Vervloet, Gabriele Carelli and others; temperas by Edoardo Dalbono with the *Eruptions of Vesuvius*; views from San Martino by Antonio Senape. The balcony commands a wonderful view over the city and the bay of Naples.

The **east and north wings** of the Chiostro Grande host a section dedicated to images and memories of the city, with a rich collection illustrating the history of Naples. Among the exhibits is the famous *Tavola Strozzi*, showing the return of the Aragonese fleet, and, in the background, a view of Naples in the 15th century. The painting is attributed to Francesco Rosselli di Lorenzo. There is also an interesting *Bird's-Eye View of Naples* by Didier Barra (1647). Others rooms are dedicated to the revolt of Masaniello (*see p. 38*), with portraits of its protagonists and paintings illustrating some episodes (note Micco Spadaro's *Revolt of 1647*); and the Parthenopean Republic of 1799 (*see p. 40*). The northernmost rooms house important collections of decorative arts. On the first floor of the south wing of the cloister, is a section on the **history of Neapolitan theatre**.

The 19th-century collection

Stairs at the left of the main entrance lead up to a series of rooms with 19th-century Neapolitan art. Here are a model for Giambattista Amendola's statue of Murat at the Palazzo Reale; a statue of Salvatore Rosa by Achille d'Orsi; portraits by Domenico Morelli; sculptures by Vincenzo Gemito; views by Frans Vervloet; and paintings by the artists of the Posillipo School (*see p. 122 below*).

VILLA FLORIDIANA:
MUSEO NAZIONALE DELLA CERAMICA

Map p. 52, 9. Gardens open daily 9–dusk; museum open daily except Tues 8.30–2; T: 081 229 2110.
The shaded gardens of the **Villa Floridiana**, beautifully sited on a spur overlooking the sea, are famous for their camellias; the view from the terrace is particularly fine. The mansion was given by Ferdinand I of Bourbon to his second wife, Lucia Magliaccio,

Duchess of Floridia (for whom it was renovated in Neoclassical style). Today it houses the Museo Nazionale della Ceramica Duca di Martina, based on the original porcelain collection of Placido de Sangro, Duke of Martina, augmented by his nephew, Count de Marzi, and presented to the city by the widow of the latter, Maria Spinelli. The museum now contains over 6,000 pieces of European and Asiatic porcelain and pottery, as well as goldsmiths' work, ivories, and 17th-, 18th- and 19th-century paintings. The porcelain collection includes pieces by Meissen, Sèvres, Delft, English porcelain (Bow, Derby, Wedgwood, Chelsea), Chinese Ming dynasty and Japanese Arita ware, as well as the famous Capodimonte porcelain from Naples itself (*see box*). Ceramics include Italian majolica from Faenza, Gubbio and Pesaro, and Turkish Iznik ware. Murano glass, Bohemian crystal and exquisite Limoges enamels are also included, as well as (in the basement) one of the most important collections in Italy of Oriental *objets d'art*, including Japanese Edo ware and Chinese porcelain and jade.

The main collections

These are housed on the first floor. Rooms 2–4 contain porcelain from Meissen, the first place in Europe to use *pâte dure*. Among the best pieces are the Augustus Rex vases, with chinoiseries on a pink background, and the figure groups (*Lovers with a Puppy Dog*; *Pair of Lovers with a Bird Cage*, by J.J. Kaendler). Room 5, the former ballroom, is dedicated to Bourbon porcelain. The collection of Capodimonte porcelain is particularly impressive; notice, among other fine pieces, the *Pietà* by Giuseppe Gricci. Other highlights include pieces from the Buen Retiro manufactory (1765–70); plates from the *Servizio Ercolanese* (which was given by Ferdinand of Bourbon to his father, then King Charles of Spain) and from the set of the Vestiture del Regno, both produced by the Real Fabbrica (royal manufactory) of Naples (1771–1806). Also displayed here are works by Filippo Tagliolini and pieces from the Doccia manufactory (1735–1838).

CAPODIMONTE PORCELAIN

The royal porcelain manufactory of Capodimonte was founded in 1739 by Charles of Bourbon, and remained in operation until 1819. His interest in porcelain came from his wife, Maria Amalia, who was the grand-daughter of Augustus the Strong, founder of the Meissen manufactory. Meissen porcelain is hard-paste porcelain, made of a mixture of kaolin and 'China stone'. Capodimonte, like Sèvres, is soft-paste ware, a mixture of local clay (from Catanzaro province) with sand and gypsum. The result is soft and grainy, as the constituents of the mix do not combine when fired, nor does the paste completely vitrify. The colour is also creamier and less pure white than 'true' porcelain. The chief modeller in Capodimonte's heyday was Filippo Tagliolini, who personally presented his famous Etruscan dinner service to King George III of England in 1785.

PARKS & PROMENADES

In the early and mid-19th century, the Romantic fashion for broad, open spaces and breathtaking views led to the construction of parks and panoramic carriage roads in and around major Italian cities, such as the Pincio in Rome and the Viale dei Colli in Florence. In Naples the old mule tracks to Posillipo were improved to make a parkway, and the waterfront at Mergellina, west of Pizzofalcone, was developed as a wooded quayside promenade, for the benefit of the smart new residential quarter on the hillside to the north. Both areas correspond extremely well to the Romantic ideal. A stroll through the park at Posillipo, in particular, is rewarding.

Villa Pignatelli

Map p. 52, 13. Museum open daily except Tues 8.30–2; T: 081 761 2356.
The Neoclassical Villa Pignatelli stands in its own little walled garden across the Riviera di Chiaia from the Villa Comunale (a popular park with an aquarium, whose tanks are fed by salt water direct from the sea). Built in 1826 for the Acton family by Pietro Valente, this once handsome mansion was acquired in 1841 by the Rothschilds, who refurbished much of the interior in the Second Empire style. It was sold in 1867 to the Pignatelli di Monteleone and bequeathed by Princess Rosina Pignatelli to the Italian state in 1952.

The villa now houses the Museo Principe Diego Aragona Pignatelli Cortes. The collection includes Italian and European porcelain; biscuit ware from Naples, Vienna and Sèvres; Chinese vases; period furniture, and some paintings and sculptures, including family portraits. Highlights include the four Japanese Edo vases in the circular vestibule; a beautiful Meissen coffee set with marine landscapes; a Doccia coffee set with pastoral landscapes, of Ginori manufacture; and a service from the Real Fabbrica di Napoli with landscape and genre scenes by Raffaele Giovine. The library has restored leather wall hangings, from the turn of the 19th century, exemplifying a fine technique of imprint decoration successively gilded *a pastiglio* (in other words with layers of raised work added, to give texture). The dining room has a table laid with a fine Limoges service made for Princess Rosina Pignatelli.

The rooms on the first floor house the Banco di Napoli collection of 16th–20th-century Neapolitan art. The villa also hosts temporary exhibitions of contemporary art. In the garden is the Museo delle Carrozze Mario d'Alessandro Marchese di Civitanova, with English, French and Italian carriages of the 19th and early 20th centuries.

Rione Amedeo

The area north (inland) of the Riviera di Chiaia is the Rione Amedeo, a modern, fashionable quarter worth a short detour. Santa Maria in Portico, a church begun in 1632, has a façade of 1862. The church of the Ascensione a Chiaia, begun in the 14th century but rebuilt by Cosimo Fanzago in 1645, contains canvases by Luca Giordano. Santa Teresa a Chiaia, designed by Cosimo Fanzago (1650–62), but ruined by later restorations, also contains paintings by Giordano.

Piedigrotta

Map p. 50, 13.

The Riviera di Chiaia passes the north side of Piazza della Repubblica, with the Monumento allo Scugnizzo by Mazzacurati (1969), commemorating the Quattro Giornate di Napoli (*see p. 44*). Shortly afterwards, it ends at Largo Torretta, an open space named after a former tower erected as a defence against pirates. Here the road divides. Via Giordano Bruno (left) leads to Piazza Sannazzaro and the harbour at Mergellina, described below. Via Piedigrotta (right) leads to Piazza Piedigrotta.

On the left of the piazza is Santa Maria di Piedigrotta, a 14th-century church remodelled in 1822 and restored at the beginning of the 20th century. The façade is by Enrico Alvino with a campanile rebuilt in 1926. Inside you can see a 15th-century Neapolitan painting on wood of the *Descent from the Cross*, and, in the large chapel near the choir, tombs of the Filangieri family. A wooden figure of the Madonna, after the manner of Tino da Camaino, heavily restored and much venerated, stands on the high altar. This forms the focal point of a lively festival celebrating the Battle of Velletri (*see p. 38*) on the night of 7th–8th September.

In Piazza Piedigrotta, beneath the railway viaduct and to the left of the entrance to the Galleria Quattro Giornate (a tunnel leading to Fuorigrotta), steps lead to the Parco Virgiliano. A pillar here marks the remains of the poet Giacomo Leopardi, moved to the park from a demolished church. Nearby is the Roman columbarium in *opus reticulatum,* restored in 1927 and known (although there is no concrete evidence to support the claim) as Virgil's tomb. Immediately below the columbarium is the mouth of the Grotta Vecchia or Crypta Neapolitana (710m long; *closed*), a remarkable feat of Roman engineering, planned by Cocceius for Agrippa and Octavian to provide a direct road from Neapolis to Puteoli (Pozzuoli). Today much the same route is followed by the Galleria della Laziale (or di Posillipo), a straight, modern tunnel 900m long (*no pedestrians*), entered from Piazza Sannazzaro.

Mergellina

Map p. 50, 13.

The little bay of Mergellina affords a good view back to Santa Lucia. Here is the lower station of the Mergellina funicular, which runs from the seafront to Via Manzoni; and here hydrofoils to/from Capri and Ischia dock. Above the south end of the bay rises the church of Santa Maria del Parto, or del Sannazzaro, founded in the 16th century by the Neapolitan poet Jacopo Sannazzaro. It contains the well-known painting nicknamed the '*Diavolo di Mergellina*' (*St Michael Overthrowing Satan*), by Leonardo da Pistoia (1542). At the back of the apse, which is decorated with paintings and stucco, is the tomb of Jacopo Sannazzaro, by Fra' Giovanni da Montorsoli (1537).

Posillipo

Map p. 134.

From Santa Maria del Parto, Via Posillipo hugs the shore for some way and then climbs away up the slopes of the hilly promontory known as Posillipo, a name said to be derived from *Pausilypon* ('the carefree'), a lavish villa belonging to the Roman patrician Vedius Pollio (*see p. 147*). The picturesque road, begun in 1808 under Murat, passes many handsome villas amid rich vegetation and commands lovely views, especially fine at sunset.

On the left side of the road is the Palazzo di Donn'Anna, built in 1642–44 by Fanzago for Anna Carafa, wife of the Duke of Medina, Viceroy of Naples. Perhaps the most ingeniously planned and dramatically situated of all Neapolitan palaces, its construction was interrupted by the death of the patron in 1642. The view becomes increasingly fine as the road climbs to Piazza San Luigi (c. 85m; restaurants), on the far side of the Parco della Rimembranza, which contains an Egyptian-style mausoleum, a memorial to victims of the First World War. The exceptional view is reflected in the name of the church, Santa Maria di Bellavista. Close to the church Via Ferdinando Russo winds down in 10mins to Capo di Posillipo (view), near which is the sumptuous Villa Rosebery, the Neapolitan residence of the President of the Republic.

Via Posillipo continues its winding course, reaching a major intersection known as the Quadrivio del Capo. To the south Via Marechiaro, a road through villas and vineyards, leads down to (1km) **Marechiaro**, an unspoilt fishing hamlet with stone houses rising in steps from the sea. From here you can take boat trips to the Grotta dei Tuoni (where the waves produce thunderous echoes) and La Gaiola, a rocky island near which the remains of Vedius Pollio's villa may be seen.

About 150m beyond the Quadrivio del Capo, Viale Tito Lucrezio Caro, to the left, winds up to the top of Monte Coroglio and the entrance to the Parco di Posillipo (153m). At the foot of the hill a byroad crosses the modern causeway to the island of Nisida, an extinct volcano known to the ancients as *Nesis*. This little isle once belonged to Lucullus, the general who served under Sulla in the Social War (*see p. 15*), and retired to live a life of ease at Neapolis. Later it became the retreat of Marcus Brutus, who was visited here by Cicero. The conspiracy against Caesar was planned at Nesis by Brutus and Cassius, and Brutus bade farewell to his wife Portia here. The castle (now a school) was used as a prison for the republican activist Carlo Poerio, whose plight horrified the visiting Gladstone.

The beautiful views and landscapes of Posillipo inspired a school of *plein-air* painters (the Posillipo School). The Dutch artist Anton Pitloo, who came to Naples in the early 19th century to teach landscape painting, was the prime mover of the school, gathering about him a group of artists who rejected the solemn formality of the academic style and embraced instead a kind of romantic spontaneity. Perhaps the greatest exponent of the school is Giacinto Gigante (1806–76).

THE RETTIFILO & ITS ENVIRONS

Map p. 51, 11.
Corso Umberto I, popularly called the Rettifilo, was laid out in 1888–94 to connect the city's civic and financial centre to the main railway station. This long, straight thor-

oughfare is grandiose in intent, but shows little regard for local needs or traditions. It dominates the area between the medieval Castel Nuovo and the Stazione Centrale, cutting through Naples' eastern districts in a merciless way, destroying the area's medieval flavour and introducing an academic, pretentious architectural style vaguely related to the Neoclassicism of the Bourbon era. A few impressive monuments of the city's past do survive, however, and amply repay a visit.

Along the Rettifilo

The Rettifilo begins at Piazza Giovanni Bovio. In the centre of the piazza is the graceful Neptune fountain, designed in 1601, probably by Domenico Fontana. The seamonsters are by Pietro Bernini, and the figure of Neptune by Michelangelo Naccherino. To the left stands the Palazzo della Borsa (1895), engulfing the 8th-century chapel of Sant'Aspreno al Porto, which was transformed in the 17th century and incorporates columns from San Pietro ad Aram (*see p. 124 below*).

A few metres up the Corso, Via Mezzocannone leads left to **San Giovanni Maggiore**. The church, built in the 6th century on the ruins of a pagan temple, but remodelled in 1685 and again in 1870, retains its basilican plan. A chapel on the south side contains an 18th-century terracotta *presepio*; the third chapel on the north side a *Baptism of Christ*, attributed to Giovanni da Nola; the fifth chapel, a late 16th-century bas-relief of the *Beheading of John the Baptist*. The magnificent high altar (1732–43) is the work of Domenico Antonio Vaccaro.

The church of **San Pietro Martire**, built in 1294–1347, stands in a small square to the right along the Corso. Much damaged during the Second World War, it contains a number of 14th–16th-century works of art, including (in the third north chapel) a naïvely realistic 15th-century Catalan painting on wood of St Vincent Ferrer, as well as paintings by Solimena and Stanzione.

Immediately opposite the church is the imposing façade of the University of Naples by Pier Paolo Quaglia and Guglielmo Melisborgo (1897–1908), with a pediment sculptured by Francesco Jerace. The university was founded in 1224 by Frederick II. In 1777 it was moved to the 16th-century rooms of the former Jesuit convent behind the present building. The Musei di Antropologia, Mineralogia, Zoologia e Paleontologia are located here, in Via Mezzocannone 8 and Largo San Marcellino 10 (*open Mon–Fri 9–1.30, Sat and Sun 9–1*). They contain the study collections of the Faculty of Science.

Three blocks further along the Corso, on the left, a crooked alley and a flight of steps lead up to the church of **Santi Severino e Sossio**, built over an earlier structure in 1494–1561 and decorated in the 17th century. The façade was restored after earthquake damage in 1731. The interior has ceiling paintings by Corenzio, who fell to his death while retouching them and is buried near the entrance to the sacristy. In the fourth chapel on the south side is a 16th-century polyptych. On the same side is the sacristy vestibule, in which are two Cicaro tombs of the 16th century, both with inscriptions by the poet Sannazzaro. The Cappella Sanseverino (right of the choir) contains the tombs, by Giovanni da Nola, of three Sanseverino brothers, all of whom were poisoned on the same day (1516) by their uncle. The choir stalls (1560–75) are by Bartolomeo Chiarini and Benvenuto Tortelli. The Chiostro del Platano, named after a plane tree said to have been planted by St Benedict, is accessible by a door to the left of the vestibule. It is frescoed by Andrea Solario.

Museo Filangieri

Map p. 53, 7. Open Mon–Sat 9–7; T: 081 203175.

Palazzo Cuomo is a severely elegant 15th-century Florentine building (1464–90) that now houses the attractive Museo Civico Gaetano Filangieri, established in 1881. The original collections of Prince Gaetano Filangieri (1824–92) were burnt by the Germans in 1943, but a new collection has since been formed. On the ground floor are objects from various excavations and Oriental arms; above, sculpture (notably a boy's head by the della Robbia family) and paintings by Ribera, Mattia Preti, Luca Giordano and others. Note particularly Ribera's gruesomely realistic head of St John the Baptist; Mattia Preti, *Meeting of Peter and Paul at the Gates of Rome;* Bernardino Lanino, *Madonna and Child;* Battistello Caracciolo *Ecce Homo.* The gallery has a good collection of porcelain, and the library has a number of manuscripts and documents dating from the 13th–19th centuries.

Four interesting churches

Sant'Agostino alla Zecca, a 14th-century church transformed in the mid-17th century by Bartolomeo Picchiatti and Giuseppe Astarita, holds the tomb of Francesco Coppola, Count Sarno. The fine 14th-century chapterhouse, opening off the Baroque cloister, is reached by a door beneath the 17th-century campanile.

The little church of **Santa Maria Egiziaca**, originally of the 14th century, but in its present form designed by Dionisio Lazzari (1684), has paintings by Andrea Vaccaro, Luca Giordano and Francesco Solimena. The oval plan is rare in Naples.

Santissima Annunziata, rebuilt by Luigi Vanvitelli and his son Carlo in 1761–82 after a fire, is important as one of the first examples of the new Classical taste in ecclesiastical architecture that was championed by Charles III. The interior is a Latin cross with barrel-vaulted nave and choir and short transepts. The nave arcade is replaced by a colonnade bearing a flat entablature. The crossing, the choir and the semicircular apse, as well as the gallery at the west end of the nave, provide interesting variants in the use of columns. The white and grey stucco underscores the severity of the design. The slender cupola, badly damaged in 1943, has been well restored. The treasury, containing frescoes (in a bad state) by Corenzio, and the sacristy, on the south side (likewise decorated by Corenzio and containing sculptured 16th-century presses), are relics of the former church of 1318, in which Joan II was buried (plain tomb before the high altar). The altars of the unusual, circular crypt are adorned with 17th-century terracotta statues.

The church of **San Pietro ad Aram** flanks the north side of the Corso. The 17th-century façade faced Via Santa Candida, but the usual entrance is by the south door from the Corso. The church stands on the site where St Peter is said to have baptised

St Candida and St Asprenus (who later became the first bishop of Naples). A fresco in the porch depicts St Peter celebrating Mass with them. The church has a finely-stuccoed interior. The high altar is decorated with mosaics, and the presbytery is adorned with early works of Luca Giordano. Restoration work in the crypt in 1930 uncovered remains of an aisled church dating from the early Christian era.

Santa Maria del Carmine and the market

The church of **Santa Maria del Carmine**, rebuilt at the end of the 13th century, has a campanile that was begun in the 15th century but not completed until 1631, when Fra' Nuvolo added the spire. The façade, by Giovanni del Gaizo, dates from 1766. The interior of the church is decorated with polychrome marble; the modern roof replaces a 17th-century coffered ceiling destroyed in 1943. On the north side is the monument, designed by the Danish sculptor Bertel Thorvaldsen, to Conradin, the last of the Hohenstaufen, who was executed in the nearby market-place in 1269, and whose remains are buried behind the altar. Under the transept arch stands a 13th-century wooden Crucifix and above it a painting, *God the Father*, by Luca Giordano. The frescoes in the north transept and in the sixth chapel on the north side, are by Solimena; in the south transept is an *Assumption*, also by Solimena. A much-venerated 14th-century painting, the *Madonna della Bruna*, occupies a 16th-century marble shrine behind the high altar. In the north transept is a 15th-century Crucifix.

West of Santa Maria del Carmine is the **Piazza del Mercato**, centre of trade in medieval Naples and still the site of the city's lively general market; the fruit and vegetable stands are particularly colourful. In

Fresco by Solimena in the north transept of the Carmine.

1269, Conradin and his kinsman, Frederick of Baden, were beheaded here by Charles I of Anjou. Here also Masaniello's rebellion against Spanish rule broke out in July 1647 (*see p. 23*). Plague victims were buried on this site in the 17th century, and the leaders of the 1799 revolution (*see p. 24*) were also executed here. A porphyry column from a chapel erected on the site of Conradin's scaffold is preserved in the church of Santa Croce al Mercato. On the west side of the piazza stands Sant'Eligio, restored after war damage, with a good Gothic doorway showing French influence. The remains of the Castello del Carmine border the south side.

Francesco Solimena (1657–1747)
Born near Avellino, Solimena came to Naples at the age of 17, and remained there for the rest of his long life. As a career painter, he was an unqualified success, achieving fame and fortune and securing the patronage of many crowned heads, both in Naples itself and elsewhere. Louis XIV of France was an enthusiastic supporter. His style owes much to the Baroque master Luca Giordano, though his sense of theatrical effect is drawn more from Lanfranco and Mattia Preti. Scholars also see his love of brown shadow as a borrowing from Preti, and note that despite the appearance of Baroque hurly burly, his compositions possess an underlying compositional rigour which has more to do with Raphael and other Classicist painters than with the true Baroque. Solimena's influence was enormous: he trained the younger artists Sebastiano Conca and Francesco de Mura; the Scottish portrait painter Allan Ramsay studied under him; and Fragonard reproduced his frescoes in San Paolo Maggiore in his *Voyage Pittoresque en Naples et Sicile*.

PRACTICAL INFORMATION

• **By air:** An airport bus (Alibus) runs between Piazza Municipio (*map p. 53, 11*) and **Naples Capodichino Airport**, 4km north of the city, at hourly intervals or less, 6.30am–11.30pm. Transit time is c. 30mins. Information from the Naples Transit Authority, ANM, www.anm.it, T: 081 531 164; or from the airport (www.gesac.it).

• **By rail:** There are four main stations for Italian Rail (Trenitalia) services: Napoli Centrale (*map p. 53, 4*); Piazza Garibaldi (in the same complex, but at a lower level); Mergellina (Piazza Mergellina, *map p. 50, 13*); and Campi Flegrei (in the suburb of Fuorigrotta). Information from Trenitalia, www.trenitalia.it, T: 89 20 21. There are also two minor stations for private railways that serve the Bay of Naples: Stazione Circumvesuviana (Corso Garibaldi 387; *map p. 53, 8*; T: 081 772 2444) for the Circumvesuviana line, which runs to Pompeii, Sarno, Sorrento, Nola, and other destinations south and east of the city; and Stazione Cumana (Piazza Montesanto; *map p. 52, 6*; T: 081 551 3328), for the Cumana and Circumflegrea lines, which run west to Pozzuoli, Cuma and Torregaveta.

• **By sea:** Naples harbour is one of the largest and busiest in the Mediterranean, with several quays. **Cruise liners** moor at the Molo Angioino (Stazione Marittima Passaggeri; *map p. 53, 11*); other vessels at the Molo Pisacane (Immacolatella Nuova; *map p. 53, 12*) or within the inner harbour between the two.

Pleasure craft may moor at Molosiglio (*map p. 53, 15*), Santa Lucia (*map p. 53, 15*), Mergellina (*map p. 50, 13*), and Posillipo. **Ferries** depart from Porto Beverello (*map p. 53, 11*) to Capri (1hr 15mins), Ischia (1hr 15mins), Pozzuoli (30mins), Procida (1hr), and Sorrento (1hr). **Hydrofoils** and **catamarans** run from Porto Beverello (*map p. 53, 11*) and from Mergellina (*map p. 50, 13*) to Capri (40–45mins), Ischia (30–45mins), Procida (35mins) and Sorrento (30mins), daily. Hydrofoils and catamarans are generally significantly more expensive than ferries. Tickets are available at the dock and from selected travel agents; schedules and other information at www.anm.it and www.campaniatrasporti.it

• **By public transport:** There is no easy way to get around Naples except, of course, to walk. Traffic is so heavy that it is practically at a standstill all day. Having said this, the underground lines, buses and trams run by ANM are very efficient. Information offices (with a map of the system) at the central railway station. *Uniconapoli* tickets (which can be used on buses, funiculars or the underground) are sold at news-stands and tobacconists. and must be stamped on board. There are two types, one lasting 90mins and the other all day. Detailed information regarding routes and schedules at www.anm.it; freephone T: 800 63 95 25.

Buses

The buses most useful to the visitor are:

  1 Centro Storico (Piazza Nazionale–Piazza Vittoria)

  R3 Lungomare (Via Medina–Via

Mergellina)

24 Capodimonte (Piazza Trieste e Trento–Via Nicolini)

140 Posillipo (Via Santa Lucia–Capo Posillipo)

C10 (Piazza della Vittoria–Città della Scienza)

Metro

1 (Yellow) Dante, Museo, Materdei, Salvator Rosa, Quattro Giornate, Vanvitelli, Medaglie d'Oro, Montedonzelli, Rione Alto, Policlinico, Colli Aminei, Frullone, Chiaiano, Piscinola.

2 (Blue) Villa Literno, Giugliano, Quarto, Pozzuoli, Bagnoli-Agnano, Cavalleggeri d'Aosta, Campi Flegrei, Leopardi, Mergellina, Piazza Amedeo, Montesanto, Piazza Cavour, Piazza Garibaldi, Gianturco, San Giovanni-Barra, Pietrarsa-San Giorgio, Portici, Ercolano, Torre del Greco, Santa Maria la Bruna, Torre Annunziata Città, Torre Annunziata Centrale, Rovigliano, Castellammare di Stabia.

A third (Red) line is under construction. Contemporary artists and architects are engaged in the design and redesign of stations; examples include Gae Aulenti (Museo and Dante), Alessandro Mendini (Salvator Rosa) and Sandro Chia (Materdei). More info at www.metro.na.it; freephone T: 800 56 88 66.

Funicular railways

Three services climb the Vomero hill from lower stations in the town: The 'Montesanto' from Piazza Montesanto (*map p. 52, 6*), the 'Chiaia' from Piazza Amedeo (*map p. 52, 9*) and the 'Centrale' from Via Toledo (*map p. 52, 10*), all with intermediate stops at Corso Vittorio Emanuele II. The fourth, the 'Mergellina', connects Posillipo (Via Manzoni) to the seafront at Mergellina and Campi Flegrei Station. Hours, stops and frequency of service are as follows:

Centrale Piazza Fuga, Petraio, Corso Vittorio Emanuele, Piazza Augusteo, in 6min every 10–15mins, 6.30am–half past midnight;

Chiaia Cimarosa, Palazzolo, Corso Vittorio Emanuele, Parco Margherita, in 5mins every 10–15mins, 7am–10pm;

Montesanto Morghen, Corso Vittorio Emanuele, Montesanto, in 5mins every 10–15mins, 7am–10pm;

Mergellina Manzoni, Parco Angelina, San Gioacchino, Sant'Antonio, Mergellina, in 7mins every 12–15mins, 7am–10pm.

Taxis

Taxis tend to get stuck in traffic, as do buses. Cabs, with ranks in all the main squares, are equipped with meters, which should be carefully watched by passengers. There are fixed supplements for holiday or night (11pm–6am) service, for luggage, and for radio calls (T: 081 570 7070, 081 556 4444 and 081 556 0202). A return fee must be paid for taxis sent beyond the city limits, and the fare from Capodichino airport is double the amount indicated on the meter.

Horsedrawn carriages

In Naples, as elsewhere in Italy, the horsedrawn *carrozza* is by no means extinct, but fares are rather high, and when hiring a vehicle it is advisable to make an exact agreement with the driver before setting off.

Country-bus services connect Naples with outlying areas. Visit www.anm.it for schedules.

INFORMATION OFFICES

Assessorato Regionale al Turismo, Via
Santa Lucia 81, T: 081 796 1111,
www.turismoregionecampania.it
Azienda Autonoma di Cura Soggiorno e
Turismo, Via San Carlo 9, T: 081 402
394; Palazzo Reale, T: 081 551 2701 or
081 402 394.
Ente Provinciale per il Turismo, Piazza
dei Martiri 58, T: 081 405 311, www.
eptnapoli.info. Branch offices at
Capodichino Airport, T: 081 780 5761;
Piazza del Gesù Nuovo 7, T: 081 552
3328; Stazione Centrale, T: 081 268
779; Stazione Mergellina, T: 081 761
2102.

The **Campania ArteCard** gives free
or reduced admission to museums and
monuments throughout the region, plus
free travel; available from the information offices and most museums, in 3- or
7-day versions.

Ask your hotel receptionist for the
useful monthly magazine *Qui Napoli,* in
Italian and English (free).

HOTELS

The best hotels in Naples are on the
waterfront overlooking Castel dell'Ovo
and the Santa Lucia yacht basin, or on
the hill above; both positions offer marvellous views over the city and its bay.
Several of the finer establishments have
roof gardens or terraces where the
Neapolitan élite gather for an aperitif on
warm evenings.

€€€ **Excelsior.** ■ A venerable establishment with a superior level of comfort and service, famous among
Neapolitans for its roof-top bar, a
favourite place for cocktails. Open all
year. Via Partenope 48, T: 081 764
0111, www.excelsior.it
€€€ **Miramare.** In a *fin-de-siècle* villa
on the waterfront, with fine views,
friendly staff and a sun-drenched terrace for fair-weather breakfasts. Via
Nazario Sauro 24, T: 081 764 7589,
www.hotelmiramare.com
€€€ **Santa Lucia.** Overlooking the
Castel dell'Ovo and Borgo Marinaro,
spacious rooms, tasteful public spaces,
helpful staff. Open all year. Via
Partenope 46, T: 081 764 0666, freephone T: 800 887 014, www.summitho-
tels.it
€€€ **Terminus.** One of Naples' historic hotels, near the station but quiet
and elegant. Open all year. Piazza
Garibaldi 91, T: 081 779 3111,
www.starhotels.it
€€€ **Vesuvio.** ■ Elegant public
spaces, including a *trompe-l'oeil* frescoed
staircase, a bounteous breakfast buffet
and rooms designed with the utmost
care (there are even specially furnished
children's rooms) make this one of
Italy's finest hotels. Open all year. Via
Partenope 45, T: 081 764 0044,
www.vesuvio.it
€€ **Britannique.** Old-world atmosphere, a shady garden, spacious rooms
with beautiful views. Open all year.
Corso Vittorio Emanuele 133, T: 081
761 4145, www.hotelbritannique.it
€€ **Chiaia Hotel de Charme.** ■ A
charming small hotel, the former home
of the Marchesi Lecaldano Sassola
Terza, just a few steps away from Piazza
del Plebiscito on Naples' fancy shopping street. Open all year. Via Chiaia
216, T: 081 415 555,
www.hotelchiaia.it

€€ **Costantinopoli 104.** Finely-appointed rooms and a luxuriant garden, right in the heart of town. Open all year. Via Santa Maria di Costantinopoli 104, T: 081 577 1035, www.costantinopoli104.it

€€ **Executive.** In a renovated convent, with nicely decorated rooms and public areas, sauna, gym and breakfast seating on a terrace in summer. Open all year. Via del Cerriglio 10, T: 081 552 0611, www.sea-hotels.com

€€ **Mercure Napoli Angioino.** Centrally located, near the castle, with light-filled rooms, double glazing, courteous staff. Open all year. Via Depretis 123, T: 081 552 9500, www.accorhotels.com

€€ **Palazzo Alabardieri.** ■ Charming small hotel in the elegant Via Chiaia-Piazza dei Martiri shopping district; elegant rooms, cosy wood-panelled bar. Via Alabardieri 38, T: 081 415 278, www.palazzoalabardieri.it

€€ **Paradiso.** Modern comfort on the Posillipo hill overlooking Mergellina harbour. Open all year. Via Catullo 11, T: 081 247 5111, www.bestwestern. it/paradiso_na

€€ **Rex.** In a turn-of-the-century town house, with period décor and sea views from some rooms. Open all year. Via Palepoli 12, T: 081 764 9389, www.hotel-rex.it

€€ **Splendid.** At Posillipo, spacious, quiet and panoramic. Open all year. Via Alessandro Manzoni 96, T: 081 714 5630, www.hotelsplendid.it

€ **Il Convento.** Small and intimate (just 14 rooms), in the Spanish Quarter adjacent to Via Toledo; all rooms are comfortable, some a bit dark due to the area's narrow streets. Open all year. Via Speranzella 137a, T: 081 403 977, www.hotelilconvento.com

€ **Parteno.** Six cosy rooms in a former villa, with sea views and lovely Vietri-tiled bathrooms. Lungomare Partenope 1, T: 081 245 2095, www.parteno.it

RESTAURANTS

€€€ **La Cantinella.** Fancy restaurant with outstanding traditional and creative cuisine. Closed Sun, late Dec–early Jan and two weeks in Aug. Via Cuma 42, T: 081 764 8684.

€€€ **La Sacrestia.** ■ One of the city's most distinguished restaurants; with outdoor summer seating and fine views. Closed Mon, Aug and late Dec. Via Orazio 116, T: 081 664 186.

€€ **A'Fenestella.** Restaurant with summer seating on a terrace overlooking the sea. Closed midday July–Aug (except Sun) and two weeks in mid-Aug. Via Marechiaro 23, T: 081 769 0020.

€€ **Bersagliera.** Where you can watch the yachts come and go while enjoying the morning's catch. Closed Tues and Jan. Borgo Marinari, Banchina Santa Lucia, T: 081 764 6016.

€€ **Valdinchenia.** A curious wedding of Campanian recipes and Lucanian (Basilicata) ingredients. Open evenings only, closed Sun and Aug. Via Pontano 21, T: 081 660 265.

€ **Da Tonino.** Old-fashioned *osteria*, lunch only except Sat, closed Sun. Via Santa Teresa a Chiaia 47, T: 081 421 533.

€ **Il Gobbetto.** Trattoria much loved by musicians from the Teatro San Carlo. Closed Sun and in Aug. Via Sergente Maggiore 8 (Quartieri Spagnoli), T: 081 411 483.

€ **La Cantina di Masaniello.** Traditional Neapolitan cuisine and great wines in a historic town house. Closed Sun and in Aug. Via Donnalbina 28, T: 081 552 8863.

€ **La Cantina di Sica.** Traditional trattoria on the Vomero hill. Closed Thur and late Aug–early Sept. Via Bernini 17, T: 081 556 7520.

€ **La Cantina di Triunfo.** Wine bar, open evenings only. Closed Sun, holidays and Aug. Riviera di Chiaia 34, T: 081 668 101.

€ **La Chiacchierata.** Traditional trattoria, open for lunch only (except Fri); closed Sun and in Aug. Piazza Matilde Serao 37, T: 081 411 465.

€ **La Mattonella.** A real, earthy *osteria*; closed Sun evening (except in summer) and two weeks in Aug. Via Nicotera 13, T: 081 416 541.

€ **La Stanza del Gusto.** ■ A tiny place in a street also known by another name (Gradini di Chiaia), known for its *sfizi* (little delicacies) and its excellent water-buffalo meat dishes prepared with creative skill by chef Mario Avallone. Evenings only, closed Sun. Vicoletto Sant'Arpino 21, T: 081 401 578.

€ **Salvatore alla Riviera.** Good traditional trattoria; closed Tues. Riviera di Chiaia 91, T: 081 680 490.

PIZZERIE

€ **Bellini.** One of the best places in town for pizza (including take-away), popular among the young artists and musicians of the nearby Accademia and Conservatorio. Closed Sun evening, all day Sun in July and Aug, and 10 days in Aug. Via Costantinopoli 79–80, T: 081 459 774.

€ **Brandi.** The city's oldest (established 1780); closed mid-Aug. Salita Sant'Anna di Palazzo 1–2, T: 081 416 928.

€ **Capasso.** Quintessentially Neapolitan, with a strong local following. Closed Tues. Via Porta San Gennaro 2, T: 081 456 421.

€ **Ciro a Mergellina.** ■ Great pizza and noisy company somehow go together here. Closed Mon. Via Mergellina 18–21, T: 081 681 780.

€ **Ciro a Santa Brigida.** Where the pizza gets a special mention from the Italian Academy of Cuisine. Closed Sun and one week in mid-Aug. Via Santa Brigida 71–74, T: 081 552 4072.

€ **Di Matteo.** Where the pizzas are so good former US President Bill Clinton had two. Closed Sun and two weeks in Aug. Via Tribunali 94, T: 081 455 262.

€ **Lombardi a Santa Chiara.** In business for over a century, in the heart of the *spaccanapoli* district. Closed Mon and three weeks in Aug. Via Benedetto Croce 59, T: 081 552 0780.

€ **Starita.** You'll be the only tourist here—the others are straight out of *L'Oro di Napoli* with Sofia Loren (which was filmed in the neighbourhood). Closed Sun and two weeks in Aug. Via Materdei 27, T: 081 544 1485.

CAFÉS & CONFECTIONERS

Acquafrescaio. The last of the vanishing breed known as *acquafrescaie*, literally 'cold water sellers', who now sell mineral water, fresh fruit juice and other exquisite drinkables. Via Chiaia 154.

Bar Ascensione. Ice creams, tiramisù, *semifreddi* and other cold specialities,

made with natural ingredients. Piazzetta
Ascensione 2.
Bar Bellavia. Sweet and savoury pas-
tries from Naples and Sicily. Via Luca
Giordano 158.
Caffè Gambrinus. ■ A historic, popu-
lar café, with excellent coffee and pas-
tries. Via Chiaia (near the Palazzo
Reale).
Dolce Idea. Confectioner with out-
standing home-made chocolates. Via
Solitaria 28.
Officine Gastronomiche Partenopee.
Home-made liqueurs and jams. Via
Rampe Brancaccio 32.
Panna, Zucchero & Cannella.
Confectioner offering assorted choco-
lates, sweets and liqueurs. Via Croce 50.
Pasticceria Girasole. Outstanding *can-
noli* and *sfogliatelle*. Via Posillipo 362.
Scaturchio. ■ One of the city's oldest
and finest *pasticceria-gelaterie*, making
pastries, cakes, ice cream, *cassate* and a
delicious *ministeriale*, or liqueur-filled
chocolate medallion. Piazza San
Domenico Maggiore 19.

OPERA, THEATRE & CONCERTS

Information on theatre performances
and concerts is carried in *Qui Napoli*,
published free every month. It is available at hotels, or from the tourist information offices. The major venues are:
  Teatro Mercadante, Piazza
Municipio 1, T: 081 552 4214, www.
teatrostabilenapoli.it
  **Teatro Mediterraneo e Arena
Flegrea**, Piazzale Tecchio 52, T: 081
725 8000, www.mostradoltremare.it
  Teatro San Carlo di Napoli, Via San
Carlo 98f, T: 081 797 2301,
www.teatrosancarlo.it

Teatro Trianon, Via Calenda 9, T:
081 225 8285, www.teatrotrianon.it
  Teatro Sannazaro, Via Chiaia 157, T:
081 411 723, www.teatrosannazaro.it
  **Centro di Musica Antica—Pietà dei
Turchini**, Via Santa Caterina da Siena
38, T: 081 402 395, www.turchini.it
  Teatro Diana, Via Giordano 64, T:
081 556 7527, www.teatrodiana.it
  Teatro di Corte di Palazzo Reale,
Piazza del Plebiscito 1, T: 081 580
8111.
  Teatro Augusteo, Via Toledo 262, T:
081 414 243, www.teatroaugusteo.com
  Teatro Bellini, Via C. di Ruvo 14, T:
081 549 1266, www.teatrobellini.it
  Teatro Politeama, Via Monte di Dio
80, T: 081 764 5001.

CULTURAL ASSOCIATIONS

Fondazione Napoli 99, Riviera di
Chiaia 202 (T: 081 667 599); **Napoli
Sotterranea** (T: 081 296 944) and
LAES, Via Santa Teresella degli
Spagnoli 24 (T: 081 400 256), are
actively involved in preserving the city's
cultural-historical heritage and making
it available to visitors. Fondazione
Napoli 99 is rehabilitating and opening
monuments and is also engaged in a
wide range of educational activities.
Napoli Sotterranea and LAES offer guided tours of underground Naples (sites
are described in the text).

FESTIVALS & EVENTS

'O Cippo 'e Sant'Antonio Horses and
other animals are blessed at
Sant'Antonio, discarded goods are gathered and burned in bonfires, 17 Jan.
Madonna del Carmine Exhibition of the

historic Crucifix and mock 'burning' of Fra' Nuvolo's campanile, 13–20 April.
Struscio Easter weekend. So called because of the rustling of the silk dresses worn on the occasion brings a great crowd into Via Roma and Via Chiaia on the Thursday and Friday before Easter to view the season's novelties in the shops. On a smaller scale, the event is repeated every Saturday evening after 6pm.

Ritorno dei Pellegrini da Montevergine Pilgrims' return from Montevergine. You can see interesting costumes and horses with beribboned harnesses in the streets near the harbour. People carry staves decorated with fruit and flowers as in the ancient Bacchanalia, Whit Monday.

Rioni Festivals Neighbourhood celebrations follow one another at frequent intervals, with processions, fireworks, sporting events and performances by local music clubs. Sat night to Sun nights in summer.

Luglio Musicale Annual music festival at Capodimonte, July.

Liquefazione del Sangue di San Gennaro When the saint's dried blood turns to liquid. The phials are borne in colourful procession (late afternoon), 19 Sept and 16 Dec in the cathedral and on the first Sat in May at Santa Chiara.

Festa di Piedigrotta New songs, specially prepared for the occasion, are sung at the Festa di Piedigrotta, at Piedigrotta, Sept.

Fiera dei Pastori Street market of Nativity figures in Via San Gregorio Armeno. Nov–Dec.

Napoli Festival Voci nel Sole Bel canto vocal music festival, Nov, Piazzetta Matilde Serao 19, www.napolifestival.it.

Festival Dissonanzen Contemporary music festival, Chiesa di Santa Caterina da Siena, Nov–May, www.dissonanzen.it

see Amalfi Coast map, p.236

CAMPANIA

ampania, the region of which Naples is the capital, is not for everyone. 'Here the beautie of all the World is gathered as it were into a bundle,' remarked the British traveller Fynes Moryson in 1617. But by 1973 another writer, Peter Nichols, could call Campania an 'Eden which produces poverty'. Indeed, although the region is strikingly beautiful, centuries of misrule have left a deep mark here, which time is only very slowly erasing. The Neapolitan hinterland is one of the most impoverished areas of Italy, with unemployment rates in certain towns and age groups reaching peaks above 80 per cent. And facilities to provide the education and training that are the keys to qualified employment are sadly lacking or, at best, dysfunctional.

Outside the more desperate areas, which lie between Naples and Caserta to the north, and along the gulf shore at the foot of Vesuvius to the south, there is a certain, carefully cultivated order to the neglect in Campania. As Leslie Stephen pointed out over a century ago, 'the squalor of [a Campanian] town surrounds monuments of incomparable beauty, and somehow does not seem altogether out of harmony with them'. As cynical as this comment may seem, it does contain an element of truth that British or North American visitors may find shocking: the people who live on the shores of the Mediterranean have a very different relationship with what we consider the 'decent draperies of human existence'.

Campania occupies the Tyrrhenian coast and the western slopes of the Apennines, between Lazio and Molise to the north, Puglia to the east and Basilicata to the south. It is a fertile region, with an astonishing variety of coast, plain and mountain. Administratively it is divided into five provinces with capitals at Avellino, Benevento, Caserta, Salerno and Naples. Anciently known as *Ausonia* or *Opicia* (after the Italic tribes who first lived here), it received its civilization from the Greeks and the Etruscans. Its present name, originally used to designate the fertile plain of Capua (the *Ager campanus*), dates from the Samnite conquest (5th century BC). Under the Romans, who occupied it after the Social War (88 BC), it rose to great prosperity and soon won the appellative *Campania felix* on account of its beauty and fertility.

With the fall of the Roman Empire the region passed to the Goths, to the Byzantines, and finally to the Lombards, who partitioned it into the duchies of Benevento, Capua, Naples and, later, Salerno. In its subsequent history the region followed the fortunes of Naples, its chief city.

THE PHLEGRAEAN FIELDS

The Phlegraean Fields or *Campi Flegrei* ('burning fields') is the name given to the volcanic region to the west of Naples, as far as Cumae. Eruptions have apparently ceased, but have left their trace in 13 low craters, some filled with water, which give the countryside its distinctive appearance. It still abounds in hot springs and *fumarole*, or steam jets, notably the Solfatara at Pozzuoli. Both Greek colonists and the Romans were quick to appreciate the glorious climate and delightful surroundings close to the sea. Innumerable villas sprang up at Baiae and Puteoli, places renowned for their unbridled luxury under the empire. Of all this nothing remains except for a few ruined buildings and the names that evoke the memory of past glories.

A tour of the principal sights may comfortably be made by car in half a day (actual driving time is just over an hour); but if you can, spend a day or two on foot exploring this delightful region. The most important sites are the Roman baths at Baia, the Greek and Roman ruins at Cumae and the Roman remains at Pozzuoli.

Agnano Terme

The first signs of volcanic activity in this rather eerie region appear as soon as you leave Naples. Agnano Terme is a spa with hot springs on the south side of the crater of Agnano. The crater, 6.5km in circumference, became flooded with water in the Middle Ages and was drained in 1866, the waters flowing out through a tunnel beneath Monte Spina, the southwest eminence. Its marshy surface abounds with mineral springs.

The spa (*open throughout the year*) and the principal springs (mostly in the southeast part of the crater) are Agnano's chief claims to fame. On the right of the central hall are the Stufe di San Germano, a series of rooms with gradually increasing temperature; to the left is a cave like the famous nearby Grotta del Cane or 'Dog Grotto', in which carbon dioxide covers the floor to the height of half a metre, instantly extinguishing lights held in it, and stupefying and killing animals. This phenomenon was once demonstrated to visitors at the expense of unhappy dogs. The most important sources are a hot spring near the spa (72.5°C), regulated in 1921, the intermittent Sprudel (70°C), further north, and the abundant Ponticello (87°C). Further on is the Fanghiera, or mud reservoir, kept moist by springs, of which the most important is the Salvatore Tommasi (70°C). About 1km north near a hot chalybeate spring (39°C) is Agnano racecourse, extending to the foot of the Astroni hills.

Adjacent to the spa are the ruins of the Roman *Thermae Anianae*, a six-storey building with passages leading to the *sudatoria* (vapour-chambers), hollowed out of the hill. Excavations have revealed mosaics and pipes for water and steam. A road skirting the east side of the Agnano crater leads to the Parco degli Astroni, another extinct volcano.

The road to Pozzuoli climbs above Bagnoli under hills anciently called *Colles Leucogaei* ('hills of white earth') because of their white soil, which was used for bleaching barley. From the base of one of them issue the Pisciarelli, hot aluminiferous springs. Out to sea appears the island of Nisida with Capri behind it, and to the west is Capo Miseno backed by Monte Epomeo on Ischia.

The road turns away from the coast and passes the convent of San Gennaro, built in the 16th century on the supposed site of the beheading of St Januarius (*see p. 68*). A stone stained with the martyr's blood, which turns bright red on the occasion of the liquefaction of his blood in Naples, is preserved in the church. There is a fine view from the convent across the gulf.

The Solfatara di Pozzuoli

The Solfatara di Pozzuoli (*open daily 8.30–dusk*) is a half-extinct volcano known to the Romans as *Forum Vulcani*. The huge elliptical crater, 752m across at its widest point, has changed little in appearance since Roman times. The path along the bottom passes (left) a well of hot water 9m deep and soon reaches the *fumarole*, a number of violent jets of steam emerging from the ground at a high temperature (c. 143°C) and charged with sulphurous vapour. The nature of the gas varies considerably. The ground is hot and makes a hollow sound when stamped on. About 100m southeast, behind a small pavilion, is the largest *fumarola*, the Bocca Grande, from which steam issues at a very high temperature (162°C) with a whistling noise. The barren northwest part of the crater is at the lowest level and was probably covered with hot muddy water until the 18th century. At various dates since, funnel-shaped cavities containing hot mud have formed here. About 240m north of the Bocca Grande are the Stufe, more *fumarole* in an artificial excavation.

POZZUOLI

Pozzuoli is a curious town standing partly on an isolated promontory of yellow tufa and partly on the landward slopes, with its main street passing between. In 1970 part of the town was damaged by a bradyseism, a 'slow earthquake', that raised the ground more than 75cm in six months. Further movement was registered in 1983.

HISTORY OF POZZUOLI

The Greek colonists from Samos called Pozzuoli *Dikaearchia*. It became a commercial post subject to Cumae and was later conquered by the Samnites. The Romans established a colony here in 194 BC and the Romanised town, renamed *Puteoli*, soon became the principal Italian port for trading with the East. It was adorned with buildings appropriate to its wealth, so that Cicero was able to describe it as *pusilla Roma* ('little Rome'). St Paul landed at Puteoli on his voyage to Rome in AD 62. The fall of Rome, the barbarian invasions, the eruption of Monte Nuovo, and the increase of malaria reduced the once prosperous port to a fishing village, and today only its ruins testify to its former glory.

The cathedral

At the east end of the town, just beyond the sea-girt Capuchin convent where the composer Pergolesi (1710–36) died of tuberculosis, is Piazza Matteotti (Porta di Città), where the buses from Naples terminate. Here, Via del Duomo ascends to the cathedral (San Procolo), which incorporates a temple erected in honour of Augustus by the architect Cocceius. The church was completely rebuilt in 1643 by Bishop Martino de León y Cardenas, but a fire in May 1964 destroyed the Baroque structure, revealing the Roman building, in marble, as well as remains of a Samnite temple, in tufa, dating from 3rd–2nd centuries BC. Pergolesi's tomb was undamaged by the fire.

Today the cathedral awaits reconstruction. It can be viewed on guided tours of the archaeological area of Rione Terra, which encompasses a considerable part of the ancient Roman city. The ruins (*open Sat and Sun 9–7; T 848 800 288 or 06 3996 7050*), which lie beneath the modern city, are reached by an underground passage behind a large, well-marked gate. Extensive areas of the *cardo* and *decumanus* have been brought to light: clearly visible are shops (*tabernae*) an industrial-scale *pistrinum* (or bakery, with flour mills), a cistern, a restaurant, and a complex of *ergastula,* originally slaves' quarters and later a brothel, now thought to have inspired the setting of Petronius Arbiter's *Satyricon.* There are also traces of mural drawings (two gladiators) and paintings (the twelve gods of Olympus, in a family *lararium*). (*NB: At the time of writing the site was closed to the public on weekdays to permit excavation to continue*).

The harbour

From the Porta di Città, Corso Vittorio Emanuele leads west and Corso Garibaldi leads north to the theatre and public gardens. Here are busts of Pergolesi and of the native composer Antonio Sacchini (1734–86). The harbour extends to the left and incorporates the surviving remains of the Roman port. The *Moles Puteolana* or *Opus Pilarum* consisted of a breakwater of 25 piers connected by arches, cleverly arranged to prevent the silting up of the harbour. At the end was a triumphal arch to Antoninus Pius, who restored the harbour in AD 120 after a violent storm. In calm weather, the foundations of a double line of piers and a number of columns can be discerned below the surface. The mooring rings by which ships were attached are now covered by more than a fathom of water, owing to the subsidence of the land. Offshore, on the south side of the town, are the remains of three submerged docks.

The Serapeum

The Serapeum (*open daily 9–dusk*) is set in a waterfront park. This was not, as the name implies, a temple dedicated to Serapis (a grain deity of Egyptian origin), but a *macellum* or rectangular market-hall (75m by 58m). It dates from the 1st century AD. Opposite the seaward entrance was an apse, preceded by four Corinthian columns, three of which still stand. They have been eroded, from 3.5m to 5.5m above ground, by a species of stone-boring shellfish, *Lithodomus lithophagus,* which still abounds in the Tyrrhenian Sea. This suggests that the columns were at some time buried for 3.5m and submerged for another 2m. Perhaps during the 1538 eruption they were again raised above sea level; they became dry at the beginning of the 20th century. Today water again covers the floor, although the 'slow quake' of 1970 raised the ground level by nearly 90cm.

Within the building is a courtyard, 32m square, surrounded by a gallery of 48 *cipollino* and granite columns beneath which were 35 booths and two marble-lined public latrines. A second storey probably existed on the same plan. The central tholos, or domed circular building, was supported by 16 columns of *giallo antico* which are now at Caserta, only their bases remaining *in situ.*

The amphitheatre

The Flavian amphitheatre (Anfiteatro Flavio; *open daily 9–dusk*) is the best preserved of the monuments of ancient Puteoli. It is extremely large, rivalling the Colosseum in Rome and the amphitheatres of Capua and Verona in size. The building you see today measures 149m by 166m. It was finished under Vespasian and replaced an older amphitheatre, whose ruins (discovered during construction work on the Direttissima railway line connecting Rome and Naples in 1926–27) may still be seen near the railway bridge to the northeast. The new amphitheatre is built on three rows of arches and was originally surrounded by a brick arcade. The cavea had three ranges of seats divided by stairs into *cunei*.

The arena (72m by 42m) has an open corridor along its greater axis, below which are substructures (dens for wild beasts and rooms for stage machinery), added under Trajan or Hadrian, in a remarkably good state of preservation. Sixty openings connecting the substructures with the arena served for letting loose the wild beasts, for ventilation and for erecting the *pegma*, a wooden scaffold on which the gladiators fought and which could be run up very quickly. In Vespasian's time, reservoirs around the amphitheatre (the largest of which, the Piscina Cardito, still exists on the right of the Solfatara road) supplied water for flooding the arena on the occasion of a *naumachia* (mock sea battle). St Januarius and his companions were imprisoned here under Diocletian before their executions near the Solfatara. Here, too, Nero amazed the Armenian king Tiridates by his exploits among the beasts in the arena.

To the northwest are remains of what was probably a Roman villa, the ruined Tempio dell'Onore, and some fragments of *thermae*, known as the Tempio di Nettuno, dating from the time of Nero.

AROUND POZZUOLI

As long as you don't do it in the torrid midsummer heat, the 16km (4hrs) walk from Pozzuoli to Cumae is well worth your while (*for the return by public transport see pp. 139–140*). Of course, you can also drive it; and the train follows more or less the same route.

Pozzuoli to Lago Lucrino

Continue north along Corso Terracciano above the town. To the right, by the church of the Annunziata, Via Provinciale Campana diverges inland, lined on either side with sepulchral monuments, more of which were discovered when the Direttissima railway was constructed parallel to the road. About 2km beyond Pozzuoli, leave the new road (which continues towards Cumae) and descend to the left, joining the old road; this, with the Cumana railway, follows the lovely coastline of the Bay of Naples.

To the right is Monte Nuovo (140m), a volcanic cone of rough *scoriae* and tufa, entered (for a small fee) from about halfway between Arco Felice and Lago Lucrino stations. It takes c. 20mins to reach the summit, and 10mins more to descend into the crater (15m above the sea). This crater was thrown up during the earthquake of 1538, when Lago Lucrino was half filled and Pozzuoli deluged with mud and *lapilli*.

Lago Lucrino (Lake Lucrine) is separated from the sea (fine beach) by a narrow strip of land, the Via Herculea whereby Hercules drove the bulls of Geryon across the swamp. The lake is much shrunken since the time (c. 100 BC) when Sergius Orata began the cultivation of oysters here. Cicero's villa, which he called the *Academia,* stood on the shore nearby.

The descent to Avernus

A road running straight inland leads to Lago d'Averno (Lake Avernus), a crater 8km around and 34m deep, entirely surrounded by hills except for a narrow opening on the south side. It has been encircled by a stone edging to prevent the formation of malarial swamps; its waters are only 40cm above sea level.

Surrounded, in the heroic age, by dense forest, which gave it a dark and gloomy atmosphere, Avernus was said to be the home of the Cimmerians (*Homer, Odyssey XI*), who lived in eternal darkness. It was also famed as the entrance to Hades, and features large in the *Aeneid*. The Greek name *Aornos* (held to mean 'without birds') gave rise to the legend that birds flying over the lake fell into it, suffocated by poisonous fumes.

Hannibal, in what was ostensibly a mark of respect for local superstition but was in fact a pretext for a reconnaissance of Puteoli, visited Lake Avernus and offered a sacrifice; the custom of making a propitiatory sacrifice to the infernal deities of Avernus lasted beyond the days of Constantine.

Agrippa completely altered the appearance of the countryside surrounding the lake. To counter the threat of Sextus Pompeius' fleet (37 BC) he cut down the forest and linked Lake Avernus to the sea by a canal, via Lake Lucrine, and to Cumae by a tunnel (*see below*), thereby constructing a military harbour of perfect security, the *Portus Julius*. This was later abandoned, and finally wrecked by the eruption of 1538. Despite Agrippa's improvements, the association between Avernus and Hades, sung by Virgil and regenerated by Pliny and Silius Italicus, survived even among 6th-century Byzantine writers.

On the east shore of the lake are ruins of *thermae*. The most remarkable remains, arbitrarily known as the Temple of Apollo, are of an octagonal building with a round interior broken by niches, the dome of which (now fallen) once spanned a space of over 36m. The overgrown ruins on the west side probably represent a shipbuilding and repair yard.

Agrippa's tunnel to Cumae, a passage more than 1km long executed by Cocceius, leads away from the northwest shore. It is known as the **Grotta della Pace**, after Pietro della Pace, who explored it in 1507. Straight and wide enough for chariots to pass, it is the most ambitious underground work attempted by the Romans and, being lighted at intervals by vertical openings, it could be travelled through with ease, even without a light, until it was damaged by fighting in 1943.

A path along the south side of the lake, rising above it to the left, leads in c. 3mins to a long gallery cut into the rock, off which opens a chamber blackened with torch smoke. Once a rival claimant to be the Sibyl's cave, this is now thought to have been part of Agrippa's defensive works.

Road and railway now follow the Via Herculea. The railway then tunnels through the Punta dell'Epitaffio, whereas the road follows the coast. Here is the site of *Bauli*, where Nero's mother Agrippina, having escaped the previous day from a planned accident at sea, was murdered, in the bedroom of her villa, on her son's orders. On the right of the road are some ruins of *thermae*, called the 'Stufe di Nerone' or 'di Tritoli', including a remarkable *sudatorium* hewn out of the tufa.

BAIA

Baia, the ancient *Baiae*, extolled by the Latin writers Horace and Martial, is a large village standing on the bay that bears its name. It enjoys a splendid view across the gulf.

HISTORY OF BAIA

In the early days of the Roman Empire, *Baiae*, which according to legend owed its name to Baius, Odysseus' navigator, was the fashionable bathing resort of Roman society. Successive emperors rivalled each other in the construction of magnificent seaside palaces, and Caligula built his famous bridge of boats here, which stretched as far as Pozzuoli. However, the reputation of the town was tarnished by Nero's murder of his mother Agrippina and his sanguinary suppression of the conspiracy of Caius Calpurnius Piso to rid Rome of its increasingly deranged emperor. Hadrian died here on 17th July 138. Baiae was plundered by the Saracens in the 8th century and gradually deserted as malaria spread. The palace ruins now extend some distance beneath the sea, owing to substantial ground subsidence of the whole area, caused by seismic activity. Finds made in the harbour in 1923–28 included statues and important architectural fragments. The finest statue, the *Aphrodite Sosandra*, was found farther up the hill. It is now displayed in the Museo Archeologico Nazionale in Naples (*see p. 84*). Other finds can be seen in the Museo Archeologico dei Campi Flegrei (*see opposite*).

The ancient ruins

The ruins of Baiae are beautiful and evocative; but their importance lies in the cluster of boldly vaulted structures, which mark an important passage in the history of western architecture. The three large, domed thermal chambers—especially the complete cupola of the Temple of Mercury, which, with its perfect hemispherical form and oculus, is the earliest of the three (possibly even as early as the late 1st century BC)—presage the grandeur of the unencumbered vaulted spaces of later Roman building, culminating in Hadrian's magnificent Pantheon in Rome, more than a century later. The stimulus to create domed spaces—especially in religious architecture from Byzantine churches to the cupola of St. Peter's—can be traced back to these early experiments.

The 'Temple of Diana' and archaeological park

Behind the station is the so-called 'Temple of Diana', one of several buildings once thought to be temples but now known to be baths. Octagonal without and circular within, it preserves four niches and part of its domed roof. From the piazza, steps ascend to the Zona Archeologica di Baia (*open daily 9–dusk*). Systematic excavations began in 1941 and were completed ten years later. A group of buildings, some of which were already known in the Middle Ages, were identified, comprising an **imperial *palatium*** built in the 1st century BC and enlarged over the following three centuries. From the entrance, a long avenue leads to a portico where architectural fragments are displayed. Here, steps lead to the upper terrace, one of several such areas set into the hillside at various levels. A row of rooms with shallow exedrae extends along the right. In the first of these the statue of *Aphrodite Sosandra* was found. The second contains a statue of Mercury, beheaded by thieves (who in Antiquity enjoyed the god's protection!) in 1978.

A staircase descends to the central terrace, along one side of which a series of rooms forming a semicircle suggests the previous existence of a theatre-nymphaeum. From here, more steps descend to the lower terrace, occupied by a large (35m by 29m) rectangular bathing pool, surrounded by a graceful portico. To the east of the pool lies the complex of buildings traditionally called the '**Bath of Venus**', which includes a large vaulted hall surrounded by apsidal openings, also believed to be a nymphaeum, and numerous smaller rooms. From the north side of the pool a corridor partially covered by arches leads to the **Temple of Mercury**. These buildings appear to have made up another thermal complex; principal among them is a great circular hall nearly 22m in diameter, similar in structure to the Pantheon in Rome (though half the size). Like the smaller halls to the rear, it is now filled with water to the base of the dome, creating the unusual acoustic effects from which it derives its nickname, 'Tempio dell'Eco'. Like the other vaulted structures of Baiae, it was built over hot thermal springs which originally rose in the pool beneath the dome.

The 'Temple of Venus'
Outside the archaeological park and across the street to the southeast is another huge structure, traditionally called the 'Temple of Venus'. It is a hall of circular plan, 26m in diameter. Although most of the vault has collapsed, the rest of the structure is intact to an impressive height. Though now separated by the modern road, this was originally an integral part of the of the Bath of Venus, mentioned above.

The Museo Archeologico dei Campi Flegrei
Beyond the excavations, the road to Capo Miseno ascends a gentle slope along the shore, passing several *columbaria* (fine view). On the left is the 16th-century Castello di Baia, built by order of viceroy Don Pedro de Toledo. The castle houses the Museo Archeologico dei Campi Flegrei (*open Tues–Sat 9–3, Sun 9–7*), with material from excavations at Baia and other sites in the area. Especially noteworthy is the reconstructed Nymphaeum of the Emperor Claudius (the original is under water off Punta Epitaffio) with statues of Ulysses and imperial family members arranged around a lighted pool. (*NB: At the time of writing the museum collections were about to be completely reinstalled, requiring the closure of some exhibits.*)

Bacoli
At the bottom of a hill is the village of Bacoli. The Via della Marina, to the left, at the entrance to the village, descends to the so-called **tomb of Agrippina**, really the ruins of a small theatre. From the main road Via Ercole and Via Sant'Anna ascend to the

church of Sant'Anna. Walking round this, you may go on (15mins) to the **Cento Camerelle** (*open daily 9–dusk, Bacoli bus stop, T: 081 523 3797*), a two-storey ruin of which the upper part was a reservoir (the function of the lower storey is not known) for the villa of Hortensius Hortalus, thought to be the most sumptuous at Baia. At Via Creco 10 you may obtain the key for the **Piscina Mirabilis**, 10mins south of the village (*open daily 9–dusk, Miseno bus stop, T: 081 855 3284, tip required*). This is the largest and best-preserved Roman reservoir known (70m by 25m). Its form recalls that of a basilica, with five pillared aisles of equal height. It once lay at the extremity of an aqueduct and was used for supplying the Roman fleet stationed at Misenum.

At the southern end of the town is the **Lago di Miseno** or Mare Morto—the 'dead' (landlocked) sea. Leave the main road heading south, following the causeway that separates the lagoon from the picturesque harbour of *Misenum*. The harbour was built by Agrippa in 41 BC as a temporary refuge for the Tyrrhenian fleet during the construction of the *Portus Julius* (*see p. 141 above*); it was while stationed here with the fleet that Pliny the Younger witnessed the fatal eruption of Vesuvius in AD 79. The port consisted of two basins, of which the inner, the Mare Morto, is now shut off from the Porto di Miseno proper by the road causeway. The colony of Misenum was founded at the same time as the harbour, but its importance diminished as Roman naval power declined. It was destroyed by the Saracens in the 9th century.

Capo Miseno

The byroad continues to the village of Miseno. Cars are not allowed beyond this point. A path turns to the right near the church, to the right again just before a farmhouse, and then to the left, passing various ruins (*see below*). The ascent (1hr there and back) leads to Capo Miseno (155m), a promontory commanding a wonderful view over the Gulfs of Pozzuoli, Naples and Gaeta, and the surrounding lakes and islands.

The headland is a segment of an ancient crater, the rest of which has sunk below the sea. The remaining portion so resembles an artificial tumulus as to have given rise to the legend that it was the burial-place of Misenus, Aeneas' trumpeter. The headland was already covered with villas when the colony was founded, and among its distinguished residents was the general Caius Marius, whose country house passed into the possession of his eminent colleague Lucullus and later to the emperors. Tiberius died there in AD 37. The ruins of Marius' villa are on the south side of the harbour; near the church are the remains of the circular baths; and to the northwest stands a theatre commanding a fine view of Ischia. On the west side of the headland is the Grotta Dragonara, an excavation supported by 12 pillars, probably a storehouse for the fleet. Walkers may follow the Spiaggia di Miliscola (the name comes from the Latin *militis schola,* roughly 'military training ground'), a narrow sandbar 2km long between the Mare Morto and the sea, and rejoin the main road c. 1km before Cappella.

Back on the main road, bear left along the north side of the Mare Morto, turning sharply right for Cappella, a village between Monte Grillo or Monte di Procida (144m) on the south, and Monte dei Salvatichi (123m). About 1km beyond Cappella a road on the left leads to (1km) **Torregaveta** (the terminus of the Cumana and

Circumflegrea railways). From here another road running south ascends to the village of **Monte di Procida** (3km; bus from Torregaveta), on a tufa hill covered with ruined villas among vineyards (which produce an excellent wine). **Acquamorta**, on the end of the promontory beyond, commands a fine view of Procida and Ischia.

Leaving the Torregaveta road on the left you reach the semicircular **Lago di Fusaro**, the ancient Acherusian Swamp, separated from the sea by a sandbar pierced by two canals, one Roman and one modern (1858). On the slopes of the hill north of Torregaveta is the ruined villa of Servilius Vatia. Since 1784 the lake has been a centre for oyster culture and fish breeding. On the lake is the **Casina**, built for Ferdinand IV by Vanvitelli (1782), now a marine biology station (*park open daily 9–sunset; Casina open Sat and Sun 10–1; T: 081 868 7080*).

CUMAE

The road crosses the railway near Cuma Fusaro station. Leaving a road to Baia on the right, follow the lake shore and then pass through vineyards to reach (15mins from the station) Cumae, perhaps the oldest Greek colony in Italy, now a mass of scattered ruins in a romantic situation where excavation fights a losing battle with nature.

HISTORY OF CUMAE

Cumae was one of the earliest colonies of Magna Graecia. By tradition, its foundation dates from c. 750 BC, the first settlers being the Chalcidians (from Chalcis, on Euboea) and the Aeolians of Kyme (in Asia Minor, modern Turkey). Its prosperity and population increased rapidly, and colonies were dispatched to Dikaearchia (Pozzuoli) and, after the conquest of Parthenope, to found the settlement of Neapolis. Cumae was a centre of Hellenic culture, and from its alphabet all other Italian alphabets were derived. According to Pliny, Tarquinius Superbus (who later died in exile at Cumae) purchased the Sibylline Books from the Cumaean Sibyl here, and regretted his attempt to bargain with her.

In 474 BC the Cumaeans, in alliance with Hieron of Syracuse, defeated an Etruscan fleet, a victory immortalised by Pindar in the first *Pythian Ode*. In 421 BC Cumae was conquered by the Samnites, passing later, with the rest of their possessions, to Rome. In the reign of Nero it was the scene of the voluntary death of Petronius Arbiter, implicated in Piso's plot to dethrone the emperor. No longer of importance, Cumae fell easy prey to the Saracens in the 9th century and was utterly destroyed by Naples and Aversa in 1207.

The ruins of the ancient city lie mainly beneath farmland; a visit requires at least two hours. A short distance before a fork, where the main road bears inland to the right, are the ruins of an amphitheatre, easily traced through the vineyards and olive groves that cover it. Taking the little road to the left, at the fork you pass (right; on cultivated land) the Temple of the Giants and, further away, the Temple of the Forum. Along the ascent towards Monte di Cuma (78m), the city's acropolis, traces of many other buildings can be seen over a wide area.

Beyond the entrance to the excavations (*open daily 9–dusk, refreshments, Cuma bus stop, T: 081 854 3060*), notice the massive walls of cyclopean stone, Greek in the lower courses, Roman above. A tunnel hewn out of the rock leads to the entrance to the **Cave of the Cumaean Sibyl**, one of the most famous of ancient sanctuaries, brought to light in 1932. Aeneas came to consult the Sibyl here, to ask whether his Trojan colony would evolve into the Roman Empire; on either side of the entrance, marble plaques now recall Virgil's account of the visit (*Aeneid VI, 42–51*). The cave consists of a *dromos*, or corridor, c. 44m long, nearly 2.5m wide and c. 5m high, ending in a rectangular chamber, all hewn out of the rock. The *dromos*, of trapezoidal cross-section, markedly Minoan in style, runs due north–south in the shoreward side of the hill, and is lit by six galleries opening to the west (so best visited in the afternoon). From the other side open three lower chambers, apparently designed for lustral (purificatory) waters and later used for Christian burials. The *oecus*, or secret chamber, at the end, probably redesigned in the 4th or 3rd century BC, has three large niches.

At a lower level (reached by a path to the left) a huge Roman crypt c. 180m long, tunnels through the hill; this lies on the same axis as the 1km-long tunnel known as the Grotta della Pace (*see p. 141*) and is probably a continuation of it. Many dark passages leading from the crypt show traces of Christian occupation.

A paved Via Sacra climbs to the first terrace where (right) some remains of the Temple of Apollo, a Greek structure altered in Augustan times and transformed into a church in the 6th or 7th century, survive. On the summit is the so-called Temple of Jupiter, a larger construction, also of Greek origin and also transformed (5th–6th century) into a Christian basilica of five aisles. Behind the presbytery are remains of a large circular pool for baptism by immersion. Here the beauty of the view and the stillness, broken only by the rustle of lizards and the murmur of the sea, make an indelible impression.

The chief necropolis, which has provided many interesting additions to the archaeological museum in Naples, lies between the acropolis and, to the north, Licola, a modern village on the site of a drained lake. From the ruins a path (which you cannot enter from the other end) leads down to the deserted shore. Towards the sea the outer wall of the town is still traceable. Torregaveta may be reached by a pleasant walk (4km) along the beach or by a well-preserved stretch of Roman road, a branch of the Via Domitiana, engineered in AD 95 to link Rome directly with Puteoli (Pozzuoli). Along its course to the north lie the Lago di Patria—once the harbour for the Roman colony of *Liternum* (scanty ruins)—where Scipio Africanus died in 184 BC; and Sinuessa (near the modern Mondragone), where it joined the Via Appia.

Arco Felice

Just 2km from Cumae is the Arco Felice, a massive brick archway, 20m high and 6m wide, in a deep cutting made in Monte Grillo by Domitian to secure direct communication between Cumae and Puteoli. To the west is a good stretch of Roman paving. Arco Felice station is 4km away.

Bagnoli

This bathing resort and spa, much frequented by the Neapolitans, is home to the new **Città della Scienza**, a multimedia science museum and planetarium occupying the 19th-century factory buildings of the former Italsider iron and steel works. Directly overlooking the Bay of Pozzuoli, the 12,000 square-metre facility offers an instructive, entertaining journey through the worlds of science and technology. (*Via Coroglio 57 and 104. Open April–May Mon–Sat 9–5, Sun 10–7; June–July Tues and Thur 9–3, Fri, Sat and Sun 6.30am–10.30pm; Sept–April Tues–Sat 9–5, Sun 10–7; closed Mon and Aug. Bus C10 from Naples, Piazza Vittoria, or train and bus, directions at www.cittadellascienza.it*).

Continuing along Via Coroglio you come shortly to the entrance to a fascinating new archaeological site, the Grotta di Seiano e Area di Pausilypon. Here are the **remains of *Pausilypon*** ('the Carefree'), the villa belonging to the Roman patrician Vedius Pollio, supporter of Octavian in his military campaigns, as well as in his bid to transform Rome from Republic to Empire. On Pollio's death the villa passed into the possession of Octavian (by then the emperor Augustus). The villa proper comprises living areas, an odeon and a large and small theatre; it is connected by the 800m Grotto of Sejanus to Marechiaro on the other side of the Posillipo promontory. In spite of its name, it is believed to have been cut in AD 37 (Lucius Aelius Sejanus, administrator of the Roman Empire for the emperor Tiberius, died in AD 31). The dig is part of an underwater archaeological park, the Parco Sommerso di Gaiola, with boat tours available (*at the time of writing the site can be entered from the Bagnoli side only; it is open Mon–Sat 9–1, with escorted tours leaving at 9.30, 10.30 & 11.30. On Mon, Wed and Fri visits are restricted to the Grotto only; T: 081 372 3760, www.areamarinaprotettagaiola.it*).

From Bagnoli the old road runs straight to Naples. The coast road (past the huge chemical works of Coroglio) climbs up to the Rotonda (with a view of Nisida) and enters Naples along the Posillipo peninsula.

PRACTICAL INFORMATION

GETTING AROUND

• **By rail:** Frequent trains are operated by the Cumana railway from Naples Montesanto station (Piazza Montesanto; *map p. 52, 6*) to Pozzuoli (20mins), Baia (30mins) and Torregaveta (40mins).

The Circumflegrea railway, also departing from Montesanto station, goes to Licola. The Metropolitana runs from Naples Piazza Garibaldi, every 8–16 mins, as far as Pozzuoli Solfatara (c. 30mins). See www.campaniatrasporti.it

• **By bus:** Country bus services are

increasingly infrequent. SEPSA buses depart Naples (Piazza Garibaldi), calling at Solfatara, Pozzuoli and Baia. From Baia, connections to Cumae, Bacoli and Capo Miseno. Be sure to check timetables (www.campaniatrasporti.it) before departing, as convenient connections are not always available. Once in Pozzuoli, you can take a city bus from the harbour (Via Roma) to Cuma (no. P9) or to the Solfatara (no. P12).

• **By sea:** There are ferry connections between Pozzuoli, Procida (30mins) and Ischia (1hr), as well as hydrofoils connecting Pozzuoli and Procida (15mins). Service is frequent enough to enable you to visit the Phlegraean Fields in the morning and the islands in the afternoon. Details at www.campaniatrasporti.it

INFORMATION OFFICES

Pozzuoli Azienda Autonoma di Cura Soggiorno e Turismo, Via Matteotti 1, T: 081 526 6639, www.icampiflegrei.it

HOTELS

Bacoli
€€ **Cala Moresca**. Nicely located at Capo Miseno, with sea views from most rooms. Open all year. Capo Miseno, Via Faro 44, T: 081 523 5595, www.calamoresca.it
€ **Villa Oteri**. ■ Elegant rooms and a very good restaurant in a lovely old villa. An excellent base for exploring the Phlegraean Fields. Open all year. Via Lungolago 174, T: 081 523 4985, www.villaoteri.it

Cuma
€€ **Villa Giulia**. ■ Six beautifully-appointed rooms and suites, pool, garden and restaurant (for guests only) in a lovely villa between the Sibyl's cave and the Arco Felice. Via Cuma Licola 178, T: 081 854 0163, www.villagiulia.it

RESTAURANTS

Bacoli
€€ **A Ridosso**. Good local fish dishes, on the road from Cuma to Capo Miseno. Closed Sun evening and Mon, in late Aug and late Dec–early Jan. Via Mercato di Sabato 320. T: 081 868 9233.
€€ **Garibaldi**. Traditional fish restaurant by the sea. Closed Mon and in Aug. Via Spiaggia 36, T: 081 523 4368.
€ **Il Casolare**. A farm serving good country meals, just a few paces away from the castle by footpath. Closed Sun evening, Mon, in late Aug and late Dec–early Jan. Via Selvatico 12, T: 081 523 5193.

Pozzuoli
€ **La Cucina Flegrea**. Restaurant-pizzeria; closed Mon and briefly in Aug. At Monterusciello, Via Monterusciello 20, T: 081 524 7481.

THE CAPUAN PLAIN

The extinct volcano of Monte Roccamonfina, today little more than a wild, wooded hill, marks the northern limit of the Capuan plain. This is the most intensively cultivated area of Campania, and although modern mechanised farming has taken away much of its original charm, it still appears as a huge, well-tended garden.

As you might expect of a place where people have lived and worked for thousands of years, sites of historic and artistic interest abound. Suffice it to mention Capua, where the museum contains a unique collection of Italic *Deae Matres* (earth goddesses); Santa Maria Capua Vetere, known for its great ancient amphitheatre; and Caserta, nicknamed the 'Versailles of Naples' after the royal palace, built here by Charles III of Bourbon. Around these major monuments are a constellation of minor sights—some, like the little church of Sant'Angelo in Formis, are equally impressive. All are easy to visit regardless of whether you arrive from Naples, or from Rome and points north.

CAPUA

Capua is situated within a narrow bend of the River Volturno, 5km west of Monte Tifata (604m). It bears the name of the ancient *Capua*, an Italic city that stood on the site today occupied by Santa Maria Capua Vetere.

HISTORY OF CAPUA

The town was founded in 856 by refugees from ancient Capua. They built a new town on the ruins of *Casilinum*, noted for its heroic defence against Hannibal in 216 BC and deserted in the 2nd century AD. The new Capua became the medieval centre of the agricultural Terra di Lavoro (which occupied most of the Capuan plain and the surrounding hills), and an important frontier town of the Norman realm of Sicily. Its famous gate, Porta delle Torri (*see overleaf*), designed by Frederick II in 1247, was destroyed in 1557.

The town fell, after a bloody siege, to the French under d'Aubigny and their ally Cesare Borgia, in 1501. Pope Honorius I (625–638) and Ettore Fieramosca (hero of Barletta, d. 1515) were both natives. The first Battle of the Volturno (1st October 1860), when Garibaldi defeated the Bourbons of Naples, took place on the plain and hills to the east of Capua. Afterwards he occupied the town.

The atmosphere of Capua combines the grace of a noble past with the hustle and bustle of a busy marketplace. The Via del Duomo crosses the town from Piazza dei

Giudici, on the south (where the façade of the town hall of 1561 displays seven marble busts from the amphitheatre at Santa Maria Capua Vetere), to Via Roma and the Museo Campano to the north. The cathedral, founded in 835 and almost completely rebuilt, was destroyed in 1942 except for part of the apse, the right outer wall, and side chapels. Of the 24 columns in the atrium (slightly damaged), 16 are original; the beautiful campanile dates from 861. The crypt, with 14 antique columns, contains mosaics.

The **Museo Provinciale Campano** occupies Palazzo Antignano, the former palace of the dukes of San Cipriano, at Via Roma 68; the portal is in a late Catalan Gothic style. The collections (*open Tues–Sun 9–1.30; closed holidays; T: 0823 961402*) focus on sculptures from ancient Capua, notably the extraordinary series of *Deae Matres*, from the Temple of Mater Matuta. Each of these small, stone women holds or suckles two to twelve stone babies, children of the Earth, who depend on her fertility and bounty for survival. In early agrarian societies such statues would have been set in a place sacred to the earth-goddess in the hope of ensuring a fruitful harvest (and providing a secure future). Uncovered in 1845 near Santa Maria Capua Vetere, the statues displayed here date from the 6th–1st centuries BC.

The museum also contains inscriptions from the amphitheatre (*see p. 152 below*), a fine series of Campanian terracottas (mostly salvaged), a colossal head of *Capua Imperiale* and medieval sculptures, notably statues from the Porta delle Torri, erected after a commission from Emperor Frederick II in 1234–39. A small picture gallery is devoted to southern Italian art from the 15th–18th centuries.

In the centre of the town is the Gothic palazzo of Ettore Fieramosca, one of the champions of the *Disfida di Barletta*, the famous contest between French and Italian knights in 1503 (*see p. 441*).

To the northeast of Capua the **Cappella dei Morti** commemorates the 5,000 victims of the French siege of 1501. Beyond the chapel, at the foot of Monte Tifata, is the 11th-century basilica of **Sant'Angelo in Formis** (*open by appointment; T: 0823 960817*), reconstructed in 1073 and adorned with 12 columns and 11th-century frescoes of scenes from the Old and New Testaments, featuring prophets, kings and saints. These are by artists of the Monte Cassino school (*see box opposite*) and show a strong Byzantine influence.

Teano and Calvi Risorta

On the eastern flank of Roccamonfina lies the town of **Teano**. Here, in 1860, Vittorio Emanuele II, on his march southward, met Garibaldi returning from the Expedition of the Thousand and the overthrow of the Bourbon dynasty of Naples. The town occupies the site of the ancient *Teanum*, capital of a pre-Roman Italic people, the Sidicini. Its main monuments are a Roman theatre and amphitheatre (near the road to the station), the Romanesque church of San Paride (just beyond), and a medieval cathedral (restored). The Museo Archeologico di Teanum (*open daily except Tues 8.30–7.30; T: 0823 657302*), in the Gothic Loggione e Cavallerizza, originally part of the Marzano castle beautifully situated at the top of the old town, displays finds from the ancient

Teanum Sidicium and its territory. Highlights include votive offerings from the sanctuaries at Loreta and Fondo Ruozzo, grave finds from the 5th century BC to the Roman Imperial age, and material unearthed during the recent excavation of the theatre.

At nearby **Calvi Risorta**, the ancient *Cales* (famous for its wine), the little Romanesque cathedral, with a Cosmatesque pulpit and bishop's throne, is intact; so are the small 10th-century castle and the Grotta dei Santi (30mins walk up the Rio de Lanzi), with its remarkable collection of 10th-century mural paintings of saints.

THE MONTE CASSINO SCHOOL

Many of the churches of southern Italy provide evidence of the coexistence of two types of monasticism: the Greek, as introduced by eastern monks and hermits in the territories controlled by the Byzantine Empire, and the Latin, as embodied by the great Benedictine abbey of Monte Cassino and its branches. Cross influences between the two can be detected not only in art and architecture, but also in the liturgy, even though the Greek followed the orthodox rite.

The abbey of Monte Cassino in Lazio, founded by St Benedict, played a crucial role for the development of art in southern Italy, particularly under Abbot Desiderius, the future Pope Victor III, who entirely rebuilt it from 1066 to 1071. With the intention of reviving the arts of Antiquity, Desiderius designed the abbey to imitate the early Christian basilicas of Rome, but invited the best mosaicists, sculptors, enamel and glass workers, as well as bronze- and silversmiths, from Constantinople. Unfortunately, next to nothing is left of the past glory of the abbey, which suffered an earthquake, was rebuilt in the 16th–18th centuries, and was eventually bombed in 1944.

However, Abbot Desiderius also founded the basilica of Sant'Angelo in Formis. It is entirely covered in frescoes which testify to the outstanding quality of craftsmanship reached by the artists in his milieu. Along the nave walls are scenes from the Old and New Testaments; on the west wall is the *Last Judgement* and in the apse is a giant figure of Christ, flanked by the symbols of the Evangelists, and sitting above Desiderius (holding a model of the church), St Benedict and three Archangels. The style and iconography of the paintings are Byzantine, as exemplified by the standard formula of Christ enthroned, with the Greek gesture of benediction (*Christ Pantocrator*).

Derivations from the style introduced at Monte Cassino and continued at Sant'Angelo in Formis can be found in the surrounding areas of Benedictine influence. The architecture of Salerno cathedral, built by the Norman Robert Guiscard and Archbishop Alfanus in 1080, closely followed the model of the abbey, while the 12th-century frescoes at Ventaroli, including a *Madonna Enthroned* dressed like a Byzantine empress, are reminiscent of Sant'Angelo in Formis. A.M.

SANTA MARIA CAPUA VETERE

Santa Maria Capua Vetere occupies the site of the ancient Capua.

HISTORY OF SANTA MARIA CAPUA VETERE

An Oscan settlement here was transformed by the Etruscans into a city called Capua. It soon became the most important place in Campania and the richest city in southern Italy. Constantly assailed and sometimes defeated by the war-like Samnites, it placed itself under the protection of Rome in 343 BC.

It was always a hotbed of unrest, however, and it opened its gates to Hannibal in 216 BC; explorations in 1976 revealed a military camp of the 2nd century BC, believed to be that of the Carthaginian forces, in the vicinity of the amphitheatre. According to the legend, the Carthaginians were so softened by the *luxuria* they learned from the Capuans that they never achieved another success. (Or, as Fynes Moryson wrote in 1617, 'the delicacies of Capua were such that the Army of Hannibal grew effeminate thereby'). The city was retaken by the Romans in 211 and severely punished.

In 73 BC the revolt of the gladiators headed by Spartacus (*see box opposite*) broke out here in the amphitheatre. Under the empire Capua was one of the wealthiest towns in southern Italy, but it was razed by the Saracens, and its inhabitants fled in 856 to found the modern Capua. The present town on this site grew from a small settlement that clustered round the church of Santa Maria, which survived the Saracen raid.

The Roman amphitheatre

Just outside the town, as you arrive from Capua, are two interesting and well pre-served Roman tombs, the second of which is the largest in Campania. The imposing **amphitheatre** (*open daily 9–dusk*) was built in the 1st century AD under Augustus, and restored by Hadrian and Antoninus Pius. Although it has been exploited for building stone over the centuries, it escaped damage in the Second World War. It measures 170m by 140m, and is second in size only to the Colosseum in Rome. It had four storeys and was surrounded by 80 arches; only two survive. Under the arena are three covered galleries, with a fourth around the circumference, and six vaulted passages lit by square apertures. Fragments of the building's sculptural decoration and other antiquities (notably a 2nd-century mosaic pavement showing Nereids and Tritons) are set in the park at the south side of the monument. Several statues (including those of Eros, Venus and Psyche) have been removed to the Museo Archeologico Nazionale in Naples, and seven of the busts of deities that adorned the keystones of the arches have been incorporated into the façade of the town hall at Capua. The **Museo dell'Antica Capua** (*Via Roberto d'Angiò 48, open as the amphitheatre*) houses an archaeological collection focusing on the history, life and artistic culture of the Etruscan, Samnite and Roman city. Highlights include bronze vases, burial treasures and polychrome architectural terracottas.

In 1923 an interesting subterranean **Mithraeum**, with well-preserved frescoes, was discovered nearby (*10mins walk; open as the amphitheatre; custodian accompanies visitors*). Further on, in Corso Umberto I, is a ruined arch erected in honour of Hadrian. The cathedral of Santa Maria contains 51 antique columns from Capuan temples.

SPARTACUS & THE THIRD SERVILE WAR

Spartacus was the leader of the slave rebellion known as the Third Servile War. His origins are uncertain; what is sure is that he was enslaved during a Roman military campaign (possibly in Thrace or Macedonia), and sent to a gladiator training school in Capua. In 73 BC he and a band of followers fled from captivity, using the crater of Vesuvius as a hideout while they gathered recruits and found weapons. The number of the rebels was swelled by other (non-gladiatorial) slaves. The resulting army, said to have been over 100,000 strong, won several victories against Roman battalions sent to crush them. They fought their way towards the Alps, and were about to cross them into safety, when for reasons unknown they turned back. The decision was to prove a fatal mistake. Spartacus reached Rhegium (Reggio Calabria), but was unable to find a ship to take him to Sicily, and was forced to turn inland again. He was defeated in Lucania (modern Basilicata). Spartacus himself died a hero's death on the field. Six thousand of his followers were crucified along the Via Appia between Capua and Rome. Their bodies were left to hang until they fell to dust.

In the environs

At **San Prisco**, 2km northeast, the church contains 5th- and 6th-century mosaics in the tomb-chapel of St Matrona, Princess of Lusitania. **Aversa**, 13km southwest, has several interesting monuments. Andrew of Hungary, Joan I's husband, was murdered in the Norman castle here in 1345 (*see p. 58*). Three years later, Charles of Durazzo, who had instigated the murder, was killed by Louis of Hungary, Andrew's brother. The cathedral preserves some original Norman work. The church of San Lorenzo has a Lombard façade and a beautiful cloister, and San Francesco houses a small collection of religious art brought here, for reasons of security, from country churches.

Aversa's white wine, called *Asprinio,* is well regarded locally. The composer Domenico Cimarosa (1749–1801) was born here. The Roman town of *Atella,* which stood nearby, was the home of the *Fabulae Atellanae,* satirical farce in the Oscan language that became a tradition in the Roman theatre. A collection of antiquities from Atella may be seen at the lovely **Museo Archeologico dell'Agro Atellano** at Succivo (*Via Roma 7; open Tues–Sun 9–7; T: 081 501 2701*).

THE ROYAL PALACE AT CASERTA

THE REGGIA OF CASERTA

Though some 69,000 people live in Caserta, the only building anyone ever visits is uninhabited. This is the famous Reggia, the most sumptuous royal palace in Italy and one of the most impressive buildings in Europe. The vast palace, originally a summer home, was begun by King Charles III of Bourbon in 1752 and completed by Ferdinand IV in 1774 from the plans of Luigi Vanvitelli. The first stone was laid by the king on his 36th birthday, 20th January 1752. For the occasion, the perimeter of the future palace was marked by regiments of infantry and squadrons of cavalry, and two cannons with artillerymen were placed at each corner. The army of workmen engaged on the building was swelled by convicts and galley-slaves.

Construction proceeded briskly until 1759, the year in which Charles left Naples to take the throne of Spain. Work then slowed, coming to a complete halt in 1764 when, in the midst of a severe plague and famine, the half-finished building was occupied by the poor and homeless. After the death of Vanvitelli in 1773, his son Carlo continued the construction, but he ran into difficulties of various kinds and was unable to complete the building according to his father's plan. Eliminated from the design were four corner towers and a central dome—which undoubtedly would have relieved the gravity of the building's present configuration—and the guards' quarters, which were to enclose the vast forecourt on all sides.

During the long reign of Ferdinand IV (Ferdinand I after the Napoleonic interlude) the palace was enlivened by balls, receptions, hunting parties and theatrical performances. It was the favourite residence of Ferdinand II and, after the Unification of Italy, it was visited by the Savoy kings. It was presented by Vittorio Emanuele III to the state in 1921. On 29th April 1945, it was the scene of the unconditional surrender of the German forces in Italy.

The two principal façades, 247m long and 36m high, are pierced by 243 windows and several monumental entrances. The palace consists of five storeys—a ground floor, mezzanine, first floor, second floor, and attic—containing 1,200 rooms served by 43 staircases, all arranged around four monumental courtyards, whose decoration was never finished. The design of the building was controversial even in its own day. Although many contemporaries regarded it as one of the noblest edifices of its kind in Europe, some considered it a megalomaniac excrescence.

The interior

Open daily 8.30–6.45; T: 0823 277 4111.

From the main portico, divided into three vestibules by 64 columns, the state stair-case ascends to the first-floor vestibule, an octagon surrounded by 24 pillars of yel-low marble. Opposite the head of the stairs is the Palatine Chapel, usually closed. Modelled on the chapel of the Palace of Versailles, it contains the finest marble orna-ments and several noteworthy paintings, including an *Immaculate Conception* by Giuseppe Bonito, a *Presentation in the Temple* by Anton Raphael Mengs and five works by Sebastiano Conca.

The royal apartments

A door on the left leads to the royal apartments, beautifully decorated with tapestries, paintings, frescoes, and period furniture. The **Room of the Halbardiers**, the first to be entered, has a Bourbon coat of arms, borne by *Virtues*, in the ceiling. The **Guard Room**, following, is decorated with the *Apotheosis of the Farnese Family* (of which King Charles's mother was an eminent member) and the *Twelve Provinces of the Kingdom*, in the ceiling. Scenes from ancient history are depicted in the bas-reliefs around the walls. On the right is a marble statuary group of *Alexander Farnese Crowned by Victory*, carved, according to tradition, out of a column from the Temple of Peace in Rome.

The adjacent **Room of Alexander**, which corresponds to the centre of the main façade, enjoys a good view of what was once the tree-lined high road to Naples. The ceil-ing fresco and the stucco reliefs show scenes from the life of Alexander Farnese; the other paintings celebrate deeds of Charles of Bourbon. The porphyry portrait medallion over the fireplace is of Alexander the Great. The room is furnished in the Empire style; particularly noteworthy is the large clock on the right wall, made in Naples in 1828.

The **New Apartment**, so called because it was the last to be completed (1845), is reached by a door on the right. It consists of three rooms, also furnished in the Empire style and decorated with paintings and reliefs of mythological subjects. Notice, in the centre of the first room, an Oriental alabaster cup presented by Pope Pius IX to Ferdinand II.

The **Throne Room**, the largest room of the palace, is adorned with a frieze con-taining medallions of the kings of Naples from Roger de Hauteville (1095–1154) to Ferdinand II (1830–59). Joseph Bonaparte and Joachim Murat have been tactfully omitted. The ceiling painting shows Charles III laying the first stone of the palace. The living quarters of the king are beyond the throne room. The **Council Room** contains a fine table given by the city of Naples to Francis I as a wedding present. An antechamber, where majolicas are displayed, gives access to **Francis II's Bedroom**, containing a magnificent mahogany bed and the first known example of a roll-top desk. The ceiling painting of *Theseus Killing the Minotaur* is by Giuseppe Cammarano. Adjoining the bedroom are the king's bathroom and study. Beyond two handsome drawing rooms decorated with mythological subjects lies the **Bedroom of Joachim Murat**, containing perhaps the finest Empire-style furniture in the palace; on the far side of the room are an antechamber and a small chapel.

Apartments of Ferdinand I

The east wing of the palace was inhabited by Ferdinand IV from 1780 until his expulsion in 1806, and again, as Ferdinand I of the Two Sicilies, from 1815 until his death in 1825. The Reception Room, Drawing Room, Dining Room, and Fumoir are decorated with *Allegories of the Four Seasons*, by Antonio de Dominici and Fedele Fischetti. Here Maria Carolina held her famous receptions, one of which is recorded by an English guest, Lady Anne Miller:

After mounting a staircase, you enter several large rooms, hung and adorned in the Italian taste with crimson damask, velvet, etc, and amply illuminated. The chairs are placed all round against the walls, and each sits down where they choose. These rooms were so full, that there was a double row of chairs placed back to back down the middle. Accident placed me exactly opposite the Queen, who took the first chair she found empty. There are no tables in any of the rooms; but every person being seated, the supper is served thus: The best looking soldiers, chosen from the King's guards, carry about the supper with as much order, regularity, and gravity as if they were performing a military manoeuvre. First appears a soldier bearing a large basket with napkins, followed by a page, who unfolds and spreads them on the lap of each of the company as they happen to sit; but when it comes to the Queen's turn to be served, a lord of the Court presents her majesty's napkin. The first soldier is immediately followed by a second, bearing a basket of silver plates; another carries knives and forkes; then follows a fourth, with a great pâté, composed of macaroni, cheese, and butter; he is accompanied by an ecuyer tranchant, or carver, armed with a knife a foot long, who cuts the pie, and lays a large slice on the plate (which has been placed on the lap of each of the company); then a fifth soldier, with an empty basket, to take away the dirty plates; others succeed in the same order, carrying wine, iced water, etc; the drinkables are served between the arrival of each eatable: the rest of the supper consisted of various dishes of fish, ragouts, game, fried and baked meats, perigord-pies, boar's-heads, etc. The dessert was formed into pyramids, and carried round in the same manner; it consisted of sweetmeats, biscuits, iced chocolate, and a great variety of iced fruits, creams, etc. The Queen ate of two things only, which were prepared particularly for her by her German cooks; she did me the singular honour to send me some of each dish.

Beyond the public rooms is the **Study**, with lacquered furniture from Frankfurt am Main, and a small drawing room. The **Bedroom of Ferdinand II** follows. From here you enter the queen's apartments: first her sewing room, with a small bathroom adjacent; then a tiny dressing room, beyond which lie the drawing room and a room for the queen's ladies-in-waiting. From the latter several richly-decorated rooms lead to the **Library**, containing some 10,000 volumes and a huge Nativity scene (*presepio*), with over 1,200 pieces made by Giuseppe Sammartino and other eminent sculptors.

The next ten rooms comprise the **Gallery**, where an extensive (but dull) collection of still-lifes, historical scenes and family portraits is displayed. The small **Museo Vanvitelliano** contains the architect's original drawings and models for the palace.

The palace is the temporary home of the Terraemotus Collection of international contemporary art (*shown hourly, 9–6*), assembled by the Neapolitan dealer/collector Lucio Amelio following the 1980 earthquake.

Return to the ground floor and cross the second courtyard to the **Palatine Theatre**. This charming 18th-century period piece hosted concerts, plays and balls. Lady Anne Miller describes the original appearance of the theatre and the use that was made of it during a ball she attended in 1771:

> *There is no precedence observed at these balls, the King and Queen go in and out promiscuously, which is the reason why the company is not so numerous as one might expect to find it. None but such as the Queen esteems proper to receive and converse with sans cérémonie are ever admitted; and there are many of the Neapolitan nobility, even to the rank of dukes, who are allowed only to see the ball from the upper boxes … The theatre is in the palace; it is approached through spacious courts, and then through large passages lined with a double row of guards under arms. The plan is circular, the proscenium appeared to me to cut off about a third from the circle; the boxes are larger than those in any other I have yet seen, they are lined, gilt, and decorated with a profusion of ornaments … The stage was covered with the musicians upon benches, rising pyramidically one above the other, the top of the pyramid is crowned by the kettle-drums. The musicians are all in a livery, their coats blue, richly laced, their waistcoats red, and almost covered with silver, small black hats, with long scarlet feathers stuck upright in them: large wax candles are placed between, so that they form a striking coup d'oeil upon our entering the theatre; the whole is so artfully illuminated that the effect is equal, and seems as if the light proceeded from a brilliant sun at the top … The pit (which is more like an antique arena) is floored with a composition coloured red, very hard, and rather slippery; here it is they dance. The boxes are appropriated to the foreign ministers and great officers belonging to the Court.*

Inaugurated by Ferdinand IV (as he then was) in 1769, the theatre has been recently restored to its original form, with a horseshoe-shaped auditorium and five tiers of boxes. The ceiling painting, by Crescenzo della Gamba, shows Apollo killing the serpents.

The gardens

From the main portico you enter the gardens (*open 8.30–dusk*), which extend to the north, east and west sides of the palace. Among the most enchanting achievements of Italian landscape architecture, they were laid out by Martin Biancour under the supervision of Luigi Vanvitelli. They are famous for their fountains and ornamental waterworks adorned with statuary groups. The crowning glory of the gardens is the great cascade, a waterfall some 75m high that can be seen clearly from the palace 3km away (shuttle bus). The central promenade leads across a broad lower garden bordered by holm oaks and camphor trees (paths diverge into the woods on the left and right) to the circular Fontana Margherita, which is linked by a bridge over a sunken road to the impressive *pescheria superiore*. Beyond, a long, narrow lawn ends at the semicircular Fontana di Aeolo, inhabited by statues of 29 zephyrs and wind-gods (54 were originally planned). This is followed by the Fontana di Cerere, containing seven stepped cascades and statues of Ceres, nymphs, tritons, and river-gods; then more lawn and the Fontana di Venere, with its group of Venus and Adonis.

From here a scenographic staircase flanked by men and women in hunting garb leads up to a basin with groups of Diana surrounded by nymphs and Actaeon being turned into a stag, into which the Great Cascade plunges. The water is brought from Monte Taburno by a lofty aqueduct. The view from the top of the wooded hill is especially fine.

To the east of the cascade is another, later garden laid out in the so-called English style; visitors are accompanied by a custodian. Here are more modest fountains and romantic groves of holm oaks, artificial ruins adorned with statues from Pompeii and Herculaneum, a large fish-pond, a miniature fort for Prince Ferdinand's mock battles, a swan lake, an apple orchard, a Classical temple, a bath of Venus, covered walks and greenhouses.

Some country excursions

San Leucio, 3km northwest of Caserta, was built as a model town and social experiment in 1789 by Ferdinand IV. He built the Casino Reale di Belvedere (also called the Casino di San Leucio) here and introduced the culture of silkworms and silk manufacture. On the outskirts northeast of Caserta lies Caserta British Military Cemetery, with 769 graves. It is immediately east of the civil cemetery.

Caserta Vecchia, 10km northeast (bus) by the road passing the cemetery, was founded in the 8th century and preserves the aspect of a medieval town. The cathedral, a fine example of southern Norman architecture, dates from 1123–53; the central cupola and campanile (the latter with a roadway through it) were added around a hundred years later. The exterior is adorned with sculptures; inside are 18 antique columns, a paschal candlestick and (in the transepts) the tombs of Count Francis II (d. 1359) and Bishop Giacomo (d. 1460), as well as many mosaic details. The ruins of the 13th-century castle lie to the east.

PRACTICAL INFORMATION

GETTING AROUND

• **By road:** The main cities in this area can be reached by car via Autostrada A1/E45 (from Rome) and A2/E45 (from Naples). Heavy traffic makes travel to and from the area on the smaller roads problematic. Country buses are slower and less frequent than trains.

• **By rail:** A choice of two routes (either the old main line to Rome via Cassino, or the line to Benevento and Foggia) provides frequent trains from Naples (Centrale) to Caserta in

30–45mins. To reach Santa Maria Capua Vetere and Capua, on the Naples–Rome line, takes an extra 10–15mins. Intercity trains from Rome stop at Caserta only (2hrs 10mins).

INFORMATION OFFICES

Caserta Palazzo Reale, T: 0823 322233.
Naples Via Santa Lucia 81, T: 081 796 1111, www.turismoregionecampania.it

HOTELS

There is a conspicuous lack of comfortable accommodation in this area of Campania, which is off the beaten tourist path. Naples hotel listings, p. 129

RESTAURANTS

The best restaurants in this thriving agricultural district are in the countryside.

Capua
€€ **Osteria a San Giovanni dei Nobiluomini**. ■ Creative cuisine and good wines, in the historic city centre. Closed Mon and two weeks in Aug. Piazza de Renzis 6, T: 0823 620062.
Casagiove (3km north of Caserta at Caserta Nord interchange)
€ **Le Quattro Fontane**. Traditional trattoria; closed Sun, in Aug and late Dec. Via Quartiere Vecchio 60, T: 0823 468970.
Caserta
€€ **Le Colonne**. Quiet, comfortable restaurant, dinner by reservation only;

closed Tues and two weeks in Aug. Via Nazionale Appia 7–13, T: 0823 467494.
€€ **Massa**. In a historic palace with garden seating in fair weather. Closed Mon and two weeks in Aug. Via Mazzini 55, T: 0823 456527.
Castel Morrone (10km north of Caserta)
€ **Il Frantoio Ducale**. The best of country cuisine in the old olive press in the ducal palace. Closed Tues and two weeks in Aug. Via Altieri 50, T: 0823 399167.
Piana di Monte Verna (15km north of Caserta)
€€ **Carpe Diem**. Traditional food and wines. Closed Sun evening, Mon and two weeks in Aug. Masserie Corte 101, T: 0823 861371.
Santa Maria Capua Vetere
€ **Ninfeo**. Simple restaurant with a strong local following. Closed Mon, two weeks in Aug and one week in Dec. Via Cappabianca, T: 0823 846700.

FESTIVALS & EVENTS

Capua
Carnevale Capuana Mardi Gras weekend. The Carnival King opens festivities on Thurs by symbolically appropriating the key to the city; masks and parades ensue, ending on the following Tues with a great public ball in Piazza del Giudici, Feb.
Caserta
Festival Settembre al Borgo di Caserta Vecchia Classical music festival in Caserta Vecchia, Sept. settembreborgo@lycos.it.

MOUNT VESUVIUS & ITS CITIES

I stood within the city disinterred
And heard the autumnal leaves like light footfalls
Of spirits passing through the streets; and heard
The mountain's slumberous voice at intervals
Thrill through those roofless halls ...
Around me gleamed many a bright sepulchre
Of whose pure beauty, Time, as if his pleasure
Were to spare Death, had never made erasure.

Percy Bysshe Shelley, Ode to Naples, 1820

Mount Vesuvius (Monte Vesuvio), the most familiar feature in the Neapolitan land-scape, is one of the smallest active volcanoes in the world (1277m; 1202m before 1944), but certainly the most famous, its development having been studied since Roman times. It is the only active volcano on the continent of Europe. In fact the name Vesuvius, or *Vesbius,* means 'the unextinguished'. It consists of a truncated cone, Monte Somma, which rises to 1152m—known as Punta del Nasone—on the north side. Within is an enormous crater, broken on the west side, called the Atrio del Cavallo and Valle dell'Inferno. From the centre of this crater rises a smaller cone, vari-able in size and shape, which is Vesuvius proper.

The volcanic activity started about 10,000 years ago. Ever since, periods of frequent eruption have alternated with periods of absolute tranquillity, sometimes lasting more than 2,000 years. Before the disastrous eruption of AD 79, the volcano had been quiet for more than 1,200 years.

Vesuvius through the ages

In ancient times the lower slopes of Vesuvius were planted with vineyards, above which was a thick belt of woods noted for their wild boar. Pliny the Elder wrote that no region on earth was more joyously touched by nature. Its volcanic nature was unsuspected except by men of science such as Diodorus Siculus, Vitruvius and, espe-cially, Strabo, who inferred its igneous nature from its conical shape and the ashy nature of its barren summit.

'In early times', he wrote, 'this district was on fire and had craters of fire, and then because the fuel gave out, was quenched' (*Geography V, 4*). To this he attributed the fertility of the lands around the mountain, saying that it had already been shown at Mount Etna that volcanic ash was particularly suited for growing vines. Today the Vesuvian soil produces grapes for the excellent wine called *Lacryma Christi.*

The peak observed by Strabo was much higher than the present summit, the now broken cone of Monte Somma. Within its seemingly dead crater, Spartacus and the rebel slaves took refuge in 73 BC (*see p. 153*), escaping via an unguarded rift from the besieging force of praetor P. Clodius Pulcher.

In AD 63 a violent earthquake, mentioned by Seneca, caused serious damage in Pompeii, Herculaneum, Naples and Pozzuoli.

THE ERUPTIONS OF VESUVIUS

Why are there active volcanoes in Italy? The theory of plate tectonics provides a convincing answer. First the collision between the African and European plates caused the Italian boot to kick back towards the Balkan peninsula, pulling the floor of the Tyrrhenian Sea along with it. As the sea floor stretched it became thinner, like pizza dough in the hands of a skilful *pizzaiolo*. This in turn created alterations both in the earth's crust, where fissures appeared, and in the mantle, which partially melted, due to the diminished pressure of the layers above. Through the cracks in the lithosphere the magma from below rose to the surface, spewing forth in the volcanic areas of Lazio, Campania and Sicily.

The activity of Vesuvius is characterised by what geologists call 'effusive' eruptions (marked by the emission of basaltic lava), and by more powerful 'explosive' eruptions. Over the past 25,000 years there have been seven eruptions like the one of AD 79. The last eruption of the explosive or 'Plinian' variety took place in 1631; the last effusive eruption in 1944. Since then Vesuvius has been 'asleep', but it is expected to reawaken any day now, with a new Plinian-type eruption that will be the more violent the longer one has to wait for it. It is important to remember, in this connection, that it was not the rain of ash or the flow of mud that killed most inhabitants of Pompeii and Herculaneum (although these caused extensive physical damage and took their toll among the early survivors). The culprit was the ring of toxic gases and incandescent dust, the 'base surge', which raced away from the crater at lightning speed, reaching the ancient cities and reaping its bitter harvest in a mere moment.

The eruption in AD 79

The earthquake of AD 63 was followed by other shocks, and in AD 79 Vesuvius's central cone blew out. Pompeii, Herculaneum, and Stabiae were destroyed, the first and last buried in cinders and *lapilli*, or small stones, whereas Herculaneum was drowned in a torrent of mud; the flow of lava does not seem to have extended very far. Catastrophe struck on the morning of 24th August, ironically only a day after the annual celebration of the *Volcanalia*, the festival of Vulcan, the god of fire and forge. History owes an inestimable debt to Pliny the Younger, who witnessed the event and left a description of his observations in two letters addressed to the historian Tacitus. This is altogether the oldest realistic description, in Western literature, of a major natural disaster. It has been reprinted here in full.

To Tacitus:

Your request that I would send you an account of my uncle's end, so that you may transmit a more exact relation of it to posterity, deserves my acknowledgments; for if his death shall be celebrated by your pen, the glory of it, I am aware, will be rendered for ever deathless ...

He was at that time with the fleet under his command at Misenum. On the 24th of August, about one in the afternoon, my mother desired him to observe a cloud of very unusual size and appearance. He had sunned himself, then taken a cold bath, and after a leisurely luncheon was engaged in the study. He immediately called for his shoes and went up an eminence from whence he might best view this very uncommon appearance. It was not at that distance discernible from what mountain this cloud issued, but it was found afterwards to be Vesuvius. I cannot give you a more exact description of its figure, than by resembling it to that of a pine tree, for it shot up a great height in the form of a trunk, which extended itself at the top into several branches; because I imagine, a momentary gust of air blew it aloft, and then falling, forsook it; thus causing the cloud to expand laterally as it dissolved, or possibly the downward pressure of its own weight produced this effect. It was at one moment white, at another dark and spotted, as if it had carried up earth or cinders.

My uncle, true savant that he was, deemed the phenomenon important and worth a nearer view. He ordered a light vessel to be got ready, and gave me the liberty, if I thought proper, to attend him. I replied I would rather study, and, as it happened, he had himself given me a theme for composition. As he was coming out of the house he received a note from Rectina, the wife of Basus, who was in the utmost alarm at the imminent danger (his villa stood just below us, and there was no way to escape but by sea); she earnestly entreated him to save her from such deadly peril. He changed his first design and what he began with a philosophical, he pursued with an heroical turn of mind. He ordered large galleys to be launched, and went himself on board one, with the intention of assisting not only Rectina, but many others; for the villas stand extremely thick upon that beautiful coast. Hastening to the place from whence others were flying, he steered his direct course to the point of danger, and with such freedom from fear, as to be able to make and dictate his observations upon the successive motions and figures of that terrific object.

And now cinders, which grew thicker and hotter the nearer he approached, fell into the ships, then pumice-stones too, with stones blackened, scorched, and cracked by fire, then the sea ebbed suddenly from under them, while the shore was blocked up by landslips from the mountains. After considering a moment whether he should retreat, he said to the captain who was urging that course, 'Fortune befriends the brave; carry me to Pomponianus.' Pomponianus was then at Stabiae, distant by half the width of the bay (for, as you know, the shore, insensibly curving in its sweep, forms here a receptacle for the sea). He had already embarked his baggage; for though at Stabiae the danger was not yet near, it was full in view, and certain to be extremely near, as soon as it spread; and he resolved to fly as soon as the contrary wind should cease. It was full favourable, how-ever, for carrying my uncle to Pomponianus. He embraces, comforts, and encourages his alarmed friend, and in order to soothe the other's fears by his own unconcern, desires to be conducted to a bathroom, and after having bathed, he sat down to supper with great cheerfulness, or at least (what is equally heroic) with all the appearance of it.

In the meanwhile Mount Vesuvius was blazing in several places with spreading and towering flames, whose refulgent brightness the darkness of the night set in high relief. But my uncle, in order to soothe apprehensions, kept saying that some fires had been left alight by the terrified country people, and what they saw were only deserted villas on fire in the abandoned district. After this he retired to rest, and it is most certain that his rest was a most genuine slumber; for his breathing, which, as he was pretty fat, was somewhat heavy and sonorous, was heard by those who attended at his chamber-door. But the court which led to his apartment now lay so deep under a mixture of pumice-stones and ashes, that if he had continued longer in his bedroom, egress would have been impossible. On being aroused, he came out, and returned to Pomponianus and the others, who had sat up all night. They consulted together as to whether they should hold out in the house, or wander about in the open. For the house now tottered under repeated and violent concussions, and seemed to rock to and fro as if torn from its foundations. In the open air, on the other hand, they dreaded the falling pumice-stones, light and porous though they were; yet this, by comparison, seemed the lesser danger of the two; a conclusion which my uncle arrived at by balancing reasons, and the others by balancing fears. They tied pillows upon their heads with napkins, and this was their whole defence against the showers that fell round them.

It was now day everywhere else, but there a deeper darkness prevailed than in the most obscure night; relieved, however, by many torches and diverse illuminations. They thought it proper to go down upon the shore to observe from close at hand if they could possibly put out to sea, but they found the waves still ran extremely high and contrary. There my uncle having thrown himself down upon a disused sail, repeatedly called for, and drank, a draught of cold water; soon after, flames, and a strong smell of sulphur, which was the forerunner of them, dispersed the rest of the company in flight; him they only aroused. He raised himself up with the assistance of two of his slaves, but instantly fell; some unusually gross vapour, as I conjecture, having obstructed his breathing and blocked his windpipe, which was not only naturally weak and constricted, but chronically inflamed. When day dawned again (the third from that he last beheld) his body was found entire and uninjured, and still fully clothed as in life; its posture was that of a sleeping, rather than a dead man.

Meanwhile my mother and I were at Misenum. But this has no connection with history, and your inquiry went no further than concerning my uncle's death. I will therefore put an end to my letter. Suffer me only to add, that I have faithfully related to you what I was either an eye-witness of myself, or heard at the time, when report speaks most truly. You will select what is most suitable to your purpose; for there is a great difference between a letter and an history; between writing to a friend, and writing for the public. Farewell.

To Tacitus:

The letter which, in compliance with your request, I wrote to you concerning the death of my uncle, has raised, you say, your curiosity to know not only what terrors, but what calamities I endured when left behind at Misenum (for there I broke off my narrative). Though my shock'd soul recoils, my tongue shall tell.

My uncle having set out, I gave the rest of the day to study—the object which had kept me at home. After which I bathed, dined, and retired to short and broken slumbers. There had been for several days before some shocks of earthquake, which the less alarmed us as they are frequent in Campania; but that night they became so violent that one might think that the world was not merely shaken, but turned topsy-turvy. My mother flew to my chamber; I was just rising; meaning on my part to awaken her, if she was asleep. We sat down in the forecourt of the house, which separated it by a short space from the sea. I know not whether I should call it courage or inexperience—I was not quite eighteen—but I called for a volume of Livy, and began to read, and even went on with the extracts I was making from it, as if nothing were the matter. Lo and behold, a friend of my uncle's, who was just come to him from Spain, appears on the scene; observing my mother and me seated, and that I have actually a book in my hand, he sharply censures her patience and my indifference; nevertheless I still went on intently with my author.

It was now six o'clock in the morning, the light still ambiguous and faint. The buildings around us already tottered, and though we stood upon open ground, yet as the place was narrow and confined, there was certain and formidable danger from their collapsing. It was not till then we resolved to quit the town. The common people follow us in the utmost consternation, preferring the judgement of others to their own (wherein the extreme of fear resembles prudence), and impel us onwards by pressing in a crowd upon our rear. Being got outside the houses, we halt in the midst of a most strange and dreadful scene. The coaches which we had ordered out, though upon the most level ground, were sliding to and fro, and could not be kept steady even when stones were put against the wheels. Then we beheld the sea sucked back, and as it were repulsed by the convulsive motion of the earth; it is certain at least the shore was considerably enlarged, and now held many sea animals captive on the dry sand. On the other side, a black and dreadful cloud bursting out in gusts of igneous serpentine vapour now and again yawned open to reveal long fantastic flames, resembling flashes of lightning but much larger.

Our Spanish friend already mentioned now spoke with more warmth and insistancy: 'If your brother—if your uncle,' said he, 'is yet alive, he wishes you both may be saved; if he has perished, it was his desire that you might survive him. Why therefore do you delay your escape?' We could never think of our own safety, we said, while we were uncertain of his. Without more ado our friend hurried off, and took himself out of danger at the top of his speed.

Soon afterwards, the cloud I have described began to descend upon the earth, and cover the sea. It had already begirt the hidden Capreae [Capri], and blotted from sight the promontory of Misenum. My mother now began to beseech, exhort, and command

me to escape as best I might; a young man could do it; she, burdened with age and cor-
pulency, would die easy if only she had not caused my death. I replied, I would not be
saved without her, and taking her by the hand, I hurried her on. She complies reluctantly
and not without reproaching herself for retarding me. Ashes now fall upon us, though as
yet in no greater quantity. I looked behind me; gross darkness pressed upon our rear, and
came rolling over the land after us like a torrent. I proposed while we yet could see, to
turn aside, lest we should be knocked down in the road by the crowd that followed us
and trampled to death in the dark. We had scarce sat down, when darkness overspread
us, not like that of a moonless or cloudy night, but of a room when it is shut up, and the
lamp put out. You could hear the shrieks of women, the crying of children, and the shouts
of men; some were seeking their children, others their parents, others their wives or husbands, and only distinguishing them by their voices; one lamenting his own fate, another that of his family; some praying to die, from the fear of dying; many lifting their
hands to the gods, but the greater part imagining that there were no gods left anywhere,
and that the last and eternal night was come upon the world.

There were even some who augmented the real perils by imaginary terrors.
Newcomers reported that such or such a building at Misenum had collapsed or taken
fire—falsely, but they were credited. By degrees it grew lighter; which we imagined to
be rather the warning of approaching fire (as in truth it was) than the return of day:
however, the fire stayed at a distance from us: then again came darkness, and a heavy
shower of ashes; we were obliged every now and then to rise and shake them off, otherwise we would have been buried and even crushed under their weight. I might have
boasted that amidst dangers so appalling, not a sigh or expression of fear escaped
from me, had not my support been founded in miserable, though strong consolation,
that all mankind were involved in the same calamity, and that I was perishing with
the world itself.

At last this dreadful darkness was attenuated by degrees to a kind of cloud or smoke,
and passed away; presently the real day returned, and even the sun appeared, though
lurid as when an eclipse is in progress. Every object that presented itself to our yet
affrighted gaze was changed, cover'd over with a drift of ashes, as with snow. We
returned to Misenum, where we refreshed ourselves as well as we could, and passed an
anxious night between hope and fear; though indeed with a much larger share of the
latter, for the earthquake still continued, and several enthusiastic people were giving a
grotesque turn to their own and their neighbours' calamities by terrible predictions.
Even then, however, my mother and I, notwithstanding the danger we had passed, and
that which still threatened us, had no thoughts of leaving the place, till we should
receive some tidings of my uncle.

And now, you will read this narrative, so far beneath the dignity of a history, without any view of transferring it to your own; and indeed you must impute it to your own
request, if it shall appear scarce worthy of a letter. Farewell.

(Melmoth–Hutchinson translation, quoted in Wolfgang Leppmann's Pompeii in
Fact and Fiction, London 1968).

Later eruptions

In the centuries that followed the eruption of AD 79 only nine comparatively unimportant eruptions are recorded, and after 1500 a period of absolute quiescence set in, during which the mountain was again cultivated up to the cone, and the crater covered with trees. On 16th December 1631, however, a violent eruption destroyed nearly all the towns at the foot of the mountain; the lava reached the sea near Portici and killed over 3,000 people.

During the next 300 years there were 23 eruptions at intervals of one to 30 years. Sir William Hamilton forecast that of 1767 and went up the mountain while it was in progress. The most serious were those of 1794, which destroyed Torre del Greco; of 1871–72, which damaged San Sebastiano and Massa di Somma; and of 1906, in which the towns of Ottaviano and San Giuseppe suffered severely. In August 1928 and in June 1929 the lava descended into the Valle dell'Inferno, menacing Terzigno. An eruption in March 1944 altered the shape of the crater; the little inner cone disappeared, and in the following month the main fissure closed.

The discovery of Pompeii and Herculaneum

With reference to the tragic end of Pompeii, Herculaneum and the other Campanian towns destroyed in AD 79, the poet Statius asked, 'Will future centuries, when new seed will have covered the waste, believe that entire cities and their inhabitants lie under their feet, and that the fields of their ancestors were drowned in a sea of flames?' As memory of the event waned and other misfortunes befell the empire, future generations did not believe because they did not know of the catastrophe. Pompeii was discovered inadvertently in 1592 and Herculaneum in 1709, but a systematic programme of excavation was not undertaken until the middle of the 19th century.

Boscoreale

Several Roman villas were unearthed between 1887 and 1907 at Boscoreale, overlooking Pompeii; they yielded a large find of silverware (now in the Louvre) and frescoes, some of which may be seen in Naples, others in the Metropolitan Museum of New York. A collection of finds from these and other sites may be seen in the Antiquarium (*Villa Regina, Via Settetermini 15, Boscoreale; open daily Apr–Oct 8.30–7.30, last entry 6; Nov–Mar 8.30–5, last entry 3.30; T: 081 536 8796, www.pompeiisites.org*), where there is a display devoted to daily life in the villas, with tools and equipment for farming and shepherding, household items, and plaster casts of animals.

THE ASCENT OF VESUVIUS

Those who wish to make the ascent of the volcano (*for a more detailed map, see p. 236*) may do so easily; the area was declared a National Park in 1991. As the expedition is most easily made by car or by public transport, via the modern town of Ercolano, it can conveniently be combined with a visit to Herculaneum.

Some historic precedents

With much difficulty I reached to the top of Mount Vesuvius, in which I saw a vast aperture full of smoak, which hindered the seeing its depth and figure. I heard within that horrid gulf certain odd sounds, which seemed to proceed from the belly of the mountain; a sort of murmuring, sighing, throbbing, churning, dashing (as it were) of waves, and between whiles, a noise, like that of thunder or cannon, which was constantly attended with a clattering, like that of tiles falling from the tops of houses on the street.

George Berkeley, British philosopher

Vesuvius is, after the glaciers, the most impressive exhibition of the energies of nature I ever saw. It has not the immeasurable greatness, the overpowering magnificence, nor, above all, the radiant beauty of the glaciers; but it has all their character of tremendous and irresistible strength. From Resina to the hermitage you wind up the mountain, and cross a vast stream of hardened lava, which is an actual image of the waves of the sea, changed into hard black stone by inchantment. The lines of the boiling flood seem to hang in the air, and it is difficult to believe that the billows which seem hurrying down upon you are not actually in motion. This plain was once a sea of liquid fire ... On the summit is a kind of irregular plain, the most horrible chaos that can be imagined; riven into ghastly chasms, and heaped up with tumuli of great stones and cinders, and enormous rocks blackened and calcined, which had been thrown from the volcano upon one another in terrible confusion. In the midst stands the conical hill from which volumes of smoke, and the fountains of liquid fire, are rolled forth for ever. The mountain is at present in a slight state of eruption; and a thick, heavy white smoke is perpetually rolled out, interrupted by enormous columns of an impenetrable black bituminous vapour, which is hurled up, fold after fold, into the sky, with a deep hollow sound, and fiery stones are rained down from its darkness, and a black shower of ashes fell even where we sat.

Percy Bysshe Shelley, letter to Thomas Love Peacock, 1818

In the same literal way in which the snows and Alpine roses of Lauterbrunnen were visible Paradise, here, in the valley of ashes and throat of lava, were visible Hell. If thus in the natural, how else should it be in the spiritual world? ... The common English Traveller, if he can gather a black bunch of grapes with his own fingers, and have his bottle of Falernian brought to him by a girl with black eyes, asks no more of this world, or the next; and declares Naples a Paradise. But I knew from the first moment when my foot furrowed volcanic ashes, that no mountain form or colour could exist in perfection, when everything was made of scoria, and that blue sea was to be little boasted of, if it broke on black sand.

John Ruskin, Praeterita (1885–89)

The way to the top

The road to the summit of Mount Vesuvius (marked) climbs to the Eremo, site of the Observatory (597m) built in 1848 on a spur of the crater of Monte Somma and so far spared by lava flows. Luigi Palmieri, curator in 1872, remained at his post throughout the eruption of that year. The building houses a library, specimens of minerals thrown up by Vesuvius, relief plans, and seismic apparatus and meteorological instruments. The road continues to a car park (1017m), from which the summit is just 10mins away on foot. Here visitors are met by an official guide (*fee*), who conducts parties by a path to the edge of the crater. If you like, you can continue around the crater to the end of the path (45mins there and back). The landscape is unsettling, to say the least; the views, spectacular. Some 3–5km below the crater floor is the first, superficial magma chamber, which was responsible for explosive eruptions like that of AD 79. There are also two smaller magma chambers deeper down (perhaps as far as 10km below the surface), responsible for the more recent effusive eruptions.

To visit the vast, beautiful Foresta Demaniale, a protected forest of oaks and maritime pines, contact the Corpo Forestale dello Stato, Via Tescione 125, 81100 Caserta; www.corpoforestale.it.

POMPEII

Pompeii (in Italian, Pompei), one of the Roman Campanian towns buried by the Vesuvian eruption of AD 79 and painstakingly brought back to light during the last two centuries, has provided fundamental knowledge of the domestic life of the ancients. 'Nothing is wanting [here] but the inhabitants,' wrote Henry Matthews in 1820. 'Still, a morning's walk through the solemn silent streets of Pompeii, will give you a livelier idea of their modes of life, than all the books in the world.' Here you see the greater part of a Roman town as it was when disaster overtook it almost 2,000 years ago, in a setting sufficiently isolated from modern surroundings to preserve the illusion of antiquity.

Unearthing and preserving the town

Between 1594 and 1600 Domenico Fontana, the Roman architect, in constructing an aqueduct from the sources of the Sarno river to Torre Annunziata, tunnelled through the Pompeian mound and discovered some ruins and inscriptions. But it was not until 1748 that antiquarian excavations were begun. These have continued ever since, with more or less activity, revealing the largest and most important half of Pompeii. In 1860 a regular plan of excavation was organised by the Italian government; however, a chronic shortage of funds has made the task of unearthing and preserving the city a slow and arduous one. The site has now been systematically photographed, and the first comprehensive catalogue of its artistic assets is in preparation. Despite efforts to protect and preserve the city, the greatest threat to Pompeii remains that of theft and the clandestine resale of artworks and artefacts.

HISTORY OF POMPEII

Although it is not known exactly when Pompeii was first established, an Oscan village probably existed on the site as early as the 8th century BC (the name *Pompeii* is of Oscan derivation). There is no archaeological or documentary evidence to support this date, however, and the oldest building that can be identified and reconstructed from its ruins—the Doric temple in the Triangular Forum—date from the 6th century, when Pompeii was already a flourishing commercial centre and one of the chief ports on the coast of Campania. Like the Greek coastal towns of Cumae and Neapolis, Pompeii fell under the domination of the Etruscans c. 530 BC. Certain aspects of the ruins, such as the layout of the oldest section and the design of the 6th-century city wall, as well as some family names (the Cuspii, for instance), are thought to be of Etruscan origin. The city fell to the Samnites c. 425 BC and remained under their dominion for more than two centuries. In 200 BC it became a subject ally of Rome, but with the outbreak of the Social War it joined the Italic League and was besieged in 89 BC.

After the war ended Pompeii sank back into the near-anonymity of provincial life. As a token of Romanisation it was now called *Colonia Cornelia Veneria Pompeianorum* after the clan name of its conqueror, L. Cornelius Sulla, and the Venus Pompeiana, patron deity of the city. In AD 59, after a brawl in the amphitheatre between the Pompeians and the citizens of Nuceria, the gladiatorial spectacles were suspended for ten years. It was possibly in compensation for this that, in AD 62, it was allowed to call itself *Colonia Neroniana.*

The following year Pompeii was devastated by an earthquake, an unwelcome token of the renewed activity of Mount Vesuvius. Heedless of this warning, however, the town continued to flourish, and even increased its wealth and influence. The final catastrophe took place on 24th August, AD 79. Pompeii, like Stabiae, was covered with a layer of fragments of pumice stone (*lapilli*), mostly very minute, and afterwards by a similar layer of ashes. The flow of lava stopped at the base of the mountain and did not reach the inhabited district.

All who had not left the city in the first hours died—from the base surge, the accumulation of volcanic debris, the collapse of buildings, or in many cases, the poisonous vapours. It is estimated that of an approximate population of 20,000, two thousand, who were trapped in the city or who for some reason chose to remain, perished. Pompeii was left a sea of ashes and *lapilli*, from which emerged the upper parts of the buildings that had not been totally destroyed. These later served as guide-posts to the inhabitants who returned to dig among the ruins, and, still later, to the searchers for treasure and building material.

'It was Goethe,' observes Norman Douglas in *Old Calabria* (1915), 'who, speaking of Pompeii, said that of the many catastrophes which have afflicted mankind, few have given greater pleasure to posterity.'

Visiting the ruins

Open daily April–Oct 8.30–7.30, last entry 6; Nov–March 8.30–5, last entry 3.30; T: 081 857 5347, www.pompeiisites.org. Entrance on the south side, by the Porta Marina or Porta Anfiteatro. Only large groups must reserve tickets. Individuals may book in advance by calling T: 081 857 5111 and asking for the Ufficio Prenotazione.

Conservation and restoration at Pompeii are ongoing processes, so expect many of the houses to be closed when you visit. The custodians, stationed in different quarters of the ancient town, will open some of the closed houses and give information. They are not supposed to accept gratuities or accompany visitors.

At least half a day is necessary for an adequate visit, which should at least touch upon the buildings around the Forum; one of the three complexes of baths; the two theatres; the Fullonica Stephani; the houses of Menander, of Loreius Tiburtinus, of the Faun, of the Vettii and of the Tragic Poet; the Villa of Julia Felix and the Villa of the Mysteries. To commemorate the excavations' 250th anniversary, two special itineraries have been marked out: one is an *extra moenia* walk, running around the outside of the walls from Porta Ercolano to Porta dell'Amfiteatro and taking in the newly excavated necropoleis; the other is the 'Circuito Borbonico', comprising the houses that were excavated between 1748, when digging began, and the end of the Bourbon reign.

The restaurant at the Posto di Ristoro (near the Forum) is a good place to stop for lunch. In hot weather the absence of shade is noticeable, and some sort of hat is a must. Be sure, also, to wear comfortable shoes: the paving-stones of the streets are notoriously uneven.

The ancient city

The elliptical form of Pompeii was determined by the configuration of the prehistoric lava flow on which it is built, the southern fortifications following the natural bulwark made by the limit of the flow. The town was first surrounded by an *agger* (earthwork), buttressed by wooden boards and crowned by a *vallum* (palisade). About 450 BC this earthwork was replaced by a rampart of tufa and limestone, 3220m in perimeter, elaborated by the Samnites in the 4th century BC and again in the 2nd century BC. In the late 2nd or early 1st century BC (just before the Social War) this was reinforced by towers. The entire enceinte has now been located, though the southwest wall remains to be excavated; all the eight gates are visible, the oldest being the Porta Stabiana.

The streets were paved in the Roman period with large polygonal blocks of Vesuvian lava, bordered by kerbed pavements. Stepping-stones for pedestrians are set at regular intervals in nearly all the roadways. These stones did not impede the heavy vehicles that have left deep ruts in the roadway, because the draught-animals, attached to the end of a pole, enjoyed great freedom of movement. When the Pompeian ladies or gentlemen did not wish to walk, they used litters.

The present names of the streets—Via di Mercurio, Via dell'Abbondanza, Vicolo del Gallo, and so on—have been taken from the street-corner public fountains, adorned with the heads of gods and goddesses, etc. You will notice numerous inscriptions on the outside walls of the houses and shops, generally in red lettering; these include recommendations of candidates for the post of *aedile* or *duumvir*, dates, records, poetical quotations or short poems, the outpourings of lovers, jests and ribaldry. The character of Pompeii as an important maritime town is indicated by the numerous shops (sometimes attached to large private houses), taverns (*cauponae*), public bars (*thermopolia*), inns (*hospitia*, one with an elephant on its sign) and stables (*stabula*), especially near the gates. The shops rarely have trade-signs, but frequently exhibit either a phallus (carved, painted, or in mosaic), intended to ward off the evil eye, or one or two painted serpents, regarded as the *genii loci*.

The principal public buildings, grouped round the Forum, lie not in the centre but in the most level part of the city, near the southwest corner. The houses built of large blocks of limestone, the Etruscan column, the Etruscan capitals, the Doric temple of the Triangular Forum, and the Porta Stabiana belong to the most ancient period of the town's history. The Samnite monuments include the other gates and the walls, the Temples of Jupiter and Apollo, the Basilica, the portico of the Forum, the Thermae Stabianae, the open-air theatre, the portico of the Triangular Forum, and the gladiatorial barracks and palaestra. The Thermae of the Forum, the *comitium* (polling booth, used for the election of civic magistrates), the covered theatre, the amphitheatre and the Temple of Zeus Meilichios are Augustan (63 BC–AD 14) or earlier. The other public buildings are of later date. The Doric temple alone corresponds to the Greek model; all the others reveal an Etruscan scheme.

The Pompeian house

The dwellings at Pompeii are a marvellous example of the evolution of domestic architecture from the 4th–3rd-century BC Italic model to the Imperial Roman one of the 1st century AD. The main feature of the Pompeian house was the atrium or interior courtyard, surrounded by a roofed arcade. On the side opposite the entrance was the *tablinum* or chief living room, where the family dined and received their guests. To the right and left were the *alae* (literally 'wings', rooms opening off the central hall), the *cubicula* (bedrooms) and the *cellae,* used for various purposes. In front of the tablinum stood the *cartibulum*, or table for the utensils used in serving meals. Near this was the *focus* or hearth. This early Italic plan was introduced by the Etruscans. Later on, the chambers adjoining the main façade, and sometimes also those at the sides, were converted into shops (*tabernae*) opening on the street. To the primitive house was added the Hellenic *peristylium* (peristyle, or porticoed courtyard). The tablinum ceased to be the general living room and was occupied by the family archives. Its former role was taken by the *triclinium*, one of the rooms opening off the peristyle. Some of the houses, even in the imperial epoch, maintained the simple original plan of atrium and tablinum. Even in the commercial districts of the last period, where its intimacy was encroached upon by shop and factory, the house remained a separate entity in Pompeii; nowhere does one find the blocks of flats typical of Ostia, the port of Rome.

The characteristic dwelling of the fully developed style shows the rooms grouped round two quadrilateral spaces, the atrium and the peristyle, usually with the tablinum between them. Air and light were admitted through openings in the roof.

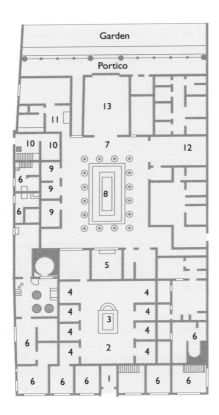

PLAN OF A
POMPEIAN HOUSE
(HOUSE OF PANSA)

1 Fauces (entranceway)
2 Atrium (entrance hall)
3 Impluvium (rainwater pool)
4 Alae (rooms leading off atrium)
5 Tablinum (living room)
6 Tabernae (street-facing shops)
7 Peristylium (colonnaded court)
8 Piscina (fish pond)
9 Cubicula (bedrooms)
10 Rooms with upper floor (for slaves or lodgers)
11 Culina (kitchen)
12 Triclinium (dining room)
13 Oecus (guest room)

The roof of the atrium sloped inwards so as to leave a quadrilateral opening in the middle (*compluvium*). Below this was the *impluvium*, a basin that received the rainwater from the gutters of the compluvium and passed it on to the *puteus* or cistern.

The commonest form of atrium, seen in the House of Lucretius Fronto, for example, is the so-called *atrium tuscanicum*. The courtyard has a roof borne by strong beams that cross from one side-wall to the other. A less common style (visible in the Houses of the Labyrinth and of the Silver Wedding) is the *atrium tetrastylum*, where the roof is sustained by four columns placed at the four corners of the impluvium. Still more rare is the Corinthian form, in which there are many columns (as seen in the Houses of Castor and Pollux and of Epidius Rufus). In some houses, as in the second atrium of the House of the Centenary, there is no opening in the roof.

Nearly every house had a second floor and some had a third; these were narrower than the first floor and were used by slaves or let out as lodgings. Few windows opening onto the street have been discovered. In some cases the floor and ceiling of the upper rooms extended to form a small pillared loggia, the so-called *cenacula*. The second floor was reached by small flights of steps, either inside or outside. A small passage adjoining and parallel to the tablinum led in to the peristyle, which was in the form of a garden (*viridarium*) surrounded by an arcade, but not always completed on all four sides.

Opening off the peristyle were smaller rooms for domestic purposes (*cubicula*, *triclinia*, *apothecae*—the latter a storeroom for food, especially wine) or for the reception of guests (*oeci*, *exedrae*). The triclinia are distinguishable by their larger size, their mosaic floors and the recesses in the lower part of their walls. The *lararium* or domestic sanctuary, in the form of an *aedicula*, or small temple, was usually found in the atrium, in an adjoining room, or in the peristyle. Sometimes it was reduced to a mere painting, even placed in the kitchen. Most houses had a second entrance (*posticum*) near the peristyle.

The shops extended along the entire front of the house and were open to the street, though they could be closed by wooden shutters or sliding doors. The counting-house or cashier's office, in front of the entrance, was often lined with marble. Many of the shops had a back room for the use of clients or a bedroom for the shopkeeper on the mezzanine floor. The number of shops lent great animation to the principal streets. Lamps hung at the doors provided lighting for the town, along with others placed on municipal altars at the street-corners.

Wall paintings

Among Pompeii's most striking attractions are the wall paintings on its interior walls. These are disposed in three horizontal bands: dado, central zone and frieze. The colours are very vivid, predominantly red and yellow. The central field is occupied by small pictures, groups of flying figures or isolated figures. August Mau, the great Pompeii expert of the late 19th century, divided the wall paintings into four categories or 'styles'. These are still used today (*defined on p. 90*). The paintings are often referred to as 'frescoes', though this is not a strictly accurate definition (*see box on p. 186 below*).

THE SITE

Pompeii is divided into an irregular chessboard of streets, the main thoroughfares being the Via Stabiana, Via di Nola and Via dell'Abbondanza. Archaeologists have devised a street plan that divides the town into nine regions (designated by Roman numerals), with varying numbers of *insulae*, or blocks (Arabic numerals). These generally consist of a group of dwellings, but may be wholly occupied by one building. The numbers given in the description below refer to the plan on pp. 176–77 below.

Via Marina

The Via Marina leads directly from the Porta Marina to the Forum. To the right you can see the remains of the **Temple of Venus Pompeiana (1)**, guardian deity of the town. This building, having been partly destroyed by the earthquake of AD 63, was in

Ox-head motif on one of the many public drinking fountains in Pompeii.

the process of restoration and enlargement when overtaken by the final catastrophe in AD 79. Further on, on the same side, is the **Basilica (2)**, the most monumental of the city's public buildings, used as a court of law. It was built in a distinctly Hellenistic style and probably dates from the 2nd century BC; the interior is divided into nave and aisles by 28 Ionic columns of brick, covered with stucco. The Corinthian pilasters in tufa, now leaning against the wall, adorned the upper storey. At the end of the hall (badly damaged by the earthquake) was the raised tribunal for the judges (*duoviri jure dicundo*).

Leave the basilica by its north door and enter the **Temple of Apollo (3)**, a Samnite structure on the site of a 6th-century *sacellum* (sacred place). The 48 columns of the portico were originally Ionic, with a Doric entablature, but after the earthquake they were converted into Corinthian columns by means of stucco, and the entablature took the form of a large zoöphorus. The stucco has now fallen off and the original design has come to light. The portico was formerly decorated with paintings of scenes from the *Iliad*. The large tripod, painted on the first pilaster of the east wing, is one of the attributes of Apollo. In the middle of the uncovered area stood a large altar of travertine. The Ionic column to the left of the steps bore a sundial, emblematic of Apollo Helios. The bases placed against the columns of the portico supported statues, now in the Museo Archeologico Nazionale in Naples. At the sides are copies of the *Apollo Sagittarius* and *Diana Sagittaria*.

The actual temple stands on a high podium, accessible by steps in front, leading to the Corinthian pronaos. This enclosed the cella, which contained the statue of Apollo and the conical *omphalos*, the symbol of the god, derived from the stone in the Temple of Apollo at Delphi, said to mark the very centre of the earth. The omphalos is still *in situ*. An Oscan inscription in the pavement of the cella records that it was laid at the instance of Oppius Campanius, the quaestor. Beside the rear door is the priest's chamber.

The Forum

The Forum, the most perfect example known of a Roman central square, is planned so that Vesuvius dominates its major axis. When the basilica was built, the opportunity was taken to furnish the square with a colonnade enclosing its two long sides and its southern extremity. Above this colonnade was a gallery, reached by small staircases (traces of which remain) designed to accommodate spectators of the fêtes and games held in the Forum before the construction of the amphitheatre. The conversion of the colonnade from tufa to travertine stone, begun in the 1st century AD, was interrupted by the earthquake. The area enclosed by the colonnade, 142m long and 38m wide, was adorned with statues of officials and other distinguished people. Twenty-two of the pedestals of these are extant, five with inscriptions. The larger base halfway down the west side is the orator's tribune. The passages leading to the central space were barred to vehicles. In a niche at no. 31 is a *tabula ponderaria* (table of weights and measures) made of travertine, showing the standard measures of capacity.

Adjacent to the Forum is the entrance to an inner court, and at no. 29 is a portico, possibly used as a vegetable market. No. 28 was a public latrine and no. 27 the municipal treasury.

At the north end of the Forum stands the **Temple of Jupiter (4)**, built in the Italic manner, with a wide cella and pronaos enclosed by Corinthian columns. Later, it became the *capitolium* of the Roman town. The pronaos is reached by a flight of 15 steps, originally flanked by equestrian statues and interrupted by a platform on which an altar stood. The cella, with its Ionic columns, had a marble pavement bordered by mosaics. Apertures in the flooring of the pronaos and cella admitted light to some lower chambers (such as the *aerarium*, or treasury), which was linked directly to the Forum. The podium against the back wall, reached by steps, is believed to have borne statues of Jupiter, Juno and Minerva. After the temple had been reduced to ruins by the earthquake, the cult of these deities was carried on at the small temple of Zeus Meilichios (*see p. 180 below*).

To the right and left of the main steps were two triumphal arches. That on the right was demolished by the ancients to open up the view of the arch behind, which had an equestrian statue of Tiberius on its top and statues of Nero and Drusus in its niches.

East of the Forum

The **Macellum (5)**, or general market, was fronted by a graceful colonnade and the shops of the *argentarii*, or money-changers. Bases for statues stand against the marble columns of the arcade and the pilasters between the shops. The interior courtyard was enclosed by another colonnade (destroyed by the earthquake). The walls were adorned with frescoes: those surviving include *Io Guarded by Argus* and *Ulysses and Penelope*. The frieze shows fish, game, amphorae of wine and the like. On the south side are shops, with an upper storey. In the open centre of the courtyard was a dome borne by 12 columns, of which only the bases remain; it probably sheltered a tank or basin for fish. A chapel at the back contained statues of the imperial family, to the right and left of this are the shops of a fishmonger and of a butcher.

The **Sacrarium of the Lares** next door **(6)** is fronted by a marble colonnade and was originally paved and lined with marble slabs. A podium in the apse bore several statues. There are niches for eight other statues around the walls, probably representing the *Lares Publici*, or tutelary deities of the town.

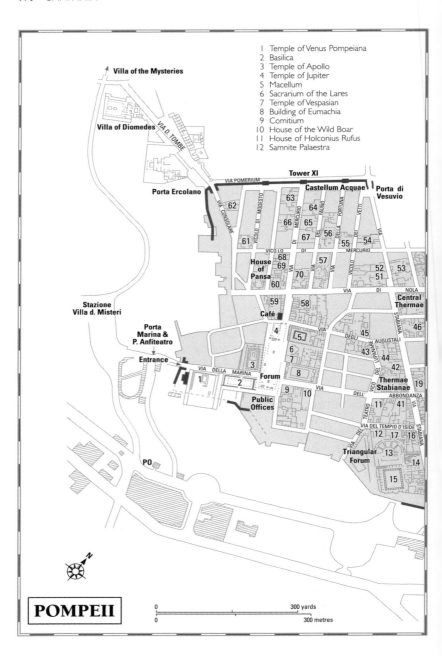

1 Temple of Venus Pompeiana
2 Basilica
3 Temple of Apollo
4 Temple of Jupiter
5 Macellum
6 Sacrarium of the Lares
7 Temple of Vespasian
8 Building of Eumachia
9 Comitium
10 House of the Wild Boar
11 House of Holconius Rufus
12 Samnite Palaestra

Villa of the Mysteries

Villa of Diomedes

Tower XI

VIA POMERIUM

Porta Ercolano

Castellum Acquae

Porta di Vesuvio

VIA CONSOLARE

62

VICOLO DI MODESTO

63

64

65

66

67

VIA DI MERCURIO

VIA DEL FAUNO

VIA DELLA FORTUNA

VIA DEI VETTI

56

55

54

VICOLO DEL MERCURIO

61

VICOLO DI

68

House of Pansa

69

57

52

53

70

VIA DELLA

51

60

59

VIA DI NOLA

Stazione
Villa d. Misteri

58

Café

Central Thermae

VIA STABIANA

46

Porta Marina &
P. Anfiteatro

Entrance

4

5

VIA DEGLI AUGUSTALI

45

43

44

VIA DEI LUPANARE

42

6

7

VIA DELLA MARINA

3

Forum

8

Thermae Stabianae

19

1

2

9

10

VIA DELL

ABBONDANZA

Public Offices

11

41

VIA STABIANA

VICO DEL TEATRO

12

17

16

VIA DEL TEMPIO D'ISIDE

PO

Triangular Forum

13

14

15

POMPEII

0   300 yards

0   300 metres

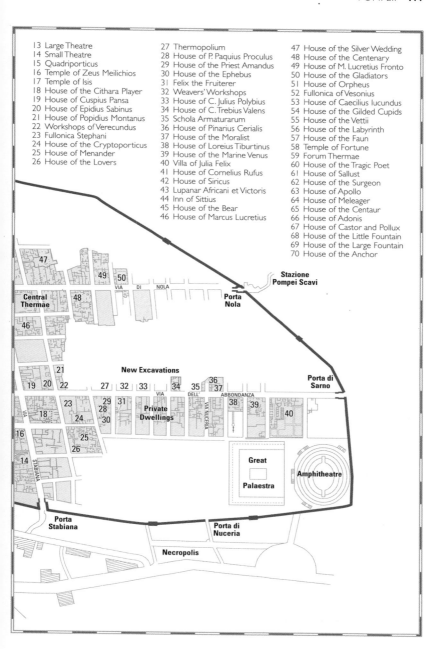

13 Large Theatre
14 Small Theatre
15 Quadriporticus
16 Temple of Zeus Meilichios
17 Temple of Isis
18 House of the Cithara Player
19 House of Cuspius Pansa
20 House of Epidius Sabinus
21 House of Popidius Montanus
22 Workshops of Verecundus
23 Fullonica Stephani
24 House of the Cryptoporticus
25 House of Menander
26 House of the Lovers

27 Thermopolium
28 House of P. Paquius Proculus
29 House of the Priest Amandus
30 House of the Ephebus
31 Felix the Fruiterer
32 Weavers' Workshops
33 House of C. Julius Polybius
34 House of C. Trebius Valens
35 Schola Armaturarum
36 House of Pinarius Cerialis
37 House of the Moralist
38 House of Loreius Tiburtinus
39 House of the Marine Venus
40 Villa of Julia Felix
41 House of Cornelius Rufus
42 House of Siricus
43 Lupanar Africani et Victoris
44 Inn of Sittius
45 House of the Bear
46 House of Marcus Lucretius

47 House of the Silver Wedding
48 House of the Centenary
49 House of M. Lucretius Fronto
50 House of the Gladiators
51 House of Orpheus
52 Fullonica of Vesonius
53 House of Caecilius Iucundus
54 House of the Gilded Cupids
55 House of the Vettii
56 House of the Labyrinth
57 House of the Faun
58 Temple of Fortune
59 Forum Thermae
60 House of the Tragic Poet
61 House of Sallust
62 House of the Surgeon
63 House of Apollo
64 House of Meleager
65 House of the Centaur
66 House of Adonis
67 House of Castor and Pollux
68 House of the Little Fountain
69 House of the Large Fountain
70 House of the Anchor

Stazione
Pompei Scavi

47

49 50
VIA DI NOLA

Central
Thermae

48

Porta
Nola

46

21

New Excavations

19 20 22

27 32 33

34 35

36
37

Porta di
Sarno

VIA DELL'   ABBONDANZA

23

29
28

31

Private
Dwellings

38

39

18

24

30

VIA NUCERIA

40

16

25

14

26

STABIANA

Great

Amphitheatre

Palaestra

Porta
Stabiana

Porta di
Nuceria

Necropolis

The **Temple of Vespasian (7)** was begun after AD 63 but never completed. It was fronted by a columned portico. An altar, with bas-reliefs depicting the sacrifice of a bull, the sacrificial utensils and a civic crown between two laurels (the symbol of the imperial house), stands in the middle of the open courtyard.

The **Building of Eumachia (8)**, an imposing structure dedicated to Concordia Augusta and Pietas, was erected by Eumachia, priestess and benefactress of the cloth-workers, acting also for her son, M. Numistrius Fronto. It was occupied by the *fullones* (fullers who shrank and thickened woollen cloth by moistening, heating and pressing). They probably used it as a saleroom. In front is a *chalcidicum* or vestibule, with a portico of two rows of columns, at the ends of which are four niches for statues of Aeneas, Romulus, Julius Caesar and Augustus. A covered corridor (*crypta*) runs round the other three sides. A marble portal with splendid acanthus leaf decoration gives access to an open courtyard (*porticus*), surrounded by a colonnade with two rows of columns on top of each other without a second storey in between. The statue of Eumachia now in the Museo Archeologico Nazionale in Naples stood at the back. At the south end of the Forum are three large halls; the central one was probably used by the *ordo decurionum* (town council), the others by the *duumviri* and *aediles*.

Via dell'Abbondanza, western section

The name Via dell'Abbondanza is due to a misinterpretation of the bust of Concordia Augusta, goddess of concord, on a fountain at the back of the Building of Eumachia. At the beginning of the street stands the **Comitium (9)**, or polling booth. Behind it a steep quarter spreads down the slope of the lava flow; this neighbourhood represents one of the last expansions of the Augustan age, when the now superfluous walls on this side were demolished to make way for terraced houses of the Herculanean type (here somewhat ruined).

The **House of the Wild Boar (10)** is named after the mosaic on the entrance floor. Further on, at the corner of Via dei Teatri, stands the **House of Holconius Rufus (11)**, home to a prominent citizen of the Augustan age, who was at once a soldier, *duumvir*, *augustalis* and patron of the city (he financed the construction of one of its theatres). He was honoured by a statue at the crossroads of Via dell'Abbondanza and Via Stabiana (now in the Museo Archeologico in Naples). The rich decoration of his elegant dwelling is unfortunately much faded.

From here, Via dei Teatri leads south to the **Triangular Forum** (Foro Triangolare). This is reached by a fine Ionic portico giving access to two gates opening onto the forum, which is surrounded by a Doric colonnade. Obliquely set within it are the ruins of a Doric temple dating from the 6th century BC, 30m in length and 20m in width. This is a heptastyle and pseudodipteral edifice, with 11 columns on each side. The remains include the elevated stylobate, a few capitals and fragments of the cella walls. Apparently dedicated to Hercules, it seems to have already been a ruin in the 2nd century BC, and was used both as a public dumping ground and a quarry of building material. Towards the end of that century, however, the area appears to have been cleared for the erection of a *sacrarium* dedicated to Athena. Near the left rear of the temple was a semicircular seat, on the back of which was a sundial. Opposite the steps leading to the pronaos is an enclosure, perhaps a heroön to Hercules. To the left are three altars and (further back) a cistern, formerly covered with a cupola raised on eight Doric columns.

Adjoining the Triangular Forum, near the corner of Via del Tempio d'Iside, lay the **Samnite Palaestra (12)**, where young men trained for the games, and where the statue of the *Doryphorus*, now in the Museo Archeologico, was found. To the south of this is a large reservoir for water used by the theatre.

Pompeii's theatres

Pompeii actually had two theatres, the larger one open-air, the smaller a roofed odeon. The **Large Theatre (13)**, which could hold 5,000 spectators, dates from the 2nd century BC. Built on the model of the Hellenic theatres and especially resembling that of Antioch, it was provided with large tanks or basins installed in the orchestra and connected to the reservoir mentioned above, making it both a theatre and a nymphaeum. The water below the stage is said to have acted as a sounding-box. The theatre was restored in the reign of Augustus.

The cavea is divided into three tiers: the topmost *summa cavea* placed above a corridor and accessible by several staircases, the *media cavea* with 15 rows of seats arranged in five wedges, all also reached from the corridor, and the *ima cavea*, accessible from the orchestra only. The ima cavea consisted of four broad, low tiers; the seats (*bisellia*) were reserved for the town councillors (*decuriones*). After the restoration of the theatre, seats for distinguished spectators were also placed in the orchestra. The stone rings at the top of the wall were for the poles supporting the *velarium*, the awning that protected the audience from the sun. The whole of the upper part overlooking the Triangular Forum is a modern reconstruction. Above the entrances to the orchestra are two small boxes (*tribunalia*), one of which was reserved for the president of the spectacle, the other (perhaps) for the priestesses. The stage (*pulpitum*), which had wooden flooring, was reached from the orchestra by flights of steps. Between the stage and the orchestra was a narrow slit for the curtain. The wall at the back of the stage (*scena*) represented the façade of a palace with three doors, the usual background of an ancient theatre.

The more recent **Small Theatre (14)**, could hold an audience of 1,000. The roof was probably pyramidal. It was constructed soon after 80 BC by the *duumviri* C. Quintius Valgus and M. Porcius, and was used as an odeon for concerts. The cavea is crossed by one *praecinctio* or corridor. The lower part consists of four wide tiers, the upper of 17 tiers, arranged in five sections. The marble pavement was presented by the *duumvir* M. Oculatius Verus.

Behind the theatre was a **Quadriporticus (15)**, a vast square piazza, surrounded by an arcade of 74 columns, that originally served as a foyer. Later, this was converted into a barracks for gladiators, with two rows of cells, the upper ones entered from a wooden gallery, part of which has been reconstructed. Here fine weapons were found (now in the Museo Archeologico Nazionale in Naples), as well as iron fetters and 63 skeletons.

The Temple of Isis and its neighbourhood

Via Stabiana leads left from the Small Theatre to the **Temple of Zeus Meilichios** (Jupiter the Placable) **(16)** on the corner of Via del Tempio d'Iside. This is the smallest temple in Pompeii. The dedication indicates a Greek cult, probably imported from Sicily. The temple had a tetrastyle vestibule. The cella had a small two-columned portico, and at the back of it were the terracotta statues of Jupiter, Juno and Minerva (now in the Museo Archeologico). A large altar stands in front of the steps.

The **Temple of Isis (17)** was almost entirely rebuilt, after the earthquake, by Numerius Popidius Celsinus. In keeping with the mysterious character of the cult of Isis (*see p. 92*), this temple is somewhat curious in form, its lateral entrance provided with a triple door. The sacred enclosure was surrounded by a colonnade, the front walk of which has a central bay formed of two pilasters with half-columns, wider than the others. Opposite was a recess, the back of which bore a painted figure of Harpocrates (now in the Museo Archeologico). In the open courtyard is a small shrine, from which steps descend to a subterranean reservoir intended for the lustral water. Small calcined bones were found on the main altar. Seven steps ascend to the pronaos, the roof of which is borne by six Corinthian columns. To the right and left of the entrance to the cells are niches for statues, and in front, to the left, is an altar. At the back, to the left, is a small staircase by which the priests entered the cella. Underneath this temple runs Domenico Fontana's aqueduct (*see p. 168 above*).

Returning to Via Stabiana, you come to the large **House of the Cithara Player (18)**, or house of Popidius Secundus Augustianus, with two atria and three peristyles. The statue of *Apollo Citharoedus*—now in the museum of Naples—was found here, hence the house's name. On reaching the intersection of the Via Stabiana with Via dell'Abbondanza (where the statue of M. Holconius Rufus stood; *see p. 178 above*), no. 20 on the right is the **House of Cuspius Pansa (19)** or of the Diadumeni and no. 22, that of **Epidius Sabinus (20)**.

The new excavations

At this point begin the new excavations (*nuovi scavi*), first undertaken in 1911. They stretch east for some 500m, to the Porta di Sarno or Urbulana, and include some of the most striking remains in the town. The original aim of these excavations was to trace the general line of the thoroughfare and to restore to their proper places the roofs, balconies, windows, stalls, doors and the like which formed the street-front. On the north side little further has been done, and though the façade is complete for much of the distance, you cannot penetrate far into any building. On the south side, however, every insula has now been excavated back to the next parallel street.

The characteristic feature of the new excavations is that the fittings and articles of domestic use, wall paintings, mosaics, statues and stucco ornamentation have all been left, as far as possible, in their original places. Fallen walls have been re-erected and rough-cast in their original colours; the painted stucco ceilings have been restored; some of the gardens have been replanted in accordance with what is known of Classical horticulture, and water plays once more in the private and public fountains.

Mural inscriptions, including unauthorised scrawls relating to the games or elections, are seen in full force. Here the ruins come nearest to capturing the atmosphere of everyday urban life in the Roman era.

The **House of Popidius Montanus (21)** was a great resort of chessplayers (*latrun-cularii*), who were responsible for the notice to the left of the portal. The door, studded with large bronze nails, was wide open at the moment of the catastrophe (plaster cast). Note also the cast of the closed door of no. 10 (left). Numbers 7–5, in front of which was a projecting penthouse, show the façade of the **Workshops of Verecundus (22)**, maker of cloth, woollen garments, and articles in felt (*coactilia*). The entrance of no. 7 is decorated by four paintings. Two of these show the patron deities of the workshops: Venus Pompeiana, in a quadriga drawn by elephants, and Mercury. The others depict the *coactiliari* or felt-makers at work (right) and the saleroom for the finished products (left). The plaster cast of the door shows the iron mechanism for fastening it.

At no. 2, also with a penthouse, and surmounted by a pillared loggia, are the **Workshops of the Dyers** (*infectores*). To the right of the threshold is one of the vats used in dyeing, projecting from a furnace bearing phallic emblems. Number 1, above which is a large balcony used as a drying-room, was also (as a notice tells us) occupied by felt-makers. The painted frieze shows busts of Apollo, Mercury, Jupiter and Diana, and the processional figure of Venus Pompeiana which was carried through the town.

The greater part of Insula 6, on the south side of the street, belonged to one owner, who lived at no. 11 and converted the neighbouring house (nos 8–9) into domestic quarters. The legs of a marble table, bearing the inscription 'P. Casca Longus', probably belonged to Casca, the conspirator who famously dealt the first blow to Julius Caesar, and may have been acquired at auction after his banishment. Number 7 is the **Fullonica Stephani (23)**. The double door was closed at the time of the eruption, but the small hatch in the right half had been left open, as is shown by the position in which its fastenings were discovered. Cloth and garments were handed in here to be washed (either in the *impluvium* or in the three tanks at the back), cleaned (in the five *saltus fullonici* adjoining the two hindmost tanks), bleached (by sulphur vapour), dried (on the wide terraces of the first floor), or pressed in the *pressorium* (by the wall to the left, on entering).

The house at no. 4 was being redecorated during the last days of Pompeii. This is suggested by the heaps of material for making stucco in the peristyle and the triclinium, the plinths still waiting for their rough-casting, the state of the rooms adjoining the entrance and the one completed frieze, in the chamber at the southeast corner of the atrium. The decorations of the cabinet (perhaps a *lararium*) to the right of the tablinum are unusually fine.

The small vaulted roof, reconstructed from hundreds of minute fragments, is adorned with scenes from the last books of the *Iliad*, executed in a band of white stucco against a blue background. At the top: Hector, driven by a Fury, resists the appeal of his parents at the Scaean Gate of Troy; Hector's combat with Achilles; Hector's corpse dragged behind the chariot-wheels of Achilles. On the sides: Priam loading his treasures on the car and setting out, under the guidance of Hermes, to offer them to

Achilles as a ransom for the body of Hector. On the south side are a large hall and cubiculum displaying the red colouring of the second style. The hall has a magnificent mosaic floor and its walls show traces of an extensive wall painting.

Number 3 on this block is the **Shop of Verus the Blacksmith**, who dealt in bronze-ware. The lamp and other objects on view here are just a few of those that were found. Among the technical instruments were the valuable fragments in bronze and iron, probably for repair, which enabled a reconstruction of the *groma*, the Roman survey-or's theodolite, to be made.

The House of Menander and its vicinity

By passing through the **House of the Cryptoporticus (24)** at no. 2 you reach the underground portico from which it takes its name, with semicircular vaulting and elaborate decoration in white stucco. Latterly, the cryptoporticus had been degraded to the status of a wine-vault (*cella vinaria*). The walls, in the second style, are divided into vertical sections by female and phallic *hermae*. The frieze showed more than 50 pictures of episodes from the Trojan War, taken not only from the *Iliad* but also from the *Aethiopis* of Arctinus and possibly other cyclic poems. Only about a score of these have been preserved, whole or mutilated. The existing chamber is just a fragment of the whole, the rest having been filled up to enlarge the garden.

Plaster casts of the impressions made by the bodies of several occupants of this house are shown in a glass case. During the eruption they took refuge under the portico but, when the rain of *lapilli* ceased, they climbed up to the garden with the aid of a ladder. The showers of ashes overwhelmed them here, and they all suffocated in one huddled group. Adjoining the east wing are some well-preserved rooms, including a striking triclinium, the vaulting of which, with fine white stucco-work, rested on painted caryatids of *rosso antico*. In the frieze are remains of paintings, in which heroic or mythical scenes alternate with banquets.

The door at the southwest corner of the cryptoporticus opens onto a little street containing the House of L. Ceius Secundus (no. 15), notable for its beautiful façade with white rustication, protected by the original overhanging roof. In the vestibule are a plaster model of the door and a ceiling, reconstructed from fragments. Beyond the tetrastyle atrium, admirably preserved and containing a plaster cast of a wooden cupboard, is a pseudoperistyle. Its walls are adorned with hunting scenes (*venationes*) and Nile landscapes with pygmies.

Across the little street is the **House of Menander (25)**, a fine dwelling belonging to a kinsman of the empress Poppaea, where silver plate—now in the Naples museum—was found in 1930. At the time of the catastrophe this house was also being redecorated. At the onset of the eruption the family, with their slaves, took refuge in the room with the strongest roof, but they were trapped by the collapse of part of the peristyle and eventually killed when the roof came down on their heads. The beautifully appointed Tuscan atrium contains a *lararium* in the form of a tiny temple. In an exedra to the left are three Trojan scenes. The peristyle has stuccoed columns, and in the centre of the mosaic floor a panel depicts a Nile scene. On the north side are two elegantly decorated *oeci*. A series of exedrae contains a rich selection of paintings, includ-ing the seated figure of the poet Menander, from which the house takes its name. The *calidarium* (warm room) of the private baths is well preserved.

Number 11 at the southwest corner of the insula is the **House of the Lovers (26)**, a charming small house with elegant decoration and a splendid inscription beneath the portico, reading *amantes ut apes vitam mellitam exigunt* ('lovers, like bees, desire a honey-sweet life').

Via dell'Abbondanza, eastern section

Return by the side lane between insulae 6 and 7 to the *compitum* (crossing) where, under a canopy, figures of the twelve *Dii Consentes* (Olympian Gods) are painted on the wall. Continue along Via dell'Abbondanza. On the north side is a **Thermopolium (27)**, or tavern, that served hot and cold drinks on the ground floor, while on the first floor the wares included the favours of such complaisant *puellae* as Asellina, Smyrna, Maria and Aegle. The objects found, including a phallic lamp, have been placed where they once might have stood. The sign, to the right of no. 4, represents large wine jars, goblets and a wine funnel.

In contrast, the opposite side of the street consists of a series of respectable middle-class houses. No. 1 is the imposing **House of P. Paquius Proculus (28)** with rich mosaics in its vestibule, atrium, tablinum, and a room adjoining the peristyle. The restoration of the first floor, behind the tablinum, is noteworthy. An exedra on the north side of the peristyle contains the skeletons of seven children caught together by the catastrophe. Beyond the modest but tasteful House of Fabius Amandio (nos 2–3) is the **House of the Priest Amandus (29)**, where the triclinium is decorated in the third style; the panels show Polyphemus with the ship of Ulysses and Galatea riding a dolphin, Perseus and Andromeda, Hercules in the garden of the Hesperides and the Fall of Icarus. The charming garden was shaded by a tree, the stump of which remains.

Entered from the side lane is the **House of the Ephebus (30)**, where the rich dec-oration added to an agglomeration of modest dwellings indicate the rise to wealth of its owner, the tradesman P. Cornelius Teges. The ephebus now in the Museo Archeologico was found here. Opposite is a dyeworks with four boilers, washing vats and pressing-tables.

On the corner of Via Abbondanza is the **Shop of Felix the Fruiterer (31)**. The sale-room, in which the fruit was exhibited on wooden shelves, is adorned with Bacchic motifs. Opposite, on the north side, are *textrinae* or **Weavers' Workshops (32)**, with a high-columned upper storey. Number 6, the Workshop of Crescens, has a painted figure of Hermes-Priapus to the right of the entrance. Continue on the north side to the next insula. The plain façade of the **House of C. Julius Polybius (33)** has carved lintels over the side doors. Adjoining the entrance of no. 5 are paintings of Aeneas, Anchises, and Ascanius (right) and of Romulus with the spoils of King Acron (left). At the corner is an *amphora urinaria* (urinal) placed there by the fullers. The contents would have been used in the cleaning and dyeing process.

On the opposite side of the street, excavations behind the frontage were resumed in 1951, revealing three interesting dwellings. The **House of the Beautiful Impluvium** (entered from no. 2) has well-preserved decoration in the atrium and tablinum. In the **House of Successus** (no. 3) the painting of the boy being chased by a duck and the statue of the boy bearing a dove probably portray a favourite child of the house. The **House of the Fruit Orchard** (no. 5) is entered through the adjacent shop, as a plaster model of the original door closes the main portal. The walls of two cubicula are finely painted in the third style, with pictures of fruit trees, including the then rare lemon. In the alley beyond is the public altar of the serpent Agathodoemon, the life-giving earth principle. Proceed past a thermopolium of the next insula, which ends with another crossroad altar, then return to the north side.

The **House of C. Trebius Valens (34)** has no shops on its front. On the façade were three announcements of forthcoming shows at the amphitheatre and numerous electoral 'posters', with the householder's recommendations of different candidates: all these were destroyed by bombs in 1943. Among the interesting features of this large house are the black-walled room at the southeast corner of the atrium; a cubiculum decorated in the second style, to the left of the atrium; the tablinum, with its fine frieze (north wall) and its reconstructed east wall; the *calidarium* behind the *praefurnium* (kitchen), to the right of the tablinum; and the reconstruction of the east door in the portico. The garden has been replanted, and the twelve jets of the fountain spout again. At the end of the garden is a summer triclinium. The skeletons of the occupants were found under the portico (reconstructed). On the same side, at no. 5 of insula 3, some carbonised fragments of mats (*tegetes*) are preserved.

The **Schola Armaturarum** at no. 6 **(35)** was probably the headquarters of a military organisation and not of the Collegium Juventutis Pompeianae, as was formerly supposed. The decorations of this building all refer to its function. On the exterior are two trophies of arms and on the door-jambs, two palm trees, the leaves of which were the reward of victory in the gymnasium. Inside are ten female *genii*, each holding a buckler (a small, circular shield) and some kind of weapon. A plaster model of one of the cupboards, which contained gymnastic apparatus and fencing gear, stands by the west wall. The modern fastening of this *armamentarium* was made from a cast of the ancient one.

Cross the narrow *cardo orientalis* or Via Nuceria, which enters the city by the Porta Nuceria. In this street to the left is the entrance (right) to the small but charming **House of Pinarius Cerialis (36)**, identified as a lapidary from 114 gems found here (some uncut). The fine decorations of a little room on the north side depict a theatrical representation of *Iphigeneia in Tauris*.

On the corner of Via Nuceria and Via dell'Abbondanza is the Tavern of Zosimus; the rest of the insula, known as the **House of the Moralist (37)**, consists of two intercommunicating houses belonging to the related families of T. Arrius Polites and M. Epidus Hymenaeus. In no. 2, two ceilings have been reconstructed: a coffered black ceiling in the triclinium, a yellow one in a cubiculum. The garden has been replanted. A wooden staircase (a reconstruction) ascends to the rooms on the upper floor, the details of which have been reproduced as far as possible. The remains of the orna-mentation have been affixed to the walls and ceilings. A small loggia, overlooking the inside garden, is almost intact. At the southeast corner is a perfectly preserved win-dow-ledge. From the foot of the staircase, pass (without re-entering the street) into no. 3, skirting a black-walled room with flying female figures (left) and a small court-yard garden (right). Below the loggia already noted, in immediate contact with the garden, is a summer triclinium in masonry, with the usual table in the middle. On the three black walls were painted, in white, three maxims for polite conduct at table. One of these was destroyed by bombs in 1943.

At the south corner of the crossroads is the **Hermes Caupona** (a tavern) with the customary downstairs bar and a first-floor balcony (reconstructed). To the left is a pri-vate cistern (*castellum aquae*), the only one yet discovered, which retains the leaden tank from which pipes conveyed the water to the neighbour-members of the *consor-tium* or user-group. On the walls of the next alley to the north are inscriptions in large white letters, 'fulminating' against committers of nuisance by invoking the thunder-bolts of Jove against offenders.

A special house

Further along Via dell'Abbondanza, on the right, between two taverns, is the **House of Loreius Tiburtinus (38)**, one of those that give us a perfect idea of patrician Pompeian life. A special charm is lent by the beautiful garden, now flourishing again after a rest of nearly 2,000 years. A wide portal, closed by a bronze door and flanked by benches, opens into the atrium where the water-jet of the impluvium plays once again. A cubiculum in the east wing contains a *Rape of Europa* and a charming medal-lion of a girl.

To the left is a room with two rows of paintings. The first, on a black ground, pres-ents a summary of the *Iliad* in a series of twelve pictures. The other shows the *Labours of Hercules*, taken from a Hercules cycle. The peristyle is bordered on the garden side by a series of communicating basins (*euripus*). At the east end is a cascade where the water gushes out between paintings of *Narcissus* and *Pyramus and Thisbe*. Below is a *biclinium* (or dining bed for two), the table of which seems to rise from the water. On the right couch of the biclinium you can glimpse the signature of the artist Lucius, who executed the adjoining paintings. When the north arm of the *euripus* was full, it overflowed through conduits, passing under the little tetrastyle temple in the middle, into another branch, crossing the garden from north to south. Beneath the temple are ornamental carvings from which issued the water for a second cascade. In the large garden numerous plaster casts have been taken of roots of ornamental plants, shrubs and trees.

The small house at no. 4 has a painted stucco relief of the imperial emblem over its entrance—a civic crown between two laurels. The **House of the Marine Venus (39)** was damaged by a bomb in 1943 and not completely excavated until 1952, when the great painting of Venus was brought to light. The stuccoed decoration of the portico around the garden was completed just before the eruption.

ANCIENT ROMAN WALL PAINTING TECHNIQUE

'Fresco' refers to a method of painting widely used in Italy in the late Middle Ages, throughout the Renaissance, and for some time thereafter. It involves the mixing of natural pigments with water, and their application into wet lime plaster: this will act as their physical binder as it dries and locks the colour particles in. The result is a slightly rough, matt finish, with no raised impasto. The surface of Pompeian painting is quite different: it is smooth, compact and slightly shiny. Close examination of its figures and decorative elements seems to show that they have been painted onto (not into) the surface: they have raised brushstrokes and areas even of thick impasto with a fluid and waxy appearance.

The literary sources for ancient painting techniques are principally Pliny's *Natural History*, Vitruvius' *De Architectura*, and a few random comments in ancient literature. Unfortunately neither Pliny nor Vitruvius was a painter. The only painting method discussed by Pliny is what he calls *encaustae picturae*, or 'encaustic paintings': he tells a number of anecdotes about great painters, which would imply that this 'encaustic' is a fluid, sensitive and expressive medium, and one in which the colours could be prepared in advance and worked with over a long period, just as a painter might use oils today.

Common knowledge has always been that encaustic involved using beeswax as a binder for pigments, because Pliny mentions the use of wax. But it is not possible to paint with beeswax alone, because it needs to be kept at a high temperature: if not, it cools on contact with the surface and becomes lumpy and unworkable. Even heating the surface, and using a hot spatula instead of a brush, does not allow the painter time to do anything subtle or sensitive. What the painter requires is an emulsifier that will make the wax fluid enough to stay on his brush and flow smoothly onto the surface, so that he can create sensitive and delicate effects.

Encaustic, as Pliny himself explains, means 'burnt in'; but 'caustic' can also refer to something that burns or corrodes by chemical action. Soap is mildly caustic and is also a good emulsifier. In ancient times it was made from heated vegetable and animal fats, compounded with alkaline bleaches derived from potash. Soaps (in particular those derived from a potassium-bleach) and warmed beeswax do, in fact, form an excellent liquid emulsion which can be diluted with water. The result would allow for the application, on an already plastered wall, of the fluid brushstrokes and thick impasto which we see in the finest Roman wall painting.

In Pompeian decoration, the large areas of background colour are blocked out in traditional wet-plaster fresco technique, and then later polished with warm wax to give them their characteristic shine. But the tiny and intricate details and many of the broader impressionistic scenes are not possible with this technique. A soap-and-wax encaustic, on the other hand, would not only make them possible, but would give them the beautiful 'enamel' quality which they so memorably possess.

N.McG.

The Villa of Julia Felix

The whole of the next insula, excavated in 1755–57 and reburied, then completely disinterred in 1952–53, is occupied by the **Villa of Julia Felix (40)** and its magnificent garden. The villa seems to have been a luxury hotel, with three sections: the residential quarter of the proprietress; a bath for public use; and an inn, a shop, and a series of rooms, some with independent street doors. The fine private rooms have big square windows overlooking the garden. They lost their wall paintings in the 18th century; that of one room (*Apollo and the Muses*) is now in the Louvre.

The portico has slender rectangular marble columns with delicate capitals; the tiled roof is a copy of the antique one. Below it the couches of the triclinium face the marble fish-ponds in the middle of the garden and the rustic stucco colonnade beyond. The baths are the most complete and perfect in Pompeii; their charming vestibule is linked to the adjacent inn by a hatch. The rented apartments, one still displaying its 'to let' notice, were on two floors.

The Amphitheatre and Great Palaestra

Behind the villa rises the **Amphitheatre**, the most ancient structure of its kind known. Begun c. 80 BC through the munificence of the *duumviri* C. Quintius Valgus and M. Porcius (who also built the Small Theatre), it was not completed until the time of Augustus (27 BC–AD 14). The inscriptions beneath the north entrance probably refer to restorations undertaken by C. Cuspius Pansa after the period of disuse that followed the fateful brawl of AD 59 (*see p. 169 above*) and the earthquake. The axes of the amphitheatre measure 135m by 107m, and it held 12,000 spectators.

The cavea was divided into three tiers, containing 5, 12 and 18 rows of seats. A space on the east side, as wide as two rows, was reserved for the president of the games. In construction it differs from later amphitheatres in that the gallery from which the first and second tiers are reached is constructed in four unconnected sections, whereas the upper gallery, reserved for women and children, is entered from a corridor reached only by an external staircase. There are no subterranean chambers beneath the arena.

To the west lies the **Great Palaestra**, a space c. 110m square once shaded by great plane trees, surrounded by a portico, with a large swimming pool in the centre. When the Samnite palaestra proved inadequate, the youth of the city exercised themselves and held their gymnastic competitions here. At the southeast corner (the latrine) were found many skeletons of youths who had fled in vain to its shelter during the eruption of Vesuvius.

From the west side you may pass between insulae 8 and 9 and, by turning left, descend to the Porta di Nuceria. Outside the gate, modern excavations have exposed a street (Via Nuceria) running east–west and flanked by sumptuous tombs that date mainly from the second half of the 1st century BC. Particularly noteworthy are (right) the painted announcements of games at neighbouring cities (Nuceria, Herculaneum and so on), tombs with portrait statues and busts, and the Sepulchre of Eumachia, the builder of the cloth market in the Forum. Just outside the gate are casts of three further victims of the disaster. To the west the extramural view of the town is impressive.

THE OLDEST WINE IN THE WORLD

Archaeological excavations and botanical studies conducted in the late 20th century uncovered remains of vine roots and stakes preserved by volcanic ash from the eruption of AD 79. Plaster casts taken of these show that vines were grown even within Pompeii's city walls, in the private gardens of patrician homes as well as in the 'suburban' area around the Amphitheatre.

In 1996 the Campanian vintner Mastroberardino was asked to revive the tradition of winemaking in Pompeii. The commission called for the establishment of experimental vineyards in five areas of the city that had been used for wine-growing in Antiquity. In 1999, after testing eight grape varieties known to have been vinified by the Romans, two reds—Piedirosso and Sciascinoso—were chosen as best suited for the site. Today the five vineyards—the *vigneti* dell'Oste Eusino, della Casa della Nave Europa, dell'Osteria del Gladiatore, del Foro Boario, and della Casa del Triclinio Estivo—occupy a total area of about a hectare (2.5 acres) and produce thousands of bottles of what is, for all practical purposes, a 2,000-year-old wine. Viticulture and vinification methods today mimic those in use before the eruption: the new vines, like the old, are arranged in densely packed rows supported by chestnut-wood stakes.

Mastroberardino Villa dei Misteri red is a Pompeian IGT wine made of 90 per cent Piedirosso and 10 per cent Sciascinoso. The grapes are harvested in late October, hand pressed, then aged in small oak barrels for 12 months and in the bottle for six months more. The first vintage (2001) produced just 1,700 bottles that were sold at auction in 2003 to benefit restoration of an ancient wine cellar in the Foro Boario vineyard (where wine was made not in oak, but in terracotta pots sunken in the floor). Unlike Roman wine, which was thick (it had to mixed with water before serving) and bitter (the stems were fermented with the grapes, making it necessary to sweeten and spice the final drink), Mastroberardino's Villa dei Misteri can be drunk 'as is'. Ruby-red in colour, it has a complex and persistent bouquet of fruit (particularly woodland berries) and spice (vanilla, cinnamon and cloves); the flavour is full and nicely balanced, displaying fine, elegant tannins. Alcohol content is 13.0 per cent. Production remains quite limited, which makes each bottle a small treasure (for which you can expect to pay €200+). But then, what would you expect from the wine of the Caesars?

Around the Thermae Stabianae

The **Thermae Stabianae**, across the street from the **House of Cornelius Rufus (41)**, were the largest baths in Pompeii. They originally date from the Samnite era, but were enlarged soon after the establishment of the Roman colony and again under the empire. The entrance leads to the palaestra, enclosed by a portico; some of the beautiful stucco decorations are visible to the left. Along this stretch are the bowling alley and the swimming pool. Opposite these are another bowling alley, a latrine and some private baths. The men's baths are to the right. These include the *apodyterium* (dressing-room), consisting of two chambers with marble floor, vaulted stucco and recesses for the clothes; the circular *frigidarium* or cold bath; the *tepidarium* with a plunge-bath; and (at the back) the *calidarium* or warm room, with a plunge-bath and a basin for washing. Hot air circulated below the tepidarium and the calidarium.

The women's baths are adjacent. From a corridor enter the dressing-room, with two entrances from the street and the usual recesses. Beyond the cold and tepid rooms is the calidarium, with hollow walls and flooring for the hot vapour to pass through. The *praefurnium,* or heating apparatus, stood between the two warm rooms (*calidaria*); you can still make out the furnace and the position of three cylindrical boilers.

Beyond the baths turn right into Vico del Lupanare. The **House of Siricus (42)** (right) is composed of two communicating apartments. On the threshold is the inscription *Salve lucru(m)*, a candid salute to lucre. The handsome triclinium contains paintings of *Neptune and Apollo Helping to Build the Walls of Troy*, *Hercules and Omphale* and *Thetis with Vulcan*. Opposite the entrance is a painting of two large serpents (*agathodoemones*), with the inscription (nearly effaced) *Otiosis locus hic non est, discede morator* ('loitering forbidden').

Further on, to the left, is the **Lupanar Africani et Victoris (43)**; the lewd paintings and inscriptions on the ground floor indicate what sort of place this was. The first floor has a balcony (carefully restored after bomb damage). Opposite is the **Inn of Sittius (44)**, the sign of which was an elephant.

Vico del Lupanare ends at Via degli Augustali, where, almost opposite, is the **House of the Bear (45)**, so called from the mosaic at the entrance. To the right is a shoemaker's shop. Keeping to the right, regain the Via Stabiana and turn left. To the right (no. 12) is a restored mill (*pistrinum*). Number 5, on the same side, is the **House of Marcus Lucretius (46)**, priest of Mars and *decurion* of Pompeii. This was once one of the more luxuriantly decorated houses in the city. In the atrium, to the right, is the *aedicula* of the two tutelary deities of the house. Opposite is the tablinum. At the back is a pretty little garden, with a fountain and some marble figures among its flowers. The best of the well-preserved paintings, in the fourth style, are now in the Museo Archeologico in Naples.

From the Central Thermae to Porta Nola

The whole of the next insula on the right is occupied by the **Central Thermae**, built between the earthquake and the eruption, with the usual features on a more sumptuous scale and, in addition, a *laconicum* or *sudatorium*, a hot-air chamber of circular shape with domed vaulting. The building was unfinished at the time of its destruction.

Leave the thermae by the north side to emerge in the Via di Nola. On the right side of the lane opposite is a tavern in which three large bronze trumpets, apparently deposited here by the gladiators of the amphitheatre fleeing from the shower of *lapilli*, were discovered.

Further on, to the right, is the entrance to the **House of the Silver Wedding (47)**, so called because the excavations were made in the presence of King Umberto and

Queen Margherita in 1893, the year of their silver wedding anniversary. This is a real Pompeian palace, with a spacious tetrastyle atrium. The front colonnade of the well-preserved peristyle is higher than the others. The triclinium is a large, handsome apartment. The *cubicula* on the south side have well preserved decorations in the third style, and their private baths have been wonderfully restored. The garden, with its stonework triclinium, is also noteworthy.

Returning to the Via di Nola and following it to the left, you soon reach (right) the large, magnificent **House of the Centenary (48)**, so named because it was excavated in 1879, the 1800th anniversary of the eruption. It has two *atria* (that on the left handsomely decorated) and a spacious peristyle. A graceful fountain plays in a small court adorned with paintings of gardens, a fish-pond and scenes of the chase. To the west are the bathrooms and two chambers adorned with paintings. A secret chamber with erotic decoration opens from one. Of interest also are the decorations of two rooms entered from the front walk of the colonnade, one with white walls, the other with black.

Off the alley opposite stands the **House of Marcus Lucretius Fronto (49)**, which dates from the early imperial period. The roof of the atrium is a modern restoration, in strict keeping with the maxims of Vitruvius. Among the notable paintings in this house are *Neoptolemus Slain by Orestes* (first room on the right), *Theseus and Ariadne*, *Toilet of Venus* (second room on the right), *Wedding of Mars and Venus*, *Triumph of Bacchus*, landscapes (tablinum), *Narcissus at the Fountain*, *Pero and her Father Micon Condemned to Death by Starvation* (room to the right of the tablinum; this story inspired the breast-feeding scene in Caravaggio's famous *Seven Acts of Mercy*; *see p. 70*), *Pyramus and Thisbe*, *Bacchus and Silenus* (first garden-room to the right).

Further on in the Via di Nola, to the left, is the **House of the Gladiators (50)** with a four-sided porticus. The Porta Nola, at the end of the street, dates from the Samnite era. It is decorated, on the side facing the city, with the head of Minerva.

Northwest of Via di Nola

At the corner of Via di Nola and Via Stabiana are a fountain, an altar to the Lares of the crossroads, and an aqueduct pillar. The House of M. Vesonius Primus is known as the **House of Orpheus (51)** from the large painting in the peristyle. In the atrium is a portrait-herm of Vesonius. Next door is the **Fullonica of Vesonius (52)**. The impluvium contains a marble table and a fountain, and there are three water tanks behind the atrium. Opposite stands the **House of L. Caecilius Iucundus (53)**, the banker, where the famous receipts, now in the Museo Archeologico, were discovered (*see p. 95*). In the atrium is a portrait-herm of the master of the house, a copy of the original at Naples; also two bas-reliefs representing respectively the north side of the Forum and the destruction of the Porta del Vesuvio by the earthquake of AD 63. The tablinum has good decorations. The sign for the Taberna Lusoria (no. 28), a vase between two phalli, indicates its business, a gambling house below with rooms for hire above.

Beyond the next crossroads on the left is the **House of the Gilded Cupids (54)**, which belonged to the Poppaei, and which demonstrates the refined tastes of the age

Wall painting of *Narcissus at the Fountain*, from the house of Marcus Lucretius Fronto.

of Nero. The porticus has been restored on its old lines. The marble sculptures in the garden remain as they were. The marble bas-reliefs in the south wing of the colonnade represent satyrs, maenads, etc. At the southeast corner of the peristyle is a shrine devoted to the cult of Egyptian deities. The *lararium* in the north colonnade has the conventional form of a small temple.

The mosaic on the floor of the interesting cubiculum to the right indicates the place occupied by the beds. On the walls, under antique glass, are the flying and gilded cupids that give the house its name. In the east colonnade is a large room with paintings of *Thetis and Vulcan, Jason and Pelias* and *Achilles in his Tent with Patroclus and Briseis.* The stucco ceilings of two *cubicula* in the west colonnade are unusually fine.

The *cardo* ends at the Porta Vesuvio, adjoining which is a *castellum aquae* or conduit-head, where water entering from an aqueduct was distributed to three channels. Outside the gate, beneath cypresses, is the tomb of the aedile Vestorius Priscus, with scenes from his life painted on the inner walls.

To the right is a terminal cippus of the ancient *pomerium* (zone of defence), set up by T. Suedius Clemens, a military tribune. Further on are the ruins of the village, with factories, reoccupied in the 2nd and 3rd centuries AD but later abandoned. Turning back, notice the fine stretch of pre-Samnite wall, which is visible to the east; to the west are three fine towers.

House of the Vettii

The **House of the Vettii (55)** belonged to Aulus Vettius Restitutus and Aulus Vettius Conviva, two wealthy merchants of the Roman colony. Its beautiful paintings (still in their original positions) and the skilful reconstruction of its apartments make it one of the most interesting houses to visit.

To the right of the entrance, under lock and key, is a characteristically salacious image of Priapus, often used in ancient Rome as a talisman to bring fertility and prosperity and ward off intruders. The atrium has delightful paintings of *amorini* and putti. To the right and left are strongrooms. Also on the right is the porter's lodge. In the corresponding little room to the left are paintings of *Ariadne Deserted, Hero and Leander,* and a fish-pond. The larger room to the left of the entrance has pictures of *Cyparissus, Eros and Pan Wrestling for the Entertainment of Bacchus and Ariadne, Leda and the Swan,* and *Jupiter Enthroned.* Opening off the atrium are two *cubicula* and the *alae,* in one of which (left) is a cleverly painted picture of a cock fight. To the right of the main atrium is a small rustic atrium (with a *lararium*), followed by the kitchen, with its fire-grate and boilers. Adjoining is a closed room with equivocal pictures and a statuette of Priapus.

The peristyle offers an enchanting spectacle. Against the columns surrounding it are statuettes from which jets of water spouted into marble basins. Two other jets rise in the middle of the colourful garden. In the east colonnade are two handsome rooms (*oeci*). In one of them are paintings of *The Infant Hercules and the Serpents, Pentheus Torn Limb from Limb by the Bacchantes, Dirce and the Wild Bull* (the story of the *Farnese Bull; see p. 79*). In the other are *Daedalus Showing Pasiphaë the Wooden Cow, Ixion on the Wheel, Bacchus and the Sleeping Ariadne,* and beautiful arabesques.

In the north colonnade is a separate group of triclinium, cubiculum, and small garden. The triclinium is the exquisite Sala Dipinta, probably used for banquets on special occasions. On a black band round the room are charming little *amorini* at work and play. On the black panels below are winged nymphs gathering flowers; *Agamemnon Forcing his Way into the Temple of Artemis to Slay the Sacred Hind; Apollo as Conqueror of the Python; Orestes and Pylades with Thoas and Iphigeneia.* On the dado, Amazons and women with sacrificial vessels and a Bacchante and satyr. On the large red panels, separated by candelabra-pilasters corresponding to the small black panels, are flying groups of *Perseus and Andromeda, Dionysus and Ariadne, Apollo and Daphne* and *Poseidon and Amymone.* On the door-jambs, *Hermaphroditus and Silenus.*

Follow Vicolo di Mercurio to the right; on the corner (left) are an aqueduct pillar and some leaden pipes. No. 10 (right) is the **House of the Labyrinth (56)**, dating from the Samnite era and taking its name from a mosaic of Theseus and the Minotaur.

House of the Faun and its neighbourhood

The famous **House of the Faun (57)**, once the residence of the Casii, is 80m long and 35m wide, and occupies the whole of its insula. Its popular name comes from the celebrated bronze statuette of the *Dancing Faun* found near the impluvium (now in the Museo Archeologico, and replaced here by a copy). On the pavement in front of the house is the salutation *have* ('welcome'). There are two *atria* and two peristyles. The beautiful stucco decoration successfully imitates marble. The fine flooring of the first peristyle is, unfortunately, badly damaged. The mosaic floors of the four *triclinia* (one for each season of the year) are now in the museum at Naples. The 28 Ionic columns of the peristyle are coated with stucco. The well-known mosaic of the *Battle of Alexander at Issus* (also at Naples) was found in the red-columned exedra. The second peristyle is in the form of a large garden, with a Doric porticus.

At its intersection of the Strada del Foro and Via di Mercurio stands the **Temple of Fortune (58)**, constructed in 3 BC by M. Tullius and restored after the earthquake of AD 79. The Corinthian pronaos has two columns on each side. The architrave of an *aedicula* in the cella bears the name of the founder. At the north (right) corner is a triumphal arch (also used as a reservoir), which bore an equestrian statue of Caligula. Refreshments are sold in the adjoining building.

Beyond the crossroad, to the left (no. 2), are the **Forum Thermae (59)**, built in the time of Sulla by the *duumvir* L. Cesius and the *aediles* C. Occius and L. Niremius. The layout resembles that of the Thermae Stabianae. The shelves in the apodyterium are decorated with a frieze of telamones. The large bronze brazier in the tepidarium and the benches were presented by M. Nigidius Vaccula. The marble basin in the calidarium was placed here in AD 3 or AD 4 and cost (according to the inscription) 5,250 *sestertii*. Inside are some more plaster casts of victims of the eruption, in glass cases.

Thieving birds: mosaic from the House of the Faun.

Opposite the baths, on the other side of Via di Nola, is the **House of the Tragic Poet (60)**, adopted by Edward Bulwer-Lytton, in his *Last Days of Pompeii*, as the house of Glaucus. Among the valuable mosaics found here was one of a theatrical rehearsal, now in the Museo Archeologico in Naples. On the threshold is a mosaic dog, with the inscription *cave canem* ('beware of the dog'). In the triclinium are paintings of a youth and maiden looking at a nest of Cupids; *Marsyas Teaching Olympus the Flute, Theseus and Ariadne, Dido and Aeneas*, and personifications of the seasons. Another important picture found here was the *Sacrifice of Iphigeneia*.

A little further on, to the right, is the large **House of Pansa**, notable for the regularity of its construction (*its plan is reproduced on p. 172 above*). Along the entrance wall and the wall to the left were rows of shops. The rooms on the right were to let.

The **House of Sallust (61)**, more properly known as the House of A. Cassius Libanus, is a fine mansion of the Samnite period damaged by a bomb in September 1943, when its well-known picture of *Diana and Actaeon* was destroyed. A partial restoration was paid for by American funds. The **House of the Surgeon (62)** is a massive structure of Sarno stone. Several surgical instruments, now at the Museo Archeologico Nazionale in Naples, were found here.

A detour outside the walls

The **Porta Ercolano** (Herculaneum Gate), at the end of Via Consolare, dates from the close of the 2nd century BC and is the most recent and most important town gate. In Antiquity it seems to have been called *Porta Salina* or *Saliniensis*. Of its three archways, that in the centre, for vehicles, was vaulted at the ends only; the lateral openings for pedestrians were vaulted throughout. Beyond the gate runs the Via delle Tombe, lined with the sepulchral monuments of prominent Pompeians.

To the right of the gate Via Pomerium skirts the walls and gives a good glimpse of Pompeii's fortifications. The **town rampart** is c. 6m thick. It consists of an outer wall (2nd century BC) and the pre-Samnite inner wall, with earth in the intervening space. The walls were originally of tufa or limestone, but they were repaired with blocks of lava shortly before the Social War. There were 12 towers between the Porta Ercolano and the Porta Marina, and several others on the north side, where the natural defences were weakest. It was this part of the wall that was chosen for attack by L. Sulla in 89 BC, and the damage caused by his missiles can still be seen.

Enter the city again through the Porta Vesuvio. Inside the wall Tower XI (which you can climb) commands an extensive panorama.

A cluster of interesting houses

The **House of Apollo (63)** has a picturesque fountain, a handsome cubiculum, a mosaic of *Achilles at Skyros* and a painting of *Apollo and Marsyas*. On the other side of the street is the **House of Meleager (64)**, with its tasteful fountain and Corinthian *oecus*. Beneath a marble table in the atrium is an apparatus for cooling wine and food in water.

The **House of the Centaur (65)** is decorated in the first style. In the **House of Adonis (66)** is a large painting of the *Wounded Adonis Tended by Venus and Cupids*. The

House of Castor and Pollux (67) has a Corinthian atrium with twelve columns and paintings of *Apollo and Daphne*, the *Birth of Adonis*, *Minos and Scylla*. Like many other dwellings, it is an amalgamation of several earlier buildings.

On the east corner of the crossroads with Vicolo di Mercurio is a *caupona* or tavern. In the back shop are scenes of tavern life. In the **House of the Little Fountain (68)**, a mosaic fountain is adorned with a boy and goose in bronze (copies). The **House of the Large Fountain (69)** has another mosaic fountain. Across the street is the **House of the Anchor (70)**, so called from a mosaic on the threshold. The garden, on a lower level, is surrounded by a cryptoporticus.

The suburban villas

To reach these two surburban villas, either walk along Via delle Tombe or take the road that leads north from Villa dei Misteri station on the Circumvesuviana line.

The famous **Villa of Diomedes** is so called on the slender grounds that the burial place of M. Arrius Diomedes is on the opposite side of the road. The villa had the largest garden in Pompeii, with a colonnade containing various chambers. Steps ascend to the peristyle, adjoining which are (right) a luxurious private bath with cold-water pool and (left) a large apsidal chamber, possibly a sitting room. The tablinum, opposite the entrance, opens onto a large terrace, from which steps and a ramp descend to the garden. In the middle are a *piscina* (tank) and a summer triclinium, with fountain, and an arbour borne by six columns.

In a vaulted cellar extending below three sides of the garden-colonnade were found amphorae of wine and 18 skeletons of adults and children who had vainly taken refuge there. The owner of the villa, probably a wine-merchant, was found near the garden door, with the key in his hand; beside him was a slave with money and valuables. A small staircase with two columns formed the main entrance from Via delle Tombe and led directly to the peristyle.

About 200m to the west of the Villa of Diomedes stands the **Villa of the Mysteries** (Villa dei Misteri), a complex dwelling that began in the 2nd century BC as a town house, developed into a manor and declined into a farmhouse. It takes its name from a hall with 24 life-size painted figures thought to have been executed by a Campanian painter in 1st century BC on a second-style background. Entrance is gained from the rear of the villa, through what was once a broad gallery with a central exedra and two lateral wings. Straight ahead is the tablinum, with black-ground paintings in a vaguely Egyptian style. Here you turn right and walk through a cubiculum adorned with Dionysiac figures (such as a dancing satyr, a hallmark of the cult of the young god of excess) to reach the marble-floored Painted Hall.

The paintings form a cycle, the meaning of which, although still under discussion, is probably connected with the initiation rites into the Dionysiac mysteries, a practice that was common in southern Italy despite prohibitory measures adopted by the Roman Senate. According to the leading interpretation, the scenes, starting on the wall to the left of the door, represent (a) a child reading the rite before a young bride and a seated matron; (b) a priestess and three female assistants making a sacrifice; (c) *sileni* playing musical instruments in a pastoral setting; (d) the flight of the frightened initiate and a group of two satyrs and a silenus with a mask; (e) the marriage of Dionysus and Ariadne (damaged); (f) a kneeling woman unveiling (or, by a differing interpretation, protecting) the sacred phallus while a winged demon raises a flagellum to strike the young initiate, who seeks refuge in the lap of a companion; (g) the orgiastic dance of Dionysus; (h) the dressing of a bride for initiation and a seated woman who has undergone the initiation rite.

Returning to the tablinum, turn right through the atrium to the peristyle, then right again to the kitchen, with its two fireplaces. The adjacent small atrium gives access to a room gracefully decorated with architectural motifs. Around the peristyle are the *vestibulum*, leading to the former main entrance (opposite the atrium), and a *torcularium*, where grapes were pressed (across from the kitchen).

Modern Pompei

The modern village of Pompei has sprung up round the pilgrimage shrine of Santa Maria del Rosario, built in 1876–91 and enlarged in 1938 as a shrine for the *Madonna of the Rosary*, an old picture, framed with gold and precious stones, that now adorns the high altar. The Museo Vesuviano (*Piazza Longo 1; open daily 9–1.30*) has Vesuvian stones, and prints and paintings representing the eruptions of the volcano.

HERCULANEUM

The excavations are entered from Corso Resina. Open daily April–Oct 8.30–7.30, last entry 6; Nov–March 8.30–5, last entry 3.30; T: 081 732 4311, www.pompeiisites.org. The great suburban Villa of the Papyri, from which many works of art in Naples museum came, was abandoned to the tufa in 1765. Pre-booked tours to a part of it, as well as to the suburban baths, run at weekends. Book through www.arethusa.net

Herculaneum (Ercolano), destroyed with Pompeii in AD 79 and rediscovered in 1709, was a residential town without Pompeii's commercial importance, surrounded by the villas of wealthy Romans. The excavations are on an attractive terraced site. Although they are small in extent compared with those of Pompeii and less immediately striking, the domestic buildings, especially their upper storeys and wooden parts, are better preserved. Gardens have been replanted, contributing to a feeling of life and humanity not always achieved at Pompeii. Herculaneum also has the interest of a richer artistic life and of contrasting styles of house construction.

Visitors who have time to see only one of the two ancient cities are advised to go to Herculaneum, where the most outstanding features can be seen in about two hours. These include the House of Opus Craticium, the House of the Wooden Partition, the Thermae, the Samnite House, the House of the Deer, and the House of the Relief of Telephus. As at Pompeii, ongoing conservation work requires the closure of certain houses from time to time. On the other hand, 'new' buildings are opened as soon as they have been made safe for visitors. Recent openings include the House of Aristides, near the House of Argus on Cardo III and, possibly, the underground theatre.

HISTORY OF HERCULANEUM

The foundation of Herculaneum, called *Heracleia* by its Greek settlers, was attributed by them to its patron deity, Hercules. The town passed through periods of Oscan and Samnite domination, before falling to Titus Didius, a lieutenant of Sulla, in 89 BC, after which a colony of veterans seems to have been established here. The damage done by an earthquake in AD 63 was being repaired, under Vespasian's patronage, when the catastrophe of AD 79 overwhelmed the town. Unlike Pompeii, Herculaneum was submerged by a torrent of mud containing sand, ashes and bits of lava, which raised the level of the soil by 12–25m and hardened into tufa, preserving many timber features and household objects that were burnt at Pompeii. Subsequent layers of volcanic matter buried the ruins to a depth of 39m and the town remained untouched for 1,630 years.

The first discoveries were made in 1709 when Emmanuel de Lorraine, Prince d'Elbeuf and cavalry commander of the Kingdom of Naples, came upon the back of the theatre's stage while sinking the shaft for a well. He distributed a large group of statues and much of the *scena* among various museums.

Charles III continued the exploration (1738–65), without any very clear plan, but the theatre, forum, and five 'temples' were located. The Villa of the Papyri was also explored and its sculptural treasures and library recovered and transferred to Naples. The Accademia Reale Ercolanese, founded in 1755 for the purpose of investigating the discoveries, published a work in eight volumes on the mural paintings and bronzes (1757–92) and a volume on the papyri (1797; by C. Rosini).

Desultory explorations were carried out in 1828–35 and in 1869–75, but systematic excavation was not begun until 1927. The excavations continue, and visitors often have the opportunity to watch a dig in progress. The new excavations have disinterred three *cardines* (III, IV and V), two roads (the *decumanus inferior* and part of the *decumanus maximus*) as well as the suburban area outside the walls, which descends towards the harbour. Houses are designated by insula (block) and street number only.

The ancient city

The extent of the city is still uncertain, but in both area and population it was probably only about one-third of the size of Pompeii. With *decumani* running parallel with the coast (then much nearer the town than it is today) and *cardines* at right angles to the *decumani* and the shore, the town suggests a Greek rather than a Roman plan and has affinities with Neapolis (Naples). The streets are paved with local volcanic stone, but are noticeably free from both the wheel ruts and the stepping-stones so characteristic of Pompeian streets. On the seaward side the town ended in a terraced promontory, lined with patrician villas, beneath which the *cardines* descended abruptly through narrow archways to the extramural quarter round the harbour.

Herculanean houses

Unlike Pompeii, which was entirely dominated by the commercial classes, Herculaneum was a city of wealthy citizens, small artisans and fishermen. The Herculanean house is more evolved, freer, and further advanced in the adoption of new ideas than the Pompeian house. The Samnite type of construction described at Pompeii also exists at Herculaneum, but frequently with the atrium daringly modified for the addition of an extra floor.

In the richer type of dwelling the Hellenistic plan of building round a peristyle is frequently followed, but the peristyle itself is often modified to a closed corridor with windows overlooking the central garden. In many middle-class houses the traditional plan has been abandoned and a central courtyard, more akin to the modern 'well', has been substituted. Finally, 'apartment houses' with several floors have been discovered (though not on the scale developed in Ostia), in which the poorer artisans lived the crowded life of their modern Neapolitan counterparts.

THE SITE

The avenue that leads from the entrance gate to the excavations commands a wonderful view across Herculaneum to the sea. This allows you to appreciate the natural beauty of the site, the magnitude of the disaster that transformed it, and the difficulties that face the excavators. Looking down on the city from above you can also see the variety of its dwellings and the topography of its streets. Lettering in the text refers to the plan overleaf.

Cardo III Inferiore

The visit begins at the west corner of the site, at the entrance to Cardo III. The **House of Argus (A)** must have been one of the finest mansions in the town: some idea of its grandeur may still be gained from the wall fronting the street and the noble columns of its peristyle. On the opposite side of Cardo III is the back entrance to the house usually (but wrongly) called the **Hotel (B)**. Occupying well over half the insula, this was the largest and perhaps the richest dwelling in the south quarter of the city. When the earlier excavations exposed its west side, it was assumed because of its proportions to be a hotel; but its plan, though complex, is almost certainly that of a private villa, designed to exploit all the advantage of its site. The house had already fallen on bad times and at the date of the catastrophe was undergoing modifications: the whole south wing had been converted into a self-contained dwelling and a room on the north side into a shop. The private bath of the Augustan period had been abandoned (hypocaust exposed). The house was badly damaged in the eruption and further mutilated by Bourbon excavators, but even in decay its extent is impressive.

Cardo IV Inferiore

Emerge by the main entrance (no. 19) into Cardo IV. Opposite is the **House of the Mosaic Atrium (C)**, a panoramic house beautifully placed for enjoying the view. From the street (no. 2), pass through the *fauces* (entrance passage) to the atrium, both of which retain their geometric mosaic floors, though the pavement was corrugated under the weight of the invading tufa. Facing the atrium are the unusual basilican tablinum, and, at right angles, a closed gallery formed by partially filling in the intercolumnar spaces of a peristyle. The door and window frames are remarkably well preserved. Off the narrow east walk are four *cubicula* with red walls, and a raised central exedra, adorned with mythological scenes, with a wooden table. This room enjoys a charming view of the garden with its marble fountain. The main living-rooms beyond, including a lofty triclinium paved in marble, open onto a terrace formerly shaded by a colonnaded roof, with a solarium, at either end of which is a *diaeta,* or siesta room, with low windows for maximum enjoyment of the view.

Continuing up Cardo IV, notice on the left the **House of the Bronze Herm (D)**, with typical though diminutive characteristics of the Samnite house. The bronze portrait head (*temporarily removed*) is presumably of the owner; the bits of ancient fabric were discovered in the House of the Cloth. The base of a staircase leading to an upper floor can be seen in the blind corridor leading off the atrium. On the other side of the street is the **House of the Alcove (E)**, its façade in *opus reticulatum* pierced with iron gratings and overhung by the remains of a first-floor balcony. The smaller door (no. 4) gave on to the stairs. The ground floor comprises two separate dwellings thrown into one, that to the left modest, and that to the right more distinguished with a tessellated atrium and a richly painted room with wooden couches. At the end of a long corridor is a small court with the alcoved room that gives the house its name.

The **House of Opus Craticium (F)** presents a unique example of the wood and plaster construction, called *opus craticium,* used for plebeian dwellings, the defects and impermanence of which were noted by Vitruvius. The building, which consists of a shop with a back-parlour or workroom, and two self-contained flats, preserves its upper floor with balcony room over the pavement. The inner rooms overlook a small yard. The staircase (restored) still has several of the original steps. The houses on the other side of the street also have interesting features; two rooms at the rear of no. 6, lit by circular windows, retain their barrel-vaulting, floors, and mural decoration (of the first period; *see p. 90*).

Next on the left is the **House of the Wooden Partition (G)**, whose façade, which rises to the second storey, offers a striking picture of the external appearance of the Roman private house. The open gallery above the cornice belonged to a second floor, added to the structure when the house declined in status; this was reached from a separate entrance in the *decumanus.* In the imposing atrium the double lining of the impluvium basin in *opus signinum* (mosaic or paving of small stones set in a rough or

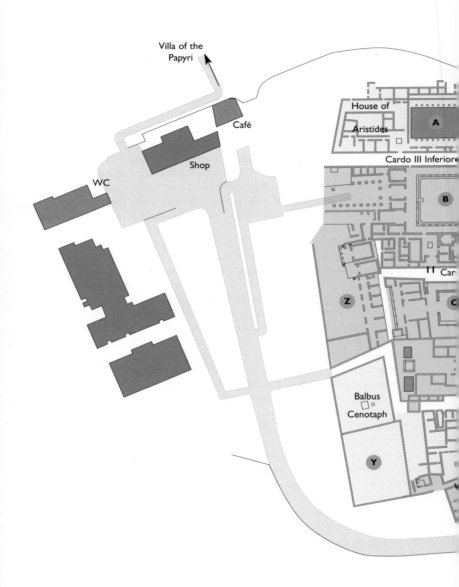

Villa of the
Papyri

Café

House of
Aristides

A

Shop

Cardo III Inferiore

WC

B

II Car

Z

C

Balbus
Cenotaph

Y

HERCULANEUM
PLAN OF THE EXCAVATIONS

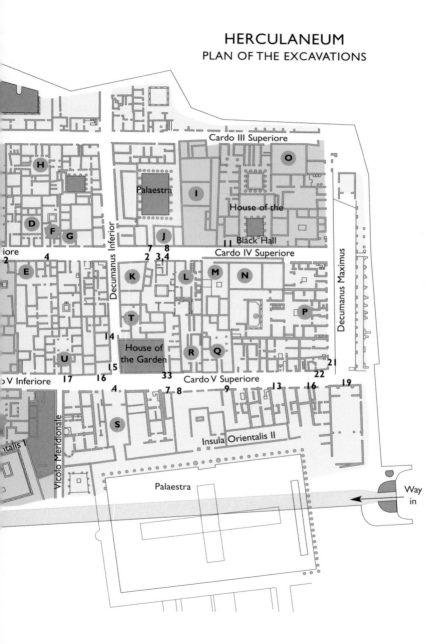

random pattern) and marble is notable; also the dogs'-head spouts (some original) of the compluviate roof. The most striking feature, giving its name to the house, is the wooden partition that closes the tablinum, reconstructed *in situ* with its ancient hinges and lamp brackets. Glass cases preserve remains of toilet articles, beans, etc, found in the house. The cubiculum to the right of the *fauces* has a geometric floor design and a marble table; the further room on the left, a well-preserved frieze. Behind the house is a charming small garden. The side of the house abutting the *decumanus inferior* was occupied by shops which, with one exception, link directly to the house. The corner shop (no. 10) contains a unique wooden clothes-press in an astonishing state of preservation.

Behind is the **House of the Skeleton (H)**, so-called from the remains discovered in 1831 on the upper floor. The small rooms are tastefully disposed and decorated.

The Thermae

Beyond the *decumanus inferior*, the greater part of Insula VI (left) is occupied by the **Thermae (I)**, public baths erected early in the reign of Augustus (c. 20 BC) on a plan similar to that used at Pompeii and decorated somewhat later. They survive, finely preserved and without modification, almost as they were planned. In the centre is the palaestra, the main entrance of which was in Cardo IV (no. 7). To the south, with separate entrances from the *decumanus*, was a covered hall with a penthouse roof, probably a *sphaeristerium*, where the ball game *pila* was played. A second entrance to the palaestra from Cardo III (no. 1), flanked by a porter's lodge and a latrine, led also to the men's baths. From the corridor you enter the *apodyterium* (dressing-room), with a convex floor in *opus segmentatum*, shelves for clothes, and vaulted stucco. A *cipollino* marble basin stands in an apse. A vestibule, to the left, leads down marble steps to the circular *frigidarium* or cold bath, the domed ceiling of which is painted with fish on a blue ground, pierced by a skylight. From the other side of the dressing-room, pass through the *tepidarium* to the *calidarium* or warm room, with the usual plunge-bath and a scalloped apse for a hand basin; the fallen vault has exposed the heating pipes and smoke vents.

The **Women's Baths (J)**, entered from Cardo IV Superiore (no. 8), though smaller and simpler, are even better preserved. You enter a waiting-room and pass through a small linen-room to the dressing-room, whose mosaic (as in the men's *tepidarium*) shows a triton surrounded by dolphins and cuttle-fish. Beyond, the small *tepidarium* and *calidarium* are virtually complete. Note the pretty marble bench with human feet. Behind (no. 10) are the service quarters, where the well can be seen, and the staircase leading up to the attendant's living quarters and down to the *praefurnium* or heating apparatus; the heavy iron door and the poker survive, though the boilers were removed by Bourbon excavators.

Further along Cardo IV (no. 11) is the **House of the Black Hall**, still largely buried, with an elegant tetrastyle portico. The paintings of the little vaulted rooms and of the black hall are particularly lively. The model temple, with wooden columns, surmounted by marble capitals, was a shrine for the *lares*.

Cardo IV Superiore

From here it is easy to visit the houses on the other side of Cardo IV, starting at the crossroads. The **Samnite House (K)**, fronted by a stretch of fine paving, has an imposing portal and an open gallery (approached by a stair from no. 2) that led to a separate apartment added at a later date. The interior decoration is beautifully executed; that of the *fauces* in the first style, of architectural imitation (*see p. 90*). The atrium has a blind gallery of graceful proportions. Beyond a simple weaver's house (nos 3–4) and workshop is the small but dignified **House of the Carbonised Furniture (L)**, in the Samnite style, with an elegantly decorated triclinium and a delightful little courtyard. The *lararium* is placed to be seen from the window of an inner room, the divan and table of which survive. Some furniture remains also in the upper rooms of the **House of the Neptune Mosaic (M)**, which stand open to the street. Below is the best-preserved shop in the town, with its specially constructed shelves for holding storage jars. A fine wooden partition separates the shop from the attractive living quarters behind, where a little court is enlivened by the fresh blues and greens of a mosaic-decorated nymphaeum (to the left as you look in), and the famous *Neptune and Amphitrite* mosaic, which gives the house its name. The **House of the Beautiful Courtyard (N)** has an unusual plan grouped around a wide hall that precedes the court. The *cardo* continues between high pavements (once arcaded, as may be seen from the remaining columns) to the crossing with the usual public fountain and altar. A painted inscription on a pillar records rules of the street police.

Herculaneum's famous *Neptune and Amphitrite* mosaic.

Turn left into the broad *decumanus maximus*, reserved for pedestrians, the far side of which still lies beneath the tufa. The **College of the Augustali (O)**, seat of the cult of the emperor established in the Augustan age, contains some very well preserved wall paintings. Retracing your steps you come, on the right, to a shop (V, 10) with a little room over the pavement. Built into the counter and sunk into the floor are the *dolia*, or large jars, in which foodstuffs could be preserved at an even temperature. This and the adjoining shops originally formed part of the **House of the Bicentenary (P)**, a rich dwelling disinterred in 1938, two hundred years after Charles III began the excavations. The ground floor preserves its original plan despite later modifications. The fine atrium still has its lattice partition and the tablinum is decorated with mythical scenes and paved in mosaic. The outline of a cross on the wall of an upstairs room suggests that a private Christian oratory existed here, although the Crucifix is not thought to have become established as a Christian symbol as early as AD 79.

Cardo V Superiore

Cardo V is admirably paved in limestone. To the left is a public fountain with a mask of Hercules; turn right, towards the sea. The corner shop (V, 21) is interesting for the wooden window-fittings remaining in the dwelling above (entered from no. 22). Beyond on the right the houses continue to be in styles already familiar; three of them, preceded by a stretch of marble pavement once shaded by a portico, have features worthy of note.

In the **House of the Corinthian Atrium (Q)**, small but in good taste, the compluviate roof, supported by six tufa columns faced with stucco, feeds a graceful fountain. A mosaic, in a room to the right, shows the sacred two-edged axe, or *labrys* in its pattern. A glass case contains a wooden table and a small basket. Note also the elegant decoration of the cubiculum, lit by three skylights (two restored). Next door is the **House of the Lararium (R)**, an earlier and smaller dwelling showing good examples of decoration in the first and third styles. Most wonderfully preserved is a wooden *sacellum*, which consists of a cupboard surmounted by a shrine in the form of a small temple in antis, with Corinthian columns, where the *lares* were kept. Beyond is the so-called House with the Garden (V, 33), though the garden probably belonged to one of the more distinguished houses in the *decumanus*.

The other side of the street is quite different, foreshadowing the style developed at Ostia a hundred years later. The whole block (**Insula Orientalis II**), c. 90m long, is of uniform construction in *opus reticulatum* and was apparently planned as a unit. The street frontage consists of shops with flats above, on a plan having no resemblance to the traditional Campanian house, but such as might be seen today. The chief interest of the plain rectangular shops is in their use and contents. Number 16 contains a marble casket and an almost perfect wooden partition door; no. 13 has a counter with remains of its vegetable wares; no. 9 preserves its stove and sink and a little painting

Finely preserved wall painting from the College of the Augustali.

of Hercules pouring a libation between Dionysus and Mercury. Number 8 was a bakery, where two mills for grinding flour, 25 bronze baking pans, the seal of the proprietor and an oven carved with a phallic emblem were found. The main staircase to the flats was at no. 7.

Behind this workaday façade a series of finely decorated and vaulted rooms overlook a huge open space surrounded by a portico, of which only the north and west sides have been unearthed. This area, the **Palaestra (S)**, where the public games were held, is approached by two great entrance halls (nos 19 and 4), each with a prostyle porch. Number 4, by which you enter, had a black tessellated floor and white walls and vault, a fitting entrance to the impressive colonnade within. Bourbon tunnels beneath the avenue give a vivid impression of the difficulties of excavation as well as of the size of the cruciform swimming-pool that occupied the centre of the palaestra. Its central fountain of bronze, cast in the form of a five-headed serpent entwined round a tree-trunk, has been re-erected.

Cardo V Inferiore

Rejoin Cardo V by the Neptune fountain, the usual rectangular basin formed of limestone slabs joined at the corners by lead clamps. On the right side of the *decumanus inferior* is the imposing entrance of the **House of the Great Portal (T)**, its engaged brick columns surmounted by Corinthian capitals carved with winged Victories and an architrave decorated in terracotta; within are several good paintings, and, in the floor of the *diaeta*, a picture executed in marble *opus sectile*. The other side of the street is occupied by shops; no. 14, a *caupona* well stocked with *amphorae*. The largest shop, on the corner (IV, 15–16), has an impressive counter, faced with polychrome marble and containing eight *dolia* for the storing of cereals.

Continuing the descent of Cardo V, note a small shop (right; IV, 17) with a priapic painting next to the counter, remains of nuts, lamps and utensils, etc, and a Judas window from the adjoining house. In the lane to the left, Vicolo Meridionale, is another *pistrinum*, or bakery, where the iron door of the oven remains closed despite the collapse of the vault, and with a stable for the asses that turned the mills. The **House of the Cloth (U)** yielded pieces of ancient fabric in which the design is still discernible. Note the unusual arrangement of the stairs. Beyond, you again approach the terraced quarter occupied by the houses of the rich.

On the right is the **House of the Deer (V)**, the grandest dwelling yet discovered at Herculaneum, with a frontage of 43m. The entrance leads into a covered atrium, from which an enclosed corridor leads to the spacious triclinium. The latter is painted with architectural motifs on black and red panels and paved in marble intarsia. Behind, in an equally elegantly-decorated *oecus*, stood a statuette of a satyr with a wineskin, removed for safekeeping to the Museo Archeologico in Naples, and represented here by a modern copy. The kitchen, latrine, and *apotheca* form a compact little block to the right. In the garden were found the two delicately executed groups of deer at bay, after which the house is named (now replaced by copies: the originals are in the Museo Archeologico). The garden is surrounded by an enclosed corridor, lit by windows and decorated with panels of cupids playing (again, most of these have been removed to the Museo Archeologico); in this, the latest development of the peristyle, the columns have finally disappeared. In the centre is a summer triclinium flanked by two lovely smaller rooms, in one of which stood the vigorously indelicate statue of the drunken Hercules urinating, now in the garden. The far walk opens onto a terrace where an arbour, flanked by flower beds and siesta rooms, overlooks a sun balcony. Originally, this terrace opened directly onto the sea, commanding a view from Posillipo to Sorrento and Capri.

Insula Orientalis I

The insula across the street consists of only two houses, both planned in an individual manner dictated by their situation; some of their rooms lie at a lower level and have yet to be explored. The **House of the Gem (W)**, named from an engraved stone found in it, has an unusual atrium with buttress-like pilasters and a side door that opens through a *dipylon* (or double door) towards the irregular sunken garden. The latrine preserves an inscription (perhaps the work of a servant) recording a visit by a famous doctor. The floor of the triclinium is 'carpeted' in fine mosaic.

The **House of the Relief of Telephus (X)**, the most extensive of the Herculanean mansions, is built around two sides of the House of the Gem and at two levels on the hillside. The walls were partially overthrown by the rush of mud that brought down the *Quadriga* reliefs (seen on either side of the entrance) from some higher public building. The atrium has colonnades on three sides. The original *oscilla*, circular marble panels depicting satyrs, have been rehung between the columns. On the north side, small doors lead to the servants' quarters and stables. Descend a steep passage to the peristyle, which surrounds the garden, at the centre of which is an azure basin. Off the south walk are the ruins of a once grand room (8.5m by 6m), with a polychrome marble floor; the reconstructed marble dado of one wall demonstrates the palatial standards of this rich dwelling. In an adjacent room is a relief of the myth of Telephus, a late work executed academically in the Classical manner.

The South Terrace

Below the terrace are the public baths known as the **Terme Suburbane (Y)**, probably of late construction and surviving in a good state. Nearby is the cenotaph of Marcus Nonius Balbus, a celebrated citizen and benefactor of the town, to whose family no fewer than ten statue bases or commemorative epigraphs have been found. A fine equestrian statue is preserved in the Museo Archeologico (*see p. 84*). Near this cenotaph another statue stood, the head of which has recently been found. The south terrace is supported by barrel vaults, formerly used as warehouses and boatyards. Three hundred skeletons of people who had tried to flee the catastrophe were found here, along with their valuables. In 1982 a Roman boat was also found, with the skeleton of the rower and a soldier. The area above the barrel vaults was a **Sacred Area (Z)**, with various rooms and two temples next to each other—one dedicated to Venus, with an altar and the remains of a fresco of a garden; to the left of the entrance is a

Detail of the Telephus relief: Achilles consults the Delphic oracle, and is told that the Greek fleet will only reach Troy with Telephus' guidance.

rudder, an attribute of Venus Fortuna, guardian of sailors. The other temple is dedicated to four gods: Minerva, Neptune, Mercury and Vulcan. Archaising reliefs, probably dating from the Augustan period, have recently been found and are displayed *in situ*.

The base of another statue to M. Nonius Balbus stands before the proscenium of the **theatre**, which lies partially buried to the west (*entrance at no. 119 Corso Ercolano; apply at the office*). The visit is interesting less for the theatre itself, the best of which was rifled by d'Elbeuf, than for the impression it gives of the daring of the 18th-century excavators.

Ercolano and its environs

Ercolano was built in the Middle Ages on the lava covering the stream of mud that overwhelmed Herculaneum. Just south of the excavations is the Miglio d'Oro, where the road is flanked by sumptuous 18th-century summer homes. One of these, Villa Campolieto, has been restored to its original splendour and occasionally hosts special events (*open Tues–Sun 10–1*).

Nearby **Portici**, smoky with factories, is the alleged birthplace of the rebel leader Masaniello (*see p. 23*). It is noted for its Palazzo Reale, begun in 1739 by Canevari, which now houses the Faculty of Agriculture of Naples University; this was the birthplace of Charles IV of Spain (1748) and was occupied by Pius IX in 1849–50. Between Naples and Portici (Granatello) the first Italian train was inaugurated on 3rd October 1839, by Ferdinand II. The Museo Ferroviario Nazionale (National Railway Museum, Corso San Giovanni a Teduccio; *open Mon–Sat 9–2, T: 081 472003, www.ferroviecampania.it*) occupies the magnificent premises of the railway works constructed by Ferdinand II in 1840 at Pietrarsa. Here are dozens of locomotives (largely steam engines), trucks and carriages, station furnishings, and static and moving model train sets. There is even the Bayard locomotive that made that first run in 1839.

CORAL FISHING AT TORRE DEL GRECO

Throughout the Vesuvian region, shops sell coral jewellery made in Torre del Greco. Though today little more than a sprawling suburb of Naples, this was once a proud, independent town with a time-honoured tradition of coral fishing and manufacturing. The *coralline* were boats that, from the 15th century until quite recently, swept the sea floor with an *ingegno*, an ingenious tool that picks up only coral. Part of the raw coral was sold at Livorno, then Italy's chief centre of coral working; but before long Torre developed its own workshops for cutting and modelling the 'red gold'. In the early 19th century, thanks to a French entrepreneur named Martin, the making of coral jewellery reached a semi-industrial level, as large numbers of master coral cutters were brought in from Trapani and Rome. A craft centre emerged, offering objects of a deliberately 'antique' nature, inspired by the finds at Pompeii and Herculaneum. Examples of these may be seen, by appointment, at Torre del Greco's Museo del Corallo (*Via Montedoro 61; T: 081 881 1225*).

Today, Torre del Greco is the only centre of coral working in Europe. Its craftsmen transform anything from 30 to 90 tonnes of raw material every year. The coral reefs of the Gulf of Naples are long gone, of course, as are most of the immense reefs discovered off the coast of Sicily in 1880. Most of the necklaces and other coral jewellery you see in the shops are made from Pacific Ocean coral. But there is no notion of sustainable growth in the coral industry, and these resources, too, will one day come to an end…

THE VESUVIAN SHORE

The Vesuvian shore, whose black sands Ruskin found so threatening, extends south and east of Naples. The area today is a big, sprawling suburb, with really only one place of interest: Torre Annunziata, the flourishing centre of the pasta industry, which was founded in 1319 beside a chapel of the Annunciation. A bathing and thermal resort, it is crowded with Neapolitans in summer. Recent excavations here have revealed two patrician villas, probably belonging to a residential suburb of Pompeii called Oplontis.

The Villa of Poppaea at Oplontis

Via Sepolcri, Torre Annunziata; open daily April–Oct 8.30–7.30, last entry 6; Nov–March 8.30–5, last entry 3.30; T: 081 857 5347, www.pompeiisites.org

Curiously, the place-name Oplontis has only been found once, in the *Tabula Peutingeriana*, a map of the road network that crossed the Roman Empire; but the town must have been of some importance, as two large buildings have been uncovered: the Villa of Craxsus (*not open to the public*), possibly a business centre, and the Villa di Poppea, thought to be the villa of Nero's second wife, Poppaea Sabina. The latter comprises a vast peristyle, baths and a monumental piscina, as well as sitting and dining rooms and a kitchen. After the emperor's death, it probably passed to another owner, who was having work done on it at the time of the eruption. The bodies of many victims were found here, along with gold jewellery and coins.

Compared to the sites of Pompeii and Herculaneum, the Villa of Poppaea, unearthed between 1964 and 1984, is on a far more intimate scale, and is a showcase for some of the finest Roman wall paintings known, their colours still remarkably vibrant and sumptuous. The atrium—the first room you and the visitor of AD 79 would enter—sets the standard for the rest of the villa, with its mosaic floor and exquisite wall decoration. Skilfully painted architectural details such as columns, architraves, colonnades, false doors and partitions created the illusion of space, a technique used throughout the villa.

The decoration of this elegant residence (the older parts date from the 1st century BC) is of the most outstanding quality. The designs in the salons or sitting rooms

present a glass bowl of pomegranates, a wicker basket of fruit covered with a fine cloth, a trolley carrying what appears to be a cake, while on a wall of the triclinium, where guests would dine lying on cots, is a remarkably realistic basket of figs. Landscapes and theatrical backdrops were another favourite device in the decorative scheme, populated with eye-catching details such as masks, peacocks and

Left and opposite: Butterfly and bird decoration, from the garden corridor at Oplontis.

musical instruments. These can be seen in the *calidarium*, *cubicula*, and sitting rooms. Even the corridors linking the various rooms of the villa were gloriously decorated with closely-observed details of birds eating fruit, with lavish fourth-style (*see p. 90*) motifs on the ceilings.

Like all high-status homes, the villa had its own baths; and further evidence of the luxury of the complex can be seen in the gardens (*viridaria*) and pool. Some of the gardens were internal, and the decoration of the walls echoed their luxuriant foliage, as well

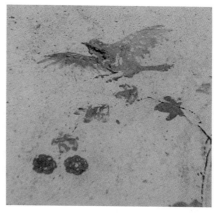

as garden features such as urns and fountains (in the second style). The huge pool, tilted south to let the water drain away (in the manner of a modern 'infinity' pool), ran down the side of the villa, overlooked by a shady corridor, the white walls of which were decorated in the fourth style with exceptionally fine still-life details: a tiny blue bird about to alight on a twig; a butterfly taking off from a blackberry bush; peacock feathers; goats, frogs and lizards in naturalistic settings. Surrounded by its tranquil gardens and overlooking the sea, the Villa of Poppaea must have been a gracious, luxurious residence away from busy Pompeii.

Castellammare di Stabia

The Sorrentine peninsula begins at this modern town, on the southeast shore of the Bay of Naples. The ancient city of *Stabiae*, northeast of the present town, was destroyed by Sulla in 89 BC but was afterwards rebuilt, only to be swallowed up by the eruption of AD 79. Pliny the Elder met his death on the beach at Stabiae. The site was repopulated, and takes its name from a 9th-century castle, which Charles I of Anjou restored when he built the town walls. In 1738 some ancient villas were brought to light by excavation, and further Roman remains are visible on the neighbouring hill of Varano.

In the centre of the town, the shady park of the Villa Comunale gives a wide vista over the gulf. To the left lies Piazza del Municipio with the observatory, the duomo (1587, much altered), and the *municipio*, formerly Palazzo Farnese. Further southwest are the harbour and the arsenal (1783), where some of the most powerful Italian warships have been built, and the Terme Stabiane, a spa. On a hill to the left is the castle, enlarged by the Swabians (1197) and again by Charles I of Anjou (1266). A pleasant walk may be taken to (2km) the Villa Quisisana (now a hotel), a royal residence from 1310 to 1860, where the park commands a fine panorama.

A turning on the left at the beginning of the road for Gragnano leads to San Marco, on the Varano plain. Here are the extensive remains of two **Roman villas** (*Via*

Passeggiata Archeologica, open daily April–Oct 8.30–7.30, last entry 6; Nov–March 8.30–5, last entry 3.30; T: 081 857 5347, www.pompeiisites.org), both with remnants of painted decoration, unfortunately damaged in the 1980 earthquake. The Antiquarium di Stabiae (*Via Marco Mario 2, closed for renovation at the time of writing; T: 081 871 4541*) contains objects from the Bronze Age to the Middle Ages, and material from the excavations in particular: frescoes, pavement fragments, Greek, Samnite, Italic and Roman vases. ·

But the best thing to do in Castellammare is leave the hustle and bustle of the town for the cool, green hills above, popular with Neapolitans seeking respite from the summer heat. The ascent of Monte Faito (1131m) by cable railway, from the Circumvesuviana station, takes roughly 8mins, services connecting with the trains. The road (15km of hairpin bends) climbs round the Villa Quisisana. The Belvedere di Monte Faito commands an extensive view; a track of 7km offers a magnificent circular walk along the ridge and round a fine wood. The ascent of Monte Sant'Angelo (1443m), the highest of the Monti Lattari, may be made (guide desirable) either from Monte Faito or from Pimonte; it takes 4–5hrs, the descent almost as much. The panorama encompasses the gulfs of Salerno and Naples, extending northwards to the Gulf of Gaeta.

PRACTICAL INFORMATION

GETTING AROUND

• **By road:** For Vesuvius from Naples or Salerno, take Autostrada A3 to the Ercolano exit, then follow the signs to the Osservatorio Vesuviano. There are buses to the Observatory from Ercolano. To Pompeii from Naples or Salerno, take Autostrada A3 to the exit marked Pompei, then follow the signs to the *scavi* (excavations). Coach excursions daily from Naples, Piazza Municipio. The modern town of Ercolano can be reached by Road 18 or Autostrada A3/E45. Once in Ercolano, Road 18 passes the entrance to the excavations.

• **By rail:** To ascend Vesuvius from Naples, take the Circumvesuviana

Railway to Pugliano, then proceed by bus. The state railway (Trenitalia) to Portici-Ercolano is more useful for visitors arriving from Salerno and the south. The Circumvesuviana railway (Sorrento line) runs from Naples to Pompei Villa dei Misteri at 35–50mins intervals. The state railway (Trenitalia) to Pompei station is more useful for visitors arriving from Salerno and the south. For Herculaneum take the Circumvesuviana railway (Sorrento line) to Pugliano station, then on foot along the wide road descending seaward from the station (10mins walk).

INFORMATION OFFICES

Naples Assessorato Regionale al Turismo,

Via Santa Lucia 81, T: 081 796 1111,
www.turismoregionecampania.it
Azienda Autonoma di Cura Soggiorno e
Turismo, Palazzo Reale, T: 081 551
2701 or 081 402 394.
Ente Provinciale per il Turismo, Piazza
dei Martiri 58, T: 081 405 311,
www.ept.napoli.it. Branch offices at
Capodichino Airport, T: 081 780 5761;
Piazza del Gesù Nuovo 7, T: 081 552
3328; Stazione Centrale, T: 081 268
779; Stazione Mergellina, T: 081 761
2102.
Castellammare di Stabia Piazza
Matteotti 34, T: 081 871 1334.
Pompeii Via Sacra 1, T: 081 850 7255.

HOTELS

See the listings for Naples (*pp. 129–30*)
or Sorrento and the Amalfi Coast (*pp.
255–56*).

RESTAURANTS

Ercolano
€ **Casa Rossa 1888 al Vesuvio**.
Restaurant-pizzeria, the little sister of
the famous Casa Rossa at Torre del
Greco. Closed Tues. Via Vesuvio 30, T:
081 777 9763.
Pompei
€€€ **Principe**. ■ Refined restaurant
offering traditional and creative cuisine.
Closed Sun evening and midday Mon.
Piazza Bartolo Longo 8, T: 081 850
5566.
€€ **Posto di Ristoro**. This is the
restaurant within the site, located
behind the Forum. Food and service are
quite acceptable. Open as the ruins.
Sant'Anastasia
€ **'E Curti**. ■ Excellent traditional

osteria; closed Sun and in Aug. Via
Garibaldi 57, T: 081 531 2797.
Somma Vesuviana
€ **La Fregola**. Simple restaurant on
the road to Santa Maria a Castello.
Closed Mon and two weeks in Nov. Via
Santa Maria a Castello 45, T: 081 893
2229.
€€ **La Lanterna**. Regional dishes and
good pizza. Closed Mon and mid-Aug.
Via Colonnello Aliperta 8, T: 081 899
1843.
Torre del Greco
€€ **Casa Rossa 1888**. ■ Restaurant
(with rooms) serving exquisite home-
made pasta and local delicacies. Via
Mortelle 60, T: 081 883 1549.

LOCAL SPECIALITIES

Torre del Greco is the leading centre
in the Mediterranean for the production
of coral jewellery and cameos. These are
available at shops throughout the
region.

FESTIVALS & EVENTS

Somma Vesuviana *Santa Maria a
Castello* Pilgrimage to the sanctuary followed by evening fireworks, first Sat
after Easter.
Torre del Greco *Festa dei Quattro Altari*
Eight days after Corpus Christi four
theatrical 'altars' are set up in the town
centre, 'paintings' of coloured powders
are made on several church floors, and
there is a procession from the church of
Santa Croce; *Immacolata Concezione* A
statue of the Madonna is carried in procession through the streets, 8 Dec.

CAPRI, ISCHIA & PROCIDA

That Capri is one of the most beautiful spots on our small planet is no secret. With its perennial sunshine, its pure air, and its luxuriant, almost tropical vegetation, it is the pearl of the Bay of Naples. The best time to visit the island is out of season (November–March), or mid-week, when the crowds are elsewhere. In all fairness it must be said that the island's appeal as a resort has been a boon as well as a burden: it was Capri's natural beauty that led an eminent Roman, probably the emperor Tiberius, to build a luxurious beach house here (the famous Villa Jovis); and Swedish physician Axel Munthe's Villa San Michele, which stands on the site of another Roman patrician home, is hardly less impressive. Development in the late 19th and early 20th centuries has given the towns of Capri and Anacapri an aristocratic air that other southern Italian resorts lack; and everywhere the views over sea and coast more than compensate for any inconvenience that sharing them with varying numbers of fellow travellers may cause.

Motor traffic on the island is severely restricted, so if you are driving, leave your car on the mainland and use the bus to get around. It is possible to visit Capri from Naples in one day by taking an early morning hydrofoil, catching the bus to Anacapri at midday and returning by a hydrofoil leaving Marina Grande in the late afternoon or evening. Even better, you could combine Capri with Sorrento by spending the night on the island and leaving for Sorrento by an early morning boat. All who can, however, should devote two or more days to Capri, to allow time for the ascent of Monte Solaro and a trip by boat along the east coast of the island.

Geography

A small island 6km long and 3km wide, Capri lies 5km from the Punta della Campanella on the Sorrentine Peninsula, of which it forms the geological continuation. It is a mountainous island, with a precipitous and almost inaccessible coast, abounding in caves and fantastic rocks.

The clearest sense of the geography of the island comes from studying it as you arrive by boat, on approaching Marina Grande. On the right hand side, to the right of the harbour moles, is a stretch of shingly beach. This, known as the 'Baths of Tiberius', still preserves a segment of Roman harbour wall. Above the shoreline stood a vast villa, the Palazzo a Mare, thought to have been a summer retreat of the emperor Augustus. There are only negligible remains, though the church of San Costanzo, built over a part of it, preserves four ancient columns. On the eminence above this, is Anacapri, with the Phoenician Steps leading up to it, crossing the modern road. The cliff rises towards the centre of the island, to the heights of Monte Solaro (589m). On the high cliff on the left stand the remains of the Villa Jovis. In the central saddle sits Capri town itself.

HISTORY OF CAPRI

Capri was inhabited in prehistoric times; later, it became Greek and then Roman. Augustus, who visited it personally, obtained it from the Neapolitans in exchange for the larger and more fertile island of Ischia. His contributions to Capri included roads, aqueducts and villas.

The wider fame of the island began with Tiberius, who retired to Capri in AD 27. The story of the magnificence, profligacy and horrors of his ten years' residence was unknown before the writings of Tacitus and Suetonius, but the publicity value of these undoubted exaggerations ensures their perpetuation. On the dominant points of the island Tiberius erected several villas, dedicated (probably) to the major deities of the Roman Pantheon. The most important of these structures was the Villa Jovis. In 182 the emperor Commodus, son of Marcus Aurelius, assigned the island as a place of exile for his wife Crispina and his sister Lucilla.

During the Middle Ages Capri was occupied by the Saracens, whose lasting influence can be seen in local building conventions, especially the barrel-vaulted roofs of many homes and churches. In 1806 the island was taken by the British fleet and strongly fortified; Sir Hudson Lowe (later governor of St Helena, during Napoleon's last exile and death) was appointed governor. In 1808 it was retaken by the French, and in 1813 it was restored to Ferdinand I of the Two Sicilies.

For more than 150 years Capri has provided a home for expatriates, artists and eccentrics. Residents have included Emil von Behring (1854–1917), discoverer of a successful inoculation against tetanus; Axel Munthe, the Swedish physician; Maxim Gorky (1868–1936), who lived here in 1907–13 and ran a school for revolutionaries visited by Lenin, Stalin, and Chaliapin; and the writer Norman Douglas (1868–1952).

CAPRI TOWN

Capri, a small, quaint town with vaulted houses and labyrinthine streets, lies 142m above sea level in the saddle between Punta del Capo and Monte Solaro. From the Marina Grande you get there by funicular railway, by road (3km), by footpath (Strada Campo di Pisco), or by steps (Via Truglio and Via San Francesco).

The road from Marina Grande

The road from the Marina Grande passes the **church of San Costanzo**, built in the 10th and 11th centuries and enlarged c. 1330. It is in the form of a Greek cross, with a Byzantine dome and small, characteristic campanile. Giant clam shells serve as stoups. Eight ancient *cipollino* columns from the nearby Palazzo a Mare once flanked the nave. Four were removed in 1755 to decorate the royal chapel at Caserta. Four remain. Little remains of Palazzo a Mare, though there is a surviving exedra below the cliff to the west. Further on, the road joins up with those from the Marina Piccola (southwest) and Anacapri (northwest), and after a few more paces ends on Piazza Umberto Primo, a broad expanse overlooking the Marina Grande.

The piazzetta

Behind Piazza Umberto Primo is the enclosed cobbled space, filled with cafés, which *capresi* call the 'piazzetta'. Here stands the 17th-century **church of Santo Stefano**, approached by a flight of steps. The interior contains, in the chapel left of the high altar, a fragment of inlaid pavement from the Villa Jovis (*see p. 220 below*) and, in the chapel to the right, the tombs of Giacomo and Vincenzo Arcucci by Naccherino.

Opposite the church entrance is the Palazzo Cerio, where Joan I used to stay. The mansion now houses a small private museum of natural history and antiquities (*open Tues, Wed, Fri, Sat 10–1, Thur 3–7; T: 081 837 0858*) displaying objects found in excavations at the turn of the century by the physician and naturalist Ignazio Cerio.

Walks around Capri

Several fine walks may be taken in the environs of Capri. To the southwest are (20mins) the ruins of the Castiglione (249m; *closed to the public*), a medieval castle constructed with ancient materials, and the **Belvedere Cannone**, which affords a superb view of the Faraglioni rocks and the Marina Piccola. To reach the latter, you ascend the steps of the church of Santo Stefano, follow (right) Via Madre Serafina and pass the church of Santa Teresa. About 500m further on, a narrow path to the right climbs to the Castiglione. Bear left. More steps and a shaded path lead to the scenic overlook. On the north slope of the hill, in 1786, the antiquary Hadrawa, secretary to the Austrian ambassador, discovered five ancient rooms with painted and marble decoration.

To reach the **Certosa di San Giacomo** (*open Tues–Sun 9–2; T: 081 837 6218*) leave the piazza by a vaulted passage in the south corner and follow Via Vittorio Emanuele to the Quisisana Hotel. Via Federico Serena, to the right of the hotel, climbs and then descends to the Carthusian monastery founded in 1371 by Giacomo Arcucci, secretary to Joan I, who dedicated the monastery to the Apostle James (Giacomo), his namesake. Its characteristic hump-backed roofscape, so typical of this whole coast, can be particularly well appreciated from Via Matteotti. The fresco above the portal of the deconsecrated Gothic church, showing the *Madonna and Child* with the founder and his queen, might be a work of Andrea Vanni, a Sienese painter and politician who acted as ambassador to the popes in Avignon. Joan was a great supporter of the Avignon papacy. When she was deposed and taken into captivity, Arcucci fell from favour. His lands were sequestered and he took refuge in this monastery, where he died and was buried. In 1553 the monastery was sacked by the Turkish corsair Dragut, 'the drawn sword of Islam', who ravaged this coast following the defeat of his great adversary Andrea Doria. The last monks left the charterhouse in 1807, when it was dissolved by Joachim Murat, brother-in-law of Napoleon. Most of the complex, including its two cloisters, is derelict today. The old refectory houses a small museum with works by the German artist Karl Wilhelm Diefenbach, who lived on Capri from

Typical 'Saracenic' hump-backed roofs of the Certosa di San Giacomo.

1900 until his death in 1913; his huge, dark canvases hang gloomily in the dilapidated space. Via Matteotti leads to **Via Krupp**, a paved path of hairpin bends built by Friedrich Krupp, the German armaments manufacturer. The path used to provide a convenient descent to Marina Piccola, but rockfalls have led to its closure (though locals do sometimes scale the gate and use it).

The **Punta di Tragara** can be reached in about 20mins. Via Camerelle, to the left of the Quisisana Hotel, skirts a series of brick vaults known as the *camerelle*, probably the arches of a road connecting the villas of Tragara and Castiglione. The vaults now operate as luxury boutiques. You ascend slightly to reach the Belvedere di Tragara; steps by the café and a path lead from here to the Punta di Tragara, from which the view includes (to the east) the flat rock, known as Il Monacone, from a species of seal once native to Capri.

What is perhaps Capri's most famous nature walk includes the **Arco Naturale** (20mins) and the **Grotta di Matromania** (10mins more). From the northeast corner of the piazzetta follow the narrow Via Botteghe, Via Fuorlovade, and Via Croce. Where the latter divides take Via Matromania (right); after 8mins keep to the left, and after 8mins more descend the steps (left) to the Arco Naturale, a fantastic archway in the rock. Returning to the path continue to descend to (10mins) the Grotta di Matromania, which opens towards the east. The cave ends in a semicircular apse, and there are various small chambers with walls in *opus reticulatum*. This is probably a sanctuary of Cybele, the *Mater Magna*; the erroneous belief that it was a Mithraeum was exploded when it was learned that a Mithraic relief in the Naples museum, supposedly discovered here, had in fact been found elsewhere on the island.

THE ISLAND OF CAPRI

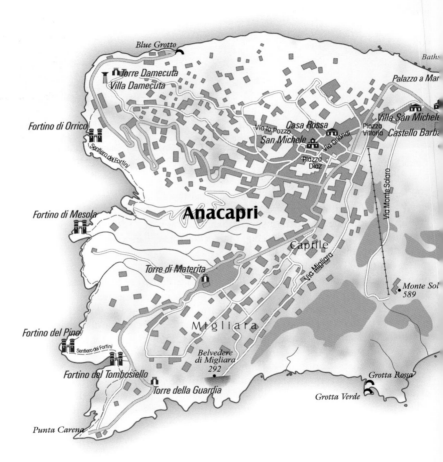

Blue Grotto

Torre Damecuta
Villa Damecuta

Baths

Palazzo a Mar

Fortino di Orrico

Villa San Michele

Casa Rossa
Via lo Pozzo
San Michele
Piazza
Vittoria
Castello Barba
Via Orlandi

Sentiero dei Fortini

Piazza
Diaz

Anacapri

Fortino di Mesola

Via Monte Solaro

Caprile

Torre di Materita

Via Migliara

Monte Sol
589

Migliara

Fortino del Pino
Sentiero dei Fortini

Belvedere
di Migliara
292

Grotta Rossa

Fortino del Tombosiello

Grotta Verde

Torre della Guardia

Punta Carena

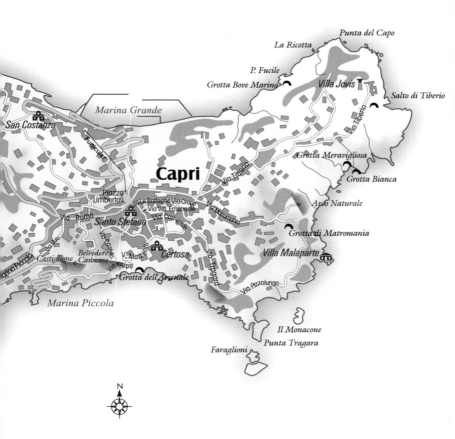

Punta del Capo

La Ricotta

P. Fucile

Grotta Bove Marino

Villa Jovis

Salto di Tiberio

Marina Grande

San Costanzo

Via Tiberio

Grotta Meravigliosa

Capri

Via Tiberio

Grotta Bianca

Piazza
Umberto I

Le Botteghe Via Croce
Via Vitt. Emanuele

Arco Naturale

Via Roma

Santo Stefano

Via Camerelle

Via Matermania

Grotta di Matromania

Via Sopramonte

Certosa

Villa Malaparte

Castiglione

Belvedere
Cannone

V. Mulo

Via Krupp

Via Tragara

Via Pizzolungo

Marina Piccola

Grotta dell'Arsenale

Il Monacone

Punta Tragara

Faraglioni

N

Villa Jovis

A lovely walk of just under an hour leads to the Villa Jovis (*open daily 9–dusk; T: 081 837 0381; www.villajovis.it*), known to the Capriots as the Palazzo di Tiberio. From Via Croce take the rising Via Tiberio (*left; follow the central strip of paving*) and pass the small church of Santa Croce. Further on bear to the right, passing near the remains of a *pharos*, or lighthouse, probably built by Augustus and overthrown by an earthquake after the death of Tiberius. Here is the **Salto di Tiberio** (296m), the almost vertical rock off which, it is fabled, Tiberius pushed his victims. A few more paces lead to the ruined villa, a residence of palatial proportions with several storeys. It was systematically explored for the first time in 1932–35, by which time most of its mosaic pave-

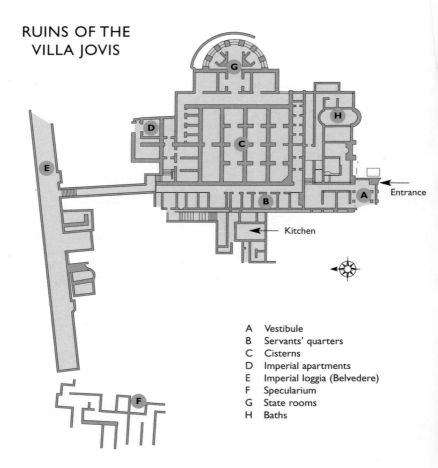

RUINS OF THE VILLA JOVIS

Entrance

Kitchen

A   Vestibule
B   Servants' quarters
C   Cisterns
D   Imperial apartments
E   Imperial loggia (Belvedere)
F   Specularium
G   State rooms
H   Baths

ments and other decorative elements had already been carried off. The ruins cover an area of 7,000m square, centering on a rectangular zone occupied by four large cisterns hewn out of the rock and divided into intercommunicating cells.

A From the entrance to the archaeological park a brick path mounts to the vestibule, a small atrium conserving the lower sections of four *cipollino* marble columns. A ramped corridor with traces of mosaic flooring leads up. From here arrows direct you anti-clockwise round the site.

B From the vestibule a corridor leads to the west wing, which was the servants' quarters, with remains of storerooms and the kitchen, set apart from the rest of the structure. It is not known whether this was the service kitchen, or the kitchen where the emperor's own meals were prepared. Tiberius was famously afraid of being poisoned, and demanded the strictest controls over the sourcing and preparation of his food.

C Adjacent are the rooms of the guard corps, converted during the Middle Ages into cisterns.

D The imperial apartments occupy only a smallish part of the complex, although the flat terrace occupying the highest point, built on an ancient substructure, was probably also part of them. The room here would have enjoyed a superb view, as the terrace does today: the little chapel of Santa Maria del Soccorso commands perhaps the finest view in Capri, embracing the island itself, the sea, the Punta della Campanella, and the two gulfs. Restored in 1979, the church stands behind an enormous bronze *Madonna*,

brought to the site by a United States Navy helicopter and solemnly blessed by Pope John Paul II.

E From the imperial apartments a corridor and steps descend to the Imperial Loggia or Belvedere, a long (92m) straight porch set into the north rim of the cliff, 20m below the level of the palace. It is thought that Tiberius would take a daily constitutional by walking along it: alcoves with the remains of benches on the landward side provided places to sit and admire the view. The view from the eastern end, down to the water far below, makes it easy to understand how legends of victims being tossed to their deaths could grow up.

F Below the loggia is the so-called Specularium, an enfilade of dank, dripping rooms thought to have been an astronomical observatory, where seers and stargazers would come to interpret the emperor's fate. In his last years Tiberius is said to have become an obsessive consulter of augurs and astrologers.

G To the east, built in a hemicycle, are the state rooms and 'entertainment area', where the emperor would have received guests.

H The baths complex consists of a dressing-room, a *frigidarium*, a *tepidarium*, a *calidarium* (with two semicircular apses), and rooms for the heating and distribution of the water.

ANACAPRI

The trip from Capri to Anacapri is a mere 3km and may be made on foot or by bus. The winding road, hewn out of the rock in 1874 and restored in 1923, ascends, affording a series of beautiful views. On the way you pass the Torre Quattro Venti, near which is the Palazzo Inglese, built c. 1750 by Sir Nathaniel Thorold, and a key point in the French assault of 1808. Formerly the only means of communication between Anacapri and the rest of the island was by the Phoenician Steps (Scala Fenicia), a flight of 800 steps attributable to the Greeks or to Augustus, descending to the Marina Grande. This (now, however, with fewer steps) crosses the road at the chapel of Sant'Antonio, above which are the ruins of the Castello di Barbarossa, destroyed in 1535 by the corsair Kheir-ed Din (known also as Barbarossa). Near the top of the steps is the Villa San Michele (*see below*).

NB: *If the Blue Grotto is closed (which happens in adverse wind conditions), tour groups tend to come to Anacapri to see the church of San Michele. If you want to admire its majolica floor in peace and tranquillity, it is best to come on a day when the boats are visiting the caves.*

Villa San Michele

Open daily Nov–Feb 9–3.30, March 9–4.30, April 9–5, May–Sept 9–6, Oct 9–5; T: 081 837 1401, www.sanmichele.org

Via San Michele leads up (15mins) from Piazza della Vittoria to the Villa San Michele, built by the Swedish doctor Axel Munthe (1857–1949) on the site of one of Tiberius' villas, where a chapel to St Michael subsequently stood (and still stands).

The building of Villa San Michele

From sunrise to sunset I was hard at work in what had been Mastro Vincenzo's garden, digging the foundations of the huge arches of the loggia outside my future home. ... The whole garden was full of thousands and thousands of polished slabs of coloured marble, *africano*, *pavonazzetto*, *giallo antico*, *verde antico*, *cipollino*, *alabastro*, all now forming the pavement of the big loggia, the chapel and some of the terraces. ... When we found the earthenware vase full of Roman coins [my fellow-workers] became tremendously excited. Every *contadino* on the island had been on the lookout for *il tesoro di Timberio* for two thousand years. It was only later on when cleaning these coins that I found amongst them the gold coin fresh as if it had been coined today, indeed the finest likeness of the old emperor I had ever seen.

Axel Munthe, from The Story of San Michele, 1929

The villa and its gardens contain a small collection of antiquities, and copies of famous pieces (mosaics from Pompeii, the bronze *Hermes* from the Villa of the

Papyri). The beautifully kept garden is one of the most luxuriant in Italy; the views from its parapets are stunning. Axel Munthe first came to Naples in his capacity as a doctor, to help with the appalling cholera epidemic that struck the city in 1884. He lived at Villa San Michele from 1896, supervising the design and construction himself, having famously remarked that 'my house must be open to the sun, to the wind, and the voice of the sea, just like a Greek temple, and light, light, light everywhere!' Ironically it was the sunlight he so loved that forced to him to leave, in 1910, following an eye complaint. He moved to the shadier Torre di Materita (*see p. 224 below*).

Anacapri village

Anacapri (284m), a village of 5,000 inhabitants, recalls Sicily with its white houses and quasi-oriental roofs. From Piazza della Vittoria the main street (Via Orlandi) bears right, past the **Casa Rossa**, a Moorish-Byzantinesque folly built by an American, Colonel J.C. MacKowen, between 1876 and 1898, with a dedication in Greek above the door: 'Hail to the city of fainéants!' A street to the right leads to Piazza San Nicola, with the octagonal **church of San Michele** (*open Nov–March 9.30–5.30, April–June 9.30–5, July–Oct 9.30–7; T: 081 837 2396*), finished in 1719. It possesses a majolica pavement showing the *Story of Eden*, executed by Leonardo Chiaiese in 1761 to a design by Solimena. You can tour the church on duckboards to view it from close

Adam and Eve are banished from the Garden. Detail of the mid-18th-century majolica pavement of the church of San Michele, Anacapri..

quarters, or climb a spiral stair to the organ loft from where the whole design can be appreciated. The plan of the church is ascribed to Domenico Antonio Vaccaro. The four sides on the main axes are slightly longer than those on the diagonals, and the vestibule and choir are deeper than the other areas leading off the central space, imparting a longitudinal emphasis to the plan. The architect also uses the pilasters at the points where the vestibule and choir join the central space to lead the eye from one area of the church to the next, placing them at an angle to the main axis.

Walks around Anacapri

The plateau of Migliara (304m), reached in 40mins, commands a striking view of the Faraglioni and the precipices of Monte Solaro. To reach it, take any one of the stony paths that climb southwards from Caprile, joining the former mule track that leads to the Belvedere di Migliara; or simply pick up the old mule track left of the Monte Solaro funicular station in Anacapri. Then return via the Torre della Guardia, above the Punta Carena, and the 15th-century Torre di Materita, where Axel Munthe lived after 1910.

A road runs west from the Chiesa Parrochiale to the Mulino a Vento and to the 12th-century **Torre di Damecuta**, once a watch-tower against pirates, commanding superb views of the sea, and subsequently also owned by Axel Munthe. Next to the tower another Roman villa (*open daily 9–dusk*), smaller but similar to the Villa Jovis, has been excavated. Damaged by ashfalls after the eruption of Vesuvius in AD 79, it was subsequently abandoned. The site was fortified by the French and British in the 19th century. Like the Villa Jovis, it had a semicircular 'entertainment area', and a belvedere on the sea. Remains of the living quarters (including a loggia perched hair-raisingly above the abyss) have been excavated (*no admission*) below the watch-tower. The view of the Phlegraean Fields is particularly fine at sunset. A path descends to the Blue Grotto (*described below*), and to the Sentiero dei Fortini, a lovely waterfront walk passing the remains of four forts.

The ascent of **Monte Solaro** (589m) may be made in about 1hr (or by chair-lift from Piazza della Vittoria in 12mins). From Via Capodimonte take Via Solaro south (left if you are coming from Villa San Michele, right from Piazza Vittoria) to reach the path (signposted) along the slope, which winds south. A steep ascent passes by remains of the English fortifications of 1806–08 to the Crocella saddle (45mins), where a shrine of the Virgin stands. It takes c. 15mins more to reach the summit of Monte Solaro, which is crowned by a ruined castle rebuilt to form a system of panoramic terraces, with a café in season. The wonderful view extends over the bays of Naples and Salerno to the Ponziane islands (northwest), the Apennines (east), and the mountains of Calabria (south).

THE BLUE GROTTO

On the north coast of the island is the Blue Grotto (Grotta Azzurra), a visit to which is the most popular excursion on Capri. The approach is made by sea (*daily 9–dusk*), except when strong north or east winds blow, making entrance to the cave impossible), from the Marina Grande, or from the landing at the base of the footpath from Anacapri (Via Lo Pozzo). The boat from Marina Grande skirts the north side of the island, affording a view of the ruins known as the Baths of Tiberius. The light effects are best between 11am and 1pm.

A marine cavern, the Blue Grotto owes its geological formation to gradual subsidence of the coast, probably since the Roman epoch. Though known in Antiquity, it seems then to have lacked the curious effects of light that are now its great charm. Its possibilities were realised in 1822 by Augusto Ferrara, a Capri fisherman, who in 1826 led August Kopisch, a German poet, and some others to its 'accidental' discovery. Kopisch entered the facts in the register of Pagano's hotel, and these were published in Hans Christian Andersen's novel *The Improvisator*.

Once a nymphaeum of Tiberius, the cavern has, in recent years, yielded a wealth of archaeological material, including several large statues. In addition, underwater explorations in 1976 revealed the existence of niches, platforms, and broad apses hewn out of the rock, in c. 2m of water. The mouth of the cave is barely 1m high, so that even in calm weather, heads have to be ducked.

The interior is 57m long, 30m wide, and 15m high. The sun's rays, entering not directly but through the water, fill the cave with a magical blue light and objects in the water have a beautiful silvery appearance. Near the middle of the grotto is a ledge where boats can land. An adjoining cleft, once supposed to be the beginning of an underground passage to the villa of Damecuta, has been proved to be a natural orifice. Outside the grotto is the beginning of a path ascending to Anacapri.

Boat trips

Those who prefer open horizons to tight spaces like caves will enjoy the *giro*, or voyage around the island by boat. The non-stop trip takes 3–4hrs and begins either from the Marina Grande or the Marina Piccola. (*Excursions daily during the season, April–Sept; on request at other times.*)

Heading east from the Marina Grande, you pass, in succession, the Grotta del Bove Marino, the strangely shaped little point of Fucile (musket), and the rock named La Ricotta (cream cheese). After doubling round Il Capo, you reach the Grotta Bianca and Grotta Meravigliosa, both with stalactites (the second accessible from the land; the first from the sea). The Grotta Bianca's stalagmite formation is described as the 'Madonna', from its resemblance to a statue of the Virgin. Further on are the Faraglione di Matromania and Il Monacone, the latter with Roman remains.

Off the Punta di Tragara are three gigantic rocks called the **Faraglioni**, one of which, La Stella (90m), is connected with the island. The outermost, Lo Scopolo (89m), resembles a sugar-loaf and is the habitat of a rare species of blue lizard.

The boat passes through a natural arch in the central rock. Next comes the Grotta dell'Arsenale, supposed to have been used for repairing ships. Beyond the Marina Piccola, at the foot of Monte Solaro, is the **Grotta Verde**, with beautiful green light effects (*best 10–11; inaccessible in a strong south wind*). Not far off is the Grotta Rossa. The voyage along the west side of the island up to the Blue Grotto is less interesting.

PRACTICAL INFORMATION

GETTING AROUND

• **By sea:** Ferries run daily from Naples (1hr 15mins), Sorrento (45mins) and Ischia (1hr, April–Oct), and seasonally from Amalfi and Positano (April–Oct). There is also a daily hydrofoil service from Naples (40–45mins), Sorrento (20mins–1hr) and Ischia (50mins, April–Oct), Positano (50mins) and Amalfi (65mins). Visit www.campaniatrasporti.it for schedules.

• **By land:** Frequent buses scurry from the main square in Capri town to Marina Grande, Marina Piccola and Anacapri; and Capri is famous for its convertible-limousine taxis, though most of the antique models are now gone. A funicular railway connects the town and its harbour (services every 15mins). Porters with electric trolleys can take your luggage around; hire them from beside the bus terminus on Via Roma.

INFORMATION OFFICES

Anacapri Ufficio Informazioni e di Accoglienza Turistica, Via G. Orlandi19/a, T: 081 837 1524.
Capri Ufficio Informazioni e di Accoglienza Turistica, Piazza Umberto I, T: 081 837 0686; Azienda Autonoma di Cura Soggiorno e Turismo, Piazzetta Ignazio Cerio 11, T: 081 837 5308, www.capritourism.com; Piazza Umberto I, T: 081 837 0686.
Marina Grande Ufficio Informazioni e di Accoglienza Turistica, Banchina del Porto, T: 081 837 0634.

HOTELS

Anacapri
€€€ **Capri Palace**. Recently renovated, transformed and promoted to a luxury hotel, with classic Mediterranean architecture, exquisite Louis XVI-style furnishings, majolica and stone paving, and stunning views over the open Mediterranean Sea and the Bay of Naples. Open all year. Via Capodimonte 2, T: 081 978 0111, www.capri-palace.com
€€ **Casa Caprile**. 24 rooms, all pleasantly furnished, and a garden with ficus, mangroves, palms, pines, cypress and other exotic plants. Open all year. Via Follicara 9, T: 081 837 3948, www.casacaprile.com
€€ **Caesar Augustus**. ■ On a cliff 300m above the sea, offering the most spectacular vistas and recently renovated interiors. Open April–Oct. Via G. Orlandi 4, T: 081 837 3395, www.caesar-augustus.com
€€ **Mulino**. A new establishment at the verdant west end of the island; each room has a private terrace with view over the surrounding park. Via La Fabbrica 9, T: 081 838 2084, www.mulino-capri.com
€€ **San Michele**. Pleasant atmosphere and comfortable rooms, pool and large garden. Open April–Oct. Via G. Orlandi 1, T: 081 837 1427, www.sanmichele-capri.com
€ **Bouganville**. Just 12 rooms with enchanting view of the centre. Open all year. Viale Tommaso de Tommaso 6, T: 081 837 3641, www.capri-bougainville.com

Capri

€€€   **Casa Morgano**. A boutique luxury hotel with luxuriant gardens, pool and private panoramic terraces. Via Tragara 6, T: 081 8370158, www.caprionline.com/morgano

€€€   **Punta Tragara**. ■ Designed by Le Corbusier, magnificently set on a clifftop amid lush gardens, two saltwater pools (one heated, with whirlpool). Open Easter–Nov. Via Tragara 57, T: 081 837 0844, www.hoteltragara.com

€€€€   **Grand Hotel Quisisana**. One of Italy's finest hotels, with sumptuous rooms, two restaurants, two pools, tennis courts, sauna, Turkish bath, and a famous bar with panoramic terrace. Open April–Oct. Via Camerelle 2, T: 081 837 0788, www.quisi.com

€€€   **La Scalinatella**. Romantic and refined, spacious rooms, splendid views, attentive staff. Open April–Oct. Via Tragara 8, T: 081 837 0633, www.scalinatella.com

€€   **La Certosella**. Comfortable rooms, excellent cuisine. Open all year. Via Tragara 13, T: 081 837 0713.

€€   **La Minerva**. Situated on the coast, in an authentic oasis of tranquillity just a few minutes' walk down the shopping streets Via Camerelle and Via Vittorio Emanuele. Open all year. Via Occhio Marino, T: 081 837 0374, www.laminervacapri.com

€€   **Luna**. Quiet and central, in a luxuriant garden with good views. Open Easter–Nov. Viale Matteotti 3, T: 081 837 0433, www.lunahotel.com

€€   **Villa Brunella**. ■ Cordial atmosphere in a renovated villa with stepped terraces leading down to pool and sea. Open Easter–Oct. Via Tragara 24,

T: 081 837 0122.

€   **Villa Krupp**. Twelve spacious rooms, in a renovated villa owned and managed by a charming family. Open March–Oct. Via Matteotti 12, T: 081 837 0362.

€€   **Villa Margherita**. Simple family-run guest-house in an old villa. Open most of the year. Via Campo di Teste 2, T: 081 837 0230.

€€   **Villa Sarah**. Family-run establishment with rooms facing sea or garden, home-made cakes and jams at breakfast. Open Easter–Oct. Via Tiberio 3a, T: 081 837 7817, www.villasarah.it

RESTAURANTS

Anacapri

€€€   **L'Olivo**. ■ At long last, gourmet cuisine is available on Capri, though at prices that would make even a Roman emperor flinch. Via Capodimonte 2, at the Capri Palace Hotel, T: 081 978 011.

€€   **Da Gelsomina**. ■ Restaurant (with rooms) serving great local dishes; closed Tues (except in summer) and Jan–Feb. At La Migliara (shuttle from Anacapri on request), T: 081 837 1499.

€€   **Lido del Faro**. Restaurant and lido. Closed Oct–March. Punta Carena, T: 081 837 1798.

€   **Rondinella**. Simple but good traditional fare, including pizza. Closed Thur (except in summer) and Feb. Via G. Orlandi 145, T: 081 837 1223.

Capri

€€€   **Quisi**. The island's most elegant (at the Hotel Quisisana), with indoor and outdoor seating, elaborate cuisine and impeccable service. Closed Nov–March. Via Camerelle 2, T: 081 837 0788.

€€ **Cantinella**. Fine cuisine and beautiful terraced garden overlooking the Faraglioni. Closed Tues, Oct and March. Viale Matteotti 8 (Giardini di Augusto), T: 081 837 0616.

€€ **La Capannina**. Traditional Neapolitan cuisine, served under a pergola in summer. Closed Wed and Nov–March. Via delle Botteghe 14, T: 081 837 0732.

€€ **Le Grottelle**. ■ A secluded restaurant serving excellent seafood, in a grotto with terrace overlooking the sea. Closed Thur except in July–Sept. Via Arco Naturale 13, T: 081 837 5719.

€€ **Pergola**. Garden restaurant with views, a good place to go for pizza. Closed Wed, Jan–Feb. Traversa Palazzo 2, T: 081 837 7414.

€€ **Villa Brunella**. ■ Good food and cordial atmosphere, with a youngish clientèle. Closed Nov–March. Via Tragara 24, T: 081 837 0122.

Marina Grande
€€ **La Scogliera**. Restaurant renowned for its fish dishes. Closed Jan–Feb. Hotel Palatium, Via Marina Grande 225, T: 081 837 6144.

Marina Piccola
€€ Below the tiny fisherman's church of St Andrew are a couple of simple restaurants with terraces over the water, and beaches attached.

FESTIVALS & EVENTS

Anacapri *Sant'Antonio* Feast of the patron, St Anthony of Padua, 13 June; *Anacapri Fa Musica* Concert series, June–Aug; *Concerti al Tramonto*, Classical music at Villa San Michele, June–Aug; Outdoor Film Series, Aug.

Capri *San Costanzo* Patron saint of the island, 14 May; *Santa Maria del Soccorso* Mass on Monte Solaro and festivities all around the island, 7–8 Sept.

PROCIDA & ISCHIA

'Capri or Ischia?' is a dilemma that faces every first-time visitor to the Naples area, and the answer might be: 'Procida'. Perhaps because it is nearer to the mainland than the other islands in the bay, or perhaps because it is the least dramatic, Procida has suffered less from the domesticating influence of tourism. For this reason it remains the most characteristic—the noisiest and most chaotic, but also the most colourful—of the three islands. Ischia, alas, is a prime destination of package tours; fortunately these focus on the thermal resorts on the north coast—Casamicciola Terme, Lacco Ameno and Forio—leaving the west and south of the island relatively untouched. You will not find Ischia as rich in history as Capri, but the geology of the island is thoroughly fascinating: its volcanic origin is responsible for the hot mineral springs that are its chief claim to fame, as well as for the rich soil that yields the excellent *Ischia Bianco* and *Ischia Rosso* wines.

PROCIDA

The island of Procida (3.5km long, pop. 11,000), the ancient *Prochyta,* was created from four craters of basaltic tufa and pumice stone, partly destroyed by the sea to form semicircular bays. The islet of Vivara represents a fifth crater. The main local industries are fishing and vine growing, and the islanders have long been famed for their seamanship. Of the three islands in the Bay of Naples, Procida alone escaped the raids, rape and ransacking of the corsair Dragut.

The town of Procida, with flat-roofed white houses of Eastern aspect flanked by steep cliffs, stretches along the north coast and rises in terraces on the hills beyond. The winding streets have changed little since the Middle Ages. Italian actor-director Massimo Troisi drew on their old charm in the urban scenes of his last film, *Il Postino* (*The Postman*), 1994.

Ferries and hydrofoils land at the marina. In Piazza dei Martiri are a tablet commemorating twelve of the inhabitants of Procida executed after the rising of 1799 (the 'Parthenopean Republic'; see p. 24), and a statue of the statesman Antonio Scialoia, who died on the island in 1877. The castle (now a prison) commands a fine view over Ischia and Monte Epomeo in one direction, and Cape Miseno and the Bay of Naples in the other. In bygone days, escaped prisoners were famous for their appetites; hence the term *sprocidato*, 'escaped from Procida' (in popular slang, 'famished'). Via San Michele climbs to the Terra Murata (91m), the highest point of the island, where the abbey church of San Michele features, in the ceiling, Luca Giordano's *St Michael Defeating Lucifer*. At the southwest end of the island, beyond the castle of Santa Margherita, is the Bay of Chiaiolella, facing Ischia and the tiny olive-clad islet of Vivara.

ISCHIA

Ischia is a collection of craters and lava streams. Its highest point is the conical Monte Epomeo (788m), the north side of an extinct volcano. Adjoining its slope are other craters—Monte Rotaro and Monte Montagnone on the northeast, Monte Trippiti on the east and Monte Imperatore and the hills extending to the Punta dell'Imperatore on the west. Lava streams also formed the promontories of Monte Caruso and Punta Cornacchia on the northwest. About 34km in circumference, Ischia is the largest island in the Bay of Naples. It has a mild climate, and its volcanic slopes are richly covered with sub-tropical vegetation.

HISTORY OF ISCHIA

According to the ancient poets, Ischia was the abode of the giant Typhoeus who, when struck by Jupiter's thunderbolts, expressed his vengeful fury in volcanoes and earthquakes. The Greeks who colonised it called it *Pithecusa* or *Pithecusae*, the Latins *Aenaria* or *Inarime*. In the 9th century it was known as *Iscla*, a corruption of *insula* or, simply, 'the Island', from which its modern name is derived.

The earliest recorded volcanic eruption on the island dates from c. 500 BC; the last was in 1301. Ischia was seized in 474 BC by Hieron of Syracuse, c. 450 by Neapolis, and by the Romans in 326. Augustus exchanged it with the Neapolitans for Capri. It was later taken by the Saracens in 813 and 947, by the Pisans in 1135, by Henry VI and by Frederick II. Finally it came to share the fortunes of Naples.

Ischia was the birthplace of the Marquis of Pescara (1489); his widow Vittoria Colonna (the great platonic love of Michelangelo) retired here in 1525. The island was sacked by the pirate Kheir-ed Din Barbarossa in 1541 and captured in 1547 by the Duke of Guise; it was occupied by Nelson, and in 1815 provided a brief refuge for Murat. The self-portrait of Scottish artist Allan Ramsay in the National Portrait Gallery in London was executed on the island in 1776, when he had come to Ischia to take the thermal cure for an injured arm. The sculptor Canova was rewarded with the title of Marquis of Ischia in 1816, after succeeding in negotiating the restitution of Italian artworks purloined by Napoleonic France.

Celebrated for its hot mineral springs (*season May–Oct; some open all year*) and for sea-bathing, boating and its delightful walks, the whole island is well supplied with hotels, restaurants and bathing establishments. A tour of the island by road (30km) may be made comfortably in half a day.

Ischia town
The *comune* of Ischia consists of the picturesque Ischia Ponte, which stretches for c. 2km along the shore, north of the castle, and the modern Ischia Porto, built around the harbour to the northwest. The two are separated by a fine beach backed by pine woods.

The town was built around a crater lake, the seaward side of which was pierced in 1854 to form the circular harbour, where ferries and hydrofoils dock. The Punta San Pietro on the east and the public park and the mole on the west side command good views. Via Roma and its continuation, Via Vittoria Colonna, lead to Ischia Ponte, beyond which the Ponte Aragonese (1438), a causeway 228m long, leads to the rocky islet fortress of Alfonso the Magnanimous (private).

On the island is the 14th-century **cathedral**, ruined when the English fleet bombarded the invading French in 1806, with a huge crypt (frescoes). The castle, where Vittoria Colonna stayed, rises 111m above the sea (*open daily 9–6; T: 081 984 340*).

The **Museo del Mare**, in the Palazzo dell'Orologio at Ischia Ponte (*open daily 10–12.30 & 5–8; T: 081 981 124*), has an entertaining collection of paintings, prints, photographs, models, tools and equipment illustrating local maritime traditions.

A road diverging to the south from the main road, about 600m west of Ischia Porto, leads (35mins walk) to Fiaiano (198m; view) and (northwest) in 10mins more to the top of Monte Montagnone (311m).

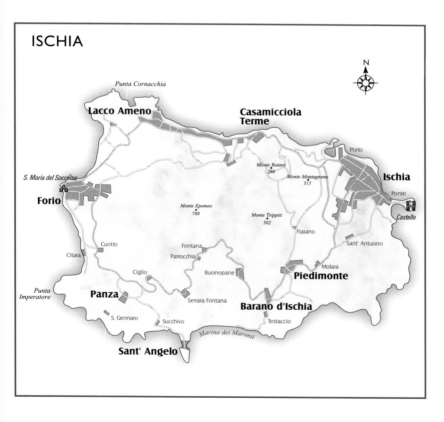

An epitome of the earth

The island ... is an epitome of the whole earth containing within the compass of eighteen miles, a wonderful variety of hills, vales, ragged rocks, fruitful plains, and barren mountains, all thrown together in a most romantic confusion. The air is, in the hottest season, constantly refreshed by cool breezes from the sea. The vales produce excellent wheat and Indian corn, but are mostly covered with vineyards intermixed with fruit-trees. Besides the common kinds, as cherries, apricot, peaches, etc, they produce oranges, limes, almonds, pomegranates, figs, water-melons, and many other fruits unknown to our climates, which lie every where open to the passenger. The hills are the greater part covered to the top with vines, some with chestnut groves, and others with thickets of myrtle and lentiscus. The fields in the northern side are divided by hedgerows of myrtle. Several fountains and rivulets add to the beauty of this landscape, which is likewise set off by the variety of some barren spots and naked rocks. But that which crowns the scene is a large mountain rising out of the middle of the island, (once a terrible volcano, by the ancients called *Mons Epomeus*). Its lower parts are adorned with vines and other fruits; the middle affords pasture to flocks of goats and sheep; and the top is a sandy pointed rock, from which you have the finest prospect in the world, surveying at one view, besides several pleasant islands, lying at your feet, a tract of Italy about three hundred miles in length, from the promontory of Antium to the Cape of Palinurus: the greater part of which hath been sung by Homer and Virgil, as making a considerable part of the travels and adventures of their two heroes.

George Berkeley, Letter to Alexander Pope, 1717

Casamicciola Terme and Lacco Ameno

Casamicciola Terme, on the north slope of Monte Epomeo, is a pleasant bathing resort and spa, the first on Ischia to be frequented for its mineral waters. The town was rebuilt after the earthquake of 1883 in which 1,700 people perished. The mineral waters (80°C) of the Gurgitello, prescribed for arthritis and rheumatism, are used in the establishments of Manzi and Belliazzi, and similar waters feed the Castagna Spa. At the Villa Ibsen (at the time, Villa Piseni) the Norwegian poet and novelist Henrik Ibsen started *Peer Gynt* in 1867. Changing exhibitions are held at the beautifully sited Museo Civico (Villa Comunale della Bellavista; *open Mon, Wed, Fri 9–1, Tues, Thur 9–1 & 3–5; T: 081 507 2535*), which also has exhibits regarding the disastrous 1883 earthquake. The Osservatorio Geofisico (*open Fri–Sun 7–11; T: 081 507 252*), with a small museum of vulcanology, commands a fine view.

Lacco Ameno is another thermal resort (considered the most select on the island) with the most radioactive waters in Italy. At the little church of Santa Restituta, dedicated to the patron saint of the island (d. 284), traces of an early sanctuary have come to light (*open daily 10–1 & 4–7; T: 081 980 538*). The 18th-century Villa

Arbusto, the former residence of media magnate Angelo Rizzoli, has been beautiful-ly renovated by eminent architect Ignazio Gardella. It now houses the Museo Archeologico di Pithecusa, containing finds from excavations of the Greek colony, remains of which occupy the gardens (*open Tues–Sun 9.30–1 & 4–8; T: 081 900 356*). In addition to Greek and Italic material, the finds include Egyptian and Syrian objects that demonstrate the colony's ancient commercial ties with the eastern Mediterranean. Highlights include Pithecusan vases from the San Montano necrop-olis, and the famous *Coppa di Nestore*, a *skyphos* bearing the oldest known Greek epi-graph (c. 725 BC), discovered in 1995.

Tour of the rest of the island

The road from Lacco Ameno ascends over the lava stream of 464 BC and descends to **Forio**, the centre of *Epomeo* wine production and the focus of the foreign (particular-ly German) community on the island. The Santuario del Soccorso, above the village, commands an enchanting view. The beautiful gardens at La Mortella (*Località Zaro; open April–Nov Tues, Thurs, Sat, Sun 9–7; T: 081 986 220*) were created by British com-poser William Walton and his wife Susana, who still maintains them. Nearby is the former summer home of Italian film-maker Luchino Visconti (1906–76), Villa La Colombaia, also with a lovely garden overlooking the sea (*open daily 9.30–12.30 & 4–7.30; T: 081 333 2147*). It now hosts concerts, theatre and cinema workshops, and other cultural events. Changing exhibitions are held at the Museo Civico Il Torrione (*Via del Torrione; T: 081 333 2934*), which also has a collection of works by the local artist and writer Giovanni Maltese.

The road passes above the radioactive sands of **Citara**, traversing Cuotto, where a path diverges to the right for the Punta dell'Imperatore (232m; lighthouse), the southwest extremity of the island. To the south lie the rich orchards of Succhivo, and **Sant'Angelo** (2.5km), a health resort with submarine springs, from whose sandy beach, the Marina dei Maronti, issue plumes of steam.

Beyond Panza the road turns east and ascends, with many turns and magnificent views all the way, to (4km) Serrara Fontana (331m); higher up is Parrocchia, a ham-let with a colour-washed church. Fontana (449m) has a church of 1374. This is the best starting place for the ascent of **Monte Epomeo** (788m; *1hr on foot; mules for hire*); the summit commands a view extending from Terracina to Capri (*a small restaurant serves light lunches, May–Oct*). The prominent iron Crucifix commemorates 44 people killed in an air crash. The descent to Forio or Casamicciola takes 2hrs. All trails are clearly marked.

Descend through a ravine to (1.5km) Buonopane (286m), separated by another ravine from (2km) Barano d'Ischia, a small town among its vineyards. To the south is the village of **Testaccio**, from which you may descend on foot to the Marina dei Maronti (*see above*). Turn northeast and Procida, Capo Miseno and the Castello d'Ischia come into view. Beyond Molara leave Sant'Antuono on the right, and follow-ing the Lava dell'Arso lava flow, join the coast once more between Ischia Ponte and Ischia Porto at the Piazzetta di Ferrocavallo.

PRACTICAL INFORMATION

GETTING AROUND

• **By sea:** Ferries sail daily to Procida from Naples (1hr), Pozzuoli (30mins), and Ischia (30mins). There is also a daily hydrofoil service from Naples (35mins), Pozzuoli (15mins) and Ischia (15mins).

Ischia is served by daily ferries from Naples (1hr 15mins), Pozzuoli (1hr), Procida (30mins), and Capri (1hr, April–Oct); and there is a daily hydro-foil service from Naples (30–45mins), Procida (15mins), and Capri (50mins, April–Oct). Details and schedules at www.campaniatrasporti.com

• **By road:** Frequent buses make a cir-cuit of Ischia, starting from Ischia Porto.

INFORMATION OFFICES

Ischia (for Ischia and Procida) Azienda Autonoma di Cura Soggiorno e Turismo, Corso Colonna 108, T: 081 507 4211, www.infoischiaprocida.it

HOTELS ON ISCHIA

Cuotto
€€ **Paradiso Terme**. ■ Quiet and pleasant, with beautiful sea views and thermal-water swimming pool. Open April–Oct. Via San Giuseppe 10, T: 081 907 014, www.hotelparadisoterme.it
Forio
€€€ **Grande Albergo Mezzatorre**. Quiet luxury in a shady park. Open April–Oct. Via Mezzatorre 23, at San Montano Nord; T: 081 986 111, www.mezzatorre.it
€€€ **Grand Hotel Punta Molino Terme**. Luxury hotel with thermal-water pool. Open April–Oct. Lungomare Cristoforo Colombo 25, T: 081 991 544, www.puntamolino.it
€€ **La Bagattella Terme**. ■ Garden setting and cordial atmosphere, away from the hustle and bustle. Open April–Oct. Via Tommaso Cigliano 8, at San Francesco, T: 081 986 072, www.labagattella.it
Ischia town
€€€€ **Grand Hotel Excelsior**. Elegant and luxurious, in a pinewood, with heated pool. Open April–Oct. Via Emanuele Gianturco 19, T: 081 991 522, www.excelsiorischia.it
€€ **La Villarosa**. In a shady garden, with thermal-water pool and excellent restaurant, open April–Oct. Via Giacinto Gigante 5, T: 081 991 316.
Lacco Ameno
€€ **San Montano**. A kilometre and a half from the village centre, in a quiet shady setting with thermal pool and outstanding restaurant. Open April–Oct. Via Monte Vico, T: 081 994 033, www.sanmontano.com
Panza
€€ **Punta Chiarito**. On a headland overlooking the sea. Open March–Nov and Dec–Jan. Via Sorgeto 35, T: 081 908 102, www.puntachiarito.it
Sant'Angelo
€€ **Miramare**. Quiet and panoramic, with tennis courts, open March–Oct. Via Commandante Maddalena 29, T: 081 999 219, www.hotelmiramare.it
€ **Il Vitigno**. B&B with restaurant, on a farm amidst olive groves and vine-yards. Open all year. Via Bocca 31, T: 081 998 307, www.ilvitigno.com, www.agriturismoilvitigno.it

Serrara Fontana
€€ **San Michele**. Garden, sea views and thermal pool. Open May–Oct. T: 081 999 276.

SPAS

Ischia The most famous are Ischia Thermal Centre in Ischia town; Terme Belliacci and Terme Piro at Casamicciola; Regina Isabella at Lacco Ameno. Many hotels on the island have thermal swimming pools.

RESTAURANTS

Chiaiolella (Procida)
€ **Crescenzo**. Restaurant with rooms by the beach. Always open. Via Marina Chiaiolella 33, T: 081 896 7255.
Casamicciola (Ischia)
€€ **Il Focolare di Loretta e Riccardo d'Ambra**. A very special family-run place in the hills above Casamicciola. Open daily except Wed, evenings only (all day Fri–Sun), closed two weeks in Nov. Via Cretaio 78, T: 081 980 604.
Forio (Ischia)
€€ **Grusoni**. Traditional fish restaurant with outdoor seating in fair weather. Closed Nov–Feb. Via Provinciale Panza 161, T: 081 907 272.
€€ **Il Melograno**. ■ Garden restaurant, known for its delicious innovative cuisine. Closed Nov. Via Mazzella 110 (Cava dell'Isola), T: 081 998 450.
€€ **La Romantica**. Nice trattoria-pizzeria; closed Wed and Nov–March. Via Marina 46, T: 081 997 345.
€ **Da Peppina**. Trattoria-pizzeria; open March–Nov evenings only, closed Wed except in summer. Via Bocca 23, T: 081 998 312.

Ischia Porto
€€ **Alberto**. Restaurant serving traditional and creative dishes, by the sea. Closed Nov–March. Passeggiata Cristoforo Colombo, T: 081 981 259.
Ischia Ponte
€€ **Cocò**. Good regional dishes, by the sea. Closed Jan–Feb. Piazzale Aragonese, T: 081 981 823.
Lacco Ameno (Ischia)
€€ **Negombo**. By the sea, with gardens, spa-pool and good views. Closed evenings and Oct–April. Spiaggia di San Montano, T: 081 986 342.

LOCAL SPECIALITIES

Procida is famous for its lace.

FESTIVALS & EVENTS

Procida *Processione del Cristo Morto* Papier-mâché creations representing Passion scenes are carried through town starting at the abbey of San Michele Arcangelo, Good Friday; *St Michael* Solemn processions, 26 Sept and 8 May.
Barano d'Ischia *'Ndrezzata* A Stravinsky-like fertility dance, attached to the feast of St John (also the summer solstice), 24 June; *Festa del Maio di Santo Stefano* A pagan winter rite, reconverted: a large chestnut tree is cut down, dragged into town and burned in a bonfire (*il focarone*), 26 Dec.
Ischia Porto *Sant'Anna* Procession of real floats—decorated rafts—in the Bay of Sant'Anna, and fireworks at the Castello Aragonese, 26 July; *Ischia Jazz* Aug–Nov, www.larryfranco.com
Lacco Ameno *St Restituta* Celebrated with fireworks and bonfires, 17 May.

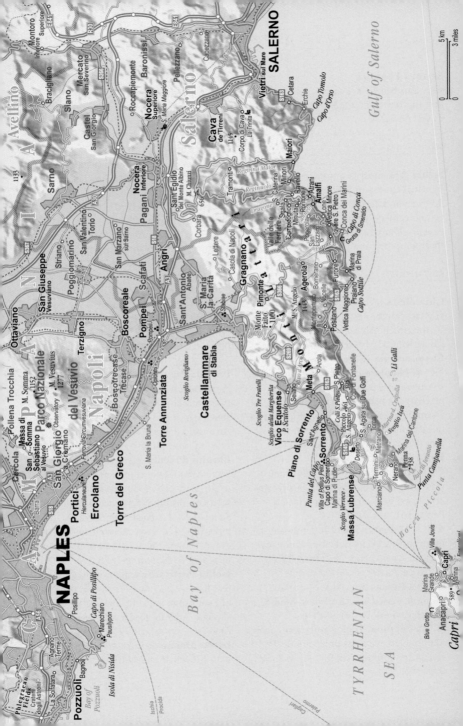

THE AMALFI COAST

This chapter focuses on Sorrento and Amalfi, two great maritime republics that once vied with Venice, Genoa and Pisa for control of trade routes in the Mediterranean. From Colli San Pietro, above Sorrento, to Vietri on the outskirts of Salerno, the road follows the rugged, lofty Costiera Amalfitana, one of the most scenic roads in Italy. The area is widely renowned for its natural beauty and is ideally suited for walking—provided you don't mind 300m elevation gains, which are quite common along its rocky, precipitous coasts—but swimmers and sunbathers might find the lack of fine beaches disappointing.

The art and architecture of the region is predominantly medieval in flavour, the cathedrals of Amalfi and Ravello being among the most impressive in the south. The vernacular architecture also hails from the Middle Ages, whereas the distinctive majolica-tiled church domes belong to the area's colourful Baroque heritage. The many lovely gardens combine Renaissance formalism with the Romantic flair for shade and seclusion.

Approaches

If you are bound for the Amalfi coast, Agerola and Amalfi can be reached by a beautiful road across the Altopiano di Agerola. From the north end of the town you climb to Gragnano, known for its excellent wine and macaroni. The road passes Pimonte, affording good views of the Monti Lattari, beneath whose crest it passes in a tunnel, c. 1km long, to emerge at Agerola, a village consisting of several *frazioni* or hamlets, all frequented by summer visitors. From here the road descends the zigzag Vallone di Furore, with vistas over the Gulf of Salerno, to join the Costiera Amalfitana road near Vettica Minore, and then on to Amalfi.

The Piano di Sorrento

Beyond Castellammare di Stabia (*see p. 211*) the road hugs the shore, passing the pleasant beaches of Pozzano and Scraio, both with sulphur springs. **Vico Equense** is the ancient *Aequana*, destroyed by the Goths and restored by Charles II of Anjou. The 14th-century ex-cathedral church of San Salvatore contains the tomb of the jurist Gaetano Filangieri (d. 1788), champion of reforms both to the Catholic Church and to the judicial procedure, and much admired by King Charles III of Bourbon. He corresponded with Benjamin Franklin, and it has been suggested that some of his ideas might have influenced the drawing up of the United States constitution. In the Palazzo Comunale is the small Antiquarium Aequano–Silio Italico (*Corso Filangieri; open Mon, Wed, Fri 9–1, Tues, Thur 3.30–6.30, Sat, Sun and holidays 9.30–12.30*) containing Etruscan, Greek and Italic material of the 7th–3rd centuries BC, discovered beneath the present town. The Museo Mineralogico Campano–Fondazione Discepolo (*Via San Ciro 2; open Tues–Sat 9–1 & 4–7, Sun and holidays 9–1; T: 081 801 5668*) has a small (1,400 pieces) but fascinating collection of minerals and fossils from around the world. Below the sheer cliff is a pleasant beach.

The road rounds the head of the pretty valley behind Seiano; beyond, it turns the promontory of Punta di Scutolo, and you get a first view of the famed **Piano di Sorrento**. This celebrated plain, about 80–100m above sea level, is a huge perennial spring garden, covered with orange, lemon and olive groves, the trees shrouded in black netting against birds and frost. The temperature is fresh and cool even in summer. It was a favourite resort of the emperors and other wealthy Romans, and its praises have been sung by numerous poets. The villages are rather closely crowded, roads can be busy and progress along them slow, but despite all this, a spirit of unhurried *festina lente* prevails, as befits an area where mankind has been holidaying for two millennia.

Meta, a pretty village, is connected by a lift with its two small harbours. The church of Santa Maria del Lauro is believed to occupy the site of a temple of Minerva. The road to Positano, Amalfi and Salerno here branches to the south. The Sorrento road winds across the plain, crosses some deep-set torrents and touches the villages of Carotto and Pozzopiano which, together with Meta, make up the *comune* of Piano di Sorrento. Sant'Agnello is now almost an extension of Sorrento, which you enter via the Corso Italia; the views are restricted by garden walls and orange groves.

SORRENTO

Sorrento, *Surriento* in Neapolitan dialect, surnamed *La Gentile* (the fair), is perched on a tufa rock rising 50m above the sea and bounded on three sides by deep ravines. Situated in an area of singular beauty, it is an enchanting place in all seasons. The district is noted for its oranges, lemons and nuts, and the town for inlaid woodwork, lace and straw-plaiting. The seat of an archbishop, Sorrento is the subject of the 19th-century song *Turna a Surriento* ('Come back to Sorrento'), popularised by Pavarotti.

HISTORY OF SORRENTO

In antiquity *Surrentum,* of Pelasgic, Etruscan or Greek origin, was never a town of importance, but the Romans frequented it for its scenic beauty and climate. In 892 it fought a naval battle with Amalfi in defence of its rights as an independent republic. Its most illustrious native is the poet Torquato Tasso (1544–95). In the 19th century Sorrento was a favourite winter residence of foreigners; here, in 1867, Henrik Ibsen finished *Peer Gynt* and, some ten years later, Wagner and Nietzsche had their famous quarrel, when Nietzsche accused Wagner of turning his *Parsifal* from a mythological epic full of grand universal truths into a banal Christian parable.

Trompe l'oeil interior of the Sedile Dominova, Sorrento's 'gentlemen's club'.

The town centre

The centre of Sorrento is the palm tree-filled **Piazza Sant'Antonino Abate**, with the Conservatorio di Santa Maria delle Grazie, behind which are the Dominican church and monastery. In the little streets near the church are some attractive early 15th-century doorways. In the centre of Piazza Sant'Antonino is a statue of St Anthony Abbot (d. 830), the patron saint of Sorrento, where he came as a refugee from Lombard persecution. The statue depicts him with a whale, referring to the tradition that he saved a child from the jaws of a sea monster. For cold-hearted sceptics some pieces of whalebone are preserved opposite the statue, in the porch of the church of Sant'Antonino; and there is a painted lunette showing the miraculous scene on Via Luigi de Maio, which ascends towards Piazza Tasso.

On the corner of Via Luigi de Maio and Via Cesareo are the walled-up remains of an old *sedile*, a covered arcade where nobles of the town would congregate for political meetings. The side facing Piazza Tasso has a clock-tower and the arms of Sorrento. Formerly there were two such buildings in Sorrento; the other survives intact, on Via Cesareo itself: the **Sedile Dominova**, a 15th-century loggia with a *trompe l'oeil* interior. Today it is the headquarters of the Società Operaia, a working men's mutual society founded in 1877. Its first members included fishermen, citrus growers and hoteliers.

The west and Marina Grande

Corso Italia continues to the west, passing the campanile, with its four columns and antique ornamentation. The vault space beneath the Arcivescovado, leading to the neglected *palazzi* of Via Pietà, was once the scene of council meetings. The **cathedral** has a marble side-portal of 1479; the façade was rebuilt in 1913–24. Inside, the first chapel on the right has reliefs of the 14th or 15th century. In the nave are the archbishop's throne with a marble canopy and a pulpit (both 1573), below which is a *Virgin with Sts John the Baptist and John the Evangelist*, a painting on panel by Silvestro Buono of Naples (1582). St John is shown holding a chalice with serpents, a reference to the Cup of Sorrows that Christ predicted he and his brother James would drink. The stalls show typical local inlay work.

Behind the cathedral is the south wall of the town, rebuilt in 1558–61 on the line of the Greek or Roman wall, after a raid by pirates; an arch from the Roman gate survives in Via Parsano. Via Tasso, opposite the cathedral, leads towards the sea. In Via San Nicola (left, no. 5) is the **Casa Fasulo** (formerly Sersale), marked by a tablet as the house of Cornelia Tasso, who received her illustrious but fugitive brother here in 1577, when he landed at the Marina Piccola disguised as a shepherd, fleeing the court of Ferrara after drawing his dagger on a pageboy, a prey to paranoia and persecution complex. Also in this street, at no. 28, is the former Palazzo Pomarici Santomasi, now the **Museo Bottega della Tarsialignea** (Wooden Intarsia Museum; *open for guided tours Tues–Sun 9.30–12 & 3–5 or 5–7; T: 081 877 1942*), which preserves some painted papier-mâché ceilings from the old palace, and exquisite intarsia work from the 15th century to the present day. In some of the old shops in town you can still see the intarsia workers at their jigsaws.

SORRENTO

Beyond the Baroque church of San Paolo is Piazza della Vittoria, which overlooks the sea. Below, on the shore, are remains of a Roman nymphaeum. To the left a road descends, the last part in steps, through an arch (?Greek) to the **Marina Grande**, where fishermen still work. Turning right you pass the Tramontano Hotel, which incorporates the remaining room of the house in which Tasso was born, and come to the **church of San Francesco d'Assisi**. The annexed convent, now an art school, preserves a 14th-century cloister with the interlaced arches so typical of this region.

The east of town

Piazza Tasso is embellished with a monument to the Sorrento-born poet, by Gennaro

Calì (1870). The square commands a view of the Marina Piccola, 48m below. From here Corso Italia leads due west to the railway station, outside which is a plaque with the full text of the famed lyric *Turna a Surriento*. Skirting past the church of Santa Maria del Carmine on the east side of Piazza Tasso, Via Correale leads to the **Museo Correale di Terranova** (*open daily 9–2 except Tues and holidays; T: 081 878 1846*) a charming old villa containing an important collection of Campanian decorative art from the 15th–18th centuries, mostly donated to the city by Alfredo Correale, Count of Terranova, and his family. The collection includes furniture, intarsia and intaglio work, and porcelain; archaeological finds from the Sorrentine peninsula; medieval sculpture and a small library of Tasso's works. Among the pictures is a unique collection of works by the Posillipo School (*see p. 122*), in particular by Giacinto Gigante. The belvedere commands a superb view.

WALKS FROM SORRENTO

The neighbourhood of Sorrento provides an opportunity for many excursions. A walk of just over an hour takes you to the Piccolo Sant'Angelo, a hill commanding wide views of the Sorrento plain and the bays of Naples and Salerno. The trail (marked) starts from Piazza Tasso in the city centre.

The walk (1hr 20mins) to Sant'Agata sui due Golfi and the Deserto combines breathtaking panoramas with local charm. Take the narrow lane along the left flank of the little church of Santa Lucia, in Sorrento. The lane winds its way steeply uphill between high walls topped by luxuriant lemon groves. The trail (waymarked) leaves the road from time to time, affording steep short cuts for strong walkers. At a T-junction turn left to (15mins) Sant'Agata sui Due Golfi (390m), a favourite summer resort and an excellent centre for excursions. The church has a Florentine altar of inlaid marble, executed in the 16th century and moved here in 1845 from the Girolamini church in Naples. The road (marked) continues to the Deserto (10mins, 454m), a suppressed convent, commanding a wonderful view of Capri and the two bays. From Sant'Agata more waymarked trails lead to Punta Campanella (through Termini), the Baia di Jeranto (Via Nerano), and the delightful little fjord known as Marina di Crapolla. Much of this area has recently come under the protection of FAI, the Italian National Trust.

Massa Lubrense

Massa Lubrense is an hour's walk away by a road (also served by bus) that runs some distance from the sea but is high up enough to afford a series of uninterrupted, delightful views. On leaving Sorrento, cross the Conca gorge. A little further on, the Strada di Capodimonte branches left. At Capo di Sorrento a track on the right descends to (7mins) the seaward extremity of the cape, with the ruins of the **Roman Villa of Pollius Felix**. The villa, praised in the *Silvae* of the poet Statius, was a graceful structure on three levels, with a secluded seawater pool for bathing. Little remains today on this exceptionally blustery spot, but the views are superb and the atmosphere evocative.

Massa Lubrense, in an exquisite setting, derives the first part of its name from Baebius Massa, a freedman of Nero, and the second from the church of the Madonna della Lobra. From the Villa Rossi, Murat watched the French assault on Capri in 1808. The lovely descent to the little harbour follows Via Palma, Via Roma (right) and Via Marina, passing the church of the Madonna della Lobra (1528), near the supposed site of the legendary Temple of the Sirens. Remains of a Roman villa lie in the fishing hamlet of Marina della Lobra. Beyond Massa Lubrense the road passes below the Annunziata and the remains of a castle (1389), leaves the attractive road to Termini on the right, and ascends to Sant'Agata (*see box opposite*). The byroad to Termini continues as a steep path (well preserved sections of Roman paving) to the **Punta della Campanella** (47m; 1hr 30mins on foot from Massa Lubrense), the *Promontorium Minervae* of the Romans, which takes its modern name from the warning bell of a tower, built in 1335 by Robert of Anjou. The lighthouse commands an enchanting view of Capri.

Over the ridge to Positano

The Sorrentine peninsula's south shore is known as the Amalfi Coast. The quickest way to get there from Sorrento is via Colli San Pietro (305m; incomparable views in both directions); the road climbs abruptly from Meta, and then drops steeply to Positano. A longer but more beautiful road passes through the little village of Sant'Agata sui due Golfi, near the peninsula's southwestern tip. Country buses ply both routes. On the peninsula's south side the road remains high above the sea, offering what may well be the most breathtaking (and heart-stopping) drive in the Mediterranean.

POSITANO & ENVIRONS

Positano is a favourite resort, where the characteristic square, white houses and luxuriant gardens descend in steep steps to the sea. In the boom years of Mediterranean trade, Positano became wealthy, and grand houses were built on the precipitous slopes. The most direct way to the harbour is down the narrow, bougainvillea-shaded Via dei Mulini, past the lovely Palazzo Murat, once the summer getaway of Joachim Murat, whom Napoleon made King of Naples (*see p. 25*). The church on the seafront has an ancient icon of the *Virgin and Child*. According to legend, it was once stolen in a Saracen raid, but spoke to its despoilers in a vision and persuaded them to return it. The raid is re-enacted every year on 14th August, the eve of the feast of the Assumption.

Positano began its career as a resort in 1943, when the newly arrived Allies established a rest and rehabilitation centre here. Later it was targeted by the international jet set—a development that was turned to advantage by canny public officials and private entrepreneurs. The result: for some time now, the local fashion industry has surpassed tourism as the town's prime source of income.

The leading players in this success story are the *pezze di Positano*, garments whose bright colours and ingenious designs have a broad, popular appeal, and a name to give them *cachet*. Cottons, linens and crêpes are the main materials; the designs, large, brightly-coloured flowers taken from the area's almost overwhelmingly sensual natural environment, or whites adorned with lace or embroidery borrowed from the traditional popular costume. The most remarkable thing about the clothes is how simple and practical they are—a fact perhaps explained by Steinbeck's amusing observations (*see box below*).

On Positano

Positano is never likely to attract the organdie-and-white linen tourist. It would be impossible to dress as a languid tourist lady: crisp, cool white dress, sandals as white and light as little clouds, picture hat of arrogant nonsense, and one red rose held in a listless, whitegloved pinky. I dare any dame to dress like this and climb the Positano stairs for a cocktail. She will arrive looking like a washcloth at a boys' camp. There is no way for her to get anywhere except by climbing. This alone eliminates one kind of tourist: the show tourist.

John Steinbeck, published in Harper's Bazaar, 1953

The road to Amalfi

The Amalfi Coast road crosses the upper part of the town. Further on, the terrace behind the solitary little church of San Pietro offers an admirable viewpoint. Beyond Vettica Maggiore the road passes through Capo Sottile by the first of a series of short tunnels.

Delightfully situated on the shore is **Marina di Praia**, a fishing village with a fine sandy beach. On the steep slopes above the road lie the scattered hamlets of Penna and Furore, and between two tunnels a viaduct crosses the Vallone di Furore, one of the most picturesque gorges in southern Italy. Narrow and fjord-like, it runs inland between imposing rocky walls that rise almost vertically below the plateau of Agerola.

The road passes close above the **Grotta di Smeraldo**. The cavern may be reached by steps or by lift; a visit takes c. 1hr (*open March–May 9–5, June–Sept 8.30–6, Oct–Feb 9–4, seas permitting*). Its name derives from the apparent colour of the interior, which glows with a remarkable green light. It was dry before the sea eroded the coast. Stalagmites may now be seen under the water, and columns have formed where stalagmites have joined to stalactites.

The main road cuts across the Capo di Conca, beyond which it offers a vista of the Amalfi coastline stretching to the Capo d'Orso. Further on you pass Tovere and Vettica Minore, two villages amid vineyards and lemon and orange groves; between them a tortuous road winds inland to Agerola.

AMALFI

Amalfi nestles in the Valle dei Mulini, the ravine of the Canneto stream. Its churches, towers and arcaded houses, grouped together with attractive irregularity, rise above a small harbour, and are backed by precipices of wild magnificence, studded with cylindrical forts.

HISTORY OF AMALFI

Though known as early as the 4th century AD, the city did not attain any degree of prosperity until the mid-6th century, in the time of the Byzantine Empire. During the early Middle Ages it developed an important Asian trade, its ships visiting the most remote seas. It has been the seat of an archbishop since 987 and its maritime republic, first established in the early 9th century and independent until 1135, once vied with Genoa and Pisa. Governed by doges, it attained great wealth and a population of 70,000, but it was subdued by King Roger of Naples in 1131 and twice captured by the Pisans soon after (1135 and 1137). Much of the ancient town was destroyed by the sea in 1343. Its maritime laws, the *Tavole Amalfitane* (on display in the Museo Civico), remained effective until 1570. Merchants from Amalfi maintained the Hospital of St John the Almoner in Jerusalem, the nucleus upon which the Crusader knights built the Order of St John after 1099. Webster's *Duchess of Malfi* is based on the life of the hapless Joanna of Aragon (c. 1478–1513), consort of Alfonso Piccolomini, Duke of Amalfi.

The duomo

From Piazza Flavio Gioia, on the waterfront, cross the main road, Via Roma. Where the traffic emerges from a tunnel, on the further side of the road, you can see the remains of the old republican naval arsenal, where Amalfi's warships were built. One of the oldest shipyards in Europe and the only surviving medieval arsenal in southern Italy, it now hosts temporary exhibitions. Here you will also see a large ceramic relief by Manuel Cargaleiro (2002) entitled *I prefer flowers*, commissioned to celebrate the quashing of Agip's plans to drill for oil off the Amalfi Coast.

From here Via del Duomo leads to Piazza del Duomo. The central fountain of 1760 has a figure of St Andrew, to whom the cathedral is dedicated. This great 9th-century edifice dominates the square, its richly coloured façade (1203) approached by a flight of steps. Both façade and steps were restored to their original Lombard-Norman style to plans by Enrico Alvino, Luigi della Corte and Guglielmo Raimondi in 1875–94. The mosaic at the top (20th century) is by Domenico Morelli. The campanile, built in 1276 and restored in 1768, is partly Romanesque and partly Saracenic in form.

The imposing porch is divided into two by columns. The magnificent bronze doors, with cross and saints in inlaid silver, were commissioned by the head of the Amalfitan

colony in Constantinople and made there before 1066 by Simeon of Syria. The head of St Andrew has been worn to a dazzling smoothness by the fingers of the faithful. The frescoes on either side of the entrance, executed in 1929 to a design by Domenico Morelli, are unfortunately stiff and academic.

Chiostro del Paradiso

The 13th-century cloister, known as the Chiostro del Paradiso (*entered from the portico, open daily 9–7 in summer; 9–1 & 3–7 in winter*) has interlaced arches of marked Saracenic appearance. It was once the burial-place of famous citizens. It is now a museum of architectural fragments, and contains exquisite 12th-century Cosmatesque mosaics of flowers, exotic birds and geometric designs. The 2nd-century sarcophagus of a Roman centurion, possibly of Greek workmanship, and showing the Rape of Proserpine, is extremely fine. There is also an interesting, though damaged, fresco of the *Crucifixion* (*pictured opposite*) by a Campanian artist (possibly Roberto d'Oderisio) of the school of Giotto. Giotto was in Naples in the 1330s, and influenced the work of many local artists (*see also p. 251 below*). The soldiers here are dressed not in Roman garb but in Angevin armour. To the left of the Cross as you view it is shown the Good Thief, his soul being borne to heaven by an angel. To the right is the Wicked Thief, with a devil's claw clamping itself to his shoulder.

The old and new cathedrals

The old cathedral, entered from the cloister, is deconsecrated and now functions as an exhibition hall. Particularly beautiful are a 14th-century Sienese School fresco of the *Madonna and Child*, and an exquisite 14th-century marble relief of the *Madonna della Neve*, whose hieratic Virgin has led some scholars to attribute it to the great Dalmatian-born master Francesco Laurana. Here, too, is the entrance to the church crypt, constructed in 1253 and restored in 1719. The crypt contains an altar by Domenico Fontana, behind which stands a bronze statue of St Andrew by Michelangelo Naccherino. Below the altar rests the body of St Andrew the Apostle, who was crucified by the Romans at Patras, and whose relics were seized in Constantinople at the time of the Fourth Crusade, and brought here in 1208. Only part of the skull is preserved here. The rest of it has returned to Patras.

From the crypt you ascend to the duomo itself. The interior, thoroughly restored, follows a three-aisled design. Highlights include the fine nave ceiling, a 16th-century silver-gilt reliquary of St Andrew holding fish (south aisle) and a lovely mother-of-pearl Crucifix from Jerusalem (west end).

The municipio and Capuchin convent

Seaward of the duomo is the *municipio*, where the *Tavole Amalfitane* (*see history, p. 245 above*) are displayed in the **Museo Civico** (*open Mon–Sat 9–8; winter Mon–Fri 9–1, Tues and Thur also 3.30–5.30*). From the main road west of the town you may climb the long

Mid-14th-century *Crucifixion* of the school of Giotto, attributed to Roberto d'Oderisio.

flight of steps mounting to the former **Convento dei Cappuccini**, now a hotel. It was founded in 1212 and was originally a Cistercian house. The cloisters are picturesque, and the beautiful flower-screened verandah commands a justly famous view.

Museo della Carta and the walk to Ravello

The main high street of Amalfi is Via Genova, becoming Via Capuano, parallel to which runs the Rua Supportico, a picturesque covered way. The road continues upwards, to become a pleasant walk through the cool Valle dei Mulini, with its water-operated paper mills (now ruined) and tall rocky sides. On the outskirts of the old town a small **Museo della Carta** (*open daily 10–6.30; T: 089 830 4561*) occupies a restored mill. Guided tours (in English) reveal the fascinating process of paper-making as it has been practised for centuries in Amalfi, and you can even make a sheet or two of your own. The museum collections include engravings, manuscripts, printed books, bills and posters, as well as tools and machines for making paper; and there is an outstanding museum shop where fine hand-made paper products are sold. Beyond the Mulino Rovinato, c. 1hr from the piazza, the trail winds through the hills to Scala and Ravello (2hrs more).

A CREATIVE INTERLUDE

No one knows for certain just when the Amalfitans started making paper, but an educated guess would be the early 12th century. The earliest client for their mills seems to have been the Curia, which used paper rather than parchment for public documents; in later years paper was adopted at the various Neapolitan courts as well. After the invention of moveable type, foreigners came to Naples from all parts of Europe to have their works printed on Amalfi paper, which was famous for its superior quality.

The oldest machinery at Amalfi's mill-cum-museum dates back half a millennium. It includes the water-powered beaters and mallets used to reduce cotton, linen and hemp rags to a fine pulp; the basin where the pulp was dissolved in water, then lifted out on fine mesh screens; the felt-covered drums on which the sheets so formed were left for the first stage of drying; and the presses in which the residual moisture was squeezed out before the paper was air-dried. Later equipment includes a 'hollander'—a machine installed in 1745, which largely automated the first phases of the process.

At the paper museum you'll acquire hands-on familiarity with many of these contraptions as you make your own sheet of Amalfi paper (though you'll have to come back to get it another day, when it has dried). You'll also have an excellent opportunity to spend more than a few pennies, as you peruse the products of hands more skilled than yours, in the museum store. Don't be surprised at how easily you succumb to the subtle appeal of this most sensual material.

View of Amalfi between the sheer cliffs of the Canneto valley, seen from the steep mule path to Scala and Ravello.

Another, more strenuous walk leads to Ravello by a steep, stepped mule path. From the cathedral square follow the signs for the Valle dei Mulini, but leave the main road opposite a bronze statue of the Franciscan Padre Pio. Turn right at the statue, and right again at a picture of the Madonna. Roughly 2,000 steps ascend from here to Pontone and the Scala villages, from where a road continues to Ravello. The ascent takes c. 2hrs 30mins. Maps are available from the lovely, muddlesome newsagent-cum-bookshop on the waterfront, opposite the bus park.

To Ravello by road

The Salerno road leaves Amalfi along the shore, passing between a 16th-century tower on the right, and the Albergo Luna, in a convent with a good 12th-century cloister. The village of **Atrani** rises in an amphitheatre shape at the end of the Dragone valley. The road spans the gorge between the village and the sea. From the bridge you descend underneath the arches, to the little piazza, with the church of San Salvatore de' Bireto (940, restored in 1810). Its name refers to the capping of the doges of the Republic of Amalfi. The handsome bronze doors, executed at Constantinople in 1086, resemble those at Amalfi. The church of La Maddalena, beyond the bridge, has an elegant campanile and a painting of the *Incredulity of St Thomas* by Andrea da Salerno.

The road to Ravello diverges to the left beyond Atrani and winds up the hillside, affording beautiful views of the Dragone valley.

RAVELLO

This isolated and markedly individual little town (350m, pop. 2,000), in a charming situation, is a bishop's see and one of the most famous beauty spots in Italy. The contrast between its dramatic situation and its seductive and richly-coloured setting, between the rusticity of its hilly streets and the delicate perfection of its works of art, the gaiety of its gardens and the melancholy of its Norman-Saracenic architecture, is extraordinarily impressive.

Walkers may shorten the distance a little (making the climb in just over an hour) by taking a mountain path from Atrani, but this is much less open than the road. Ascend the steps to the right of the church of La Maddalena, turn to the right, pass another church, follow a vaulted lane and climb a long flight of steps. Then enter the Dragone valley and join the road, profiting by various short cuts. At a fork, turn to the right around the small church of Santa Maria a Gradillo: here you get your first view of Ravello. Passing below the ruined castle, you then reach the piazza.

HISTORY OF RAVELLO

The origins of Ravello are obscure, though stories persist of patrician Roman founders, driven to these hilly fastnesses by barbarian incursions further north. Ravello's noble families were keen to point out their illustrious lineage: the Rufolo, for example, maintained descent from a 2nd-century BC consul, Rutilius Rufo; the d'Afflitto claimed as ancestor a Roman general named Placidus, later martyred under the Christian name of Eustachio. What is certain is that by the 9th century Ravello had come under the rule of Amalfi, and that it became independent in 1086, maintaining its liberty until 1813. It enjoyed great prosperity in the 13th century, deriving its wealth not from wool, as did the communities of Scala on the opposite side of the Dragone valley, but from maritime trade. Its prosperous citizens formed relations with Sicily and the East, and introduced the Norman-Saracenic style of architecture to their native town. Characteristic of many doorways in Ravello are the antique colonnettes, on either side, which give them the appearance of the Graeco-Roman *prothyrum*.

The duomo

The duomo (San Pantaleone), built in 1086, was remodelled in 1786. The façade has three portals and four ancient columns. The fine bronze doors in the middle (*under restoration at the time of writing*), by Barisano da Trani from Puglia (1179), are divided into 54 panels with saints, scenes of the Passion, and inscriptions. They are protected on the inside as well as the outside by a double set of wooden doors, and are shown on request by the sacristan. In the nave (right) is a magnificent marble ambo, borne by six spiral columns resting on lions, three male and three female, and adorned with mosaics. It was executed in 1272 by Niccolò da Foggia at the order of Niccolò Rufolo, husband of Sigilgaida della Marra. The beautiful 13th-century bust purported to be of Sigilgaida, which was above the door of the stairs, is now in the museum in the crypt. A smaller ambo on the left, of earlier date (c. 1131), has a mosaic of *Jonah and the Whale*. The chapel to the left of the high altar is dedicated to St Pantaleon, whose blood (preserved here) liquefies on 19th May and 27th August. The sacristy hosts a Byzantine *Madonna* and two pictures by Andrea da Salerno. Fresco fragments at the west end of the nave and in the south aisle are thought to owe debts of inspiration to Simone Martini and to Giotto. Martini was at the court of Robert of Anjou, and Giotto worked in Naples in the early 14th century. Stairs lead from the south aisle to the crypt (*open 9–7; fee*), which contains a small collection of 12th- and 13th-century sculpture and metalwork.

Villa Rufolo and the grand hotels

Pass to the south side of the cathedral, noting its fine 13th-century campanile, and enter the tower gateway of the **Villa Rufolo** (*open daily, summer 9–8, winter 9–6; T: 089 857657*), begun in the 11th century for one of Ravello's foremost families. The palace has hosted Pope Hadrian IV (1156; Nicholas Breakspear, the only English pope), Charles of Anjou, Robert the Wise and Vittorio Emanuele III, not to mention a galaxy of later stars and celebrities. An ensemble of Norman-Saracenic buildings, partly in ruins, it is enhanced by tropical gardens; here Wagner found his inspiration for the magic garden of Klingsor in *Parsifal*. The arcading of the tiny cloister-like court is striking, and the little anti-quarium set up in the chapel displays items found by the villa's late 19th-century owner, the Scottish botanist Francis Neville Reid. The terrace (339m) commands an extensive panorama. The palace houses a small collection of antiquities and fragments from the cathedral.

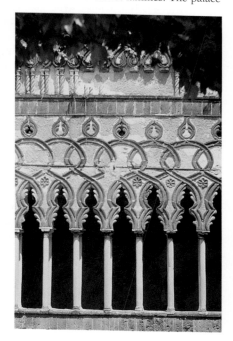

The Villa Rufolo's 'Moorish cloister'.

On leaving the garden turn right and immediately right again, to Via dell'Episcopio, which climbs the low hill behind the cathedral. The house at no. 4 was home to two eminent 20th-century writers: André Gide (who wrote *L'Immoraliste* here in 1902) and E.M. Forster (who wrote *The Story of a Picnic* in 1928). Next door is the old bishop's palace, with its typical colonnette portal (*see history, p. 250 above*). The road continues as Via San Giovanni del Toro, past the Hotel Palumbo (Palazzo Confalone) to the **Belvedere Principessa di Piemonte**, with magnificent views across the Gulf of Salerno towards Paestum. After Palazzo Sasso (another luxury hotel), the road passes under an archway to Piazza San Giovanni del Toro, with the Hotel Caruso (the former Palazzo d'Afflitto) and Restaurant Belvedere. Opposite the hotel is **San Giovanni del Toro** (*under restoration at the time of writing*), a 12th-century church with a characteristic low campanile. The epithet *toro* ('bull') comes from the former fortress of ancient Ravello, nicknamed 'the bull' for its impregnability. Inside the church, the nave is borne by ancient columns. The ambo, resembling that in the duomo, has mosaics, Persian majolica tiles (1175) and ancient frescoes. A chapel off the south aisle contains a statue of St Catherine, in stucco.

Villa Cimbrone

From the cathedral square, Via San Francesco leads to the area of town dominated by two foundations of the Franciscan order: the church of San Francesco (in the house next to which D.H. Lawrence wrote *Lady Chatterley's Lover*) and the Poor Clares convent of Santa Chiara. Beyond is **Palazzo Cimbrone** (now a hotel), with famous gardens open to the public (*open summer 9–8, winter 9–dusk; T: 089 858072*). The villa and its gardens were created by an Englishman, Lord Grimthorpe, who fell in love with the spot and acquired it in 1904, instructing his valet, the former tailor Nicola Mansi, to fashion formal gardens for him, as well as to turn the ramshackle farmhouse on the site into a fanciful palace, with a tiny mock cloister. At the extreme edge of the gardens is the Belvedere Cimbrone, the furthest point of the ridge on which Ravello lies. The open view of Atrani and the gulf is unrivalled. The palace was frequented in the early 20th century by the Bloomsbury Circle of English writers, whose rejection of the informality of Romantic gardens is said to have inspired the Renaissance-like formalism of these. A plaque on the palazzo wall commemorates the 'divine' Greta Garbo, who fled Hollywood to find 'a few moments of peace' here with Leopold Stokowski. Other plaques throughout the garden reproduce snatches of romantic verse, by authors as diverse (in time, if not in their fixations) as Catullus and D.H. Lawrence. There are copies of famous statues, too, including Verrocchio's *David*, and of the famous *Hermes Resting*, from the Villa of the Papyri at Herculaneum.

Scala and its villages

A short (1.5km) walk may be taken from Ravello round the head of the valley to Scala (374m), once a populous, flourishing town, but ruined by pestilence and the rivalry of Ravello. The cathedral has a handsome Romanesque portal and contains a mosaic ambo, a mitre with enamels of the 13th century, and a spacious crypt. The nearby vil-

View of the villages of Pontone and Minuta, above the Dragone valley.

lages of Santa Caterina, Campidoglio and Minuta all have interesting medieval churches, though that of Campidoglio has been extensively altered by Baroque additions. From Minuta walkers may cross Via Pontone into the Valle dei Mulini (*see p. 248 above*) to reach Amalfi. Above the village of Pontone is the impressive ruin of the basilica of Sant'Eustachio, with its Saracenic apse. The Scala villages made their living from the wool trade. Their prosperity waned earlier than that of Ravello, and never knew a resurgence. No writer set enchanted gardens here, and the cloth halls have not been turned into hostelries for artists and film stars. The contrast between Pontone, for example, and Ravello, is extraordinary. There are no shops selling souvenirs, crafts and artisanal headscarves, no five-star luxury hotels, just a single bar in the village square and boys riding ponies bareback through the streets.

Towards Salerno

From Atrani the road skirts the shore to **Minori**, a delightful village at the mouth of the Reginuolo. To the left of the road lie the remains of a 1st-century Roman villa (*custodian opens daily 8–dusk; T: 089 852893*), excavated in 1954. The large peristyle, the nymphaeum, and some vaulted rooms with frescoes are worthy of inspection. The antiquarium houses paintings found in the ruins of other Roman villas destroyed by the eruption of Vesuvius in AD 79, a *lararium* from Scafati, assorted pottery and architectural fragments.

At **Maiori**, a fortified village with a sandy beach at the mouth of the Tramonti valley, the church of Santa Maria a Mare has a majolica-tiled cupola and an English alabaster altar-frontal. The inland road leads across the Valico di Chiunzi to Angri.

The scenery becomes wilder as the road twists away from the sea and back again round the Capo d'Orso, passing through a rocky defile. Beyond Capo Tomolo it makes a long detour round the savage Erchie valley, affording the first glimpse of Salerno. The road crosses the wooded Vallone di San Nicola. From Cetara, a colourful fishing village, the road is so high up that it commands the whole gulf as far as Punta Licosa, with a glorious prospect of Vietri and Salerno.

Vietri sul Mare is entered by a lofty bridge. The Museo Provinciale della Ceramica, in the Villa Guariglia at Raito di Vietri (*open May–Sept daily 9–dusk, closed Mon; T: 089 211835*) contains ceramics from Vietri and the province of Salerno, from the 17th century to the present day, with a particularly rich collection of modern designs from the 1920s–40s. The Fondazione Museo Artistico-Industriale Manuel Cargaleiro, opened in 2004 in the Palazzo dei Duchi Carosino (*Corso Umberto 5; open Tues–Sun 10–1 & 4–8; T: 089 763076*) features work by the Portuguese ceramicist Cargaleiro, and other contemporary artists. Beyond Vietri the road approaches Salerno through scattered suburbs.

PRACTICAL INFORMATION

GETTING AROUND

• **By rail:** The Circumvesuviana Railway goes hourly from Naples to Sorrento in 60–80mins. Fast Intercity and Eurostar trains connect Salerno to Naples in about 40mins, and to Reggio Calabria in 3hrs 30mins–4hrs.

• **By road:** Frequent buses run between Naples (Piazza Municipio), Salerno (Piazza della Concordia) and the Sorrentine peninsula. Country buses (SITA) make a circular tour of the Sorrentine peninsula, closely following the itinerary described here. They leave from Piazza Municipio, in Naples, in the early morning, returning in the evening. For travellers without their own transport, a tour of the Sorrentine peninsula may conveniently be combined with

Capri; the night is spent at Sorrento, with departure next day by ferry or hydrofoil to Capri, returning from there to Naples. This journey may also be made in reverse, spending the night on Capri.

• **By sea:** Hydrofoils run several times daily, in 30mins, from Naples (Mergellina) to Sorrento, from where there are daily hydrofoil and ferry connections to Capri. Visit www.campaniatrasporti.it for information and schedules. In the holiday season (June–Sept) boat trips run daily from Salerno (Molo Mattuccio Salernitano) to the Amalfi Coast.

INFORMATION OFFICES

Amalfi Corso Roma 19, T: 089 871107, www.amalfitouristoffice.it

Maiori Corso Regina 71, T: 089 877452, www.aziendaturismo-maiori.it
Positano Via del Saracino 4, T: 089 875067, www.positanonline.it
Ravello Piazza Duomo 10, T: 089 857096; www.ravellotime.it
Sorrento Via L. de Maio 35, T: 081 807 4033, www.sorrentotourism.com
Vico Equense Via San Ciro 16, T: 081 879 8826.

HOTELS

Amalfi

€€€ **Santa Caterina**. An elegant, luxurious place with terraced gardens, spacious rooms, great food and enchanting views. Open all year. Strada Statale Amalfitana 9, T: 089 871012, www.hotelsantacaterina.it
€€ **Luna Convento**. In a 700-year-old monastery, with sea views from most rooms and breakfast in a Byzantine cloister. Open all year. Via P. Comite 33, T: 089 871002, www.lunahotel.it
€€ **Villa Lara**. In the former villa of Baron Pierre Beauchamp, a tiny (7 rooms) *hôtel de charme* set among lemon groves and bougainvillea on high ground overlooking Amalfi and the sea. Via delle Cartiere 1/bis, T: 0898 736358, www.villalara.it

Furore

€ **Sant'Alfonso**. This former convent on the terraced slopes of Furore offers 10 rooms of monastic simplicity. The excellent little restaurant has summer seating with breathtaking views of coast and sea. Closed Nov. Via Sant'Alfonso 6, T: 089 830515, www.agriturismosantalfonso.it

Maiori

€ **Casa Raffaele Conforti**. Raffaele

Conforti was a wealthy lemon farmer, and staying in his (9-bedroom) villa is a trip back in time: everything, from the coloured-tile floors, to the furniture, to the frescoed ceilings, is original (and comfy). Open March–Nov. Via Casa Mannini 10, T: 089 853547, www.casaraffaeleconforti.it

Massa Lubrense

€€ **Delfino**. Quiet and comfortable, on a lovely little bay overlooking Capri and the sea. Open April–Dec. Via Nastro d'Oro 2, T: 081 878 9261, www.hoteldelfino.com

Positano

€€€ **Le Agavi**. Outside the town, with marvellous views and private beach. Open April–Oct. Via Marconi at Belvedere Fornillo, T: 089 875733, www.leagavi.it
€€€ **Le Sirenuse**. ■ A superb place with spacious rooms, lovely terraces, magnificent sea views, stupendous pool, excellent restaurant (cooking lessons in April and Nov). Open all year. Via Cristoforo Colombo 30, T: 089 875066, www.sirenuse.it
€€€ **Poseidon**. In a lush garden with magnificent views over the town and sea, restaurant seating on a vine-shaded terrace, heated pool, sauna, gym. Open April–Oct. Via Pasitea 148, T: 089 811111, www.hotelposeidonpositano.it
€€€ **San Pietro**. ■ Possibly the most spectacular hotel in Italy (though not the most discreet), with glass-walled rooms descending in flowering terraces to the sea and the highest level of luxury; also an excellent restaurant. Open April–Oct. Via Laurito 2, T: 089 875455, www.ilsanpietro.it
€€ **Casa Albertina**. Small but comfortable, with good rooms and pleasant

atmosphere. Open all year. Via della Tavolozza 3, T: 089 875143, www.casalbertina.it

€€ **Palazzo Murat**. This beautifully restored Baroque town house, with spacious rooms and public areas, excellent restaurant and lush tropical garden, was once Murat's summer mansion. Open all year. Via dei Mulini 23, T: 089 875 177, www.palazzomurat.it

€€ **Villa Rosa**. ■ All rooms have private terraces and breakfast in bed is free. Open March–Nov. Via C. Colombo 127, T: 089 811955, www.villarosapositano.it

Ravello

€€€ **Palazzo Sasso**. Simply one of Europe's top hotels: quiet luxury, unforgettable views, impeccable service. Open March–Nov. Via San Giovanni del Toro 28, T: 089 818 181, www.palazzosasso.com

€€€ **Palumbo**. A small (13 rooms) but elegant establishment in a 12th-century building, known for the breathtaking views from its garden terrace. Open March–Dec. T: 089 857244, www.hotelpalumbo.it

€€€ **Villa Cimbrone**. ■ In a mock-medieval palace set in magnificent gardens. Open April–Oct. Via Santa Chiara 26, T: 089 857459, www.villacimbrone.it

€€ **Rufolo**. Near the gardens of the same name, in a lovely part of town. Open March–Nov. Via San Francesco 1, T: 089 857133, www.hotelrufolo.it

Sant'Agnello

€€€ **Grand Hotel Cocumella**. Exquisite luxury hotel in a former Jesuit monastery, with large luxuriant gardens, beach, pool, sea view, and a Classical concert series, May–Sept. Open

April–Oct. Via Cocumella 7, T: 081 878 2933, www.cocumella.com

Sorrento

€€€ **Bellevue Syrene**. ■ Quiet and comfortable, with wrought-iron beds and breathtaking views from lovely rooms facing the sea. Open all year. Piazza della Vittoria 5, T: 081 878 1024, www.bellevuesyrene.it

€€€ **Excelsior Vittoria**. A charming place with a venerable past and spacious rooms enjoying marvellous views. Open all year. Piazza Tasso 34, T: 081 8071044, free phone T: 800 890053, www.exvitt.it

Vico Equense

€€ **Capo la Gala**. A charming place in a panoramic position just outside the town, with thermal-water pool, private beach, majolica-tiled bathrooms. Open April–Oct. Via L. Serio 8, T: 081 801 5758, www.capolagala.com

---

RESTAURANTS

Amalfi

€€ **Ciccio Cielo, Mare e Terra**. Restaurant known for its fresh, simple cuisine and its marvellous views; closed Tues and Feb. Via Nazionale per Sorrento 17, at Vettica Ovest, T: 089 831265.

€€ **Da Gemma**. Old-fashioned trattoria overlooking the duomo. Closed Wed and mid-Jan–mid-Feb, Aug open evenings only. Via Fra' Gerardo Sasso 9, T: 089 871345.

€€ **La Caravella**. Excellent fish restaurant; closed Tues (except July–Aug) and Nov–Dec. Via Matteo Camera 12, T: 089 871029.

€€ **Eolo**. Fish restaurant by the sea; closed Tues and Jan–Feb. Via Omite 3,

T: 089 871241.

Atrani

€€ **A Paranza**. Locally famous trattoria (and rightly so). Closed Tues (except in summer) and Dec. Via Dragone 1–2, T: 089 871840.

Cetara

€€ **Acquapazza**. Traditional *osteria* in the Amalfi Coast's last remaining fishing village. Closed Mon (except in summer) and Jan. Corso Garibaldi 38, T: 089 261606.

€€ **San Pietro**. Family-run trattoria with rooms. Closed Tues (except in summer) and Jan–Feb. Piazza San Francesco 2, T: 089 261091.

Furore

€€ **Hosteria di Bacco**. Restaurant with rooms on a cliff overlooking the sea. Closed Fri (except in summer) and Nov–Dec. At San Giacomo, Via G.B. Lama 9, T: 089 830360.

Massa Lubrense

€ **La Primavera**. Restaurant with 10 rooms overlooking Capri and the Bay of Naples. Closed Tues and Jan. Via IV Novembre 3/4, T: 081 8789125.

€€ **Antico Francischiello**. Restaurant (with rooms) much renowned among locals. Closed Wed (except June–Sept). Via Villazzano 27, T: 081 5339780.

Nerano

€€ **Quattro Passi**. Garden restaurant (with rooms) serving delicious regional food. Closed Wed, Nov–Dec and Feb. Via Vespucci 13, T: 081 808 1271.

€€ **Salvatore**. Garden restaurant with seasonal menu. Closed Wed and Dec–Feb. Piazza Santa Croce 8, at Termini, T: 081 808 1107.

€€ **Taverna del Capitano**. Exceptionally good seaside restaurant with 16 sunny rooms facing the Gulf of Salerno. Open March–Dec. Piazza delle Sirene 10/11, at Marina del Cantone, T: 081 808 1892.

Positano

€€ **Bucca di Baco**. Traditional fish restaurant by the sea. Closed Tues and Nov. Via Rampa Teglia 8, T: 089 875699.

€€ **Donna Rosa**. Informal, family-run restaurant. Closed Tues and Jan–March. Via Montepertuso 97–99, at Montepertuso, T: 089 811806.

€€ **Il Ritrovo**. ■ Trattoria offering delicious home-made pasta dishes under a cool pergola in summer. Closed Wed (except in summer) and Jan–Feb. Via Montepertuso 77, at Montepertuso, T: 089 875453.

€€ **Le Tre Sorelle**. Traditional fish restaurant, on the beach. Closed Nov–Dec. Via Marina 5, T: 089 811922.

Praiano

€ **La Brace**. Good local restaurant, closed Wed (except April–Sept). Via Capriglione 146, T: 089 874 226.

Sant'Agata sui Due Golfi

€€€ **Don Alfonso 1890**. ■ Restaurant (with rooms) featuring traditional cuisine with a creative twist, a spectacular selection of wines (in a cellar possibly of Etruscan construction) and a boutique selling products from the owners' organic farm. Closed Mon June–Sept, Mon and Tues other months, closed Jan–Feb. Corso Sant'Agata 11, T: 081 878 0026.

Sorrento

€€ **Caruso**. Excellent food, both traditional and creative, and pleasant atmosphere. Closed Wed (except in summer) and Nov–March. Via Sant'Antonio 12, T: 081 807 3156.

€€ **Tasso**. Restaurant in the pedestrian district, with fair-weather seating outdoors. Via Correale 11/d, T: 081 878 5809.

€€ **Vela Bianca**. Once a sailors' tavern, the restaurant at Hotel Il Faro fills up with locals at lunch time; outdoor seating in summer. Marina Piccola 5, T: 081 878 1144.

Vico Equense

€€ **Torre del Saracino**. The best the sea has to offer, imaginatively prepared by a young chef and served outside, overlooking the water, in summer. Closed Sun evening and Mon, Jan and early Feb. Via Torretta 9, T: 081 802 8555.

LOCAL SPECIALITIES

Agerola is famous for its cheeses, especially the exquisite *fior di latte*, best at Caseificio Belfiore, Via Belvedere 35; Fior di Agerola, Via Galli 74; Agerolina, Via Tutti i Santi 6. In **Amalfi**, visit Andrea Pansa, at the foot of the cathedral steps, for candied fruit and pastries (try the *delizia al limone*). Amalfi is also famous for its hand-made paper; the best selection is probably at the Museo della Carta, though shops in the town proper may sell more original designs.

Cetara is famous for its canned tuna and sardines, which can be purchased at Pescheria Battista Delfino, Via Umberto I, 78 and Pescheria San Pietro, Via Umberto I, 72. The most famous of Campanian ceramics, which display colourful designs on white backgrounds, are made at **Vietri sul Mare** and sold all over the Amalfi Coast.

Positano is famous for its casual-chic fashions. **Sorrento's** leading craft item—apart from inlaid wood—is the delicious lemon liqueur, *limoncello*, made by hand from the large, plump lemons that grow locally. Try to find one that is greenish and translucent; the very yellow ones are less nice.

FESTIVALS & EVENTS

Amalfi *Sant'Andrea* 7 June, 30 Nov; *Regatta delle Antiche Repubbliche Marinare* every four years (alternating with Venice, Genoa and Pisa), third Sun in June (at Amalfi in 2009, 2013, 2017); Lemon Festival, Sept.

Cetara *San Pietro,* statue of the saint carried in procession over streets strewn with flower petals, 29 June.

Positano *Sbarco dei Saraceni,* when a mock landing from the sea is defeated amid fireworks, 14 Aug.

Ravello Classical music festival June–July; concert series March–Sept and New Year's Day.

Sorrento *Processione del Venerdì Santo,* particularly colourful processions, from dawn to dusk, Good Friday; *Incontri Internazionali del Cinema,* film festival, Sept.

Vico Equense *Le Pacchianelle,* itinerant living Nativity; *pacchianelle* in dialect refers to the children who dress as peasants, 6 Jan; *Sacra Rappresentazione,* procession in costume, on foot and horseback, every three years (2009, 2012), Good Friday.

Vietri sul Mare Amalfi Coast Music Festival, classical music in locations on the Amalfi Coast, June–July, T: 089. 349878, www.jacoponapoli.it

SALERNO & BENEVENTO

Salerno is the main place in southern Campania and one of Italy's leading university cities (pop. 151,000). Though somewhat overshadowed by Naples, it possesses a strong individual character, which is expressed with particular flair in its handsome cathedral and two fine museums. It is beautifully situated on the gulf to which it gives its name (the Roman *Paestanus Sinus*). The old quarter, inland, has narrow streets, and the modern quarter extends along the shore behind an excellent beach.

HISTORY OF SALERNO

Salerno succeeds the ancient *Salernum*, which became a Roman colony in 194 BC. In the early Middle Ages it was subject to the Lombard duchy of Benevento, but from the 9th to the 11th centuries it was practically an independent principality until it fell to the Normans in 1076. Pope Gregory VII, rescued by Robert Guiscard from the Castel Sant'Angelo in Rome, took refuge in Salerno, where he died in 1085. The city was destroyed by Henry VI in 1198, and soon after that it became part of the Kingdom of Naples.

Salerno is considered by many to be the cradle of modern medicine. The famous medical school of this *Civitas Hippocratica* reached its zenith in the 12th century, before the rise of Arabic medicine. Petrarch calls it *Fons Medicinae* (the 'Fount of all Medicine') and St Thomas Aquinas mentions it as being as pre-eminent in medicine as Paris was in science and Bologna in law. Salerno was the native town of the painter Andrea Sabatini (Andrea da Salerno; 1480–1545).

During the Second World War, Salerno was the site of the Allied invasion of the southern Italian mainland, and much of the town was destroyed. The city's misfortunes continued in the post-war period. Salerno suffered from an eruption of Vesuvius, two serious floods (that of 1954 caused 460 deaths and left 20,000 homeless), and an earthquake (in 1980). The need for new homes was desperate, and *abusivismo*, as unauthorised building is known, was a serious problem until 1990, when the city council decided to re-draw the zoning plan, calling in several renowned town-planners. Among them was the Catalan architect Oriol Bohigas (who redesigned Barcelona's seafront for the 1992 Olympics). With Bohigas as a leading force, work is now underway to restore the historic centre and to improve conditions in the upper part of the town. New parks, streets and pedestrian areas are being designed in the empty areas left over from the war, and a sophisticated rapid-transit system is to be implemented. The master plan was completed in December 2002 and international competitions have been announced for 17 ancillary projects.

The cathedral and Museo Diocesano

From the waterfront, Via del Duomo leads into the old town, between the churches of Sant'Agostino (right) and San Giorgio (left), both of which contain paintings by Andrea da Salerno. The cathedral (San Matteo) was founded in 845 and rebuilt by Robert Guiscard in 1076–85. The Porta dei Leoni, a fine Romanesque doorway, leads to the atrium, the 28 columns of which were brought from Paestum. To the right, the detached 12th-century campanile (55m) rises above the colonnade. The central doorway, decorated in 1077, has a bronze door with crosses and figures of *niello* work, made at Constantinople in 1099. In the nave are two splendid ambones (1173–81) and a paschal candlestick, in their mixture of Saracen and Byzantine styles resembling those in Palermo. The north aisle contains the tombs of Margaret of Durazzo (d. 1412), wife of the Angevin Charles III of Naples (her cousin), by Baboccio da Piperno, and of Bishop Nicolò Piscicelli (d. 1471), by Jacopo della Pila.

The east end terminates in three apsidal chapels; in the one on the left is a *Pietà* by Andrea da Salerno; the one on the right contains, beneath a mosaic vault, the tomb of Pope Gregory VII, enemy of the emperor and friend of the Normans, who died in exile

Detail of the atrium of Salerno's cathedral of San Matteo, with Moorish arches surmounting ancient columns from Paestum.

in 1085 while the guest of Robert Guiscard. To the left is the funeral monument of Archbishop Gregorio Carafa (d. 1675), attributed to Cosimo Fanzago. The base of the composition is a pagan sarcophagus showing a relief of the *Rape of Proserpine*. There are other interesting tombs at the end of the south aisle. The little door, beside a curious relief of a ship unloading, leads to the crypt, preserving the body of St Matthew, the cathedral's titular saint, brought here in 954.

The **Museo Diocesano**, in the Episcopio (*Via Monsignor Monterisi 2; open daily 9–12.30, Sun also 3–6.30; T: 089 239126*), contains a large *paliotto*, or altar-front, of 54 ivory panels (late 11th century), the largest known work of its kind. The high altar is decorated with 12th-century mosaic.

Behind the cathedral, Via San Benedetto leads southeast to the **Museo Archeologico Provinciale e Galleria Provinciale d'Arte** (*Via San Benedetto 28; open daily 9–8, Sun 9–1.30; T: 089 231135*), where a variety of finds from excavations in the surrounding province may be seen. The museum occupies two floors of the Lombard Romanesque convent of San Benedetto and contains medieval coins, paintings and a folklore section, as well as antiquities ranging in date from prehistory to late Antiquity. The star of the collection is a bronze head of Apollo from the 1st century AD, fished out of the gulf by chance in 1930; also notable is a late 5th- or early 4th-century burial treasure from Roscigno, with over 40 objects including a magnificent silver and gold crown.

Other sights in Salerno

The Via dei Mercanti, typical of the old quarter, leads west from the Via del Duomo to the **Arco Arechi**, part of an 8th-century building, beneath which the road continues to the Fontana dei Delfini. From here a street to the right leads to the church of Sant'Andrea, with a small 12th-century belfry. The view from the old **Castello degli Arechi** (273m; *open daily 9–2 & 4–dusk; T: 089 227237*) beyond the *autostrada* to the north, makes the climb well worthwhile. This Byzantine, Lombard and Norman fortress, whose recently restored interior has been reopened to the public, now houses a small collection of ceramics.

The **Area Archeologica di Fratte**, in Via Fratte (*open Mon–Sat 9–dusk, Sun and holidays 9–1.30; T: 098 481014*) has remains of a pre-Roman sanctuary (an Etruscan acropolis and Samnite necropolis) dating from the 6th century BC.

EXCURSIONS FROM SALERNO

To the east of Salerno rise the sparsely populated **Monti Picentini**, which derive their name from Picentine settlers who fled here (c. 268 BC) before the Roman advance in the Marches. Their chief city, *Picentia*, sided with Hannibal in the Second Punic War, and its people took refuge in the foothills on his defeat. At **Pontecagnano**, just outside Salerno, excavations have brought to light 3,000 tombs in a large necropolis of the 9th–4th centuries BC. Much of the material found during the digs (ceramics, arms and armour, Neolithic and Iron Age tools) is now visible in the Museo Nazionale dell'Agro Picentino (*Piazza del Risorgimento 14; open daily 9–1.30 & 2.30–7; T: 089 383505*). A few kilometres further east is the site of Salerno British Military Cemetery, with 1,850 graves of those who fell in the landings of 1943.

To the northwest of Salerno, **Cava de' Tirreni** is a busy town frequented by Neapolitans in summer. The cylindrical towers on the surrounding hills were used for netting wild pigeons by a curious local method, now rarely seen. The main street, Corso Italia, is arcaded. The principal place of interest is the Benedictine abbey of La Trinita di Cava, 4km southwest, romantically situated near the hamlet of Corpo di Cava beneath a crag on the Bonea torrent. The abbey, founded by the Cluniac St Alferius, was built in 1011–25 and consecrated in 1092 by Urban II in the presence of Roger I of Sicily, whose second wife Sibylla is buried here. So too are the founder and the antipope Theodoric (d. 1102). The structure was radically altered in 1796; the campanile dates from 1622. The church contains a fine Cosmatesque ambo and a candlestick from the original building, as well as the 11th-century altar frontal. The crypt has 14th-century frescoes. The chapter house has carved and inlaid stalls, perhaps designed by Andrea da Salerno. An earlier chapter house is reached from the beautiful 13th-century cloister. The library now houses a museum (*open Mon–Sat 8.30–1*) containing items from the archives, which, with c. 15,000 Lombard and Norman documents, make this one of the most important centres for the study of local medieval history.

Nocera Inferiore, the *Nuceria Alfaterna* destroyed by Hannibal in 216 BC, is now an agricultural centre of some 48,000 inhabitants. Queen Beatrice, first wife of Charles of Anjou, died here in 1267. Helena, Manfred's Byzantine queen, died in 1271 in captivity in the castle, where Urban VI put six cardinals to torture and was himself kept a prisoner by Charles of Durazzo (1384). Francesco Solimena the painter (*see p. 126*) was born here. The Museo Archeologico dell'Agro Nocerino Sarnese (*open Mon–Sat 9–1 & 4–8, Sun 9–1; T: 081 929880*) occupies the 14th-century church and convent of Sant'Antonio. Opened in 1965, it houses the Pisani collection of prehistoric material from the Sarno valley and material from recent local excavations. Highlights include a Roman marble statue of Athena.

More finds may be seen in the Museo Archeologico at **Nocera Superiore** (*Palazzo del Municipio; open Mon–Fri 9–1; T: 081 929880*). Just outside Nocera is the village of Santa Maria Maggiore, which has a round church of the 4th or 5th century, probably built as a baptistery. The double cupola, resting on 32 monolithic columns, covers a large octagonal font.

BENEVENTO

The train journey from Naples to Benevento is particularly lovely. Beyond Caserta, the line passes under the Ponti della Valle, the colossal bridge that carries the Acquedotto Carolino across the Maddaloni valley. The bridge was designed by Luigi Vanvitelli and has three tiers of arches (96 in all); its height is 65m. The 48km aqueduct carries spring waters from Monte Taburno (1394m) to feed the park of the palace at Caserta. Beyond Frasso Telesino-Dugenta the line approaches the Volturno and shortly after crosses the River Calore near its confluence with the Volturno. After that it follows the lovely Calore and Miscano valleys to Benevento.

The roads are equally beautiful, especially the one that connects Benevento with Foggia, in Puglia, winding its way amid verdant hills and touching upon little medieval towns like Buonalbergo (*see p. 265 below*).

Benevento, roughly translated, means 'fair breeze', and on some days, when the cool north gusts blow down from the high, green Apennines, the name rings true. It is a city of ancient importance, whose 65,000 inhabitants live on a ridge between the Calore and Sabato rivers in an amphitheatre of mountains. It was badly damaged in the Second World War, the lower town and the cathedral being almost completely destroyed.

HISTORY OF BENEVENTO

This is the Oscan or Samnite city of *Malies*. Latinised as *Maleventum*, supposedly because of the bad air of the place, it changed its name to *Beneventum* on its establishment as a Roman colony, soon after the decisive defeat nearby in 275 BC of Pyrrhus at the hands of Curius Dentatus. An important place under the Empire, it stood at the end of the first extension from Capua of the Via Appia, which was later continued as far as Brundisium. It rose again to fame in 571 as the first independent Lombard duchy, and preserved its autonomy until 1053, when it passed to the Church. It has been the see of an archbishop since the 10th century. On 26th February 1266 Manfred of Hohenstaufen was defeated here by Charles of Anjou and sought a voluntary death in battle after the treacherous defection of his allies. The title of Prince de Bénévent was conferred on Talleyrand by Napoleon in 1806. As a consequence of continuous neglect in recent years, the present city is one of the least hospitable in Italy.

Santa Sofia and the Museo del Sannio

The principal artery of the city centre, Corso Garibaldi, crosses the town from east to west. At its east end stands the **castle** (Rocca dei Rettori), built in 1321 by John XXII; here Attendolo, first of the Sforza, and father of Francesco, was once imprisoned. The historical section of the Museo del Sannio, housed in the castle, contains material relating to the town's past. The adjoining public garden affords a good view.

In a little piazza on the right of the corso stands the **church of Santa Sofia**. Built in 760 and rebuilt in 1668, it has a dome borne by antique Corinthian columns and a 12th-century cloister with interesting columns, capitals and carved impost blocks. The decorative scheme is the work of local masters and combines late Roman, Moorish, Byzantine and Lombard motifs in Old and New Testament, mythological and historical scenes. Adjoining the cloister is the **Museo del Sannio** (*open Tues–Sun 9–1 & 2–8; T: 0824 21818*), with a collection of Greek, Daunian and Samnite antiquities; sculpture from a Temple of Isis erected by Domitian in AD 88; arms, armour and other objects from Lombard tombs discovered in the environs; paintings from the Middle Ages to the contemporary period (chiefly by local artists); and prints and drawings.

The Arch of Trajan

Via Arco Traiano leads (right) to the Arch of Trajan, or Porta Aurea, a single triumphal arch of Parian marble, 15m high. It was erected across the Via Appia in honour of Trajan (114–166) and is one of the finest and best preserved arches of its kind. The bas-reliefs, set between composite columns, depict scenes from the life of the emperor and mythological subjects. The side facing Beneventum and Rome bears a glorification of Trajan's home policy, including, in the attic level, Roman consuls receiving Trajan and Hadrian, and Jupiter offering the emperor his thunderbolt; in the middle level, Trajan conferring benefits on the Roman people; in the lower level, the emperor's triumphal return after the Germanic campaign. The façade facing Brundisium and the overseas provinces celebrates Trajan's provincial policy and benefits, including, in the top registers, river gods welcoming the emperor; in the middle level, Trajan recruiting troops and forming new colonies; and in the lower levels, foreign peoples swearing loyalty or bearing gifts. A continuous frieze in the form of a triumphal procession runs around all four sides of the monument. Beneath the arch are personifications of cities, and scenes of Trajan inaugurating a new road and distributing funds to the poor.

Continuing along Corso Garibaldi you reach the tiny Piazza Papiniano, with an Egyptian obelisk of red granite from the Temple of Isis, found nearby in 1872.

The duomo and corso

The duomo is a 13th-century Romanesque building shattered by bombardment in the Second World War. Its richly sculptured façade, badly damaged, and its campanile of 1279, still standing, incorporate fragments of Roman and Lombard architecture. The famous bronze doors, possibly of Byzantine workmanship, were injured beyond repair, but two-thirds of their plaques were saved and placed in the seminary. The treasury is notable for a golden rose and a bronze coffer of the 11th or 12th century, and the chapter library includes interesting Lombard manuscripts, illuminated choir-books, and the 13th-century death registry, the *Necrologio di Santo Spirito*. The 12th-century *Benevento Missal*, which disappeared in the chaos of the Second World War, and surfaced again in England (it was sold to the British Library), may soon be returned to Italy. Negotiations were underway at the time of writing.

To the north, Corso Vittorio Emanuele descends to the **Ponte Vanvitelli**, which crosses the Calore river. The bridge, built by Luigi Vanvitelli, has been restored several times; remains of a medieval bridge survive 100m upstream. Corso Garibaldi continues, changing its name to Corso Dante and then Viale San Lorenzo, towards the

Madonna delle Grazie, a huge 19th-century church containing a 6th-century wooden statue; in front of the church stands a granite bull from the Temple of Isis.

The Roman theatre

Below the duomo to the southwest are the pillaged remains of another triumphal arch and the Roman theatre, built in the reign of Hadrian and enlarged by Caracalla to accommodate 20,000 spectators. The first and part of the second of three tiers survive, the remainder having been destroyed to make way for the modern buildings that encroach on its perimeter. Beyond the stage ran a peristyle, possibly intended as a promenade for spectators, which was reached from the exterior by three flights of steps. A lower corridor behind the auditorium remains intact. Notice also the extant fragments of the stage buildings.

Further west are the ancient Port'Arsa; the Torre della Catena, part of a Lombard fortress; and, beyond the railway, four arches of the Ponte Leproso, by which the ancient Via Appia crossed the Sabato.

AROUND BENEVENTO

Through the hills to Puglia

A pleasant road winds in a northeasterly direction towards Foggia, offering good views back over Benevento and its plain. Each of the small villages visible in the surrounding hills has a castle of some interest. The road descends to the broad Calore valley in a region rich in the remains of Roman towns (the ancient *Hirpinia*). It crosses the Calore near a ruined Roman bridge of the Via Traiana, then ascends the gentle slope of Monte Sacro, through olive and oak groves. A turning on the left leads to **Paduli**, the ancient *Batulum*, on the ridgetop between the Tammaro and Calore rivers. Once the seat of a duchy, it is now an important farming town, known for its olive oil.

Buonalbergo, in the highlands of Monte San Silvestre, consists of two distinct towns: Terravecchia, to the south, and Terranova, to the north. The latter, with its rectilinear street plan, is thought to be the Roman *Forum Novum*. The town preserves a 7th-century Lombard fortress known as the Castello di Boemondo, and remains of a bridge from the Via Traiana, the Ponte delle Chianche. The little 17th-century church of the Madonna della Macchia, just beyond the town, contains a wooden *Madonna and Child* of the late 12th century, supposedly found in the woods (*macchia*).

A road on the right (no. 414) diverges south to **Ariano Irpino**, a town on a ridge, with an imposing castle of Norman origin. On the way is **Montecalvo Irpino**, where the Collegiata dates from the 14th century and the Cappella Carafa contains a curious baptismal font consisting of a sarcophagus borne by pillars carved by local craftsmen.

A turning on the left ascends to **Montaguto** (*map p. 438*), in a wonderful position enjoying broad views over the highlands of Irpinia, the Monti del Matese and the Tavoliere di Puglia to the Adriatic Sea. You enter Puglia near Stazione Orsara, where the valley widens.

Avellino

Avellino (pop. 56,000) lies in a wide basin surrounded by mountains, at the junction of several important roads. The town ultimately derives its name from *Abellinum*, an ancient city of the Hirpini, whose site is 4km east. Raised to the status of provincial capital in 1806, it has a spacious, modern aspect, having been devastated by earthquakes many times.

In the town are the scanty remains of the Lombard castle, where the antipope Anacletus II recognised Count Roger as King of Sicily in 1130; and the Palazzo della Dogana, rebuilt in 1657 and adorned with antique statues. The duomo has a Romanesque crypt and is adjoined by a museum (*open daily 9–1*) containing works of religious art from throughout the province, brought here and restored after the earthquake of 1980. The collections of the **Museo Irpino** are housed in a modern building in Corso Europa (*open Mon–Thur 8–2 & 4–7: T: 0825 782382*). These include archaeological finds from the Neolithic to the late Roman age, from Mirabella Eclano, Iriano Irpino, Cairano and other sites in the Ofanto valley; as well as a collection of 15th–19th-century paintings, ceramics of Neapolitan and foreign manufacture, a *presepio*, and a section dedicated to the Risorgimento.

THE PLACE OF HAZELNUTS

The hazel (or filbert) tree is found throughout Europe, in Asia Minor and in North Africa. It was well known to prehistoric man, for whom its nuts were a very useful resource, given that they do not spoil in winter. But the Romans alleged that they caused headaches, stomach problems and lethargy. They called hazelnuts *abellanae* because they were a speciality of that Campanian city. When Abella later became Avellino, the French called large hazelnuts *avelines* (Italian *avellane,* Spanish *avellanas*), a word later substituted by *noisette* (little nut), in Italian, *nocciola* (in Spanish it remains *avellana*). Today, country cuisine around Avellino uses hazelnuts to make everything from breads, to stuffings, to sweets.

Just below the summit of Monte Partenio, to the northwest, stands the **sanctuary of Montevergine** (1493m; reached by a tortuous road of 18km), celebrated for a greatly-venerated picture of the Virgin Mary and visited by pilgrims at Whitsuntide and on 8th September (Nativity of the Virgin). The head of the Virgin, in Byzantine style, was rescued in 1265 from Constantinople by Baldwin II and brought here in 1310 by Catherine of Valois, bride of Philip of Taranto, younger son of Charles II of Naples. It is reputed to have been painted by St Luke. The remainder was executed in 1310 by Montano d'Arezzo. The church in which it is honoured, built by William of Vercelli in 1119–24 on the ruins of a temple of Cybele and rebuilt in the 17th century after an earthquake, contains 14th-century tombs. Here are buried Catherine of Valois (d. 1347) and her son, Louis of Taranto (d. 1362), second husband of Joan I. Below the sanctuary is the Convento di Loreto (Campania), the winter residence of the abbot, designed in 1735 by Domenico Antonio Vaccaro, where 16th-century Flemish tapestries and the important archives may be seen.

FINE WINES OF CAMPANIA

The most famous wine of all Antiquity came from Campania: Falernian, praised by Pliny the Elder and the poet Martial. In the Middle Ages Naples harbour was filled with wine merchants' ships, taking Campanian wine to every corner of the civilised world. It is something of a surprise, then, that today the region only has a handful of world-class cellars. Nevertheless, world-class wine is being made here: the red Taurasi, and the white Fiano d'Avellino, which the Romans called *vitis apiana*, because its flowers are peculiarly attractive to bees.

Taurasi is Campanian wine par excellence, made of the region's finest red-wine grape, Aglianico. The name is a corruption of Hellenico, and the variety is almost certainly of Greek origin. It is a very late-ripening grape, which cannot be grown further north: it does best in the hills around the village of Taurasi (hence its name). Harvested almost in winter, it is high in acid, but modern winemaking ensures malolactic fermentation, resulting in a soft, seductive end product. Antonio Caggiano is one of the first Taurasi producers—he was the first to bring the wine into the DOCG category.

Fiano d'Avellino is a lovely, subtle white, light and easy to drink but capable of great complexity. Two of the best producers are Feudi di San Gregorio (which also makes Taurasi) and Terredora di Paola. Other Campanian cellars to look out for are Gaggiano, Molettieri and Mastroberardino.

J.K.

PRACTICAL INFORMATION

GETTING AROUND

• **By rail:** Fast Intercity and Eurostar trains connect Salerno to Naples in about 40mins, and to Reggio Calabria in 3hrs 30mins–4hrs. Benevento is located midway along the Naples–Foggia line (c. 1hr 20mins–2hrs from each city).
• **By road:** To reach Salerno you can use any number of combinations of Autostrada A3/E45, main roads 18, 267, 447, 562, and local roads. Bear in mind that traffic can be quite slow during the summer, even on the motorway, when the beaches are crowded. Buses connect Salerno to destinations throughout the province. Visit www.campaniatrasporti.it for more details.
• **By sea:** Boats ply daily, May–Oct, from Salerno (Molo Mattuccio Salernitano) to the Amalfi Coast; hydrofoils (Molo Manfredi), to Capri and Ischia. Tickets at the quay; schedules at www.campaniatrasporti.it

INFORMATION OFFICES

Avellino Ente Provinciale per il Turismo, Via Due Principati 5, T: 0825 74695;
Ufficio Informazioni, Piazza Libertà 50, T: 0825 74731.
Benevento Ufficio Informazioni e di Accoglienza Turistica, Piazza Roma 11, T: 0824 319938, www.eptbenevento.it
Ente Provinciale per il Turismo, Via N. Sala 31, T: 0824 319911, www.eptbenevento.it
Salerno Ente Provinciale per il Turismo, Piazza Vittorio Veneto, T: 089 231432, and Via Velia 15, T: 089 230411;
Azienda Autonoma di Cura Soggiorno e Turismo, Via Roma 258, T: 089 224744.

HOTELS

Avellino
€€ **Hermitage**. An 18th-century villa with garden outside the city, with comfortable rooms and pool. Open April–Oct. 5km southwest on Road 88, T: 0825 674788, www.hotelhermitage.av.it

Salerno
€€ **Plaza**. Simple and friendly, across the square from the station and on the edge of the pedestrian district. Open all year. Piazza Vittorio Veneto 42, T: 089 224477, www.plazasalerno.it

RESTAURANTS

Atripalda (4km east of Avellino)
€€ **La Tavola del Duca**. At the Hotel Civita—traditional regional cuisine, indoor and outdoor seating. Via Manfredi 124, T: 0825 610471.

€ **Valleverde**. Family-run trattoria (with rooms). Closed Sun and Aug. Via Pianodardine 112, T: 0825 626115.
Ariano Irpino
€€ **Pignata**. Rustic charm and good wines. Closed Tues and two weeks in Sept. Via Due Tigli 7, T: 0825 872571.
Avellino
€€ **Antica Trattoria Martella**. Trattoria just off the main square, known for its genuine *cucina avellinese*. Closed Sun evening and Mon, Aug and late Dec. Via Chiesa Conservatorio 10, T: 0825 31117.
€€ **Malaga**. Good fish restaurant, closed Tues. Via Francesco Tedesco 347, T: 0825 626045.
€€ **La Maschera Locanda d'Autore**. Regional cuisine served in a garden or in the cellar of an old church. Closed Sun evening, Mon and two weeks in Aug. Rampa San Modestino 1, T: 0825 37603.
€ **Evoè**. Wine bar with broad selection of Italian and foreign wines and light lunches. Via del Gaizo Modestino 12–14, T: 0825 74951.
Benevento
€ **Nunzia**. Traditional trattoria run by a dynasty of women chefs. Closed Sun and Aug. Via Annunziata 152, T: 0824 29431.
€ **Traiano**. Trattoria-pizzeria in the old town centre. Closed Tues and mid-Aug. Via Manciotti 48, T: 0824 25013.
Cava de' Tirreni
€€ **Incanto**. Reserved and romantic, with views. Closed Tues and Dec–Jan. Via Pineta La Serra, at Annunziata di Cava dei Tirreni, T: 089 561820.
€ **L'Arcara**. Traditional restaurant-pizzeria. Closed midday (except in summer), Mon and Nov. Via Lambiase

7, T: 089 345177.

€ **Le Bistrot**. Good simple restaurant. Closed Mon and two weeks in Aug. Corso Umberto I, 203, T: 089 341617.

€ **Taverna Scacciaventi**. Straightforward *osteria*. Closed Mon and two weeks in Jan. Corso Umberto I 38–40, T: 089 443173.

Manocalzati (7km north of Avellino)
€ **Antichi Sapori**. Trattoria-pizzeria. Closed Mon. Via Calzisi, T: 0825 675441.

Moschiano (15km southwest of Avellino)
€ **Santa Cristina**. Restaurant known for its good country cooking. Closed Mon. Vicolo San Rocco 3, T: 081 824 0383.

Nocera Superiore
€€ **Terrasanta**. Friendly *osteria* beneath the basilica. Open evenings (also midday on Sun), closed Tues, Aug and Dec–Jan. Piazza Materdomini 46, at Materdomini, T: 081 933562.

€€ **Carmelo**. Traditional fish restaurant with good grill. Closed Wed (except in summer) and late Jan. Strada Statale 562, at Isca, T: 0974 931138.

Ospedaletto d'Alpinolo (8km north of Avellino on road 374d).
€ **Osteria del Gallo e della Volpe**. *Osteria* in the green heart of Irpinia. Closed Mon two weeks in July and Dec. Piazza Umberto I 12, T: 0825 691225.

Salerno
€€ **Cenacolo**. Delicate, refined cuisine in a historic setting. Closed Sun evening, Mon and Aug. Piazza Alfano I, 4–6, T: 089 238818.

€ **Antica Pizzeria del Vicolo della Neve**. The oldest wood-oven pizzeria in the city. Open evenings only, closed Wed, mid-Aug and late Dec. Vicolo

della Neve 24, T: 089 225705.

€ **Hostaria il Brigante**. Traditional *osteria* by the cathedral. Open evenings only (lunch by reservation). Closed Mon and Aug. Via Fratelli Linguiti 4, T: 089 226592:

€ **La Botte Piccola**. Tiny but good, open for dinner only (lunch by reservation). Closed Sun and Aug. Traversa E. da Corbilia 7, T: 089 254101.

€ **Santa Lucia**. Restaurant-pizzeria (with rooms) much loved by Salernitans. Closed Mon and early Jan. Via Roma 182, T: 089 225696.

LOCAL SPECIALITIES

San Lorenzello and **Cerreto Sannita**, both northwest of Benevento (*map p. 386*), are known for their ceramics inspired by 18th-century designs. At **Salerno**, Manzoni (Corso Garibaldi 248), is a great bakery and wine shop.

FESTIVALS & EVENTS

Benevento
Città Spettacolo Drama festival, Sept.
Cava de' Tirreni
Disfida dei Trombonieri Mock combat among medieval soldiers, first week in July; *Festival di Musica da Camera le Corti dell'Arte* Chamber music festival, July, T: 089 349878, www.jacoponapoli.it,
Mercogliano (Montevergine)
Madonna di Montevergine Pilgrimage to the sanctuary throughout Sept, especially Sept 1 and 8.
Nocera Superiore
Sagra dell'Assunta Music, song and dance at the church of Materdomini, 15 Aug.

EASTERN CAMPANIA
& THE CILENTO

Salerno is a perfect starting point for exploring the Cilento, one of the most beautiful and unspoilt areas of the south (much of it national park). Local journeys are sometimes still made by mule or by the traditional cart along this broad mountainous peninsula. The coast, known in ancient times for its unpredictable winds and currents, is particularly rich in literary allusions to Homer and Virgil. The Cilento is also the site of two important colonies of Magna Graecia, Paestum and Velia.

PAESTUM

South of Salerno extends the alluvial plain of the River Sele, one of the prime areas of Greek colonisation in Antiquity. Here stands Paestum, for a thousand years a romantic ruin in the midst of a solemn wilderness. Its Doric temples, unsurpassed even by those of Athens in noble simplicity and good preservation, produce an incomparable effect of majesty and grandeur.

HISTORY OF PAESTUM

Originally called *Poseidonia*, city of Poseidon, Paestum was founded by Greeks from Sybaris around 600 BC together with a sanctuary (the Heraion) further north at the mouth of the River Sele. Its situation next to tradeways, water courses and fertile lands rapidly turned the city into a thriving agricultural and maritime centre whose wealth led to the construction in less than a century (530–450 BC) of its three magnificent Doric temples. In 410 BC the city was taken by the Lucanians and in 273 BC by the Romans, who Latinised its name to *Paestum* and enriched it with a forum, an amphitheatre, baths, and the so-called Temple of Peace.

Paestum was famed in Antiquity for its roses, which flowered twice a year, and for its violets, from which scented oils were made. The city decayed during the late Empire when the political centre of the Roman world shifted to Constantinople, and Paestum was reduced to a little Christian community concentrated in the area of the Temple of Ceres (turned into a church). The majority of the people fled to the surrounding hills founding the town of *Caput Aquis* (Capaccio) to escape malaria and the incursions of the Saracens, who destroyed Paestum in AD 877.

All but overgrown by tangled vegetation, it was rediscovered during the building of the coach-road in the 18th century and became the myth of writers and artists such as Goethe, Shelley, Canova and Piranesi, and the must of any traveller engaged in the Grand Tour that completed a fashionable gentleman's education.

The site

Open daily 9–dusk (last admission 2hrs before sunset). A complete visit requires about 3hrs. T: 0828 811023; information and reservations, T: 06 841 2312; plan on p. 275.

The ancient ruins comprise remains of numerous public, private and religious buildings, including four major temples, a forum and an extensive residential quarter. The town walls are constructed of square blocks of travertine and are 4750m in circumference. Their extant ruins rise to a height of 5–15m and include four gates (of which the most important is the Porta Sirena on the east side) and several towers. The town is crossed by a *cardo* and a *decumanus*, both of which preserve paved segments. Recent excavations have shown that the temples belong to two groups: that to the south (dedicated to Hera) including the so-called basilica and Temple of Neptune and 11 smaller temples, and that to the north (dedicated to Athena) focusing on the Temple of Ceres. Between the two ran the Via Sacra, now excavated. In the middle, immediately east of this main street, are the forum and a few public buildings; the residential area develops to the north and west. Botanists have restored some of the antique rosebeds, and in May and June the flowers' soft colours and delicate scents offer a fitting complement to Paestum's venerable old stones.

Temple of Hera

From the Porta della Giustizia, on the south side of the excavations, the Via Sacra leads first to the Temple of Hera, the earliest temple at Paestum. It was misnamed the 'basilica' by its 18th-century discoverers who, judging by its lack of traditional tem-

Paestum: Temple of Hera.

Paestum: Temple of Neptune.

ple fronts at either end, thought it was used for civic, not religious functions. Measuring 54m by 24m, it is an enneastyle peripteros with 50 fluted columns, nine at the ends and 18 along the sides. The colonnade is still standing, as are the entablature and part of the inside of the frieze. The columns are 6.5m high, with a lower diameter of 146cm and an upper diameter of 98cm. They belong to the Doric order and show distinct features of the early style: rapid tapering, a marked entasis (or swelling profile) and a bulging moulding of the capital. These and other features enable archaeologists to date the temple to c. 530 BC.

Inside the colonnade stood the cella, or sanctuary, approached via a porch-like structure (pronaos in antis) formed by three columns standing between two great pilasters at the ends of the cella walls. A colonnade at the centre of the cella divided the interior into two small naves, suggesting that two deities, not one, were worshipped here. Three columns are still standing and the capital of two others are lying on the ground. There were probably seven in all, and also perhaps a half-column against the end wall, which separated the cella from the treasury.

Temple of Neptune

About 50m further north stands the Temple of Neptune. This temple, built in the 5th century BC, is the largest in Paestum and ranks with the Temple of Hephaistos at Athens and the Temple of Concord at Agrigento as one of the three best preserved temples in Europe. It stands on a stylobate of three steps and is 60m long by 24m wide. It is a hexastyle peripteros with 36 fluted columns (14 at the sides, six at the ends). These are 9m in height and taper from 270cm at the base to 146cm at the top. The cella, with a pronaos in antis, and opisthodomos, is divided into three aisles by two rows of two pilasters and seven columns 1m in diameter, with smaller columns above, of which three remain on the north side and five on the south. The entablature is well preserved and the pediments are almost intact. The roof, however, has gone. Shelley, the English Romantic poet, wrote that 'the effect of the jagged outline of the mountains through the groups of enormous columns on one side, and on the other the level horizon of the sea, is inexpressibly grand'. To the east are the remains of a large sacrificial altar.

The forum

Continuing to the north, the Via Sacra crosses the *decumanus maximus* (which joins the Porta Sirena to the Porta Marina) on the site of the forum, which replaced the earlier Greek agora. Measuring 15m by 57m, it was surrounded on all four sides by a fine Doric portico, of which some fragments are still visible on the three remaining sides. The two long sides of the forum were lined with *tabernae*; behind those, on the south side, are the remains of Roman Imperial baths, a basilica of the late 1st century AD (the so-called **Curia**) with a long semicircular seat in the centre, and the **Macellum** (covered market). To the southeast, unfortunately crossed by the modern road, is the **Asclepieion**, the sanctuary of the healing god Asclepius, built around 300 BC and made into a farm in Roman times. The building included a series of rooms providing shelter for the sick and possibly functioning as school of medicine, as was customary in the great sanctuaries of Asclepius.

On the north side of the forum is the so-called **Temple of Peace**, actually dedicated to *Mens Bona*, erected around the beginning of the 1st century BC with a north–south orientation and an entrance directly on the square. The temple encroaches on the adjoining **Comitium** (2nd century BC). This was the most important public building of the Latin colony, the one where elections and trials took place. It consisted of a stepped circular structure (the cavea), flanked on the north side by the Curia. The temple of Mens Bona was later built above a section of the cavea thereby considerably reducing the number of seats. Further to the right and partly under the modern road built by the Bourbons in 1829 is the Roman **Amphitheatre** of the 1st century AD.

Adjoining the Via Sacra just north of the forum are the ruins of the **Sanctuary of Fortuna Virilis** (3rd century BC) consisting in a square courtyard with a central pool (*natatio*) and a platform rising on one side (of which only the foundation survives). These were used during the *Veneralia*, festivities in honour of Venus, whose statue was taken in procession, immersed in the water, then placed upon the platform (thereby re-enacting the birth of the goddess). This was performed as a propitiatory rite by married and pregnant women in order to ensure happy childbirth. The pool was interred during the imperial age and the sanctuary transformed into a Caesaraeum (a temple for the cult of the emperors).

From here the Via Sacra leads north past an underground *sacellum*, a tomb-like structure whose exact significance has long been a matter of dispute among archaeol-

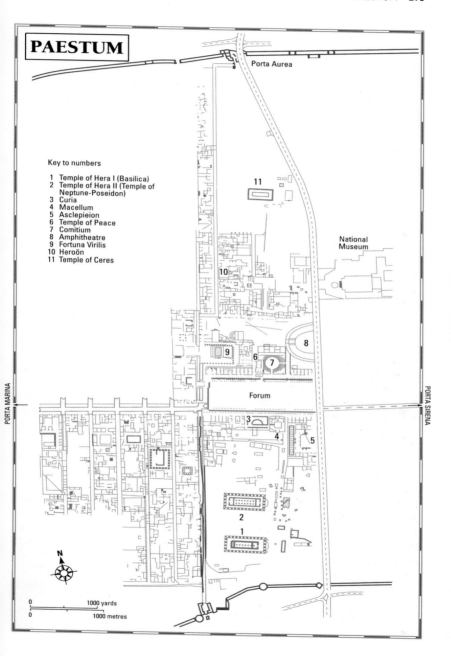

PAESTUM

Porta Aurea

Key to numbers

1 Temple of Hera I (Basilica)
2 Temple of Hera II (Temple of
  Neptune-Poseidon)
3 Curia
4 Macellum
5 Asclepieion
6 Temple of Peace
7 Comitium
8 Amphitheatre
9 Fortuna Virilis
10 Heroön
11 Temple of Ceres

11

10

National
Museum

9
6
7
8

Forum

3
4
5

2

1

PORTA MARINA

PORTA SIRENA

N

0   1000 yards
0   1000 metres

ogists. It is now believed to have been a **Heroön**, an empty tomb consecrated to the cult of a hero, possibly Is, the mythical founder of Sybaris, erected at Paestum by Sybarite refugees after their city was destroyed in 509 BC. Inside the tomb were found six *hydriae*, two extraordinary bronze *amphorae*, and a black-figure vase from Attica representing the apotheosis of Hercules.

Temple of Ceres

Further north along the Via Sacra stands the Temple of Ceres, more accurately an Athenaion (a temple dedicated to the goddess Athena), of a date intermediate between the two surviving southern temples. It is the smallest of the three, a hexastyle peripteros of 34 fluted columns (6 by 13), 6m high; it is raised on a stylobate of two steps and measures 33m by 14m. The cella is quite simple and the pronaos of unusual depth. The architrave is the only remaining part of the entablature, but much remains of the pediments

In front of the temple are the remains of a large sacrificial altar and a votive column, suggesting that the temple once stood at the centre of a small sanctuary. To the southeast are traces of a small Archaic temple, possibly the first Athenaion and the oldest structure of the whole town.

Excavations on the west side of the Via Sacra have brought to light an extensive residential quarter in which some homes appear to have been quite luxurious; at least one had a private *piscina*, probably of Hellenistic workmanship.

Paestum: Temple of Ceres.

The city walls

The atmosphere of Paestum may best be appreciated by a tour of the walls (c. 4km). The lower and outer courses date from the 5th century BC, the inner parts date from the Lucanian period. The Porta Sirena retains its arch and the Porta Marina its towers and bastions. From the latter the Torre di Pesto, a medieval watch-tower, lies c. 1km southwest. It commands a good view of the magnificent sandy beach, unfortunately marred by bathing establishments, extending in both directions. About 9km to the north, near the mouth of the Sele, lie the remains of another Greek temple, referred to by Strabo and Pliny but undiscovered until 1934.

The Sanctuary of Hera

This sanctuary outside the walls was built during the 6th century BC in honour of Argive Hera and as a defence against the Etruscans, who had settled on the other side of the Sele. The sanctuary became famous throughout the Greek world and its construction, as told by Strabo (63 BC–AD 26) and Pliny the Elder (23 BC–AD 79) was attributed to Jason and his Argonauts. The cult of Hera outlived the site and was transposed in the Christian cult of the *Madonna del Granato* ('Madonna of the Pomegranate', the fruit being the traditional symbol of Hera/Juno) that is still venerated in nearby Capaccio.

Although very little is visible today, inside the sacred precinct (*temenos*) were an Archaic building (a treasury or temple) of the mid-6th century BC; the main temple of a later date (end of the 6th century BC); two sacrificial altars and possibly a number of minor temples, treasuries and other functional structures. The Archaic building was decorated with a magnificent Doric frieze of triglyphs and metopes (33 of these survive in the museum). The main temple was pseudodipteral with pronaos and opisthodomos. It measured 38m by 18m and originally had 50 Doric columns (8 by 17) and a sandstone frieze, of which 12 metopes are exhibited in the museum. Unfortunately only the foundations survive, as the temple was damaged by earthquakes, fires and the eruption of Vesuvius of AD 79. During the 2nd century BC, as the terrain became increasingly marshy, the sanctuary fell into disuse and much of the sandstone was re-employed for the production of lime. Over time the sanctuary was completely forgotten. It was searched for in vain during the 18th century, only to be found in 1934 by two tenacious archaeologists, Paola Zancani Montuoro and Umberto Zanotti Bianco.

A museum (*open Tues–Sat 9–2.30*) has audio-visual material as well as a virtual reconstruction of the sanctuary and the friezes, casts of the metopes and a thematic study of the different myths that these represent.

The museum

Open daily 8.45–7.45, last admission 7, closed first and third Mon of every month; combined ticket with the archaeological site.

The National Museum, adjoining the archaeological area, was designed in 1952 to display many fine objects from recent excavations, including prehistoric and proto-historic material, burial treasures, an important group of tomb paintings, architectur-

Bearded man and his youthful lover: banquet scene from the Tomb of the Diver (5th century BC).

al and sculptural fragments, and votive terracottas of Greek, Lucanian and Roman provenance. Most notable is the collection of Archaic sculpture from the sanctuary of Argive Hera at the mouth of the Sele, including 33 metopes with Homeric and other scenes; and the truly extraordinary cycle of mural paintings from the so-called **Tomb of the Diver**, perhaps the only extant examples of Greek painting (c. 480 BC). The four panels forming the coffin are decorated with a funeral banqueting scene in which singing, games, love, and music accompany the deceased into the other world. The fifth panel, the lid, shows the diver from whom the tomb takes its name—a naked youth who executes a perfect dive into a blue sea—in an unusual allegory of death.

ENVIRONS OF PAESTUM

Grotte di Castelcivita

About 30km northeast of Paestum are the Grotte di Castelcivita, an impressive complex of limestone caverns situated at the foot of the Monti Alburni. They are 4.8km long, though only 1.7km are open to the public. They were inhabited in prehistoric times and present some fantastic stalactite and stalagmite formations.

Through the interior to Sapri

The traditional route across the Cilento to Sapri (and into Calabria) crosses the mountainous interior of the peninsula, where some of the wildest landscape in Campania is to be found. Although the driving is slow and difficult, the scenery is magnificent.

South of Paestum the road (no. 18) climbs away from the Sele plain to Ogliastro Cilento (350m), which commands a view over the Gulf of Salerno to Amalfi and Capri. Prignano Cilento was the birthplace of Urban VI (Bartolomeo Prignano, 1378–89), a quarrelsome, schismatic pope who enjoyed a bad relationship with Charles of Durazzo (Charles III of Naples) and Margaret his queen. The road descends the west side of the Alento valley. After Procoio, the main road climbs to **Vallo della Lucania**, where the church of Santa Maria delle Grazie contains a polyptych by Andrea da Salerno. To the east rises Monte Sacro (1705m) with a sanctuary, already a place of pilgrimage before 1323. Beyond the town, the view over the hills to the sea opens up to embrace Pioppi and the Torre di Punta.

The road continues through oak woods to Laurito, perched on a spur of Monte Bulgheria. Torre Orsaia is known for its textile industry. Beyond, the main road descends to Policastro Bussentino (the Greek *Pixous*), set against a beautiful backdrop of hills. The cathedral of Santa Maria Assunta dates from 1177.

The southern Campanian seaboard

The scenic coast road from Paestum touches places of Homeric and Virgilian fame. Across the River Solofrone from Paestum lies **Agropoli**, a popular resort. The medieval town stands on a headland above a small, picturesque bay. A short distance to the west is the convent of San Francesco, situated on a cliff 60m above the sea.

San Marco di Castellabate, a fishing village and a growing resort, has remains of ancient walls and, in the sea, of a Roman breakwater carved out of the rock. Mule tracks lead along the coast past (3.5km) **Punta Licosa** (the ancient *Enipeum* or *Posidium Promontorium*), which takes its name from the siren Leucosia, who threw herself from the headland into the sea after failing to enchant Ulysses. The tracks continue to (3.5km) Ogliastro Marina, on the south side of the peninsula. Opposite the point stands the tiny isle of Licosa, containing remains of ancient walls and the modern navigational light, visible at a distance of 19 kilometres.

Acciaroli, on a lovely promontory, was a favourite resort of Ernest Hemingway. Leave the town to the right and wind past the houses of Pioppi, where there are fine views of Capo Palinuro. At Marina di Casal Velino, you cross the valley of the Alento (the *Hales* of the ancients). Above the river, now marked by a medieval ruin, lie the remains of the ancient Velia.

VELIA & PALINURO

Elea, as ancient Velia was called by the Greeks, was founded in the mid-6th century BC by Phocaean colonists driven from their homeland by the attacking Persians. One of the last Greek colonies to be founded on the Italian peninsula, it retains the typically Phocaean system of town planning, by which residential quarters were divided into independent zones separated by walls. The town derived its livelihood from fishing and commerce, as the rocky, arid hinterland was unsuitable for agriculture. Its ties with *Massalia* (the modern Marseilles) developed to such an extent that at one time Elea was considered a sub-colony of the latter. In the 3rd century BC the inhabitants threw in their lot with Rome; nevertheless the city retained its Hellenic culture, language and customs, supplying the capital with priestesses of Ceres, whom tradition dictated must be Greek. Although it never attained great civic or economic importance, Elea became a leading intellectual centre, giving its name to the Eleatic School of philosophy of Xenophanes, Parmenides and Zeno. Its decline became evident in Roman times, as its harbours (there were apparently two, on the north and south sides of the headland, which once projected into the sea) filled with silt. By the 12th century it had disappeared altogether, and the medieval town of Castellammare della Bruca had grown up in its place. This in turn was abandoned in the 17th century.

The ruins

Open daily 9–dusk; T: 0974 972134. A visit can be comfortably accomplished in about 2hrs.
The city was surrounded by walls (about 4.5km long) and was organised in quarters north and south of the headland, scenically exploiting the natural terracing of the hill. On the highest point, looking out over the sea, was the acropolis, today replaced by the ruins of a medieval castle. On the south side of the archaeological site, close to the entrance, are the remains of a Roman necropolis which, according to Roman burial customs, was placed outside the city walls. Here you can see a section of the seaward walls, built of sandstone blocks and later fortified when the area beyond filled with silt. Just beyond stands the **Porta Marina Sud**, one of the two gates (the other is at the north end of the town) which initially opened onto the harbours. Within extends the south quarter, the centre of residential and political life. Facing a large paved road with pedestrian sidewalks are the living quarters of 'Insula I' and a large building of the Augustan age conventionally termed 'Insula II'. It consists of a triporticus with an altar in the centre and a U-shaped cryptoporticus; notice, near the entrance to the latter, the collection of bricks, of a type peculiar to Velia, impressed with the town's mark. Numerous statues, including a portrait of Parmenides, were found here.

Further along the road, in an olive grove to the east, are **Roman baths** dating from the 2nd century AD, of which some rooms preserve their mosaic floors. Going uphill, on the right are the remains of a monumental complex of the 3rd century BC that once consisted of three terraces with porticoes and fountains. Only the lowest terrace is visible today. This was probably a sanctuary dedicated to Asclepius, god of medicine, whose statue was found nearby. The cult had a particular relevance at Elea, which was famous for hydrotherapy.

The main street now ascends more sharply. Near the top of the hill stand the **Porta Arcaica**, built in the 6th century BC in a position of obvious defensive importance, and the **Porta Rosa**, a remarkable structure of the 4th century BC. Towards the end of the same century the lofty arch was walled up and this tract of the road, threatened by landslides, was replaced by another road that runs along the viaduct above.

To reach the acropolis you have to double back and return to a pathway leading west off the main street. This is located opposite the ruins of Hellenistic baths. Along the pathway are the foundations of Elea's oldest settlement (6th century BC) built in small polygonal blocks of sandstone. The houses were abandoned in the 5th century BC when the hill was entirely devoted to religious and public functions and the residential quarters moved further south. On the terrace above lie the remains of a **Greek theatre**, of the 4th century BC but heavily restored in Roman times. It could hold up to 2,000 spectators and remained in use until the 5th century AD. Behind the cavea, and replaced today by a 12th-century chapel, was the *propylon*, the monumental entrance to the **acropolis**. Here remains of an Angevin tower overlie the foundations of an Ionic temple dating from the second half of the 5th century BC and possibly dedicated to Athena.

Two small **museums** exhibit finds from the site. The Cappella Palatina holds stone inscriptions and Roman material; the 18th-century church of Santa Maria di Porto Salvo has Greek material pertaining to the Archaic, Classical and Hellenistic phases of Elea.

On the ridge to the east excavations have revealed a small Hellenistic temple and an open sanctuary dedicated to Poseidon. From here it is possible to continue the ridge walk and to follow the course of the walls. These come together at the northeast corner of the site to form the Castelluccio, a tall tower dating from the 4th century BC and subsequently rebuilt. Alternatively, a path descends directly from the acropolis towards the main entrance, passing the so-called House of the Frescoes, of the early 2nd century BC.

Palinuro and points south

A series of curves leads through wild valleys and groves of giant olives, past the villages of Ascea and Pisciotta, to **Palinuro**, a fishing centre and a popular resort splendidly set in a small bay. An antiquarium (*open by appointment; T: 0974 918003*) contains finds from the necropolis of Molpa. At the entrance to the harbour you can see the ruins of what popular belief holds to be the cenotaph erected to Palinurus, helmsman of Aeneas, who, overtaken by sleep, fell into the sea and drowned, appearing to the hero here, asking to be buried (*Aeneid, V, 838–71; VI, 337–83*).

A walk along the coast may be made to the ruins of **Molpa** (2km, 30mins). Originally an outpost of the Greek colony at Velia, it was later converted into a castle, where Emperor Maximian withdrew after renouncing his title (AD 305). The path, which runs through olive groves and along the beach, is difficult in places. The Capo Palinuro headland contains numerous caves accessible from the sea (boats may be hired at the harbour), some of which were occupied in prehistoric times. Also of interest are the natural arches at Foce del Mingardo and Archetiello.

Sapri, beyond Policastro, is a pleasant resort on a sheltered bay, known for its fine beaches, its olive oil, and its wood and marble industries. It achieved a certain notoriety during the Risorgimento, giving its name to the ill-fated expedition of Carlo Pisacane and Giovanni Nicotera, who landed on the beach to the west of the town in 1857 with a handful of adherents, freed from the political prison on the Isle of Ponza, in the hope of stirring a popular rebellion against the Bourbons. Though they planned their mission meticulously, they grossly misjudged the psychological inclination of those they were to liberate; after a brief clash with the Bourbon troops the party dispersed and was largely cut down by local peasants.

THE VALLO DI DIANO

Beyond Salerno, Autostrada A3/E45 proceeds east-southeast, leaving the road to Potenza on the left and entering the lovely, long Vallo di Diano, once a lake, drained when the River Tanagro was canalised.

Near the north end of the valley, **Eboli** stands on a hill to the left of the road. The village was made famous by Carlo Levi's tale of southern Italian rural life, *Christ Stopped at Eboli*, an unsentimental portrait of a region where the milk of human kindness can seem to flow quite thin. The Collegiata church contains an *Assumption* by Andrea da Salerno, and San Pietro alli Marmi has a plain Romanesque interior (restored). The motorway follows the Diano valley, crossing first the River Sele, then the Tanagro. Signs mark the way to the **Grotta di Pertosa** (*open daily March–Oct 9–7; Nov–Feb 9–4; T: 0975 397037*), an extensive cavern 2.5km long that may be explored by boat and on foot; the stalactites are impressive.

In the hillside village of **Teggiano**, the cathedral, rebuilt after an earthquake of 1857, has a richly carved portal, ambo and paschal candlestick, all of the 13th century; the 14th-century tomb is by followers of Tino da Camaino. Above the town stands the castle, erected by the Sanseverino (*see opposite*) in 1285 but later rebuilt.

Sala Consilina, dominated by its castle, is set against a backdrop of mountains rising well above 1200m. The Museo Archeologico (*Via Cappuccini; open daily 9–7*) contains finds from local excavations dating from the 9th–6th centuries BC.

THE CERTOSA DI SAN LORENZO

Open daily May–Oct 9–7.30, Nov–April 9–6.30, last entry 1hr before closing; T: 0975 778549. A storyteller provides unusual official tours, in Italian.

The magnificent Certosa di San Lorenzo, on the plain just below the town of Padula, is one of the largest religious buildings in Europe and, together with the Certosa di San Martino in Naples, the finest expression of Carthusian architecture in Italy. Its plan follows the standard pattern of a Carthusian monastery, in keeping with the order's religious and administrative organisation. A long wall, once acting as an enceinte, encloses the complex. The arrangement of the building within is determined by the rigorous division between 'lower' and 'upper' houses—or, in lay terms, between communal and secluded activity.

The outer buildings

The main gate opens onto the outer courtyard, which gave access to the pharmacy, the vegetable garden, the stables and storage rooms. In the right wing, which is decorated by an 18th-century fountain imitating a grotto, were the living quarters of the *conversi*, or lay brothers. These were the only monks, apart from the prior and the *procuratore*, who could have contact with the outside world to provide for the community's practical needs and the sale of its products. In the left wing were lodgings for pilgrims. The second entrance, the principal one in architectural terms, leads into the monastery itself, where visitors were only rarely admitted. One eminent visitor was Charles V, who stayed here in 1535, on his way from Naples to Reggio Calabria. For the occasion the monks are said to have prepared the emperor and his train an omelette made with a thousand eggs.

The main façade, built in the second half of the 16th century, has more the appearance of a secular building than of a religious one. It has a two-storeyed, rusticated front with engaged Tuscan columns. The statues in the niches represent St Bruno, founder of the Carthusian order, St Lawrence to whom Padula is dedicated, St Peter and St Paul. The busts on the second storey represent the four Evangelists, the Virgin with St Anne and the Virgin and Child. The figurative decoration as well as the attic balustrade, the urns, the pinnacles and the elaborate crowning niche with a statue of the Virgin and Child are all 17th-century additions. They reflect a Neapolitan tradition of terminating a façade with a horizontal line broken in the centre by an emphatic vertical element.

HISTORY OF SAN LORENZO

San Lorenzo was founded in 1306 by Tommaso Sanseverino, who paid for and erected the Carthusian monastery on his own land. The decision to found a monastery for a French order is likely to have been made for political reasons, as Tommaso was close to the Angevin kings of Naples; and the valley—situated between the capital and the remote province of Calabria—was of considerable strategic importance: through the feudal organisation of its land, the Certosa maintained a strong influence over the entire area. For similar reasons the Angevins favoured other Carthusian foundations, such as those at Guglionesi in the region of Molise (1338), at Chiaromonte in Basilicata (1334), as well as the splendid San Martino at Naples (1325) and the Certosa at Capri (1356). San Lorenzo retained its importance until its suppression by Napoleon in 1810. It was used during the Second World War as a concentration camp and afterwards as an orphanage.

The inner complex

Inside, to the right, is the small **Chiostro della Foresteria**, or guest cloister, made up of a double loggia with a fountain in the middle. On the upper floor are ten guest rooms for distinguished visitors, the only outsiders to be admitted within the monastery (pilgrims found accommodation in the outer courtyard). Other illustrious people who stopped here, besides Charles V, include Frederick of Aragon, Alfonso Duke of Calabria and Ferdinand of Bourbon.

Carthusian monasteries often shared building plans, architects and decorative artists: not surprisingly the architecture of the *chiostro* recalls the work of G. Antonio Dosio, who had been active in the Neapolitan Certosa di San Martino in the late 16th century. Upstairs are lovely 17th-century landscapes by Domenico Gargiulo, the Neapolitan artist who had also been employed at San Martino in Naples (*see p. 116*). Also on the upper floor is the richly-decorated **Cappella di Sant'Anna** with 18th-century gilded stucco work of Sicilian inspiration. The lower loggia and some of the rooms beyond are decorated with frescoes of sacred and secular themes by Francesco de Martino (early 18th century).

The church

The church is entered from the courtyard through a wooden door dated 1374 and carved with reliefs of the *Annunciation* (on the left) and the *Life of St Lawrence* (on the right). The single-aisled interior has cross-vaults borne by ogival arches. Its Baroque decorations fortunately do not mask its simple Gothic structure, dating from the 14th century. Magnificent intarsia choir stalls (c. 1507) grace the nave and chancel. The Coro dei Conversi has 24 stalls decorated with the four Evangelists, bishops, martyrs and saints who founded religious orders, as well as landscapes and architecture. The work is signed (above the last three stalls to the left of the entrance) with the name Giovanni Gallo and dated 1507. Beyond is the Coro dei Padri, with 36 stalls reserved for the monastic brothers who led a fully secluded life. It depicts episodes from the New Testament, saints and hermits, stories of martyrs and illusionistic architecture.

The fine 18th-century majolica floor comes from the same workshop that produced the beautiful cloister of Santa Chiara in Naples. The high altar, executed around 1680, is made of *scagliola* (plaster inlaid with powdered coloured marbles bound together with glues), here enriched with mother of pearl and fragments of stones, set in swirling floral patterns. Even though the altar was designed by the Neapolitan Giovanni Domenico Vinaccia, the technique, rather than coming from a Campanian milieu, was first used in northern Italy (in Emilia Romagna and Tuscany) in the 16th century and was adopted at Padula for all the altarpieces of the monastery. Scagliola is cheaper in terms of material than marble inlay, but technically more difficult; so it is likely that the actual execution was left to the patience of the monks. The stucco work and ceiling frescoes, representing scenes from the Old Testament, were originally executed toward the end of the 17th century, although the painted surface was heavily retouched in the mid-19th century by the Neapolitan Salvatore Brancaccio, a Carthusian monk who is also the author of the three canvases at the sides of the altar with the *Martyrdom of St Lawrence*, the *Death of St Bruno* and the apotheosis of both saints. Other paintings were stolen after Napoleon's suppression of the monasteries, as testified by the seven empty fields framed by stucco decorations.

The door to the sacristy has intarsia panels depicting the entrance to the monastery and church as it was at the beginning of the 16th century. Inside the sacristy is a fine bronze tabernacle that had been lost in 1813 and only recently identified in the Museum of Capodimonte. It has been attributed to Jacopo del Duca, a pupil of

Michelangelo, whose influence is clear in the reliefs showing the *Passion of Christ*. The vault has an 18th-century fresco of the *Assumption of the Virgin*.

The chapels, treasury and chapter room

To the right of the church is a series of small chapels, the most interesting of which is the **Chapel of the Relics**. These are kept in a reliquary conceived like a Spanish *retablo* and closely influenced by the reliquaries of the church of Gesù Nuovo at Naples. Restoration has brought to light a 15th-century fresco of St John the Baptist that had been painted over in the Baroque refurbishment of the complex.

To the left of the church is the **treasury**, with fine Baroque stucco work. It once housed fabulous riches including gold chalices, silver crosses and busts covered in gems by Neapolitan silversmiths, as well as a famous ivory Crucifix attributed to Michelangelo. All of these disappeared during and after the suppression of 1810. Passing out of the treasury you come to the small 'room of the bells', named after the bell-tower that rises above it. It was actually a recreational antechamber where the monks met and exchanged a few words (elsewhere they observed silence) before entering the chapter room. Particularly interesting is the notice board with letters indicating the location of the monks and the office they attended to.

Beyond is the Sala del Capitolo, or **chapter room**, with more stucco work executed by Neapolitan artists at the beginning of the 18th century and statues of St Lawrence, Tobias with the Angel, St John and St Joseph. The latter two refer to the coexistence in the monastery of the contemplative life of the hermit monks and the active life of the *conversi*. All the stucco frames remained empty after the Napoleonic spoliation: as Abbé Saint-Non recounts in his *Voyage Pittoresque* (1781–86), there once was a marvellous painting of the *Virgin and Sleeping Child* by Luca Giordano. The only extant canvas of the room is the altarpiece by Ippolito Borghese, an artist of the Counter-Reformation, representing the *Madonna and Child with Sts Lawrence and Bruno*. The frescoes decorating the vault, of modest quality, represent the *Miracles of Christ* and were executed at the end of the 18th century. The putti with flowers belong to an earlier phase (early 18th century) and follow the style of Francesco de Martino.

The old cemetery and adjacent rooms

From the antechamber, access is gained to the old cemetery (1522), rebuilt in the 18th century after the cemetery was moved to the great cloister, and featuring architectural elements derived from Antonio Vaccaro. Around the portico are antique architectural fragments found on the site during building work. The **Cappella del Fondatore**, at the far end, contains the 16th-century tomb of Tommaso Sanseverino. Next to the chapel is the refectory with a splendid 18th-century portal, a much worn majolica floor, a marble pulpit and a fresco of the *Wedding at Cana* by Alessio d'Elia (1749), following the style of his master Francesco Solimena. The refectory was used on Sundays and feast days only, for a communal meal that was taken in absolute silence. All other meals were consumed by the hermit monks in their own cells. The lay brothers used the refectory of the *conversi*, which today houses a museum (*see below*).

The old cemetery also gives access to the interesting and well-preserved **kitchen complex**, with storage rooms, a mill and a giant oak press (1785). Originally the kitchen served a different function. It may have been a chapter house, as is testified by the incongruous presence of a 17th-century fresco of the *Deposition*.

Chiostro dei Procuratori and prior's apartments

Adjoining the storage rooms is the main corridor of the monastery. From here you enter the 18th-century **Chiostro dei Procuratori**, with a fountain in the centre and symmetrically arranged flower beds planted with lemon and orange trees. The architecture is reminiscent of the work of Ferdinando Sanfelice. Here were the apartments and offices of the *procuratore*, the monk who was entrusted with the economic and practical administration of the monastery. Depending on the size of the property, there could be more than one *procuratore*. This was the case at Padula, whose community owned land and buildings as far afield as Naples.

Looking out onto the cloister, on the right hand side, are the **apartments of the prior**, the head and spiritual leader of the convent. These can be entered from the main corridor and consisted of ten rooms with additional services and a private chapel. The chapel is dedicated to the Archangel Michael, patron of Padula, whose wooden statue is signed and dated 'Gioseppe Feriello 1649'. The four paintings on the walls illustrate the apparitions of the Archangel and were executed by an unknown artist from the circle of Solimena. There is also an interesting wall cupboard decorated with prints of imaginary landscapes. The loggia, opening out to the garden, is beautifully painted with *trompe l'oeil* landscapes showing strong analogies with the frescoes on the upper floor of the Chiostro della Foresteria. A pathway in *opus spicatum* leads through the recently restored Italian garden.

The library and great cloister

On the left in the main corridor is a boldly designed, narrow staircase (*closed at the time of writing*) winding up like a ribbon without balustrades. At the top is the **library**, with exquisite Baroque doors of inlaid coloured marbles and a good majolica floor. The ceiling is decorated with allegorical canvases from the 18th century. Today only 1,940 volumes survive at Padula: most of the library's collection was sent to Naples shortly after the suppression, ending in what has meanwhile become the National Library.

Now descend to the immense **great cloister**, which measures a staggering 104m by 109m and is articulated by 84 pilasters of smoothly rusticated stone. A heavy Doric frieze, decorated with scenes of martyrdom and of the *Passion of Christ*, runs between the upper and lower storeys. In the centre is a fountain, and on the south side the monks' cemetery, enclosed by an elegant balustrade. Although its architects are unknown, they owe much to Giovanni Antonio Dosio and Cosimo Fanzago, who had been architects at San Martino in the late 16th and early 17th centuries. The sense of space, peace and melancholy that the cloister imparts is memorable. Its atmosphere and poetic charm were recorded by François Lenormant in 1883:

I went to sit in the Great Cloister. There were many clouds, driven by a violent wind, passing swiftly in front of the full moon, producing continuous sudden changes that ranged from profound darkness to brilliant light... There is nothing more enchanting than the effect of these drops of nocturnal light which at times reveal the architecture in all its extraordinary purity down to the smallest detail, and at times conceal it completely. These sudden changes in light seemed to conjure up white phantoms in the depths of the porticoes, as though the ghosts of the old inhabitants of the monastery had risen, as was their custom, to celebrate night office.

Off the great cloister are the **monks' quarters**. The 26 cells consisted of two rooms, a portico, an open loggia and a garden with a fountain. Each monk had his own little plot of land where he would grow his own fruit and vegetables, as well as herbs and flowers carrying a symbolic meaning (lilies, violets, etc). Because nature was considered an emanation of God, the gardens were conceived as an aid to contemplation. They opened out onto a communal park.

On the north side of the cloister is an octagonal tower containing the elliptical grand staircase by Gaetano Barba (1761–63), a structure of singular elegance leading to an upper gallery (*now closed to the public*). Also accessible from the cloister is the **Museo Archeologico della Lucania Occidentale** (*opening times as for the Certosa*), set up in 1957 to display material from local sites. It contains interesting finds from a nearby Villanovan necropolis.

PRACTICAL INFORMATION

GETTING AROUND

• **By road:** To reach Salerno and the Cilento you can use any number of combinations of Autostrada A3/E45, main roads 18, 267, 447, 562, and local roads. Bear in mind that traffic can be quite slow during the summer, even on the motorway, when the beaches are crowded. Buses connect Salerno to destinations throughout the province. The most useful services are those from Piazza della Concordia to Paestum and the Amalfi Coast, and from Piazza Ferrovia to Pompeii. Visit www.campaniatrasporti.it for more details.

• **By rail:** Fast Intercity and Eurostar trains connect Salerno to Naples in about 40mins, and to Reggio Calabria in 3hrs 30mins–4hrs. Most Intercity trains stop at Battipaglia (where you can change onto a local train to Paestum), Agropoli and Sapri; Eurostars stop at Sapri only. Benevento is located midway along the Naples–Foggia line (c. 1hr 20mins–2hrs from each city).

• **By sea:** Boats ply daily, May–Oct, from Salerno (Molo Mattuccio Salernitano) to the Amalfi Coast; hydrofoils (Molo Manfredi), to Capri and Ischia. Tickets at the quay; schedules at www.campaniatrasporti.it

INFORMATION OFFICES

Paestum Via Magna Grecia 151,
T: 0828 811016, www.infopaestum.it

HOTELS

Agropoli
€ **La Colombaia**. Country villa with
garden and pool. Open March–Oct. Via
La Vecchia 12, T: 0974 821800,
www.lacolombaiahotel.it

Centola
€ **Sant'Agata**. Seven rooms on a beautiful farm (olives, vines, prickly pears)
in a panoramic position in the hills
above Palinuro. Open Feb–Dec, restaurant evenings only. Contrada Sant'Agata,
T: 0974 931716.

Paestum
€ **Tenuta Seliano**. An estate just a few
kilometres from the temples, with 12
guest rooms, a lovely garden with patio
and pool, and excellent cuisine featuring home-grown olives and vegetables,
and fresh mozzarella. Closed Nov–Feb.
Via Seliano at Borgo Antico, T: 0828
724544.

Palinuro
€€ **King's Residence**. A restful place
with splendid views of the sea and
coast. Open Easter–Oct and Dec–Jan.
T: 0974 931324, www.hotelkings.it

San Marco di Castellabate
€ **Giacaranda**. Green and restful B&B
with a high cultural profile (seminars
on topical issues, cuisine). Open all
year. Conrada Cenito, T: 0974 966130,
giaca@costacilento.it

Santa Maria di Castellabate
€€€ **Palazzo Belmonte**. On the
beach in a quaint little fishing village:
spacious rooms, suites and apartments
in the 17th-century hunting lodge of
the Prince of Belmonte. Via Flavio Gioia
25, T: 0974 960211,
www.palazzobelmonte.com

Sala Consilina
€ **La Pergola**. Restaurant with rooms,
once a coach station on the old road to
Calabria. Open daily. Trinità 239,
T: 0975 45054.

RESTAURANTS

Centola
€ **Sant'Agata**. Farm in the hills
between Palinuro and Marina di
Camerota. Outdoor seating with sea
views; open daily, evenings only. Closed
Jan. Contrada Sant'Agata, T: 0974
931716.

Marina di Camerota
€€ **Pepè**. Simple but good fish restau-
rant. Closed Tues. Via delle Sirene 41,
T: 0974 932461.
€€ **Valentone**. Family-run trattoria
known for its grilled fish. Closed Sun
(except in summer) and Oct–Dec. Via
Marina di Camerota, T: 0974 932004.

Paestum
€€ **La Pergola**. Restaurant-pizzeria
with garden seating in summer. Closed
Mon and Sept. Via Nazionale 1, at
Capaccio, T: 0828 723377.
€€ **Nettuno**. ■ Restaurant adjoining
the excavations near the south gate,
with good views over the temples.
Closed evenings and Mon from
Sept–June. Via Nettuno 2 (Zona
Archeologica), T: 0828 811028.

Pisciotta
€ **Perbacco**. *Osteria* and wine bar.
Closed Oct–May. Contrada Marina
Campagna 5, T: 0974 973849.

€ **Angiolina**. Restaurant with garden seating, crowded in summer. Open evenings, closed Nov and Easter. Via Passeriello 2, at Pisciotta Marina, T: 0974 973188.

Pollica (Celso)
€ **Costantinopoli**. Family-run restaurant in the hills between Acciaroli and Pioppi. Open weekends (daily in summer), closed Oct–March. Contrada Costantinopoli 6, T: 0974 901134.

San Giovanni a Piro
€ **U' Zifaro**. Traditional fish restaurant by the sea; open weekends (daily in summer), closed Dec–Jan. Lungomare Marconi 43, at Scario, T: 0974 986397:

Sapri
€€ **'A Cantina i Mustazzo**. Simple trattoria with a staff of one. Closed Wed (except in summer) and late Sept. Piazza Plebiscito 27, T: 0973 604010.

FESTIVALS & EVENTS

Agropoli
Madonna di Costantinopoli Statue of the Madonna carried in colourful boat procession, 24 July.

Teggiano
San Cono Procession, marching bands, fireworks, 1–3 June.

BASILICATA

NB: The first part of this chapter is covered by the map on p. 270. Most of the rest opposite. The eastern coast with Metapontum is on p. 470; and the southern Mont region, in its entirety, is on p. 318.

The landscape of Basilicata is out of the ordinary, even for the very well travelled and so striking at every turn that it can make the heart race. Places like Matera make an indelible impression, and the richness of its ancient heritage comes as a surprise. After a visit to this region, the spicy tang of sun-dried tomatoes and the rich fruitiness of Cirò wine will return to mind for years to come. But do heed Norman Douglas's advice: when you come here, bring a friend.

A region corresponding roughly to the ancient *Lucania*, Basilicata occupies a three-cornered area between the Gulf of Taranto, the Tyrrhenian Sea and the lowlands of Puglia. The country is almost entirely composed of steep parallel ranges of limestone and dolomitic mountains, preventing easy communication. It was colonised from Greece in the 7th century BC and reached a high degree of prosperity, but was later drawn into the struggles between Rome and the Samnites and the campaign against Pyrrhus and Hannibal (3rd century BC), and in the Middle Ages it suffered from the continual vicissitudes of the Kingdom of Naples.

Its present name was assumed in honour of Emperor Basil II (976–1025), who overthrew Saracen power in Sicily and southern Italy. Despite recent progress, the region is one of the poorest in Italy: the soil is unproductive, and industries remain undeveloped. Potenza and Matera, the only towns of any size, are the provincial capitals. In the forests, wild boar and wolves are not uncommon.

NORTHERN BASILICATA

There is a distinctly northern European feel to this area: with its broad horizons, neatly tilled fields and imposing castles, northern Basilicata clearly reflects its Norman heritage. This and recent industrial development—there is a Fiat factory at Melfi, and Agip petrochemical works at Candela (*map p. 438*)—have brought a gradual influx of wealth to the region, which has been skilfully invested in pleasant (though by no means luxurious) hotels and fine restaurants serving traditional dishes based on lamb, game and mushrooms. It was a land much loved by Frederick II, who left two of his finest architectural achievements at Melfi and Lagopesole. Walkers, bird-watchers and nature-lovers in general will enjoy the wild woodlands of Monte Vulture, an extinct volcano. Dozens of windmills, on the hilltops between Venosa, Atella and Acerenza, provide clean, renewable electrical power.

ttural fortress, was the first Norman capital. It
velopment scheme in the South. In the castle
onfirmed by Pope Nicholas II in 1059, at the
lfi between that year and 1101. The First
id during his sojourn at Melfi, Frederick II
he *Constitutiones Augustales* (*see box below*).
.n Mon 2–8, *Tues–Sun 9–8; T: 0972 238726*),
...ciiensive archaeological profile of Melfi and the Monte
...um prehistoric to Roman times. Here Bronze and Iron Age finds, Greek
and Roman objects, burial treasures from a Daunian necropolis etc, testify to the
sophistication of indigenous peoples and their contacts with Greek, Etruscan and
Roman civilization. Highlights include the *Sarcophago di Rapolla*, an extraordinary
marble sarcophagus of a woman, of the 2nd century AD, displayed in one of the towers. The reliefs, ascribed to artists from Asia Minor, represent the deceased asleep (on
the lid) and the Roman heroes who represented the mythic 'references' of her aristocratic family (in niches).

A little further up the hill is the church of **Sant'Antonio di Padova**, with its pleasing rose window. It contains two amusing holy-water stoups; the one on the left, dating from the 16th century, is the more complete.

THE CONSTITUTIONS OF MELFI

The *Constitutiones Regni Siciliae*, also called *Liber constitutionum* or *Liber augustalis*, were compiled for Frederick II by Pier della Vigna and by James, Bishop of
Capua, and promulgated in the general parliament of Melfi of August 1231. The
constitutions include the most important legislation of the Norman kings of
Sicily, and the constitutions published earlier by Frederick II himself (those published after 1231 were added to the code as the *Novae constitutiones*). There are
three books. The first regards public law in general, with particular regard to
judges, state finances and the police; the second deals with court procedure; the
third presents various articles of private, feudal and criminal law. Celebrated for
their balanced sense of justice and their ingenious blend of old and new,
Frederick's constitutions are the greatest secular legislative achievement of the
Middle Ages.

Via Garibaldi leads on towards the cathedral, passing on the right the 13th-century
portal of the former church of Santa Maria la Nuova (now a cinema), with its dog-
tooth carving. The **duomo** has a campanile of 1153 with fine decorative brickwork,
including the representations of two griffins (emblems of the Norman dynasty in

Sicily); the pyramidal top is a modern addition. The interior has a wooden ceiling and a Baroque high altar and surround. The latter also encloses an elaborate bishop's throne of gilded and painted wood. At the end of the north aisle is a fresco of the enthroned Madonna and Child, a late imitation of a Byzantine model; and in the second chapel on the south side is the much revered *Madonna dell'Assunta*, protectress of the city. Holy objects from the cathedral and other churches in the town can be seen in the adjoining bishop's palace.

Around Melfi

The district around Melfi contains several painted chapels hollowed in the rock (*apply to the municipio to visit*), of which one of the most easily accessible is to be found on the road to Venosa. About 1km outside Melfi a small lane leads left towards the cemetery and, almost at once, a track leads left again to the **Cappella Santa Margherita**, containing 13th-century frescoes.

From here it is a short drive to **Rapolla**, a thermal resort, where the cathedral dates from the late 13th century. Set into the south wall are two bas-reliefs, one representing *Original Sin*, and the other the *Annunciation*. Both date from the early 13th century and show a marked Byzantine spirit. The church of Santa Lucia, a beautiful little building with two cupolas, is built to a Byzantine plan (*key from the cathedral sacristan*).

Monte Vulture

Rionero in Vulture, located 11km south of Melfi and 20km east of Venosa, is the starting point for excursions to Monte Vulture, an extinct volcano whose summit commands nearly all Puglia.

The area to the west, now much frequented by local tourists, is renowned for its natural beauty. Its main attractions are the beautiful little **Laghi di Monticchio**. Near the point where these two nearly-circular lakes meet are the ruins of the Abbazia di Sant'Ippolito, dating from the 11th and 12th centuries. On the heights above the smaller of the two lakes you can see the late 17th-century Abbazia di San Michele, of little interest. The **Bosco di Monticchio**, a splendid forest, contains over 970 varieties of flora, some rare.

A small road from Rionero leads (in about 8km) to the village of **Ripacandida**, in a commanding position at the top of a hill. Just beyond the village stands the Santuario di San Donato, where the small church is almost completely covered with 14th-century frescoes (repainted) depicting scenes from the Old and New Testaments, figures of saints and representations of miracles.

Barile is an Albanian colony founded in the 15th century; the inhabitants retain their ethnic and linguistic traditions. Weddings and funerals are particularly interesting, as are the ceremonies for religious holidays. In the Scescio and Solagna del Fico areas are a number of curious caves carved in the tufa, formerly inhabited, now used as wine cellars. A troglodytic settlement has been found in the area of San Pietro.

THE LEGACY OF FREDERICK II

When Frederick died, his concept of empire died with him. Central to this concept was the notion of the deification of the prince, drawn from the imperial tradition of Rome and from Eastern cults of the sovereign; and although the notion of a universal monarchy did not survive Frederick, his endeavour to create a state emancipated from the Church did live on. In fact it was much admired—and imitated—by later generations.

Frederick's political actions were conditioned by the traditions and experiences of his Norman ancestors. He had no understanding of nascent city-states and their determination to defend their republican ideals. Aspirations to civic autonomy were harshly repressed in the Kingdom of Sicily, and in Germany, too, after 1230, Frederick allied with the princes against the cities.

Frederick's plan to join the Italian regions of the empire with the kingdom of Sicily to form a single political entity south of the Alps called for more resources than the kingdom could offer. Undoubtedly the reforms carried out between 1220 and 1246 set Sicily leagues ahead of other states in matters of local administration, taxation and jurisprudence. Similarly, the decision to train judges and other public officials in a state university, and to control their activities through a central court, was unprecedented. However, the sovereign's arbitrary administration of punishment often contrasted with the law proclaimed in the constitutions. Moreover, his subjects suffered high fiscal pressure, the absorption of economic resources by state monopolies, and control over civic life and religious expression.

Frederick devoted himself to art, literature and science with a fervour that deeply impressed his contemporaries, although the coexistence at his court (as at the courts of other European princes) of rational propositions and occult theories gave rise to misunderstandings. Frederick possessed a gift for discovering talent and for capturing the interest of philosophers, mathematicians and scientists—especially through his queries, a sort of oral exam to which he subjected them—which transformed his thirst for knowledge into a force of attraction few could resist. Michael Scotus, recruited as court astrologer, and Theodore of Antioch, his translator, spilled rivers of ink in writings and translations for their sovereign. Previously unknown works by Aristotle, Averroës and Avicenna, in translations from the Arabic and from the Greek, changed the course of Western philosophy.

Frederick participated personally in the famous Sicilian school of poetry. Although his own poetry is somewhat stiff and lifeless, his example encouraged more gifted writers to experiment with the Sicilian vernacular as a poetic language, giving rise to the first example of literature created in an Italian vulgate.

The stylistic models of ancient Capua and the Roman Curia inspired the official writings of the Sicilian chancellery. After Frederick's first trip to Germany, the chancellery took on a new character alongside its administrative functions, becoming a high school of Latin style. With Pier della Vigna and his disciples it competed with the papal chancellery for beauty of expression. In the syntactic constructions, the rhythms and the rhetorical figures of the new school of writers, the Latin language took on an unprecedented expressive capacity and a stylistic flexibility that won the emperor's proclamations and political papers widespread admiration.

Frederick also expressed the Roman character of his empire in other ways. He collected antique sculpture, and had sculptors execute copies of ancient works. The Porte del Ponte at Capua, whose design incorporated antique sculptural fragments and new sculptures of Classical inspiration, announced the values that inspired his monarchy to all those who entered from the north; and the stunning, octagonal Castel del Monte revealed the full originality of his ideas to those who arrived from the south and east. Even the *augustale*, the gold coin circulated after 1231 as the reserve currency of the Mediterranean market, represented the emperor in the Classical manner—as a Caesar crowned with laurel.

Frederick was considered a sceptic in his time, whose tolerance derived from his relativistic conception of religion and the articles of faith. Yet he was by no means an Enlightenment figure *ante litteram*. There is plenty of reason to believe that he considered himself a devout Christian true to precepts of the Church. And although pagan and Oriental elements were present in his conception of empire, he was convinced his sovereign power came from the God of the Christians. In his conflict with the popes he never questioned the institution of the papacy itself, though he contested its supremacy over the empire and claimed for the latter the same *plenitudo potestatis* that the popes claimed for themselves.

During his lifetime, laws and proclamations, letters and literary works, sermons and prophecies, not to mention the invectives of his adversaries, ascribed supernatural powers such as ubiquity and immortality to Frederick. He was *Stupor mundi*, the 'Wonder of the World', and when his life came to an end, doubts arose over whether he was really dead. False Fredericks popped up, demanding obeisance, first in Sicily and then in Germany—and their following, initially, was considerable. In Sicily the story spread that Frederick had thrown himself into Etna; in Germany it was rumoured that he had gone to sleep in a mountain (the Kyffhäuser in Thüringia) and that he would awaken at the end of time to restore order to the world.

Opinions of Frederick have always been controversial. Burckhardt saw him as the first modern monarch. The 20th-century biographer Ernst Kantorowicz was more cautious, but still raised Frederick above his historical context, giving him personal credit for developments that, in reality, were firmly rooted in the political and social situation of his time. What cannot be dismissed are the fascination and fear Frederick inspired in his own and later generations, to whom his uncommon deeds and exceptional stature inspired that myth of the emperor as *Stupor mundi*, which still accompanies his name today.

Lagopesole

At **Atella**, 6km south of Rionero Vulture, the Puglian aqueduct crosses the valley. The village has a 14th-century Romanesque-Gothic cathedral. Fourteen kilometres further south stands **Lagopesole** (829m), huddled at the foot of the last of Frederick II's great castles, begun in 1242. The emperor spent the last summer of his life here. The castle was built as a mountain retreat and as a bulwark against the rebellions that became frequent in Basilicata towards the end of his reign. It was also frequented by Manfred, and by Charles of Anjou, who restored it in 1266, after Manfred's defeat at the Battle of Benevento, and made it the prison of Helena, Manfred's wife.

The reddish tone of the walls is due to the oxidation of iron salts in the rock. The entrance, on the west side (*open daily summer 9.30–1 & 4–7; winter 9.30–1 & 3–5; T: 0971 86083*), leads to a vaulted hall and then to the imposing courtyard, flanked on the north and west by the royal apartments and containing a series of fine mullioned windows. The chapel, in the southeast corner, is linked by a covered gallery to the emperor's apartments. A double staircase on the south side ascends to a smaller court, at the centre of which stands the massive square keep. The entrance, 8m above ground, is marked by corbels that at one time supported an external platform. The roof was carried on the two carved heads visible above, one of which is traditionally said to represent Beatrice, second wife of Emperor Barbarossa, and the other, with ass's ears, to be a likeness of the emperor himself.

VENOSA & ENVIRONS

Venosa (*map p. 290*), the ancient *Venusia,* is famous as the birthplace of the Roman poet and satirist Horace (Q. Horatius Flaccus, 65–8 BC), whose statue adorns the piazza; and of Manfred (born 1232), son of Frederick II and King of Sicily.

HISTORY OF VENOSA

The surrounding territory was inhabited in prehistoric times and constitutes one of the richest archaeological areas in Basilicata. Traces of Chellean and Acheulean settlements (Palaeolithic period) have been found at the borders of the Venosa basin, which at one time probably held a large lake. Some of the objects brought to light by recent excavations may be seen in the Museo Archeologico (*described below*), although the bulk of the material is distributed among the museums of Potenza, Matera, Rome, Florence and Milan. *Venusia*, originally an Apulian town, became the largest colony in the Roman world in 290 BC; Hannibal ambushed and killed the celebrated Roman general Marcellus here in 208 BC.

In Piazza Umberto I stands the great 15th-century castle, with cylindrical corner towers, a broad moat and a lovely arcaded courtyard. The interior hosts the **Museo**

Archeologico Nazionale (*open Tues 2–8, Wed–Mon 9–8; T: 0972 36095*) ⋎. nating display of Greek, Italic, Roman and medieval antiquities from excavat⋏ Venosa and its territories. The collection focuses on the Roman colony of Venusi⋏, with epigraphs, coins, architectural fragments and ceramics documenting the city's political and cultural history (including the presence of a large Jewish population that buried its dead in catacombs adjoining those of the Christians). Also interesting are the bone fragments and other traces of *homo erectus* (who lived c. 300,000 years ago), among the oldest such finds in Europe; and finds including Acheulean hand-axes and some implements of the so-called Clactonian culture (early Palaeolithic), the third phase of which is named after Venosa.

Across the square from the castle is a 13th-century monumental fountain built by order of Charles II of Anjou and guarded by two Roman lions. To the west the undistinguished remains of the supposed tomb of Marcellus can be seen. The **cathedral** dates from the 16th century; its walls contain fragments of Roman buildings. The church is entered by a rustic Renaissance portal and contains a painting of the *Martyrdom of St Felix* attributed to Carlo Maratta. Behind the cathedral to the north are the 15th-century fountain of San Marco (which takes its name from a demolished church) and an interesting early 20th-century public laundry.

The abbeys of La Trinita and Santa Maria

To the northeast of the town (at Località San Rocco) lie the considerable remains of **La Trinita Abbey**, one of the most impressive monastic complexes in Basilicata. Founded by the Benedictines c. 1046, the abbey predates the Norman invasion. It stands on the ruins of an early Christian church, which in turn overlies a Roman temple. The new church (incomplete) dates from 1063. Notice the Cluniac form of the building, including a splendid ambulatory; also the beginnings of two *campanili* and the fine carvings of the capitals. To the south of this part of the group can be seen the remains of an early Christian baptistery. The earlier church dates from the time of the abbey's foundation, but was later enlarged and redecorated. It has a fine façade with a beautifully carved second portal with horseshoe arch, inside the first porch. Many carved pieces belonging to the buildings are displayed to the right.

The interior contains what is said to be the tomb of Robert Guiscard (d. 1085) and of his first wife Alberada, divorced on the grounds of consanguinity. Robert's sarcophagus also contains the remains of his half-brothers, William Bras-de-Fer, first Count of Apulia (d. 1046), Drogo (murdered in 1051), and Humphrey (d. 1057). Numerous frescoes decorate the walls, including one that is possibly a portrait of Joan I of Naples, under which is a 14th-century *Pietà* attributed to Roberto d'Odiserio. The extensive remains of Roman baths, including walls in *opus reticulatum* and some fine mosaic pavements, flank the baptistery. Across the road (*in an archaeological park; open 9–dusk*) are remains of a Roman amphitheatre and, further on, Jewish catacombs hewn out of the rock c. 50m above the road.

Time permitting, a further excursion can be made from Venosa to another ruined abbey. Head for the town of **Banzi**, 25km southeast, where the parish church encloses

ey of Santa Maria. These can be seen from the sacristy;
of the north aisle; and in the walls of the adjoining hous-
rances (an arch leading from the main street). The church
el to the left of the high altar, a 12th- or 13th-century wood-
f the Madonna and Child and the remains of a triptych attrib-
.lerno. Over the high altar is a *Madonna* in the Byzantine style.

Ove₁ of the church is a relief of the Madonna and Child.

About ·, ₁rtheast of Potenza, with a station on the Potenza–Bari line, stands **Acerenza**, a s₁₋all town splendidly situated on a calcareous hill. The Romanesque cathedral, rebuilt in 1281, has an ambulatory with three radiating chapels and a splendid west portal. The crypt contains early 16th-century frescoes of rustic charm. Within the church is a small museum with a marble bust, said by some to represent Julian the Apostate and by others (more doubtfully) to be a likeness of Frederick II. The curious cylindrical tower is a later addition.

POTENZA & THE ROUTE EAST

Potenza (pop. 68,000), the highest provincial capital of mainland Italy (820m; only Enna, in Sicily, is higher), has suffered much from war and earthquakes, and its architecture is undistinguished. The overall atmosphere of the city is nevertheless quite pleasant. In Via Lazio is the **Museo Archeologico Provinciale Lucano** (*entrance in Via Cicotto; open Sun and Mon 9–1, Tues–Sat 9–1 & 4–7; T: 0971 444833*), with a fine collection of objects from Metapontum (*see p. 310*) and other Lucanian excavations, notably local antique ceramic ware, Archaic bronze statuettes, terracottas, a bronze helmet from Vaglio, an early 5th-century *kouros* and a 5th-century marble *tempietto* from Metapontum. Look closely and you will notice that some of the terracottas, made from clay quarried in gold-rich riverbeds, contain tiny specks of the precious metal.

South of the museum stands the church of Santa Maria del Sepulcro, originally 13th-century but altered in the 14th and 17th centuries, and now restored to its original state. The church contains a fine polyptych attributed to Andrea Solario.

East of Potenza

The area east of Potenza is studded with small sleepy villages in a magnificent landscape. **Vaglio Basilicata** is the first of the little towns of medieval aspect that crown small hills above the highway (Road 7) that rises and falls along the wooded north slopes of the wide valley of the Basento river. At the entrance to the village is a piazza containing two fountains. To the right is a pleasing Renaissance portal, near to which stands an ex-Franciscan monastery (now an orphanage) enclosing the church of Sant'Antonio (*ring at convent for admittance*), which contains many excellent examples of Baroque gilded and painted woodwork, including a particularly outstanding 17th-century carved and painted wooden pulpit. There are also several statues, among the best of which is a terracotta of St Anthony Abbot, in the centre of the screen behind the high altar.

Just outside **Tricarico** lie the monasteries of the Carm
Sant'Antonio is of little interest, but the Carmine contains a
frescoes (much damaged) and, in the church, 17th-century fr
tain liveliness in content and execution, the best being those i
figures of saints on the choir arch. In the town itself is the fine
Norman castle. The church of Santa Chiara, entered through ....g a
17th-century Crucifix, has a fine gilded ceiling. The duome, ...cted by Robert
Guiscard but many times restored, contains interesting woodwork, exuberant
Baroque stucco in the chapel to the right of the high altar and the tomb of Diomedo
Carafa (1639), a member of the powerful southern Italian family which in its time has
provided the Church with numerous cardinals, and a pope (Paul IV).

The road climbs away from the Basento to **Miglionico**. The impressive castle is
thought to be the place where Antonello Sanseverino and his barons hatched their
unsuccessful conspiracy against Alfonso of Aragon in 1481. Alfonso, son of King
Ferdinand I, was Duke of Calabria. And though he had successfully retaken Otranto
from the Turks, the rule that he instituted in his domains was greatly to the distaste
of the feudal lords. The church of San Francesco contains a splendid *Madonna and
Child with Saints* by Cima da Conegliano (1499). The Crucifix over the high altar is
flanked on one side by the Madonna and on the other by St Francis. The *Chiesa
Matrice* has a Romanesque campanile, with sculptured figures set into its higher
regions, and a Renaissance-Baroque portal with a *Pietà* in the lunette.

MATERA

Beyond the Bradano, which runs through a deep gorge here, and Lago San Giuliano,
a lake made by damming the river, you climb through ever-wilder scenery scarred by
deep ravines carved out of the chalk. Matera, capital of its province, is beautifully situated (399m) on the edge of a ravine.

HISTORY OF MATERA

The environs of Matera appear to have been inhabited since Palaeolithic times,
and for this reason make up one of the most important archaeological zones of
southern Italy. However, little is known of the city's ancient history. Although
Greek tombs have been discovered in the area of the old town or *civita*, it is generally agreed that the Greek settlement at Matera was of little importance. The
town was destroyed by the Saracens in 944 and its inhabitants killed or dispersed. In 1638 it became the capital of Basilicata, a position which it retained
until Potenza rose to primacy in 1806. Today Matera is a very pleasant modern
city; a few of its 55,000 inhabitants have moved back to the *Sassi*, ancient cave
dwellings, recently renovated.

Museo Ridola to the duomo

...r the town by Via Ridola. A little way down on the left stands the church of Santa Chiara, with 18th-century woodwork of a certain rustic charm. Next to this, in the former Poor Clares convent, is the **Museo Nazionale Domenico Ridola** (*open June–Sept Tues–Sun 9–8, Mon 2–8, Sat 9–11; T: 0835 310058*), which contains changing displays of material from the local excavations, including Corinthian helmets in bronze dating from 5th century BC, Roman bronze vases, Greek vases, etc; and an extraordinary prehistoric collection, ranging from Palaeolithic finds from Matera and its environs, to late Bronze Age material from Timmari, 14km west. The ambience of the museum is very pleasant, and the exhibits are well displayed and clearly marked.

Further on, to the left, stands the **church of the Purgatorio**, with its charming Baroque façade decorated, in part, with strange, somewhat gruesome 18th-century sculptures. Piazza San Francesco has the **church of St Francis**, dating from the 17th century, also with a decorative façade. The second south chapel contains an 18th-century Baroque altar and the 16th-century tomb of Eustachio Pavlicello. Set into the organ case behind the high altar are panels from a polyptych by the 15th-century painter Bartolomeo Vivarini. In the fifth chapel on the north side is the entrance to the earlier church of Santi Pietro e Paolo (*closed*), over which the present church stands. In the first north chapel stands a polychrome wood statue of St Francis.

The street on the south side of San Francesco leads into Piazza Vittorio Emanuele. The decorative entrance to the Conservatorio di Musica can be seen on the right. From here Via del Duomo leads into Piazza del Duomo; along the way, notice the fine palace on the right, opposite which there is a splendid view along the Sasso Barisano valley.

The duomo

The duomo of Matera dates from the 13th century and is Apulian Romanesque in style. The west end has a large rose window carried by angels, and the central portal has fine basket-work carving and a sculptural group representing the Madonna and Child with Sts Peter and Paul. The south side has a carved central window. The door to the west (Porta della Piazza) has another good surround and a carved central relief of monks with the word 'Abraham' inscribed above it. The Porta dei Leoni (the east door; *pictured opposite*) take its name from the two lions at its base.

The interior is built to a Latin-cross plan with a tall nave of typically Lombard conception, and aisles divided by columns (some from Metapontum) with extraordinary capitals. In the first north chapel are a 13th-century *Madonna and Child* of Byzantine style, and the finest inlaid altar in the church. Further on is the Cappella dell'Annunciata, a sumptuously decorated 16th-century edifice containing good sculpture by Altobello Persio, a local artist, and helpers. At the end of the north aisle, set into an elaborate carved surround, are other figures by Persio and Sannazzaro

Matera duomo: Porta dei Leoni (13th century).

d'Alessandro. To the left of this is a chapel containing an immense *Nativity* with a host of sculpted figures, also by Altobello Persio and Sannazaro d'Alessandro (1534). The choir contains 15th-century inlaid stalls by Giovanni Tantino da Ariano Irpino, above which hangs a great painting of the *Assumption and Saints,* of the early 17th-century Venetian school. Over the third south altar is a *Madonna and Child with St Anne* attributed to the Polish artist Sebastiano Majeski (1632), and over the first altar on the same side an *Assumption of the Virgin with Saints* by Giovanni Donato Oppido di Matera; both are in fine carved frames. Next to the Cappella dell'Annunciata a door leads into a passageway, at the end of which the portal of the small church of **Santa Maria di Constantinopoli** can be seen, with worn carving and a 13th-century relief in the lunette showing the carriage procession of the *Madonna della Bruna* (*see p. 316 below*).

Piazza Vittorio Veneto

The Piazza del Duomo (from which there is a fine view over the Sasso Barisano) and Via del Duomo split the *Sassi* into two parts. You can enter both the Sasso Barisano and the Sasso Caveoso from the piazza, or from Via Ridola.

Retrace your steps along Via del Duomo, branching off to the right along Via Margherita. This leads into Piazza Vittorio Veneto, which divides the old town from the new. Just off the piazza is **San Domenico**, a 13th-century church with a rustic façade. The interior contains a repainted statue of the Madonna and Child, of indeterminate date. Above the first altar on the south side hangs a 17th-century copy of Raphael's *Holy Family*, near which is the tomb of the dramatist Orazio Persio (d. 1649). Beyond the church Via San Biagio leads to the church of San Rocco, which contains a brutally realistic Crucifix of the early 17th century.

Almost opposite stands the early 13th-century **church of San Giovanni Battista**, with a fine carved portal on the south side (through which you enter the church) with delicate foliate decoration of Byzantine inspiration and a Saracenic arch embedded in the door recess. The interior is of a strangely inarticulate nature, with interesting carved capitals and an extremely high central elevation, showing signs of early northern Gothic inspiration.

From the opposite end of Piazza Vittorio Veneto, Via Lavista leads southwest to a public garden, from which steps ascend to the unfinished **Angevin castle**. Its builder, the tyrannical Count Tramontano, was killed in a popular revolt on his way out of the cathedral in 1515, in the sidestreet still known as Via del Riscatto, 'street of vengeance'.

Palazzo Lanfranchi in the central Piazza Pascoli, a former seminary and superb example of local 17th-century architecture, now houses the **Museo Nazionale dell'Arte Medievale e Moderna** (*open 9–1 & 4–7; T: 0835 256262*). Highlights here are the Pinacoteca d'Errico, a collection of c. 300 paintings and 400 prints by Neapolitan painters of the 17th and 18th centuries (notably Mattia Preti, Massimo Stanzione, Francesco Solimena, Francesco de Mura, Domenico Antonio Vaccaro and Salvatore Rosa), amassed in the 19th century by Camillo d'Errico, who was mayor of Matera for three decades. The Collezione Carlo Levi is a beautiful group of works by the celebrated 20th-century artist and writer confined to Basilicata by the Fascists.

The Sassi

Tours of the Sassi may be arranged through the Information Office and the affiliated Cooperativa Turistica. The area is divided into 22 work sites, some of which will be closed to the public on any given day.

In this strange valley are to be found habitations, churches and frescoed chapels, some of which are conventionally built, but most of which are carved out of the rock itself. The *Sassi*, which recently came under the protection of UNESCO, are undergoing systematic restoration and rehabilitation; the municipality has begun assigning the renovated homes to newly-weds.

Tours rarely enter all the rock churches (there are simply too many of them). Well worth visiting are **Santa Maria d'Idris** and **Santa Lucia**, both of which contain 13th-century wall paintings, the latter having a particularly fine fresco of *St Michael* and architectural devices carved on the rough stone pillars. Of the churches constructed in a more conventional way (identifiable by their *campanili*), the most interesting are those of San Pietro Caveoso (constructed in

Thirteenth-century fresco of St Michael in the rock church of Santa Lucia.

the 17th and 18th centuries) and San Pietro Barisano (dating from the 12th–13th centuries). The Sasso Barisano is home to the **Museo Laboratorio della Civiltà Contadina** (*Via San Giovanni Vecchio 60, open summer daily 9–1 & 4–8; winter Sat, Sun and holidays by appointment; T: 0835 344057*), documenting material culture in the Materan countryside up to the 1950s.

Many more chapels are cut into the hillsides elsewhere in the ravine; some of them contain frescoes of a surprisingly high quality but a guide is necessary. Of particular interest are **Santa Maria della Valle**, popularly called 'La Voglia', carved out of the rock near the Altamura road, with an interesting façade of 1280 and 17th-century frescoes within; the **Cristo alla Gravinella**, a crypt-church of which the façade and frescoes were reworked in the 17th century; and **Santa Maria della Colomba** (or Santo Spirito), popularly 'La Palomba', in a picturesque position overlooking the Gravina di Matera, with a Romanesque façade incorporating a rose window and 15th-century bas-reliefs.

The well-preserved church of **Santa Barbara**, on the opposite side of the town, is entered through an arched portal flanked by columns, and contains 13th-century frescoes, an iconostasis and, in the ceiling, false domes carved out of the rock.

Neolithic trench villages

The area around Matera is also noted for its Neolithic trench villages, curious settlements centering around circular or elliptical trenches, up to 3m in depth, which originally held hut-like habitations and burial chambers—excavated with the sole aid of simple stone wedges. The material gathered from these sites, now chiefly at the Museo Ridola, includes incised and painted ceramic ware, the latter of a type peculiar to Matera; and numerous broken or discarded tools. Excavations in the area have also brought to light a burial ground with Villanovan cinerary urns and objects decorated in bronze; a Greek necropolis with Apulo-Peucetian tombs of the 4th and 3rd centuries BC containing ceramic ware, bronzes, votive vases and statues; and a sanctuary dedicated to Persephone. (*Further information and guides from the Museo Ridola.*)

Montescaglioso

A pleasant side-trip may be made from Matera to Montescaglioso, a large, mostly whitewashed village (25km south by Road 175). The **Chiesa Maggiore** has an imposing Baroque façade and inlaid altars, of which the high altar is particularly fine. At the top of the village stands the imposing abbey of **San Michele Arcangelo**, a monastic foundation dating from the 11th century, reconstructed by Charles II of Anjou and again partly rebuilt in the late 15th century. The exterior now has the look of a Renaissance building. It contains two interesting cloisters and a small museum of material culture. The territory around Montescaglioso has yielded traces of Lucanian settlements dating from the 6th century BC. Beyond Montescaglioso, you may rejoin the main road leading to Metaponto and the coast (*see map on p. 470*).

View over the *Sassi* at Matera.

SOUTHERN BASILICATA

One of the chief attractions of this rugged, mountainous region (*mainly mapped on pp. 290 and 318*) is the variety of beautiful back roads connecting the Tyrrhenian and Ionian coasts, providing endless possibilities for leisurely exploration. Maratea, on the west coast, is one of Italy's pleasantest seaside resorts, famous at home but unknown abroad.

Ancient Grumentum

A few kilometres south of the Certosa di San Lorenzo (*see p. 282*), near Montesano station, Road 103 crosses into Basilicata by the Sella Cessuta (1028m) to **Moliterno** (*map p. 290*) an interesting old town with a much altered Lombard castle. Beyond Grumento Nova, above the River Agri (right) is the **Roman *Grumentum***, site of two Carthaginian defeats in the Second Punic War. The extensive ruins (*open daily 9–dusk*) were once thought to have yielded the bronze *Armento Rider* (now in the British Museum); it is now thought that the findspot was more likely to have been Armento, some way to the northeast. Other finds may be seen in the small Museo Nazionale Archeologico dell'Alta Val d'Agri (*open Mon 2–8, Tues–Sun 9–8; T: 0975 65074*). Highlights include Greek and Italic burial treasures, and a sculptural portrait of Livia, wife of Augustus Caesar. The road continues steeply left to **Stigliano**, a superbly sited old town, then descends via Montalbano Ionico to Scanzano, on the Ionian seaboard. Alternatively, Road 598, an expressway, bears east after Grumentum, skirting the north shore of the lovely **Lago di Pietra del Pertusillo**, past a turn for Armento, and following the Agri valley to Scanzano. Both roads are remarkable for the dramatic quality of the landscape, which increases its power and beauty as you near the sea. (*See p. 309 below for the Ionian coast of Basilicata.*)

The Sinni valley

Lagonegro is a small town somewhat bleakly situated high in the mountains. In the wooded Piazza Grande are three Baroque churches: Sant'Anna (1665), San Nicola (1779–1839), and the Madonna del Sirino, flanked by an open chapel containing Romanesque pillars and two lions from another building. Monna Lisa del Giocondo (Leonardo da Vinci's 'Mona Lisa') is said to be buried in the 10th-century church of San Nicola, in the old town. According to the story—to which local people cling with extreme tenacity—the Florentine merchant's daughter had accompanied her husband on a business trip to the South, was taken ill at Lagonegro, and died here in 1505. Monte del Papa (2005m), to the east (ascent in 3–4hrs), commands views of both the Tyrrhenian and Ionian seas.

Road 653 runs across southern Basilicata to the Ionian Sea at Nova Siri. It commands exceptional views down the Sinni valley to the coast, passing through **Chiaromonte**, where the parish church contains a medieval Crucifix, two paintings of the Neapolitan school and a good inlaid marble altar; and **Senise**, where the church of San Francesco has a polyptych by Simone da Firenze and good choir stalls. Senise stands on a lake formed by Europe's first earthwork dam, visible from the road just east of the town.

Roughly halfway between the lake and the coast a minor roa.
In the lower town is the cathedral, which has two interesting repres...
Annunciation, a good painted ceiling, and a majolica floor. A fine monstranc. ,
can be admired in the sacristy. In the upper town, reached by a stiff climb, the Chiesa
della Rabatana, once the cathedral, dates from the 16th century but was much altered
in the 18th. It has a fine inlaid marble high altar and a 14th-century triptych representing the *Madonna dell'Icona*, with scenes from the life of Christ and the Virgin.
Steps lead down to an earlier crypt, where a chapel contains 16th-century frescoes
and, in an adjoining room, a *Nativity* composed of carved stone figures. It dates from
the 16th century and has great—though somewhat naïve—charm.

On a ridge between the Sinni and Agri valleys, near the coast, is the isolated church
of **Santa Maria di Anglona**, a Romanesque construction initiated in the 11th century, but today consisting mainly of alterations and additions from later centuries. It has
a good west portal, a fine apse and a number of interesting but crude carvings let into
different parts of the building. The interior contains 11th-, 12th- and 13th-century
frescoes and the curious *Madonna Nera*, of uncertain date and provenance.

The Tyrrhenian coast

Rivello is a small town perched on a hill, scenically dominating the valley of the River
Noce. Founded by a Basilian community, it was the object of a long dispute among
Lombards and Byzantines. While the Lombards conquered and fortified the lower
town, the Greeks retreated to the top of the hill, with the result that the inhabited centre was divided in two parts: one following the Latin rite and concentrating around
the church of Santa Maria Maggiore, the other, of Greek rite, concentrating around the
fortress-like church of San Nicola. The division, which lasted until the 17th century
when the Greek rite was abolished, has left its traces in the names of streets, squares
and fountains. Byzantine traces are also visible in the architectural structure and the
tiled cupolas of some churches, like San Michele dei Greci, Sant'Antonio (*see below*)
and Santa Barbara, which is decorated with frescoes of saints by the local 16th-cen-
tury painter Antonio Ajello. Unfortunately, a great part of the lower town was heavily damaged by the earthquake of 1998; nevertheless it maintains the charm of its narrow streets enlivened with balconies, loggias and architectural decorations.

Below the historic centre lies the interesting **monastery of Sant'Antonio**. Begun as a
Basilian foundation, it was turned into a Benedictine and later a Franciscan convent. The
entrance porch has 16th–17th-century frescoes and a Catalan door flanked by two lions.
The interior, refurbished in the Baroque style, is decorated with stucco work and 17th-
century paintings. Behind the altar are choir stalls (1623–53) charmingly carved with
religious and lay themes ranging from saints and episodes from the Old Testament, to
amusing genre scenes of everyday life, hunting, seasonal arts and crafts and fantastic animals. They were executed and signed by a Benedictine monk, Fra' Ilario da Montalbano,
and provide a provincial counterpart to the much earlier and more refined choir stalls
of the Certosa di San Lorenzo (*see p. 282*). The adjacent cloister has 17th-century frescoes, and the refectory a colourful *Last Supper* animated by a wealth of anecdotal details.

The clustering houses of Maratea, in the hills above the Tyrrhenian shore.

From Lagonegro Road 19 winds southwards towards Lauria; from a junction 5km north of the village (take the Lauria Sud exit if you come by *autostrada*), a fine new road (No. 653) runs east via Latronico and the Parco Nazionale del Monte Pollino (*see p. 321*).

Maratea

Maratea, pleasantly situated on a hill-slope above the villages of Acquafredda, Fiumicello and Marina di Maratea, is Basilicata's finest seaside resort. The town commands a marvellous view of Policastro bay. At Maratea Inferiore is the church of Santa Maria Maggiore, containing very fine 15th-century Gothic choir stalls, a marble *Virgin in Glory*, and paintings of the Neapolitan school. The former church of the Franciscans has an interesting cloister. From Maratea Superiore the road continues for about a kilometre to the sanctuary of San Biagio, with good views back into Campania to Capo Palinuro and Monte Bulgheria.

Local roads and a short stretch of Road 585 link Maratea with Lauria, from where Road 19 winds along the south slopes of the Pollino Massif to Calabria. The landscape is a harmonious medley of forest, pasture and fields of grain.

THROUGH ANCIENT LUCANIA

NB: This area is covered by the map on p. 470.

Before the Byzantine Emperor Basil II (976–1025) evicted the Saracens from southern Italy, Basilicata (the 'land of Basil') was known by its ancient name, *Lucania*. Today numerous excavations testify to the importance of this region in the Greek and Roman world. The major archaeological sites of Metapontum and Heracleia, lying on a plain near the sea, have excellent museums affording insight into life in the Greek colonies of Magna Graecia.

HERACLEIA

The Pantano di Policoro, a thicket of myrtle, oleander and lentiscus, extends along the north shore of the River Sinni (formerly the *Siris*), the boundary between Basilicata and Calabria. The hills come close to the sea near Rocca Imperiale (*map p. 290*), with a castle built by Frederick II on an eminence 4km west of the road. Just west of Policoro, excavations after magnetic soundings in 1961–67 have located the site of *Heracleia*, a joint colony of *Taras* (Taranto) and *Thurii*, founded in 433 BC at the end of a ten-year struggle for control of the fertile Siri valley. The painter Zeuxis was born here in the 5th century BC, and Pyrrhus achieved his first victory over the Romans (who were terrified by the appearance of a herd of elephants) in 280 BC.

The museum

The Museo Archeologico Nazionale della Siritide (*open Tues 2–8, Wed–Mon 9–8; T: 0835 972154*), close by the ruins, contains the result of excavations from the site of Siris-Heracleia and others in the Valle d'Agri (including Roccanova, Sant'Andrea, Castranova, Chiaromonte). The museum is customarily used as a way-station for burial treasures excavated in the environs and awaiting restoration: the entrance hall sometimes holds entire tombs, complete with earth, in open crates. The exhibits follow an open plan: the rooms to the left of the entrance are mostly concerned with diggings from Siris-Heracleia, and those to the right with the Valle d'Agri excavations. The rooms are well laid out and clearly labelled, with an abundance of plans and photographs to show the sources of the finds.

To the left are terracottas from the 6th–1st centuries BC, including a disc with a votive inscription; an ivory figure (4th century BC); a fictile bust of Hephaistos (second half of the 4th century BC); results of excavations in the Sanctuary of Demeter at Heracleia, including heads of divinities, fragments of painted vases, several bronze plates with dedicatory inscriptions and the representation of the divinity Eleusinie (late 5th century BC); a large Laconic *krater* (Archaic) used in Classical times for libations and filled with small votive vases, coins, etc.

To the right are two fine burial treasures, one from the tomb of a man, the other from that of a woman; a Corinthian helmet, remains of armour and other bronze ware

uries BC; Roman glass; the skull of a young girl still bearing her
̦ure *lekythos* by the Painter of Edinburgh; coins from the
and Bendis; Greek vases, including a *hydria* showing a conver-
̦g people in the presence of Eros, by the Painter of Amykos (5th
, of vases by the Painter of Policoro (late 5th–early 4th century BC);
and a sup̦ ̦ portraying Poseidon and Athena, attributed by some to the Painter
of the Carnee, and by others to the Painter of Policoro.

A brief turn inland

The Agri valley road (no. 595), between Heracleia and Metapontum, is one of the most
spectacular in southern Italy; the landscape, deeply eroded by wind and rain, affords
views of a strange, wild beauty that certainly merit a short detour (20mins up and
20mins back are sufficient to get a taste of what the countryside can offer). Along the
road are numerous villages, of little artistic merit but fascinating by virtue of their strong
intrinsic character. Another road worth exploring (no. 63) runs up the Sinni valley.

METAPONTUM

The River Bradano marks the border between Puglia and Basilicata. On the river bank,
to the north of the road, is the acropolis of the ancient *Metapontum*, the entrance to
which is marked by the disused antiquarium.

HISTORY OF METAPONTUM

Founded in the 7th century BC, possibly from Pylos in the western Peloponnese,
Metapontum may have served initially as a buffer state between the Achaean
colony at *Sybaris* and the Spartan *Taras* (Taranto). Archaeological evidence suggests that it was built on the site of an earlier, indigenous settlement. The city prospered due to the suitability of the surrounding land to agriculture and its excellent
location for trade with *Poseidonia* (Paestum) and the Tyrrhenian colonies.

Pythagoras transferred his school here after his expulsion from Croton (*see p.
327*), giving rise to a philosophical tradition that was carried on long after his
death in 497. Alexander, King of Epirus, killed in battle against the Bruttians and
Lucanians, was buried at Metapontum. During the Second Punic War the city
sided with Hannibal, who, on his retirement from Italy in 207 BC, evacuated the
inhabitants to save them from Roman vengeance. Later, the city was sacked by
Spartacus.

Air surveys of the area have revealed the limits of the city walls (c. 6km in circumference); the grid-like street plan, with wide avenues at regular intervals and
rectangular *insulae* measuring c. 190m by 38m; the agora; and an artificial harbour at the mouth of the Basento, linked to the town by a canal.

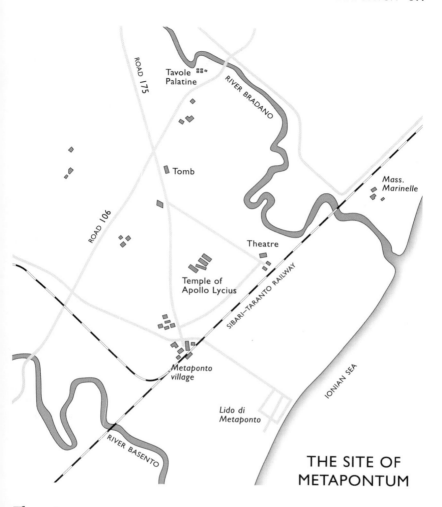

THE SITE OF
METAPONTUM

The ruins

The **Tavole Palatine**, a peripteral hexastyle temple of the Doric order, is the most
extensive remnant of the ancient colony and one of the best preserved monuments of
Magna Graecia. Built in the late 6th century as a sanctuary, probably dedicated to
Hera, it stands 3km from the urban centre. Of its 32 Doric columns, 15 are still
upright; some bear traces of their original stucco. Although parts of the lower course
of the architrave have been preserved, the entablature has disappeared altogether.
Much remains, however, of the stylobate and the foundations of the cella, which
seems to have been divided into two unequal parts.

The remainder of the town may be reached by following Road 106 c. 2km south to the junction with Road 175 and turning left (immediately on the left, remains of a monumental tomb from the Hellenistic period; further on, on the right, another tomb from the 5th century). From the modern village of Metaponto, where there is a modern **antiquarium** (*open Tues–Sun 9–8, Mon 2–8; T: 0835 745327*) with temporary exhibitions of finds from the excavations, a country road follows the railway north to (c. 3km, left) the theatre and the **Temple of Apollo Lycius**, a Doric construction of the 6th century BC. From the fragmentary remains archaeologists have deduced that this temple, like that of the Tavole Palatine, had 32 columns, 6m high. Numerous sections of these, as well as several Doric capitals and pieces of the architrave, have been found on the site, and a reconstruction is underway. Excavations around the perimeter of the temple have revealed traces of smaller religious buildings and numerous Archaic votive statuettes.

PRACTICAL INFORMATION

GETTING AROUND

• **By road:** Melfi and its region is best reached via Autostrada A16 and Road 658, an expressway that follows roughly the same route as the older (and slower) state highway, Road 96. Road 658 also provides access from the south via Potenza, which has its own fast road link to Autostrada A3/E45 (Salerno–Reggio Calabria). Two good roads link Potenza with Matera: the older and slower one is the old Via Appia; the other is an expressway along the valley of the Basento, Road 407. It terminates at Metaponto, on the Ionian coast.

Country buses provide infrequent but punctual services throughout the region Fast north–south access to the area is provided from Naples and Reggio Calabria by Autostrada A3/E45. Road 106, which is being widened at the time of writing to make a four-lane expressway, runs along the Ionian coast. The many minor roads are safe and well maintained, but not for those who suffer motion sickness.

• **By rail:** Travelling to northern Basilicata by train is a problem. The main Salerno–Taranto line serves Potenza, with fast Eurostar trains making the run from Salerno in c. 1hr 30mins, or from Taranto in 1hr 50mins. From Taranto to Metaponto, junction for Potenza and Naples, 44km in c. 30mins. There is no line in the Melfi area, and you have to get a bus at Ferrandina for Matera. The Taranto–Reggio line hugs the Ionian coast. Slow regional trains cover the 76km from Bari to Matera via Altamura in c. 1hr 40mins. There are also slow trains from Altamura to Potenza. Potenza has two railway stations: Inferiore (Trenitalia) on the main Salerno–Taranto line, with a branch to Foggia, and Città for Altamura and Bari. Maratea has a station on the main Salerno–Reggio Calabria railway

INFORMATION OFFICES

Maratea Piazza del Gesù 40, Fiumicello di Santa Venere, T: 0973 876908.
Matera Via de Viti de Marco 9, T: 0835 331983 and Piazza del Gesù 32, T: 0973 876908, www.aptbasilicata.it
Potenza Via del Gallitello 89, T: 0971 507611, www.aptbasilicata.it, and Via Anzio 44, T: 0971 448647, www.regione.basilicata.it

HOTELS

Acerenza
€ **Il Casone**. Modern, quiet and comfortable, in the wooded countryside of the upper Bradano valley. Open all year. 6km northwest at Bosco San Giuliano, T: 0971 741141.

Bernalda
€ **Relais Masseria Cardillo**. Ten beautifully-furnished rooms (with restaurant) in a fortified farm complex a stone's throw from Metapontum and the beach. Open April–Oct. Strada Statale 407, km 98, T: 0835 748 992, www.masseriacardillo.it

Maratea and coastal Basilicata
€€€ **Santavenere**. Overlooking the sea from a lovely garden, with large luminous rooms, pool and tennis courts. Open April–Oct. Via Santavenere 28, T: 0973 876910.
€€ **Locanda delle Donne Monache**. In a former convent, with four-poster beds, private garden, magnificent views. Open April–Oct. Via Mazzzei 4, T: 0973 877487, locdonnemonache@tiscalinet.it
€€ **Villa Cheta Elite**. ■ Quietly elegant turn-of-the-century villa in a superb garden with magnificent sea views and good restaurant. Open all year. Via Timpone 46, Acquafredda, T:

0973 878134, www.villacheta.it
€ **La Tana**. In a pleasant garden 10km south of Maratea, with good views over the bay of Policastro, shuttle service to the best beaches, and an excellent restaurant. Open Feb–Dec. Via Nazionale 26, at Castrocucco, T: 0973 871770, latana@tiscalinet.it

Matera
€€ **Italia**. An old-established place near the *Sassi* and the archaeological museum. Open all year. Via Ridola 5, T: 0835 333561, www.albergoitalia.it
€€ **La Casa di Lucio**. ■ Beautiful, romantic small hotel in the heart of the historic Sasso Caveoso. Open all year. Via San Pietro Caveoso 66, T: 0835 312798.
€ **Il Piccolo Albergo**. Small and atmospheric, in a former patrician town house. Open all year. Via de Sariis 11, T: 0835 330201.
€ **I Sassi**. Central and comfortable, with views of the cathedral and the Sassi. Via San Giovanni Vecchio 89, T: 0835 331009, hotelsassi@virgilio.it

Pietrapertosa (42km southeast of Potenza)
€ **Il Frantoio**. A simple place with just 12 rooms, overlooking the village and the mountains of central Basilicata. Open all year. Via M. Torraca 15/17, T: 0971 983190.

Policoro
€ **Callà 2**. A modest, Mediterranean-style establishment with 20 luminous rooms. Open all year. Via Lazio; T: 0835 981098, www.hotelcalla.it

Potenza
€ **Vittoria**. A comfortable place, with hardwood floors and good bathrooms, just outside the city centre. Via della Tecnica 11, T: 0971 56632.

Rifreddo (12km south of Potenza)
€ **Giubileo**. A quiet place in a shady
garden in the hills near Potenza; good
restaurant. Open all year. Strada Statale
92, T: 0971 479910, hgiubileo@tin.it
Rionero in Vulture
€ **Masseria delle Sorgenti**. ■
Beautifully-situated farm with simple
rooms, good food and excellent home-
made *Aglianico* wine. Road 167 km
13.50, at Monticchio, T: 0972 731300.
Trivigno (southeast of Potenza)
€ **La Foresteria di San Leo**. Six rooms
in a former Benedictine monastery, with
restaurant and good views over the
Lucanian Dolomites. Open April–Dec.
Contrada San Leo, T: 0971 981157.
Venosa
€ **Orazio**. In a 17th-century palace,
with antique majolica and inlaid marble
floors. Open all year. Corso Vittorio
Emanuele II 142, T: 0972 31135.

RESTAURANTS

Acerenza
€ **Palazzo Gal.** Refined restaurant in
the historic centre conscientiously managed by two brothers. Closed Mon. Largo
Consigliere Gala 14, T: 0971 741163.
Avigliano (26km northwest of Potenza
on Road 7)
€ **Pietra del Sale**. Good trattoria in a
former hunting lodge of the Doria family. Closed Mon. Strada Provinciale 50, at
Frusci-Monte Carmine, T: 0971 87063.
€ **Vecchio Lume**. Trattoria, closed Fri
and Sept. Sarnelli, T: 0971 87080.
Barile
€€ **Locanda del Palazzo**. Refined
restaurant serving the best local ingredients prepared with skill and imagination, offers an excellent wine list. Also

rooms. Closed Sun evening and Mon,
and two weeks in Feb and July. Piazza
Caracciolo 7, T: 0972 771051, www.
locandadelpalazzo.com
Bernalda
€ **Da Fifina**. Simple family-run tratto-
ria. Closed Sun (except in Aug) and
Sept. Corso Umberto 63, T: 0835
543134.
Castelmezzano (42km southeast of
Potenza on Road 407)
€€ **Dolomiti**. Restaurant offering good
grilled meats and wines. Also rooms.
Closed Mon. Via Volini 7, T: 0971
986075.
€ **Al Becco della Civetta**, *Osteria* with
great home cooking in the heart of the
'Lucanian Dolomites'. Closed Tues.
Vicolo I Maglietta 7, T: 0971 986249.
Francavilla in Sinni
€ **Fontana del Tasso**. A farm in the
Monte Pollino National Park, traditional
dishes prepared with flair. Closed Tues
and in autumn. Contrada Scaldaferri 40,
T: 0973 644566.
Lagonegro
€ **Valsirino**. Country cooking on a
beautiful farm between Lagonegro and
Maratea. Always open. Contrada Niello
at Monte Sirino, T: 338 8158496.
Marsico Vetere (47km south of Potenza
near Road 276)
€ **Osteria del Gallo**. *Osteria* in the
Agri valley, at the foot of Monte
Vulturino. Closed Tues (except in sum-
mer). Largo Nazionale 2, Villa d'Agri, T:
0975 352045.
Maratea
€ **Zu Pascali**. Simple country trattoria.
Closed Oct–Easter. Via Varacia 4, at
Massa, T: 0973 870242.
Matera
€€ **La Buca**. Restaurant on the out-

skirts of town, famous for dishes using the delicious local variety of veal (called *podolico*). Closed Sun evening, Mon and July. Via San Pardo 95, T: 0835 261984.

€ **La Stalla**. Trattoria in a former stable carved out of the rock and overlooking the Sasso Barisano. Closed Mon and one week in Aug. Via Rosario 73, T: 0835 240455.

€ **Le Botteghe**. Trattoria in the heart of the Sasso Barisano, with outdoor seating in summer. Closed Wed. Piazza San Pietro Barisano 22, T: 0835 344072.

€ **Lucanerie**. Materan country cooking in a restaurant in the historic centre. Closed Sun evening, Mon and Aug. Via Santo Stefano 61, T: 0835 332133.

€€ **Tommaso**. Quiet, refined, panoramic traditional restaurant. Closed Wed and mid-Aug. Via degli Aragonesi 31, T: 0835 261971.

Melfi

€ **Farese**. Restaurant with rooms at the foot of Monte Vulture. Always open. Via Foggianello 1 at Fogianello, T: 0972 236478.

€ **Novecento**. Low-key popular trattoria. Closed Sun evening, Mon and late July. Contrada Incoronata, T: 0972 237470.

Nemoli (southeast of Lagonegro)

€ **Da Mimì**. Restaurant with rooms by the lovely little Lago Sirino, along the old highway (road 19) from Naples to Calabria. Contrada Lago Sirino, T: 0973 40586.

Pignola (10km south of Potenza on Road 92)

€€ **La Fattoria sotto il Cielo**. Sheep farm and fruit farm serving and selling home-grown products. Closed Wed. Contrada Lago di Piglona, T: 0971 420166.

€ **Amici Miei**. Simple but good, popular with the locals. Closed Mon. Strada Comunale Pantano 6, T: 0971 420488.

Potenza

€€ **Antica Osteria Marconi**. *Osteria* offering tratitional Lucanian cuisine. Closed Sun evening, Mon and mid-Aug. Viale Marconi 233–235, T: 0971 56900.

€ **Da Mimmo il Ciclista**. Trattoria lovingly managed by a passionate cyclist. Closed Sun and mid-Aug. Via Vaccaro 47, T: 0971 54840.

€ **Fuori le Mura**. Restaurant just outside the old city walls, near the churches of San Francesco and San Michele. Via IV Novembre 34, T: 0971 25409.

€ **Triminedd'**. Home cooking in a fine country trattoria. Closed Mon and Aug. Contrada Bucaletto 127, T: 0971 55746.

€ **Zi Mingo**. Excellent inexpensive trattoria often crowded with locals. Closed Mon. Contrada Botte 2, T: 0971 442984.

Rionero in Vulture

€€ **Pescatore**. Restaurant offering great traditional food (and fine views). Closed Wed and Feb. Località Monticchio Bagni, T: 0972 731036.

Rotondella

€ **La Mangiatoia**. Restaurant in a village (near Roads 380 and 106) known as the 'Balcony of the Ionian'. Closed Mon. Via Giotto 23, T: 0835 504440.

Trecchina (southwest of Lauria)

€ **Aia dei Cappellani**. Farm serving home-grown products on a panoramic terrace in summer. Closed Tues (except June–Sept) and Nov. Contrada Maurino, T: 0973 826937.

€ **Da Mamma**. Family-run place offering old-time Lucanian fare. Closed Wed. Piazza del Popolo 17, T: 0973 826129.

€ **Lanterna Verde**. Family-run restaurant in a pleasant little village above Maratea. Closed Mon (except in summer) and Nov–March. Piazza del Popolo 22, T: 0973 826216.

LOCAL SPECIALITIES

Avigliano La Radice at Via Colle San Martino 5 is a delicatessen known for its fresh and conserved truffles, meat and vegetable pâtés and other goodies. The *pasticcerie* in Via Coluzzi and Via Petruccelli make delicious traditional sweets: try the almond *mustazzuol* and anise-glazed *raffioli con naspro*. Avigliano is also an important centre for carved wood and hand-made rugs.

Matera produces imaginatively shaped and coloured bread figures and the distinctive terracotta whistles called *cuccù*. Forno a Legna Cifarelli is a wood-oven bakery making excellent bread and *foccacia* (Via Istria 17). Il Buongustaio is a delicatessen selling local specialities and a good selection of wines (Piazza Vittorio Veneto 1). Matera's craftsmen are famous for their work in terracotta and papier-mâché. The two materials are often combined in the locally crafted Christmas crêches.

Potenza Latteria Capece sells homemade cheeses in Via Vaccaro near Zi Mingo. Panetteria Giovanna Salvatore (Contrada Poggio Cavallo 84b) and Forno di Lucia Pace (Contrada Dragonara) are wood-oven bakeries producing bread, focaccia and sweet and savoury pastries.

Basilicata's finest ceramics are made at **Calvello**, **Grottole**, **Lavello** (*map p. 438*) and **Venosa**. **Rivello** and **Tricarico** are known for their coppersmiths, Policoro for its wrought iron,

Stigliano for its blacksmiths and **Trecchina** for its tinsmiths. People in **San Paolo Albanese** make household textiles from broom.

FESTIVALS & EVENTS

Acettura (Matera) *Matrimonio degli Alberi* A tall, straight *cerro* is cut down in the woods, stripped of its branches and dragged into town. At the same time a crown of *agrifoglio* is cut and formed. On Pentecost the naked trunk is erected and the circular 'crown' placed over its top, symbolising the 'marriage of trees' (reconciliation of opposites, resolution of dualities, and fertile coitus). During the feast days the statue of the patron saint, Julian, is carried in procession, young girls wearing garlands of flowers parade through the streets, music and food abound, and the more courageous youths attempt to climb the pole, Pentecost.

Barile *Passione di Cristo* With children in costume interpreting the Passion, Good Friday; *Sagra del Vino Aglianico e della Castagna* Aglianico Wine and chestnut festival, Sept.

Bernalda *San Bernardino* Statue of the saint carried in procession, fourth Sun in Aug.

Calciano (Potenza) Calciano Jazz festival, Aug. www.comune.calciano.it

Lagonegro *Madonna di Sirino* A statue of the Madonna is carried up to the mountain sanctuary of the Madonna della Neve in June, venerated there in August, then carried back down to town and celebrated with a full carnet of events for three days in Sept (third Sun).

Latronico *Muse Briganti* Jazz festival,

July. www.termelucane.it

Maratea *Maratea Musica Festival*
Classical music in various spaces around
the town, July, T: 0971 37457; Drama
festival, Aug.

Matera *Madonna della Bruna* An annual
religious festival commemorating the
recovery of a Byzantine Madonna stolen
by the Turks and consisting of a colourful triumphal procession, ending in the
destruction of the papier-mâché float on
which the image is borne through the
streets, 2 July; *Lucania Opera Festival*
Teatro Duni (Matera) and Auditorium
del Conservatorio (Potenza), May–June,
www.orchestralucana.it

Melfi *Festa dello Spirito Santo*
Commemoration of the French sack of
Melfi of 23 March 1528, when the populace fled to the Santo Spirito Forest: a
statue of the Trinity is carried up Monte
Vulture in a procession in historic costume, Pentecost.

Montescaglioso *Mardi Gras* A procession featuring personifications of
Carnevalone (Fat Carnival), *Quaremm*
(Lent, his wife, who cries because her
husband will die that day), *U Piccin*
(their newborn child) and *Parca*
(Death), winds its way through town
from the early morning hours knocking
on doors and asking for donations of
food or cash for the evening feast,
which rages until midnight when slow-
tolling church bells announce
Carnevalone's demise, Feb; *Processione
dei Misteri* Procession of the penitents,
led by the *mamuni,* hooded and thorn-
crowned cross-bearers, followed by six
heavy, hand-held wooden floats of
Passion scenes, Good Friday; *San Rocco*
With horse-drawn floats and procession,
20 Aug.

Potenza *Presepe Vivente* The Magi, on
horseback, visit the Christ Child in
Piazza della Prefettura, 6 Jan; *Sacra
Rappresentazione del Venerdì Santo* Re-
enactment of Christ's Passion, Good
Friday; *Maggio Potentino* With artistic,
cultural, and sports events, culminating
in the *Sagra di San Gerardo & Sfilata dei
Turchi,* with four *tableaux vivants* illustrating how the bishop-saint saved the
city from the Turks, May, ending May
29; *Lucania Opera Festival* Teatro Duni
(Matera) and Auditorium del
Conservatorio (Potenza), May–June,
www.orchestralucana.it; *Sagra di San
Rocco* With traditional celebrations, 16
Aug; *Festival Internazionale di Arti
Pirotecniche* International fireworks display competition, first Sun in Sept.

Rionero in Vulture *Via Crucis* Four
Tableaux vivants representing episodes of
Christ's Passion, in four different places
around town, Good Friday.

Tricarico *Mardi Gras* Every town in
Basilicata, it seems, has its own, particular way of representing Carnival. Here
the *Romita* (Hermit), clothed in ivy, and
the *Orso* (Bear), wearing a sheepskin, go
from house to house asking for in-kind
donations for the evening's feast, Feb.

CALABRIA

Calabria, the mountainous peninsula between the Tyrrhenian and the Ionian seas, is the toe of the Italian 'boot'. Roughly 223km long, its northern point culminates in Monte Pollino (2248m), and in the south it terminates in the Aspromonte group (1955m). Central Calabria expands into the granite plateau of the Sila (1928m). The rivers are short but copious. The vegetation along the coast is typically southern, but fine forests and mountain flora prevail inland.

Calabria enjoyed an age of prosperity as part of Magna Graecia, and Croton (where Pythagoras taught), Sybaris, Locri and Rhegion were flourishing cities. Many traces of the past have been destroyed by frequent earthquakes. The chief towns of the region are Cosenza, Catanzaro and Reggio.

On the whole Calabria is now a poor region, though emigration to northern Italy, the United States and Australia has largely been halted. The work of the post-war development programme known as the *Cassa per il Mezzogiorno*, in particular in encouraging hydro-electric schemes in the Sila, has brought considerable improvement; an excellent olive oil is produced in several places (the olive groves at Gioia Tauro are amongst the best in Italy); and a blossoming tourist trade along the Tyrrhenian riviera has actually led to over-development, especially around Reggio and between Praia a Mare and Amantea. In spite of its charms, Calabria is still little known to the English-speaking traveller, though improvements in accommodation have brought most of the area within reach.

On Calabria

Calabria is not a land to traverse alone. It is too wistful and stricken; too deficient in those externals that conduce to comfort. Its charms do not appeal to the eye of romance, and the man who would perambulate Magna Graecia as he does the Alps would soon regret his choice ... The joys of Calabria are not to be bought, like those of Switzerland, for gold.

Norman Douglas: Old Calabria, 1915

Norman Douglas's classic work remains one of the most brilliant, incisive portraits of this rough, wild region—as true to life today as when it was written. Calabria, indeed, is a severe land, a place of steep, harsh mountains, cactus and agave. Noisy and lively along the coast, inland it is silent and sometimes mournfully desolate. Yet it is precisely this disquieting, haunted character that makes it a land of such fascination. Like the summer temperatures, emotions run high here, and the thrill of reaching the peaks of the Pollino massif on foot, or of the first glimpse of Stilo in its desert landscape as you descend from the wooded shades of Serra San Bruno, is truly memorable.

THE TYRRHENIAN COAST TO PAOLA

The Tyrrhenian coast of Calabria is famous in Italy for its superb beaches and picturesque villages. Beyond the lovely resort of Maratea, in Basilicata, the highway and railway run the whole length of Calabria beside the sea. To the east steep mountains separate the seaboard from the rest of the region, rising to heights of well over 1000m. Motorists should bear in mind that traffic can be quite slow during the summer, when the seaside resorts are crowded.

Regardless of whether you arrive from Maratea or from Lagonegro, you enter Calabria just before **Praia a Mare**. Above the town you can see the Santuario della Madonna della Grotta (reached by steps), containing a medieval wooden statue of the Madonna and Child, and another marble *Madonna* of the school of Gagini. Off the coast lies the Isola di Dino, a triangular plateau rising 65m above the sea, with grottoes showing the same light effect as at the Blue Grotto of Capri. The island may be reached by boat from Praia a Mare in c. 20mins.

The road continues beside the sea to **San Nicola Arcella**, a charming little town on a hilltop; then it crosses Capo Scalea and descends once again to the sea. A turning on the left ascends to **Scalea**, an attractive old town rising in steps above a good beach, now largely spoilt by development, but commanding good views of the cape, the sea and the fertile Lao delta. The latter is believed to be the site of the Sybarite colony of *Laos*, a flourishing commercial centre of the 6th and 5th centuries BC that later fell to the Lucanians. Some Greek and Roman remains can be seen at the Antiquarium Torre Cimalonga (*Largo Cimalonga 11; open Tues–Sun 9–7.30; T: 0985 920069*). A Lucanian necropolis has recently come to light south of the river, near the site of the Roman *Lavinium*, remains of which are no longer visible. The church of San Nicola contains a tomb of 1343 that recalls the Pisan style of Tino da Camaino.

On the road from Scalea to Mormanno, deep in the hills, lies **Papasidero**, near which (*car park; marked*) is the rock shelter of Il Romito, with Palaeolithic graffiti depicting bulls and oxen (c. 10,000 BC), discovered in 1961. **Mormanno** itself is a popular refuge from the heat of summer, where the church of Santa Maria del Colle contains much good gilded and carved woodwork, fine Baroque altars, a Tuscan relief to the right of the main altar and, in the sacristy, a good painting of the 18th-century Neapolitan school. The narrow sidestreets are well worth wandering down.

South to Paola

Above Cirella, the ruined medieval town of Cirella Vecchia, destroyed by the French in 1806, is prominent on its hill. South of the town, on the beach before the fortified Isola di Cirella, are the remains of a Roman tomb. Beyond the fishing resort of Diamante (known for its cedar trees) the road hugs the narrow coastal plain to **Belvedere Marittimo**, which commands a splendid view of the sea and the coast. The *Chiesa Matrice* has a 15th-century Tuscan relief above the main door, and the Chiesa del Crocifisso (as the name suggests) a great wooden Crucifix. The ruined medieval castle also merits a glance.

Cetraro has three statues by Giovanni Battista Mazzola (1533) in the church of the Ritiro. Guardia Piemontese and Montalto Uffugo, in the hills to the southeast, were colonised by Waldensians in the late 14th century, but these Protestant colonies were destroyed with great cruelty in 1559–61.

Paola (*map p. 326*), once an attractive town, has been entirely transformed by unchecked development as a resort. It was the birthplace of St Francesco da Paola (1416–1507), founder of the Minims, the strictest order of the Franciscans. The Santuario di San Francesco, above the town to the north, dates from 1435 and is fronted by a long piazza with a modern statue and an obelisk commemorating the Holy Year of 1950. The basilica, dedicated to Santa Maria degli Angeli, has recently been restored; its façade is an unusual mixture of Renaissance and Baroque motifs. The interior contains the 16th-century Cappella del Santo and 15th- and 16th-century artworks of the Neapolitan school; adjacent is a small cloister. In central Paola are several churches of minor interest. The Santissima Annunziata, high in the town, built in the 13th century and later redecorated in the Baroque manner, has been restored to its former state. Above the high altar, with its marble inlay, is a 16th-century painting of the *Annunciation*. A descent may be made by steps (left), passing a pleasing Baroque fountain, through the Porta San Francesco, with another fountain at its centre. Rising at the back you can see the Baroque façade of the church of Santa Maria di Monte Vergine. Santa Caterina, with a Gothic portal of 1493, houses a painting of the *Madonna delle Grazie*, attributed to Domencio Beccafumi.

ACROSS THE APENNINES

The Apennines create a formidable barrier between southwestern Italy's Tyrrhenian and Ionian coasts, creating two distinct bio-regions. On the Tyrrhenian side the moist west wind brings abundant rainfall. The vegetation is therefore quite lush, and where they have not been felled for firewood or pasture, tall shady forests still grow. In summer these provide welcome relief from the sweltering heat on the coast.

The prevailing westerlies are blocked by the peaks of the Maddalena, Pollino and Serra Calabra ranges, leaving the Ionian shores of Basilicata and Calabria in a state of semi-aridity. Only relatively recently has large-scale irrigation made it possible to convert areas of the Ionian bio-region from sheep-grazing to agriculture.

To cross this natural bulwark has always been an arduous undertaking. But if you're not in a rush, it can actually be one of the highlights of a trip to the south.

MONTE POLLINO

There are two explanations for the name Pollino: the first is based on the Latin *pullus* (young animal), whence *Mons Pullinus*, the 'Mountain of the Young Animals', referring to the ancient custom of driving new-born cattle up to graze on the massif's high pastures in spring; the second derives Monte Pollino from the Latin *Mons Apollineus*, the

'Mountain of Apollo', god of health and the first physician, because of the great variety of medicinal herbs that grow on its slopes.

Whatever the case may be, Monte Pollino is one of southern Italy's highest, wildest and most beautiful mountain systems. If you arrive from the south by *autostrada*, it appears as an immense rocky wall running 'across the grain' of the Apennine chain. For centuries it has formed the boundary between Calabria and Basilicata, isolating the latter from the rest of Italy.

Formed largely of limestone, dolomitic limestone, flysch and ophiolite, and populated by wolves, eagles and a unique variety of pine, *Pino loricato*, it is one of the last remaining wilderness areas in the Mediterranean. Myth and mystery come together here, in a setting of rugged natural beauty punctuated by austere stone hamlets and villages. Together, the variety and beauty of its landscape, the unspoilt character of its natural environment, its broad, open horizons and bright, crystalline skies make Monte Pollino an ideal place for walking.

MONTE POLLINO WALKS

Here are three suggested itineraries. The trails are loosely waymarked, so be sure to obtain a map and ideally a local guide. Park office at Rotonda, Via Mordini, 20, T: 0973 661692 or 0973 667802.

1. Pedarreto—Piano Ermite—Monte Grasta circular walk
This 6.5km circuit (4hrs) entails an elevation gain of just 200m. It starts and ends on the highland known as Piano Pedarreto (1350m), a broad, panoramic terrace overlooking the Valle del Mercure. The plateau is made up of a series of rolling, grassy hills backed by the superb beech forests of the Coppola di Paola and bordered on the north by the spectacular Vallone di Mauro. The numerous cold springs, copious even in late summer, make it an excellent place to picnic.

2. Colle dell'Impiso—Serra del Prete circular walk
4hrs 30mins, moderately strenuous. This is a more challenging, 8km circuit with an altitude gain of 670m, overlooking the broad, beautiful Valle del Frido. It starts from Colle dell'Impiso (1570m), the pass between the Timpone di Mezzo and Serra del Prete (*Colle dell'Impiso* means Hangman's Hill in dialect—a haunting reminder of the times of brigandage). The nearest towns are San Severino Lucano and Viggianello.

3. Colle d'Impiso to Monte Pollino by the northeast crest
5hrs 30mins, strenuous. This is a tough but rewarding climb (3.5km up and 2km back) to the top of Monte Pollino (2241m), elevation gain 800m. It goes via the Piani di Vacquarro, the Piani di Pollino, and climbs to the peak towards the top of the gully that marks the mountain's northeast face. For the best views, stick to the more exposed part of the spur all the way to the summit.

THE COSCILE & CRATI VALLEYS

From Mormanno (*see p. 320 above*) the road crosses the Passo di Campotenese, a rich pastoral plateau nearly 900m high. The road descends abruptly, into the valley of the Coscile, passing just east of **Morano Calabro**, dominated on its conical hill by the church of San Pietro, which contains, at the first altars on the north and south sides, marble statues of St Catherine and St Lucy by Pietro Bernini; and, to the left and right of the high altar, statues of St Peter and St Paul by followers of Bernini. Also of fine workmanship are the late 18th-century and early 19th-century choir stalls by the local artist Agostino Fusco, and a beautiful processional Cross, dated 1445, from the Abruzzese workshop of the Guardiagrele. At the bottom of the hill stand the churches of San Bernardino, with a superb carved wooden pulpit of 1611, and La Maddalena, with its tiled cupola, a beautiful 18th-century organ, and a polyptych by Bartolomeo Vivarini, signed and dated 1477, temporarily moved here from San Bernardino.

Castrovillari

Castrovillari stands on an upland plain at the southern end of the Pollino massif. The old town or *civita* has a massive **castle** built in 1490 by Ferdinand I of Aragon to keep the citizens of Castrovillari under his thumb. It was used as a prison by the Spinelli, dukes of Castrovillari—a function it retained until recently.

A small collection of finds from local excavations, including prehistoric, protohistoric, Roman and medieval material, can be seen at the **Museo Civico** in Corso Garibaldi (*open daily 8.30–1, Tues and Thur 8.30–1 & 3–6; T: 0981 25249*). Highlights include a group of 5th-century BC votive statuettes from a temple site at Colle della Madonna del Castello, ceramics from a Roman villa at Camerelle (2nd century BC–2nd century AD); finds from the Italic necropoleis of Bello Luce (8th–7th centuries BC) and Ferrocinte (4th century BC), and treasures from the Lombard necropolis of Celimarro (7th century AD). The museum's other facility, in the 18th-century Palazzo Gallo in Piazza Vittorio Emanuele II, has paintings by A. Alfano and others. The restaurant in **La Locanda di Alia** (*see p. 339*) is said by some to be the finest in Calabria.

A long winding road leads on, past the church of San Giuliano, with its pleasing Renaissance façade, to **Santa Maria del Castello**, a church dating from the 11th century and reconstructed in the 14th. Here, in the Cappella del Sacramento, a fine Baroque altar encloses a fresco of the *Madonna del Castello*, a much revered image in the Byzantine style. On the right wall of the staircase leading up to the cantoria you can see the remains of frescoes, possibly dating from the 13th century. The church also contains two paintings by Pietro Negroni, 17th-century choir stalls and, on a pillar in the south aisle, a 17th-century olive-wood figure of the Crucified Christ. The Baroque high altar and the bishop's throne likewise warrant attention. The sacristy houses a minute museum, which includes a 15th-century copper plate made in Nuremburg and a cope given to the church by Pope Pius IV.

Altomonte and Spezzano Albanese

Road 105 winds south from Castrovillari to Firmo, beyond which a turning on the left leads to **Altomonte** (9km), and the splendid Gothic church of Santa Maria della Consolazione. This is one of the most interesting Gothic buildings in Calabria, constructed, possibly by Sienese architects, under the patronage of Filippo Sangineto, Count of Altomonte, during the Angevin period. The simple façade, which dates from 1380, contains a large rose window. Within is the splendid tomb of the founder, by a follower of Tino da Camaino (c. 1350). The former Dominican convent adjoining the church houses a small museum (Museo Civico di Santa Maria della Consolazione; *open Tues–Sat 8–8, Mon and holidays 10–1 & 4–7; T: 0981 948464*) with works of art removed from the church during a recent restoration. These include small remains of frescoes, three parts of a triptych by an artist close to Bernardo Daddi, a *Madonna and Child* of the 15th-century Neapolitan-Catalan school, and two small panels in alabaster of 1380, related to French art of the period.

On the Ionian side of the *autostrada* is **Spezzano Albanese**, pleasantly spread out on a hillside. The local medicinal springs are exploited as a spa. The costume and dialect of the inhabitants proclaim their descent from Albanian refugees who fled before the Turks and settled here in the 15th century. The people are noticeably tall and fair among the small, dark Calabrians.

A few kilometres south of Spezzano on Road 19, another road (no. 106b) leads east to **Terranova**, where the convent of Sant'Antonio contains rich Baroque work and the cloister has charming rustic frescoes.

The Crati valley

The Autostrada A3 runs south along the Crati valley, notable for its wide expanses of gravel. In summer, the temperature here can reach scorching heights. In the hills to the east lie Bisignano and Acri, both towns of growing importance in the Calabrian hydroelectric scheme. At **Bisignano** remains of a Byzanto-Norman castle can be seen and, in the church of the Riformati, a *Madonna della Grazia* of the school of Antonello Gagini (1537).

Isolated in the mountains 15km north of Acri is **San Demetrio Corone**, the most important Albanian colony in Calabria, with an Italo-Albanian college founded in 1791 by Ferdinand IV. The 11th- or 12th-century church of Sant'Adriano contains a Norman font with a representation of a monkey sitting on two dragons (?) and four pieces of pavement with snakes, birds and leopards, also dating from the Norman construction.

AROUND THE GULF OF CORIGLIANO

South of Trebisacce is the large alluvial **plain of Sibari** surrounding the mouth of the River Crati. The ancient *Sybaris*, from which Sibari takes its name, probably stood on the left bank of the Crati (*Crathis*). This Achaean colony, whose luxury and corruption have become a byword (sybaritic), was destroyed by the men of Croton (510 BC), who flooded it with the waters of the Crathis. The descendants of the survivors, with the help of a band of Athenian colonists, founded *Thurii* in c. 443 BC, 6km further inland. Among the Athenians were the orator Lysias (d. 402), and Herodotus, who died at Thurii between 430 and 425 BC.

Romanised after 290 BC under the name of *Copiae*, the town lasted until the decline of the Empire. Recent drainage operations, which have greatly improved the former malarial condition of the plain, have brought some traces of Copiae to light, though the exact site of Greek Sybaris remains a mystery. Some of the material discovered to date may be seen in the **Museo della Sibaritide e Parco Archeologico** (*on Road 106 at Contrada Casoni; open daily 9–7.30; closed first and third Mon of the month; T: 0981 79391*).

To the south there is a splendid view of the mountains of the Sila area and, to the north, the steep limestone crags of Monte Pollino, snowcapped except in the height of summer.

The Ionian coast to Cariati

At **Corigliano Calabro** the large church of Sant'Antonio di Padova has a decorative Baroque interior and a good inlaid marble high altar. In the hills southeast of the town lies the Convento del Patire (Santa Maria del Patirion), founded by St Nilus (*see below*) on a rugged peak in magnificent surroundings. In the 12th century it rivalled Mount Athos in Greece as a seat of monastic learning; the church preserves traces of a mosaic pavement.

Rossano lies 6km south of the coast road. The little town was the birthplace of St Nilus (910–1001), founder of the convents of Patire and of Grottaferrata, near Rome. The cathedral has a wooden ceiling and a Baroque altar, attached to a pillar on the north side of the nave, which encloses a Byzantine *Madonna* of the 8th or 9th century. In the archbishop's palace is the Museo Diocesano (*open July–Sept daily 9–12.30 & 4–7; Oct–June Tues–Sat 9.30–12.30 & 4–7, Sun 10–12 & 4.30–6, closed Mon; T: 0983 525263*) in which you can see the celebrated *Codex Purpureus Rossanensis*, an extremely rare Greek work of the 6th century, consisting of 188 sheets of purple parchment bearing gospels copied and illuminated at Caesarea, in Palestine. There are also other parchments, codices, vestments, liturgical objects, and a 15th-century Greek icon, the *Nuova Odigitria*.

The narrow Via Arcivescovado, to the right of the cathedral, leads down to the small church of the Panaglia, a 12th-century building with an interesting apse containing *opus spicatum*. Within is a fresco of St John Chrysostom. At the top of the town stands the 10th-century church of San Marco, built to a Byzantine plan with five domes and three apses. The Passeggiata di Santo Stefano commands a view across the Gulf of Taranto.

Further along the coast, at **Cariati**, you can make a circuit of the old city walls and bastions, into which houses have been built. The cathedral, whose tiled cupola can be seen from the marina, has an impressive interior and contains 18th-century choir stalls by Girolamo Franceschi. The cemetery church (just outside the town) is a bare and pleasing late Gothic building with a well proportioned ribbed dome, completely decorated inside with patterned tiles of Moorish inspiration.

CROTONE

South of the River Neto lies the Marchesato, a former fief of the Ruffo family. Its main city, Crotone, stands on a promontory c. 2km east of the road. An industrial centre of some importance, it has the only harbour between Taranto and Reggio. George Gissing wrote much of his *Ionian Sea* here in 1897.

HISTORY OF CROTONE

The Achaean colony of *Croton*, founded in 710 BC by settlers sent, as legend narrates, by the Oracle of Delphi, became the most important city of the Bruttians. Its dominion, together with that of Sybaris, extended over much of Magna Graecia and included colonies on both the Ionian and the Tyrrhenian coasts. Pythagoras (c. 540 BC) made it the chief centre of his school of philosophy, but was expelled some 30 years later when the oligarchy that he supported and justified was overthrown. In the same century, Croton was conquered by the Locrians but, thanks to the prowess of its champion, Milo (one of a series of famous Crotonian athletes), it vanquished the Sybarites in 510. It submitted to Agathocles of Syracuse in 299. Hannibal embarked here after his retreat from Rome.

In the 13th century its status was revived, and it became the capital of the Marchesato. Most of its ancient buildings were used by Don Pedro of Toledo in the construction of his castle. From the 11th century to 1929 the town was known as Cotrone.

On the road to the town are storehouses for olives, oranges and liquorice. The castle dates from the 16th century. The church of San Giuseppe has a decorative façade with two domed chapels. Nearby is the excellent **Museo Archeologico Nazionale** (*open daily 9–7.30; closed first and third Mon of the month; T: 0962 23082*). The museum was established in 1910 and its collection largely constructed by the early 20th-century archaeologist Paolo Orsi. It has been enriched by maps, plans and photographs of archaeological sites in and around Crotone. The ground floor documents the development of Crotone from prehistoric times to the Middle Ages, with particular emphasis on the founding of the city and the School of Pythagoras. The first floor is devoted to the surrounding territory; the finds include tomb treasures, red- and black-figure Attic pottery, terracotta votive statuettes and architectural details. On the top floor are some extraordinary jewellery (*Gioielli della Dea del Lacinio*) and an assortment of votive offerings from the newest dig, at Capo Colonna. The visit culminates in the room devoted to the *Tesoro di Hera*, a group of bronze, silver and gold objects including a splendid gold diadem.

The Castello Aragonese has a small **Museo Civico** (*open Tues–Sat 9–1 & 4–8, Sun 9–1; T: 0962 921535*) illustrating the history of Crotone with prints, drawings and photographs, coins, weapons and ceramics.

A hilly peninsula lies south of Crotone. Calypso's island of Ogygia was supposed to lie off the coast here. Isola di Capo Rizzato was one of the centres of the 1948 agrarian reform, when large feudal estates were broken up and redistributed. This was one of the first social reforms of the Italian Republic. Capo Colonna (11km) takes its name from the scant remains of a Greek temple (notably a single standing column). The little antiquarium in the 16th-century watch-tower at Torre Nao (*closed at the time of writing; T: 0962 23082*) preserves the cargo of a Roman ship of the 3rd century AD that had set out from Asia Minor but sank off Punta Scifo. Le Castella (25km) is named after the Aragonese fortress built on an island just offshore.

Catanzaro

Catanzaro is an animated city of 104,000 inhabitants, capital of its province. Situated high up between the gorges of two mountain torrents, it boasts a glorious record of opposition to tyranny.

From Catanzaro station a funicular tramway ascends through a tunnel to Piazza Roma and crosses Corso Mazzini. To the west of the corso, near the rebuilt cathedral, is the church of the Rosario (or San Domenico), a Baroque edifice with paintings of the *Madonna del Rosario* and the *Madonna della Vittoria*, celebrating the victory of Lepanto; as well as some marble altars, all 17th century. On the south side of the church is the Oratorio della Congrega del Rosario, with elaborate stucco work. The **Museo Provinciale**, in the public gardens of the Villa Margherita (*open Tues–Fri 9.30–1 & 3.30–5.30, Sat–Sun 9–1; T: 0961 720019*), contains antiquities from Catanzaro and its province: some 8,000 coins (for which it is hugely famous among specialists); the remains of an equestrian monument of the 2nd century AD; prehistoric material; a marble head from Strongoli and a Greek helmet from Tiriolo, of fine workmanship. Adjacent to the museum is the Villa Margherita, a public park commanding exceptional sea views.

On Catanzaro

The sun was setting when I alighted at the Marina, and as I waited for the branch train my eyes feasted upon a glory of colour which made me forget aching weariness. All around lay orchards of orange trees, the finest I had ever seen, and over their solid masses of dark foliage, thick hung with ripening fruit, poured the splendour of the western sky. It was a picture unsurpassable in richness of tone; the dense leafage of deepest, warmest green glowed and flashed, its magnificence heightened by the blaze of the countless golden spheres adorning it. Beyond, the magic sea, purple and crimson as the sun descended upon the vanishing horizon. Eastward, above the slopes of Sila, stood a moon almost at its full, the yellow of an autumn leaf, on a sky soft-flushed with rose. In my geography it is written that between Catanzaro and the sea lie the gardens of the Hesperides.

George Gissing: By the Ionian Sea, 1901

Santa Maria della Roccella and Squillace

Catanzaro Marina is an important industrial town and a crowded, built-up resort. Just 2km south of it is one of the region's most majestic monuments, the ruined church of **Santa Maria della Roccella** (*open 9–dusk*). Although its date of construction is disputed, the church is generally believed to be an 11th-century building modelled on the large Cluniac churches of the north and conditioned by local building traditions. It is built to a Latin cross plan, with a simple nave, three semicircular apses, and a broad transept. The crypt follows the plan of the presbytery and apses. The façade, nave walls and transept have largely fallen down, and access to the crypt is difficult; nevertheless the contrast between the warm red brick of the remaining walls and the cool silver-green of the olives that grow around the ruin is striking. Excavations nearby have begun to bring to light the ruins (forum and theatre) of a Roman settlement.

Squillace, the Greek city of *Schilletion*, later the Roman *Scolacium*, was the birthplace of both Cassiodorus (480–575), secretary to the Byzantine emperor Theodoric, and General Guglielmo Pepe (1782–1855), revolutionary commander of a Neapolitan army (*see p. 25*), and leader of a corps who fought the Austrians in the Venetian revolt of 1848. The cathedral contains 16th-century sculptures and the castle commands a view.

Sant'Eufemia Lamezia and environs

From Catanzaro a fast road runs toward the Tyrrhenian coast, reaching it at Sant'Eufemia Lamezia, which lies in an intensely cultivated plain encircled by beautiful mountains, the lower slopes of which are covered with olive groves. A modern town, and the road and railway junction for the Ionian resort areas, Sant'Eufemia is the sum of five distinct villages, the most impressive being **Nicastro** (11km northeast), the old *Neocastrum* of Byzantine or Norman origin, almost entirely destroyed by an earthquake in 1638. Charmingly built, on the mountainside, it is dominated by the ruins of one of Frederick II's castles, the prison of his rebellious son Henry, who escaped only to die mysteriously at Martirano, 16km northwest. The local costumes worn by the women are beautiful.

MAIDA VALE

East of Lamezia rises the plateau of Maida. The Battle of Maida, by which the British, under Sir John Stuart, expelled the French from Calabria in 1806, gave its name to Maida Vale in London. This battle proved the value of the rifle and the 'thin red line' tactics put to successful use in the Peninsular War.

From Capo Suvero, on the coast, you have a view of the whole curve of the Gulf of Sant'Eufemia and, on a clear day, of Stromboli and the Aeolian Islands. **Amantea** extends downward from its ruined castle to the beach. A modest centre in Roman times, the town has been identified with the *Clampetia* of Livy. It was vehemently defended against the French under Verdier in 1806, but has resisted the recent onslaught of builders and holiday-makers less successfully. The ruins of the medieval church and convent of San Francesco d'Assisi, in the upper part of the town, and those of the vast castle on its hilltop, offer splendid views of the sea and the coastline. In the lower town, the 15th-century church of San Bernardino da Siena is fronted by a portico with five Gothic arches on octagonal piers, with ceramic decorations. The first north chapel contains a *Madonna* by Antonello Gagini (dated 1505) and other sculpture.

In **Fiumefreddo Bruzio**, parts of the medieval town walls and two gates can still be seen. The church of Santa Chiara has a wooden coffered ceiling, coloured majolica-tile floors and three carved and gilded wooden altars. The church of the Carmine, on a hill east of the village, has a 15th-century Gothic portal and remains of a cloister. A dirt track to the north leads in c. 1 hour to the ruined abbey of San Domenico or Fonte Laurato, originally dating from 1020–35, interesting for its mixture of Byzantine and Norman architectural elements.

San Lucido further north is a charming little town on a promontory overlooking the sea. Cardinal Fabrizio Ruffo (1744–1827) was born in the castle here. Ruffo, a Bourbon politician, was the collaborator of Fra' Diavolo, leader of the peasant army assembled to wage war on France's Parthenopean Republic (*see p. 40*).

COSENZA & ENVIRONS

Road 107 runs inland from Paola (*see p. 321 above*) to Cosenza (32km). The appeal of this route lies in the striking views from the high mountains of the Catena Costiera, the range that separates the Tyrrhenian seaboard from the plain formed by the rivers Crati and Busento. After leaving Paola the road climbs steeply up the west slope of the Catena Costiera among vineyards and orchards, and through dense forests of oak, chestnut and beech trees. There are splendid views through the trees to the sea. The **Passo della Crocetta** (950m) offers a breathtaking panorama that extends from the volcanic cone of Stromboli and the other Aeolian Islands to the west across the broad Crati valley and east to the Sila. The descent to Cosenza begins here, through the fields and forests that dominate the Crati valley.

San Fili enjoys a good location on a hilltop, among woods and farms. The Chiesa Parrochiale dell'Assunta has a Baroque portal and interesting choir stalls of inlaid wood (1801). After 7km a road diverges right to **Rende**, where the Palazzo Municipale was built in the 12th or 13th century by remodelling a castle initially dating from 1095. The Palazzo Zagarese (*Via del Bartolo; open Mon–Fri 9–1, Tues and Thur 9–1 & 3–6; T: 0984 443593*) contains a small museum of folk art and ethnography: some 3,000 objects document farming and sheep farming, spinning and weaving, vernacular architecture, domestic, social and religious life, folk music and the Calabrian diaspora.

The descent continues among woodlands and olive groves to the valley floor. After 10km turn right onto Road 19, and enter Cosenza from the north.

COSENZA

Cosenza (pop. 104,000), a provincial capital of Calabria, stands at the confluence of two rivers. The old town, overshadowed by its castle, descends to the River Crati, whereas the growing modern city lies to the north, beyond the Busento, on level ground. The historic city centre is crossed by the winding Corso Telesio. Even the humblest of the medieval sidestreets has a certain appeal—a rare quality in the cities of Calabria.

HISTORY OF COSENZA

Cosenza succeeds *Cosentia*, the capital of the Bruttians, which came early under the influence of the Greek settlements of Magna Graecia. Taken by Rome in 204 BC, in imperial times it was an important stop on the Via Popilia, linking Rome with Reggio and Sicily. Alaric the Visigoth died here in AD 412 (probably of malaria) on his way back to Sicily after the sack of Rome. Legend holds that he was buried along with his treasure in the bed of the Busento river, the waters having been diverted for the occasion and then restored to their natural channel. Twice destroyed by the Saracens, the town was conquered by Robert Guiscard, but it rebelled against the rule of his half-brother Roger, who managed to restore his authority only after a siege (1087). In the 13th, 14th, and 15th centuries the city shifted its loyalties several times in the struggle between the Aragonese and the Angevins, and Louis III of Anjou died here in 1434 while campaigning against the Aragonese.

A notable centre of humanistic culture in the 16th century, Cosenza was the birthplace of the philosopher Bernardino Telesio (1509–88), whose ideas were instrumental in freeing scientific research from theological restrictions. The city contributed freely to the liberal movement in the 19th century and participated in the uprisings of 1848 and 1860. It was damaged by earthquakes in 1783, 1854, 1870 and 1905, and frequently bombed in 1943. Today it is an important commercial and agricultural centre. The University of Calabria lies on the outskirts to the north.

The cathedral

Old Cosenza retains much of the charm that so struck George Gissing (*see box overleaf*). The cathedral, in the Gothic style of Provence, was consecrated in 1222 in the presence of Frederick II. The interior was reworked in the Baroque style in 1750, and the façade made over in 1831; both, however, have been restored to their original states. The façade, with its three Gothic portals, large central rose window and two smaller rose windows at the sides, is one of the most graceful in Calabria. It is ideally complemented by its surroundings.

The interior is simple, with a nave and two aisles divided by piers, and an elevated presbytery. The apse was restored in a Gothic Revival manner and frescoed at the end of the 19th century. In the south aisle, at the foot of the stairs to the presbytery, is a Roman sarcophagus; in the north transept is the lovely tomb of Isabella, wife of Philippe le Hardi, who died in 1270 after falling from her horse while returning to France from Sicily (some authorities say her body was returned to Saint-Denis).

On Cosenza

To call the town picturesque is to use an inadequate word. At every step, from the opening of the main street at the hill-foot up to the stern medieval castle crowning its height, one marvels and admires. So narrow are the ways that a cart drives the pedestrian into shop or alley; two vehicles (but perhaps the thing never happened) would with difficulty pass each other. As in all towns of southern Italy, the number of hairdressers is astonishing, and they hang out the barber's basin—the very basin (of shining brass and with a semicircle cut out of the rim) which the Knight of La Mancha took as substitute for his damaged helmet.

George Gissing: By the Ionian Sea, 1901

Museo Civico Archeologico

Behind the cathedral, beyond the Provincial Office Building, extends the newly restored **Villa Comunale**, a lovely public garden with native and exotic plants, arranged and lit (for evening viewing) with great care. In the nearby Piazza XXV Marzo, with monuments commemorating Telesio and the brothers Bandiera, heroes of the Calabrian rising of 1844, stand the Biblioteca Civica and the **Museo Civico Archeologico** (*open Mon–Fri 8–2, Mon and Thur 8–2 & 3.30–6.30; T: 0984 813324*), housing a modest collection of antiquities from excavations in the city and environs. Notable exhibits include protohistoric burial treasures from the Italic settlements of Torre Mordillo and Michelicchio di Cerchiara (9th–8th centuries BC), from the necropolis of San Mauro di Corigliano (8th–6th century BC), and from a group of pit tombs in Contrada Moio (4th–3rd centuries BC). There is also some early (3rd century BC) Roman material from the necropolis at Cannuzze.

The old town

From a point in Via Telesio opposite the cathedral, Via del Seggio climbs to an old quarter with many interesting details. The church of **San Francesco d'Assisi** has a 13th-century doorway and a plain cloister. Within (*open daily 9–1*) is a small display of paintings by southern Italian artists of the 15th–18th centuries (Mattia Preti, Luca Giordano), a gold-laminate reliquary of the Holy Cross (the *Stauroteca*, 12th century), and a 13th-century painting of the *Madonna del Pilerio*. The adjoining offices of the Soprintendenza contain an extraordinary Byzantine reliquary cross in gold and enamel work with Greek lettering, presented by Frederick II on the occasion of the consecration of the cathedral (*viewable on request*). The small enamel panels depict the four Evangelists, the Madonna, and the symbols of Christ. The pedestal dates from the 18th century. The ruined **castle** (383m) was the site of Louis III of Anjou's marriage to Margaret of Savoy (1434). It commands good views. A steep staircase to the right of the church of San Francesco descends to the point at which the two rivers meet. The 16th-century church of San Francesco da Paola stands beyond the River Crati.

LA SILA

The Sila plateau, inhabited by descendants of the Bruttians, is an irregular expanse of gneiss and granite 1000–1300m above sea level. It occupies the area between the Ionian Sea on the east, the steep Crati valley on the north and west, and the Marcellinara ridge beyond the Corace valley on the southwest. It is divided into three parts: the Sila Greca to the north (which includes the Albanian colonies in Calabria); the Sila Grande and the Sila Piccola to the south, divided roughly by the Rogliano–Crotone road. The highest peak is Monte Botte Donato (1928m).

The forests of the Sila plateau were renowned by the ancients for the wood they supplied for shipbuilding, but deforestation has left much of the area free for pasture. This condition is being slowly corrected by controlled cutting and careful replanting. The climate is harsh in winter (snow does not disappear from the mountain tops until May) and mild in summer, offering a pleasant escape from the often stifling heat of the Calabrian coast. Olive, oak, poplar and fruit trees grow at the lower altitudes, intermixed with vineyards and the typical, low-growing *macchia mediterranea*. Above 700m these give way to chestnut, turkey oak and broad expanses of cereal crops. The area above 1200m is characterised by alders, aspens, maples and a native pine (*Pino laricio calabrico*) that grows to over 40m in height, often in dense groves. On the higher peaks are beech trees and, in some areas, silver fir, once much more common. Snowdrops bloom in February–March, followed, in late April–June by daffodils, jonquils, violets and small orchids. In June–July the pine forests abound with wild strawberries, and in September–October, with exquisite mushrooms. In autumn, the contrast of red beech trees against dark firs is splendid. Woodland animals, particularly foxes, hares, martens, wild boar, roe deer, squirrels and a rather ferocious variety of wolf, are still present in large numbers. Wildfowl include interesting native species of partridge. Vipers may be found in all the wilder areas, and the lakes and streams abound with trout.

SILA GRANDE

The route over the Sila from Cosenza to the Ionian coast crosses some of the finest countryside in Calabria. The first part of the journey passes through rolling green highlands, touching upon the lovely Lago di Cecita and running near Lago Arvo. Beyond San Giovanni in Fiore the landscape becomes more arid and dramatic as the road descends to the sea and town of Crotone.

From Cosenza the road winds up the west slope of the Sila. The air becomes notice-ably cooler on approaching **Celico**, birthplace of the Abbot Gioacchino da Fiore, a her-mit and mystic whose writings are still important today in the study of theology and depth psychology (*see box below*). Immediately afterwards, you touch upon **Spezzano della Sila**, a locally important centre in a splendid position overlooking Cosenza.

Gioacchino da Fiore (1130–1202)

The theologian and mystic Gioacchino da Fiore (b. Celico, c. 1130, d. San Giovanni in Fiore, 1202) lived at roughly the same time as St Francis of Assisi and Frederick II of Hohenstaufen. Originally a Cistercian monk, he soon came into conflict with the order, leaving it in 1190 to form the Florensi Order. Considered for centuries the work of a visionary or a prophet, his writings are among the highest achievements of monastic theology. They are still important today, because of their interpretation of the relationship between the godhead and the three persons of the Trinity as demonstrated in *Libellus de unitate et essentia Trinitatis* (now lost), and their critique of the Christocentric notion of history in favour of a markedly Trinitarian conception (explained in *Liber con-cordiae Novi et Veteris Testamenti*, in which the 'end of history' is not perceived as the Second Coming of Christ, but as an age of freedom and harmony on earth ushered in by the Holy Spirit). Da Fiore accused those who held the traditional views of his time of *quarternitas*: of considering the divine substance as disjoined from the three persons, constituting an independent, fourth element. His posi-tion was formally condemned in 1215 by the Fourth Lateran Council.

Camigliatello Silano (1275m) is a summer and winter sports resort. From here a minor road leads west to Fago del Soldato, a village of small wooden houses among pine woods, from which the Botte San Donato may be climbed in c. 3hrs. Springs along the way offer excellent mineral waters. The combined use of timber and corru-gated steel is characteristic of local architecture.

A few kilometres north of Camigliatello, **Lago di Cecita**, also called Lago di Mucone, sits in a wide valley among pastures and fields of grain, at an altitude of 1135m. It was created by damming the Mucone, and like Lakes Arvo and Ampollino, its waters are used to generate electricity. To the south lies Monte Botte Donato, to the east Monte Pettinascura, to the north Monti Altare and Sordello, to the west the Serra la Guardia. The road from Camigliatello winds along the east shore. At Forge di Cecita a turning on the right leads through dense forests to (4km) **La Fossiata**, a hamlet named after the nearby torrent. Planted with a variety of Silan flora, it is the showcase of the Forest Administration and a starting point for the ascent of the Serra Ripollata (1682m).

The road to San Giovanni in Fiore and Crotone leaves Camigliatello from the south. Woods gradually give way to broad fields of grain and pasture, affording views to the left of Lago di Cecita and the magnificent wood, Bosco di Gallopane, beyond. Further to the right the verdant slopes of Monte Pettinascura can be seen. The landscape is relatively flat here—you are crossing the highland plain at an altitude of roughly 1350m. From the small hamlet of Croce di Magara a secondary road follows the Neto valley to Germano, at the foot of Monte Ruggiero. The route continues through rolling countryside, running parallel to the one-track railway. The road is joined by the road from Lorica, beyond which you follow the valley of the Garga. A few kilometres further on, a turning on the right winds southwest to Lago Arvo, shortly after entering the valley of the Arvo river, and the vista opens up to the Ionian Sea.

San Giovanni in Fiore, the chief town of the Sila, is somewhat mean and shabby in appearance. It grew up in the 12th century around the Badia Florense, founded by Abbot Gioacchino, who enjoyed a wide local reputation as a prophet (*see box opposite*). The women of the town still wear attractive local costumes, and the town is famous for its textile trade. The abbey, a 13th-century Cistercian Gothic edifice of bare aspect, stands in the lower part of the town.

Continuing to the east, you cross the River Neto (the *Neaethus* of Theocritus) and reach (10km) the turning for Caccuri, birthplace of Cecco Simonetta, secretary to the Milanese warlord Francesco Sforza, and of his brother Giovanni, who wrote a biography of the prince. After 12km bear right, leaving the new road for Crotone on the left. The deeply eroded landscape is known for its conical formations of clay, called *timpe*.

Santa Severina

Santa Severina, on an isolated outcrop of sheer rock, was a Byzantine and Norman fortress with a scholastic tradition. John of Salisbury (c. 1115–80) notes that its inhabitants helped him with difficult passages of Aristotle. The sainted 8th-century pope Zacharias (d. 752) was a native. He successfully negotiated peace between the Lombards and the Greeks, supported Pepin the Short's assumption of the Frankish crown, and had much influence on the reconstruction of Europe. In 1950 the expropriation of landed estates began here under the Sila reform act. The church of **San Filomeno** is built to a Byzantine plan, with three apses (only one visible from the exterior). The high cupola is reminiscent of Armenian constructions. Underneath is the church of the Pozzolio, the exterior of which is adorned with good carved surrounds. The Norman **cathedral** has been largely rebuilt; it has a main portal of the 13th century enclosed in a later surround showing provincial Renaissance-Baroque taste. A Byzantine baptistery (8th–9th century), built to a circular plan and incorporating pillars from a pagan edifice, is attached to the north side of the church; and there is a small collection of liturgical objects in the former Palazzo Arcivescovile. The old cathedral, or Addolorata, dates from the 10th century. The **castle**, of the same period (now a school), was rebuilt by Robert Guiscard.

SILA PICCOLA

From Camigliatello there are any number of routes you can take to reach Lake Arvo (1280m). The most scenic passes near the summit of Monte Botte Donato (1928m); the easiest involves following Road 107 eastwards for a few kilometres. Lake Arvo was created by damming the River Arvo near Nacelle. Tunnels convey its waters, together with those of Lago Ampollino, to the hydroelectric plants at Orichella, Timpa Grande and Caluria, on the River Neto.

Twenty-two kilometres west lies **Aprigliano**, the medieval *Aprilianum*, birthplace of the poet Domenico Piro (1664–96). Nearby is the hermitage of San Martino, where the Abbot Gioacchino (*see p. 334 above*) is believed to have died. The church, with its single nave, wide transept and three semicircular apses, recalls French monastic architecture of the 11th century.

The view opens up on all sides as you reach Colle Ascione (1384m). Beyond, you descend through forest to the valley of the River Savuto. Here Road 179d branches south towards Taverna and the Sila Piccola. Bearing left soon after the Colle Ascione pass you follow the Savuto valley east to its source, crossing woods, pastures and fields planted with wheat and rye. You then descend the wooded Ampollino valley, which widens below the forested summit of Montenero (1881m) to form **Lago Ampollino** (1279m). The lake, created by damming the Ampollino at the foot of Monte Zingomarru, is approximately 13km long and its waters are used to generate electricity. The road winds around the wooded south bank. The view over the water is splendid. At the east end of the lake you leave a road to (19km) Cotronei on the left and loop around the south shore of the lake to the junction with Road 179d. The road descends through dense pine woods, then climbs to Villaggio Racise, a much-frequented summer resort.

Taverna

Taverna is set among the foothills of the Sila Piccola. Its name suggests that the village might have been a staging post on the road from the Ionian coast to the Sila. The old town, which was located to the east of the present centre, was destroyed once by the Saracens and again by the *condottiere* Francesco Sforza.

Mattia Preti (1613–99), the 'Cavalier Calabrese', one of the most renowned painters of the 17th-century Neapolitan school, was a native of Taverna, and several of the town's churches contain paintings by him. The former conventual church of **San Domenico** houses the most notable of these, including, on the north side (first altar), *St John the Baptist*, in the lower right corner of which is a self-portrait of the artist dressed as a Knight of Malta (an honour bestowed on him by Pope Urban VIII after he had worked in the cathedral on the island); second altar, *Madonna with Saints*; third altar, *Crucifixion*; fifth altar, *Madonna of the Rosary*; behind the main altar, *Christ in Majesty*, possibly inspired by Michelangelo's Christ of the *Last Judgement*; on the south side (first altar), *Martyrdom of St Peter*; second altar, *St Francesco da Paola*, resembling the painting of the same subject in the church of Sant'Agata degli Scalzi in Naples; third altar, *St Sebastian* (patron saint of the town); fourth altar, *Madonna and Saints*, an early work; fifth altar, the *Infant Christ*. The furnishings of the church also merit inspection, as does the wooden ceiling.

Above the high altar in the nearby church of **San Nicola** is the handsome *Madonna della Purità*, commissioned by Giovanni Antonio Peorio and Lucrezia Teutonica, his wife, and probably executed in Emilia between 1636 and 1644. The painting is mov-

Madonna della Purità, by Mattia Preti and his brother Gregorio.

able; in a niche behind is a large carved and painted bust of St Nicholas of Bari (1699).

The church of **Santa Barbara**, which formerly belonged to the Order of the Minims, contains several more of Preti's paintings, including a *Baptism of Christ*, *St Barbara Received into Heaven* (reminiscent of Guercino) and the large *Patrocinio*, sent by the artist from Malta, in which the dead Christ is supported in the arms of his Father. In the lower part of the painting appears a portrait of Marcello Anania, Bishop of Sutri and Nepi, once priest at Santa Barbara and Preti's first master. The church also contains finely-crafted Baroque altars and figures, especially that of St Sebastian to the right of the entrance; and a Crucifix of the school of Fra' Umile da Petralia. On the outskirts of the village, in the church of San Martino, is a panel by Preti and his school.

East of Taverna

At Taverna Road 109 leads east to the little village of **San Pietro**, where the church of Santa Maria della Luce contains an interesting 17th-century wooden Crucifix. At **Zagarise**, the church of the Assunta has a fine Gothic façade of local granite, with an ogival portal and rose window. Beyond, the road winds among the hills, with good views at times to the coast. **Sersale** enjoys a position dominating the hills of the Marchesato.

Mesoraca, to the north, is built on a ridge between two mountain torrents. The former conventual church of the Ritiro (the monastery was destroyed by an earthquake in 1783) contains some unusual paintings of the late Neapolitan school. At the church of the Annunziata a good 16th-century *Madonna and Child* graces the central portal. The church contains a series of marble inlaid Baroque altars, of which the finest is the high altar, upon which stands a silver tabernacle. The sacristy has 18th-century woodwork. In the environs are the ruins of the Basilian monastery of Sant'Angelo di Frigilo and the Santuario del Santissimo Ecce Homo, which contains a *Madonna and Child* by Antonello Gagini (1504) and, in a chapel to the right, a venerated wooden figure of Christ attributed to the Sicilian friar Fra' Umile da Petralia (1600).

The town visible on the horizon beyond Mesoraca is Petilia Policastro. It was initially called simply Policastro (from the Byzantine *palaiokastron*, 'old castle'). The second name was added in the mistaken belief that the town stood on the site of the Greek settlement of *Petilia*, which, faithful to Rome, held out against Hannibal in 206 BC. This is now believed to have been located near Strongoli.

PRACTICAL INFORMATION

GETTING AROUND

• **By air:** Southern Basilicata and northern Calabria are served by flights via Lamezia Terme Airport, www.sacal.it. Airport buses to/from Cosenza are operated by Fratelli Romano, T: 0962 21709, and Ferrovie della Calabria, T: 0961 896111. Both companies make the run four or five times a day in c. 1hr.

• **By road:** Fast north–south access to the area is provided from Naples and Reggio Calabria by Autostrada A3/E45. Road 106 along the Ionian coast is being widened at the time of writing to make a four-lane expressway. Minor roads are safe and well maintained, but not for those who suffer motion sickness. The best routes across the highlands are from Cosenza to Crotone (126km) by Roads 107/E93 and 106; and from Camigliatello or San Giovanni in Fiore to Catanzaro (c. 100km) by Roads 107, 108b, 179d, 109b and local roads.

• **By rail:** A branch of the main Salerno–Reggio Calabria railway connects Cosenza to the west coast at Paola. The Taranto–Reggio line hugs the Ionian coast. Cosenza has three railway stations: Centrale and Casali (www.trenitalia.it) and Città (www.ferroviedellacalabria.it). From Maratea to Reggio, 283km in c. 3hrs 20mins. To (139km) Lamezia Terme Centrale, junction for Catanzaro, in c. 1hr 10mins. With a few exceptions, fast trains bear inland after Lamezia.

INFORMATION OFFICES

Castrovillari Autostrada A3, IP Service Area, T: 0981 32710.
Catanzaro Via San Nicola 8, T: 0961 720260, www.regione.calabria.it
Via Spasari 3, Galleria Mancuso, T: 0961 743961.
Crotone Via Torino 148, T: 0962 23185.
Cosenza Corso Mazzini 92, T: 098 427271.
Web: www.turismo.regione.calabria.it

HOTELS

Altomonte
€€ **Castello di Altomonte**. Eleven quietly luxurious rooms in a historic setting at the very top of the town. Open all year. Piazza Castello 6, T: 0981 948933, www.altomonte.it
€ **Barbieri**. A homely place owned and managed by the Barbieri family, with comfortable rooms, particularly fine breakfasts and one of the region's best restaurants. Open all year. Via Italo Barbieri 30, T: 0981 948072.

Amantea

€ **Mediterraneo**. In a former town house in the historic centre of Amantea, with private beach. Open all year. Via Dogana 64, T: 0982 426364.

Camigliatello Silano

€ **Aquila-Edelweiss**. A modest place with adequate rooms and excellent restaurant, open all year. Via Stazione 11, T: 0984 578044, haquila@fidad.it

Castrovillari

€€ **La Locanda di Alia**. ■ A charming, romantic hotel with just 14 rooms, set in a beautifully scented garden; the restaurant is the best in Calabria. Open all year. Via Jetticelle 55, T: 0981 46370, www.alia.it

Cetraro

€€ **Grand Hotel San Michele**. In an early-20th-century villa overlooking the sea, with private beach, windsurfing, golf, tennis, pool. Open Dec–Oct. SS18 at Bosco, T: 0982 91012, www.sanmichele.it

Crotone

€€ **Costa Tiziana**. Large, modern hotel in a garden near the sea a few kilometres outside the town, with tennis courts and two pools. Open all year. Via per Capocolonna, T: 0962 25601, www.costatiziana.it

Frascineto (Monte Pollino)

€ **Skanderbeg**. A small (16-room) family hotel with comfortable rooms, offering hiking, riding, mountain-biking. Open all year. Via Arcuri 24, T: 0981 32117.

Gizzeria Lido

€€ **Marechiaro**. Small (8 rooms), tasteful and on the sea, with outstanding breakfasts and restaurant. Closed mid-Dec–mid-Jan. Strada Statale 18, T: 0968 51251.

Pianopoli (east of Nicastro)

€ **Le Carolee**. Seven recently-renovated rooms in a fortified manor house amid olive-clad hills overlooking the sea. Contrada Gabella 1, T: 0968 35076.

Scalea

€€ **Grand Hotel de Rose**. A quiet place with comfortable rooms, garden and pool. Closed Nov–March. T: 0985 20273, www.hotelderose.it

Sellia Marina (east of Catanzaro)

€ **Contrada Guido**. A citrus and olive estate with 12 lovely rooms and a fine restaurant serving delicious local cuisine; also a pool and private beach. Closed Jan, restaurant closed Mon. Località Contrada Guido, Strada Statale 106 km 202, T: 0961 961495, www.contradaguido.it

Terranova di Pollino

€ **Picchio Nero**. A small place frequented by hikers, in the Monte Pollino National Park. Open all year. Via Mulino 1, T: 0973 93170.

RESTAURANTS

Amantea

€ **Locanda di Mare**. Trattoria run by a family of fishermen. Closed Mon. Via Stromboli 20, T: 0982 428262.

Belvedere Marittimo

€ **Sabbia d'Oro**. Good seafood, by the water. Closed Tues and Nov. Piano delle Donne, T: 0985 88456.

Borgia (north of Squillace)

€€ **L'Ovile**. Seasonal regional cuisine in a historic farmhouse with garden and views, on an archaeological site. Closed Nov. Contrada Giordano, at Roccelletta, T: 0961 391418.

Buonvicino (inland from Diamante)

€ **Il Mulino**. A farm serving local delicacies in a shady vale by a mill-stream. Open July–Aug, daily except Mon. Contrada Maucera, T: 0985 85188.

Camigliatello Silano

€ **La Tavernetta**. Tasty dishes prepared with native Sila mushrooms (and more). Closed Wed (except in summer) and late Nov–early Dec. Contrada Campo San Lorenzo 14, T: 0984 579026.

Castelluccio Inferiore

€ **Beccaccino**. Country restaurant serving excellent regional dishes, especially lamb. Closed Tues and Nov. Via Marconi 2, T: 0973 663213.

Castrovillari

€€ **La Locanda di Alia**. ■ Superb restaurant, in a renovated farmhouse. Closed Sun. Via Jetticelle 69, T: 0981 46370.

Catanzaro

€ **Da Filippo**. Popular *osteria*. Closed Sat. Via Domenico Marincola Pistoia 247, T: 0961 751067:

€ **Da Salvatore**. Trattoria-pizzeria in the tradition of the *putica*—a simple establishment serving wine and the pitta-bread tripe sandwich known as *morzeddu*. Closed Mon, in Aug and late Dec–early Jan. Salita I del Rosario 28, T: 0961 724318.

€ **Da Teresa**. Popular *osteria*. Closed Sun and early Sept. Via degli Angioini 81, no telephone.

Cerva

€ **Mundial 82**. Trattoria-pizzeria in a quiet village of the Sila Piccola, between Mesoraca and Sersale. Closed Tues (except in summer). Via Daniele 221, T: 0961 939481.

Civita (east of Castrovillari)

€ **Agorà**. ■ Restaurant specialising in Calabro-Albanian dishes. Closed Mon and Nov. Piazza Municipio 30, T: 0981 73410.

€ **La Kamastra**. ■ A good place for *arbreshe* (Albanian) fare. Closed Wed.

Piazza Municipio 3–6, T: 0981 73387.

Crotone

€€ **Casa di Rosa**. Traditional restaurant known for its meat and fish dishes, and its traditional Calabrian sweets. Closed Sun and Dec–Jan. Via Cristoforo Colombo 117, T: 0962 21946.

€€ **Hostaria Le Lanterne**. Fine country cooking in a former farmhouse. Closed Mon and late Sept. Road 106, at Poggio Pudano, T: 09662 948004.

€€ **Peppone**. Friendly and hospitable, with good regional food. Closed Sun and Dec–Jan. Via Santa Maria delle Grazie, T: 0962 23855.

€€ **Sosta da Marcello**. Delicious traditional dishes, refined ambience. Closed Sun (except May–Sept). Via Corrado Alvaro, Palazzo Merigliano, T: 0962 23831.

€€ **Sparviero Due**. Restaurant near the harbour, run by a family of fishermen. Closed Mon and late Aug–early Sept. Via Interna Marina 39, T: 0962 25009.

Firmo (south of Castrovillari)

€ **La Capricciosa**. A genuine academy of Calabro-Albanian cuisine. Closed Mon. Via Angelo Viscardi, at Piano dello Schiavo T: 0981 940247.

Isola di Capo Rizzuto

€€ **La Scogliera**. Excellent fish restaurant romantically situated on a rock overlooking the sea. Closed Nov–March. Via Fosso, at Le Castella, T: 0962 795071.

Scalea

€ **La Rondinella**. Family-run trattoria with summer seating outside. Closed Sun (except in summer). Via Vittorio Emanuele III 31, T: 0985 91092.

Taverna

€€ **Sila**. Good home cooking in a small hotel restaurant. Closed Tues. Via Villaggio Mancuso 3, at Villaggio

Mancuso, T: 0961 922032.
Trebisacce (on the Gulf of Corigliano)
€ **Trattoria del Sole**. Trattoria crowded
with locals. Closed Sun (except in summer). Via Piave 14bis, T: 0981 51797.

LOCAL SPECIALITIES

Rossano and **Crotone** are famous for
their goldsmiths. **Terranova di Pollino** is
famous for its rustic country knives in
wooden sheaths. Beautiful silk items are
manufactured at **Longobucco** and at
Tiriolo, which is especially known for its
silk/wool-blend scarves, called *vancali*.
San Giovanni in Fiore is famous for its
rugmakers and its goldsmiths, though the
latter risk extinction. Woodworkers at
Castelsilano still make beautiful beech
looms for weaving. Furniture is made
throughout the Sila.

FESTIVALS & EVENTS

Altomonte
Festival Mediterraneo dei Due Mari
Classical music series. Anfiteatro di
Altomonte, July–Aug, T: 0981 948329,
redazione@n2b.it; *Presepe Vivente* The
Nativity is re-enacted in a cave; on the
Epiphany the Magi arrive on horseback,
25 Dec, 6 Jan.
Castrovillari *Mardi Gras* More a celebration of Calabrian folk culture than a religious event: displays of traditional costumes, musical instruments, dances, food
and wines, Feb.
Catanzaro *La Naca* Deposition of Christ
re-enacted, on a rotating basis, in the
churches of the Carmine, San Giovanni,
Rosario and Immacolata, Good Friday.
Cetraro *San Benedetto Abate* The statue of
the saint is carried to sea in a boat procession, then dunked in the water to bring
luck to fishermen, 11 July; *Torneo dei
Rioni* The town's neighbourhoods, associated with animals as in the more famous
Palio di Siena (here the characters are the
Eagle, Dolphin, Dragon, Falcon, Wolf,
Panda and Fox), compete in various
colourful events, second Sun in Aug.
Crotone *Madonna di Capo Colonna* The
celebrated Black Virgin is carried in procession from the duomo to the sanctuary
at Capo Colonna, and great amounts of
local delicacies are consumed, second and
third Sun in May.
Morano Calabro *Festa della Bandiera*
Historic pageant centering around the city
standard (*bandiera*) commemorating a
9th-century rebellion against the Saracens,
Sun around 20 May.
Paola *San Francesco da Paola*. Francesco
da Paola (1416–1507) is the patron saint
of Calabria: each year he is honoured
with a different series of events, always
involving copious supplies of food and
wine, late April.
Rossano *Passion* Celebrated in two separate processions: in the morning, a prayer
march to seven churches; in the afternoon
bearing the *Misteri*, wooden sculptures of
episodes from the Passion, Good Friday;
Fuochi di San Marco Bonfires commemorating the miraculous intervention of St
Mark, who spared Rossano from the devastating earthquake of 1836, 24 April.
San Demetrio Corone *Festa Pasquale*
On Easter Eve residents of Albanian
descent dress in traditional costume and
walk in utter silence to a spring in the
countryside, drink the waters, exchange
greetings and return to town singing; a
bonfire is lit in the main square and to
chants, in Greek, of *Christos anesti* ('Christ
has risen'), Easter Sunday.

SOUTHERN CALABRIA

VIBO VALENTIA

The Greeks called Vibo Valentia (pop. 34,000) *Hipponion*, after the horses they bred on the high pastures of the Monte Poro plateau. It was a place of some military importance, described by Cicero as an '*illustre et nobile municipium*'. An important intellectual centre in the late 18th century, it was the provincial capital under Murat, a status it has recently regained. It contributed enthusiastically to the cause of unity during the Risorgimento.

The **church of Leoluca** (or Santa Maria Maggiore) is splendidly decorated with fine 18th-century stucco work and large bas-reliefs of an excellent Baroque exuberance. The last chapel on the north side contains a superb marble group of the Madonna between St John the Evangelist and Mary Magdalen (notice the fine bas-reliefs on the bases). These are the last works of Antonello Gagini (1534). In the chapel opposite can be seen statues of the Madonna and Child and St Luke, of the Gagini school. On the high altar is a *Madonna and Child* attributed to Girolamo Santacroce. Two Romanesque lions in the sacristy once formed part of an earlier façade of the church.

The **Chiesa del Rosario** (1280, rebuilt in the 18th century) contains a strange Baroque wooden pulpit rising from a confessional. Beyond the balustrade to the high altar, on the right, stands the Cappella Crispo, a Gothic construction dating from the 14th century. **San Michele** is an exquisite little Renaissance church dating from the early 16th century, with a fine but somewhat overshadowing campanile of 1671.

The magnificently restored Castello Normanno-Svevo, on a hilltop overlooking the town, houses the **Museo Archeologico Statale Vito Capialbi**. The museum (*open daily 9–7; T: 0963 43350*) preserves a fascinating collection of finds from the necropoleis of Hipponion, beautifully displayed and lit. The visit begins on the first floor, with rooms devoted to the Greek sanctuaries at Scrimbia (7th–5th centuries BC) and Cofino (6th–4th centuries BC), and the city walls of Hipponion (6th–3rd centuries BC). Highlights include a splendid group of bronze helmets on the first floor, and a fascinating gold lamina bearing an Orphic inscription (*cf Naples, p. 95*), on the ground floor. The other ground-floor rooms host temporary exhibitions.

A cypress-lined road at the north edge of the town leads to the cemetery; halfway along on the left are the imposing remains of the **Greek walls** (best seen at sunset), which include the foundations of several large towers. The huge sandstone blocks are weathering badly and have been enclosed in a temporary pavilion. On the other side of the road, in the Parco della Rimembranza or Belvedere, can be seen the somewhat scanty remains of a late 6th- or early 5th-century Doric temple.

The Tyrrhenian coast beyond Vibo Valentia

Pizzo, a prosperous little town traditionally engaged in fishing for tuna and swordfish, is now also a resort. In the old castle (erected in 1486 by Ferdinand I of Aragon and partially restored) Joachim Murat, ex-king of Naples, was tried by court-martial and shot on 13th October 1815, five days after he had landed in an attempt to recover his throne. The church of San Giorgio contains a number of marble statues, among which may be noted a 16th-century *St John the Baptist* and a regal figure of St Catherine of Alexandria. From the narrow streets of the medieval town there are extensive views of the coast; below, the rock on which the settlement stands (*Lu Pizzo* in local dialect) plunges straight into the sea.

The coast road continues along the sea, past the busy industrial port of Vibo Marina to **Briatico**, a farming and fishing town located between two lovely beaches, La Rocchetta to the north and Le Galere to the south. From here the road follows the railway to Tropea, still perhaps the most picturesque of the several small fishing towns that line the rocky coast between Sant'Eufemia Lamezia and Gioia Tauro.

TROPEA & ENVIRONS

Huddled on a cliff above the sea, Tropea commands stunning views of the coast and, on clear days, of the Aeolian Islands. Below, broad white sandy beaches extend to the north and south for more than 4km.

HISTORY OF TROPEA

The origin of the town is uncertain. The most likely hypothesis holds that it was founded by the Greeks, whose initial interest probably focused on its natural harbour (which Pliny the Elder calls *Portus Hercules*, in reference to the popular belief that the hero was the first to realise its importance). Excavations have revealed remains of Greek and Roman settlements, now chiefly in the archaeological museum in Reggio Calabria, as well as an extensive proto-Villanovan necropolis. A Siculan centre has been identified at Torre Galli, c. 4km southeast of the town. During the Middle Ages Tropea provided a natural fortress for those members of the lesser nobility and the middle class who sought respite from their feudal obligations. The numerous extant palaces, with fine sculpted doorways, attest to this tradition.

From Piazza Ercole, at the centre of the town, Via Roma leads north to Largo Duomo and the **cathedral**, a Norman construction rebuilt several times in the 17th and 18th centuries and restored to its 'original' state in 1926–32. The east flank, with its false arcade and inlaid ornamentation, and the Gothic arcade adjoining the main façade, give the church a rare grace and beauty. The three-aisled interior is impressive in its simplicity. It contains a 14th-century wooden Crucifix, a marble ciborium of Tuscan workmanship and an interesting double tomb with effigies of a brother and sister, to which the *tondi* representing the *Annunciation*, now mounted on the interior walls, also belonged. At the end of the south aisle stands an extremely fine *Madonna and Child*, a statue by Giovanni Angelo Montorsoli. Behind the high altar, enclosed in a silver frame, can be seen the *Madonna di Romania*, supposedly painted by St Luke.

Throughout the old town are the once luxurious residences constructed by the lesser nobility and the rising middle class, now largely reduced to flats. The houses, distinguished by their carved granite doorways (often crowned by grotesque masks to ward off the evil eye) follow a common plan, with living quarters on the second and third floors and a spacious atrium on the ground floor. Although originally medieval, most were redesigned and rebuilt to Baroque canons; some, like **Palazzo Toraldo**, Via Glorizio 2, have beautiful courtyards with dramatic open staircases. Others, such as the **Palazzo Toraldo di Francia** (Via Lauro 12), were renovated at the turn of the 19th century in the Liberty style, an austere variant of Art Nouveau. More such designs may be seen in the early modern villas at the southwest edge of the old town.

GROCERY SHOPPING IN TROPEA

It's no secret that underdevelopment has its positive side, especially where the production and distribution of food is concerned. Generally speaking, the less you do to a fruit, vegetable, meat or cheese, the better (and more nutritional) it is. Calabria's slow entry into the 21st century has meant that many traditional products arrive in the shops with their flavours (and nutrients) intact: Calabrian beef, for instance, is among the best in Italy. What is more, the younger and more sensitive farmers of the region have been quick to capitalise on the fact that chemical fertilizers have never been used on their lands. They're now among the country's leading producers of organic fruits and vegetables and their spin-offs— jams, marmalades, olive spreads, sun-dried tomatoes, etc. Many of these products are whisked away to northern Europe. Others, however, can be found in the places where northern Europeans congregate in Calabria, and especially in Tropea, where there are several shops that sell nothing else.

Corso Vittorio Emanuele, the main street of Tropea, connects Piazza Ercole with the *affaccio*, a scenic overlook on a clifftop at the seaward end of the town. Opposite, on a steep rock, are the remains of the Benedictine sanctuary of **Santa Maria dell'Isola**. This is reached from the Belvedere del Canone, another scenic overlook just a few blocks south of the *affaccio*, from where steps descend to the beach. The path that climbs to the church is lined with fishermen's caves; the garden behind offers outstanding views of the town, the coast and the Aeolian Islands. In mid-August the sun sets directly over Stromboli.

A DAY TRIP TO SERRA SAN BRUNO

A good day trip can be made from Tropea to Serra San Bruno, 59km east by Roads 522, 18, and 182. From here you have the further option of descending to the Ionian coast.

Leave Tropea by the road to the station, passing beneath the railway and bearing left into open country, with good views back to the town and the sea. The road winds upward through switchback turns amid woods and farmland; to the northeast the Serre Calabre range, dominated by the wedge-like mass of Monte Cocuzzo, is visible in the distance. A small road leads left to Drapia; further on, another leads right to Brattirò, known for its vineyards. At Caria, follow a sharp bend to the left and climb through a second series of curves to the Monte Poro plateau, an isolated formation rising a little over 700m above the sea, particularly rich in archaeological finds. At Torre Galli, excavations conducted in 1922–23 revealed an extensive necropolis dating initially from the 9th century BC and used for some 300 years thereafter. Over 330 trench or pit tombs were unearthed, as well as a few instances of cremation attributed to the infiltration of Greek influences. The artefacts found at the site are now in the National Museum in Reggio Calabria.

The road is crossed by another leading to Zungri and Spilinga. At the former airport of Vibo Valentia (now a military airfield) turn left on Road 18 then right onto Road 182 to Soriano Calabro.

Soriano Calabro

The town is an important centre for agriculture and handicrafts, founded by the Normans and acquired in fee by the Dominicans in the mid-17th century. The monastery of San Domenico, founded in 1501, was one of the wealthiest and most illustrious Dominican houses in Europe; it produced four popes and was visited by Charles V on his return from Tunisia (1535). The convent was destroyed by an earthquake in 1659 and again in 1753, rebuilt and destroyed by fire in 1917, and restored on a smaller scale in the 1920s. The earthquake of 1783 also devastated the town, causing extensive landslides and altering the river course.

The main street ascends to the town hall, then turns abruptly left. Steps at the right of the turning descend to the former main façade of the monastery, now a solitary ruin. The new church of **San Domenico**, constructed in the 19th century, contains portraits of Benedict XIII and Innocent II (two of the four monks from Soriano who became pope) by a follower of Caravaggio, handsomely carved choir stalls and a painting depicting St Dominic dating from the late 15th or early 16th century. The road continues to the village of Sorianello (in the church of San Giovanni is a wooden Crucifix by the Flemish artist David Müller), then it ascends, in a series of curves, through dense forests of chestnut and holm oak. Higher up, firs and pines predominate.

Serra San Bruno

Serra San Bruno lies on a broad, wooded plateau. Founded in the late 11th century by Bruno of Cologne, founder of the Carthusian Order, the town was originally intended to house the families of the lay dependants of the nearby monastery of Santo Stefano del Bosco and was held in fee by the latter until 1765. It now enjoys relative prosperity as a result of its woodworking industry. Its small wood and stone houses, often entered from external steps; the lace-like decoration around eaves and gables; and the graceful balconies with 17th-century ironwork make this one of the most charming mountain towns of Calabria.

The Baroque churches are notable for their carved granite façades. Chief among them is the **Chiesa Matrice** (also called San Biagio) at the north end of the wide main street, constructed in 1795. Within, marble statues of St Stephen, St Bruno of Cologne, the Madonna and Child, and St John the Baptist, originally in the Charterhouse, stand against the first and third piers on either side of the nave. On their bases are bas-reliefs depicting the *Stoning of St Stephen*, *St Bruno Making Peace between Count Roger and Robert Guiscard*, the *Nativity*, and scenes from the life of St John the Baptist, signed by David Müller and dated 1611. The figure of the *Matrice* (above the high altar), a fertility figure identified by the fruit or grain that she holds or that decorates her image, is rich in pagan allusions.

Further along the main street stands the **church of the Addolorata**, built in 1794. The bold curvilinear façade, with its broken lines and unusual proportions, reflects a taste that prevailed earlier in the century in more cosmopolitan centres. The interior contains a ciborium with bronzes and coloured marble reconstructed from the one designed for the Charterhouse by Cosimo Fanzago in 1631 and destroyed by earthquake in 1783 (other fragments are in the cathedral of Vibo Valentia). Continue down the main street to the **church of the Assunta** (also called San Giovanni), which dates from the 13th century. The Baroque façade, with its campanile and clock, was added in the 18th century.

The abbey of **Santi Stefano e Brunone** enjoys a splendid location in a valley 2km southwest. Founded by St Bruno of Cologne at the end of the 11th century on land donated by Roger, brother of Robert Guiscard, it houses an independent community of Carthusians. The members are bound by vows of silence, poverty and solitude, in emulation of the primitive monks of Egypt and Palestine. The present abbey, with its low walls and cylindrical towers, was built in the late 18th and early 19th centuries. It adheres to the canons of Carthusian architecture, with two cloisters adjoining the church, surrounded by the living quarters of the lay brothers and the monks' cells. The visitable areas are entered from the museum (*entrance marked; open 9–1 & 3–6.30 or 7.30; T: 0963 70608*). There are displays on St Bruno and monastic life, and the ruins of the magnificent buildings of the earlier monastery destroyed by the earthquake of 1783. On top of the free-standing Doric façade of the former abbey church stand two massive stone pinnacles, turned out somewhat by the tremors. Behind rise the first two arches of the nave arcade (the church was built to a Greek-cross plan with three aisles on double Doric piers and a dome at the crossing); in front and to one side stand the remains of the cloister. The new abbey (*generally closed to visitors*) is built in an austere Gothic Revival style. The church contains interesting woodwork by local craftsmen and a silver bust of St Bruno, containing the saint's skull.

Further along the road that leads from the village to the abbey is the little church of **Santa Maria del Bosco**, set in a charming valley and surrounded by a dense fir forest (*paid parking, refreshments*). Here Bruno of Cologne lived and died, in the company of a handful of followers from the Chartreuse of Grenoble. At the foot of the broad stairway before the church is the pool into which the saint plunged as penance. The waters of the pool are held to be miraculous. More walks, through lush vegetation and offering splendid views, may be made to Colle di Arena (locally, La Crista, 1104m) in c. 3hrs and to Monte Crocco (1268m), in c. 4 hrs; both with broad views of the Serre, Monte Poro and the bays of Gioia Tauro and Sant'Eufemia.

To drive on to **Stilo**, on the Ionian coast, return towards the village, bearing sharply right at the Parco della Rimembranza onto Road 110 for Monasterace. The road ascends through a magnificent forest of firs, pines and beech to a broad, open plateau occupied chiefly by farm and pasture land. At Passo di Pietra Spada (1335m) the descent to the Ionian sea begins, with spectacular views of the rocky, arid landscape that characterises the east side of the Serre. A road on the right diverges to Nardodipace (1086m), a new town built in 1955 to accommodate the inhabitants of a village destroyed by floods. The descent continues; after crossing a beech wood the road winds through some of the wildest and most dramatic landscapes in Italy. On a clear day the view stretches as far as the sea, with good prospects of Monte Consolino to the northeast and the steep slopes of Monte Stella, ahead. Mount Pazzano (410m) develops vertically along the slope of the latter. Leave Road 110 on the left for Stilo (*described on pp. 359–60*).

AROUND THE CAPO VATICANO

Head south from Tropea along the coast, following the road signs for Capo Vaticano. On the outskirts of the town, leave the cemetery on the right, following the road around to the left through verdant farmland, with good views to the sea, to **Santa Domenica**, where pleasant excursions may be made along the beaches at the base of the cliffs (footpath from the station). Soon after the road turns inland toward Ricadi, a village among fields of olives, wheat and onions. **Capo Vaticano**, a magnificent headland with good bathing beaches, lies to the southwest. After Coccorino the road hugs the coast, the cliffs falling straight into the sea on the right. The view is one of the most striking in all of Calabria. Joppolo is a charming little village with a splendid prospect over the coastline to the south.

Nicotera, an old town on a hill, has magnificent views of the sea and Gioia plain. Built on its present location by Robert Guiscard, its name, recorded in ancient itineraries, remains unaltered. A walk through its winding streets can be rewarding. The cathedral (1785) has a *Madonna della Grazia* by Antonello Gagini, some fragments of bas-reliefs, and a wooden Crucifix, often displayed in the Museo Diocesano di Arte Sacra (*Piazza Duomo 10; open Mon–Sat June–Sept 9–12 & 4–7; Oct–May 9–12.30 & 3–6; T: 0963 81308*). The Museo Civico Archeologico (*open Mon–Sat 8–1; T: 0963 886166*), on the main road, houses a collection of objects unearthed nearby, in the area between Marina di Nicotera (6km, bus) and the mouth of the River Mesima. Here archaeologists hypothesise the existence of a Roman emporium that may have served the Greek *Medma* (Rosarno); remains can be seen in the small *area archeologica* at Piano delle Vigne (*see below*). Iron Age tombs similar to those at Torre Galli have also been found in the area.

The Gioia Plain

Beyond Nicotera you leave the coast and descend to the plain of Gioia Tauro, entering an area (extending south to Scilla) devastated by earthquake in 1783. After 11km the road meets up with Road 18 and enters **Rosarno**, a busy modern town much ruined by unchecked building. The ancient colony of *Medma* is believed to have stood at Piano delle Vigne, nearby (*open daily 8.30–1.30 & 2.30–dusk*). Founded by the Locrians in the 6th century BC, it passed back and forth between its parent city and Croton before finally gaining independence in the late 5th century. It was the home of Philip of Medma, friend of Plato and possibly the author of the latter's posthumous works.

Across the plain lies **Gioia Tauro**, a sprawling city with a small harbour and a popular beach, known principally for its olive production. The city is thought to stand on or near the site of the Locrian colony of *Metauron,* and excavations have revealed traces of the Greek necropolis and remains of Roman buildings.

On a hill, 15km south of Gioia Tauro, lies **Seminara**, once the most formidable fortress in Calabria. Here, in 1495, the Sieur d'Aubigny, Charles VIII's general, defeated Gonzalo de Córdoba in the only battle that the *Gran Capitán* ever lost, and in 1503 was himself defeated by the Spaniard Hugo de Cardona. The battles are commemorated in four contemporary bas-reliefs in the Casa del Comune. Now a centre of ceramic production, Seminara commands good views.

Sinopoli, 12km further on the same road, is a starting point for the ascent, by bridle path and footpath, of Montalto (1955m), the highest peak of the Aspromonte.

PALMI & THE ASPROMONTE FOOTHILLS

Heavy traffic characterises the route from Gioia to Reggio Calabria. Beyond the Petrace the foothills of the Aspromonte (a wild, mountainous area; *see p. 357*) reach to the sea. The road, offering wide views across the Straits of Messina to Sicily, passes east of **Palmi**, which lies among olive groves halfway up the north slope of Monte Sant'Elia. Some early 20th-century Liberty designs can be seen here. The centrally located Casa della Cultura Leonida Règpaci (*open Mon–Fri 8–2, Mon and Thur also 3–6, T: 0996 262250*) houses several museums. The Museo Calabrese di Etnografia e Folklore Raffaele Corso has an extensive collection of ceramic materials, hunting and fishing equipment, tools and articles related to shepherdry, and sections devoted to religious life, popular superstitions, weaving and costumes. In the same building is a museum dedicated to Francesco Cilea (1866–1950), composer of the opera *Adriana Lecouvreur*, born in Palmi in 1866; and to Nicola Antonio Manfroce (1791–1813). Also of interest are the Gipsoteca Guerrisi, with works by the local sculptor Michele Guerrisi (1893–1963) and the Antiquarium, with a collection of materials from *Taurianum*, an ancient city destroyed by the Saracens, of which scant remains are visible between Palmi and Lido di Palmi. The Pinacoteca has works by Guercino, Manet, Corot, Giovanni Fattori, Renato Guttuso, and sculptures by Giacomo Manzù, among others.

Five kilometres south of Palmi a road (marked) on the right climbs to the summit of Monte Sant'Elia, commanding a splendid view across the Straits of Messina to Sicily. On a clear day, Stromboli is also visible. To the south the high cliffs drop sheer into the sea.

Bagnara Calabra, in a lovely position on steep slopes terraced and planted with vineyards, is known for its sword-fishing in April–June. It has been destroyed several times by earthquakes, most recently in 1908. The Museo Angelo Versace (*open daily except Thur 9–12.30 & 3.30–7.30; T: 0966 376007*) houses a modest collection of antiquities from the Stone Age to Norman times, and religious art.

Scilla

Scilla is built on a spur behind the famous rock of Scylla. Crowned by a castle (now a youth hostel), it rises 73m sheer from the sea. It faces the Punto del Faro, in Sicily, across the Straits of Messina, which are four nautical miles wide at this point. The castle fell to the Saracens in the 9th century and to the Normans in the 11th. It was fortified by Pietro Ruffo in 1225, and in 1282 the fleet of Charles I of Anjou took shelter here after failing to take Messina. The castle was occupied by the British after the Battle of Maida (*see p. 329*) and defended for 18 months against the French.

Huddled around the northernmost of the two small bays is the fishermen's quarter; the main bathing beach is on the south side of the headland. The recently rebuilt church of the Immacolata, at the foot of the road leading to the castle, was once an important Basilian monastery.

MARINERS BEWARE

Although the rock of Scylla—personified in the *Odyssey* as a marine monster with seven heads—and the whirlpool of Charybdis were placed by the ancient poets exactly opposite each other, modern geographers have transferred Charybdis to a spot nearer the harbour of Messina. At certain tides there are still strong currents and whirlpools off the Faro point, but these are not very dangerous, even to small craft. The conditions may have been changed since Antiquity by earthquakes. An alternative explanation is that 'Charybdis' was the collective name given to the waterspouts that commonly form off the Sicilian coast. Seafarers know that in days of old, when ships navigated along the coast by dead reckoning, these could very well 'devour' them, as a rock like Scylla could 'grab' them, especially in fog or darkness.

Beyond Scilla the scenery, with its luxuriant vegetation characterised by aloes, prickly pears and orange groves, becomes even more beautiful. At Villa San Giovanni there are train and car ferries to Messina (see *Blue Guide Sicily*). Habitation is continuous from here to Reggio Calabria.

REGGIO CALABRIA

Reggio Calabria is the regional capital and the last major city on the Italian peninsula before crossing to Sicily. A flourishing city (pop. 178,000), with wide streets and low buildings constructed in reinforced concrete, it is known above all for its Museo Nazionale della Magna Grecia, which houses an extraordinary collection of prehistoric, Graeco-Roman and medieval antiquities. The city stands at the foot of the Aspromonte, a wild, mountainous region, for centuries isolated from the rest of the world. In some villages, the dialect spoken is still based on ancient Greek. Interesting day trips may be made from Reggio and its environs, the usual starting points being Melito di Porto Salvo on the south coast, and Bagnara Calabra to the north.

HISTORY OF REGGIO CALABRIA

Reggio Calabria still carries a reference to *Rhegion* or *Rhegium*, founded c. 723 BC by the Chalcidians, who were afterwards joined by the Messenians. The colony grew in size and wealth under Anaxilas, but it was sacked by Dionysius the Elder of Syracuse in 387 BC and was later subject to the Mamertines and repopulated by the Romans. Its propitious situation secured it continuous prosperity and enabled it to survive the repeated ravages of both pirates and earthquakes.

Reggio was rebuilt with wide and regular streets after the earthquake of 1783, only to be practically demolished again on 28th December 1908, when 5,000 of its 35,000 inhabitants perished and every house that was not completely ruined was seriously damaged. Heavily bombed in 1943, it was occupied by the Allies, who crossed the Straits of Messina practically unopposed.

The Museo Nazionale della Magna Grecia

Palazzo Piacentini, Piazza de Nava. Open daily 9–8, closed first and third Mon of the month; T: 0965 812255.

By far Reggio's chief attraction for the visitor, this museum occupies a monumental early Modernist building designed by the foremost Italian architect of the 1930s, Marcello Piacentini. One of the largest museums of Greek antiquities in the world, it contains an extensive collection of artworks from Sibari, Locri, Medma and other Calabrian sites. The museum is open on a rotating gallery basis; displays on the mezzanine and first floors may be closed; the hall of the Riace Bronzes, however, is always open.

NB: For information on Magna Graecia, its people and colonies, see pp. 10–13.

Ground floor

Paleolithic, Neolithic, Iron and Bronze Age collections: Flint implements, iron

and bronze swords, spear heads, pottery and bones are well displayed and clearly labelled in the ground-floor rooms. At the beginning of the section are large cases containing scale models of prehistoric villages and a cast of a *graffito* representing a bovid (*Bos primigenius*) from Papasidero, the only such Italian find dating from the Upper Palaeolithic period (11,000 years ago). The rooms that follow display material from localities throughout the region.

Greek collection: This starts with a small sampling of the treasures unearthed at Locri Epizephyrii: terracottas, ointment jars, mirrors, *fibulae*, jewellery and bronze statuettes, dating from the 7th–4th centuries BC. A highlight here is the extraordinary **collection of *pinakes*** (clay tablets intended as ex-voto offerings, once brightly painted) from the Sanctuary of Persephone, the most famous shrine of the goddess in Magna Graecia. These small clay bas-reliefs were manufactured in Locri and distributed throughout the Greek world. Archaeologists have counted 176 different types representing ten basic subjects. The reliefs displayed have been assembled from fragments: they were found in a 'bank' where offerings were deposited after being ritually broken. Although they have lost most of their colouring and are marred by chips and cracks, the refinement of their forms and liveliness of their compositions still testify to the enormous skill of the Locrian craftsmen, who worked between 490 and 450 BC.

Here too are 38 **bronze tablets** (account books) inscribed in Locrian dialect (350–250 BC) from the archive of the Temple of Zeus. Another work of the greatest importance is the **terracotta equestrian group** from Locri's Marafioti temple. Believed to be a pediment sculpture, it shows a nude horseman riding above a winged sphinx. The latter supports the horseman's feet with her hands and his steed with her head, suggesting to scholars that the group may represent one of the Dioscuri, the twin sons of Zeus, who were thought to have led the Locrians to victory against superior forces from Croton, around 550 BC. The sculpture is notable not only for its artistic value, but also because it suggests that clay was considered an acceptable alternative to marble (which was not available locally) or bronze (prohibitively expensive) by early settlers in Magna Graecia.

Set against a beautiful green ground in a room of their own are the most celebrated ancient representations of this subject, the **Parian marble *Dioscuri*** from the Ionic Sanctuary of

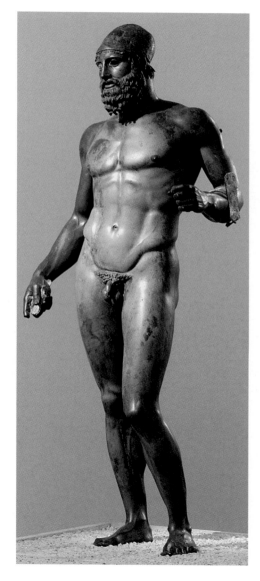

The celebrated *Riace Bronzes*, Greek originals of the 5th century BC (*see overleaf for description*). Opposite: Statue A; below: Statue B.

Contrada Marasà. Here Castor and Pollux are shown leaping off their mounts to rush to the aid of the Locrians. The horses this time are carried by tritons, who raise their front hoofs to make horse and rider fit the ideal triangle of the pediment. The centre of the composition is believed to have held a winged Victory, a considerable part of which survives. The sculptures, it seems, were made in Greece around 400 BC and imported to Locri; discovered in the late 19th century, the original fragments were 'integrated' with plaster reconstructions, as was the custom of the time.

Basement

Marine archaeology collection: This displays the museum's most famous treasures. Beyond an atrium with Greek, Punic and Roman *amphorae*, anchors and other objects recovered from wrecks along the Calabrian coast and in the treacherous Straits of Messina, glass doors lead to the climate-controlled main hall. Here you are immediately greeted by two splendid **bronze heads** recovered near Porticello, at the north entrance to the Straits of Messina. That nearest the door, labelled *Bearded Mask,* shows the idealised features characteristic of the Severe Style (the face is symmetrical, arranged horizontally around the double arch of the eyebrows and vertically around the straight, strong axis of the nose; hair and beard are stereotyped). It is thought to represent a god or an aristocrat and has been dated to the early 5th century BC. The adjacent *Head of a Philosopher* is much more naturalistic (the face's inherent asymmetries have been preserved, as have distinctive traits such as the long beard and thinning hair). It is ascribed to the Classical period of Greek sculpture (450–400 BC) and is considered the only Greek portrait head in existence. Both heads show signs of damage inflicted by violent impact: they are thought to have belonged to a cargo of deliberately smashed sculptures on their way to the foundry to be recycled.

The hall is dominated by the celebrated heroic nude statues discovered off Riace, on Calabria's Ionian shore, in 1972 (the **Riace Bronzes;** *pictured on previous page*). Standing high above the floor on special anti-seismic plinths, they are among the very few surviving examples of Classical Greek bronze statuary. They spent eight years in Italy's most sophisticated restoration laboratories before being revealed to the public in Florence in 1980. Produced by the lost-wax method, in which molten bronze 'chases' a wax simulacrum of the sculpture out of a clay mould, both figures stand over 2m tall and weigh around 160kg. They are finished in ivory and glass (eyes), silver (teeth) and copper (lips and nipples), and signs suggest they each held a shield and lance. The statues have been attributed both to Pheidias (460 BC) and to Polyclitus (430 BC), and they have been associated with the Temple at Delphi, built by the Athenians to commemorate the victory of Marathon. In the absence of documentary evidence, however, any hypothesis regarding the provenance of the statues remains just an educated guess. Mystery also shrouds the issue of how the statues got to be where they were. X-ray analysis has shown that Statue B was altered after the initial casting to resemble its companion (the right arm and left forearm are not original). On this basis some experts suggest that the sculptures were en-route to a new (perhaps Roman) location when they were thrown overboard from a ship in distress.

First floor

Landing: Here is displayed more **material from Locri**: mainly architectural fragments from the Temple of Zeus (5th century BC). Here also is a fine collection of coins, nearly all Greek and Roman, well displayed, and representative of all sites. It includes the silver *stater*, typical of Magna Graecia, of standard weight (8g), stamped with the symbol of the mint and the name of the city where it was made (tripod = Croton; bull = Sybaris; hippogriff = Locri; eagle and serpent = Hipponion; wheat = Metapontum).

Material from other colonies: The following rooms display material from the Greek colonies at Rhegion, Metauron, Medma, Laos and Caulonia. The finds from **Rhegion** include architectural terracottas, some bearing traces of the original painting; a large Hellenistic sarcophagus in the form of a foot (the deceased was buried in a sitting position); and a goblet of Alexandrian glass with hunting scenes in gold leaf. The best displays from **Metauron** include imported ceramics from Attica and Chalcis. From **Medma** come an interesting group of fictile votive offerings and the moulds for making them (notice the small statue of a seated deity holding a dove); bronze objects, including a mirror handle with Silenus approaching a seated nude youth. The finest material from **Laos** is the treasure from a 4th-century chamber tomb used for the burial of a Lucanian warrior and his wife, including a fine ceremonial suit of armour and diadem. From **Caulonia** notice the clay lion-head decoration of a temple, head of a statue, and coloured mosaic with a sea monster from a patrician house. The last room houses finds from the **Temple of Apollo Alaios** that stood alone on the headland now known as Punta Alice, near Cirò Marina. Notable are a 5th-century Head of Apollo attributed to Pythagoras of Rhegion, and fragments of feet and hands.

Second floor

Works that the National Museum inherited from the Provincial Gallery it superseded are displayed here. Byzantine artefacts: reliquary crosses and medals of the 6th–11th centuries. Arabo-Norman gesso-work: columns and panels with peacocks. Two small panel paintings by Antonello da Messina: *St Jerome* and *Three Angels*. Two late 15th-century panels by Pietro Cararo. A fine, but small, late 14th-century *St Lucy*. Mattia Preti, *Return of the Prodigal Son*. Fede Galizia, *Judith and Holofernes*. Various 17th-century canvases, dark and anonymous. Paintings of the 18th–19th centuries.

Other sights in Reggio Calabria

Corso Garibaldi, roughly parallel to the sea, forms the main thoroughfare of the city, with Piazza Italia at its centre. To the northeast of the piazza the severe Tempio della Vittoria (1939) serves as a war memorial. Two massive towers of the castle survive, further south, with a fine view over the city and the straits. There is a mosaic pavement of the Norman period, taken from two ancient Calabrian churches destroyed, like so many others, by earthquakes, in the nearby Chiesa degli Ottimati.

Near the post office are remains of the Greek walls and a Roman bath. The Lungomare, described by Gabriele d'Annunzio as the most beautiful kilometre in Italy, though now busy with traffic, commands a magnificent panorama.

ASPROMONTE: THE GREAT SOUTHERN SPUR

The Aspromonte, the last great spur of the Apennines, is an old massif with soft contours descending in several terraces to the sea. The Aspromonte district is bounded by the Tyrrhenian Sea, the Straits of Messina and the Ionian Sea, and by the Petrace, Plati and Careri rivers. At the centre rises Montalto (1955m), the highest peak of southern Calabria; from here numerous ridges radiate out, most of these dropping abruptly into the sea. The longest ridge, which extends to the northeast, forms the main watershed.

The four terraces or Piani dell'Aspromonte, as they are known locally, were made by bradyseisms and reflect successive alterations in the relative levels of land and sea. Earthquakes have afflicted the area with uncommon frequency, the most disastrous being that of 1783, which destroyed much of the inhabited area between Reggio and Palmi, 46km up the west coast.

Almonds, peaches, figs and citrus fruit flourish in the coastal areas, and the lowlands between Scilla and Capo Spartivento are famous for their plantations of bergamot orange, used for scent and eau de cologne. Jasmine is also grown in the area around Brancaleone. In the hill zones are groves of giant olives. Above 650m chestnuts and oaks prevail, then beech and conifers. The highland areas were once covered by dense forest, unfortunately destroyed over the centuries, so that much of the region is now given over to pastures and to the cultivation of grain and potatoes. The forests of the Aspromonte are constantly expanding, however, due to an active reafforestation programme. The region's main attractions are the spectacular views—which at some points span the north and west coasts of Sicily—winter sports at Gambarie, and its woodlands. A considerable part of the area was set aside as a National Park in 1991.

Garibaldi's untimely advance on Rome (he had been ordered to attack Austria in the Balkans, but decided instead to attack the Papal States, without the approval of king and cabinet) was checked by Cialdini at the Battle of Aspromonte in September 1862 (*see overleaf*). In later years its fastnesses were the haunt of Musolino, a 19th-century Robin Hood; even today, the mountains are a favourite hiding-place of fugitives from the law.

Detail from *Three Angels*, by Antonello da Messina (1460), in the museum of Reggio Calabria.

GIUSEPPE GARIBALDI & THE CONQUEST OF THE SOUTH

The second son of a merchant-marine captain, the young Giuseppe Garibaldi had a passion for the sea. In 1833 in the Crimea, while serving in the navy of the kingdom of Piedmont-Sardinia, he learned of Giuseppe Mazzini's plan to form an Italian republic. This was his 'initiation' (as he himself called it) to the 'sublime mysteries of the homeland'. He immediately decided to take up the cause of Italian nationhood and joined Mazzini's revolutionary group, *Giovine Italia*.

He met Mazzini later that same year, in Marseilles, and took part in a mutiny intended to provoke a republican revolution in Piedmont. The plot failed, and he was condemned to death by a Genoese court. From 1836–48 Garibaldi lived as an exile in South America, where he immersed himself in the turmoil and revolution that characterised the continent in those years.

In April 1848 Garibaldi led 60 members of his Italian Legion back to Italy to fight for for Carlo Alberto, the king of Piedmont-Sardinia, in the war of independence against the Austrians. The king gave him a lukewarm welcome, for Garibaldi's conviction as a rebel in 1834 was still remembered; moreover, the regular army despised the self-taught guerrilla leader. Therefore, Garibaldi went to the aid of the city of Milan, where Mazzini had already arrived and had given the war a more republican and radical turn. After defeat by the Austrians at Custoza, Carlo Alberto agreed to an armistice, but Garibaldi continued in the name of Milan what had become his private war, and won engagements with the Austrians at Luino, Varese and Morazzone. Then Camillo Cavour, the prime minister of Piedmont, invited him to talk, in the belief he could prise him away from the republican Mazzini. Following a secret meeting on 13th August 1856, Garibaldi announced, to the utter shock of his republican friends, that monarchy would be the basis of Italian unity.

In May 1860 Garibaldi set out to conquer Sicily and Naples. With at least the tacit approval of Cavour and Vittorio Emanuele he sailed from near Genoa on 6th May with about 1,000 men (the 'Thousand' or '*I Mille*' of Risorgimento lore). At the end of May he captured Palermo. The autumn found him back on the mainland where, with 30,000 men under his command, he fought the biggest battle of his career on the Volturno river, north of Naples (1st–2nd October). After his victory, he held plebiscites in Sicily and Naples to establish the sovereignty of Vittorio Emanuele over southern Italy. When the two met (at Teano, on 26th October), Garibaldi was the first person to hail Vittorio Emanuele as king of a united Italy.

In 1861 a new Kingdom of Italy came into existence. Early in 1862 Vittorio Emanuele again persuaded Garibaldi to lead a revolutionary expedition, this time to attack Austria in the Balkans. However, he decided to use this army to attack the Papal States. Not wanting to jeopardise its relations with France, the Italian government ordered its own forces to stop him. At the Battle of Aspromonte (29th August), he was wounded and taken prisoner.

Reggio Calabria to Gambarie

A pleasant excursion climbs through the foothills of the Aspromonte, offering good views across the Straits of Messina and along the densely populated coast.

Sambatello (286m) is known for its dry rosé wine. Beyond, the road follows the Gallico valley, dominated by the ruined castle of **Calanna**, a structure of strategic importance in Byzantine, Norman and Swabian times. Below, the river-bed is strewn with small orchards protected by dykes against the violent winter currents. The road crosses the river and is joined by the road from Calanna, perched on the ridge above. The village enjoys a splendid view. The parish church displays fragments of medieval sculpture from a ruined Byzantine church, a 15th-century bell and sculptural fragments dating from the 16th and 17th centuries. Excavations conducted nearby, in 1953, revealed a necropolis dating from the 9th–6th centuries BC. The material recovered is now in the Museo Nazionale in Reggio.

The ascent becomes more tortuous as the valley narrows. Laganadi is set among olive groves. The road crosses a deep ravine, then resumes its climb, with views of the villages of Cerasi and Ortì in the distance. Beyond Sant'Alessio, you continue through wooded glens and past a river-bed graced by flowering junipers in summer to **Santo Stefano in Aspromonte**, a small town with a distinctive mountain character (the upper floors of many houses are in wood), the birthplace of the outlaw Musolino. Beyond, the road loops back to the west. The view spans the Straits of Messina and the Sicilian coast from Punto Faro to Mount Etna. The road ends at **Gambarie** (1300m), a popular summer and winter resort in a magnificent position among beech and fir forests.

Among the many pretty side trips from Gambarie, the following are particularly pleasant; all have good views. **Puntone di Scirocco**, 1660m, is c. 2km by chairlift from Bivio di Gambarie, where the roads from Gallico and Dellanuova meet. The summit of **Montalto**, 1955m, can be reached on foot in 4hrs by a steep mule-track (also on mule-back, May–Oct, conditions permitting). It is crowned by a large bronze *Christ* turned towards Reggio in benediction. The Straits of Messina are out of sight from the top of the mountain, and Sicily and Calabria appear to form a single, continuous land mass. Just below the summit, a track to the north leads to (3hrs) Dellanuova. A steep path to the northeast winds through forests of beech, fir, oak and chestnut to the **Santuario di Santa Maria dei Polsi**, of Byzanto–Norman origin. The **Cippo di Garibaldi** commemorates the Battle of Aspromonte. From Bivio di Gambarie, Road 183 crosses a plateau. A signpost indicates a way through the woods to a modern marker (1204m) on the site where the general was captured.

THE SOUTHERN IONIAN COAST

Stilo and environs

Stilo is beautifully situated on the side of Monte Consolino. The philosopher Tommaso Campanella (1568–1639) was born here, and its environs were a favourite resort of Basilian anchorites. Emperor Otho II was defeated by the Sicilian Saracens here in 982.

The town is overlooked by the **Cattolica**, a gem of Byzantine architecture resembling the church of San Marco at Rossano, and perhaps the best preserved monument of its kind in Europe. The Cattolica was the church of all those who lived as monastic hermits in the surrounding hills. It was built in the 10th century, survived the earthquake of 1783, which destroyed much of the town, and was restored in the first quarter of the 20th century. Built to a square plan, it has five conical domes on circular drums. The interior measures 6m by 6m and is divided into nine quadrants by four rough columns. The latter, taken from antique buildings, have been placed on top of their capitals to symbolise the defeat of paganism. The first column on the right bears the Greek inscription, 'God is the Lord who appeared to us', surmounted by a carved cross. On the walls and ceiling can be seen traces of Byzantine frescoes in three strata, corresponding to three different epochs, discovered and restored in 1927. You can glimpse the remains of other domed churches from the vantage point of the Cattolica. These include the ruined convent of San Domenico, where Campanella lived and worked.

South of Stilo, in the valley of the Allaro, the former *Sagras*, 10,000 Locrians defeated 130,000 Crotonians c. 540 BC. **Caulonia**, 8km inland, was founded by the refugees from ancient *Caulonia*. The church has a Carafa tomb of 1488. At **Roccella Ionica**, the ruined castle stands on a striking cliff overlooking the sea. There are remains of a small Roman theatre near the station at **Gioiosa Ionica**. Plantations of bergamot trees line the coast between here and Siderno, a sprawling modern town with a popular beach.

LOCRI & GERACE

Locri lies 5km north of the ruins of its ancient namesake, the famous *Locri Epizephyrii*. The latter was founded by colonists, probably from the Opuntian Locris in Greece, in either 710 or 683 BC, on a site that had already been inhabited by native Siculian peoples for several centuries.

HISTORY OF LOCRI

The Greek colony flourished, perhaps by virtue of its location on a major road (the *dromos*, which bisects the site) and its contacts with Sicily and Tyrrhenian colonies. Locri was the first Greek city to possess a written code of laws, attributed to Zaleucus (664 BC), and it was praised by Pindar as a model of good government. Religious life centred on the goddess Persephone, and the city contained a celebrated sanctuary dedicated to her. The Locrians conquered the Crotonians (*see above*), allied themselves with Dionysius I and finally surrendered to Rome (205 BC). The town dwindled and was eventually destroyed by the Saracens.

Although the finest remains from the site are housed in the Museo Archeologico Nazionale in Reggio Calabria, the **Antiquarium Statale di Locri** (*open daily 9–7; Sat*

9–7; *June-Sept 9–12; closed first and third Mon of the month; T: 0964 390023*) contains clear plans and photographs illustrating the history and artistic development of the city, a well-displayed collection of pottery and bronzes from Greek and indigenous tombs, architectural fragments, a vast assortment of small votive statues (the crafts-men of Locri specialised in producing these), Roman inscriptions and Locrian and Greek coins. There is also a fine collection of 5th-century BC *pinakes*, clay tablets with painted reliefs of Hades and Persephone, an item for which the craftsmen of Locri were famous throughout the Greek world. They were used as grave offerings.

The ruins
Open daily 9–7; closed first and third Mon of the month; T: 0964 390023.
Visits begin at the museum, from where a dirt path leads inland to (500m) the remains of an **Ionic temple** believed to have been dedicated to Zeus. Originally con-structed in the 7th century BC, it was enlarged in the 6th century and completely rebuilt in the following century.

ANCIENT LOCRI

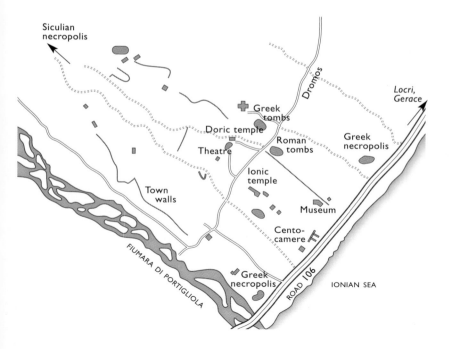

Further on, a footpath leads from a modern hamlet situated on the *dromos* to a **Doric temple** (called Marafioti) and the neighbouring **Hellenistic theatre**, much altered in Roman times. The 4th–3rd-century BC bronze tablets recording civic expenditures, now in Reggio museum, were found here. The visible stretches of the **town walls** (behind the antiquarium and c. 1km further south, along a track perpendicular to the coast road) probably date from the 6th century. Traces of the earlier walls may be seen at the **Centocamere**, an area only partially excavated, entered from a dirt track (marked *Locri scavi*) c. 500m south of the museum on Road 106. Here too are the foundations of houses and parts of a water system, as well as the beaten-earth streets dividing the *insulae*. The **Shrine of Persephone** stands in a ravine outside the city wall, just above which are the foundations of a small Temple of Athena. Little, however, remains to be seen of these monuments, and access is difficult. Greek and Roman tombs lie close to the *dromos*, and a Siculian necropolis further inland.

Gerace

From the centre of modern Locri, Road 111 climbs inland through olive groves to (9km) Gerace, situated on an impregnable crag overlooking the road. Founded by refugees from Locri in the 9th century, it possesses a remarkable **cathedral**, the largest church in Calabria. Consecrated in 1045, this was rebuilt under Swabian rule and restored after an earthquake in the 18th century. The spacious interior is built to a Latin cross plan. The nave and aisles are divided by 20 granite and coloured marble columns, possibly from Locri, above which rounded arches of differing heights spring from high stilt-blocks. At the end of the south aisle is the Gothic Cappella del Sacramento (1431); in the adjacent south transept the 14th-century tomb of Giovanni and Battista Caracciolo and of Niccolò Palazzi can be seen. Antique columns also support the vault of the much-restored crypt.

The **church of the Sacro Cuore** has a distinctive dome and contains pretty Baroque decoration. **San Francesco d'Assisi** (1252) has two fine portals, of which the larger bears Arabic and Norman decorative elements. Within are a tomb of Niccolò Ruggo (d. 1372), of Pisan influence, and a marvellous inlaid marble high altar. The small church of **San Giovanello** is also of Byzanto-Norman construction.

On to Reggio

Continuing south along the coast, just before Ardore Marina, a road turns inland to (5km) **Bombile**, near which lies the Santuario di Bombile, constructed in a most astonishing way inside a large cave. The sanctuary, reached by a track through olive groves, has a charming façade into which an attractive Baroque portal, dated 1758, is set. Inside, the edifice is completely built and vaulted as would be any free-standing church and exhibits somewhat later decoration. Over the high altar stands the *Madonna della Grotta*, a fine marble statue, possibly by a close follower of Antonello Gagini.

At Bovalino Marina a turning on the right mounts to (5km) **Bovalino Superiore**, where the church of the *Matrice* contains a marble *Madonna della Neve* by the Gagini school. Set into the south wall is a fragment of a marble *Madonna and Child*, mutilated by Turkish pirates. Also to be noted is the *Madonna of the Rosary*, clothed in fine 18th-century garments.

Beyond Brancaleone you round Capo Spartivento, the Roman *Heracleum Promontorium*, at the southeast extremity of Calabria. Some of the villagers in this area retain a dialect of Greek origin, though scholars dispute whether it originates from Antiquity or the Middle Ages.

Garibaldi landed in 1860 and again in 1862 at **Melito di Porto Salvo**, the southernmost town on the mainland. A beautiful mountain road ascends to Gambarie. Mount Etna and the east coast of Sicily come into view. On the right rises the five-pronged crag of Pentedattilo, whose name translates from the Greek as 'five fingers', with a picturesque ruined village at its foot. Further on, the road winds around the Punta di Pellaro to Reggio (*see p. 351*) and Messina is visible across the strait.

PRACTICAL INFORMATION

GETTING AROUND

• **By air:** Most of the places in this chapter are served by domestic and international flights via Lamezia Terme Airport, on the Tyrrhenian coast, www.sacal.it. Buses (operated by Ferrovie della Calabria, T: 0961 896111) connect the airport with Vibo Valentia 3–4 times daily in 40mins.

Points from Gioia Tauro south are served by Ravagnese Airport, 4km east of Reggio Calabria, www.sogas.it. Airport buses connect to central Reggio in 20min (ATAM, T: 800 433310, www.atam-rc.it). From here trains and buses run to Villa San Giovanni and points north.

• **By road:** Road 106 covers the entire 500km from Taranto to Reggio Calabria. Motorists should bear in mind that the road is perennially under construction, and roadwork can cause major delays. Where there is no interruption, the flow of traffic is fast and

wild, an oncoming vehicle rarely being viewed as an obstacle to overtaking.

• **By rail:** From Naples (Campi Flegrei, Mergellina, Centrale or Porta Garibaldi) to Reggio Calabria (Centrale), 476km in 4hrs 20mins by Eurostar or Intercity, stopping at Paola, Lamezia Terme, Vibo Valentia-Pizzo, Gioia Tauro and Villa San Giovanni. To Villa San Giovanni (where through trains to Sicily cross the Straits of Messina), in c. 10mins less. From Taranto to Reggio Calabria, 471km in c. 5hrs 30mins. From Maratea to Reggio, 283km in c. 3hrs 20mins. With a few exceptions, fast trains bear inland after Lamezia, returning to the coast at Gioia Tauro. A branch line serves Tropea and the picturesque towns of the Monte Poro headland.

Reggio has three train stations: Centrale, Piazza Garibaldi, at the south end of the town, for all trains; Lido, more centrally placed near the hotels and the museum is served by most; Marittima is the terminus of trains from the east, but is not served from the north.

• **By sea:** Ferries and hydrofoils run throughout the year from Messina, in Sicily, to Reggio Calabria and Villa San Giovanni (20mins). There are also daily hydrofoils between Reggio Calabria, Messina and the Aeolian Islands (15mins–c. 2hrs). For information and tickets, Trenitalia Reggio Calabria, T: 0965 97957 (ferries to Messina); Aliscafi SNAV, Stazione Marittima, T: 0965 892 012 (hydrofoils). In summer (June–Sept) boats run between the Aeolian Islands and Tropea and Vibo Marina. Contact the information office in Vibo Valentia for details.

INFORMATION OFFICES

Gerace Piazza Tribuna 10, T: 0964 356888.
Locri Via Fiume 1, T: 0964 29600.
Palmi Piazza 1 Maggio, T: 0966 22192
Reggio Calabria Ufficio Informazioni e di Accoglienza Turistica, Corso Garibaldi 329, T: 0965 892012; branch offices at Ravagnese Airport, T: 0965 643291; Stazione Centrale, T: 0965 27120.
Azienda di Promozione Turistica, Via Roma 3, T: 0965 21171, www.netonline.it/apt
Santo Stefano in Aspromonte–Gambarie Piazzale Mangeruca, T: 0965 743295.
Vibo Valentia Ufficio Informazioni e di Accoglienza Turistica, Via Forgiani 1, T: 0963 42008, www.costadei.net
Azienda di Promozione Turistica, Via Forgiani 8, T: 0963 42008,

www.costadei.net
Web: www.turismo.regione.calabria.it

HOTELS

Gerace
€ **La Casa di Gianna.** ◼ Ten rooms (and a good restaurant) in a lovely old home in the historic centre of this gem of a town make this one of the most attractive venues on Calabria's Ionian coast. Via Paolo Frascà 4, T: 0964 355024, www.lacasadigianna.it
Parghelia (above Tropea)
€€€ **Baia Paraelios.** ◼ Set in a luxuriant garden on the sea, with outdoor dining, private beach, three pools, tennis, windsurfing, sailing, diving and waterskiing. All rooms are suites with private patio. Open Easter–Sept. Contrada Fornaci, T: 0963 600300, www.baiaparaelios.it
€€€ **Porto Pirgos.** A faux village set in luxuriant surroundings with pool, outdoor dining, private beach. Open Easter–Sept. Marina di Bordila, Contrada Fornaci, T: 0963 600351, www.portopirgos.com
Reggio Calabria
€€ **Excelsior.** A classic place across the street from the national museum. Open all year. Via Vittorio Veneto 66; T: 0965 812211, info.excelsior@ montesanohotels.it
€€ **Miramare.** Sober but comfortable, on the Lungomare. Open all year. Via Fata Morgana 1, T: 0965 812444, info.miramare@montesanohotels.it
€€ **Palace Masoanri's.** Pleasant, centrally located near the national museum. Open all year. Via Vittorio Veneto 95, T: 0965 26433.
€ **Fata Morgana.** Simple but comfort-

able. Open all year. Via Lungomare, at Gallico Marina (8km north of the city centre), T: 0965 370008.

€ **Lido**. Near the sea between the Lido station and the national museum. Open all year. Via Tre Settembre 1943 6, T: 0965 25001, www.hotellidorc.it

Stilo

€ **San Giorgio**. Well-decorated rooms in the 17th-century Palazzo Lamberti, with stunning views across the Stilaro valley to the sea; garden and small pool, fireplaces in public rooms. Open all year. Via Citarelli 1, T: 0964 775047.

Tropea

€ **Punta Faro**. A small (25-room), family-run place overlooking the rocky headland and white sandy beaches of Capo Vaticano. Open June–Sept. San Nicolò di Ricadi (Capo Vaticano), T: 0963 663139, www.hotelpuntafaro.it

Villa San Giovanni

€€€ **Altafiumara**. A luxury establishment occupying a one-time Bourbon fortress in a vast park with restaurant, pool, fitness centre, magnificent views over the Calabrian and Sicilian coasts, and a respectable collection of art by modern and contemporary masters. Località Santa Trada-Cannitello, T: 0965 759804, www.altafiumarahotel

RESTAURANTS

Bagnara Calabra

€ **Taverna Kerkira**. Restaurant serving Greek-Calabrian dishes. Closed Mon, Tues and Dec–Jan. Via Vittorio Emanuele 217, T: 0966 372260.

Bivongi (near Stilo)

€ **La Vecchia Miniera**. Country restaurant not far from Stilo. Closed Mon. Contrada Perrocalli at Lavaria,

T: 0964 731869.

Canolo (northwest of Gerace)

€ **Da Cosimo**. Regional dishes of the Aspromonte in a village near Gerace. Closed Wed (except in Aug) and Sept. Via Pertini 1, T: 0964 385931.

Caulonia

€ **Da Giglio**. Classic *osteria* halfway between Roccella Ionica and Caulonia itself. Closed Mon (except in summer) and Nov. Contrada Carrubara 20, T: 0964 861572.

€ **Trattoria del Pesce Fresco**. Trattoria run by a former ship's cook, between Roccella and Marina di Caulonia. Closed Sun (except in summer). Road 106, Contrada Canne, at Marina di Caulonia, T: 0964 82746.

Gerace

€ **La Tavernetta**. Trattoria on the road from Gerace to Antonimina. Closed Tues (except in summer). Road 112, at Azzuria, T: 0964 356020.

Melito di Porto Salvo

€€ **Casina dei Mille**. Restaurant with rooms (Garibaldi slept here). Closed Sun evening (except in summer) and late Dec. Strada Statale Ionica 106, at Annà, T: 0965 787434.

Nicotera

€ **Da Vittoria**. Homely trattoria popular with the locals. Open daily. Via Stazione 16, Nicotera Scalo, T: 0963 81358.

Palmi

€€ **Rosa dei Venti**. Seasonal and fish dishes, with summer seating outdoors; closed Wed (except in summer), Aug and late Dec. Strada Provinciale per Marinella, T: 0966 21080.

Pizzo

€ **A Casa Janca**. Farm serving traditional local cuisine. Closed Wed (except in summer) and Nov, Jan, Feb. Via Riviera Prangi at Marinella, T: 0963 264364.

Reggio Calabria

€€ **Cantuccio Club**. Warm, genuine restaurant with a strong local following. Closed Sun, Mon and June–Sept. Via Nuova Friuli 9, T: 0965 891614.

€€ **Garden**. Restaurant at the Hotel Miramare, with good traditional cuisine. Open all year. Via Fata Morgana 1, T: 0965 812444.

€€ **Fuori Porta Club**. Creative cuisine in a pleasant garden restaurant. Closed midday, Sun (in summer), Wed (in winter) and Sept. Via Vecchia Provinciale 37, at Archi, T: 0965 45199.

€€ **Gabbiano**. Seaside restaurant with good views and food. Closed Sept–May. Contrada San Gregorio, T: 0965 758174.

€€ **Galà**. Restaurant at the Grand Hotel Excelsior, with good panorama. Open all year. Via Vittorio Veneto 66, T: 0965 812211.

€€ **London Bistro**. Creative cuisine. Closed Mon, midday Sat and Aug. Via Osanna 2f, T: 0965 892908.

€ **Taverna degli Ulivi**. Trattoria-pizzeria. Closed Sun. Via Eremo Botte 32, T: 0965 891461.

Rizziconi (east of Gioia Tauro)

€ **Osteria Campagnola della Spina**. Simple country trattoria. Closed Mon and mid-Aug–mid-Sept. Contrada Audelleria 2, T: 0966 580223.

Roccella Ionica

€ **Giare**. Restaurant with rooms and pool, on a farm by the sea. Closed Nov–March. Strada Statale 106, km 111, T: 0964 85170.

Santo Stefano in Aspromonte

€ **Villa Rosa**. Good simple trattoria.

Open all year. Road 184, at Schiccio, T: 0965 740500.

Scilla

€€ **Glauco**. Family-run trattoria by the sea, with summer seating outside. Closed Tues and Oct–March. At Chianalea di Scilla, T: 0965 754026.

€€ **Grotta Azzurra**. Good fish restaurant with outdoor seating and sea views. Closed Mon and Dec. Lungomare Cristoforo Colombo, T: 0965 754889.

Serra San Bruno

€ **Roseto**. Lovely farm serving great country meals. Open May–Oct. At Roseto in Agro, T: 0963 70670.

Siderno Superiore

€ **Zio Salvatore**. Simple trattoria in the old town centre. Closed Tues. Via Annunziata 1–3, T: 0964 385330.

Soverato

€€ **La Perla**. Traditional seafood restaurant. Closed Mon (except in summer) and Nov. Via Cristoforo Colombo 6, T: 0967 25815.

€€ **Riviera**. Restaurant belonging to the hotel of the same name. Closed Mon and late Dec–early Jan. Via Regina Elena 4–6, T: 0967 25738.

Tropea

€€ **El Sol**. ■ Good regional cuisine with outdoor seating in summer. Open all year. Largo Mercato, T: 0963 61174.

€€ **Pimm's**. The fanciest place in town, overlooking the sea from a clifftop. Closed Mon (except in summer) and Jan. Largo Migliarese 2, T: 0963 666105.

€ **Osteria del Pescatore**. Good fish (but slow service) in a simple *osteria* in a picturesque lane near the cathedral. Closed Wed (except in summer) and Nov–March. Via del Monte 7, T: 0963 603018.

Vibo Valentia Marina
€€ **L'Approdo**. ■ The best fish restaurant on the coast. Closed Mon (except in summer). Via Roma 22, T: 0963 572640.

Villa San Giovanni
€€ **Antica Osteria Vecchia Villa**. Old-fashioned trattoria just off the station square. Closed Wed and Aug. Via Garibaldi 104, T: 0965 751125.

LOCAL SPECIALITIES

Palmi is a good places to go if you're in the market for hand-made furniture; **Seminara** makes Calabria's most famous ceramics, though the potters in neighbouring towns (especially Bagnara Calabra) are also skilled. Beautiful ceramics are also produced by craftsmen in **Squillace**, **Locri** and **Gerace**. Lace and embroidery are made throughout Calabria. At **Reggio Calabria** the Torrone Giuseppe Malavenda confectioners produces almond paste and *torroncini* flavoured with mandarin oranges, orange blossom honey, etc. Via Santa Caterina 85–91.

FESTIVALS & EVENTS

Palmi *Madonna dell'Alto Mare* Statue of the Madonna borne in procession by boats, then by hand, with fireworks, Last Sun in July; *Madonna della Sacra Lettera* The *Varia*, a representation of the Assumption of the Virgin, 16m tall and weighing 20 tonnes, is drawn through the town followed by the *Animella*, a young girl playing the Blessing Virgin, last Sun in Aug; *San Rocco* St Roch of Montpellier (1350–80), on the death of his wealthy parents, cast off his riches to become a mendicant pilgrim, but was arrested for vagrancy and died in prison. Our collective guilt is expiated by the *Spinati*, penitents who wear a crown of thorns (women) or a cloak of prickly wild juniper (men), in procession until the thorns draw blood, 16 Aug.

Reggio Calabria *Madonna della Consolazione* Statue of the Madonna on a float weighing three tonnes is borne by hand from the sanctuary of the Madonna della Consolazione, on the outskirts of Reggio, to the cathedral; the event is celebrated with music and craft fairs, second Sat in Sept.

Serra San Bruno *San Bruno* Procession with the bust of the saint, Pentecost, 6 Oct; *Festa della Montagna* Featuring porcini mushrooms and other woodland foods, 14 Aug.

Tropea *Sagra del Cammello* Commemoration of a historic victory over the Saracens, whose commander was burnt alive on his camel; celebrated with due violence by the *Esplosioe della Galera* (blowing up his ship) and *Scopio del Cammello* (blowing up his camel), both with fireworks, 3 May; Theatre and classical music series at the cathedral and other locations, July–Aug.

Vibo Valentia *Affruntata* Historic re-enactment of the annunciation to the Virgin of Christ's resurrection, Easter Sunday.

ADRIATIC

SEA

Tortoreto
Tortoreto Lido
Giulianova
Mosciano
S.Angelo
Notaresco
Morro
d'Oro
Roseto degli Abruzzi
Cellino Attanasio
Atri
Pineto
Montefino
Silvi
ABRUZZO
Castlienti
Silvi Marina
Castiglione
Messer Raimondo
Elice
Città
S.Angelo
Montesilvano
Piccano
Cappelle
sul Tavo
Penne
Collecorvino
Spoltore
PESCARA
Loreto
Aprutino
Moscufo
S.M. del Lago
Francavilla al Mare
Montebello
di Bertona
Pianella
S.Giovanni
Teatino
Villa Celiera
Cepagatti
Torrevecchia
Teatina
P. di Ferruccio
Civitella
Casanova
Chieti Scalo
CHIETI
Ripa
Teatina
Migliantco
Tollo
Ortona
Carpineto
della Nora
Catignano
Nocciano
Rosciano
S.Maria
Arabona
Villamagna
Bucchianico
Giuliano
Teatino
P. di Acquabella
Brittoli
Civitaquana
Cugnoli
Alanno
Vacri
Crecchio
S.Vito Chietino
Corvara
Pietranico
Scafa
Turri-Via
lignani
Casalin-
contrada
Serramo-
nacesca
Fara
Filiorum
Petri
Capasa
Sannita
Frisa
S.Giovanni
Treglio
Rocca
Poggiofiorito
P. Cavalluccio
Fossacesia Marina
escosan-
onesco-
Torre
de'Passeri
S.Valentino
in Abr Cit.
Letto-
manoppello
Casacanditella
S.Martino
Filetto
Lanciano
Fossacesia
Torino di
Sangro Marina
Manoppello
Abbateggio
Roccamorice
Rapino
Marrucina
Orsogna
Mozzagrogna
S.Maria
Imbaro
Castiglione
a Casauria
S.Clemente
in Casauria
Bolognano
Tocco
da Casauria
R. Lanciano
1306
Guardiagrele
Castel
Frentano
Torino
di Sangro
Madonna
d'
Paglieta Miracoli
Salle
Caramanico
Terme
Bocca
di Valle
S.Eusanio
d. Sangro
Villalfonsina
Casalbordino
Roccacasale
S.Eufemia
a Maiella
Pennapiedimonte
Palombaro
Pollutri
Vasto
Pratola
Peligna
M. Morrone
2061
M. Acquaviva
2737
2259
Fara
S.Martino
Casoli
Altino
Perano
Archi
Scerni
Monteodorisio
Cupello
S.Salvo
Badia Morronese
Parco Naz.
M. Amaro
2793
Civitella
Messer Raimondo
Bugnara
Pacentro
Lama
dei Peligni
Gessopalena
Rocca
scalegna
1020
Tornareccio
Bomba
Casalanguida
Atessa
La Montagna
Gissi
Furci
Lentella
Sulmona
Introdacqua
Taranta
Peligna
Letto-
palena
Torricella
Peligna
Pennadomo
Iuvanum
Carpineto
Sinello
S.Buono
Fresa-
grandinaria
Montenero
di Bisacce
Malfada
Pettorano
sul Gizio
Campo
di Giove
Palena
M. Porrara
2136
Colle
di macine
Montebello
sul Sangro
Montelapiano
Colledimezzo
Guilmi
Liscia
Dogliola
Tufillo
M. Genzana
2170
Cansano
Montenerodomo
Villa S. Maria
Fallo
Pietraferrazzana
Monte-
ferrante
Montazzoli
Rocca
spinalveti
Carunchio
S. Felice
del Molise
Villalago
d'Maiella
Pizzoferrato
Civitaluparella
Quadri
Borrello
Roio
del Sangro
Fraine
Celenza
s. Trigno
Montemitro
Acquaviva
Collecroce
Scanno
Rocca Pia
M. Secine
1885
Gamberale
Rosello
Pescopennataro
Castel Fraiano
1415
Castiglione
Messer Marino
Torrebruna
S.Giovanni
Lipioni
Montefalcone
nel Sannio
M. Marsicano
2242
Pescocostanzo
Rivisondoli
S. Angelo
del Pesco
Belmonte
del Sannio
Castelguidone
Roccavivara
Guarda
Parco
Naz.
d'Abruzzo
M. Greco
2283
Roccaraso
Ateleta
Castel del Giudice
Capracotta
Schiavi
d'Abruzzo
Trivento
MOLISE
Lucito
M. Pratello
2056
M. Mauro
1043
Castel
M. Marsicano
2242
Villetta Barrea
Castel
di Sangro
S.Pietro
Avellana
Vastogirardi
M. Cantaro
1730
Agnone
Poggio
Sannita
Salcito
S.Biase
Civitampom
Lupara
Mor
Cas
Petrella
Tifernina
Castelb
Civitella
Alfedena
2247
M.Petroso
Barrea
Scontrone
Alfedena
Rionero
Sannitico
Carovilli
Castelverrino
Pietrabbondante
S.Angelo
Limosano
Pietracupa
Limosano
S.Mauro
LAZIO
M. di
Meta
Aufidena
Montenero
Val Cocchiara
M.Curvale
1760
Forli
del Sannio
Roccasicura
Pescolanciano
Chiauci
Bagnoli
del Trigno
Fossalto
S.Angelo
Limosano
M. della Meta
2241

ABRUZZO & MOLISE

The east and centre of the Abruzzo region is covered by the map opposite. The whole of Molise is covered by the map on p. 386. L'Aquila, the Gran Sasso and mountain regions of Abruzzo are shown on p. 396.

A bruzzo and Molise represent a hidden treasure, a land of mountains at once rugged and soft, clothed here in a mantle of dark forest, there in a golden cloak of grain. Whatever you think of the towns, which in the more remote areas can be rather grim, you will be favourably impressed by the particular character of the landscape, 'these impressive Abruzzi ridges that combined in so special a way hard temper with soft color—as if there were steel underneath blue silver, yet a blue so etherealized that one peak, with its pencilled veins of snow, seemed to merge into the slate-blue heavens' (Edmund Wilson, *Europe without Baedeker,* 1947).

These two relatively small regions occupy the east centre of the Italian peninsula, with their seaboard on the Adriatic. They are bordered on the north by the Marche, on the west by Lazio and on the south by Campania and Puglia, and comprise the hilly provinces of L'Aquila, Teramo, Pescara, Chieti, Campobasso and Isernia. Formerly a single region, they became administratively independent in 1963.

The highest peaks of the Apennines are to be found in Abruzzo. They diverge slightly from the main northwest–southeast axis here to form the Meta Massif, in the Abruzzo National Park. The Lago-Gran Sasso-Maiella range—which culminates in the Corno Grande (2912m), the 'roof' of the peninsula—divides the region into two fundamentally different landscapes and climates: one maritime, the other alpine. Between this and the central range lies the so-called Abruzzo Highland, with the basins of L'Aquila and Sulmona.

The first human presence in Abruzzo seems to date from the Lower Palaeolithic period. Evidence from the Upper Palaeolithic and Neolithic periods has been found throughout the region, particularly in the Fucino basin, rich in cave finds, and at Corropoli, where the so-called Ripoli culture, distinguished by a particular type of painted ceramics, appears to have lasted over a millennium. The Neolithic Apennine culture was introduced at a fairly advanced stage, in the Middle Bronze Age, probably by small groups of shepherds from Apulia or the Marches; and Neolithic traditions persisted even in the later, sub-Apennine phase. Especially in the mountain areas, the sub-Apennine cultures maintained their autonomy, contributing later to the formation of numerous allied tribes, of mixed origin, who were subdued by the Romans only after a long, bitter struggle culminating in the Social War (91–82 BC).

After the fall of the Roman Empire, the region was partitioned between the dukes of Spoleto and Benevento and was later united by the Normans to the Duchy of Apulia. Frederick II of Hohenstaufen transformed Abruzzo into an independent province with Sulmona as its capital, but after the arrival in the mid-13th century of the Angevins, the region followed the fortunes of the Kingdom of Naples. The Bourbons in 1684 divided it into Abruzzo Citeriore, Ulteriore Primo and Ulteriore Secondo (corresponding to the three northern provinces of today), and Molise.

The name, Abruzzo, originally *Aprutium*, seems to be derived from the Praetuttii, one of the aboriginal tribes. The Tronto river, which today separates Abruzzo from the Marche, is the historical border between the Kingdom of Naples and the Papal States. On the west, the boundary with Lazio still follows the dividing line between the ancient *IV Regio Samnium* and *I Regio Latium*. The title of Duke of Abruzzi was borne by Luigi Amedeo (1873–1933), the distinguished explorer and mountaineer, and grandson of Vittorio Emanuele II.

Medieval Abruzzan art is characterised by severe simplicity, and Abruzzan churches are distinguished by their flat, gableless façades. The origin of the name Molise, which is first mentioned as a region in the 13th century, is uncertain.

WHITE SANDS & PINES

The Adriatic coast of Abruzzo and Molise is flat and unremarkable, but just a few kilometres inland are areas known for their natural beauty, for magnificent castles and austere medieval churches; particularly fine examples of the latter may be seen at Atri and Lanciano. The little resorts by the sea are good starting points for exploring these areas—as well as Abruzzo's mountainous interior. Day trips can easily be made to L'Aquila and to the Gran Sasso, or to the churches, castles and archaeological sites of the western highlands. Whatever you do, don't miss the archaeological museum in Chieti, which won a European Union award for its excellent layout in 1984. Chieti itself is a lively, pleasant town. Pescara is a busy provincial capital.

Most of the towns along the coast have become summer resorts, usually with sandy beaches backed by cool pinewoods. The towns can be curiously quiet in low season, which here extends from mid-September to mid-June.

Giulianova

Giulianova, a seaside resort, was founded in 1470 by the people of San Flaviano (the ancient *Castrum Novum*) and named in honour of Giulio Antonio Acquaviva, Duke of Atri. It consists of a medieval town set on a hill a kilometre from the coast and a new quarter, Giulianova Lido, by the sea. The Renaissance **duomo**, built to an octagonal plan, contains a 14th-century reliquary. The fine Romanesque church of Santa Maria a Mare was ruined in 1944, but has been restored. The **Pinacoteca Comunale Vincenzo Bindi** (*Via Garibaldi 14; open Mon–Fri, in summer 9–12.30 & 3–6.30 & 9–11pm; winter 9–12.30 & 3–6.30; T: 085 802 1215*) has a modest collection of Neapolitan School paintings (17th–18th centuries), Posillipo School paintings (19th century) and Capodimonte ceramics; and there is a small collection of modern art in the former convent of the **Madonna dello Splendore** (*open Tues–Sun, in summer 10–1 & 5–8; winter 10–1 & 4–7; T: 085 800 7157*).

Atri

Pineto lies near Atri, on a hill to the west. This is the legendary *Hatria*, which became a Roman colony in 282 BC. Its coins are among the heaviest known, exceeding the oldest Roman coins in weight. The **cathedral** (1285), with a graceful campanile and a beautiful, though simple façade, contains 15th-century frescoes of Old and New Testament scenes, and of Evangelists, doctors, and saints, by Andrea Delitio, and a fine tabernacle (1503) by Paolo de Garvi. The crypt, entered from the handsome cloister behind the church, is a Roman *piscina*; in the sacristy are two carved polyptychs. The Museo Capitolare (*open June–Sept daily 10–12 & 4–8; Oct–May daily except Wed 10–12 & 3–5; T: 085 879 8140*), also in the cloister, houses a small but beautiful collection of medieval art. There are also a glazed majolica *Madonna and Child* attributed to Luca della Robbia, and exhibits of ceramics made in Abruzzo between the 16th and 20th centuries.

The churches of Sant'Agostino and Sant'Andrea have good portals. The severe façade of the **Palazzo Acquaviva dei Duchi** (town hall and post office) masks an attractive 14th-century courtyard. The Museo Civico Etnografico (*Piazza San Pietro, open July–Aug Tues–Sun 4.30–7; Sept–June Tues–Sat 10–1; T: 085 879 1210*) and Museo Didattico di Strumenti Antichi (*Piazza Duchi di Acquaviva, open by appointment; T: 085 879 1210*) document local material culture (farm tools, craft tools, household utensils and furniture) of the 18th and 19th centuries.

Inland to Penne

From Montesilvano country roads run west to **Città Sant'Angelo**, with a 14th-century church, and southwest to Penne. **Moscufo** is situated on a hilltop with views over the sea and mountains, from the Gran Sasso to the Maiella. The church of Santa Maria del Lago, 5km south of the road, has a fine pulpit of 1158. To the south of **Loreto Aprutino**, the church of Santa Maria in Piano contains notable frescoes (*Last Judgement*, stories from the life of St Thomas Aquinas, New Testament scenes and saints) by 13th- and 14th-century artists. **Penne** is an ancient city of the Vestini. The church of San Giovanni contains a processional cross attributed to Nicola da Guardiagrele (in the treasury). The 14th-century cathedral, almost completely destroyed in 1944, has been restored. Santa Maria in Colleromano, 1km southeast, has fragmentary 15th- and 16th-century frescoes; and at **Pianella**, 18km southeast near the road to Chieti, is an interesting little Romanesque church.

PESCARA

Pescara (pop. 129,000), capital of the province of Pescara, is the most active commercial town in Abruzzo as well as an important fishing port and a popular bathing resort. The completely modern town, charmingly situated among pinewoods, is divided into two parts by the River Pescara. The northern section, known as Pescara Riviera, was formerly the separate *comune* of Castellammare Adriatico. Pescara proper, to the south, is on the site of the Classical *Aternum*, the common port of the Vestini, Marrucini and Peligni, and at the seaward end of the Via Valeria (today Road 5).

Pescara was the birthplace of Gabriele d'Annunzio (1863–1938), the controversial early 20th-century writer and politician, whose life and work may be admired in the **Museo Gabriele d'Annunzio** (*Corso Manthoné 101; open Mon–Fri 9–1, last admission 30mins before closing; T: 085 60391*). The **Museo Civico e Pinacoteca Basilio Cascella** (*Via Guglielmo Marconi 45; open daily, summer 9–1 & 4–7, winter 9–1; T: 0854 283515*) contains paintings, sculpture, and prints by three generations of the Cascella family, also natives. The **Museo delle Genti d'Abruzzo** (*Via delle Caserme 22; open June–Sept Mon–Fri 9–1, Tues–Sun 9pm–12.30am; Oct–May Mon–Sat 9–1, Tues, Thur, Sun 4–7; T: 085 451 0026*) has sections devoted to ethnography, prehistory and protohistory, religion, popular festivities, and agriculture. It occupies the former Bourbon *bagno penale* (gaol).

Gabriele d'Annunzio (1863–1938)

Gabriele d'Annunzio is known as much for his political activism as for his dark, turbulent literary works. He was born in Pescara on 12th March 1863. He studied literature in Rome, where he also wrote for several magazines and soon distinguished himself as a socialite. Elected to parliament in 1897 (his home district was Ortona), on a whim he suddenly swung from the extreme right to the extreme left. In the same year he took a villa at Settignano near Florence, but at the insistence of his creditors, fled to France in 1910.

He returned to Italy in 1915 as an ardent champion of Italian intervention against Austria in the First World War. Convinced (rightly) that the example of an internationally famous poet would be influential, he flew over Austrian-held Trento and Trieste in 1915, lost an eye in a forced landing near Grado, took part in the Italian bombings of Pula and Kotor in 1917, and rode Italy's infamous manned torpedos (MAS) against Austrian warships. In 1919, he led a band of irregulars to occupy Rijeka (formerly Fiume, on the Dalmatian coast), which had been denied to Italy at the Paris peace conference, holding the city until the arrival of the Italian army in 1920. A firm supporter of Fascism in its early stages, in 1921 he retired from public life to his villa, the Vittoriale, at Gardone Riviera, where he remained until his death on 1st March 1938. His most famous literary achievements are the four volumes of verses known as the *Laudi del Cielo, del Mare, della Terra e degli Eroi*, composed between 1899 and 1912.

Francavilla and Ortona

Francavilla al Mare, just south of Pescara, was the home of the painter Francesco Paolo Michetti (d. 1929), whose work is the focus of the Museo Mumi (*open summer Tues–Sun 6pm–midnight*) in the former town hall. In the treasury of the modern church of Santa Maria Maggiore is a monstrance by Nicola da Guardiagrele (*see p. 377*).

Ortona, several times devastated by earthquakes and badly damaged in the Second World War, is the most important port of Abruzzo. The cathedral (San Tommaso) is a restoration, having been half demolished in the Second World War. The Palazzo

Farnese, begun in 1584 by Giacomo della Porta for Margaret of Parma, was left unfinished on her death here in 1586. It lies between the *municipio* and a piazzetta named after the composer Francesco Paolo Tosti (1846–1916), a native of Ortona. The palazzo is home to the pinacoteca and museum, with works by regional artists and material from local archaeological sites, which are opened on request (*T: 085 906723*). More interesting, perhaps, is the Museo Musicale d'Abruzzo in the Palazzo Corvi (*open Mon–Fri 9.30–1.30, Tues and Thur also 3–6 and, in summer, 7–11; T: 085 906 6310*), dedicated to Tosti, the composer of the classical 'Neapolitan' songs *A Vucchella* and *A Marechiare*. Several other well-known local songwriters and performers (Gaetano Braga, Primo Ricitelli, Bonaventura Baratelli, Giuseppe de Luca) are also represented.

About 3km south of the town, beyond the Moro river, is the **Moro River Canadian War Cemetery**, with 1,615 graves of Canadian, British and other Allied dead.

CHIETI

Chieti (pop. 58,000), capital of the province of the same name, is a lively little town, famous for its wide views of Abruzzo, from the Gran Sasso and the Maiella to the sea. Chieti railway station is at Chieti Scalo, 5km west (bus connection). The town stands on the site of the ancient *Theate Marrucinorum*. Gian Pietro Carafa, Bishop of Chieti (afterwards Paul IV), gave the name of his see to the Theatines, the religious order that he founded in 1524, with Gaetano da Thiene (St Cajetan).

National Archaeological Museum of Abruzzo

Villa Comunale. Open Tues–Sun 9–7.30; T: 0871 331668.

This superb museum won the European Museum of the Year award in 1984 for its superb collections of Italic and Graeco-Roman antiquities.

The collection

Rooms 1, 3 and 4 are devoted to **burial cults in pre-Roman Abruzzo**, ranging from the 9th–4th centuries BC. The objects displayed were found at grave sites throughout the region; their provenance is labelled and they are numbered progressively. Although most are made of inorganic materials (which do not decay), rare fragments of fabric, leather and wood also survive. The finds include vessels for food and drink, arms and armour, jewellery and personal adornments, which indicate the social status of the deceased, and the commercial and cultural ties that the Italic communities in Abruzzo enjoyed with other Mediterranean and continental European peoples.

Room 1: Especially interesting are two of the 272 **tombs excavated at Campovalano** (Province of Teramo). The first, belonging to a man, yielded a Corinthian-type bronze helmet and a bronze shin-guard; the second, of a woman, contained embossed bronze sandals imported from Etruria and a glass sceptre. Both are 'patrician' tombs of the 7th or 8th century BC. In the same room are **burial treasures from Penna Sant'Andrea** (Teramo) in 1973, including masks and pearls of Phoenician–Punic origin; similar objects have been found only at Carthage, in Spain and in Sardinia. Particular importance is given to the stone stelae from the same site, which bear the first written evidence (7th or 6th century BC) of the ethnic term *Safin* (Sabines).

Room 2: Devoted to Italic sculpture, and holds the famous **Warrior of Capestrano**, the burial stele of an Italic monarch of the 6th century BC, flanked by a series of presumably contemporary Archaic sculptures: the so-called *Devil's Legs* from Collelongo (L'Aquila), the *Atessa Torso* (Chieti), the *Leopardi Head* from Loreto Aprutino (Pescara), and a fragment from Rapino (Chieti).

Room 3: Contains a variety of material from Iron Age necropoleis, notably the treasures of several tombs unearthed at Capestrano (one is probably that of the warrior); a stele from Guardiagrele (Chieti); material from Paglieta and Torricella Peligna (excavated in the 19th century but never before displayed); finds from the necropolis of Alfedena (L'Aquila); an iron sword and bronze belt with traces of fabric from the necropolis of Pennapiedimente (Chieti), dating from the 4th century BC, and treasures from two of the 300 tombs identified in 1983 at Le Castagne, dating from the 7th or 6th century BC and representing one of the largest necropoleis of Abruzzo.

The museum also houses a number of important human remains, mainly from Iron Age necropoleis, housed in the **anthropological section** (Room 5). Explanatory panels outline how knowledge about a person (sex, age at death, state of health, blood group, nutritional habits, etc) is obtained centuries or even millennia after the individual's death by examining his or her bones. Fundamental in evolutionary terms is the Ortucchio jaw (8000–9000 BC), which demonstrates a marked decrease in the size of teeth compared to other specimens of the late Iron Age.

The **Pansa Collection** (Rooms 10–11), a private collection recently left to the museum, reflects the tastes and interests of an amateur of the late 19th and early 20th century, an eminent local solicitor with a predilection for small bronzes, objects from daily life, jewels, glass, and ivory. In the **numismatic collection** (Rooms 12–13), the exhibits have been selected from among c. 15,000 coins from various areas of Abruzzo, ranging in date from the 4th century BC to the 18th century AD. The coins have been arranged to reflect the economic history of the region from pre-Roman times onward; the thematic display cases and panels show the provenance, technical characteristics, and site of each find. The coins are also colour-coded for clarity (yellow = Greece and Magna Graecia, red = Republican Rome, and so on). Especially interesting are the Roman *Aureo of Gauda* (Case 7), one of three known examples of this type (the other two are in the British Museum); and the medieval pieces, many of which were minted in northern Italy and illustrate the prosperity brought to the

The *Warrior of Capestrano*, royal grave stele from the 6th century BC.

region by the trade in wool, silk and spices. Magnifying glasses are provided on request. **Roman portraiture**, public, private and funerary is displayed in Rooms 14–16; Rooms 17–18 constitute the **lapidarium**, with Roman funerary and honorary epigraphy, including two extraordinary burial beds in bone and ivory.

Other sights in Chieti

The **cathedral**, many times rebuilt, has a graceful campanile (1335–1498); within are a Baroque pulpit and stalls, and (in the treasury) a silver statue of St Justin, by Nicola da Guardiagrele. Behind the post office are interesting remains of three small Roman temples. The Palazzo Municipale, in the cathedral square, was erected in 1517, as the palace of the Valignani, and rebuilt in a Neoclassical style in the 19th century.

The **Museo d'Arte Costantino Barbella** (*open Tues–Sat 9–1, Tues and Thur also 4–7, first Sun of every month 9–12; T: 0871 33 0873*) occupies the Palazzo Martinetti-Bianchi, a former Jesuit college, in the central Via Cesare de Lollis. It has a few paintings by Francesco Paolo Michetti, and other works, of painting and ceramics, dating from the 16th century to the present. The 16th–18th-century Castelli majolicas are particularly fine. The **Museo di Arte Sacra**, adjoining the Baroque church of San Domenico (1642), is mainly notable for its examples of local woodcarving (*open daily 8–12 & 4.30–7*). Santa Maria Mater Domini (to the southeast) contains a *Madonna* carved in wood, by Gagliardelli.

At the eastern edge of the town, in the shadow of a high-rise development, lie the remains of **Roman thermae**, consisting of a large (60m by 14m) cistern and numerous rooms, one of which retains its mosaic pavement. The complex probably dates from the early imperial period.

Excursions from Chieti

The Roman Via Valeria (now Road 5) ascends the valley of the River Pescara, linking the Adriatic coast with Rome. A bit further west of Chieti, on the south side of the valley, is the Cistercian church of **Santa Maria d'Arabona** (1208), containing a noteworthy aumbry and paschal candlestick (*the way is marked; ring for admittance*).

Torre de' Passeri is a picturesque village, bypassed by the main road. About 2km south (marked) is another fine church, **San Clemente in Casauria**, rebuilt by the Cistercians in the 12th century, but retaining its original crypt of 871, the date of its foundation by Emperor Louis II. The façade is fronted by a magnificent portico, with three broad arches (that at the centre is rounded, whereas the others are slightly pointed) on compound piers. The capitals and archivolts are richly carved. Above, two orders of attached shafts terminate in a delicate band of arched corbels, above which rises the fenestrated upper storey, an addition of 1448. The main portal, with its complex sculptural programme, is a splendid work of the 12th century. The bronze doors, with 72 relief panels (some missing), are roughly contemporary. The interior, built to a Latin-cross plan with shallow transepts, ends in a semicircular apse, unusual in Cistercian architecture, but in keeping with the Romanesque tradition. The first four bays of the nave arcade are taller than the others and are lighted by clerestory windows. Above the door is a Gothic loggia. The magnificent ambo (right), candlestick (left) and altar canopy are of the same date as the sculptures of the portal. Steps lead down to the crypt.

Caramanico Terme, to the south, is a summer resort with sulphur baths on the west slopes of the Maiella range. Its church of Santa Maria Maggiore has a fine portal of 1476 and a reliquary by Nicola da Guardiagrele; San Domenico has two good doorways.

LANCIANO & ENVIRONS

Lanciano is the Roman *Anxanum*, originally a city inhabited by the Frentani. The handsome cathedral, with its 17th-century campanile, is built on a bridge dating from the time of Diocletian and restored in 1088. The church has been closed indefinitely for restoration. **Santa Maria Maggiore**, a Cistercian edifice of 1227, has a Gothic portal of 1317 and, in the handsome Burgundian Gothic interior, a crucifix by Nicola da Guardiagrele (1422) and a triptych by Polidoro di Renzo (1549). Sant'Agostino contains other interesting examples of goldsmiths' work. The 13th-century church of **San Francesco** is traditionally held to contain evidence of the first eucharistic miracle recorded by the Church, which took place around the year 700 during a mass celebrated by a Basilian monk who doubted the eucharistic presence. The reliquary is kept in a marble tabernacle over the ciborium and is composed of a silver monstrance (1713) and a chalice below it in crystal, the former containing the flesh, the latter the blood into which the bread and wine were transubstantiated. The 11th-century **Porta San Biagio** is the only remaining town gate; near it is the 14th-century campanile of the disused church of San Biagio.

Guardiagrele

Road 363, with good views, leads from Lanciano to **Guardiagrele**, a little town noted in the 15th century for its goldsmiths, of whom Nicola di Andrea (Nicola da Guardiagrele, c. 1390–1459) was the most famous. Born in Guardiagrele, he knew Ghiberti, and worked in Abruzzo and Rome. The 14th-century Romanesque church of Santa Maria Maggiore was damaged in 1943, but the external fresco of St Christopher, by Andrea Delitio (1473), survived. The noted silver Crucifix by Nicola da Guardiagrele (1431), stolen from the treasury and dismembered, has been almost entirely recovered and is now the focus of a Museo di Arte Sacra (*open by appointment; T: 0871 82117*). The 14th-century church of San Francesco has a carved Romanesque-Gothic portal and a 15th-century cloister. The Biblioteca Comunale has a small collection of architectural fragments and sculptures from churches in the area.

A scenic road (no. 81) leads to Chieti via the **Bocca di Valle**, where a huge inscription on a cliff and a cave chapel serve as the Abruzzo Memorial to the First World War. At **Fara Filiorum Petri** the Feast of St Anthony Abbot (16th January) is celebrated by burning a forest of *farchie*, bamboo columns up to 12m high. To the south rises the Maielletta.

The castle at **Crecchio** (reached by a turning on the right) gave refuge to Vittorio Emanuele III and the Italian Command when they escaped from Rome following the armistice of 8th September 1943. Today the castle hosts the **Museo dell'Abruzzo Bizantino ed Altomedievale** (*open daily July–Sept 10–12 & 3–7; Oct–June Sat 3–7, Sun 10–12 & 3–7; T: 087 194 1392*), which displays an extraordinary collection of early medieval artefacts, mainly of Byzantine and Lombard origin. The gilded bronze Ostrogoth helmet from Torricella Peligna is the highlight.

The conspicuous lack of cultivated fields draws attention to Abruzzo's historic vocation: pasturage.

ALONG THE SANGRO

South of Lanciano, the road winds south to join the valley of the River Sangro, winding down for 74km to Castel di Sangro (*see below*). It passes **Bomba**, with a Museo Etnografico documenting rural culture in Abruzzo (*open summer Sat–Sun 6–8; winter Sat–Sun 3.30–5.30; T: 087 286 0128*) and remains of cyclopean walls. From here a winding country road ascends to **Fallascoso**, near which lie the ruins of the Roman *Iuvanum*. The extensive remains include a forum, a theatre, foundations of several temples and numerous houses and streets. A parallel road on the east (Road 364) passes **Atessa**, where the church of San Leucio contains a monstrance by Nicola da Guardiagrele.

Roccaraso, with its ruined castle, is a pleasant summer resort and winter sports centre, connected by rail with Sulmona. About 2km northwest of the town, Road 17 bears west and Road 84 north. The magnificent views afforded by the latter road on its descent have won for it the name of *Ringhiera dell'Abruzzo* ('Balcony of Abruzzo').

Just north of the fork lie **Rivisondoli** (1320m), a summer and winter resort, and **Pescocostanzo** (1395m), once famous for its lace and other local arts. The little town, with its characteristic deep eaves and porches, is now also a popular summer and winter holiday centre. The church of Santa Maria del Colle, a remarkable work of the

16th, 17th and 18th centuries, has elaborately carved wood detailing. Particularly noteworthy are the ceiling of the nave and the high altar, the latter incorporating, in a central niche, an 11th-century *Madonna and Child*, the so-called *Madonna del Colle*. A station on the Sulmona railway serves both resorts.

Castel di Sangro

Castel di Sangro is a picturesque town situated partly on a hill and partly on level ground, at the confluence of the Sangro and the Zittola rivers. A developing resort, it is also known for its traditional ironworking, woodworking and woollen industries. The town was reduced to ruins during the Second World War and has been largely rebuilt. The 16th-century Convento della Maddalena houses the **Museo Civico Aufinenate** (*open 10.30–12.30 & 5–8 in Aug; other summer months as above except Mon and Tues; winter Wed–Sun 10–1 & 5–7; T: 0864 840826*), with the municipal archaeological collection: two headless Roman statues, architectural fragments and a collection of antique bronzes unearthed along the River Zittola in 1957. In the central Piazza del Plebiscito stands the church of the Annunziata (or San Domenico), originally 15th-century and rebuilt after the Second World War. Steps opposite ascend to the upper town.

Here the two-towered church of **Santa Maria Assunta**, rebuilt in 1695–1727 over an earlier edifice, escaped the war with minor injuries. The Baroque façade incorporates modern statues. At the far end of the portico on the right is a 14th-century *Pietà* in a Gothic aedicule. The interior, entered from the sides, is built to a Greek-cross plan with four small domes in the arms and a large dome at the crossing. In the south arm are a *Madonna and Child with Saints* by Paolo de Matteis, and *Adoration of the Shepherds* and *Disputa* by Domenico Antonio Vaccaro. Behind the marble high altar (1738), *Last Supper* by de Matteis, *Ecce Homo* and *Christ at Calvary* by Francesco de Mura. In the north transept are a painted wooden altar frontal of the 16th century, and minor paintings.

Several medieval and Renaissance houses can be seen in the upper town. A mule track leads through pine woods up to the ruined castle, near which are traces of cyclopean walls.

INTO MOLISE

The village of **Fossacesia** lies 4km inland from Fossacesia Marina. Here the magnificent conventual church of San Giovanni in Venere overlooks the Adriatic above the railway station. Documented from the 8th century, it was rebuilt in 1015 by Trasmondo II, Count of Chieti, and after 1165 it was enlarged in the Cistercian style by Abbot Oderisio II. The lower part of the façade is in stone, the upper part in brick. The remarkable marble Portale della Luna (1225–30) has a tall quatrefoil archivolt, and in its lunette, *Christ Enthroned between the Virgin and St John*; below are the remains of small statues of St Benedict and Abbot Rainaldo. At the sides of the door stand broad, flat engaged pilasters with bas-reliefs depicting Old and New Testament scenes, of Apulian Romanesque inspiration. Above rises the tympanum, divided into three parts like a triptych and probably conceived in relation to a group of frescoes that was never executed. The basilican interior (1165) has a nave and aisles separated by cruciform piers. Above these, in the nave, are attached shafts designed to support a vaulted ceiling that was never carried out. The raised presbytery is covered by cross-vaults; in the apses are 12th-, 13th- and 14th-century frescoes. Steps in the aisles descend to the crypt, which contains some late 12th-century frescoes and columns from a temple of Venus that occupied this site in Antiquity. At the rear of the church the three elegant apses are visible. The cloister (*ring for entrance*) was rebuilt in 1932–35.

Across the River Sangro on Road 16 is Torino di Sangro Marina, south of which lies the **Sangro River British Military Cemetery**, with 2,619 graves. Beyond Casalbordino station a road diverges for the much-visited **Santuario della Madonna dei Miracoli** (festival, 11th June).

Vasto

Vasto is a pleasant town 3km from its railway station. It is the mythical *Histonium*, and for centuries was subject to the powerful d'Avalos family. The painter and poet Dante Gabriel Rossetti was the son of a blacksmith from Vasto. He is honoured by a statue in Piazza Diomede. The **church of San Pietro** contains a picture painted at the age of 80 by Filippo Palizzi (1818–99), a native of the town. The castle dates from the 13th century. The plain duomo (1293) has a Gothic portal. Across the square, the **Museo e Pinacoteca Civici**, in the 18th-century Palazzo d'Avalos (*open July–Aug Tues–Sun 10.30–12.30 & 6–12; Sept–June Thur–Sun 9.30–12.30 & 4.30–8.30, Tues and Wed 4.30–8.30: T: 087 336 7773*) contains antiquities, including Oscan inscriptions, a costume collection, and works by Filippo Palizzi. The double sarcophagus of Pacuius Sceva and his wife Flavia, the glassware from the burial treasure of a young Roman woman, and the traditional dresses of Abruzzo, are especially remarkable. The River Trigno forms the boundary between Abruzzo and Molise.

PRACTICAL INFORMATION

GETTING AROUND

• **By air:** GTM Bus 38 runs between Pasquale Liberi Airport (www.abruzzo-airport.it) 6km north of Pescara and the central Corso Vittorio Emanuele in 15min at 10–30min intervals, 6am–10.30pm.

• **By road:** Autostrada A14 follows the coast closely, and is the best road to use when visiting the area. Highway 16, parallel to the *autostrada*, is satisfactory for short hops but may prove tiresome over long distances.

• **By rail:** The main line connecting Milan with Bari, Brindisi and Lecce keeps close to the road all the way. Fast Eurostar trains stop at Pescara; slow local trains stop at most other towns on the line. There is also a local service from Rome to Pescara (240km in c. 3hrs 35mins). Pescara has two railway stations: Centrale, the main station and the terminus of the line from Rome, and Porta Nuova, for the south of the town.

• **By sea:** Ortona and Vasto are connected by boats and hydrofoils to the Tremiti Islands. To/from Vasto: daily hydrofoils June–Sept in 1hr. Ortona: daily hydrofoils June–Sept, 2hrs. For further details contact offices in Ortona: Adriatica di Navigazione, c/o Agenzia Fratino, Via Porto 34, T: 085 906 3855; Vasto, Adriatica di Navigazione, c/o Agenzia Massacesi, Piazza Diomede 3, T: 0873 362680.

INFORMATION OFFICES

Chieti Amministrazione Provinciale, Settore Turismo, Corso Marruccino, T: 0871 408282; Ufficio Informazioni e di Accoglienza Turistica, Via Spaventa 29–31; T: 0871 63640.

Francavilla al Mare Viale Nettuno 107, T: 085 817169.

Giulianova Via Mamiani 16, T: 085 800 3013.

Lanciano Piazza Plebiscito, T: 0872 714959.

Ortona Piazza della Repubblica 9, T: 085 906 3841.

Pescara Ufficio Informazioni e di Accoglienza Turistica, Via Nicola Fabrizi 171, T: 085 4290 0212; Via Mazzini 146, T: 085 421 5933 and Corso Vittorio Emanuele 301, T: 085 429001.

Roccaraso Palazzo del Comune, Via Mori 1, T: 0864 62210.

Vasto Piazza del Popolo 18, T: 0873 367312.

HOTELS

Chieti
€€ **Abruzzo**. The traditional place to stay in Chieti, with comfortable rooms and cordial staff. Via A. Herio 20, T: 0871 41940, gaa@alicom.com

Città Sant'Angelo
€€€ **Villa Nacalua**. In the country near the *autostrada* at Pescara Nord. Elegant rooms, marble baths, pool. Contrada Fonte Umano, T: 085 959225, www.nacalua.com

€ **Giardino dei Principi**. Simple but comfortable, with an excellent restaurant. Viale Petruzzi 30, at Moscarola, T: 085 950235, www.hotelgiardinodeiprincipi.it

Francavilla al Mare
€€ **Sporting Hotel Villa Maria**. ■ Distinguished establishment with lovely rooms, pool and shady gardens. Contrada Pretaro, T: 085 451 1001, www.sportingvillamaria.it

Lanciano
€ **Anxanum**. A modern place with spacious rooms, pool and sauna. Via San Francesco d'Assisi 8, T: 0872 715142, hotelanxanum@tin.it

Loreto Aprutino
€€ **Castello Chiola**. Refined and comfortable, in a historic building. Via degli Aquino 12, T: 085 829 0690, www.castellochiolahotel.com

€ **La Bilancia**. In the hills 5km from the town, with an excellent restaurant. Closed mid-Dec–mid-Jan. Contrada Palazzo 11, T: 085 828 9321, www.hotellabilancia.it

Ortona
€ **Ideale**. Simple and quiet, with good views. Via Garibaldi 65, T: 085 906 3735, www.hotel-ideale.it

Pescara
€€ **Esplanade**. Refined and comfortable, with an excellent restaurant, in the very centre of town. Piazza Primo Maggio 46, T: 085 292141, www.esplanade.net

€ **Ambra**. Central and comfortable. Closed mid-Dec–mid-Jan. Via Quarto dei Mille 28–30, T: 085 378247, www.hotelambrapalace.it

Roccaraso
€ **Grande Albergo**. A comfortable, family-run establishment in the town centre. Closing times vary. Via Roma 21, T: 0864 6023523, www.grandealbergo.it

€ **Iris**. Owner-managed, clean and cordial. Viale Iris 5, T: 0864 602366, iris@roccaraso.net.

Spoltore (8km west of Pescara)
€€ **Montinope**. ■ Just 18 rooms and 2 suites, with good views and an excellent restaurant. Via Montinope, T: 085 496 2836, www.hotelmontinope.it

RESTAURANTS

Chieti
€€ **Caminetto d'Oro**. Restaurant offering good regional fish and meat dishes. Closed Mon and late Aug. Via Aterno 36, T: 0871 561349.

Città Sant'Angelo
€ **La Locanda dell'Arte**. The art of cooking *farro* (spelt), in a simple *osteria*. Closed Sun (except in summer). Vico II Santa Chiara 7, T: 085 96669.

Civitella Casanova (west of Chieti)
€ **La Bandiera**. ■ Authentic regional cuisine at its best, in the countryside miles from anywhere. Closed Wed, Jan and July. Contrada Pastini 32, T: 085 845219.

Fara Filiorum Petri
€€ **Belvedere**. Traditional restaurant with great regional food and wines. Closed Mon and Nov. Via San Giacomo

50, T: 0871 70282.

Giulianova

€€ **Osteria dal Moro**. Trattoria with good fish. Closed Mon and Tues, Thur and Sat evening, late Sept–early Oct and late Feb–early March. Lungomare Spalato 74, at Giulianova Lido, T: 085 800 4973.

€€ **Osteria della Stracciavocc'**. *Osteria* serving delicious regional seafood. Closed Mon and 10 days in Oct. Via Trieste 159, at Giulianova Lido; T: 085 8005326.

€ **Beccaceci**. ■ Traditional fish restaurant. Closed Mon evening, Tues and Dec–Jan. Via Zola 28, T: 085 800 7073.

Guardiagrele

€ **Santa Chiara**. Delicious regional cuisine in the heart of the historic town centre. Closed Tues and late July. Via Roma 10, T: 0871 801139.

€ **Villa Maiella**. ■ Locally famous restaurant offering outstanding regional cuisine and good ambience. Closed Mon and late July. Via Sette Dolori 30, T: 0871 809319.

Lanciano

€€ **Ruota**. Restaurant known for its good regional cuisine, especially fish. Closed Sun. Via per Fossacesia 40, T: 0872 44590.

Loreto Aprutino

€ **La Bilancia**. ■ Small hotel restaurant with great local cooking, often crowded. Closed Mon and Dec–Jan. Contrada Palazzo 10, T: 085 828 9321.

Notaresco (north of Atri)

€€ **Tre Archi**. ■ Great old-fashioned country cooking in the hills above the coast. Closed Wed and Nov. Via Pianura Vomano 36, at Guardia Vomano, T: 085 898140.

Ortona

€€ **Cantina Aragonese**. Good traditional restaurant. Closed Sun evening and

Mon. Corso Matteotti 88, T: 085 906 3217.

€€ **Il Sestante**. Pleasant restaurant and pizzeria near the harbour. Closed Mon (except in summer) and Nov. Via Marina 72, T: 085 9061878.

Pescara

€€ **Michele al Sea River Club**. ■ Outstanding fish restaurant overlooking the River Pescara. Closed Sun evening, Mon and Jan. Via Roveto 37, T: 085 28056.

€€ **Da Attilio**. Good seafood reasonably priced. Closed Sun evening and Mon and late Aug–early Sept. Viale La Figlia di Iorio 20, T: 085 451 4920.

€€ **Franco**. ■ Delicious traditional fish dishes. Closed Mon. Via Andrea Doria 28, T: 085 66390.

€€ **Guerino**. Good fish restaurant with outdoor seating by the sea. Closed Thur and Dec–Jan. Viale della Riviera 4, T: 085 421 2065.

€€ **La Locanda Manthoné**. Refined, friendly *osteria* in the heart of Pescara's restaurant district. Open evenings only, closed Sun. Corso Manthoné 58, T: 085 454 9034.

€ **Enoteca-Osteria Visaggio**. Wine bar with a wide selection of wines and cold snacks. Via de Cesaris 44, T: 085 421 6692.

€ **La Figlia di Attilio**. Reasonably priced family-run fish restaurant. Closed Sun evening, Mon and Aug. Via Pepe 117, T: 085 451 1500.

€ **La Lumaca**. *Osteria* with an excellent wine list and good local cheeses; open evenings only, closed Tues. Via delle Caserme 51, T: 085 451 0880.

€ **Osteria dei Miracoli**. *Osteria* with a strong local following, known for its seasonal cooking. Open evenings only, closed

Tues and late July–early Aug. Corso Manthoné 57, T: 085 66986.

€ **Taverna 58**. Authentic trattoria offering good seasonal cuisine. Closed midday Sat, Sun, holidays and Aug. Corso Manthoné 58, T: 085 690724.

Pianella

€€ **Il Club dei Buongustai**. ■ Family-run restaurant with good regional food, especially fish. Closed Sun evening, Mon and Nov. Via Francesco Verrotti 10, T: 085 973393.

Pineto

€€ **Italia**. Good fish restaurant by the sea. Closed Mon and Nov. Via al Mare 8, T: 085 946 2117.

€ **Al Bacucco d'Oro**. Restaurant-pizzeria in the hills above Pineto. Closed Wed (except in summer) and Nov. Via del Pozzo 6, at Mutignano, T: 085 936227.

Ripa Teatina (between Chieti and Francavilla)

€ **Casa di Filippo**. Good regional cooking in a historic setting, with garden. Closed Mon and mid-Aug. Contrada Santo Stefano 152, T: 0871 398007.

Rivisondoli

€€ **Giocondo**. Traditional dishes of Abruzzo in a small, amiable restaurant. Closed Tues. Via del Suffragio 2, T: 0864 69123.

San Salvo (near Vasto)

€ **Osteria delle Spezie**. Fine *osteria* in an otherwise uninteresting village. Closed Wed and late Sept. Corso Garibaldi 44, T: 0873 341602.

San Valentino in Abruzzo Citeriore (north of Caramanico Terme)

€ **Antichi Sapori**. Excellent local trattoria. Closed Wed (except in summer). Contrada Cerrone 4, T: 085 854 4053.

San Vito Chietino (on the coast near Ortona)

€€ **L'Angolino di Filippo**. ■ Good, elegant fish restaurant by the sea, in the same family for over a hundred years. Closed Mon and late Dec–early Jan. Via Nazionale Adriatica, T: 0872 61632.

Silvi Marina (between Pineto and Pescara)

€€ **Gabbiani del Faro**. Good fish restaurant by the sea. Closed Mon and Oct–Nov. Via Garibaldi 196, T: 085 930 0589.

€ **Don Ambrosio**. Restaurant (with rooms) offering regional food and good wines, at Piomba Alta, in the hills above Silvi. Closed Tues and Nov. Contrada Piomba 49, T: 085 935 1060.

€ **Vecchia Silvi**. Traditional recipes from mountain and shore; closed Tues. Via Circonvallazione Boreale 22, at Silvi Alta, T: 085 930141.

Vasto

€€ **All'Hosteria del Pavone**. Warm, friendly trattoria in the historic town centre. Closed Tues (except in summer) and Jan–Feb. Via Barbarotta 15–17, T: 0873 60227.

€€ **Villa Vignola**. Restaurant with 5 rooms, on the sea just outside the town. Open all year (except a few days in late Dec). Strada Statale 16 at Marina di Vasto, T: 0873 310050.

LOCAL SPECIALITIES

Loreto Aprutino and **Guardiagrele** are important places for coppersmithing, an art still extensively practised in Abruzzo. **Pescocostanzo** has been famous for its goldsmiths since the 13th century, and also for its blacksmiths. The women produce beautiful lace.

FESTIVALS & EVENTS

Atri *Passione di Gesù* Grand evocation of the Passion of Christ in several locations around the town, Wed before Easter; *Sfilata dei Carri Aprutini* Parade of hand-painted oxcarts, 15 Aug; *Festival Europeo dei Duchi d'Acquaviva* Classical music festival, Aug–Sept, T: 0858 709147, www.amicidellamusica2000.it

Chieti *Processione del Cristo Morto* Generally considered the largest and oldest Good Friday procession in Italy (est. AD 842), with symbolic sculptures representing themes from the Passion and local religious lore in the morning, followed by afternoon processions in historic costume; Francesco Selecchy composed his famous *Miserere* for the event in 1735; *Theate Mvsica Antiqva Festival* Antique music series, July; *Vivi l'Estate* Cultural and folk events, July–Aug; *Stagione di Prosa e di Musica* Music and theatre, Nov–May.

Fara Filiorum Petri *Sagra di Sant'Antonio Abate* Celebrated by burning a forest of *farchie,* bamboo columns up to 12m high. The event commemorates a forest fire, reputedly set by the saint, that prevented invading Napoleonic troops from attacking the town, 16 Jan.

Giulianova *Madonna del Porto Salvo* The protectress of sailors and fishermen is borne to sea in a boat procession, a crown of flowers is cast to the waves and food (especially fried fish) and wine flow freely for days, 4–10 Aug.

Lanciano *Marti Gras* On the last day of Carnival effigies of public figures who have achieved a bit too much notoriety are tossed on a bonfire; *Estate Musicale Frentana* Classical music festival, July–Aug, T: 0872 710241,

www.lanciano.it; *Il Dono e la Festa della Madonna del Ponte* A double feast, partly pagan and partly Christian in origin: *Il Dono* (the Gift) is probably a pre-Christian offering to the divinity who was replaced by Mary, associated with the Nativity of the Virgin; the *Madonna del Ponte* is a terracotta statue of the Virgin found during repairs made to Lanciano's Roman bridge following an earthquake of 1088. On 8 Sept men and women in historical costume bring the Virgin gifts of produce; the Madonna del Ponte is celebrated with horse races, music, dancing, a fireworks competition and a solemn procession. A sort of vege-tarian pizza is sold on the streets for the occasion, 8, 14 and 16 Sept; *La Squilla* All the church bells in town ring for an hour (6–7) in celebration of the coming Birth of Christ, 23 Dec.

Loreto Aprutino *San Zopito* A proces-sion led by a white ox bearing a child dressed as an angel threads its way through town to the church of San Pietro Apostolo, where the ox kneels, Mon after Pentecost.

Pescara *Stagione Estiva di Prosa* Open-air theatre, July–Aug; *Pescara Jazz* July, www.pescarajazz.com; *Stagione Teatrale e Musicale* Theatre and music, Nov–May; *Mostra Mercato dell'Artigianato* Large craft fair, by the marina, last week in July; *Sant'Andrea* The patron saint of fishermen is borne to sea, a laurel wreath commemorating those who died at sea is cast to the waves, and the saint is brought back to the church of Sant'Andrea, late July.

Pineto *Pineto Accordion Jazz Festival* July, www.pinetoaccordionjazzfestival.com

Rivisondoli *Presepe Vivente* Tableaux vivants representing the Nativity, Jan 5.

MOLISE

TERMOLI & LARINO

Termoli (*map p. 426*) is probably the ancient *Buca* of the Frentani, Samnites who lived on the Adriatic coast between the *Sagrus* (Sangro; *map p. 368*) on the north and the *Frento* (Fortore; *map p. 426*) on the south. It has suffered repeatedly from earthquakes and was largely destroyed by the Turks in 1566, though it was little damaged in the Second World War. The town, with 27,000 inhabitants, has medieval walls, a castle built in 1247 by Frederick II, and a 13th-century duomo. The striking stone façade, in the Apulian Romanesque manner, dates from the 12th–15th centuries; the arcading continues along the right flank of the church to the apse. The views from the promontory on which the old town stands are exceptional: to the west is the Maiella range; to the east the mountainous Gargano promontory; seaward, 25m distant, the Tremiti Islands (*see p. 434*), for which Termoli is a major departure point.

Larino

Larino (bus from the station in 5mins), in charming surroundings, is the ancient *Larinum*, a town of the Frentani. The medieval town, damaged by earthquake in 1300, was destroyed by the Saracens shortly thereafter. It was rebuilt in 1316, but in 1656 plague claimed the lives of 9,625 of its 10,000 inhabitants.

The **duomo** (1319), with an attractive façade, has a 16th-century campanile and a fine Gothic portal by Francesco Petrini, the sculptor of the portal of Santa Maria Maggiore in Lanciano. In the lunette, *Crucifixion with the Virgin and St John*. The large rose window is similar to those that characterise Apulian churches; the mullioned windows on either side open above the level of the aisle roofs. The interior has three tall, narrow aisles separated by pointed arches (six on the south side, five on the north) on cruciform piers with carved capitals. In the south aisle is an *Immaculate Conception* attributed to Francesco Solimena. The chapter house contains a marble altar, built to a design by Andrea Vaccaro, and other interesting objects.

The **Palazzo Comunale**, in the cathedral square, contains a monumental staircase of 1818, adorned with Roman architectural fragments and, in the library, mosaic floors from Roman villas discovered in the environs of the amphitheatre (*see below*). Also of interest are a 14th-century wooden *Madonna* and numerous ceramic and bronze objects, some dating from the second millennium BC.

The wooded avenue that ascends to the station passes (left) the so-called *Ara Frentana*, a cylindrical altar of pre-Roman origin, and other archaeological material (chiefly inscriptions and architectural and sculptural fragments) from nearby excavations. The **ruins of Larinum**, including the conspicuous remains of an amphitheatre of the late 1st or early 2nd century BC, lie northeast of the station, in and around Piazza San Lorenzo, and in the vicinity of the Torre Sant'Anna and Torre de Gennaro.

SOUTHERN MOLISE

Campobasso

Campobasso (*map p. 386*), with 51,000 inhabitants, is the chief town of the province of the same name, formerly the county of Molise. The local cutlery industry has dwindled to a handful of artisans who make and engrave scissors and knives. The *Sagra dei Misteri* (Corpus Domini) is celebrated with 18th-century iron contrivances in which children assume impossible poses (flying angels, etc) depicting Christian mysteries or miracles of the saints. These human sculptural configurations are borne through the streets on wooden platforms.

MOLISAN METALWORKING

In many Molisan villages Christmas Eve culminates with torchlit processions or with bonfires of wood and grass, and at Agnone, to the northwest, carnival fires 'burn away' the end of winter. In a spiritual context, fire is an element of purification and transformation but a popular saying says, 'fire is the father of metals,' and in these parts the culture of fire is accompanied by that of metals. Metalworking in Molise, in fact, dates as far back as the ancient Samnites (c. 600 BC).

The working of iron, copper and bronze is common throughout the region. Campobasso's goldsmiths are famous for creations that still echo Spanish (Aragonese) designs—and more often than not, they are made for the statues that adorn religious feasts rather than for flesh-and-blood clients.

Other famous centres are Agnone, where Molisans have been producing bronze church bells for over a thousand years, and Frosolone, from which knives and scissors are exported throughout Europe. The beautiful horn-handled jack-knives are particularly popular in rural Italy. Not least of Molisan metal crafts is copper-working, practised throughout the region thanks to the cheese industry, which still uses immense copper cauldrons in which to boil the milk.

In the old upper town are two churches preserving Romanesque portions: San Bartolomeo, with a fine 14th-century portal, and San Giorgio, with delicate 12th-century bas-reliefs. The **Nuovo Museo Provinciale Sannitico** occupies the 19th-century Palazzo Mazzarotta, at Via Chiarizia 12 (*open daily 8.30–7, T: 087 441 2265*). Here you will find material ranging in date from the dawn of history to the Samnite age, all found in Molise. The museum is divided into four sections: clothing and accessories (bronze belts, helmets, spear points, bracelets and jewellery); housewares (vases, lamps, keys, etc), tools and equipment (knives, weights, bricks and tiles), religious and burial cults (bronze and clay votive statues, burial treasures). There are also a reconstructed tomb from the Lombard necropolis at Campochiaro, and some epigraphs.

Above rises the 15th-century **Castello Monforte**, square in plan with six rampart towers. The square before the entrance offers good views over the town and the surrounding countryside. On the south of the castle hill is the **church of Sant'Antonio**, with a painting of St Benedict by Fabrizio Santafede. An inscription beneath the portico of the **town hall**, in the lower town, records the death, in 1383 near Campobasso, of Amedeo VI, the 'Green Count' of Savoy, who conquered Abruzzo and Apulia for Louis I of Anjou, titular king of Naples. His predilection for dressing in green earned him his soubriquet. Nearby, in Piazza Vittoria, is a Museo Internazionale del Presepio in Miniatura, containing a fine private collection of Italian and foreign Nativity scenes (*open by appointment, T: 0874 413672*).

SAEPINUM

Rolling hills separate Campobasso from Vinchiaturo, an attractive little town rebuilt after the earthquake of 1805. A road to the east leads through more splendid landscape to Cercemaggiore. Above the latter, near the summit of Monte Saraceno (1086m) are the walls of a Samnite village intermingled with the ruins of medieval fortifications. The view from the summit spans vast areas of Molise, Campania and Apulia.

Beyond Vinchiaturo, Road 17 (the Benevento–Isernia road) bears southeast. **Sepino**, on a hill 4km south, is the successor of the Roman *Saepinum*, the ruins of which lie along the road on the right. Later named *Atilia*, Saepinum was founded by survivors from the Samnite *Saipins*, destroyed in 293 BC. Its history was not particularly eventful; it was destroyed by the Saracens in the 9th century.

The ruins

Open daily 9–dusk: T: 0874 790207.
The defensive walls, 1250m in circumference, still surround the ancient town. Fortified by 27 bastions, they are pierced by four gates, today known as the Porta di Bojano (northwest), Porta del Tammaro (northeast), Porta di Benevento (southeast) and Porta di Terravecchia (southwest).

Enter by the Porta del Tammaro and cross the site to the Porta di Terravecchia, outside which is an improvised car park surrounded by low walls in *opus reticulatum*. Within, the *cardo maximus* leads past modern farmhouses built with the stones of the ancient city. Further on, the road preserves its ancient pavement. The **basilica**, on the left, has a peristyle made up of 20 slender Ionic columns. Turning right, follow the *decumanus* past the forum and a series of public buildings that includes the *curia*, or town hall, and a temple believed to have been dedicated to the Capitoline triad (Jupiter, Juno and Minerva).

Further on, on the left, are the **Casa del Frantoio**, an olive press (note the brick-lined wells for storing the oil); the *Mulino Idraulico* or water mill; and the so-called **Casa dell'Impluvio Sannitico**, a house with a graceful fountain, built to the typical Samnite plan around an atrium with impluvium, preceded by shops. Beyond the Porta di Benevento stands a monumental tomb with an inscription describing the civic and military career of the defunct. To the left is a small **museum** (*open Tues–Sun 9–1*) with photographs and texts describing the town and its discovery and a collection of Roman inscriptions.

Returning to the centre of the town, pass behind the basilica to the octagonal market and what appears to be a small temple. Beyond are the remains of private dwellings and, at the end of the street, the imposing **Porta di Bojano**, in *opus tessellatum*, flanked by cylindrical bastions, another of which can be seen along the wall to the north. At the sides of the arch are statues of prisoners on plinths. The keystone is carved with a bearded head, possibly of Hercules; the inscription above the arch tells that the fortification of the town was financed by the future emperor Tiberius and his brother Drusus.

Steps ascend to the top of the gate, from where there is a fine view over the excavations; the rectangular tomb of the Numisi, in a field to the north, and the **thermae**, the remains of which extend along the town wall between the *decumanus* and the **theatre**. The latter is reached by a minor gate, an unusual feature suggesting that theatrical performances were combined with fairs held outside the walls. Surrounded by farmhouses, it preserves large portions of the cavea and orchestra. On the stage, another farm building houses a beautiful **collection of finds** (*open as above*) from the site and the vicinity, chiefly funerary sculpture from a necropolis brought to light along the extramural portion of the *decumanus*. Photographs and texts explain the finds. On the first floor are numerous maps and plans describing the territory, the town and its monuments.

THROUGH WESTERN MOLISE

Molise's southwestern boundary is formed by the Monti del Matese, a large, high massif extending crescent-like between the rivers Volturno (north), Calore (south), Tammaro (east) and Biferno (northeast). The lofty, forested massif is one of the most beautiful and unspoilt areas of southern Italy. On the south, or Campanian side, it rises like a steep wall, whereas the north slopes ascend more gradually. The central region, which contains highland plains at altitudes of 1400–1900m, culminates in the triple peaks of Colle Tamburo (1982m), Monte Gallinola (1923m) and Monte Miletto (2050m). The latter is the *Tifernus Mons* of Livy and the site of the last Samnite struggle against the Romans.

The valleys and gorges of the interior are largely calcareous, and the porosity of the rock permits the absorption of large quantities of water, giving rise to numerous springs at various altitudes and, on the south side, to the large Lago del Matese. The smaller lakes of Gallo and Latino are man-made. The Matese is covered by vast beech woods, with lesser numbers of oaks, maples, ashes, spruces, chestnuts, walnuts, hazel-trees, hornbeams, etc; and by pastures. The native fauna include wild pigs, roe deer (rare), wolves, foxes, badgers, wildcats, hares, weasels, martens and squirrels. Eagles nest on the Miletto and Gallinola as well as in the Tre Finestre district.

Moorhens, ducks, lapwings, woodcocks and snipe inhabit the areas along the lakes and streams, and trout abound.

Campitello Matese, Bojano and San Massimo (in Molise) and Piedimonte Matese, San Gregorio and Letino (in Campania) are the best starting points for excursions and climbs. San Gregorio and Campitello are year-round resorts.

Campochiaro and Bojano

Campochiaro, in the foothills of the Matese, is a walled medieval village with an Angevin keep. Excavations have brought to light a nearby Italic sanctuary of the 2nd century BC, incorporating the largest known Samnite temple after that of Pietrabbondante (*see p. 392 below*). Evidence of earlier buildings, dating from the 4th–3rd centuries BC, has also been found.

Bojano, a chilly place, is the ancient *Bovianum*, one of the main centres of the Samnites and the meeting place of the Italic chiefs during the last phase of the Social War, before the capital was moved to Isernia. The upper town preserves some megalithic walls and remains of a castle. From Bojano you can climb Monte La Gallinola (1923m) in c. 2hrs. A road mounts to the Rifugio Sant'Egidio, from where a steep trail, later a footpath, climbs through the forest to the Costa Alta, a pass 1680m high (view). The way crosses ski slopes at Sogli di Bojano to the base of Monte La Gallinola. A narrow path climbs to the summit. The view is extraordinary, embracing the entire peninsula from the Gulf of Naples to the Adriatic, with the Lago del Matese directly below. You may also climb Monte Miletto in c. 3hrs from Sogli di Bojano; or in c. 1hr from Campitello Matese. The latter, a winter sports centre (1417m), has a refuge maintained year-round by the APT in Campobasso.

Northwest of Bojano, reached by Road 17, are **Cantalupo del Sannio**, whose name means 'wolfsong'; **Carpinone**, with a handsome castle belonging to the Caldora family, and **Pesche**, presenting medieval walls with cylindrical bastions.

ISERNIA & THE ANCIENT HILL TOWNS

Isernia is the Samnite *Aesernium*, headquarters of the Italics after the fall of *Corfinium* (89 BC). Though a provincial capital, it is a modest town, producing onions and lace, with only one main street. The Romanesque Fontana Fraterna was damaged in the Second World War. Bomb damage to the church of **Santa Maria delle Monache** exposed a 14th-century fresco of the *Last Judgement* that was covered with 18th-century plaster. The church complex now houses a museum documenting prehistoric, Samnite and Roman settlements in the area, the **Museo Archeologico Sannitico Romano** (*open daily except Mon morning, 8.30–7.40; T: 086 541 5179*). The cathedral tower stands on a medieval archway. One of the Roman bridges is partially intact. Recent excavations nearby have revealed some monumental tombs.

From Isernia Road 85 turns southwest past Macchia d'Isernia and Monteroduni, both with fine castles, to Ponte a Venticinque Archi (25 arches), by which you cross the Volturno.

Venafro

Venafro, with its cyclopean walls and the remains of an amphitheatre, is the ancient *Venafrum*, praised by Horace for its olive oil. The 18th-century **Chiesa del Purgatorio** contains a *Madonna and Child with Saints* by Fedele Fischetti (1860–1935). In the adjacent Piazza Cimorelli is the 15th-century **Palazzo Caracciolo**, a fortified residence built by Mary of Durazzo, who also enlarged the castle. Beneath the Baroque veneer of the **church of the Annunziata** is a Romanesque building of 1387. Within, the second south altar incorporates seven English alabasters dating from the 15th century representing scenes from the Passion. The former convent of Santa Chiara houses the **Museo Archeologico di Venafro** (*open Tues–Sat 9–7, Sun 8.30–1.30; T: 0865 900742*), containing inscriptions, statues, architectural fragments and miscellaneous objects relating to the Roman colony of Venafrum. On the southwest edge of the town is the 15th-century **cathedral**; in a transitional Romanesque-Gothic style, it is a conglomerate of several churches, the oldest of which dates from the 5th century. Recent excavations have revealed remains of a Roman theatre on Monte Croce, near the ancient walls.

The far west

Stunningly situated in the hills 28km northeast of Isernia are the ruins of **Pietrabbondante** (*open 9–dusk*). Excavations here have revealed a religious sanctuary of Samnite construction, the largest yet discovered, consisting of two temples and a theatre, and dating from the 2nd century BC. At nearby **Agnone** the cathedral has a good Romanesque portal. At **Schiavi di Abruzzo**, where St Anselm retired in 1098 after his attendances at the conclave of Bari, you can see two Italic temples of the 3rd and 2nd centuries BC.

Road 17 climbs north from Isernia through splendid countryside to **Rionero Sannitico**, where dairy cattle are raised. A turning leads south to **Cerro al Volturno**, with a ruined castle in an imposing position above the town; the nearby **Badia di San Vincenzo**, a Benedictine abbey dating from the 8th century, possesses a small crypt containing frescoes of the life of Christ and martyrdom of Sts Lawrence and Stephen, the only surviving examples of the 9th-century Benedictine school. In the hills to the west lies the beautiful lake of Castel San Vincenzo.

From Rionero Sannitico there is a descent to Ponte Zittola. From here, Road 83 runs west to **Alfedena**, on the Sangro, with a 15th-century church. On the opposite side of the river are the cyclopean walls of the Samnite town of *Aufidena* and, beyond the station, the Madonna del Campo, with frescoes by Cola dell'Amatrice. Beyond the Vallico de Barrea, a pass 1164m high, lies the Parco Nazionale d'Abruzzo (*described in the following section*).

PRACTICAL INFORMATION

GETTING AROUND

• **By rail** Most of the places in this chapter are served by slow local trains. One possible itinerary, touching upon the major sights, is Campobasso to Isernia, 59km in c. 1hr.

• **By sea** Termoli is connected by boats and hydrofoils to the Tremiti Islands. To/from Termoli: daily ferries 1hr to 1hr 40mins, hydrofoils 50mins. For further details contact Navigazione Libera del Golfo, at the harbour, T: 0875 704859 (ferries) and Adriatica di Navigazione, c/o Agenzia Adriashipping, at the harbour, T: 0875 705343 (hydrofoils).

INFORMATION OFFICES

Campobasso Assessorato Regionale al Turismo, Via Mazzini 94, T: 0874 4291; Ente Provinciale per il Turismo, Piazza della Vittoria 14, T: 0874 415662.
Isernia Via Farinacci 9, T: 0865 3992.
Termoli Azienda Autonoma di Soggiorno e Turismo, Piazza Bega, T: 0875 706754; Ufficio Informazioni, Via Capua 3, T: 0875 706120.

HOTELS

Molise is not well endowed with places to stay. See the listings on pp. 382 and 419 for accommodation in Abruzzo.

RESTAURANTS

Bojano

€ **Filomena**. Good, old-fashioned *osteria*. Open midday (and Fri and Sat evenings), closed Mon and July. Via Garibaldi 16, T: 0874 773078.

Campobasso

€ **Da Concetta**. Good home cooking and attentive service. Closed Sat, Sun and Aug. Via Larino 9, T: 0874 311378.

€ **Da Nonno Cecchino**. Trattoria serving largely local fare in the old town centre. Closed Sun evening (except in summer). Via Larino 32, T: 0874 311778.

€ **Miseria e Nobiltà**. Rustic country restaurant, with garden. Closed Sun and July–Aug. Viale del Castello 16–18, T: 0874 94268.

€ **Sagittario**. Creative interpretations of local recipes, in the historic town centre. Closed Tues and July. Via Ziccardi 74, T: 0874 698413.

€ **Vecchia Trattoria da Tonino**. Good selection of local delicacies. Closed Sun and late Aug. Corso Vittorio Emanuele 8, T: 0874 415200.

Campomarino (near Termoli)

€ **Nonna Rosa**. Tiny trattoria in the historic town centre. Closed Tues (except in July–Aug) and first two weeks of Oct. Via Biferno 41, T: 0875 539948.

Cantalupo del Sannio

€ **Trattoria del Riccio**. Trattoria, open for lunch only. Closed Mon, 10 days in June and 10 days in Sept. Via Sannio 7, T: 0865 814246.

Casacalenda

€€ **Villa Continelli**. Fine country restaurant with views. Closed Mon. Road 87, Contrada Monte.

Ferrazzano

€ **Da Emilio**. Restaurant serving local dishes with a creative twist, in the main square of this panoramic village near Campobasso. Closed Tues and July. Via Spensieri 21, T: 0874 416576.

Guglionesi (near Termoli)

€€ **Ribo**. Restaurant known for its creative interpretations of traditional fish and game dishes. Closed Mon. Contrada Malecoste, T: 0875 680655.

€ **Il Pagatore**. Good local recipes in a pleasant hill town. Closed Sun (except in Aug) and two weeks in Nov. Corso Conte di Torino 71, T: 0875 680550.

Isernia

€ **Dai Due Vagabondi**. Lamb in every possible manner, and more. Closed Mon. Via Berta 131, T: 0865 410233.

€ **Taverna Maresca**. Delicious traditional food, in the heart of the old town. Closed Sun, Aug and late Dec–early Jan. Corso Marcelli 186, T: 0865 3976.

San Martino in Pensilis (near Termoli)

€ **Castello**. Fine local dishes from the hills and mountains, in a historic setting. Closed Wed and Sept. Piazza Vittoria 23, T: 0875 604902.

Schiavi di Abruzzo

€ **Templi Italici**. Café-restaurant by the archaeological site. Open evenings only, closed Wed. Contrada Taverna 1, T: 0873 976173.

Sepino

€ **L'Imperatrice**. ■ Trattoria near the archaeological site offering great local cooking. Closed Wed. Contrada Rio Verdaro 18, T: 0874 790005.

Termoli

€€ **Cian**. Another good seafood restaurant, on the water. Closed Mon and Nov. Lungomare Cristoforo Colombo 48, T: 0875 704436.

€€ **San Carlo**. ■ Excellent regional cuisine in a historic building in central Termoli. Closed Tues (except in summer). Via Giudicato Vecchio 24, T: 0875 705295.

€€ **Torre Saracena**. Good fish restaurant with sea views, in a historic setting. Closed Mon and Nov. Strada Statale 16, T: 0875 703318.

€€ **Z'Bass**. Warm, sometimes crowded trattoria known for its outstanding seafood. Closed Mon (except in summer). Via Oberdan 8, T: 0875 706703.

€ **Carlo**. Seafood restaurant with good service and fine views. Closed Mon and Sept. Via Alcide de Gasperi 1, T: 0875 82610.

Vastogirardi (west of Agnone)

€ **La Taverna**. Trattoria with delicious mountain cooking. Closed Mon. Via Mazzini 13, T: 0865 836156.

Vinchiaturo

€ **Hotel Residence Le Cupolette**. Hotel restaurant known for its delicate cuisine and attentive service. Road 87 at Santa Maria delle Macchie, T: 0874 340030.

LOCAL SPECIALITIES

Isernia Dolciaria Valentino is a pastry shop selling traditional Molise sweets (Contrada Pettoranello).

Molise in general is known for its beautiful hand-woven textiles: prevalently wool at Agnone, Carovilli, Castelverrino, Capracotta, Pescopennataro and San Pietro Avellana, linen and cotton at Montemitro, San Felice del Molise and Acquaviva Collecroce.

The leading centres of Molisan knife- and scissor-makers are Frosolone and Campobasso. Oratino and Riccia are famous for their coppersmiths, and bells have been made at Agnone since the Middle Ages.

FESTIVALS & EVENTS

Agnone *I Fuochi di San Michele*
Immense bonfires are set to mark the
return of spring, 8 May; *'Ndocciata*
Torchlight procession in which the
'torches' are fir trees 3–4m tall carried
by groups of men, women and children
representing the various neighbourhoods and outlying areas; in the central
square the *'ndocce* are thrown together
to form a bonfire, at the foot of a
tableau vivant of the Nativity, while
other fires burn in the hills around the
town, 24 Dec.

Campobasso *Processione dei Misteri*
Celebrated with 18th-century iron con-
trivances (*ingegni*) in which children
assume impossible poses depicting
Christian mysteries or miracles of the
saints: St Isidore, St Crispin, St
Januarius, Abraham, Mary Magdalene,
St Anthony Abbot, the Immaculate
Conception, St Leonard, St Roch, the
Assumption of the Virgin, St Michael, St
Nicholas and the Sacred Heart, Corpus
Domini; *Autumn Jazz Festival* Oct.
www.autumnjazzfestival.it; *Rassegna di
Musica Antica–Musica di Corte* Classical
music festival, Oct–Nov.

Isernia *Processione del Venerdì Santo*
Hooded and thorn-crowned *penitenti*
carry in procession the Holy Cross and
statues representing the Passion and
Death of Christ, Good Friday; *Focata
d'Inverno* Singing and dancing around
fires set in the city streets; also, exhibition and sale of locally-made laces, 17
Jan; *Fiera di San Pietro delle Cipolle*
Farmer's market dating from 1254, Late
June; *Sant'Antonio di Padova* Procession
featuring the saint on a hand-carried
float, followed by a local *Zigana*
(Gitane) community, in costume on lav-
ishly decorated horses, 13 June; *Festa
dei Santi Cosma e Damiano* The chapel
dedicated to these two saints was erected over a pagan sanctuary of Priapus;
the tradition of carrying to the chapel
phallic votive offerings to ward off
impotence and sterility has continued
to the present, 28–29 Dec; *Maitunate*
Jeering, satirical players roam the streets
to 'sing the praise' of public figures on
New Year's Eve, 31 Jan.

Larino *Sagra di San Pardo* A torchlight
procession of elaborately decorated
plaustri or pseudo-Roman ox carts,
25–27 May.

Termoli *Sagra del Pesce* Summer is
brought to a close with this gigantic
fish-fry (using pans 4m in diameter),
accompanied by music, dancing and
fireworks, last Sun in Aug; *San Basso*
The saint's statue is carried to sea and
back (with an overnight stay at the fish
market) in a boat procession, 3 Aug.

Venafro *San Nicandro* The saint is fêted
with a procession, a *tableau vivant* of his
martyrdom, and a donkey race, third
Sun in June; *Presepe Vivente* and
Passione di Gesù The two key events
from the life of Christ are celebrated
with *tableaux vivants* in the castle and
the olive grove adjoining the cathedral,
respectively, 24 Dec, Good Friday.

Vinchiaturo *Lancio del Cacio* Race in
which two teams of four youths roll
15kg cheese wheels uphill over an
obstacle course; winners, losers and
spectators then celebrate with wine and
cheese, Shrove Tuesday.

THE WESTERN HIGHLANDS

Welcome to the most spectacular natural environment in south-central Italy, an area of wooded mountains and fertile valleys—wild countryside punctuated with medieval castles and villages that economic development has not yet had time to spoil. Even the most sedentary will feel the temptation to explore the region on foot, and with good reason: the cool, pine-scented air and magnificent views more than compensate for the effort of walking. And the more adventurous have excellent chances of encountering the small wolves and brown bear native to the region, as well as deer and chamois. The drive from L'Aquila to Teramo offers unequalled views over the Gran Sasso d'Italia and the Vomano valley. Roccaraso, Sulmona, Popoli and Campli are fine old cities that are well worth strolling round, and L'Aquila and Teramo remain pleasant places despite being bustling provincial capitals.

THE PARCO NAZIONALE D'ABRUZZO

Visitor's centre at Pescasseroli, with an excellent small museum and wildlife area (open daily in summer 10–1 & 3–7; in winter 10–1 & 2–5; T: 0863 91131). Maps and camping permits from the Ufficio di Zona, Via Santa Lucia. Other museums and wildlife areas, open as above, at Civitella Alfedena (map p. 386; Museo del Lupo Appenninico: wolves); Opi (map p. 386; Museo del Camoscio: chamois); San Sebastiano (Museo degli Insetti: insects) and Villavallelonga (Museo del Cervo: deer).

Italy's second-oldest national park was established in 1923 and enlarged in 1925 and 1976. It now occupies an area of 400km square in one of the wildest and most spectacularly beautiful zones of the Apennines. Its grassy valleys, vast beechwoods and alpine meadows compare favourably with those of the Alps or the Pyrenees. Its rare wildlife, which includes the Abruzzo brown bear (*Ursus arctos marsicanus altobelli*), the highest concentration of wolves in Italy and a sub-species of the chamois (about 500 of which inhabit the so-called Camosciara between Monte Amaro and the Meta Massif) is known to naturalists throughout the world. Within the park lie the sources and upper valleys of the Sangro, Giovenco and Melfa. The eastern boundary is formed by the Montagna Grande range, the south and south-west boundary by the watershed between the Sangro and the Liri, which also includes the highest peak of the park, Monte Petroso (2247m).

Hunting, fishing and the gathering of native flora are forbidden, and special hunting regulations are enforced in a wide area around the park. The park is a refuge for golden eagles, wrynecks, firecrests, Sardinian warblers, blue rock thrushes, alpine choughs, snow finches and the most southerly breeding population of dotterel in Europe. It is also rich in wild flowers and butterflies.

Benedetto Croce (1866–1952)

Born in Pescasseroli, Benedetto Croce is arguably the most important Italian philosopher, historian and literary critic of the 20th century. He established his idealist philosophical system in the first decade of the century, with seminal works dedicated to aesthetics, logic, economics and ethics. In the journal *La Critica* he carried out a sharp critique of Positivism and other dominant schools of thought of his time. The journal evolved from his friendship with another early 20th-century luminary, Giovanni Gentile; but their friendship was broken after political choices led the two philosophers in opposite directions—Gentile becoming an ideologue of the Fascist movement, Croce of liberal anti-Fascism. Today Croce is studied chiefly for his critique of Hegelian dialectics, his aesthetics, and his works on the relationship between philosophy and history, notably *La Storia come Pensiero e come Azione* (History as Thought and Action), which gives a philosophical basis to the struggle against Fascism.

SULMONA

Sulmona (405m) is a pleasant town with a population of 25,000, delightfully situated in a ring of mountains, on a ridge between two small streams. Its many attractive old houses, medieval or later, give it a charming air of antiquity.

HISTORY OF SULMONA

Sulmona, the *Sulmo* of the Paeligni, was the birthplace of the poet Ovid (P. Ovidius Naso, 43 BC–AD 17) and of Innocent VII (Cosimo de' Migliorati, 1339–1406), collector of Peter's Pence (the regular payment to the papacy) in England in 1376–86. Emperor Frederick II made Sulmona the capital of an independent province. It was bestowed by Charles V as a principality upon Charles de Lannoy (1487–1527), Viceroy of Naples, to whom the French king Francis I surrendered at Pavia (1525). In the 14th and 15th centuries, the goldsmiths of Sulmona were famous. Today it is renowned for its sweets and liqueurs.

The **duomo** (San Panfilo), at the north end of the town, is built on the ruins of a Roman temple and has a Gothic portal and an 11th-century crypt. Beyond the Villa Comunale the Corso Ovidio, the main street of the town, leads to (right) Via Ciofano, where the 15th-century Palazzo Tabassi (no. 44) has a fine Gothic window.

In the Corso are the **church and palazzo of the Annunziata**, founded in 1320 and showing a happy combination of Gothic and Renaissance elements. The left portal is surmounted by a richly carved Gothic arch embracing statues of St Michael and, in the lunette, the *Madonna and Child*, originally gilded, painted and set against a fresco background. Inscribed in the architrave is the date 1415. The monumental central portal recalls the Tuscan Renaissance style. It dates from 1483, as does the central portion of the façade. The smaller right portal is somewhat later.

Along the base of the façade, on tall plinths, are statues of the doctors of the Church (Sts Gregory the Great, Jerome, Ambrose and Augustine), St Pamphilus, titular of the cathedral, and the Apostles Peter and Paul. Above, a delicately carved frieze runs the length of the façade, forming the base of the ornamental windows, which offer the same interesting contrast of styles as the portals below. The **Museo Archeologico in Situ** (*open Tues–Sun 10–1; T: 0864 210216*) displays Roman archaeological finds from excavations conducted beneath the 14th-century church complex: walls, architectural details, mosaics and fragmentary frescoes. The church, rebuilt after an earthquake in 1706, preserves a campanile of 1565–90. More archaeological finds, from Italic, Roman and medieval sites in and around Sulmona, can be seen in the little **Museo Civico** (*Corso Ovidio; open May–Nov Mon–Sat 9–1, Sun 9–1 & 4–7; T: 0864 210216*).

A 20th-century statue of Ovid stands in the nearby Piazza XX Settembre. Further on, opposite a fountain of 1474, is a rich Romanesque portal leading to the presbytery of the church of San Francesco della Scarpa. The aqueduct that powered local industries during the Middle Ages terminates here.

Around Sulmona

About 6km north of here is the abbey of Santo Spirito, or **Badia Morronese**, founded in the 13th century by Pietro Angeleri, afterwards St Celestine V (*see p. 409*), who lived in a hermitage high up on the Montagna del Morrone. The convent (dating from the 17th and 18th centuries, with a fine chapel of the original foundation) and hermitage can be visited by appointment with the Ufficio Informazioni e di Accoglienza Turistica (*Corso Ovidio 208; T: 0864 53276*). On the way to the hermitage are the remains of a Temple of Hercules, called Ovid's Villa. The undulating upland plain of Sulmona was referred to by Ovid in his lament for his homeland as the 'fresh land of copious springs'. Poplars are a feature of the landscape here, their growth encouraged by the many streams.

Anversa degli Abruzzi and Scanno

A brief excursion (31km) can be made from Sulmona to Scanno, a village forgotten by time in a beautiful, rugged setting due south of the city. Leave Sulmona by the imposing 14th-century Porta Napoli and cross the River Gizio. Near Anversa–Scanno station the road passes beneath a lofty railway viaduct. At **Anversa degli Abruzzi** the church of the Madonna delle Grazie in the piazza has a doorway dated 1540 and *Sts Michael and Francis*, a painting of the 15th-century Sulmona school, in the sacristy. San Marcello has a Gothic portal. The road beyond Anversa threads through the deep, narrow gorge known as the Gola del Sagittario. A bit further on, the Lago di Scanno (c. 2km long) is stocked with trout.

Scanno (1015m), an ancient little town in a striking situation, is popular for summer holidays. The local women still wear their handsome traditional costume. The country New Year, 11th November (St Martin's Day), is celebrated by igniting immense bonfires (the *Glorie di San Martino*) in the hills around the town.

The Piana del Fucino

Between Pratola Peligna and Popoli the Via Valeria turns westwards, passing the village of **Corfinio**, known until 1928 as Pentima and given the name of the ancient Italic capital (*Corfinium; see p. 15*) by Mussolini. Beyond the village is the 13th-century Romanesque Basilica of San Pelino, with a characteristic apse and a finely carved ambo. The adjoining church of Sant'Alessandro incorporates antique architectural fragments. The former seminary, on the north side of the church, contains the small Museo delle Antichità Corfiniensi (*open by appointment; T: 0864 728350*), with antiquities from the widely scattered ruins of Corfinium, the chief town of the Paeligni. In 91 BC, at the beginning of the Social War, it became the capital of the insurgent Italic tribes, who renamed it *Italica* and intended that it should supplant Rome. In 49 BC, after Julius Caesar had crossed the Rubicon, L. Domitius Ahenobarbus, leader of the conservative senatorial aristocracy that opposed his claim to power, held out against him for a short time here.

At Molina Aterno the Via Valeria turns southwest past Castelvecchio Subequo, after which, rising in sharp curves, it reaches the summit at Forca Caruso (1107m). At Collarmele you cross the Pescara–Rome railway and motorway and descend to the north side of the **Piana del Fucino**, the dried-up basin of Lake Fucino.

A LAKE WITHOUT WATER

The ancient *Lacus Fucinus* was the largest lake in central Italy (155km square); it had no visible outlet and was subject to sudden variations, often flooding the countryside. Emperor Claudius first attempted to drain it by digging a tunnel to connect it with the basin of the Liri, 6km south. The tunnel was opened with great rejoicing in AD 52, but without much result; a second attempt met with equal failure, and the tunnel, the most important work of underground engineering until the construction of the Mont Cenis Tunnel, became blocked.

Frederick II attempted to reopen it in 1240, but it was not until 1852 that work was seriously undertaken. A company was formed which entrusted the plans to Hutton Gregory, an English engineer, and later operations passed under the control of Alessandro Torlonia, a wealthy Roman, who was aided by Swiss and French engineers. The old route was more or less followed, but the new tunnel is nearly 500m longer than the old one. The work was successfully finished in 1875. The outflow is used by electrical installations at Capistrello, to the southwest. In the spring of 1951 the reclaimed lake area, which formed part of the Torlonia estate, was expropriated. About 14,000 hectares were handed over to 8,000 families.

CELANO

Celano, which stands on a hill (800m) crowned by a castle of the Piccolomini, was the birthplace of Thomas of Celano (d. 1253), the first biographer of St Francis of Assisi and author of the hymn *Dies Irae*. Its churches have been well restored after an earthquake in 1915, as has the imposing castle. This was begun in 1392 and completed after 1463, and consists of a rectangular core with four square towers and projecting battlements, surrounded by an irregular enceinte with cylindrical towers at the corners and square bastions along the ramparts. The attached *logge* and mullioned windows were added in the 15th century, possibly by Antonio Piccolomini. Within, a ramp ascends to the keep, at the centre of which is a courtyard encircled by a Gothic portico, and above, a fine *loggiato* with rounded arches carried by columns bearing the Piccolomini seal in the capitals. The ramparts command good views over the surrounding countryside.

Museo Marsicana di Arte Sacra
Open summer daily 9–7; winter Mon–Fri 9–1.30, Sat and Sun 9–7; T: 0863 792922.
The museum, situated on the castle's gallery floor, houses examples of religious art from western Abruzzo. The exhibits are introduced by panels illustrating the history, economy and art of the region; there is also a model representing the Marsica area before the draining of Lake Fucino. A computer gives general information about the works displayed, their media, and the techniques used in their restoration.

Room 1: Early medieval **sculptural fragments**, most from the church of San Pietro at Alba Fucens (*see p. 404*), where they were found after the earthquake of 1915. Of particular interest is the little pillar, once part of an iconostasis now lost, inscribed with the names of its patron and makers. Other fragments from the iconostasis include a lion and a capital with acanthus leaves and human and animal figures.

Room 2: Two sets of **wooden doors**, one from the church of Santa Maria in Cellis, Carsoli (1132), the other from the church of San Pietro at Albe (late 12th century). Beautifully carved plant motifs divide the Carsoli doors into ten panels carrying New Testament scenes (*Annunciation, Nativity, Adoration of the Magi, Presentation at the Temple*, an unidentified scene, *Visitation, Annunciation to the Shepherds, Massacre of the Innocents, Disputa* and unidentified figures). The Albe doors are undated but affinities with others suggest they may have been carved at the same time and perhaps even by the same artist. The 28 relief panels (much ruined, but showing Evangelists, fantastic animals, knights and a monk) were probably painted.

Room 3: The *Albe Triptych* is a beautifully carved and painted work of 14th-century Venetian school depicting the Madonna and Child with Christ the Redeemer, Evangelists and saints, and adorned with silver gilt, pearls, gems and enamels; the ten lateral niches carry scenes from the life of Christ. Severely damaged in the 1915 earthquake, the altarpiece was restored in Rome and installed here in 1995. Also here are a panel painting from the church of Santa Maria delle Grazie at Collelongo (13th century); two sculptures representing the Madonna and Child, from Carsoli and Colli di Monte Bove (13th century); panel painting of the *Madonna del Latte* from Carsoli; some detached frescoes from the church of San Pietro at Albe (14th–15th century); two panels representing the Virgin and St John, ascribed to Giovanni da Sulmona (15th century); and an interesting fragment representing the Virgin, from Cese di Avezzano, recently attributed to Andrea Delitio (1439–42).

Rooms 4–5: Tabernacle with scenes from the life of Christ, from Scurcola Marsicana; small wooden saint from Magliano dei Marsi; paintings, by an unknown artist, of *Christ Carrying the Cross*, *Assumption of the Virgin*, and *Resurrection of Christ* from the church of Sant'Angelo, Celano; 15th-century frescoed *Crucifixion* from the Palazzo Ducale, Tagliacozzo; four wooden sculptures representing St Peter, St Paul, St Benedict and St Andrew, from the church of Santa Maria at Luco dei Marsi; two 17th-century paintings, of the *Holy Trinity* and the *Crucifixion*; 16th-century wooden tabernacle from the church of Santa Maria della Vittoria at Scurcola Marsicana, painted with scenes from the life of Christ.

Rooms 6–7: Goldsmiths' art, including precious objects formerly kept at the Museo di Palazzo Venezia in Rome, notably a cross-shaped Byzantine reliquary (13th century), a gilded chalice from Celano (14th century), the silver *Croce degli Orsini* with enamels (dated 1334), a small ivory box of the Embriachi school, two silver Crucifixes from the church of San Nicola in Albe (15th century), and a silver Crucifix from Magliano dei Marsi (17th century); around the walls are more 15th-century frescoes from the Palazzo Ducale, Tagliacozzo. Room 7 was the private chapel of Antonio Piccolomini and his family.

Rooms 8–9: Vestments dating from the 15th–19th centuries, notably two silk hempen chasubles from the church of San Cesidio in Trasacco (15th–16th century). Silk was especially valued for this kind of garment because of its luminosity and the permanence of its dyes.

Ovindoli and Avezzano

A scenic mountain road winds northward from Celano to **Ovindoli** (1379m), situated at the foot of a rock-girt, grassy valley. The village is a starting point for the ascent of Monte Velino (2487m) reached in c. 4hrs via the CAI Sebastiani Refuge (1996m; key at Ovindoli), and the Colle di Pezza (2070m). The road (no. 5b) continues northwards to L'Aquila, winding at a high level between Monte Velino and Monte Sirente (2349m).

Road 5 skirts the north side of the Piana del Fucino, closely followed by Autostrada A25. **Avezzano** (695m), a town of 37,000 inhabitants, was completely destroyed by an earthquake on 13th January 1915, but, in common with the surrounding villages, it has been rebuilt and has the atmosphere of a garden city. It suffered further damage in the Second World War, when the Palazzo Torlonia, used by the Germans as a headquarters, was bombed. The Castello degli Orsini dates from 1490. The present building has been largely reconstructed. The Museo Lapidario Marsicano (*closed at the time of writing; T: 086 35011*) contains tomb inscriptions and sculptural and architectural fragments from sites in the ancient Marsica (Alba Fucens, Marruvium, Ortona dei Marsi).

The Roman Town of Alba Fucens

Alba Fucens, also called *Alba Fucentia*, lies near the village of Albe, 8km north of Avezzano. It is reached by a minor road (marked). Alba received a colony of 6,000 citizens from Rome in 304 BC and became the chief Roman stronghold in the uplands of central Italy. Its three hilltops, the northeast one of which is occupied by the old village (ruined by the earthquake of 1915), were united by a strong wall of polygonal masonry, constructed in the 3rd and 2nd centuries BC, part of which was incorporated in the medieval town wall on the west. Another well-preserved stretch, reinforced by an external rampart and a rectangular platform probably built during the Social War, is visible to the northwest of the modern village.

ALBA FUCENS

1 Forum
2 Basilica
3 Market
4 Baths
5 Theatre
6 Amphitheatre
7 San Pietro

Excavations conducted jointly by a Belgian mission and the Soprintendenza Archeologica di Chieti have brought to light a considerable stretch of the ancient Via Valeria, the main street of the town, as well as part of the parallel Via dei Pilastri—so called after the tall shafts (rebuilt) that line the north side of the road. Also excavated were a forum and remains of numerous buildings, including the basilica, the market, shops and the partially-excavated baths, opposite which stands a much-ruined theatre.

The amphitheatre lies on the east slope of the Collina di San Pietro. At the top of the hill stands the church of San Pietro, with Corinthian columns and Cosmatesque ornament, which has been expertly restored; on the hill of Pettorino (southeast) are further remains of walls and the houses of the rebuilt village. It is interesting to note that the walls of Alba Fucens had no towers or bastions other than those at the four gates.

THROUGH THE HILLS TO ROME

West of Avezzano **Scurcola Marsicana**, dominated by a castle of the Orsini (1269), preserves in its parish church a fine polychrome wooden *Madonna*, a relic of the ruined church of Santa Maria della Vittoria built by Charles of Anjou to mark the site of his victory over Conradin, last of the Hohenstaufen, at the battle of Tagliacozzo (12th August 1268). **Tagliacozzo** itself (823m) is an attractive town built on a slope above the Salto river. The Palazzo Ducale, in the imposing piazza, is a fine building of the 14th and 15th centuries. The first floor loggia has 15th-century frescoes (partially ruined). More frescoes are in the adjoining chapel. San Francesco, a 14th-century convent of Franciscan simplicity, has a Gothic portal and rose window of the mid-15th century and a fine frescoed cloister. Within are a 16th-century wooden Crucifix and a 15th-century *Madonna and Child*. There are two other churches with 13th-century doorways and many interesting old houses in the town.

Carsoli, further west, stands beneath an ivied keep. The name derives from *Carseoli*, a stopping place on the Via Valeria. The charming medieval houses in the principal square were completely destroyed in the Second World War, but the 12th-century church of Santa Maria in Cellis, southwest of the station, escaped injury.

ABRUZZO'S GREEN HEART

Popoli, with its mantle of emerald fields and dark forests, marks the heart of Abruzzo. The little town is dominated by the ruined castle of the Cantelmi, dukes of Popoli. The war-damaged church of San Francesco preserves its important façade and a good medieval *Crucifixion* group above the high altar. The 14th-century Gothic Taverna Ducale was built as a storehouse for ducal tithes.

Near Popoli station Road 17 begins an immediate, steep and winding ascent, called the Strada delle Svolte, reaching a height of 746m. From Navelli (760m) a byroad descends on the right to **Capestrano**, the birthplace of St John Capistran (1386–1456), an early reformer of the Catholic church. The fine castle, built by the Piccolomini, dates from the 15th century, as does the nearby Convento di San Giovanni.

From here a country road descends to Bussi, passing near (right) the ruined abbey of Santa Maria di Cartignano and (left) the lonely Romanesque church of **San Pietro ad Oratorium**, with 12th-century frescoes and 13th-century sculptures.

Frescoes in the forest

Just north of Navelli, a turning ascends westwards to **Bominaco** (3km), where two remarkable churches, relics of a fortified monastery, have been preserved (*if closed, call the custodian, T: 0862 93765; a small donation will be appreciated*). The lower church, **San Pellegrino**, was rebuilt in 1263 and has a small porch with three rounded arches. The rectangular interior is covered by a pointed barrel vault divided into four bays by transverse arches and reflects on a humble scale the Burgundian Gothic style introduced to southern Italy with the abbey of Fossanova. The walls and ceiling are completely decorated with murals of the period, of which the most extraordinary are those above the cornice, a cycle representing the *Calendar of the Diocese of Valva*, with the months, the signs of the Zodiac and feast days. Two stone plutei, carved with a dragon (left) and a griffin (right), and originally painted, separate the nave from the sanctuary. Hidden on the north side of the altar is a small hole through which, according to tradition, you can hear the heartbeat of the saint, buried below. The upper church, **Santa Maria Assunta**, is a splendid example of 12th-century architecture, with some superb sculptural decoration. It contains a contemporary pulpit, signed and dated 1180.

The small 13th-century church of San Pellegrino at Bominaco.

L'AQUILA

L'Aquila (pop. 68,000) is a regional capital in a setting of great natural beauty. Its air of detached serenity is still largely unspoilt, notwithstanding Baroque and Neoclassical attempts to redesign the city and the modern building that has invaded the surrounding countryside. In the city and its environs you can see some of the finest churches in Abruzzo, notably Santa Maria di Collemaggio, the highest achievement of Abruzzan religious architecture. The 16th-century castle houses a truly outstanding collection of polychrome wooden statues removed for safekeeping from these churches, many of which are in a state of partial or total abandon. The Gran Sasso d'Italia rises above the city, and is largely responsible for L'Aquila's chilly climate. The peaks of this chain are the highest in the Apennines, rising to 2912m at the Corno Grande.

HISTORY OF L'AQUILA

Founded in 1240 by Frederick II as a barrier to the encroachments of the popes, L'Aquila was peopled with the inhabitants of the numerous castles and fortified villages that had grown up in the valley and on the surrounding hills following the destruction of the ancient centres of *Amiternum*, *Forcona*, *Foruli* and *Peltuinum*. In 1423, the combined armies of Joan II, Pope Martin V and the Duke of Milan successfully assaulted the town, and Braccio Fortebraccio, the *condottiere* who held the place for Alfonso of Aragon, was killed. In the same battle while fighting for the allies, Attendolo, first of the Sforza (later lords of Milan), was drowned in the nearby Pescara river.

In later years L'Aquila became, on the strength of its wool trade, one of the chief cities of the Kingdom of Naples, extending its commercial ties to the major centres of north Italy and Europe. It was at this time that the Franciscan saints Bernardino of Siena, John Capistran and James of the Marches came to the town, increasing its importance as a centre of religious activity. L'Aquila suffered especially severely from the earthquakes of 1461 and 1703.

A famous fountain

Inside Porta Rivera is the Fontana delle Novantanove Cannelle, a singular fountain with 99 spouts (an allusion to the 99 castles from which the town was formed) in the shape of a courtyard of red and white stone. The water issues from 93 grotesque masks (six of the spouts are unadorned) of human, animal and fantastic figures, each of which differs from the others. Set into the end wall is a tablet inscribed *Magis. Tangredus de Pontoma de Valva fecit hoc opus* and dated 1272. Tancred's fountain is believed to have included two sides only; the third, that on the left of the entrance, is generally thought to have been added in 1582. The complex was restored and the right wall rebuilt in the 18th century (as the Baroque character of the masks attests),

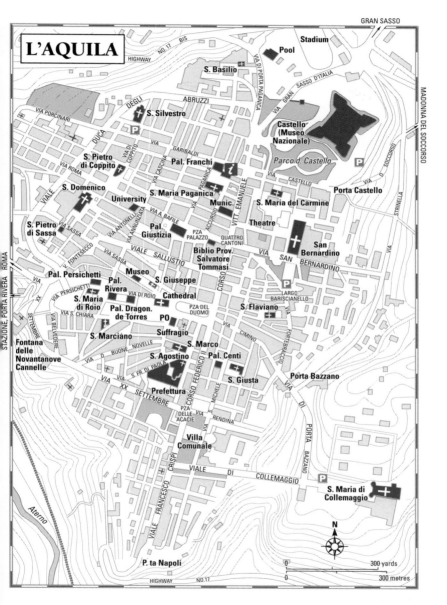

probably following damage in the earthquake of 1703. Further restorations were carried out in 1871 and 1934.

Santa Maria di Collemaggio

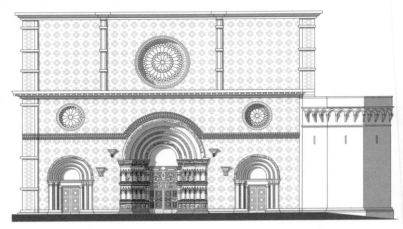

SANTA MARIA DI COLLEMAGGIO

This majestic Romanesque church (1287), in the south of town, was founded by Pietro Angeleri (or Pietro del Morrone; 1215–96), who was crowned here as Pope Celestine V (*see box opposite*) in 1294 and canonised as St Peter Celestine in 1313. The façade is a graceful composition of red and white stone, with three doors and three rose windows; the central one is particularly splendid. The large central portal, embellished with spiral moulding and delicate carvings, is flanked by Gothic niches, some of which retain fragments of statues. The wooden door dates from 1688. Carved surrounds also adorn the lateral portals. The façade is divided horizontally by a prominent frieze, the linear value of which lends emphasis to the flat roofline, a recurrent characteristic of the churches of Abruzzo. The low octagonal tower at the south corner was possibly intended for open-air benedictions. On the north side of the church is a Holy Door, unusual outside Rome.

The impressive interior was restored in 1973. The floor is paved with red and white stones in square and diamond patterns. The graceful nave arcade consists of broad pointed arches on massive piers, supporting a wooden ceiling. In the aisles are 15th-century frescoes revealed during the restoration, a 15th-century terracotta statue of the Madonna and paintings by the 17th-century artist Karl Ruther. The church also contains the Renaissance tomb (1517) of Celestine V, in a chapel at the right of the apse.

Piazza del Duomo and district

On the west side of Piazza del Duomo is the cathedral (San Massimo), dating from 1257 and rebuilt after 1703. The Neoclassical façade is a 19th-century work; the upper storey, with its twin bell-towers, was added in 1928. The original wooden doors are covered by an awkward bronze composition of 1976. Traces of the 13th-century church can be seen along the right flank. Within is a monument to Cardinal Amico Agnifili by Silvestro dall'Aquila (1480), reconstructed after the earthquake of 1703. Other fragments of this work may be seen at the left of the door to the sacristy and above the portal in the south flank of the church of San Marciano (*see below*). On the south side of the square stands the 18th-century church of the Suffragio.

On the immediate right of the cathedral Via di Roio leads past three 18th-century mansions: Palazzo Dragonetti de Torres and Palazzo Rivera (left) and Palazzo Persichetti. Other fine houses from this and earlier centuries may be seen in the neighbourhood. The churches of Santa Maria di Roio, across the street from Palazzo Persichetti, and San Marciano, behind Palazzo Rivera, have plain Romanesque façades.

The church of **San Marco** preserves two portals from the 14th and 15th centuries. **Santa Giusta** (1257), on the other side of Corso Federico II, has a simple façade incorporating a Romanesque portal and a splendid rose window adorned with grotesque figures. The uninteresting interior contains, in the first south chapel, a *Martyrdom of St Stephen* by Cavaliere d'Arpino. In the choir are Gothic stalls. Opposite the church is the 18th-century Palazzo Conti, a sumptuous building with an unusual balcony.

Pope Celestine V (1215–96)

Pietro Angeleri was born into a humble peasant family in Molise, the eleventh of twelve children. Of saintly disposition and an eremitical turn of mind, he became a Benedictine monk at the age of 17, and retreated into the mountain fastnesses of the Maiella, to live a life of solitude and contemplation. He was known for the rigour of his fasts, and for the coarseness of his hair shirt. Only once did he stray into the public eye, to berate the cardinals in Rome for taking so long to elect a new pope (the throne of St Peter having been vacant for two years). The result was that the conclave immediately elected Pietro: one July morning the peace of his hermitage was shattered by a troop of Vatican delegates, bearing the news of his election. Unwillingly Pietro accepted his destiny, and rode into L'Aquila on a donkey, to be crowned in Santa Maria di Collemaggio, taking the name Celestine V. King Charles II of Anjou was all agog at the prospect of a Neapolitan pope. He exercised a pernicious influence over the humble dotard, making him appoint numerous new cardinals, all either Frenchmen (and thus pro-Angevin) or from Neapolitan families. Celestine even transferrerd the Curia from Rome to the Castel Nuovo at Naples, building a tiny cell there, to resemble his hovel on the Maiella. Celestine hated being pope, and was fully aware of how ill-suited to the role he was. He resigned after only five months, the only pope ever to renounce the pontificate. His successor, Boniface VIII, treated him with great unkindness, refusing to let him return to his mountain cell and shutting him up in a castle in Campania, where he died in 1296. He was canonised in 1313, and is the patron saint of bookbinders. The Order of the Celestines is his lasting legacy.

San Bernardino and vicinity

The imposing church of San Bernardino (1454–72) rises at the head of a flight of steps. The elaborate Renaissance façade is by Cola dell'Amatrice (1524). The Baroque interior, with a splendid, 18th-century carved ceiling by Ferdinando Mosca, contains (second south chapel) a *Coronation of the Virgin, Resurrection*, and saints by Andrea della Robbia; further on are the tomb of San Bernardino (1505) and (in the apse) the monument of Maria Pereira (1496), two fine works in stone by Silvestro dall'Aquila, the latter showing the influence of Antonio Rossellino.

From the piazza in front of the church, Via San Bernardino leads left to a busy cross-roads called Quattro Cantoni. Beyond the Corso is to Piazza del Palazzo, with a statue of the historian Sallust (Sallustius Crispus, 86–34 BC), a native of *Amiternum*, by Cesare Zocchi (1903). Palazzo di Giustizia and its bell-tower dominate the piazza; the bell sounds 99 strokes every day at Vespers. The palace was rebuilt in 1573 for Margaret of Austria, illegitimate daughter of Charles V, wife of both Alessandro de' Medici and Ottavio Farnese, and Governess of the Abruzzi.

On the opposite side of the square is the **Biblioteca Provinciale Salvatore Tommasi**, the most important library in Abruzzo, with over 100,000 volumes, among them two books printed at L'Aquila in 1482. Adjacent is the Convitto Nazionale, in which St Bernardino of Siena died in 1444. The **Casa Museo Signorini Corsi** (*Via Patini 27, near Piazza del Palazzo; open Tues–Sun 4–7, Sat–Sun 10–1 & 4–7; T: 0862 241 0900*) preserves the appearance of a patrician house of the early 18th century, with interesting period furniture, as well as a coin collection, icons from Russia, Crete and Dalmatia, and paintings from the 14th–20th centuries.

On L'Aquila's architecture

The town looked as if it were constructed of hard panes of light and shade that made the most violent contrasts. Above white blinding sidewalkless streets stood façades built of local stone that had a richness despite their austerity, with their juxtaposed orange and sepia, burnt siena and *café au lait*, neutral liver and green-ish grey, that made a double scale of colors, one darkened and cold, one glowing. The tall doorways were impressively hooded with heavy ornamental archi-traves, and the windows, well-proportioned and brown-shuttered, were capped with a variety of pediments that resembled now triangular crests, now crowns with twin peaks, now coronets, and contributed to a standard of dignity that [...] attained something akin to grandeur: [...] Aquila had a unity and harmony which made it seem all to have been built in one piece like those wasps'-nests in the hills that had given her the creeps, but which here imposed themselves upon her and compelled her to respect and admire. This, she saw, was what architecture could do—not merely lay out a plan as at Washington, but dominate a whole city and actually provide the medium in which human beings lived.

Edmund Wilson: Europe without Baedeker, 1947

The Museo Nazionale d'Abruzzo

Open Tues–Sun 8.30–7.30, last entry 30mins before closing; T: 0862 6331.
The castle, built by Pier Luigi Scrivà in 1530, now houses the museum and the Auditorium, one of the halls used by the Società Aquilana dei Concerti. The museum, the finest in east-central Italy, incorporates the collections formerly held by the Museo Civico and the Museo Diocesano d'Arte Sacra, as well as works from ruined churches throughout the region.

Ground floor

You enter through a monumental doorway surmounted by the arms of Charles V and huge horns of plenty carved by Salvato Salvati and Pietro di Stefano and dated 1543. Beyond the entrance hall lies the large, rectangular court; turn right and proceed beneath a vaulted portico to the large, domed room in the southeast bastion, at the centre of which stands a prehistoric elephant (*Archidiscodon meridionalis vastinus*), partly reconstructed with plaster casts, found at Scoppito, 14km west of L'Aquila. Plant fossils are exhibited on the wall. In an adjoining room is a group of works donated to the museum in 1993 by the contemporary artist Emilio Greco.

The nearby **Sala del Gonfalone** displays the banner of the city of L'Aquila, a curious work painted in 1579 by the local artist Giovanni Paolo Cardone. The banner shows L'Aquila as it looked before the 1703 earthquake, presented to Christ the Redeemer by the four patrons of the city (Sts Maximus, Equitius, Bernardino and Celestine). At the sides of the Saviour are the Virgin, interceding for the city, and an angel holding an amphora. The influence of Roman Mannerism is particularly evident in the figure of Christ holding the Cross, which seems to be derived from the *Resurrected Christ* sculpted by Michelangelo for the church of Santa Maria sopra Minerva in Rome.

Return to the courtyard and, passing the entrance, turn right to the **archaeological collection**. Outside the entrance are various architectural fragments of Roman manufacture and a large Roman *Hercules* (1st century AD). Highlights of the collection include inscriptions, a tomb relief from Coppito (*Pitinum*), a stele of Q. Pomponius Proculus, from Scoppito (*Foruli*), a calendar from Amiternum, a milestone of the Via Claudia Nova (*Foruli*), a tympanum with head of Medusa from Preturo, a headless lion holding the head of a ram, a bas-relief with a funeral procession, a tympanum with butcher's tools and another with a relief of carpenter's tools, vases in terracotta and impasto, bronze jewellery, painted vases, Etruscan ware in *bucchero* and clay (6th century BC); terracotta votive statues (3rd–2nd centuries BC), and a fine collection of small cups, plates and bowls (1st century BC–1st century AD).

First floor

The **religious art collection** is arranged in the corridor and in the adjoining rooms. In the corridor are (left) a fresco of Christ with the Virgin and St John by Armanino da Modena, for an apse (the work is dated 1237 and signed by the artist, which was unusual at the time); below, a stone altar frontal with plant and animal reliefs; nearby, a large *Baptism of St Augustine* by Mattia Preti; a polychrome wooden sculpture of the Virgin and Child by an anonymous local artist of the 16th century; and (right) detached frescoes from ruined churches of Abruzzo: *Madonna del Latte* (14th–15th century); a Byzantine fresco with the Madonna and Child, St Sebastian, and a mandorla with the *Virgin in Glory* (15th century), a Byzantine fresco with the Madonna and Child, saints and an Archangel; a fresco with a *Crucifixion* by Francesco da Montereale (16th century).

Room 1: Polychrome wooden Crucifix (13th century); enthroned Madonna and Child (13th century); 12th–13th-century fresco fragments, notably *Deposition* by an anonymous 13th-century artist, from the church of San Pietro in Valle at Caporciano.

Room 2: Polychrome wooden figure group of the Madonna and Child (dated 1262); polychrome *Madonna and Child* (13th century); Byzantine panel painting of the *Madonna del Latte* (1270–80); panel of the Madonna and Child (signed Gentile da Rocca and dated 1283); a wooden figure of the Deposed Christ (early 15th century).

Room 3: *St Balbina*, a polychrome wood statue from Pizzoli; polychrome Madonna and Child (early 14th century); wooden statue of St Catherine of Alexandria between panels representing episodes from her life; *Enthroned Madonna*; polychrome wooden statue of St Leonard (15th century); wooden figure of St Bartholomew, showing French influence.

Room 4: More polychrome wooden statues, including a poorly preserved but evocative *Santa Coronata*; in the glass case, gilded silver processional Cross (dated 1434 and signed by Nicola da Guardiagrele).

Room 5: *Tree of the Cross* (early 15th century), by the Master of the Beffi Triptych, from Santa Maria a Paganica, L'Aquila; *Madonna and Child*, the 'Beffi Triptych' (15th century), from Santa Maria del Ponte, Tione; *Madonna and Child with Saints*, altarpiece by Jacobello del Fiore (15th century); *St Bernardino of Siena*, by Sano di Pietro; triptych, with the enthroned Madonna and Child, *Nativity*, *Annunciation to the Shepherds* and *Assumption*, showing Sienese influence (15th century).

Room 6: Polychrome wood sculpture of the Madonna and Child, by Silvestro dall'Aquila (late 15th century); minor sculptural works, including a marble statue of St Peter Celestine from Santa Maria di Collemaggio; *St Sebastian* (1478) by Silvestro dall'Aquila, showing the influence of Verrocchio; panel paintings of the 15th and 16th centuries; fragmentary panel of the Virgin by Andrea Delitio, showing the strong influence of Piero della Francesca and Benozzo Gozzoli. Note the **painted ceilings** in this and the following room. The ceiling of Room 6 represents mythological scenes, including the rape of Ganymede and the story of Cupid and Psyche, from Ovid's *Metamorphoses*; the ceiling of Room 7 is adorned with heads of Roman emperors.

Room 7: Fifteenth-century panel paintings: *St John Capistran* with episodes from the life of the saint, and *Stigmatisation of St Francis*, both by the Master of St John Capistran (15th century); a poorly preserved terracotta Madonna and Child (16th century); at the centre, terracotta *Nativity* (late 15th century).

Room 8: Fifteenth- and 16th-century stained glass and church furnishings.

Rooms 9–10: Assorted paintings by local artists of the 15th–16th centuries, including three paintings (two Madonnas and *St Anthony of Padua*), by one of Carlo Crivelli's disciples, and two paintings attributed to Saturnino Gatti.

The recently established **coin collection**, also reached from the first-floor loggia, displays over a hundred pieces offering a good sample of Abruzzan numismatics from the 4th century BC to the Unification of Italy. The gold room, on the landing between the first and second floors, contains an arrangement of objects (notably processional crosses and shrines) from Sulmona, Teramo and L'Aquila.

Second floor

The first two rooms, off the corridor on the right, are dedicated to artists native to L'Aquila, notably Francesco da Montereale, Giovanni Paolo Cardone and his master, Pompeo Cesura, all active in the 16th century. In the third room are Flemish painters, followed by the 17th-century artist Giulio Cesare Bedeschini in the fourth room. Next are works by 17th-century Neapolitan and Roman artists, and paintings by Karl Ruther, a Benedictine monk of German origin and member of the community of Santa Maria di Collemaggio. Rooms 7 and 8 host paintings by locally famous artists Antonio di Giovanni d'Enrico (called Tanzio da Varallo) and Michelangelo Bonocore.

Andrea Vaccaro: *St Agatha.*

Jusepe Ribera: *Mary Magdalene.*

Return to the corridor from the far end to view the **Cappelli collection**, featuring works by Neapolitan artists. The best include a *Madonna and Child* by Fabrizio Santafede; *St Agatha* by Andrea Vaccaro; *Mary Magdalene* by Jusepe de Ribera; *Tribute Money, Christ and the Adulteress, Martyrdom of St Bartholomew* and *Job in the Dung Pile* by Mattia Preti; and *The Triumph of Charles of Bourbon* by Francesco Solimena.

Other sights in L'Aquila

The road to the right of the castle leads to (15mins) the Madonna del Soccorso, with a good Renaissance façade (1496) and two early 16th-century tombs in the style of Silvestro dall'Aquila. From the end of Corso Vittorio Emanuele, Via Garibaldi leads northwest to the 14th-century church of **San Silvestro**, with an elegant rose window in its simple façade and 15th-century frescoes in the apse. Of the many 18th-century mansions, perhaps the most interesting is the **Palazzo Benedetti**, in Via Accursio (near Santa Maria Paganica), with its finely proportioned courtyard. The Convento di San Giuliano, just outside the town, houses a small natural history museum (*Museo di Scienze Naturali; open Tues–Sun, 10–1 & 3–6: T: 0862 314201*).

The **Museo Sperimentale d'Arte Contemporanea Muspac** (*Via Paganica 17, open daily 5.30–8.30, closed two weeks in July, T: 0862 410505*), has a small but outstanding permanent collection of works by well-known international contemporary artists.

THE GRAN SASSO D'ITALIA

The Gran Sasso d'Italia, a predominantly limestone formation, containing the highest mountains in Italy (apart from Etna), is part of the east wall of the Abruzzo mountain group. Icy in spring or autumn, it can be cool even in midsummer. With an average depth of c. 15km, it extends in a west-northwest–east-southeast direction for c. 35km from the Passo delle Capannelle, on Road 80 from L'Aquila to Teramo, to Forca di Penne, on a secondary road from Popoli to Penne.

The Gran Sasso comprises two almost parallel chains separated by a central depression interrupted by peaks of its own. The south chain is a uniform rampart extending from Monte San Franco (2132m) in the west to Monte Bolza (1904m) in the east, with the Pizzo Cefalone (2533m) in the centre. The north chain includes the formidable peaks of Monte Corvo (2623m): the Pizzo Intermesoli (2635m), the Corno Piccolo (2655m), the Corno Grande with its three summits, one of them the highest of all (2912m). Deep valleys extend from this chain to the north. To the south are the Passo di Portella (2260m) and the Vado di Corno (1924m).

Much of the central depression consists of the Campo Imperatore, a vast tableland (2130m) inhabited by herds of wild horses. It is connected with the road from L'Aquila by cableway. Other approaches include those from La Provvidenza, on Road 80 from L'Aquila to Teramo; Pietracamela, at the foot of the Corno Piccolo; Isola del Gran Sasso, below the Corno Grande; and Castelli, below Monte Prena.

ASCENT OF THE GRAN SASSO

The Gran Sasso cableway (*runs 8–5 except in high winds*) enables travellers to reach the Campo Imperatore and return to L'Aquila in a day. An alternative approach to the Campo Imperatore may be made in fair weather by an extension of Road 17b, which links the upper and lower stations of the cableway.

The lower station is at Fonte Cerreto, above Assergi: take the Viale del Gran Sasso d'Italia out of L'Aquila, past the castle, heading east along Road 17b to Paganica (660m). Alternatively, leave L'Aquila by the Porta Napoli and take Road 17 to Bazzano and from there by a secondary road to Paganica. From Paganica the road ascends northeast to tiny Assergi (867m); its church has a Gothic façade and a 12th-century crypt. Beyond Assergi the road climbs sharply to Fonte Cerreto (1120m) and the lower station of the cableway (Stazione Inferiore Funivia). Autostrada A24 follows roughly the same course to Assergi. Buses from L'Aquila (50–60mins) connect with the cableway services.

The cableway climbs several times daily to Campo Imperatore in 30mins. Above the terminus is the Albergo di Campo Imperatore. The hotel is at the top of a ski-lift (*sciovia*), 600m long, which ascends from Le Fontari (1980m) during the winter season (Dec–April). It was the scene of the daring Nazi 'rescue' of Mussolini on 12th September 1943. Now it is the usual starting point for walks and ascents.

From the Albergo di Campo Imperatore there are several recognised hiking trails across the Gran Sasso and up to its various summits. The hotel sells trail maps. Those who would like a guide should apply to the Ufficio Informazioni e di Accoglienza Turistica, in L'Aquila. Detailed information about the area is given in the *Guida dei Monti d'Italia, Volume Gran Sasso*, published by the CAI (Club Alpino Italiano) and TCI (Touring Club Italiano).

MUSSOLINI ON THE GRAN SASSO

Following talks between Mussolini and Hitler at Feltre (19th July 1943), at which Mussolini endured one of Hitler's famous monologues and failed to find the courage to resist demands for full Italian co-operation, the Gran Consiglio del Fascismo voted to remove the *Duce*. King Vittorio Emanuele III accordingly dismissed Mussolini and had him arrested. He was taken into custody on the heights of the Gran Sasso. The next day a new cabinet, formed under General Pietro Badoglio, disbanded the Fascist Party (28th July) and, while publicly expressing the wish to remain loyal to Germany, secretly began talks with the Allies. After the announcement of the armistice, signed in Sicily on 3rd September between the Allied Command and the Italian government, on 8th September the Germans occupied the principal strategic points of northern and central Italy, and Rome. The disorientated Italian troops were largely disarmed or taken prisoner. The Badoglio government, without making any provision for armed resistance against the Nazis, fled with the royal family to Brindisi, where they found Allied protection.

On 12th September an SS assault team freed Mussolini from his prison on Campo Imperatore and flew him away to Salò, on Lake Garda. Here, with Hitler's support, Mussolini formed the Repubblica Sociale di Salò, a puppet state of Nazi Germany. On 13th October the Badoglio government declared war on Germany.

The road to Teramo

The route from L'Aquila to Teramo (not the shortest, but incomparably the most beautiful) climbs over the Gran Sasso by the Passo delle Capannelle (1299m). Road 80 branches to the right of Road 17 just west of L'Aquila and ascends the valley of the Aterno. **San Vittorino**, a 12th-century village on a hill, is reached by a turning on the right. Beneath the Romanesque church of San Michele (1170, rebuilt 1528), you can see the Catacomba di San Vittorino, with walls in *opus reticulatum* and *opus incertum*, 14th- and 15th-century frescoes and the presumed tomb of the saint. The church, which is broken into two parts by a dividing wall, contains 13th-century frescoes and reliefs.

Near Ponte Cermone are the **ruins of *Amiternum***, comprising a theatre, an amphitheatre, and the remains of a building with frescoes and mosaics, excavated in 1978. This ancient Sabine town was the birthplace of Sallust.

At Arischia, you begin to ascend the northwest flank of the Gran Sasso. Taverna della Croce (1270m) marks the beginning of a saddle preceding the road's summit-level at the Passo delle Capannelle, the west–northwest limit of the Gran Sasso range. Four kilometres beyond, a secondary road leads left to the lovely **Lago di Campotosto**, an artificial lake 64km round, taking its name from the village of Campotosto, on the north shore. The fishing in the lake is excellent.

Beyond La Provvidenza (1100m), a starting point for the ascent of the Gran Sasso, the descent of the narrow, picturesque Vomano valley begins. A by-road climbs south to Pietracamela (1005m), passing the village of **Fano Adriano**, where the 12th-century church of San Pietro has a simple, characteristic façade of 1550. Monte Corvo and other peaks of the Gran Sasso appear on the right. **Montorio al Vomano** is dominated by its ruined castle. In the main square stands the church of San Rocco, with a curious composite façade, added piecemeal over the centuries. About 16km south, on a by-road, is Isola del Gran Sasso, one of the approaches to the Gran Sasso. To the southeast is Castelli, a centre of pottery-making. From Montorio the road climbs out again, then descends, in view of the Monti della Laga, to Teramo.

TERAMO & ENVIRONS

Teramo (pop. 52,000), the modern-looking capital of the province of the same name, is situated between the Tordino and the Vezzola rivers. It was the ancient *Interamnia Praetuttiorum*, which became a Roman city in 268 BC. Under the Angevin dukes of Puglia it flourished in the 14th century; but later, distracted by feuds between the Melatini and the Antonelli, it became part of the Kingdom of Naples.

The cathedral

The cathedral, at the centre of the town, has a handsome campanile and a singular Romanesque-Gothic portal incorporating mosaic decoration, a rose window, and statues of *Sts Bernard and John the Baptist*, and *Christ Blessing*. In the architrave is the date 1332. On either side of the door are statues of the Archangel Gabriel and the Virgin Annunciate, by Nicola da Guardiagrele, on columns borne by lions; several other lions scattered about the façade probably belonged to the porches of the lateral doorways, now destroyed.

The austere interior was begun in the 13th century and extended in the following century. The two parts meet at a slight angle, with steps separating the earlier church from the Gothic addition. The high altar is faced with a fine silver frontal by Nicola da Guardiagrele (1433–48), with 34 relief panels depicting New Testament scenes, apostles and saints. On the south wall of the presbytery is a notable polyptych by Jacobello del Fiore, formerly in the church of Sant'Agostino; and in the south transept, a fine, 13th-century wooden *Madonna* set in a marble tabernacle. The church incorporates numerous antique architectural fragments and part of the wooden ceiling of the original building. Above the arches of the nave are the arms of the churchmen who helped in its reconstruction. The holy-water stoups at the west end of the nave arcade have been reassembled from medieval sculptural fragments.

Museo Archeologico

Via Delfico 30. Open daily except Mon, July–Aug 9.30–1 & 5–10; Sept–June 9.30–1 & 3–7; T: 0861 247772.

Opened in 2001, just a few blocks from the cathedral, the museum collections, on two floors, document human settlement in the Teramo area, with particular emphasis on the Roman city of *Interamnia*. Highlights include statuary and architectural fragments from the forum, the theatre and three villas, plus burial treasures from the necropolis at Ponte Messato. In the basement is an *in situ* exhibit of just a few of the many Roman mosaics found beneath the cathedral and other buildings in the historic city centre.

The eastern districts

Near the east end of the town are the **Madonna delle Grazie**, with a 15th-century wooden *Virgin* attributed to Silvestro dall'Aquila; Sant'Antonio, with a portal of 1309; and the 14th-century Casa dei Melatini. Remains of the walls of a **Roman amphitheatre** may be seen in Via San Bernardo, on the left side of the cathedral, and in Via Vincenzo Irelli, which branches south to the recently excavated Roman theatre. In the Villa Comunale is the **Pinacoteca Civica** (*open Tues–Sun, July–Aug 10–12 & 5–12; Sept–Jun 9–1 & 3–7; T: 0861 247772*) containing 15th-century works by local artists and 17th- and 18th-century works by Roman and Neapolitan artists (Luca Giordano, Francesco de Mura and Corrado Giaquinto).

NORTH OF TERAMO

Campli

In the hills to the north of Teramo lies the little town of Campli (393m), where the lovely central Piazza Vittorio Emanuele is paved with brick and marble. The **cathedral of Santa Maria in Platea** dates from the 14th century. Within are a painted wooden ceiling and a good reproduction of Raphael's *Visitation* (original now in the Prado in Madrid). The crypt has 15th-century frescoes. Opposite the church stands the Palazzo Farnese, the former *Palazzo Parlamentare*, erected in the 14th century, rebuilt in 1520 and restored in 1888. It has a portico on heavy piers and mullioned windows. Along the main street are the Casa della Farmacia with a 16th-century loggia, and the Casa del Medico, of the same date.

A museum in the former convent of San Francesco, the **Museo Archeologico Nazionale** (*open Tues–Sun 9–8; T: 0861 569158*), houses material from an Italic necropolis discovered at Campovalano nearby. This is the largest known pre-Roman necropolis in Italy. Excavation of the site, which began in 1967, has revealed more than 20,000 pit tombs dating from the 7th–5th centuries BC. The church, an early-14th-century Romanesque building, has a fine portal and simple but elegant decorative details. Within are a 14th-century Crucifix, 15th-century frescoes, and a panel of *St Anthony of Padua* by Cola dell'Amatrice (1510).

The little **church of San Giovanni** also dates from the 14th century and contains a 14th-century wooden Crucifix and 15th-century frescoes, as well as two 16th-century wooden altars. Just beyond is the Porta Orientale, part of the medieval walls.

From the centre of the town a country road leads to (c. 1km) the **church of San Pietro**, founded—together with the adjacent ruined Benedictine convent—in the 8th century and rebuilt at the beginning of the 13th. The three-aisled interior, restored 1960–68, has votive frescoes on the piers and, on the north wall, a panel from an early Christian sarcophagus, with bas-reliefs of biblical scenes.

North to the border with the Marche

Further north, **Civitella del Tronto** rises in a magnificent position on a hillside below its ruined castle, which was almost the last stronghold of the Bourbons to yield to the Italian troops (1861). It also resisted Guise's attack in 1557 after he had taken Campli in his campaign against Alva's Spaniards. Civitella is interesting for its Renaissance mansions.

The road to the lovely town of Ascoli Piceno (*see Blue Guide Marche & San Marino*) descends, with good views back towards Civitella, crossing the Salinello river by a tall bridge. A road branches left to **Ripe**, near which caves inhabited from the Upper Palaeolithic to the Bronze Age have been found. Beyond Lempa you enter the Marche, and begin a long, winding descent.

PRACTICAL INFORMATION

GETTING AROUND

• **By road:** Throughout the region, the driving may be difficult in winter because of snow. Bus connections, sadly, are too infrequent to be useful.
• **By rail:** Sulmona to L'Aquila, 60km in 1hr. For L'Aquila the Rome–Antrodoco route is followed by a secondary railway linking it to the Rome–Ancona main line (Rome to L'Aquila in c. 3hrs, with a change of trains at Terni).

INFORMATION OFFICES

L'Aquila Amministrazione Provinciale Settore Turismo, Piazza Santa Maria di Collemaggio 4, T: 0862 2991; Ufficio Informazioni e di Accoglienza Turistica, Via XX Settembre 8, T: 0862 22306 and Piazza Santa Maria di Paganica 5, T: 0862 410808.
Pescasseroli Via Piave 2, T: 0863 910461.
Scanno Piazza Santa Maria della Valle 12, T: 0864 74317.
Sulmona Corso Ovidio 208, T: 0864 53276.
Tagliacozzo Via Veneto 6, T: 0863 610318.
Teramo Amministrazione Provinciale Settore Turismo, Via G. Milli 2, T: 0861 3311; Ufficio Informazioni e di Accoglienza Turistica, Via del Castello 10, T: 0861 244222.

HOTELS

Assergi
€€ **Campo Imperatore**. In a splendid

position (2130m; 10mins by chairlift) at the foot of the Gran Sasso, with an excellent restaurant. T: 0862 400 000.

€ **Rifugio Campo Imperatore**. Simple lodge next to the hotel Campo Imperatore. Via Campo Imperatore 1, T: 0862 400011.

Ceppo

€ **Ostello del Ceppo**. Hostel serving the Parco Nazionale del Gran Sasso, managed by Cooperative Iride. Via Vidacillo 16, Ascoli Piceno, T: 0736 256417.

L'Aquila

€ **Duca degli Abruzzi**. Large, quiet rooms and restaurant with views over the city centre. Open all year. Viale Giovanni XXIII 10, T: 0862 28341, www.ducadegliabruzzi.com

€ **Duomo**. Centrally located, in a renovated 18th century palazzo with terracotta floors and wrought-iron beds. Open all year. Via Dragonetti 6/10, T: 0862 410893, www.hotel-duomo.it

Leofara

€ **Ostello di Leofara**. Hostel serving the Parco Nazionale del Gran Sasso, managed by Cooperative Iride. Via Vidacillo 16, Ascoli Piceno, T: 0736 256417.

Paganica

€€ **Villa Dragonetti**. ■ Beautiful 18th-century villa in a park, with delightful frescoed interiors, antique furniture, impeccable service and one of the best restaurants in L'Aquila and environs. Via Oberdan 4, T: 0862 680222, www.villadragonetti.it

Pescasseroli

€€ **Duca degli Abruzzi**. ■ Delightful small hotel with excellent restaurant, in the centre of the village. Piazza Duca degli Abruzzi, T: 0863 911082,

www.pescasseroli.net/ducadegliabruzzi

€€ **Daniel**. Modern and tidy, with pool and private balconies. Viale Colli dell'Oro, T: 0863 912896, www.hoteldaniel.it

€€ **Edelweis**. Comfortable family-run establishment in a garden, known also for its delicious food. Viale Colli dell'Oro, T: 0863 912577, www.edelweisshotel.biz

€€ **Paradiso**. Friendly, quiet and restful, with a large garden a short walk from the village. Via Fonte Fracassi, T: 0863 910422.

€ **Pagnani**. In a wooded garden just outside the village; warm, quiet, luminous rooms, indoor pool and gym. Open all year. Viale Colli dell'Oro 5, T: 0863 912866, www.hotelpagnani.it

Teramo

€€ **Sporting**. ■ Modern and comfortable, with an excellent restaurant. Via de Gasperi 41, T: 0861 210285, www.hotelsporting.teramo.it

RESTAURANTS

Anversa degli Abruzzi

€ **La Fiaccola**. Warm, rustic trattoria on the road from Sulmona to Scanno. Closed Mon. Via Duca degli Abruzzi 12, T: 0864 49474.

Avezzano

€€ **Jardin**. Garden restaurant offering delicious traditional dishes. Closed Tues and Aug. Via Sabotino 36, T: 0863 414710.

€ **Il Gioco dell'Uva**. Wine bar with cold meals. Closed Mon. Corso Garibaldi 133, T: 0863 25441.

Bellante

€ **Casale**. The best ingredients intelligently cooked and presented; on the

road from Teramo to the coast. Closed
Tues. Via de Luca 1, T: 0861 611925.
Campli
€€ **Locanda del Pompa**. ■ Trattoria
with rooms just outside the town, on
the road to Ascoli. Closed Wed and one
week in Jan. Bivio Campli 5, T: 0861
569011.
Campotosto
€ **Barilotto**. Simple trattoria with
rooms, closed Tues and Feb. Via Roma
18, T: 0862 900141.
€ **Trattoria del Pescatore**. Simple
trattoria, closed Mon (except in sum-
mer). Via Rio Fucino, T: 0862 900227.
Canzano
€ **La Tacchinella**. Best place around
for *tacchino alla canzanese*, the famous
(turkey) delicacy of this town between
Teramo and the coast. Closed Mon
(except in summer). Via Roma 18,
T: 0861 555107.
Carpineto della Nora
€ **La Roccia**. Good country trattoria.
Closed Tues (except in July–Aug) and
two weeks in Oct. Contrada Versante al
Bosco, T: 085 849142.
Carsoli
€€ **L'Angolo d'Abruzzo**. Outstanding
regional cuisine and good wine list.
Closed Mon and early July. Piazza Aldo
Moro 8, T: 0863 997429.
€ **Al Caminetto**. No-nonsense home-
style restaurant. Closed Mon (except in
Aug) and early July. Via degli Alpini 95,
T: 0863 995105.
Castel del Monte (at the foot of the
Gran Sasso, 41km east of L'Aquila)
€ **Il Gattone**. Traditional trattoria.
Closed Wed. Via Campo della Fiera 9,
T: 0862 938446.
Castelnuovo (at the foot of the Gran
Sasso, 23km southeast of L'Aquila)

€€ **La Cabina**. Small hotel restaurant.
Closed Mon (except in Aug), Jan–Feb.
Via Aufinate 1, T: 0862 93567.
Civitella del Tronto
€ **Zunica**. Restaurant with rooms.
Closed Wed and late Nov. T: 0861
91319.
Colonnella (border of Abruzzo and
Marche)
€ **Zenobi**. ■ Farm serving excellent
country meals. Closed Tues (except in
summer) and Nov. Contrada Rio Moro,
T: 0861 70581.
Controguerra (border of Abruzzo and
Marche)
€ **La Credenza**. Wine estate
(Controguerra DOC) and farm serving
country meals. Open for dinner (lunch
by reservation). Closed Mon and Jan.
Via Pianura del Tronto 80, T: 0861
89757.
Corropoli (border of Abruzzo and
Marche)
€ **Locanda della Tradizione
Abruzzese**. Restaurant-pizzeria in a for-
mer farmhouse. Closed Wed (except in
summer) and a few days in Oct and
Dec. Via Piane, at Piane, T: 0861
810129.
Fonte Cerreto
€ **Geranio**. Good food and wines, and
unique ambience, in the old station of
the Gran Sasso cableway. Closing times
vary. T: 0862 606678.
Gagliano Aterno (between Popoli and
Ovindoli)
€ **Sotto le Finestre**. Traditional restau-
rant with a strong local following.
Closed Mon. Via Fontana 3, T: 0864
79125.
Isola del Gran Sasso (at the foot of
the Gran Sasso, 37km south of Teramo)
€ **Il Mandrone**. Uncomplicated coun-

try trattoria. Closed Tues and Wed (except in Aug), late Nov–early Dec and late Jan–early Feb. at San Pietro, T: 0861 976152.

L'Aquila

€€€ **Tre Marie**. ■ The only place in town where the menu, as well as the décor, is landmarked. Closed Sun evening, Mon and late Dec–early Jan. Via Tre Marie 3, T: 0862 413191.

€€ **Elodia**. ■ Fabulous country cooking, just outside the city on the Gran Sasso road. Closed Sun evening, Mon and Oct. Road 17 at Camarda, T: 0862 606219.

€ **Antiche Mura**. Warm, friendly *osteria*. Closed Sun. Via XXV Aprile 2, T: 0862 62422.

€ **Il Caminetto**. Exquisite renditions of traditional recipes from the city and its environs. Closed Mon and Jan. Via Antica Arischia, at Cansatessa, T: 0862 311410.

€ **Mangiatoie**. Warm atmosphere, good food and great wines in the historic city centre. Closed Tues and Nov. Via Dragonetti 22, T: 0862 24639.

€ **Matriciana**. Fine old-fashioned trattoria with *fin-de-siècle* interiors. Closed Wed and late June–early July. Via Arcivescovado 5a, T: 0862 26065.

€ **Taverna del Duomo**. Good, simple home cooking. Closed Wed. Via Roio 45, T: 0862 25392.

Magliano de' Marsi (near Alba Fucens)

€ **Laghetto di Magliano**. Friendly family-run restaurant. Closed Mon and early Sept. Piazza Uno del Serpentone, T: 0863 517346.

€ **Massa d'Albe La Conca**. Trattoria known for its wholesome country cooking. Closed Wed. Corso Umberto I 30,

T: 0863 510249.

Martinsicuro (border of Abruzzo and Marche),

€€ **Il Sestante**. Excellent fresh fish in a locally famous restaurant. Closed Sun evening and Mon, and late July–early Aug. Lungomare Italia, at Villa Rosa, T: 0861 713268.

€€ **Mare**. Good choice for fresh fish. Closed Sun evening and Mon, and late Oct–early Nov. Lungomare Europa 40, T: 0861 762100.

Montereale (west of Campotosto)

€€ **Palazzetto**. Refined restaurant in a small hotel, serving original interpretations of traditional dishes. Closed Mon. Largo San Lorenzo 1, T: 0862 901340.

Montorio al Vomano

€ **Totò**. Restaurant and pizzeria with good local recipes. Closed Mon. Via Gramsci 3, T: 0861 598508.

Ovindoli

€ **Il Pozzo**. Warm, friendly restaurant in a former stable carved out of the rock. Closed Wed and late Sept–early Oct. Via Monumento all'Alpino, T: 0863 710191.

Pacentro (near Sulmona)

€€ **Taverna de li Caldora**. ■ Fine traditional trattoria in the town centre, with outdoor seating in summer. Closed Sun evening, Tues and mid-Jan–mid-Feb. Piazza Umberto I, T: 0864 41139.

Pescasseroli

€€ **Alle Vecchie Arcate**. Warm, cosy, family-run restaurant in the centre of the village. Via della Chiesa 41, T: 0863 910781.

€€ **Plistia**. Small, family-run hotel-restaurant. Closed Mon. Via Principe di Napoli 28, T: 0863 910732.

€ **A Cavu't**. Simple, rustic trattoria known for its fresh pasta and grilled meats. Closed Mon except in July–Aug. Piazza Vittorio Veneto 17, T: 338 267 2842.

Poggio Picenze (20 km east of L'Aquila on SS 17)

€ **Osteria della Posta**. Lovely warm country trattoria, with good food and atmosphere. Open evenings (and midday Sat and Sun), closed Tues, July and Nov. Via Palombaia 1, T: 0862 80474.

€ **Poggio del Sole**. Creative interpretations of local dishes, with fair-weather seating outdoors. Closed Mon and Sept. Contrada Nardangelo 12, T: 085 972233.

Prata d'Ansidonia (south of L'Aquila)

€€ **Casa Baroni Cappa**. ■ Restaurant in a historic building, offering innovative interpretations of traditional dishes. Closed Mon and Nov. Via della Fonte 33, at San Nicandro, T: 0862 93419.

Scanno

€€ **La Fonte**. Delicious local cooking in the heart of old Scanno. Closed Wed and Oct–Nov. Via Fontana Saracco 3, T: 0864 747390.

€ **La Volpe e l'Uva**. Wine bar with cold meals, open for lunch. Closed Wed (except in summer) and Feb. Piazza San Rocco 6, T: 0360 526529.

Sulmona

€ **Clemente**. Traditional restaurant in the 14th-century Palazzo Sardi de Letto. Closed Thur and a few days in June and Dec. Osteria della Quercia, Vico Quercia 5, T: 0864 52284.

€ **Frangiò**. Delicious regional cuisine in a historic setting, with garden seating in summer. Closed Mon and Nov. Via Ercole Ciofano 51, T: 0864 212773.

€ **Gino**. Old-fashioned *osteria* in the centre of town. Open midday only, closed Sun. Piazza Plebiscito 12,

T: 0864 52289.

€€ **Rigoletto**. Warm, traditional restaurant with outdoor seating in summer. Closed Mon. Via Stazione Introdacqua 46, T: 0864 55529.

Teramo

€ **Angolo Divino**. Creative interpretations of traditional recipes. Closed Sun evening, Tues and Aug–Sept. Via Crucioli 10, T: 0861 247354.

€ **Antico Cantinone**. Quiet, traditional restaurant. Closed Sun and Aug. Via Ciotti 5, T: 0861 248863.

€ **Duomo**. ■ Excellent family-run restaurant in a historic building. Closed Mon. Via Stazio 9, T: 0861 241774.

€ **Enoteca Centrale**. Wine bar offering light meals. Closed Sun and two weeks in Aug. Corso Cerulli 24–26, T: 0861 243633.

€ **Gran Sasso**. Good regional dishes from hills and shore. Closed Sun evening. Via Vinciguerra 12, T: 0861 24530.

€ **Moderno**. Fine regional cuisine. Closed Mon and Aug. Costa Sant'Agostino, T: 0861 414559.

Torano Nuovo (border of Abruzzo and Marche)

€ **La Sosta**. Good trattoria-pizzeria in the Montepulciano and Trebbiano d'Abruzzo wine country. Closed Tues and late Aug–early Sept. Via Regina Margherita 34, T: 0861 82085.

Valle Castellana

€ **Remigio II**. Hotel restaurant with great mountain food and views. Closed Mon. Valle Castellana—Monte Pisello, T: 0861 930123.

LOCAL SPECIALITIES

Sulmona The Confetti Pelino confectioner's has a wide assortment of Sulmona's famous candies (Via Introdacqua 55). Reginella d'Abruzzo, at Via Aroto 1, has fresh and matured cheeses made with milk from local pastures. Sulmona has also been famous for its goldsmiths since the 13th century. **Castelli** is the historic centre of ceramics in Abruzzo. **L'Aquila** is justly famous for its wrought iron. Not surprisingly, the main crafts of Abruzzo's western highlands are woodworking, notably at **Popoli**, **Scoppito**, **Ovindoli** and **Arischia**; and metalworking, which traditionally requires wood fuel.

FESTIVALS & EVENTS

Civitella del Tronto *A la Corte de lo Governatore* Evocation, in historic costume, of the lifting of a French siege of 1557, with three days of banqueting, song and dance in the castle, mid-Aug.
Cocullo (5km north of Anversa degli Abruzzi) *Processione dei Serpari* Pliny the Elder recounts that the ancient inhabitants of Abruzzo, the Marsi, whose name means 'handlers of serpents', were skilled at capturing and training snakes, which they venerated as holy; by another tradition, it was St Dominic of Foligno (951–1051) who agreed to protect the inhabitants of Cocullo from the snakes that infested the area. Since the 1600s the saint (in effigy), completely covered with writhing snakes (real) has been paraded through town by the *serpari,* who hunt the reptiles down at winter's end and train them for the event; the statue-bearers are closely followed by young women bearing baskets brimming with *ciambelletti,* ring-like cakes adorned with hard candies, which

they offer to the *serpari*. Well worth a special trip if you're in the area, first Thurs in May.
L'Aquila *Teatro Internazionale dei Burattini* International puppet theatre, June–July; *Rassegna Musica e Architettura* Music and architecture review, July–Aug; *Perdonanza Papale* Historical-religious pageant celebrating Celestine V's *Bolla del Perdono* of 29 Sept 1294, by which plenary indulgence is granted to all those duly penitent *aquilani* who enter the basilica of Santa Maria di Collemaggio between vespers of Aug 28 and vespers of Aug 29.
Montorio al Vomano *La Congiura dei Baroni* Two days of food, wine, pageantry and competitive games between the town's four neighbourhoods; highlights include the *Corsa Pazza Nuda* (Crazy Naked Race), re-enacting an event of 1486, third Sat and Sun in June.
Scanno *Le Glorie di San Martino* Celebrated by igniting immense bonfires (the 'glories') in the hills around the town, 11 Nov.
Sulmona *La Madonna che Scappa in Piazza* Statues of Christ (resurrected), St John and St Peter are placed in the piazza outside the church of San Filippo Neri; after a while, a statue of the Madonna, wearing a black veil in mourning, is carried out of the church by a group of swift-footed *portatori;* the veil is torn from her face as she 'runs' toward her resurrected Son, Easter; *Giostra Cavalleresca* Medieval tournament among rival neighbourhoods, last Sun in July.
Teramo *Luoghi Sonori* Concert series in various locations around town, Jan–Dec, T: 0861 248866,

www.istitutobraga.it; *Sacre Rappresentazioni* Processions bearing statues of Our Lady of Sorrow (during the night) and the Dead Christ (in the morning), Good Friday; *Sagra delle Virtù* The 'virtues' here are spring vegetables, which are cooked up in an immense pot in the cathedral square, to make a sort of minestrone; the celebration is mentioned by Poggio Bracciolini in his *Liber Facetiarum* (1438–52), 1 May; *Giugno Teramano* Theatre, opera, folklore and cuisine, June; *La Teramo Ignorata* Chamber music concerts in various locations around town, June, T: 347 197 8357, www.quintettocherubino.it; *Stagione Lirica e del Balletto* Opera and ballet, Nov–Dec.

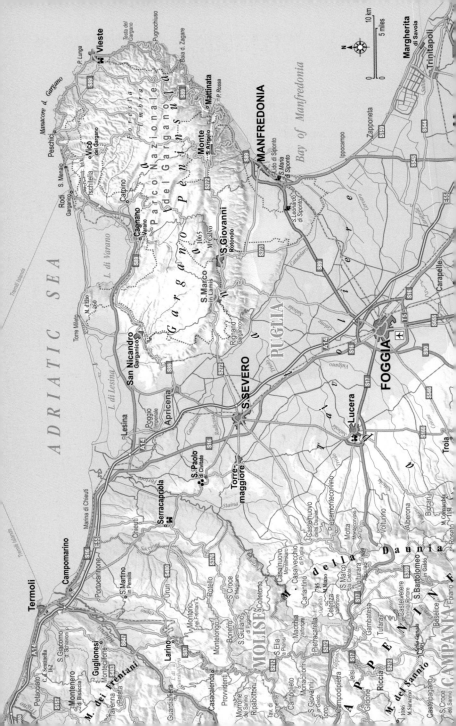

PUGLIA

Maps of Puglia are shown opposite (Foggia and the Gargano); on p. 438 (the coast to Bari); p. 470 (Alberobello, Taranto and the Murge), and p. 494 (Brindisi, Lecce and the Salentine peninsula.

Puglia occupies the extreme southeast of the Italian peninsula, from the 'spur' (Monte Gargano) to the 'heel' (Salentine peninsula) of the boot. For the most part it is flat, rising gently inland to a long plateau (Le Murge), with no considerable elevations except the Gargano promontory. It is the ancient *Apulia*, originally inhabited by the Pelasgians and the Oscans. Among its towns were several Greek colonies, including *Taras*. It flourished under the Roman rule which followed the defeat of Pyrrhus, and with the rest of southern Italy it has passed through the hands of innumerable overlords, its most prosperous period being under the Swabians.

The great period of church-building in Puglia was under the Normans, who combined diverse influences from France, Pisa, the Lombards and the Orient into the style known loosely as Apulian Romanesque (*see p. 455*).

As in Abruzzo and Lazio, there are still nomad shepherds in parts of Puglia. In these three provinces together there are about 3,000 kilometres of grassy drove-roads, known as *tratturi* (with side-tracks known as *tratturelli* or *bracci*), under the administration of the state, by which the sheep are driven up to the lofty pastures of Abruzzo in spring, returning to the Puglian lowlands in autumn.

Puglia largely consists of flat expanses of limestone, almost destitute of rivers, as the surface water disappears into the limestone fissures. The rainfall is very light, and the region deserves its epithet of *seticulosa* or thirsty. However, the soil is well cultivated. Wheat is the chief crop in the almost treeless plain of the Tavoliere della Puglia, known also as the Capitanata, around Foggia. Further south, vineyards predominate, with groves of olives, almonds and figs. The great Puglian aqueduct, the largest in the world, with 2,700 kilometres of channels, supplies drinking water to 268 communes in the region. From the sources of the Sele, on the west side of the Apennine watershed, it carries c. 15,000,000 litres of water per hour into Puglia.

FOGGIA & THE GARGANO

Entering Puglia from the north, by the motorway or railway that runs along the Adriatic shore, you gradually leave the rolling hills of Molise for much flatter country. Ahead stretches the great plain of Foggia, an area rich in prehistoric sites, few of which have been systematically excavated. In Roman times the plain was centuriated—that is, partitioned into farms of uniform area with a regular network of roads between them. This pattern, which can still be traced, gives the district its popular nickname, *tavoliere* (chessboard). Its modern prosperity was greatly increased by an improvement scheme of 1934–38. Photographic reconnaissance in 1945 revealed upwards of 2,000 settlements, many confirmed as Neolithic on excavation. Passo di Corvo, which is the largest known Neolithic site in Europe, has yielded tools, implements and masses of pottery.

Standing watch over Puglia's northern gateway are the fabulous Gargano peninsula and its offshoot, the quiet little archipelago known as the Tremiti Islands. Here you'll find respite from the hustle and bustle of the Puglian coast, as well as immense natural beauty. The region has more in common geologically with the eastern Adriatic than with the rest of Italy: the Gargano and the Tremiti Islands in fact form a single geological unit, composed largely of white limestone identical to that of southern Croatia. Unlike the neighbouring plain, they are densely forested, and the combination of glistening stone, dark forest and azure sea is unforgettable.

FOGGIA

Foggia (pop. 160,000), Puglia's northern gateway, is a city of modern aspect with important paper and textile mills. As the marketing centre of a vast agricultural region, it is also the focus of communication for northern Puglia.

HISTORY OF FOGGIA

Founded by the people of the abandoned Italic town of *Arpi* (the site of which may be traced 3km north), Foggia probably takes its name from the *foveae*, or trenches made to store grain. Frederick II often resided here; on Palm Sunday in 1240 he summoned the Third Estate to a *colloquia*, an event almost certainly noted by Simon de Montfort, who passed through Puglia shortly afterwards, embarking from Brindisi to join the crusade led by Richard of Cornwall, second son of King John of England. Frederick's third wife, Isabella, daughter of King John of England, died here in 1241, as did Charles I of Anjou in 1285.

In 1528 the French Viscount Lautrec took the town and massacred the inhabitants. It was almost totally destroyed by an earthquake in 1731, when the casket containing Frederick's heart was lost. Foggia became an important airbase in the Second World War and was much damaged by bombing, the remaining portions of Frederick's palace being destroyed.

The cathedral

From Piazza Cavour, the older part of the city lies to the northwest. Follow Via Lanza and Corso Vittorio Emanuele to Via Garibaldi. Here turn left, then immediately right into Via Duomo. The cathedral, built in 1172, retains part of its Romanesque façade and crypt; the remainder, shattered in 1731, was rebuilt in the Baroque style. An interesting portal with primitive bas-reliefs, brought to light in 1943 when bombs levelled the building which adjoined the cathedral, can be seen along the north flank.

The interior, built to a Latin-cross plan with a single nave, has modern (1932) stained-glass windows and, above the door, a painting of the *Miracle of the Loaves*, by Francesco de Mura. The Cappella dell'Icona Vetere, to the right of the presbytery, contains a Byzantine icon that was found in a pond in 1073, according to tradition. The restored crypt has vaulted ceilings and stout columns with delicate Romanesque capitals, possibly by Nicola di Bartolomeo da Foggia.

Museo Civico

Via Arpi, to the north, leads (right) to Piazza Nigri, where the small **Museo Civico** (*open Tues–Sat 9–1, Tues and Thur also 4–7, Sun 9–1; T: 0881 726245*) has sections on archaeology and painting. The archaeology rooms focus mainly on Daunian culture, with finds from Arpi, Ascoli Satriano (*Ausculum*), Lucera, Ordona (*Herdoniae*) and San Paolo di Civitate (*Teanum Apulum*), though there are also Neolithic ceramics, Gnathian ware (*see p. 486*) and tomb treasures of diverse provenance. The pinacoteca features the Neapolitan School (de Mura, Morelli, Palizzi), a group of local artists active in the 19th century (Altamura, Caldara, Dattoli, Parisi), and works by the Italian Modernists Carlo Levi and Renato Guttuso. A room dedicated to Umberto Giordano holds the local-born composer's piano, diaries, and the score of his best-known oeuvre, *Andrea Chénier*.

ENVIRONS OF FOGGIA

Several of the towns in the environs of Foggia warrant a visit. **San Severo**, the ancient centre of the area known as the Capitanata, is noted for its vines (Sansevero white is particularly dry and delicate). It is a starting point for exploring the Gargano. The church of San Severino has an elegant rose window in its Romanesque façade. The Biblioteca Comunale (Via Zannotti) includes the small Museo Alessandro Minuziano (*open daily 8.30–2 & 4–7; T: 0882 334409*), with Stone, Bronze and Iron Age finds, Daunian material of the 4th and 3rd centuries BC, Roman inscriptions (from *Teanum Apulum*), and medieval ceramics. There is also a section dedicated to the Grotta Paglicci and the Gargano in general, in the Stone Age.

Serracapriola, with a castle, stands on a hill near the border with Molise. Between the Ponte di Civitate, over the River Fortore, and San Paolo di Civitate lie the scanty ruins of the Roman *Teanum Apulum*, and, higher up, those of the medieval *Civitate*, where the Normans defeated and captured Pope Leo IX in 1053, immediately afterwards imploring his pardon, which was accorded and accompanied with a grant of the suzerainty of Puglia, Calabria and Sicily to Humphrey and Robert Guiscard.

LUCERA & TROIA

Lucera, a town with a magnificent castle, was a provincial capital until 1806 and preserves many relics of its former greatness.

HISTORY OF LUCERA

Luceria Augusta, already Roman in 314 BC, became a *colonia* under Augustus. Destroyed in 663 by Constans II, Emperor of Byzantium, it was rebuilt in 1233 by Frederick II, who repopulated it with 20,000 Saracens from Sicily, to whom he granted liberty of worship. It then took on the appearance of an Arab town. It became the stronghold of the Ghibellines in southern Italy and in 1254 was the refuge of Manfred and, later, of his widow. The city was taken in 1269 by Charles I of Anjou. After the revolt of 1300 Charles II massacred all the Saracens that he could not forcibly convert and repopulated the town with Provençal families.

The cathedral

The cathedral (Santa Maria Assunta), a curious blend of Romanesque and Gothic, was founded by Charles II of Anjou and built in 1300–17. It is one of the less altered monuments of its age. The simple façade has three Gothic portals, that at the centre incorporates Roman columns and sculptural representations of St Michael and the Madonna and Child. The low campanile is crowned by an octagonal lantern of the 16th century. The streets at the sides of the church lead round the protruding transepts to the magnificent **apse**, attributed to Pierre d'Agincourt, where massive buttresses and tall lancet windows betray an unmistakably French design.

The **interior** is built to a Latin-cross plan, with a tall nave and aisles separated by pointed arches on rectangular piers with attached columnar shafts. The nave and aisle ceilings are in wood, whereas those of the three polygonal apses are vaulted and ribbed. In the south aisle are a *Last Supper*, attributed to Palma Giovane, and an elegant pulpit of 1560, obtained by reworking a tomb of the Scassa family. The south apse contains two cenotaphs, one of 14th-century Neapolitan workmanship; and a 14th-century wooden Crucifix. Above the altar is a 15th-century fresco of the *Pietà*; on the walls are martyrs, apostles and saints frescoed by Belisario Corenzio.

The stone **high altar** came in part from Castel Fiorentino, the castle (14km northwest; now a ruin) where Frederick II died on 13th December 1250; the choir stalls date from the 17th century, the frescoes of the apse from the 18th century. In the north apse are a 17th-century tomb and a heavily repainted 14th-century wooden statue of the *Madonna della Vittoria*, commemorating the Angevin rise to power. In the north aisle can be seen a *Madonna with Sts Nicholas and John the Baptist*, by Fabrizio Santafede; a fine baptismal font with Renaissance baldachin; and a 15th-century tabernacle. Below the organ is the *Madonna delle Stelle*, a late 14th-century sculpture. To the right of the entrance is a relief of *God the Father*, of the 16th-century Neapolitan school.

The Museo Civico and castle

Opposite the cathedral stand the bishop's palace and Palazzo Lombardi, both 18th century. Via de' Nicastri, at the rear of the church, leads to the **Museo Civico Giuseppe**

Fiorelli (*closed at the time of writing*), which contains a Roman *Venus*, a fine mosaic pavement (1st century), terracottas (3rd century BC) and ceramics of the Saracen and Angevin period, as well as 17th-century paintings and ethnographical exhibits.

About 500m west of the town on an eminence (250m) stands the **castle** (*open Tues–Sun 9–2*), the most magnificent in Puglia, built by Frederick II in 1233 and enlarged by Charles I (1269–83). The enceinte of nearly 1km, with 24 towers, is still complete, and encloses the ruins of the Swabian palace. To the northeast of the town (10mins) are the ruins of a **Roman amphitheatre** (*closed for reconstruction at the time of writing*) of the Augustan period with two imposing entrance arches (reconstructed).

Troia

Troia, a small town founded in 1017 as a Byzantine fortress on the site of the ancient *Aecae*, commands a wide view. The **cathedral** (1093–1125) is perhaps the most remarkable example of the successful Puglian marriage of Byzantine sculptural ornament of Saracen inspiration to the Pisan Romanesque style. The well-proportioned façade, plain below (with blind arcades and lozenge motifs that continue around the sides and rear of the church) and of singular richness above (note the projecting lion and bull consoles and the beautifully carved moulding of the arch beneath the gable), is pierced by a rose window. The west and south doors (1119 and 1127), by Oderisius of Benevento, are in bronze; some panels are executed in high relief, others are incised. They show both Eastern and Classical influences, as do the reliefs of the lintel and the capitals above the main door. The apse has double tiers of free-standing columns. The sombre interior has three aisles separated by semicircular arches on columns with singularly rich capitals. In the penultimate bay is an ambo of 1169 with curious sculptures, formerly in the nearby domed 11th-century church of San Basilio (*shown by the cathedral sacristan*). The rich treasury contains various silver statues and liturgical objects, including a chalice by followers of the famous Florentine goldsmith Benvenuto Cellini (1521).

THE GARGANO

A mountainous peninsula rising in Monte Calvo to 1065m, the Gargano is still thickly wooded, especially with oak. These forested highlands were declared a National Park in 1991. The whole of the promontory is streaked with limestone, and the streams have no outlet except in the fissures, where they are swallowed up. There are many unexplored pot-holes and stalactite grottoes. The Gargano has the same geological composition as Dalmatia and in the Tertiary period was separated from Italy by a narrow stretch of water.

The most common approach to the Gargano is from Foggia by Road 89. Near the coast, on the south side of the road, are the ruins of an abbey whose 11th-century church (San Leonardo) has a simple façade with blind arcades, a plain portal and a small rose window. Along the left flank of the church is a richly sculptured doorway, probably 13th century, in a shallow porch with griffins in the impost blocks and (modern) columns supported by lions.

Santa Maria di Siponto

Sipontum, northeast of Foggia, was an ancient coastal town abandoned in 1256 probably on account of malaria. Conrad landed here in 1252 to claim the crown of Sicily. An important Daunian centre, it was conquered by Hannibal and, soon after, by the Romans. By the early Middle Ages it had become the chief port of northern Puglia and attracted the attention of the Lombard princes of Benevento, under whose dominion it remained from the 7th–11th centuries. It was occupied in 1039 by the Normans, under whom its influence extended over most of the Gargano promontory. In the 13th century the slow-quake phenomenon known as *bradyseism* caused much of its territory to degenerate into swampland, and the earthquake of 1223 virtually levelled the town. The inhabitants and the diocese were transferred to the new town of Manfredonia.

Little remains of the town proper, other than the scanty ruins visible from the road. But a few metres before the archaeological zone, in a small pine grove, stands **Santa Maria di Siponto**, the beautiful 12th-century cathedral, built above an underground church dating probably from the 5th century and modified in the 13th and later centuries. The simple but elegant façade, restored in 1975, has a fine doorway of local workmanship framed by a shallow porch and flanked by columns borne by lions. At the sides are blind arcades enclosing rhomboid decorative motifs, which are carried around to the south and east walls.

The interior, built to a square plan with two small apses and a central vault (reconstructed) carried by four rectangular piers, has a distinctly Oriental flavour. On three of the four walls are blind arcades with attached shafts, like those of the exterior. On the north wall you can see mosaic fragments from an early Christian basilica found nearby. The high altar is made from an early Christian sarcophagus; above is a copy of the *Madonna and Child* in the cathedral of Manfredonia. The circular chapel to the right of the altar is, in all probability, a later addition.

Steps on the north side of the church descend to the crypt, with a vaulted ceiling, four squat columns corresponding to the piers above, and 16 small columns, some ancient, with sculptured capitals of Classical and Byzantine design. Remains of a still earlier (4th–7th century) church—chiefly bases, capitals and fragments of columns—as well as some Roman and medieval tombs, have been discovered nearby.

Manfredonia

Manfredonia, on the bay of the same name, stands at the foot of the Gargano promontory. It was founded in 1256 by Manfred (1231–66), King of Sicily and Naples, and peopled by the inhabitants of Sipontum. Much of the town was destroyed by the Turks in 1620. The first act of Austrian aggression against Italy was carried out here in 1915, with the bombing of the railway station and the sinking of the *Turbine* in the bay. Now a developing industrial centre, Manfredonia is not a particularly pleasant place; however, it is an excellent starting point for excursions in the Gargano.

The **Castello Svevo-Angioino**, begun by Manfred in 1256, originally stood outside the town walls. The primitive core, which is still visible today, is a square plan with massive bastions—three cylindrical and one rectangular—at the corners and a tall enceinte surrounding a central court entered by archways in the east and west walls. Charles of Anjou enclosed this earlier fortification within a new set of walls, also built to a rectangular plan with cylindrical towers at the corners. The great spear-head bastion was added in the 16th century. The castle houses the **Museo Archeologico Nazionale del Gargano Meridionale** (*open daily 8.30–7.30; T: 0884 587838*), with an interesting collection of material from local excavations, notably 6th-century bronze and ceramic objects of Daunian workmanship and an unusual series of 6th- and 5th-century Daunian grave slabs, carved to represent people and animals. The church of **San Domenico** (1299, rebuilt in later centuries) has a Gothic doorway and 14th-century frescoes. The late 17th-century **cathedral**, of little architectural interest, contains a 12th-century wooden Crucifix.

Gargano limestone head of a warrior from a Daunian grave, one of 1,500 such pieces in the museum of Manfredonia.

Monte Sant'Angelo and the Foresta Umbra

This town of 16,000, situated on a south spur (884m) of Monte Gargano, owes its origin to the foundation of the **Santuario di San Michele Arcangelo** in a grotto, now in the centre of the town (*open daily, summer 7.30–7.30, winter 7.30–12.30 & 2.30–7.30, T: 0884 561150*). From the portico with two Gothic doorways (that on the right dates from 1395; the other is a modern imitation), flanked by a fine octagonal belfry of 1281, 89 steps descend to the inner vestibule built by Charles I of Anjou, where a bronze door made in Constantinople in 1076 fills the Romanesque portal. From here you enter the church, built of stone (1273), and finally the grotto, consecrated, according to tradition, by the archangel Michael himself, when he revealed it to St Laurence, Bishop of Sipontum, on 8th May 490. The grotto contains a 16th-century statue of St Michael and an 11th-century stone bishop's throne.

In front of the campanile steps lead down (left) to the ruined church of San Pietro, through which you enter the so-called **Tomba di Rotari**, probably a baptistery, with a cupola and 12th-century decorations. To the right is the church of **Santa Maria Maggiore** (1198). Above the town the massive ruined castle, started by the Normans, affords a wide view. In the lower town, the church of San Francesco contains the supposed tomb of Joan I. Here also is the **Museo delle Arti e Tradizioni Popolari del Gargano** (*open daily 9–1 & 2–7; T: 0884 562098*), with a collection of folk art.

From Monte Sant'Angelo you can follow the Valle Carbonara (leaving to the left a road that runs along the spine of the promontory via San Giovanni Rotondo to San Severo) then climb over the arid Piano della Castagna towards the **Foresta Umbra** (marked). The Rifugio Foresta Umbra (29km) is a charmingly situated shelter in the heart of the forest. Descend by Vico del Gargano, through olive and orange groves, and through the splendid Marzini pine forest to the coast road.

San Giovanni Rotondo

This small village stands on a plateau below Monte Calvo (1065m), the highest peak of the Gargano. In 1177 it belonged to Joan Plantagenet, wife of William II of Sicily. The 14th-century church of **Sant'Onofrio** and the contemporary towers are interesting, but the **Rotonda di San Giovanni**, a baptistery of uncertain date, is more mysterious. It was reputedly built on the ruins of a Temple of Jupiter. At the west end of the village, the tree-lined Viale dei Cappuccini leads to the 16th-century convent of **Santa Maria delle Grazie**. The conventual church, consecrated in 1629, contains a much-venerated *Madonna delle Grazie*. In the crypt of the modern church nearby is buried Padre Pio da Pietralcina (1887–1969), the Franciscan monk canonised in 2002, whose reputation for working miracles has made the village a centre of pilgrimage. The Fiorello La Guardia Hospital, named after a mayor of New York City, is supported largely by American funds. Renzo Piano designed the dramatic church of San Pio da Pietralcina.

Along the coast

Beyond Manfredonia the coast road winds its way through stunning scenery to Mattinata, in rocky, wooded country, and the modern **Vieste**, a small town with a castle in a fine position on the northeast tip of the Gargano. Celestine V was arrested here in 1295 by order of Boniface VIII. **Peschici** is a picturesque village perched above a rocky cliff. Beyond, the headland of Monte Pucci commands an admirable view along the coast. San Menaio has a sandy beach that extends to **Rodi Garganico**, a fishing village below hills ringed with orange groves and pine woods. The **Lago di Varano** is a shallow lagoon separated from the sea by a strip of sand dominated by Cagnano Varano. From here a new, fast road flanks the shallow lake, Lago di Lesina, to Termoli. Road 89 bears inland via San Nicandro Garganico and the last foothills of the Gargano to Foggia.

THE TREMITI ISLANDS

The Isole Tremiti, a group of small limestone islands 22km north of the Gargano peninsula (*see map on pp. 4–5*), are known throughout Italy for their natural beauty, clear waters and mild climate. These are the *Insulae Diomediae* of Classical mythology, where the companions of Diomedes, hero of Troy, allegedly changed into herons.

Of the three main islands, the largest, **San Domino**, was the scene of the death of Julia, daughter of Augustus. In recent years the island has experienced a sudden rush of 'green' tourists drawn by its pine forests, marine caves, and other natural assets.

San Nicola, though smaller than San Domino, is the administrative centre of the group and is of greater interest from a historical point of view. From the marina at the southwest tip of the island, a narrow, walled road passes through two medieval gates to the town proper and the abbey church of **Santa Maria a Mare**, founded in 1045 and rebuilt in the 15th, 17th and 18th centuries. From the abbey's foundation, in the 8th century, to the mid-12th century, it was governed by the Benedictines of Monte Cassino. In the 12th century it passed to the Cistercian Order and was fortified by Charles II of Anjou. In the 14th century corsairs, who managed to enter the convent by trickery, laid waste to it and massacred the monks; it was not until 1412 that the Laterans of San Frediano di Lucca, by concession of Gregory XII, took over the complex, embellishing the church and building a new defensive system. Their monastic fortress successfully held off an assault by Süleyman II in 1567.

In 1783, after a period of gradual decline, Ferdinand IV of Naples suppressed the abbey, the possessions of which had once included vast areas of the Gargano, the Terra di Bari, Molise and Abruzzo, establishing in its place a prison. From 1926–1945 it was used for the detention of political prisoners.

The 15th-century façade of the church incorporates a Renaissance doorway (1473) flanked by double Corinthian columns and surmounted by weather-worn sculptures. The interior has retained its original 11th-century plan, with a rectangular nave preceded by a double narthex. The painted wooden ceiling dates from the 18th century and replaces an earlier dome. The colourful mosaic pavement, of which substantial areas remain, was executed c. 1100. The church contains a 12th-century painted Graeco-Byzantine *Crucifixion* and a fine, early 15th-century Venetian polyptych. The island of **Capraia** (also called Caprara or Capperara), to the north of San Nicola, is interesting for its many small rock arches or *archetielli*. **Pianosa**, 20km northeast, is not served by commercial passenger craft.

PRACTICAL INFORMATION

GETTING AROUND

• **By air:** Helicopters fly twice daily in summer and around Christmas and Easter, from Foggia to the Tremiti Islands. Contact Alidaunia, www.alidaunia.it; or airport information, T: 881 650539, freephone T: 800 949 944.
• **By road:** You can make a 223km circuit of the Gargano peninsula from Foggia via Manfredonia, Vieste and Peschici (short cut: Foggia to Peschici via Monte Sant Angelo) to Rodi Garganico and back to Foggia. Travel time is 3hrs 30mins, plus stops.
• **By rail:** Fast Intercity trains run to Foggia from Pescara in c. 2hrs and from Bari in c. 1hr. Eurostar trains run from Rome via Caserta in c. 3hrs 30mins; and from Naples in c. 3hrs. Local trains from Foggia to Manfredonia, 36km in c. 25 mins, with bus connections to Vieste.
• **By sea:** The Tremiti Islands are best reached by hydrofoil from Ortona (*map p.*

368; daily June–Sept, 2hrs), Vasto (daily June–Sept, 1hr), Termoli (daily all year, 50mins), and Rodi Garganico (daily June–Sept, 50mins). Ferries daily from Termoli (1hr 40mins). Details in Rodi Garganico from Adriatica di Navigazione, c/o VI.PI, Piazza Garibaldi 10, T: 0884 966357; on San Domino, from Adriatica di Navigazione, c/o Cafiero, Via degli Abbati 10, T: 0882 463008. Also, Ortona: Adriatica di Navigazione, c/o Agenzia Fratino, Via Porto 34, T: 085 906 3855; Termoli: Navigazione Libera del Golfo, at the harbour, T: 0875 704859 (ferries) and Adriatica di Navigazione, c/o Agenzia Adriashipping, at the harbour, T: 0875 705343 (hydrofoils); Vasto, Adriatica di Navigazione, c/o Agenzia Massacesi, Piazza Diomede 3, T: 0873 362680.

INFORMATION OFFICES

Foggia Via Senatore Emilio Perrone 17, T: 0881 723650, ww.pugliaturismo.com, www.gargano.it
Manfredonia Piazza del Popolo 11, T: 0884 581998.
Vieste Corso Fazzini 38, T: 0884 707495 and Piazza Kennedy, T: 0884 708806.

HOTELS

Foggia
€€ **Cicolella**. Traditional, central, quiet and comfortable, with a good restaurant. open all year. Viale XXIV Maggio 60, T: 0881 566111, www.hotelcicolella.isnet.it
Manfredonia
€€ **Gargano**. Overlooking the sea, with antiques, plants and flowers, pool, tastefully furnished rooms, and an excellent restaurant. Viale Beccarini, 2, T: 0884 587621.

Mattinata
€€ **Baia delle Zagare**. In an olive grove overlooking the sea, with private beach. Open June–Sept. At Baia dei Mergoli, 17km northeast, T: 0884 4115, www.hotelbaiadellezagare.it
€€ **Dei Faraglioni**. As above, with views of the Faraglioni rocks. Open June–Sept. At Baia dei Mergoli, 17km northeast, T: 0884 49584.
€ **Apeneste**. On the outskirts of the town, surrounded by oleander, olive and lemon trees; good views, great cuisine. Piazza Turati 3, T: 0884 550743, www.hotelapeneste.it
Monte Sant'Angelo
€€ **Michael**. Simple but comfortable rooms and a scrumptious breakfast buffet on a terrace enjoying magnificent views. Via Reale Basilica 86, T: 0884 565 519, www.hotelmichael.com
Peschici
€ **Solemar**. In a pine grove 3km outside the town, towards Vieste; private beach, pool, cinema; closing time varies. At Baia San Nicola, 3km northeast, T: 0884 964186, hotel.solemar@tiscalinet.it
Tremiti Islands (San Domino)
€€ **Kyrie**. Quiet and comfortable, in a pine grove. Open April–Sept, T: 0882 663241.
€€ **Gabbiano**. Panoramic location, courteous staff, wholesome local cuisine, shuttle to harbour and beach. Open all year. T: 0882 463410, www.hotel-gabbiano.com
€ **San Domino**. Small, friendly and tranquil. Open all year. T: 0882 663404, hdomino@tiscalinet.it
Vieste
€ **Seggio**. In the old town hall, on a cliff above the sea, at the heart of the pedestrian district; pool and private beach. Open April–Oct. Via Vieste 7, T: 0884 708123.

RESTAURANTS

Foggia

€€ **Il Baraccio**. Trattoria famous for its skilfully prepared local delicacies. Closed Thur and 10 days in July. Corso Roma 38, T: 0884 583874.

€€ **Chacaito**. *Osteria* near a wonderful fruit and vegetable market. Closed Sun and Aug. Via Arpi 62, T: 0881 708104.

€€ **Da Pompeo**. Traditional trattoria in the historic city centre. Closed Sun and Aug. Vico al Piano 14, T: 0881 724640.

€€ **La Locanda di Malì**. Romantic restaurant offering fine creative cooking. Closed Mon, Tues and Aug. Via Arpi 86, T: 0881 723937.

€ **Zia Marinella**. Warm, friendly, central *osteria*. Closed Sun and mid-Aug. Via Saverio Altamura 23-31, T: 330 654510.

Mattinata

€ **Montesacro**. Farm serving country meals, in a grove of olives and almonds near the sea. Open daily, Jan and Feb by reservation only. Contrada Stinco, T: 0884 558941.

Monte Sant'Angelo

€ **Da Costanza**. Simple trattoria. Closed Fri (except in summer) and in winter. Via Garibaldi 67, T: 0884 561313.

€ **Medioevo**. Traditional restaurant. Closed Mon (except in summer) and Nov. Via Castello 21, T: 0884 565356.

San Giovanni Rotondo

€ **Antica Piazzetta**. Restaurant known for its regional food. Closed Wed, July and Jan. Via al Mercato 13, T: 0882 451920.

San Severo

€€ **Fossa del Grano**. *Osteria*, with good wine list, in an old granary. Closed Tues, Sat, Sun in July–Aug. Via Minuziano 63, T: 0882 241122.

LOCAL SPECIALITIES

Textiles are made by hand at **Carpino** (near Foggia) and throughout the Gargano; **Troia** is famous for its lace and embroidery. The best ceramics in the area are found at **Serracapriola** and **Torremaggiore**. The fishermen of **Vieste** are famous for their basketwork nets, called *nasse*.

FESTIVALS & EVENTS

Foggia *Festa dell'Incoronata* The Santuario Madre di Dio Incoronata, on the outskirts of town, marks the spot where the Virgin appeared to a peasant farmer in 1001; celebrated with floats, an all-night vigil and morning Mass, last Sat in April.

Lucera *Torneo delle Chiavi* Re-enactment of a medieval tournament, 14 Aug.

Manfredonia *Carnevale Dauno* Processions, folk theatre, dancing, and widespread consumption of a ricotta and wheat cake, the *farrata*, 17 Jan; *Mostra dell'Artigianato del Gargano* Superb local crafts fair, first week in Aug; *Sagra della Pizza Rustica* Not a traditional pizza, but a sort of vegetable pie, is served up with grilled lamb while youths compete in games and donkeys are raced, mid-Sept.

Monte Sant'Angelo *Pellegrinaggio in Onore di San Michele* A huge crowd of pilgrims converges, largely on foot, on the little sanctuary, 7–8 May.

Vico del Gargano *Messa Pazza* Unusual Mass marked by loud shouts and other forms of profanity symbolising the overturning of the order of nature caused by the death of Christ, Good Friday.

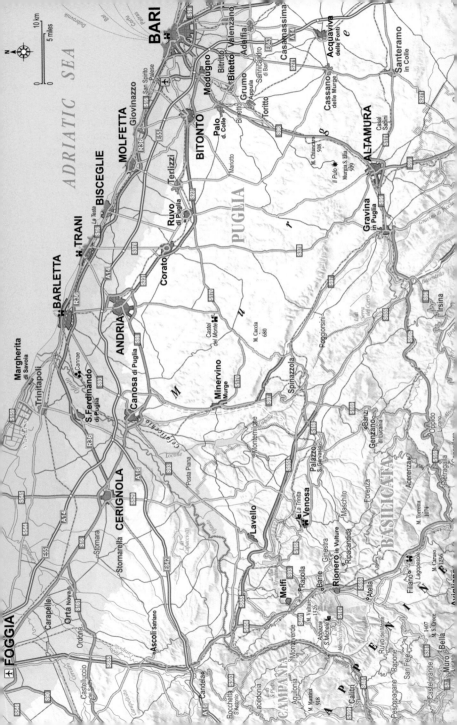

THE TERRA DI BARI

The area between Barletta and Bari possesses the richest architectural heritage on the Adriatic south of Venice. Here are the splendid Terra di Bari cathedrals, great churches that combine northern and eastern influences in a unique way, giving rise to a characteristic local style broadly referred to as the Apulian Romanesque (*see p. 455*).

BARLETTA

Barletta, an agricultural centre and port, with a considerable trade in vegetables and wine, has recently regained some of the prosperity it enjoyed in the Middle Ages, when it was Manfred of Hohenstaufen's favourite residence.

HISTORY OF BARLETTA

Archaeological evidence has demonstrated the existence of an indigenous centre on the site dating from the 4th or 3rd century BC. However, the first mention of the town—which was variously known as *Barduli*, *Baruli*, *Bardulo*, *Baretum* and finally *Barletta*—dates from Roman times. Under the Normans it became an important trade centre and fortress. Its population increased in 1083 with refugees from Cannae, who fled when the city was destroyed by Robert Guiscard.

Frederick II proclaimed his son Henry heir to the throne here in 1228, before embarking on a crusade. The inhabitants rebelled after the king's death, but the uprising was put down by Manfred, who established his court here. The city was the seat of the Archbishop of Nazareth from 1291 until 1818. It reached its greatest prosperity under the Angevins, and during this period traded actively with the Orient. Its merchant fleet was one of the finest in the region.

Here in 1459 Ferdinand I of Aragon was crowned King of Naples. In February 1503, while the French were besieging the town, the famous Challenge or *Disfida di Barletta* was staged as a means of ending the conflict (*see p. 441 below*).

Barletta was damaged by earthquakes in 1689 and 1731, and stricken by plague in 1656–57, after which it suffered a long period of decay. Since 1860 it has grown rapidly in wealth and size and it now hosts important electrical, chemical, automobile manufacture, leather-working and food-processing industries.

San Giacomo and San Sepolcro

From the west side of town, follow Corso Vittorio Emanuele, passing (right) **San Giacomo**, with its eccentric plan, pyramidal tower, and pointed arches. At the far end of the avenue stands (right) the *Colosso*, a 5th-century bronze statue, over 5m high, possibly representing the Emperor Marcian. The head and torso are original; the hands and legs were recast, somewhat clumsily, in the 15th century. The statue was restored in 1980.

Behind is the 13th-century **Chiesa del San Sepolcro**, built over an earlier church documented from the 11th century. The north flank has blind arcades with pointed arches enclosing monoforum windows and a good Gothic portal. The Baroque façade conserves, on the right, a small Gothic doorway; at the left corner stand the remains of the campanile brought down by the earthquake of 1456. The church was completely restored in 1972. The interior is built in the Burgundian Gothic style with three aisles, three apses and a shallow transept preceded by a vestibule or narthex incorporating a gallery in the upper part. The aisle ceilings have simple cross-vaults, whereas those of the nave and transept are ribbed. Over the presbytery is an octagonal dome, possibly of Byzantine inspiration. In the gallery are 14th-century frescoes representing the life of St Anthony Abbot, the *Annunciation*, and saints. The south apse contains a 16th-century Byzantine-style panel portraying the *Madonna di Costantinopoli*. The baptismal font, near the entrance door, dates from the 13th century.

The duomo

The duomo, nestled among the narrow streets at the end of Corso Garibaldi, was built in the 12th century, enlarged in 1307 and again in the 15th century; it underwent a thorough restoration in 1996. The tripartite façade has blind arcades, a rose window and a profusely carved monoforum window in the central section flanked by elegant bifora windows on either side. The main entrance dates from the 16th century. The lateral entrances, which belong to the original building, have historiated arches. An inscription above the left portal records the participation of Richard Coeur-de-Lion in the building's construction. The Romanesque campanile has monoforum, bifora and trifora windows on successive levels. The campanile, with its octagonal spire, was added in 1743.

The first four bays of the basilican **interior**, carried on antique columns, are built in the Apulian Romanesque style, with decorative bifora above the nave arcade. They date from the 12th century and reflect the plan and character of the original church. The remaining bays, which date from the 14th century, have pointed or rounded arches on compound piers and ribbed cross-vaults. The polygonal apse, with its ambulatory and shallow radiating chapels, was erected during the following century and shows French Gothic influence. It contains carved tomb slabs of various ages. The 13th-century tabernacle above the high altar was dismantled in the 17th century and reassembled, with modern additions, in 1844. The *Madonna della Disfida* (*see box opposite*) by Paolo de' Serafini da Modena (1387), the only signed work of that artist, hangs in the ambulatory. The fine pulpit on the south side of the nave was executed in 1267. Steps at the end of the north aisle descend to the crypt, where the semicircular apses of the 12th-century cathedral have been revealed by recent excavations.

In a room adjoining the church (*usually closed*) is a small collection of paintings and ecclesiastical objects, including some 13th-century illuminated codices.

THE DISFIDA DI BARLETTA

In 1503, at a time when the French and the Spanish were disputing possession of the territories of southern Italy, a French army besieged Barletta. When one of the French soldiers, Charles de la Motte, spoke slightingly of the valour of the Italians involved in defending the city, it was decided to try who was more valorous in mortal combat. Thirteen Italians and 13 Frenchmen met in deadly battle. Prospero Colonna and Bayard umpired the struggle, which ended in victory for the Italians. The champions were greeted by the clergy in procession, bearing aloft Serafini's *Madonna*, now in the cathedral. On the last Sunday in July the citizens of Barletta re-enact the (locally) famous Challenge for control of the besieged town. The Italians win today as they did then, amid a flurry of medieval pageantry.

The castle

To the northwest of the cathedral is the little **church of Sant'Andrea**, with a fine 13th-century portal signed by Simeone da Ragusa, and a *Madonna* by Alvise Vivarini (1483). The massive **castle**, to the east, was built in the 13th century on top of the earlier construction that hosted both the court of Manfred and Frederick II's assembly of barons and prelates at the time of the Third Crusade (1191–92). Later in the 13th century it was enlarged by Charles of Anjou to a design by Pierre d'Agincourt, and fortified again some 200 years later by the Aragonese, in the face of the impending Saracen invasion. The four corner bastions were erected in 1532–37 by Charles V to a plan by Evangelista Menga, architect of the castle of Copertino.

Within, the impressive court is lined by vaulted rooms, no doubt used as workshops, stables and barracks. On the east side a ramp mounts to the bastions. A fine staircase gives access to the first-floor rooms. Along the walls are three 13th-century windows, two of which bear reliefs of eagles in the tympana. The inner halls of the castle house the **Museo Giuseppe de Nittis** (*open Tues–Sun 9–1 & 3–7; T: 0883 578613*), displaying mainly finds from the battlefield at Cannae, and some interesting pieces of Daunian, Messapian and Apulian ceramics. A room overlooking the parade ground holds a 13th-century bust of Emperor Frederick II, possibly the only extant contemporary portrait of the emperor. The **Pinacoteca** in Palazzo della Marra (*open Tues–Sun 10–7; T: 800 961993*) has a modest collection of southern Italian painting, ranging from the 14th–19th centuries; some early modern paintings from northern Italy, and a fine collection of paintings, drawings and prints by Giuseppe de Nittis (1846–84), a native.

ENVIRONS OF BARLETTA

Andria

Four kilometres south of the motorway is Andria (pop. 90,000), the largest city in the province after Bari. Founded by the Normans c. 1046, it was sacked by the French in

1527 and again in 1799. Its earlier fidelity to Frederick II is recalled by the inscription on the Porta Sant'Andrea. The Gothic **cathedral** (*closed for restoration, yet again, at the time of writing*) is several times restored (the façade is a modern reconstruction), and has a large crypt with remains of sculptures and frescoes; here lie Yolande of Jerusalem and Isabella of England, two of Frederick's consorts. The Museo Diocesano (*closed at the time of writing; T: 0883 593032*) houses paintings, sculptures and decorative objects from several of the town's churches. Sant'Agostino (1230) has a highly individual 14th-century portal with rich decoration. In San Domenico is a bust of Francesco II del Balzo (1442), perhaps by Francesco Laurana.

Canosa

Canosa di Puglia, a flourishing agricultural and trade centre on a hilltop overlooking the Tavoliere, is the ancient *Canusium* which, according to legend, was founded by Diomedes after the Trojan War. It may well have been of Greek origin, as archaeological evidence (chiefly silver and bronze coins inscribed in Greek) and later records (its inhabitants were bilingual at the time of Augustus) suggest. In Antiquity the town was well known for its polychrome and red-figure pottery and large *askoi* decorated with relief figures, examples of which may be seen in the museums of Ruvo, Bari and Taranto. An early and steadfast ally of Rome, it supported her in the wars against Hannibal, taking in survivors from the Battle of Cannae (216 BC). This was its most prosperous period, with commercial activities at their peak. The town retained its importance after the opening of the Via Traiana, and in the 4th century AD it became the capital of the region. Its diocese, documented from AD 343 but moved to Bari following the destruction of the town by the Saracens, is the oldest in Puglia.

The **cathedral**, dating from the 11th century, is uninteresting externally. Within, the *chiesa antica* or old church is readily identifiable despite 17th-century alterations and modern additions (the latter corresponding to the first three bays of the nave). It is built to a Latin-cross plan, with five domes in the Byzantine manner and cross-vaults, in the aisles, carried on arches that spring from 18 antique columns. The columns, taken from the ancient monuments of Canusium, have beautiful white marble capitals with carved volutes and acanthus leaves. On the north side of the nave stands a masterfully carved pulpit of the 11th century. Behind the altar, with its modern tabernacle and 13th-century silver-gilt icon of the *Madonna della Fonte*, is a splendid **bishop's throne** borne by elephants and decorated with plant and animal motifs, carved by the sculptor Romualdo for Urso, Bishop of Bari and Canosa (1079–89). Steps in the aisles descend to the crypt, rebuilt in the 16th century. A door in the south transept leads to a small court where the remarkable **tomb of Bohemond** (d. 1111), son of Robert Guiscard, has a fine door fashioned from solid bronze by Roger of Melfi. The walls of the tomb are faced with marble. Within are two columns with good capitals and the simple tomb slab, inscribed 'Boamundus'. Around the walls of the court architectural fragments, inscriptions, and a Greek torso of the 4th century BC can be seen.

Adjacent to the church are the public gardens of the Villa Comunale, containing more architectural fragments. Across the town, Via Cadorna leads to the three **Ipogei**

Lagrasta, underground burial chambers excavated in 1843, which yielded a number of gold, ivory and glass objects, and a variety of vases, including the famous *Anfora dei Persiani*, now in the Museo Archeologico in Naples. The largest of the tombs has nine chambers and an interesting atrium with painted and stuccoed Ionic columns.

The **Museo Civico Archeologico** (*open June–Sept Tues–Sun 9–1 & 5–7; Oct–May 9–1 & 4–6; T: 0883 663685*) has a small collection of Canosan ceramic ware (the *askoi* are especially interesting for the reliefs that decorate their mouths), Greek and Roman material from the district, and finds from the nearby Tomba d'Urso (bronze helmet, jewellery, glassware), which also yielded objects now in the Museo Nazionale in Taranto. The ruined medieval **castle** incorporates large (1.5m by 1m) blocks of tufa from the ancient acropolis; the view ranges across the Tavoliere from the mountains of the Basilicata to those of the Gargano.

Ancient Cannae

On the banks of the Ofanto, the ancient *Aufidus*, some 10km nearer the sea, lies the site of *Cannae* (*open daily 8–7.45; T: 0883 510993*) where, in 216 BC, Aemilius Paullus and Terentius Varro, the Roman consuls, were defeated by Hannibal. Many Romans perished in the battle. The **Antiquarium di Canne della Battaglia** (*open as the archaeological site*) houses finds from the immense necropolis and the scanty remains of the ancient city, including native Apulian painted vases (among the oldest painted ceramic ware in Italy), ivories, bronzes and coins, and numerous other objects demonstrating the continuous importance of the site from prehistoric times to the Middle Ages. The Cittadella di Canne, situated on a hill above the museum, has been excavated in the more superficial strata only and shows mainly medieval remains.

To the north of Canosa is **San Ferdinando di Puglia**, a wine-producing centre. West of this is **Cerignola**, where Gonzalo de Córdoba defeated the French in 1503, two months after the Challenge of Barletta. **Margherita di Savoia**, on the coast, has an important salt field (the bromo-iodide salts are used for medicinal cures) and a good beach. **Minervino Murge**, south of Canosa, is known as the 'Balcony of Puglia' on account of its panorama.

Castel del Monte

Castel del Monte is by far the most important monument in this area. A massive octagonal castle with Gothic corner towers, it crowns an isolated peak (540m) of the Murge and is known as the 'Spy-tower of Puglia'. It was built by Frederick II c. 1240, and for 30 years was the prison of Manfred's sons. It is notable for its harmony of proportion, its fine windows in the Italian style and the principal entrance in the form of a Roman triumphal arch, most unusual for the 13th century. The interior (*open daily, summer 10.15–7.15, winter 9.15–6.15*) is built round an octagonal courtyard and has two storeys with spacious rooms, virtually identical in plan and decoration. The capitals of the pillars are remarkable for their beauty and variety. (*Official guides offer free tours in English, gratuity welcome. They can be found, in summer, at the information hut at the car park; in winter the information office in Andria, T: 0883 592283, can arrange a tour.*)

TRANI

Trani, a pleasant town with whitewashed buildings and a small harbour, is an important centre of the wine trade, its strong, dark red wines being mostly exported for blending.

HISTORY OF TRANI

The modern city succeeds the ancient *Tirenum* or *Turenum*, which probably dates from the 3rd or 4th century AD, although legend attributes its foundation to Tirenus, son of Diomedes, the Greek hero of Troy who ended his days in Daunia. Before the year 1000 it was, together with Bari, one of the easternmost outposts of the Roman Church. Under the Normans it was an important embarkation point for the Orient. Its commercial activity attracted considerable colonies of merchants from Genoa, Pisa, Ravello and Amalfi, as well as a large Jewish community. Its *Ordinamenta Maris* (1063) is the earliest maritime code of the Middle Ages.

The town enjoyed its greatest prosperity at the time of Frederick II, when it rivalled Bari in importance. Here in 1259 Manfred married his second wife, Helena of Epirus; here also (a few days after Conradin's execution) Charles of Anjou married Margaret of Burgundy. Trani suffered greatly from the struggle that shook Puglia under the Angevins, and in 1308–16 it engaged in a political and economic conflict with Venice. It repeatedly shifted its loyalty between the Angevins and the Aragonese, finally siding with the latter in 1435.

The cathedral

The cathedral (San Nicola Pellegrino), next to the sea, was begun at the end of the 11th century, over the earlier church of Santa Maria della Scala. Its imposing form and refined decoration, together with the dramatic beauty of its location (best appreciated at dawn) make it one of the most striking churches of Puglia.

The façade, reached by a flight of steps, has a richly sculptured portal with bronze doors by the native sculptor Barisano da Trani (1175–79), who also cast the doors of the cathedrals of Ravello, and of Monreale in Sicily. The iconographic and decorative schemes of both the bronze and the stone reliefs reflect Byzantine, Saracenic and Romanesque models. The door jambs are decorated with bas-reliefs of biblical scenes, plant and animal motifs, and geometric patterns that are carried over into the arch above. To either side, blind arcades with cylindrical shafts and finely carved capitals traverse the façade to enclose the lateral portals. The upper storey consists of a broad, smooth surface of warm stone pierced by a fine rose window and four smaller windows with carved surrounds. The beautiful, tall, 13th-century campanile stands upon a graceful archway open to the sea. The octagonal belfry and spire date from 1353–65.

The 12th-century cathedral of Trani, with its 13th-century campanile.

The flanks of the church are traversed by prominent blind arcading surmounted by a double clerestory. High up on the south transept are a second rose window and two large bifora, above a curious sculpture of two men and a bull. The triple apsidal ending, like the transepts, has finely-carved eaves with projecting animal corbels and, at the centre, a great window with a rich surround. More windows and carving can be seen on the north transept.

The **interior**, restored to its original Romanesque form, has a nave arcade of six semicircular arches supported by double columns. Above runs a triforium, the left and right halves of which are joined by a characteristic gallery spanning the west façade; and a clerestory with simple monoforum windows. The ceilings of the nave and transept are in wood, whereas those of the aisles have stone cross-vaults.

At the sides of the presbytery you can see fragments of a 12th-century mosaic pavement; in the chapel on the north side is a 13th-century relief of the *Crucifixion*. The crypt has an interesting vaulted ceiling carried on 28 marble columns with intricately carved capitals.

A door in the west wall admits to the lower church of **Santa Maria della Scala**, which may also be entered from the archway beneath the porch of the façade. The area of this church corresponds to that of

Detail of relief carving on Trani cathedral.

the nave above, and is divided into three narrow aisles by Roman columns, probably brought here from Canosa, supporting low cross-vaults. Here a Gothic tomb, Lombard sarcophagi (under the porch), some 14th- and 15th-century frescoes and fragments of an early mosaic pavement are to be seen. Beneath is the interesting **Ipogeo di San Leucio**, a burial area preserving fresco fragments. At Piazza del Duomo 4 is the **Museo Diocesano** (*open Tues–Fri 9.30–1 & 3.30–7, Sat–Sun 10–1; T: 0883 582470*), with Corinthian, Attic and Apulian ceramics, bronzes and ivories; and architectural and sculptural fragments and paintings, chiefly from the Middle Ages. Highlights are a 14th-century Burgundian ebony altar made for Charles of Anjou, and a contemporary icon representing St Nicholas and episodes from his life.

Other sights of Trani

Use as a prison has spoilt much of the **castle** (*open daily 8.30–7.30*), which was built for Frederick II in 1233–49 by Phillip Chinard, Stefano di Trani and Romualdo di Bari, as an inscription on the sea-wall records.

Near the harbour are the 15th-century Palazzo Caccetta, the Baroque chapel of Santa Teresa (adjacent); and by an arch over the street, the church of **Ognissanti**, erected by the Knights Templar in the 12th century. The latter is preceded by a sort of pronaos with a double file of piers and columns, beyond which three sculpted 13th-century doorways admit to the simple interior.

Of the four surviving Romanesque churches, Sant'Andrea, in the form of a Greek cross, is the oldest. San Francesco has a quaint, pleasant façade with a modest portal and an oculus; the interior has been redecorated in a Baroque style and contains three little Byzantine domes. Both churches flank Via Mario Pagano. Rising from the shore at the south edge of the town is the 11th-century Benedictine abbey of Santa Maria della Colonna, now a hall for temporary exhibitions.

BISCEGLIE & MOLFETTA

Bisceglie, a town that exports excellent cherries, has a Romanesque **cathedral**, begun in 1073 and completed in 1295. The façade, altered by Baroque additions, has an ornate central portal with a shallow porch borne by griffins on columns. Along the south flank is a Renaissance doorway with crude sculptures; more interesting is the apsidal end, with its richly decorated window and blind arcades. The interior, completely restored in 1965–72, is basilican in plan with compound piers and a graceful triforium above the nave arcade. Over the main entrance is a 13th-century relief of Christ with Sts Peter and Paul. The Renaissance choir stalls, brought here from the destroyed abbey of Santa Maria dei Miracoli, are carved with the likeness of 70 eminent figures of the Benedictine order.

The **Museo Civico Archeologico** is in the former monastery of Santa Croce (*Via Frisari 5; open Tues–Fri 8.45–12.45, Tues and Thur 8.45–12.45 & 3.45–5.30; T: 080 395 7576*). Highlights are the Palaeolithic and Neolithic tools and ceramics from the Grotta di Santa Croce and Cave Mastrodonato. The little church of **Santa Margherita** (1197), set in a courtyard in Via Santa Margherita, is one of the simplest achievements of the Apulian Romanesque style (*see p. 455*). Along the south side are three tombs of the Falcone family, the largest of which dates from the 13th century.

Molfetta's waterfront and west façade of the Duomo Vecchio.

Molfetta

Molfetta is an active commercial centre with light industries and one of the largest fishing fleets on the Adriatic. On the sea at the edge of the old town stands the **Duomo Vecchio** (San Corrado), an unusual building begun in 1150 but not completed until the end of the 13th century. The highly original design, probably of Byzantine inspiration, has a short nave covered by three domes, on polygonal drums, with pyramidal roofs. Compound piers with rounded arches separate nave and aisles; on top of the engaged columns are intricately carved capitals. More carvings (dating from the 13th century) may be seen in the second chapel on the south side. The west front of the church is without a façade, whereas the apsidal end, which presents, as elsewhere in Puglia, a flat wall masking the semicircular apse, has delicate interlacing blind arches, a fine window with a sculptured archivolt flanked by columns supported by lions, and two tall *campanili* of Romanesque design. You enter the church from the adjacent bishop's palace.

The Baroque **Duomo Nuovo** dates from 1785. The interior, asymmetrical in plan, is of harmonious design. The Museo Diocesano (in the bishop's palace) and the Museo

Archeologico (Seminario Regionale Pugliese) house local archaeological finds including Peucetian and Hellenistic ceramics (*open by appointment; T: 080 397 1559*).

Ruvo di Puglia

Ruvo di Puglia succeeded the ancient *Rubi*, famous for its terracotta vases (5th–3rd centuries BC). An excellent collection of these may be seen in the beautifully appointed **Museo Archeologico Nazionale Jatta** (*Piazza Giovanni Bovio 35; open Sun–Weds 8.30–1.30, Thur–Sat 8.30–7.30; T: 080 361 2848*). Exhibits range from the Iron Age to Archaic, Classical and Hellenistic Greece. Imported Corinthian and Attic ware of the 6th–4th centuries BC is particularly abundant, as are the Apulian red-figure vases of which Ruvo was the most important centre of production in the 4th and 3rd centuries BC. There are several large Canosan vases, an Athenian *krater* with the death of Thalos (late 5th century BC), Apulian *amphorae* with the story of Antigone (4th century BC), a Proto-Italic *krater* with stories of Hercules, and some amusing cups (*rhyton*) with human or zoömorphic shapes.

RUVO DI PUGLIA: CATHEDRAL

The 13th-century **cathedral** is a fine example of the late, richly ornamented Apulian Romanesque style. The vertical thrust of the façade, evident in the tall central gable and steep roof line, has been somewhat lessened by the widening of its base to accommodate the chapels added to the interior in later centuries. Along the edges of the roof, blind arcades spring from delicate human- or animal-head corbels, a motif that continues along the right flank of the building. High up at the centre of the façade is a superb 16th-century rose window, surmounted by a seated figure that some identify with Frederick II, others with an Apocalyptic personage. Below are a mullioned window (in the lunette, *St Michael* in bas-relief) and an oculus surrounded by angels' heads. On the ground level, the three portals stand beneath supporting arches that redistribute part of the weight of the massive wall above. The jambs and archivolts of the doorways are carved with figurative and decorative reliefs by local artists, in a style that fuses Lombard, French and Oriental elements. On either side of the main entrance are unusually slender columns borne by crouching telamones and surmounted by griffins. The sculptural decoration of the apse, transept and south flank of the church also merits close inspection. The campanile, set apart at the rear of the church, was originally a defensive tower.

The interior, like the façade, foreshadows the Gothic sensibility for soaring height and delicate ornamentation. It is built to a basilican plan with semicircular apses and high wooden ceilings in the nave and transept. Above the nave arcade runs a balcony on sculptured corbels; higher up is a graceful triforium articulated, as is the nave arcade, by pilaster strips. Recent restoration has closed off all but two of the lateral chapels. The tabernacle above the main altar is a modern construction.

Bitonto

Bitonto produces olive oil. Free tours of Bitonto are given, in English, by the police (!), who have been cross-trained as official guides (*T: 080 375 1014*). The town is renowned for its Romanesque **cathedral** (1175–1200), the most complete and harmonious in Puglia. The church follows a T-plan, the apse being concealed behind a single uniform wall surface that unites the arms of the transept and that is a recurrent characteristic of the Apulian Romanesque style. The façade, the design of which faithfully follows that of San Nicola in Bari (*see p. 456 below*), is divided into three parts by bold pilaster strips. Blind arcades surmounted by a chessboard cornice run along the pointed gable and the eaves above the aisles. The upper portion of the façade is dominated by the magnificent rose window, protected by a foliated archivolt on hanging columns. Below are bifora windows. The central portal has strongly projecting foliated arches resting on griffins surmounting columns borne by lions and topped by the pelican pecking her breast, a symbol of the Passion. Above the door, in the lintel, are reliefs of the *Annunciation, Visitation, Epiphany* and *Presentation at the Temple*; and, in the lunette, of the *Descent into Limbo*. The lateral portals have door-joints and architraves carved with plant motifs. A loggia on the left connects the façade with the 16th-century Palazzo de Lerma, now a tenement. Along the right flank, deep arches enclose lancet windows and, in the last bay, the Gothic Porta della Scomunica, with sawtooth mouldings of Siculo-Norman workmanship. Above runs a graceful hexaform gallery, with splendidly carved arches, columns and capitals; and a clerestory with intricate tracery in the windows.

The south transept is adorned with tall blind arcades surmounted by bifora and a rose window, with a handsomely carved architrave. On the east wall is a finely carved window, similar in form and workmanship to the main portal, and, higher up, a broad Moorish arch. The 13th-century campanile was remodelled in 1488 and in 1630.

The interior, simple and dignified, is built to a Latin-cross plan with three semicircular apses and a shallow transept. The nave arcade is borne by columns alternating with compound piers in a rhythmic order of two to one. The capitals are profusely carved. Along the aisle walls are half columns from which spring simple cross-vaults. The nave arcade is surmounted by a triforium, the two parts of which are joined by a 19th-century balcony on the west wall. Along the south side of the nave are a pulpit made with fragments of the high altar of 1240 and a magnificent ambo by Maestro Nicola (1229) with a bas-relief representing Frederick II and his family. Stairs in the aisles descend to the crypt with 30 fine columns.

In the alleys behind the cathedral, the church of **San Francesco** has a façade of 1286; that of the **Purgatorio**, bizarre reliefs of human skeletons above the portal (cf Gravina in Puglia; *p 455*). Several Renaissance *palazzi* survive in the town. The **Museo Civico Eustachio Rogadeo** (*Via Rogadeo 52; open Mon–Fri 9.30–1.30, Tues and Thur 9.30–1.30 & 3.30–6.30; T: 080 375 1877*) houses a small collection of antiquities from local excavations as well as a gallery of paintings by 19th- and 20th-century regional artists.

BARI

Bari, the capital of Puglia, is the second largest town in southern Italy (pop. 353,000) and a frequent port of call for ships bound for the eastern Mediterranean. It has important oil refineries.

Bari has grown steadily in wealth and population over the last century and a half, expanding to over ten times its previous size. The present city consists of three parts; the old town, new town and industrial area. The **Città Vecchia**, where the major medieval monuments are located, stands compactly on a peninsula. It is characterised by a maze of narrow, winding streets where life is still closely tied to the maritime activities of the adjacent port. Its peculiar, baffling town plan (it is almost impossible to wind your way from one end of the quarter to the other without getting lost) protected the inhabitants from the wind as well as from their enemies (Saracen invaders were lured into the narrow streets and blind alleys and attacked from the windows and rooftops).

The **Città Nuova** or modern quarter, broadly laid out to a chessboard plan with wide, straight avenues, is the financial and administrative centre of the city. The museums, theatres, concert halls and university (one of two in Puglia, the other being at Lecce) are also located here. The industrial area spreads inland, sandwiched between the city proper and the semicircular ring of satellite towns.

Via Sparano da Bari—the high street—bisects the new town, connecting the Città Vecchia at one end with Piazza Umberto I and the railway station at the other. Corso Vittorio Emanuele II, running east and west, divides the modern city from the old town. In Piazza della Libertà, an expansion of the corso, are the Municipio, the Teatro Puccini, the *prefettura* and a monument to Puccini.

HISTORY OF BARI

The ancient *Barium* was founded by the Illyrians, civilized by the Greeks and developed as a commercial centre under the Roman Empire. Seized from the Romans by the Ostrogoths, who in turn lost it to the Byzantines, it eventually came under the rule of the Lombard dukes of Benevento. In 847 it became a Saracen emirate, only to be liberated, some 34 years later, by Emperor Louis II. After the fall of Sicily to the Saracens it became the capital of the Byzantine province of Lombardy and, in 975, the seat of the 'catapan' or Byzantine governor.

In the 11th century the city became one of the more important Adriatic ports in Italy, rivalling Venice, with whose help it was freed from a Saracen siege in 1003. The anti-Byzantine revolts that shook the town and much of north-central Puglia in the first half of the century paved the way for the Norman conquest of the region, which was made final in 1071 with the fall of Bari to Robert Guiscard. In 1087 the remains of St Nicholas of Myra, patron saint of Russia, stolen from Asia Minor by sailors from Bari, were brought here to be deposited in the basilica of San Nicola (begun in 1089). In the following years the city became a major religious centre: at the Council of Bari in 1098, St Anselm of Canterbury defended the doctrine of the procession of the Holy Ghost against the Greek Church. In 1156 the town rose against the Normans. As a reprisal William the Bad levelled it to the ground, except for the shrine of St Nicholas.

Bari flourished under Frederick II (who granted it considerable powers and privileges, despite the dubious loyalty of the townspeople), but it declined under the Angevins. At the end of the 15th century it passed into the hands of the Sforza, and Isabella of Aragon, widow of Galeazzo Sforza, held her court here. At her daughter Bona's death in 1558 it became part of the Kingdom of Naples and, like many southern Italian towns, suffered the grievous effects of absentee government. Torn by famine (in 1570 and 1607), class strife and internal political struggles, it fell into a century-long period of decay. The plague of 1656–57 claimed the lives of four out of five inhabitants, reducing the population to a mere 3,000. In the 18th century Bari was subject to the Austrians, then to the Bourbons; the latter, under Ferdinand IV, drew up an ambitious plan for enlarging the city. This, however, was not to be carried out until 1813, when Joachim Murat issued a decree authorising construction of a Borgo Nuovo outside the old town walls.

The castle

To the north, beyond Piazza Massari, is the Castello Normanno-Svevo. The castle was built by Frederick II over an earlier fortress, in 1233–39 and extended with massive bastions by Isabella of Aragon in the 16th century. It is frequently used for special

exhibitions (*open daily except Wed 9–7; T: 080 528 6111*). Its predecessor saw the traditional meeting of Frederick and St Francis in 1221. The earlier structure, which
stands at the centre of the complex, is readily distinguishable from the 16th-century
additions. It is trapezoidal in plan, with a tall enceinte made of warm brown tufa laid
in rusticated rows, and block-like corner towers. You reach it by crossing the moat
(now a public garden) to a vaulted entrance hall, from where an archway on the right
leads to the outer courtyard. Here the walkway leads around the massive south tower
to a second archway with 13th-century bas-reliefs, the entrance to the elegant atrium.
Beyond lies the inner courtyard. The more monumental rooms are used to house the
Gipsoteca del Castello (*open as the castle*). The vaulted hall on the west side contains
a collection of plaster-cast reproductions of sculptural and architectural fragments
from Romanesque monuments in Puglia. On the floor above are the offices of the
Soprintendenza ai Monumenti e Gallerie di Puglia and laboratories for the restoration
of paintings.

The cathedral

To the east lie the narrow streets of the old town. One block west is the cathedral, an
apsidal church of the 12th century, built over the remains of an earlier church
destroyed by William the Bad in 1156. Basilican in plan, with shallow transepts surmounted by an octagonal drum, it is one of the most noteworthy medieval cathedrals
of Puglia. The façade is Romanesque in spirit, with a modern rose window and three
Baroque portals incorporating the simpler 12th-century doorways. Deep arcades run
along both flanks, surmounted by a gallery that corresponds to the triforium level of
the interior. Two towers, of which that on the south side was damaged by earthquake
in 1613, rise just east of the transepts and are joined at the rear of the church by a
wall that masks the apse. The east window, a masterpiece of Apulian sculpture, is set
beneath a hanging baldachin and ornamented with plant and animal motifs of Eastern
inspiration. The cylindrical structure on the north side, now the sacristy, was built in
the 11th century as a baptistery and converted to its present function in 1618.

The **interior** has been restored to its original simplicity, with a nave and two aisles
supported by tall, slender columns probably taken from the earlier church. Above the
rounded arches of the nave arcade runs a false matroneum, which opens directly onto
the side aisles. The nave contains remains of a 14th-century marble pavement with a
rose design matching that of the façade. Steps in the crossing mount to the raised
presbytery; the dome above rises to a height of 35m.

In the semicircular main apse marble choir stalls and a bishop's throne recomposed
from fragments of the original can be seen. The ciborium on the high altar and the
marble pulpit in the nave are likewise modern reconstructions. The north apse contains remains of 13th- and 14th-century frescoes and the tomb of Bishop Romualdo
Grisone (d. 1309). A door in the north aisle opens onto the sacristy, and steps at the
ends of both aisles descend to the Baroque crypt.

Excavations below the church floor have brought to light an early Christian basilica dating from the 8th–10th centuries, with extensive remains of a mosaic pavement,

now visible in the south apse. In the archives is a precious early 11th-century *Exultet*, an illuminated scroll with medallions of Greek saints and liturgical scenes on the verso. Also of interest are the late 11th-century *Benedizionario* of Apulian workmanship and two smaller *Exultets*. More works from the cathedral and the diocese are preserved in the bishop's palace (*shown by appointment; T: 080 521 2725*).

THE APULIAN ROMANESQUE

The Norman unification of southern Italy was to have important consequences for the architecture of the region. By 1056 Robert Guiscard had conquered Calabria and Apulia, while his brother Roger annexed Sicily (under Arab dominion), thus preparing the ground for the Kingdom of the Two Sicilies (instituted in 1130). The Normans favoured a programme of 'Latinisation', pursued by the Church of Rome in territories that were heavily imbued with Greek culture. They were responsible for the diffusion of Benedictine monasticism on the one hand, and the reconstruction of several town cathedrals on the other. The art of this period is defined as Romanesque and is characterised by a deliberate rediscovery of Classical forms. Yet it remained a unique kind of Romanesque, particularly in Apulia. The style has the massive solidity, rounded arches and flat ceilings found in the contemporary architecture of northern Europe, though here embellished with delicately detailed ornamental features of Byzantine or Saracen origin. In its last phase, the Apulian Romanesque aspired to an elegance and grace which in northern Europe was to become a guiding aesthetic principle. This architectural taste is coupled with rich and eclectic decorative schemes that unabashedly combine Byzantine, Norman, Pisan, Lombard and Provençal motifs.

The most typical expression of the style is the magnificent Basilica of San Nicola in Bari, built after the arrival of the saint's relics from Turkey in 1087. The sanctuary soon became an important site for pilgrims and crusaders leaving the port of Bari for the Holy Land. At the same time it was also a palatial church of the Norman princes, reflecting northern European building types, particularly in the façade. It was to this model that the builders of later churches turned for inspiration, at least initially. The new principles introduced at San Nicola served as a model for the cathedrals of Trani, Bari and Barletta and, at the very end of the 12th century, for Ruvo and Bitonto. The influence of Byzantium was never forgotten, however, as is shown in the cathedrals of Canosa, Siponto, Troia (which also follows Pisan models) and, somewhat later, Molfetta.

Painting at this period remained attached to Byzantine prototypes, and Romanesque art is best illustrated in sculpture. Most of the sculptural output was linked to the architectural fabric of the cathedrals or applied to church fittings such as episcopal thrones, pulpits, altar screens and paschal candelabra. The marble throne in the cathedral of Canosa (1079–89; *see p. 442*) is of interest, being supported by two elephants, inspired by Islamic bronzes (possibly from Iran). Of a different character and outstanding quality is the throne in San Nicola di Bari, commemorating Bishop Elia (founder of the church): the three caryatid figures holding the throne at the front, the two lions at the back, and the overall decoration are reminiscent of Classical sculpture and represent the most mature expression of Romanesque art in the south. A.M.

The Basilica di San Nicola

From the north flank of the cathedral follow Strada del Carmine and Strada delle Crociate to (right) the **Arco di San Nicola**, a large Gothic arch adorned with a relief of the saint (this is an area of town dear to pickpockets: watch out). Pass beneath and emerge in a small piazza dominated by the Romanesque basilica of San Nicola, the first great church built by the Normans in Puglia.

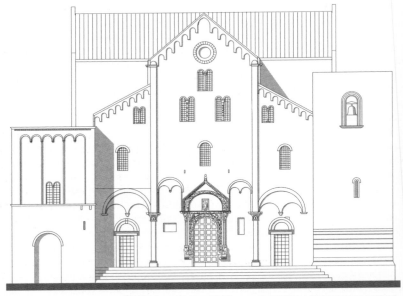

SAN NICOLA DI BARI: MAIN FAÇADE

The basilica was founded in 1087 to receive the relics of St Nicholas, stolen from Myra in Lycia by 47 sailors from Bari. It stands in the centre of four *piazze*, known as the Corti del Catapano, after the Byzantine governor's (catapan's) palace, which once stood here. Owing something to the churches of Caen, but deriving more from Lombard models, San Nicola became the model for the cathedral and the inspiration of later Apulian churches.

The exterior

The majestic façade, flanked by unfinished towers, is clearly divided into three parts reflecting the tripartite division of the interior. The tall central section terminates in a steep gable, whereas the lateral sections end in gently sloping semi-gables. The entire roofline is edged with blind arcading that culminates in the large, slightly pointed arch at the apex. The vast surface of the façade is enlivened by an oculus and eight arched windows, of which the uppermost are mullioned. Lower down its flatness is relieved by blind arches and attached columns. The central portal is set beneath a shallow porch with a pointed gable surmounted by a sphinx and carried by two bulls. The surface surrounding the door and the arch and gable above are richly carved with ornamental and symbolic motifs combining Arabian, Byzantine and Classical influences.

Tall, deep arcades, which become noticeably shallower in the arms of the transept, run along both flanks of the church, surmounted by a graceful gallery below the eaves of the roof. In the third arch on the north side is the magnificent **Porta dei Leoni**, so called after the lions that support the columns at the sides of the doorway. The sculptural decoration, including two figures of months on the impost blocks and scenes of chivalry below the arch, are signed by the sculptor Basilio. Another fine doorway is to be seen on the south side. The east wall, like that of the cathedral, masks the apsidal endings of the nave and aisles. The bas-relief of the miracles of St Nicholas below the central window dates from the 15th century.

The interior

The nave and aisles of the interior are separated by tall, stilted arches on marble columns with elaborately carved capitals. The three great transverse arches were added in 1451; the church seems to have been completed c. 1105, although it was not consecrated until 1197. An arched choir screen on tall columns with fine Romanesque capitals (note particularly that on the left) separates the nave from the transept. Beyond it is the high altar. The **bishop's throne**, probably made for the council of 1098, stands in the apse below the monument (1593) of Bona Sforza, Queen of Poland and Duchess of Bari.

The crypt, reached by steps in the aisles, has 28 columns with diverse capitals; the vaulted ceiling was freed of its stuccoes in 1957. The altar contains the relics of St Nicholas, said to exude a 'manna' to which miraculous powers are attributed; the silver and gold reliefs were executed in 1684 by Domenico Marinelli and Antonio Avitabili over a Byzantine icon donated in 1319 by the King of Serbia. Notice the mosaic detail of the floor and the low bench in the apse. In the galleries above the aisles are housed the remains of the Treasure of St Nicholas, together with fragments of paintings and sculpture brought to light during the recent restoration.

San Gregorio

On the north side of San Nicola is San Gregorio, an 11th-century church with fine windows and façade, and three semicircular apses. The Romanesque interior has particularly good capitals. The Museo di San Nicola (*Largo Abate Elia 13; open by appointment; T: 080 573 7254*) preserves a small collection of religious and historical objects.

Pinacoteca Provinciale

Lungomare Nazario Sauro leads southeast to the Palazzo della Provincia. On the top floor is the **Pinacoteca Provinciale** (*open Tues–Sat 9.30–1 & 4–7, Sun 9.30–1; T: 080 541 2421*) containing 11th–19th-century works, mainly by southern Italian artists.

Room 1: Medieval sculptural fragments and paintings of local provenance, including low reliefs, fragments of capitals, a charming polychrome wood *Madonna and Child* from Basilicata, and two fine icons of the 13th century, representing St Margaret and St Nicholas, from Santa Margherita, Bisceglie.

Room 2: In the first part of the room are 11th-, 12th- and 13th-century sculpture and paintings, notably architectural details that fell from the rose window of San Nicola in 1943, when an American ammunition ship blew up in the harbour. The second part of the room hosts 15th-century panels for altarpieces produced by the Venetian painters Antonio and Bartolomeo Vivarini for the churches of Surbo, Altamura, Andria and Modugno; especially noteworthy is Bartolomeo Vivarini's *Annunciation* for the Chiesa Matrice, Modugno, a small work commissioned by the Venetian clergyman Alvise Canco; at the end of the room is a *presepio* composed of fragmentary figures that were once painted in naturalistic colours, by the Puglian sculptor Stefano da Putignano.

Room 3: Dominant here is Giovanni Bellini's *St Peter Martyr*, painted for the Indelli Chapel in the church of San Domenico in Naples; the painting is set away from the wall to give a glimpse of the fine drawings by the artist on the back. Also in the room are a small *St Peter*, a *Pietà with Saints*, a *Head of a Saint* and minor paintings by anonymous artists.

Room 4: Devoted to Renaissance painting in Puglia, showing affinities with Neapolitan trends of the period.

Room 5: The display highlights a fascinating neo-Byzantine trend fostered in the Terra di Bari during the 16th century by artists who came to the area from the eastern Mediterranean after the fall of Constantinople, and their followers. The works include a *Madonna and Saints* by Donato Bizamano, showing a mixture of Eastern and Venetian elements, a fine panel with miniatures of the lives of Christ and the Virgin by Giovanni Maria Scupula; and a polyptych by an anonymous eastern Adriatic artist known by the initials ZT. The other great 16th-century trend, Mannerism, is represented by Marco Pino (*Holy Trinity*).

Room 6: The Venetian school returns with three outstanding paintings executed for Bari cathedral: *Sacra Conversazione* by Paris Bordone, *Virgin in Glory with Saints* by Paolo Veronese and a *St Roch* by Jacopo Tintoretto, completed in 1594 (after the artist's death) by Leonardo Corona.

Rooms 7–9: Seventeenth-century painting by Neapolitan artists and local painters trained in Naples, which eventually replaced Venice as the leading point of reference for the cultural élite of Puglia. Conventional painters working in the tradition of Domenichino, for whom local patrons expressed a preference, and the more radical *caravaggeschi* (Andrea Vaccaro, Matthias Stomer) are both represented.

Ecstasy of St Francis, by Luca Giordano.

Rooms 10–11: Room 10 is a corridor lined with glass cases displaying examples of popular ceramics. Room 11 has a (wood-block) printed tapestry by Petrus Wouthers of Antwerp.

Room 12: Here are two large genre scenes by the early 18th-century Neapolitan painter Giuseppe Bonito and, in a small showcase, a composition of statuettes (of shepherds) possibly inspired by the paintings.

Room 13: Dramatically placed so that it is framed by the marble doorway is Luca Giordano's painting of *St Peter of Alcantara*, who was Puglian by birth. The original study for the painting is also displayed here. The room contains other works by Giordano (*Deposition of Christ*, *Departure of Rebecca*) and by his follower Andrea Miglionico, altarpieces by the local painter Nicola Gliri, and, in a large glass case, an *Adoration of the Magi* with putti and shepherds from the Caleno Presepio.

Rooms 14–15: Rococo painting, represented in particular by the Puglian artists Corrado Giaquinto (who worked in Rome, Naples, Madrid, Turin and Vienna) and Oronzo Tiso, a follower of the Neapolitan master Francesco Solimena.

Room 16: The tone changes abruptly as you enter this room, which hosts 19th-century works of more secular subjects on a smaller scale, for middle-class patrons. There are several paintings by the local artist Francesco Netti (1832–94), as well as works by Telemaco Signorini, the Macchiaiolo School, Francesco Galante of the Posillipo School, and a small *Wooded Landscape* attributed to Corot.

A separate section of the gallery, dedicated to the **Anna and Luigi Grieco collection**, provides an outstanding panorama of 19th- and early 20th-century Italian painting by a number of distinguished artists including Giuseppe de Nittis, Telemaco Signorini, Massimo Campigli, Giorgio Morandi, Giorgio de Chirico and Mario Sironi.

Other sights in Bari

The Museo Archeologico, formerly in the Palazzo dell'Università (or dell'Ateneo), is being moved to new quarters at Santa Scolastica, in the Città Vecchia. It is not known when it will re-open.

The Facoltà di Agraria (Via Amendola) has a modest botanical garden (*open by appointment; T: 080 242152*); and the Museo Etnografico Africa Mozambico (*Convento Cappuccini, Via Gen. Beltomo 9, at Poggiofranco; open by appointment; T: 080 551 0037*), houses a small but interesting collection of ethnographical material from East Africa.

In the southern suburbs (Via Bitetto) is Renzo Piano's brilliant white **Stadio San Nicola** (designed 1987, completed 1990). Its unabashedly modern design has won it the nickname *Astronave* ('Spaceship'). One of the finest examples of late 20th-century architecture in Italy, it is well worth driving by even if you are not a football fan. Those who do attend a game will find the stunning sail-like awnings, inspired by those that shaded ancient Roman amphitheatres, offer welcome shelter from the Mediterranean sun.

Bari Military Cemetery, west of the city, is the burial place of 2,000 officers and men killed in local fighting.

NB: For Ostuni and the coast beyond Bari, see p. 484.

SOUTH OF BARI

Several places of interest along the coast and in the hills lie just outside the city limits of Bari. **Modugno** is a large town with a 17th-century campanile. The ancient church of San Pietro (or San Felice), 3km southeast on the Bitetto road, is the sole survival of the medieval town of Balsignano. **Palo del Colle** has a 12th-century cathedral. Its railway station also serves **Bitetto**, where the cathedral (San Michele), originally 11th century, was remodelled in 1335 using Romanesque forms. The handsome façade has a richly-decorated central doorway, with reliefs of the Madonna and Child in the lunette, Christ and the Apostles on the architrave, and New Testament scenes on the doorposts. At the northeast corner of the church stands a Romanesque campanile, probably belonging to the original building. The Baroque bell-tower to the left of the façade probably dates from 1764. The interior has been extensively altered, especially in the 16th century, but recent restoration has returned it more or less to its 14th-century form. It is basilican in plan, with long, narrow aisles, wooden ceilings, slightly pointed arches and a triforium. Behind the main altar is an *Assunta* by Carlo Rosa (1656).

ALTAMURA

In the midst of a lonely landscape lies Altamura, a flourishing agricultural and industrial centre built along the top of a ridge.

HISTORY OF ALTAMURA

Altamura was a Peucetian centre of considerable importance, the name of which is still unknown. The ancient city was destroyed by the Saracens and the area remained uninhabited until 1230, when Frederick II founded a new town on the site of the former acropolis, with a population of Italians, Greeks and Jews drawn from neighbouring villages by the concession of special privileges.

In the centuries that followed, the town was granted in fee to the del Balzo and Farnese families, among others. In 1799 it was ruthlessly sacked and burned by the *Sanfredisti* under Cardinal Ruffo (*see p. 24*) for its adherence to the Parthenopean Republic. It became a major intellectual centre in the 18th century and possessed its own university from 1748 until the end of the century. Altamura was the seat of the first provisional government of Puglia during the Risorgimento.

Piazza Unità d'Italia marks the entrance to the town. From here Viale Regina Margherita descends to the station, passing the Strada Panoramica, from which considerable remains of the 5th-century BC Peucetian city walls may be seen. Approximately 3700m in circumference, the walls stand over 4m high in some areas, with an average thickness of c. 5m.

The **Porta di Bari**, originally a medieval gateway, was later absorbed by the massive Palazzo del Balzo. Corso Federico II di Svevia, beyond, leads to the heart of the old town. To the left of the gateway are remains of the 13th-century walls that give the town its name (*Altamura*, 'high walls'). Pass, on the left, the little church of **San Niccolo dei Greci**, erected in the 13th century by Greek colonists, where the Orthodox rite was celebrated until 1601. The simple but attractive façade has a rose window and an interesting portal decorated with Old and New Testament scenes in bas-relief. Beyond, the corso ends in Piazza Duomo, with its monument to the citizens of Altamura who were slain in the sack of 1799.

The cathedral

The cathedral of the Assunta is one of the four Palatine basilicas of Puglia (the others are San Nicola di Bari and the cathedrals of Barletta and Acquaviva delle Fonti). Begun by Frederick II in 1232 and rebuilt after the earthquake of 1316, it was further altered in 1534, when its orientation was inverted and the main portal and rose window were dismantled and reassembled in their present position, on what was formerly the apse.

The façade stands between two 16th-century *campanili*, to which Baroque pinnacles were added in 1729. In a loggia beneath the pediment can be seen a figure of the *Assunta*, flanked by *St Peter* and *St Paul* above the arch. Below is the beautiful recessed **rose window**, with delicate fretted stonework and multiple bands of ornate carving. The Gothic window of 1232, which originally stood in the apse wall and which was removed to make way for the rose window, is now located in the left portion of the façade, next to three coats of arms, the largest of which bears the arms of Charles V.

The 14th–15th-century **main portal** is one of the most richly decorated doorways of Puglia. It is set beneath a shallow porch with four slender columns and a pointed gable, within which bands of moulding carved with foliate motifs and scenes from the life of Christ establish a formal and visual link between the doorposts and the delicately pointed arches above. In the lintel is a relief of the *Last Supper*. The lunette contains an exquisitely carved *Madonna and Child with Angels*.

Along the unaltered north flank of the church, broad semicircular blind arches enclose slender lancet windows and the elegant Porta Angioina, named after Robert of Anjou whose arms, together with a Gothic inscription commemorating its construction, appear above. Between the tops of the arches and the roof run 12 trefoil windows with intertwining arches. The transept, a 16th-century addition to the church, incorporates a tall Gothic window from the earlier façade.

The vast, sombre three-aisled basilican **interior** retains its original flavour despite the 19th-century additions. The nave is divided into three broad bays by semicircular arches on piers alternating with columns with good capitals. Above the nave arcade is a triforium with semicircular arches on slender columns, also bearing interesting capitals. The aisles contain a number of paintings, chiefly by local artists. The inlaid choir stalls, the bishop's throne and the carved marble pulpit all date from the mid-16th century.

Museo Archeologico

Via Santeramo 88. Open Mon–Sat 8.30–7.30, Sun and holidays 8.30–1.30; T: 080 311 7679.

The museum contains material from excavations at Belmonte, Modugno, Paolo del Colle and the Pulo di Altamura (*see below*). There are some intriguing Bronze Age pots, bronze and ceramic ware from tombs dating from the 8th–5th centuries BC, locally painted pottery from the 6th–5th centuries, a bronze helmet and Gnathian and Peucetian ware; also medieval exhibits, notably a French enamel box of the 13th century.

Around Altamura

In the environs of Altamura you can visit numerous *specchie*, free-standing sepulchral monuments of a type quite common in prehistoric Puglia. Interesting excursions may be made to the **Pulo**, 7km northeast of Altamura, a circular sinkhole 500m in diameter and c. 75m deep, inhabited in the Stone Age; and to **Casal Sabini**, a village 9km east on the Santeramo road, where there are several Bronze Age rock-cut tombs, as well as Peucetian trench-graves dating from the 6th–3rd centuries BC. The site lies to the right of the road just beyond the village.

GRAVINA IN PUGLIA

Gravina in Puglia is set in a breathtaking position on the edge of a deep ravine. It succeeds the Peucetian centre of *Sidion*, which in Roman times became known as *Silvium*, probably located on the nearby hill of Petramagna, today known as Botromagno. During the Barbarian invasions its inhabitants took refuge in the *gravina* or ravine, and many continued to live in its limestone caves even after the present town began to take shape around the 5th century. This town was destroyed in the 10th century by Saracen mercenaries, and was occupied in the following century by the Normans. In 1420 it passed to the Roman Orsini family, who held it in fee until 1807. The old town is interesting for its winding streets and ancient houses with balconies supported by corbels.

The old centre

In the centre of town is Piazza della Repubblica, flanked by the much-altered Palazzo Orsini. From here Corso Matteotti leads to Piazza Notar Domenico, where the **church of the Purgatorio** (or Santa Maria dei Morti) has a bizarre portal with a *memento mori* of reclining skeletons in the tympanum. The columns, carried by bears, allude to the Orsini family (*orso* = bear) who commissioned the building in 1649. Within are a painting of the *Madonna and Saints* by Francesco Solimena and the tomb of Ferdinando III Orsini (d. 1660).

To the left of the church is the Biblioteca Finya, founded by Cardinal Angelo Antonio Finya (1669–1743). From here a narrow street on the left descends to the Rione Fondovico, the oldest quarter of the town, where the church of **San Michele di Grotti** is hewn entirely out of the rock. The interior has five aisles and a flat ceiling borne by monolithic piers. There are scant remains of frescoes, and in one corner, human bones which tradition attributes to the victims of the Saracen attack of 983. More of these are heaped together in the Grotta di San Marco, above.

The duomo and Museo Civico

In Piazza Benedetto XIII is the **duomo**, originally of 1092, enlarged in 1420, destroyed by fire in 1447 and rebuilt in 1482. The basilican interior has three aisles separated by semicircular arches on columns with finely carved capitals. The gilded wooden ceiling incorporates rather indifferent paintings. Above the fourth altar on the south side is a 16th-century relief of the *Presentation of the Virgin*. The wooden choir stalls date from 1561. The former seminary now houses a small but fascinating **Museo Civico Archeologico** (*open Tues–Sun 9–1 & 4–8; T: 080 322 1040*) featuring full-scale reconstructions of the tombs of two Peucetian warriors, complete with their weapons and burial treasures, and another reconstruction, of a 3rd-century BC family cave-tomb.

Palazzo Pomarici Santomasi and district

Returning to Piazza Notar Domenico, take Via Ambrazzo d'Ales and Via Lelio Orsi to **Palazzo Pomarici Santomasi**. Here are the collections (*open Tues–Fri 9–1 & 4–7, Sat 9.30–12.30 & 4.30–6.30, Sun 9.30–12.30; T: 080 325 1021*) donated to the city by this prominent local baron in 1917. They include archaeological material from Botromagno, coins and medallions, a section devoted to rural life, a reconstruction of the Byzantine crypt of San Vito Vecchio with 13th-century frescoes of local workmanship, as well as architectural fragments and ethnographical collections. The pinacoteca has works by 17th- and 18th-century artists, notably Ludovico Carracci and Francesco Guarino.

Nearby is the small church of **Santa Sofia**, in the presbytery of which you can glimpse the tomb of Angela Castriata Scanderbeg, wife of Ferdinand I Orsini (d. 1518). The Renaissance church of **San Francesco** has a fine rose window and sculptured portals; the Baroque campanile dates from 1766. Also worthy of attention is the church of the **Madonna delle Grazie**, near the station, the unique façade (1602) of which incorporates three crenellated towers in rusticated stone and an enormous eagle with outspread wings in low relief.

PRACTICAL INFORMATION

• **By air:** AMTAB Bus 16 runs hourly from 5am–11pm from Piazza Moro, in Bari, to Palese Airport, 8km west of the city, in 35–40 mins. There is also a shuttle (Tempesta) which makes the run in 5–10mins less. Airport website, www.seap-puglia.it, or T: 080 580 0200, freephone T: 800 949 944.
• **By road:** Autostrada A16 from Naples to Bari crosses extraordinarily beautiful countryside, offering broad, open horizons and dramatic skies in addition to gently rolling hills and vast forests. From Cerignola the coastal towns are conveniently reached by a new road (16b) running parallel to the old coast road to Bari and slowly being extended southwards. It has replaced Road 16 beyond Bari, and some parts are open as far as Maglie, in the Salentine peninsula. The A14 is also the quickest way to reach the area from Taranto and the Ionian region. Be aware that highway robbery is still common in the area, and the Carabinieri discourage visitors from travelling the more isolated country roads.
• **By rail:** The towns in this section lie on the main rail lines from Rome, Naples and Milan to Bari, Brindisi and Lecce. Eurostars make the run from Rome to Bari in 4hrs 34mins, stopping at Barletta; Intercity trains from Pescara reach Bari in 2hrs 50mins, stopping at Barletta and Trani. The main line from Bari to Taranto touches upon Modugno. Secondary lines run from Gioia to Altamura and Gravina in Puglia, and from Bari to Altamura and Matera. Schedules and fares at www.trenitalia.it.

Bari Assessorato Regionale al Turismo, Corso Sonnino 177, T: 080 540111, www.pugliaturismo.com; Azienda per la Promozione Turistica, Piazza Moro 33a, T: 080 524 2361; Ufficio Informazioni e di Accoglienza Turistica, Piazza Moro 32a, T: 080 524 2244.
Barletta Corso Garibaldi 208, T: 0883 531555.
Trani Piazza Trieste 10, T: 0883 588830.

Andria
€ **Lama di Luna**. Nine bright rooms in a historic farm complex renovated to Feng Shui bioarchitectural standards, with a restaurant serving natural foods. Closed Jan–March. At Montegrossa, T: 0883 569505, www.lamadiluna.com
Bari
€€€ **Palace**. An elegant and well-managed hotel conveniently located on the edge of the old town. Open all year. Via Lombardi 13, T: 080 521 6551, palaceh@tin.it
€€ **Mercure**. A registered landmark encompassing a Neoclassical villa and a large park; comfortable, refined rooms, competent staff, pool, sauna, gym. Open all year. Villa Romanazzi Carducci, Via Capruzzi 326, T: 080 542 7400, mercure@villaromazzi.com
€€ **Vittoria Parc**. In a garden in a

northern suburb of Bari; modern and comfortable, with a shuttle van to the city centre. Open all year. Via Nazionale 10f, Palese, T: 080 530 6300, avasi@tin.it

Bisceglie

€€ **Salsello**. A modern, well-managed place in a large park on the beach just outside the town. Open all year. Via V. Siciliani 32, T: 080 395 5953, www.hotelsalsello.com

Margherita di Savoia

€€ **Delle Term**. Large and somewhat impersonal, but on the sea with great views, luminous well-furnished rooms, spa and private beach. Open April–Oct. Via Garibaldi 1, T: 0883 656888.

Trani

€€ **San Paolo al Convento**. Simple but elegant rooms in a former monastery of the 15th century, on the waterfront. Open all year. Via Statuti Marittimi 111, T: 0883 482949.

€ **Royal**. Centrally located in a Liberty-style town house; quiet, comfortable rooms. Open all year. Via de Robertis 29, T: 0883 588777.

RESTAURANTS

Andria

€€ **Antica Cucina**. Very good regional cuisine and wines. Closed Mon and July. Via Milano 73, T: 0883 521718.

€€ **Arco Marchese**, *Osteria* serving great seasonal dishes. Closed Tues and two weeks in Aug. Via Arco Marchese 1, T: 0883 557826.

€€ **Madama Camilla**. Lovely old farm serving local delicacies, outside in summer, on the road to Castel del Monte. Closed Mon and Jan. SS 170, T: 0883 546545.

€€ **Masseria Barbera**. Fine old farm with great local fare, on the road to Minervino. Closed Mon and late Aug. SS 97, T: 0883 692095.

€€ **Taverna Sforza**. Trattoria-pizzeria with rooms and good views. Closed Tues and late Jan. SS 170, T: 0883 569996.

€€ **Tenuta Cocevola**. Good county restaurant with garden and views. Closed Mon. SS 170, at Cocevola.

€ **Antichi Sapori**. Wholesome family-run trattoria. Closed Mon and a few days in July and Aug. Piazza Sant'Isidoro 12, at Montegrosso, T: 0883 569529.

€ **Au Coq d'Or**. *Osteria* in the hills just outside of town. Closed Mon and mid-Aug. Via Santa Maria dei Miracoli 259, T: 0883 291361.

€ **Locanda de la Poste**. Creative interpretations of seasonal dishes of the region. Closed Wed and two weeks in Aug. Via Bovio 49, T: 0883 558655.

Bari

€€€ **Santa Lucia**. Haute cuisine *alla pugliese*, famous especially for its creative renderings of traditional fish dishes. Closed Mon and late Dec–early Jan. Lungomare Starita 9, T: 080 534 7579.

€ **Al Focolare da Emilio**. Restaurant-pizzeria serving simple but delicious food. Closed Sun evening, Mon and Aug. Via Principe Amedeo 173, T: 080 523 5887.

€ **Osteria delle Travi**. Simple, traditional trattoria in the old town. Closed Sun evening, Mon and two weeks in Aug. Largo Chiurlia 12, T: 330 840438.

€ **Verde**. Simple restaurant-pizzeria. Closed Sun and mid-Aug. Largo Adua 19, T: 080 554 0870.

Barletta

€€ **Baccosteria**. Warm atmosphere, delicious food, excellent wines. Closed Sun evening, Mon and Aug. Via San Giorgio 5, T: 0883 534000.

€€ **Il Brigantino Uno**. Good fish restaurant by the sea, with panoramic terrace, garden and pool. Open all year. Viale Regina Elena 19, T: 0883 533345.

€€ **Cascina del Borgo**. Lovely garden restaurant known for its fresh seasonal cooking. Closed Mon. Via Canosa 315, at Palombaro, T: 0883 510940.

Corato

€€ **Corte Bracco dei Germani**. Country estate offering great seasonal dishes. Closed Tues. Via Ruvo, T: 080 872 5344.

€€ **Il Mulino**. Characteristic restaurant. Closed Mon and Jan. Via Castel del Monte 135, T: 080 872 3925.

Gravina in Puglia

€ **Osteria di Salvatore Cucco**. Simple *osteria* on the edge of the old town. Closed Sun evening, Mon and mid-Aug. Piazza Pellicciari 4, T: 080 326 1872.

Minervino Murge

€ **La Tradizione**. Trattoria with good traditional fare. Closed Thur, Sun evening and a few days in Sept and Feb. Via Imbriani 13, T: 0883 691690.

Molfetta

€ **Bistrot**. Simple, straightforward cooking in the old town, near the harbour. Closed Wed, Sun evening and Aug. Corso Dante 33, T: 080 397 5812.

€€ **Borgo Antico**. Fine seafood restaurant by the water. Closed Mon and Nov. Piazza Municipio 20, T: 080 397 4379.

Palo del Colle

€ **La Stalla del Nonno**. Wine-bar serving hot and cold meals. Open evenings only, closed Sun and Aug. Via XXIV

Maggio 26–28; T: 080 629598.

Ruvo di Puglia

€ **L'Angolo Divino**. Wine-bar serving hot and cold meals, including good vegetarian dishes. Open evenings only, closed Mon and two weeks in Aug. Corso Giovanni Jatta 11, T: 080 362 8544.

€€ **Ristor**. Restaurant offering country cooking from the Murge. Closed Mon and July. Via Alberto Mario 38, T: 080 361 3736.

Trani

€€ **La Nicchia**. Excellent seafood restaurant with a strong local following. Closed Thur, Sun evening and July. Via San Gervasio 69, T: 0883 482020.

€€ **Melograno**. Good regional cooking in a warm atmosphere. Closed Wed and Jan. Via G. Bovio 187, T: 0883 486966.

€€ **Torrente Antico**. Good creative cooking and great wines. Closed Sun evening, Mon, July and early Jan. Via Fusco 3, T: 0883 487911.

€ **Ai Platini**. Fresh seafood in an *osteria* in the old city centre. Closed Mon and Oct. Via Commeno 16, T: 0883 482421.

LOCAL SPECIALITIES

Bari Stoppani, at Via Roberto da Bari 79, is a famous pastry-maker. De Carne, at Via Calefati 128, is a venerable old delicatessen with fine regional specialities and ready-made takeaway dishes. The Enoteca de Pasquale, at Via Marchese di Montrone 91, is a wine shop with an extraordinarily wide variety of Puglian wines. Il Germoglio, at Via Puntignani 204, has organic foods, from jams to cheeses to pasta. Marazia, at Via Manzoni 217, and Veneto, at

Corso Cavour 125, are two bakeries selling traditional breads, *pizze* and *foccace*.

Gravina in Puglia is known for its ceramics, as well as for baskets and other straw goods.

Molfetta Pasticceria Barese, at Via Cavallotti 15, is the place for *bocconotti, spume di mandorla, cassatine, postaccioli* and other local pastries.

FESTIVALS & EVENTS

Andria *Processione dei Misteri* Procession featuring the town's relic—a piece of the Crown of Thorns—and wooden sculptures representing scenes from Christ's Passion, Good Friday.

Bari *Festival Organistico Internazionale* International organ-music festival, Jan–May, at Parrocchia Santa Croce, Piazzetta dei Frati Cappuccini 2, organfestivalbari@libero.it;
Take Five Jazz festival, Feb–March;
San Nicola Celebrated with a colourful historical parade of St Nicholas and the *Processione dei Pelligrini* (procession on the sea) on 8 May, in commemoration of the arrival in the city of the saint's relics. Bari also honours the saint's traditional feast day, 6 Dec; it was his legendary generosity (mentioned by Dante in *Purgatorio* XX, 31–33) and the nearness of his feast to Christmas that led Sanctus Nicolaus (Santa Claus) to be associated with Father Christmas;
Fiera del Levante Inaugurated in 1930 to increase Bari's trade with the Levant, this international trade fair is held annually near the Punta San Cataldo, Sept;
Festival Internazionale Time Zones Sulla Via delle Musiche Possibili

Contemporary music festival, Oct–Nov, info from Via Abbrescia 970, T: 080 5581587, www.timezones.it;
I Lunedì della Musica Music festival, Oct–May at Parrocchia Santa Croce, Piazzetta dei Frati Cappuccini 2, organfestivalbari@libero.it

Barletta *Certame Cavalleresco* Also known as the *Disfida*, this festival re-enacts the celebrated 16th-century contest between French and Italian knights (*see p. 441*), 13 Feb.

Bitonto *Processione dei Misteri* Overnight procession of the Mysteries of the Passion, from dusk on Good Friday to dawn on Easter Saturday. It moves at a snail's pace through the town;
Santi Cosma e Damiano Immense historiated *cerri* (candlesticks) and statues of the saints are carried in procession, 26 Sept.

Cerignola *Madonna di Ripalta* To celebrate the Virgin's role in saving a group of children kidnapped by brigands, her statue and children dressed as angels are paraded through town on a colourful float, second Sun in May;
Festa del Lavoro Giuseppe di Vittorio, the founder of Italy's labour unions and a native of Cerignola, is celebrated, appropriately enough, on Labour Day. His image is paraded through the streets by representatives of the various trades, including farmers on tractors adorned with olive branches and sprigs of wheat, 1 May.

Molfetta *Vergine dei Martiri* A noisy crowd, playing music and setting off fireworks, accompanies a bejewelled statue of the Virgin on a procession over land and sea, 8 Sept.

Ruvo di Puglia *Settimana Santa* (Holy

Week) The Easter Week celebrations in Ruvo include three days of processions—the Eight Saints (representing figures from the Holy Sepulchre) on Thurs, Christ bearing the Cross followed by barefoot *penitenti* on Fri, and the Resurrected Christ on Sunday—when the *Quarantene*, allegorical figures of Lent, are blown up with fireworks, Maundy Thursday–Easter Sunday.

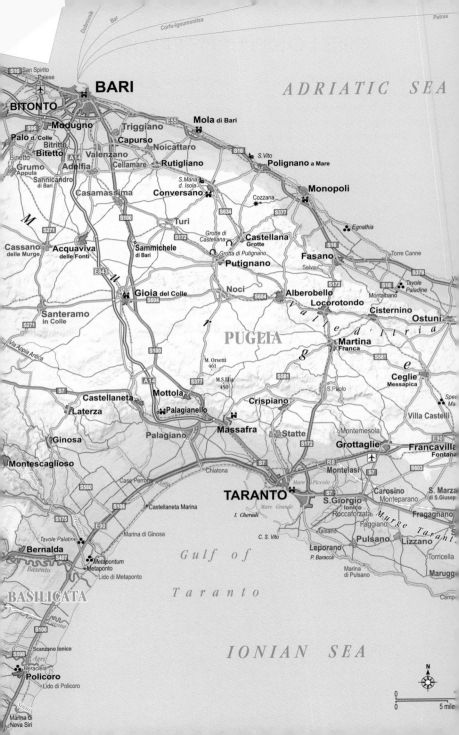

THE LONELY INTERIOR

This region embraces the rocky highlands between Bari and Taranto, the inhabitants of which took refuge in the Middle Ages in caves in the deep, narrow ravines (*gravine* in Italian) to escape the Saracen massacres. Later, as more conventional settlements grew up on the cliff-tops nearby, the caves were frequently made into chapels and decorated with rough frescoes or carved designs. The finest examples of this unusual architectural genre are to be found at Matera, in neighbouring Basilicata (*see p. 299*); but there are many others strewn about the region, such as those at Massafra. Between the two towns, in the country around Castellaneta (which, with its pristine whitewashed houses is well worth a stop) is another fascinating form of local architecture, the *masseria fortificata*, or fortified farm. Many of these walled agricultural complexes, which usually include a noble residence for the landowner, simple but harmonious peasant homes, and barns and other outbuildings, are now being turned into country inns.

SOUTH ACROSS THE PLATEAU

Capurso has a Renaissance baronial palace and a venerated icon of the Madonna (reputedly found in a well) in the 18th-century church of the Madonna del Pozzo. At **Sammichele di Bari**, a former Serbian colony, the 17th-century castle houses the Museo della Civiltà Contadina Dino Bianco (*open Tues–Fri 4–8 or 9, Sat–Sun 9–12 & 5–10 or 11; T: 080 891 8157*) with over 5,000 exhibits documenting rural life and peasant culture in the 18th and 19th centuries.

Gioia del Colle

Gioia del Colle is a busy market town of strong medieval character, with a massive, austere **castle** that was begun at the end of the 11th century and enlarged by Frederick II, who used it mainly as a hunting lodge. The fortress is built to a rectangular plan with the four walls of the enceinte facing the cardinal points. The walls and towers are heavily rusticated and originally displayed a single, impregnable surface to the outside, the windows being later additions. The interior has been extensively altered; nevertheless, the grace and refinement of the original structure and of the Angevin and Aragonese additions are still visible. According to tradition, the castle was the birthplace of Manfred, son of Frederick II and Bianca Lancia, whom the emperor, out of jealousy, imprisoned in the smaller of the two towers.

The rooms now house the Biblioteca Comunale and the small **Museo Archeologico Nazionale** (*open daily 8.30–7.30; T: 080 348 1305*), displaying material from the nearby excavations at Monte Sannace, where explorations in 1957 and 1961 revealed an unidentified Apulian settlement, believed to be a major Peucetian town. The extensive site (*open Wed–Sun 8.30–3*) includes remains of houses, public buildings, city walls and an acropolis, and in some places the street plan can be discerned. The defensive walls (including the remains of a gate) average 4m in width and reach 6m in height. The necropolis, in part composed of small tombs beneath the floors of houses, also extends beyond the city walls. It has yielded much material now in the museums of Gioia, Bari and Taranto.

Acquaviva delle Fonti

The name of Acquaviva reflects the abundant and accessible water supply that distinguishes this now-prosperous agricultural district from neighbouring areas. The elegant **cathedral**, a Norman edifice begun under Roger II, was transformed in the 16th century in a late Renaissance style. The bipartite façade has a delicate rose window, bold pilasters and a triangular pediment surmounted by statues of the Madonna and Child at the apex, and of saints at the ends. Free-standing columns borne by lions, a vestige of the earlier Romanesque building, support the broken pediment above the tall central doorway. In the lunette is *St Eustace with the Stag*, in bas-relief. The **Municipio**, formerly the Palazzo dei Principi, erected in the 17th century by the de Mari family, has an open loggia crowned by a decorative course of niches and masks running the length of the façade. The two towers belong to the Norman castle that originally stood on the site.

Cave-churches of the Gravine

Linked to Matera and Basilicata (*map p. 290*) by the Roman Via Appia, now Road 7, **Laterza** is an agricultural town huddled on the brink of a ravine that is lined with cave dwellings and churches carved from the rock. The ancient castle, situated at the north end of the old town, has been extensively rebuilt. The main entrance, on the north side, consists of two double-pointed archways preceded by a stone bridge; on the south side a similar doorway gives access to the maze of narrow, winding streets that make up the old town. The Romanesque church of the Assunta is the last remaining vestige of the Cistercian monastery of Santa Maria la Grande. Within is an interesting baptismal font with 12th-century sculptural decoration. The *Chiesa Matrice* (also called San Lorenzo) has a curious Veneto-Dalmatian façade dating from the 15th century.

Ginosa, 7km south, is the ancient *Genusia* mentioned by Pliny, and the site of important archaeological finds. It is surrounded on three sides by a deep ravine containing cave-churches with frescoes dating from the 12th–14th centuries.

Castellaneta, dramatically perched on a spur above its ravine, is the birthplace of the silent-movie star Rudolph Valentino (Rodolfo Guglielmi, 1895–1926). The old town is divided into two quarters, known locally as Sacco and Muricello, on either side of the cathedral. Begun in the 13th century and rebuilt in the 17th century, the cathedral has a façade of 1771. The campanile retains blind arcades and mullioned windows belonging to the original Romanesque structure. Via Seminario, on the right of the church, leads to the bishop's palace, where there is a fine polyptych, the *Madonna with Saints, Angels and Apostles*, signed by Girolamo da Santacroce and dated

1531. Reached by a dirt track on the south edge of the town is the little church of the Assunta, recently restored to its original 14th-century appearance. The Romanesque façade contains a finely crafted portal and rose window. Within are 14th- and 15th-century frescoes. More fresco fragments can be seen in the ruins adjoining the church.

At **Palagianello** the castle, rectangular in plan with sharp corner bastions, dates from the 18th century. It stands in a dominant position on the outskirts of the village. To the left of the castle can be seen the *gravina*, which holds several cave-churches. San Nicola, to the south of the village, contains remains of 14th-century frescoes. San Girolamo, the largest in the area, has a badly damaged fresco of the Madonna dating from the 15th century.

There are numerous cave-churches in the environs of **Mottola**, some with 12th–15th-century frescoes.

MASSAFRA

Massafra, situated at the top of a deep ravine, is divided into two distinct parts: the Terra, or old town, on the west, and the more modern Borgo Santa Caterina on the east. Two lofty bridges—the Viadotto Superiore or Ponte Nuovo, and the Viadotto Inferiore or Ponte Vecchio—span the abyss between the two quarters.

To see Massafra to full advantage, arrange for a free guided tour (in English). Many of the monuments are open sporadically, but tour guides (Via Vittorio Veneto 15; T: 099 880 4695) have the keys.

The castle

From Piazza Vittorio Emanuele, at the centre of the modern Borgo, Corso Italia bears across the Ponte Vecchio (spectacular view of the ravine with its caves and terraces) to the ancient Terra. Here Via La Terra leads to the imposing castle, built in the mid-15th century on the site of a Norman fortification and rebuilt in the late 17th or early 18th century for Michele Imperiali, whose eagle emblem can be seen on the entrance wall. Rectangular in plan with cylindrical towers and a massive octagonal bastion at the southeast corner, it incorporates in one rampart the church of San Lorenzo (or *Chiesa Matrice*), built in the 15th century and remodelled in 1533. The terrace below commands a view of the entire coastal plain west of Taranto.

Farmacia del Mago Greguro

Returning to Piazza Garibaldi at the foot of the bridge, follow Via Vittorio Veneto then Via del Santuario to a terrace on the outskirts of the town, from which a monumental staircase descends to the sanctuary of the **Madonna della Scala**. Built in 1731, the church contains an unusual 12th- or 13th-century fresco of the Madonna and Child with two kneeling deer from the Basilian crypt over which it stands. The latter, believed to date from the 8th or 9th century, is reached by steps in the atrium. Several incised crosses can be seen on the walls and piers. The adjacent **Cripta della Buona**

Nuova, partially ruined by the building of the sanctuary, contains a 13th-century representation of the *Madonna della Buona Nuova* and a large frescoed *Christ Pantocrator*. At the bottom of the valley, c. 200m distant, lies the so-called **Farmacia del Mago Greguro**, a complex of adjoining caves, the walls of which contain hundreds of small hollows where, according to tradition, the monks stored their medicinal herbs.

Crypt churches and chapels

Returning to the town, take Viale Marconi to Via Frappietri (also called Via del Cimitero). Here turn left (300m) to the 13th-century **crypt of San Lorenzo**. The primitive church, only partially intact, contains frescoes of saints on the arches of the presbytery, and a *Christ Enthroned* in the apse. Viale Marconi leads on to the Ponte Nuovo, near which three arches cut in the rock mark the entrance to the **Cappella-Cripta della Candelora**. Located in a private garden, the chapel may be reached from Via dei Canali. Six metres wide and 8.5m long, it has three aisles, a low dome, and arched niches in the walls. On the capitals are incised Greek crosses. The walls also bear extensive remains of 13th- and 14th-century frescoes with Greek and Latin inscriptions, including a well-preserved *Presentation in the Temple*.

In the east wall of the ravine is the unusually well-preserved **Chiesa-Cripta di San Marco**, of uncertain date. Access is afforded through a gate at the end of Via Fratelli Bandiera (reached by crossing the bridge to Via Scarano and turning right, then right again; *ring for key at the house next door*). A stairway carved out of the rock descends to the church. Entry is through a vestibule; on the left is a well, presumably a primitive baptismal font; on the right, a large fresco depicting St Mark. Piers with rough carvings, inscribed in Greek and Latin and surmounted by rounded arches, divide the church into nave and aisles. Steps lead to the raised presbytery and the main apse; another apse, on the right, is closed off by a parapet, possibly used as a pulpit. In the walls are carved niches that may have served as *arcosolia*. Of the frescoes they once contained, only a 13th-century representation of Sts Cosmas and Damian remains, the others having been destroyed by humidity.

Just outside Massafra, to the south, stands the 10th-century Byzantine chapel of **Santa Lucia**. Parts of the original building can still be seen; of particular interest are the distinctive cupolas, pyramidal on the outside but rounded within.

THE MURGE

The Murge is a great limestone plateau (473m above sea level) that extends southeast of Bari. Here are two jewels of Puglian architecture, medieval Conversano and Baroque Martina Franca. Over much of this area run the *parietoni*, imposing dry stone walls

The Massafra ravine, between the new town of Borgo Santa Caterina and the old town of Terra, containing ancient crypt-churches.

originally hundreds of kilometres long—mysterious vestiges left by the region's early Italic residents. Archaeologists believe they functioned as divisions among tribes or peoples—as Hadrian's Wall did in a different place at a later date. Early (19th-century) scholars suggested a link between the *parietoni* of Puglia and the tholos architecture of the Mycenaeans—a hypothesis that is still under consideration today. A study conducted in the 1980s by A. Ambrosi and E. Degano points out that the fortifications are particularly common around Oria, Manduria, Ceglie Messapico, Carovigno and Brindisi, and suggests they were erected by the Messapians against their arch-enemies, the Tarentines. The walls are still in use today as property boundaries.

ON THE MURGE

The Italic tribes of Puglia considered the long, low massif of the Murge an ideal place to live: close to the Adriatic, but high enough above it to be out of the sight of travellers passing by land or sea.

Rutigliano stands on the site of an ancient Apulian settlement 22km southeast of Bari. The church of Santa Maria della Colonna, founded by the Normans, was consecrated in 1108. The main portal retains the original carved architrave with *Christ and the Apostles*, and the *Annunciation*; the Gothic porch dates from the 13th or 14th century. Within is a polyptych of 1450 by Alvise Vivarini.

Some 8km southeast of the town is the conventual church of **Santa Maria dell'Isola**, built to an unusual plan with two aisles, Gothic arches and vaults and three domes in a row. The church contains the tomb of Giulio Antonio Acquaviva, Duke of Atri, executed in 1482 by Nuzzo Barba di Galatina.

Conversano

Conversano stands on a hill overlooking the Adriatic. It appears to have been a Peucetian town, possibly the *Norba* described in the *Tabula Peutingeriana*, an Italic document in the Oscan language, as lying on the inland route from Bitonto to Egnathia. It was bitterly contested by the Normans and Byzantines during the late Middle Ages. It changed hands several times in the following centuries, ending up among the possessions of the Acquaviva, Counts of Conversano, who retained it until 1806.

From the public gardens of the Villa Garibaldi, at the edge of the town, the view embraces the coastal plain to Bari. Nearby, at the centre of a sloping piazza, stands the **castle**, originally Norman, transformed over the centuries into a lordly manor with numerous wings and towers. Above the tiled roofs rises the rectangular Norman keep: the low polygonal bastion and the taller cylindrical one, respectively located at the northeast and northwest corners, date from the 15th century; the remaining structures are chiefly 17th-century. The main entrance, which faces Piazza della Conciliazione, and the elegant gallery in the atrium, were built in 1710 by order of Countess Dorotea Acquaviva. The interior contains private dwellings and the Biblioteca Civica.

The **duomo** was restored after a fire in 1911. The 14th-century façade combines Romanesque and Gothic forms, with interesting sculptural decoration above the main portal. At the ends of the transept are two low *campanili*. The interior, with nave and aisles divided by piers, a trefoil matroneum and triple apse, contains a 13th-century icon of the Virgin (left aisle), a 14th-century wooden Crucifix, traces of frescoes and a modern pulpit.

From the rear of the cathedral, Via San Benedetto, to the left, leads to the ancient **Convento dei Benedettini**. Founded, according to tradition, by St Mauro or St Placid, it is documented from the 10th century onward. The conventual church, erected in the late 11th century and extensively altered in the 16th and 17th centuries, stands beneath a Baroque campanile of 1655. Part of its original decoration can be seen in the rough mosaic frieze that runs along the top of the entrance wall. The richly decorated interior has a nave surmounted by three consecutive domes with 17th-century frescoes. Along the left flank of the church is a pleasing 11th-century cloister with trefoil arches and delicately carved capitals. From here you may enter the crypt, originally a 6th–9th-century Byzantine cenobium. In the apse are some repainted frescoes. The small **Museo Civico** (*open Tues–Sat 9–12 & 4–7, Sun 9–12; T: 080 495 1975*), houses archaeological material from local excavations, medieval art, and paintings ranging in date from the Middle Ages to the 18th century.

About 1km northeast of the town stands the unusual little church of **Santa Caterina**, with four semicircular arms arranged in a clover-leaf pattern around a central dome. The building is believed to date from the 12th century.

Castellana Grotte

Castellana Grotte takes its name from the spectacular caverns 2km southwest of the town, the Grotte di Castellana. Possibly the most exciting series of caverns in the whole of Italy, they are 1.5km long with an average depth of c. 65m. A series of corridors connects various chambers, rich in stalagmites and stalactites, in alabaster and other coloured stones. The short guided tour (*open for tours April–Sept at 11, 1, 4 and 7; in English at 11 and 4; T: 080 499 8211*), which terminates at the Grave al Precipizio, takes about an hour. The full tour to the **Grotta Bianca** (considered by some the most beautiful cavern in the world because of its brilliant crystalline formations (*tours hourly April–Sept 9–7.30; Oct–March 9–1*) takes two hours. The temperature inside the caverns remains constant at around 15°C. The nearby observation tower offers good views over the surrounding countryside.

Other interesting caverns, the **Grotta di Putignano**, chiefly in pink alabaster (*open 9–12 & 3–6*), can be seen 1km northwest of Putignano, a busy market and manufacturing town.

Alberobello

Alberobello is a small town with a quarter wholly composed of story-book *trulli*, flanking narrow streets. The name, Alberobello, derives from the *Sylva Arboris Belli*, the vast oak forest that once covered the area. The town was probably founded by the Acquaviva, Counts of Conversano, in the 15th century. In the following century it grew up around a mill and a tavern built by Count Gian Girolamo II. The area comprising the Rioni Monti and the Aia Piccola, composed of over 1,000 *trulli*, has been declared a national monument. Although it is now crowded with tourists from May to October, with shops selling trinkets that only vaguely recall the region's rural craft tradition, it nevertheless remains a fascinating place to visit.

THE TRULLI OF THE MURGE

Trulli are curious dwellings, built without mortar from local limestone and usually whitewashed. Their conical roofs, formed from flat-pitched, spiral courses of the same stone, are capped with diverse finials. They are found all over the region, isolated or in groups, and their origin is very remote. It is no doubt related to the rocky nature of the soil, and in many cases the same limestone used for the *trulli* is also adopted in the drywork walls used as boundary markers, which give the agrarian landscape of this area its distinctive appearance.

Religious or folk symbols are traced in white on many of the grey conical roofs. Inside, the rooms are small and usually windowless; the interior walls, like those of the exterior, in most cases receive one or two coats of whitewash each year, which accounts for their immaculate appearance. In Alberobello the Trullo Sovrano, in Piazza Sacramento, has two storeys; and the pretty church of Sant'Antonio derives its inspiration from the *trullo* style.

Locorotondo and the Valle d'Itria

Locorotondo is a strikingly beautiful town, designed in a circular plan (hence the name, 'round place') and set on a hilltop at the heart of the Murge. From the Villa Comunale at the top of the hill there are splendid views over the Itria valley, with its constellations of *trulli*, to Martina Franca (*see below*). The church of San Marco della Greca, a late Gothic building erected by Piero del Balzo, Prince of Taranto, has pilasters and half-columns with interesting capitals and bases. A road to the east connects Locorotondo to Ostuni via Cisternino, a town of almost Greek appearance, made up of white terraced houses with external staircases.

South of Locorotondo stretches the **Valle d'Itria**, one of the most beautiful and exotic areas of southern Italy, where the neat *trulli*, low stone walls, and small, meticulously planted farms all combine to create a truly distinctive atmosphere.

Martina Franca

Martina Franca is a graceful 18th-century town known for its strong white wine (used in preparing vermouth and *spumanti*) and for its many Baroque and Rococo buildings. The town was established in the 10th century by refugees from Taranto, forced inland by the Saracen invasions. It was enlarged in the early 14th century by Philip of Anjou, who granted it the fiscal immunities from which it derives its appellative, *franca*. In the years that followed it was given defensive walls and no fewer than 24 bastions, to which Raimondello del Balzo Orsini added a castle in 1388. The town was held in fee by a branch of the Caracciolo family of Naples from 1506 to the extinction of the line in 1827.

The central **Piazza XX Settembre** is flanked by the Villa Comunale, beyond which stands the 15th-century Gothic church of Sant'Antonio. Across the square rises the Porta Sant'Antonio, an 18th-century structure surmounted by an equestrian statue of St Martin, patron of the city. In the triangular **Piazza Roma**, beyond, stands the former Palazzo Ducale, now the town hall, attributed to Bernini (1668), with a fine ironwork balcony running the length of its façade. The building stands on the site of the Orsini castle. The Palazzo Martucci, across the square, has an elegant, restrained Baroque façade.

The narrow Corso Vittorio Emanuele winds past charming Baroque and Rococo town houses to the collegiate church of **San Martino** (1747–75), its tall, graceful façade dominated by the sculptural group of St Martin and the Beggar above the main door. The Romanesque-Gothic campanile is from a 15th-century church, over which the present edifice was built. The richly adorned interior consists of a single nave with transept. The main altar, in coloured marble, has 18th-century statues of *Charity* and *Maternity*. The paintings above the minor altars are by local artists. The Palazzo della Corte (1763) and the Torre dell'Orologio (1734) stand at the left of the church.

From nearby Piazza Plebiscito, Via Cavour leads past some more 17th- and 18th-century town houses to Piazza Maria Immacolata. From here, Via Principe Umberto runs past the church of San Domenico and the Conservatorio di Santa Maria della Misericordia (both 18th-century). Further on, in Via Pergolesi outside the town gates, is a terrace offering marvellous views over the Valle d'Itria.

From Martina Franca road and railway descend the southern edge of the Murge, crossing the plateau abundant with grain, vines and olive groves. Near **Crispiano** are Basilian cave-churches with 13th-century frescoes, and a small but well-displayed collection of traditional agricultural tools (at the 16th-century Masserie Lupoli). The Ionian Sea and Taranto, preceded by the Mare Piccolo, stretch out before you as you cross the last low foothills to the coast.

TARANTO

Taranto, at the northern extremity of the gulf that bears its name, is an important commercial port and industrial centre (pop. 244,000) and the second naval dockyard in Italy after La Spezia.

HISTORY OF TARANTO

The Spartan colony of *Taras*, founded in 708 BC after successful struggles against the Messapians and Lucanians, became the greatest city in Magna Graecia, famous especially for the purple dye it produced from the murex, a marine mollusc, for the wool of its flocks, and for its wine, figs and salt. It was also a centre of Pythagorean philosophy. The mathematician Archytas, president of the town (430–365), was visited by Plato here, and Aristoxenes (4th century BC), author of the earliest known treatise on music, was also a Tarantine.

Threatened by Rome in the 3rd century BC, the city summoned Pyrrhus, King of Epirus to its aid, but after ten years of war it lost its independence (272 BC). In 209 BC the city surrendered to Hannibal, for which, after being taken by Fabius Maximus, it was severely punished. It was subsequently Latinised as *Tarentum*.

Of little importance under the Roman Empire, it was destroyed by the Saracens (927), but rebuilt by Nicephorus Phocas, the Byzantine emperor, in 967. It retained its importance under the Normans, Swabians and Angevins, and by the 14th century its territory included much of Puglia and Basilicata. Although it was made an independent *signoria* under Raimondello Orsini (1393–1406), it was captured by Gonzalo de Córdoba in 1502. In 1647–48 it was torn by a popular uprising inspired by that of Masaniello in Naples.

The town came under Bourbon rule in 1734 and adhered to the Parthenopean Republic (*see p. 24*) in 1799. Occupied by the French in 1801, it proved to be one of Napoleon's strongest bases against the English and the Russians. With the opening of the Suez Canal, it grew to be one of the newly united Kingdom of Italy's strategic harbours. During the First World War the port was used by British troops en route to and from the Eastern Fronts. In September 1943, the Royal Navy entered the harbour and landed troops unopposed.

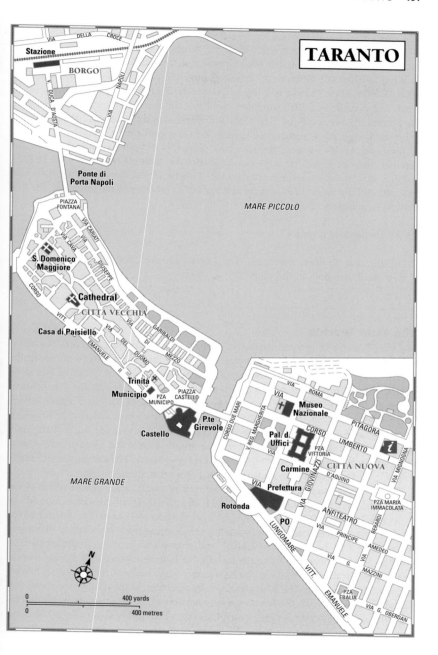

TARANTO

Stazione

VIA DELLA CROCE

BORGO

V. DUCA D'AOSTA

VIA NAPOLI

Ponte di
Porta Napoli

MARE PICCOLO

PIAZZA
FONTANA

VIA CARIATI

VIA CAVA

VIA GIUSEPPE

S. Domenico
Maggiore

CORSO

Cathedral

CITTÀ VECCHIA

VITT.

VIA DEL DUOMO

VIA DI MEZZO

VIA GARIBALDI

Casa di Paisiello

EMANUELE II

Trinità

Municipio

PZA
MUNICIPO

PIAZZA
CASTELLO

P.te
Girevole

Castello

CORSO DUE MARI

V. REG. MARGHERITA

VIA ROMA

VIA

Museo
Nazionale

PITAGORA

CORSO UMBERTO

Pal. d.
Uffici

PZA
VITTORIA

CITTÀ NUOVA

VIA MIGNOGNA

i

VIA GIOVINAZZI

Carmine

D'AQUINO

MARE GRANDE

VIA

Prefettura

PZA MARIA
IMMACOLATA

Rotonda

PO

ANFITEATRO

VIA BERARDI

LUNGOMARE

VIA

PRINCIPE

VITT.

VIA G.

AMEDEO

VIA G.

MAZZINI

EMANUELE

PZA
EBALIA

VIA G. OBERDAN

N

0   400 yards

0   400 metres

The town occupies an unusual site. The industrial Borgo, with the railway station, is on the mainland to the northwest. The Città Vecchia stands on the site of the Roman citadel on an island between the Mare Grande and the Mare Piccolo. The Mare Grande is a bay in the Gulf of Taranto, separated from the open sea by the fortified Isole Cheradi. The Mare Piccolo is a large lagoon extending some 8km northeast of the town and divided by a peninsula into two bays; the first is used as a naval harbour, the second for oyster culture. The Città Nuova, separated by a navigable canal dating from the Middle Ages, stands on a peninsula to the southeast.

Taranto gives its name to the tarantula, a species of spider, whose bite was the reputed cause of a peculiar contagious melancholy madness (tarantism; *see p. 520*), curable only by music and violent dancing. This hysterical mania reached its height in southern Italy in the 17th century and has left its memory in the *tarantella*, the folk dance of the region.

All the fault of a spider?

In Taranto it is always afternoon. 'The Tarentines', says Strabo, 'have more holidays than workdays in the year'

Norman Douglas, Old Calabria, 1915

The Città Vecchia

The Città Vecchia, connected with the Borgo by the long Ponte di Porta Napoli, is oblong in plan and crossed by four parallel avenues and many narrow alleys. In the animated Via Duomo is the **duomo**, dedicated to San Cataldo (St Cathal of Munster), who remained at Taranto after a pilgrimage to the Holy Land in the 7th century. Constructed in the 11th century over an earlier building, it has been rebuilt several times, most notably in 1596 and 1657. The Baroque façade was added in 1713. Much of the building has been restored to its original form. The outside walls of the nave and transept are decorated with charming geometric motifs and blind arcading, as is the cylindrical drum of the Byzantine cupola at the crossing. The campanile, originally of 1413, was completely rebuilt during the recent restoration.

The church is entered through a 15th-century vestibule, at the left of which is the **baptistery**, containing a covered font (1571) incorporating antique columns, and the 17th-century tomb of Tommaso Caracciolo, Archbishop of Taranto. The interior of the church, a three-aisled basilica, has rounded arches rising from 16 columns of ancient marble (the first on the left is fluted) and marvellous capitals of Byzantine and Romanesque craftsmanship (note particularly the figures of birds with foliage, second on the left). On the right of the entrance is a holy-water basin carried by female herms, one of which is missing. The 17th-century coffered ceiling of the nave bears reliefs of St Cathal and the Virgin. In the floor are scanty remains of the original mosaic pavement. From the aisles, steps mount to the raised transept, which has vaulted ceilings and blind arcading high up on the walls. The cupola, rebuilt in 1657, rises above the crossing.

To the right of the apse, the Baroque **Cappella di San Cataldo**, with inlaid marble walls, 18th-century statues and a richly frescoed ceiling, is enclosed by ornate bronze- and iron-work gates. The statue of the saint on the altar dates from 1984, replacing an earlier piece that was stolen. Steps in front of the high altar descend to the Gothic **crypt**, built on low columns belonging to the first phase of the building. On the walls are fragments of Byzantine frescoes dating from the 12th–14th centuries. Also in the crypt is an early Christian sarcophagus.

Behind the duomo is the church of **San Domenico Maggiore** (also called San Pietro Imperiale), built in the late 11th century and remodelled in the Gothic style in 1302. It is preceded by a high Baroque double staircase. The façade has a fine main portal with a baldachin, a graceful rose window and blind arcading. The interior is built to a Latin cross plan with a single nave and a rectangular apse. Along the north wall are 16th-century chapels with coloured marble decoration; the third of these contains a painting of the *Circumcision* by Marco Pino.

At the east end of the island, preceded by two antique columns thought to have belonged to a 6th-century Greek temple dedicated to Neptune, stands the **castle**, built by Ferdinand of Aragon in 1480, enlarged by the Spaniards in the 16th century, and further modified in the 19th century. It is now home to the Taranto naval command.

The castle of Taranto, originally built by Ferdinand of Aragon in the late 15th century.

The Città Nuova

A swing bridge crosses the channel to the Città Nuova. Here, in Piazza Archita, its principal square, are the imposing Palazzo degli Uffizi and the **Museo Archeologico Nazionale**, containing the largest collection of antiquities in southern Italy after that of the Museo Archeologico in Naples. (*At the time of writing, the museum was being rearranged. Parts of the collection on view at Palazzo Pantaleo, Corso Vittorio Emanuele II; open daily 8.30–7.15; T: 099 471 8492.*) Installed on a rotating basis, the displays range from prehistory to the 1st century BC. The exhibits are articulated in sections regarding prehistory, small mass sculptures and, most significantly, Greece and Magna Graecia, with a beautiful selection of pottery, gold and jewellery. Highlights include proto-Corinthian and Corinthian ceramics (dating from the 8th–6th centuries BC), Laconic ceramics (7th–6th centuries BC), and superb examples of Attic black- and red-figure pottery (5th–3rd centuries BC). Most of the gold objects are of Tarentine workmanship.

THE ADRIATIC COAST TO OSTUNI

Though the coast beyond Bari is flat and monotonous, the beaches are generally quite good. Monopoli and Ostuni are pleasant places to stay if you are looking for a central base from which to explore Puglia; Monopoli is closer to Bari and the main roads leading north and west, whereas Ostuni, an attractive town with a distinct Oriental air, is nearer Alberobello and the Valle d'Itria. All around Alberobello the rolling countryside is planted with vines, olives and almond trees and dotted everwhere by clusters of *trulli* (*see p. 478*). **Mola di Bari** was a crusader port. Today it consists of an old town on a headland and a new quarter that extends inland to the railway. The cathedral, erected in the mid-16th century on the site of an earlier church, combines Romanesque and Dalmatian architectural motifs. The rose window is probably a remnant of the earlier structure. Within is a curious nave arcade, taller at the east end and shorter, with a gallery in the walls above the arches (again a vestige of the old church), at the west. In the south aisle can be seen a baptismal font with dancing putti. Near the head of the promontory rises the castle, built by Pierre d'Agincourt for Charles of Anjou in 1278. Irregular in plan, it has a tall enceinte and polygonal corner bastions with steep scarps.

Near Polignano a Mare is the former **abbey of San Vito**, which dates from the 9th century but has been repeatedly altered, particularly in the 16th century. The abbey church, preceded by a porch, has an unusual nave surmounted by three domes. A medieval watch-tower stands nearby.

Polignano a Mare rises abruptly from the rocks. The *Chiesa Matrice*, in Piazza Vittorio Emanuele, was consecrated in 1295. The 16th-century interior contains a contemporary stone *presepio* by Stefano da Putignano, 17th-century choir stalls and, in the sacristy, several panels of a polyptych by Bartolomeo Vivarini (1472). Steps descend from the village to two large (25–30m in diameter) caves collectively called the Grotta Palazzese; these and the Museo di Paleontologia, may be seen on request (*T: 080 742253*).

Monopoli

Monopoli, a large, busy town, derives its livelihood from fishing, farming and industry. The polygonal **castle** was built in 1552 and remodelled in 1660. Beyond is the harbour, frequented by merchant and fishing vessels. The **cathedral**, founded in 1107 and rebuilt in 1742–70, is one of the most prominent Baroque buildings in the district. It has a tall façade of grey stone connected, on the right, to a blank wall with statues in niches, a scenographic addition to the piazza. The interior is a Latin cross with nave and aisles faced in coloured marble. It contains paintings by several prominent artists, including (first south altar) *Fall of the Rebel Angels* by Palma Giovane; (south transept) *Last Supper* and (in *tondi* on the walls) *Sacrifice of Abraham* and *Supper at Emmaus*, by Francesco de Mura; (further on) *Madonna in Glory with Sts Roch and Sebastian*, attributed to Palma Giovane, and *Circumcision*, by Marco da Siena (Marco Pino). Steps mount to the presbytery; above the altar is a 13th-century Byzantine *Madonna*, possibly by a Campanian painter.

In the sacristy and the adjoining room you can see architectural fragments from the 12th-century church, including an architrave with bas-reliefs and a capital bearing a representation of *Daniel in the Lion's Den*. The treasury contains an extraordinary 10th- or 11th-century reliquary, possibly from Constantinople, with panels that open to form a triptych representing the *Crucifixion*, with Sts Peter and Paul; a 17th-century processional cross of Neapolitan workmanship and other precious objects. In the Vescovado are a *Crowning of the Virgin* by Palma Giovane, and a *Madonna and Saints* by Paolo Veronese and pupils.

The church of **San Domenico** is distinguished by an elegant Renaissance façade. Within is Palma Giovane's canvas of the *Miracle of Soriano*, one of the most noteworthy of the artist's Puglian paintings. The graceful chapel of **Santa Maria Amalfitana**, erected in the 12th century by merchants from Amalfi, stands over a Basilian cave-church. The apse and the south flank belong to the original Romanesque structure; later additions were made in the Gothic and Baroque styles. The interior has a nave and two aisles divided by compound piers with good Romanesque capitals. Above, semicircular arches support the nave walls and simple wooden ceiling. From the south aisle, steps descend to the Basilian *laura*, now the crypt. A doorway at the end of the aisle opens onto a small court, from which may be seen the east end of the church (restored). The largest of the three apses is adorned with slender half-columns, grotesque consoles and a fine window framed between two small columns—motifs that link the chapel to the Lombard Romanesque churches of northern Italy.

In the suburb of Cozzana, on the Conversano road, the private **Villa Meo-Evoli** has a collection of antiquities (*closed at the time of writing; T: 080 803052*) from sites in Puglia and Campania.

Ancient Egnathia

On the coast 18km south of Monopoli are the ruins of Egnathia (*Egnazia in Italian; open daily 8.30–dusk*), a Graeco-Messapian town set on the frontier between Messapia and Peucetia, where Horace and his companions were amused at a pretended miracle (*credat Judaeus Apella, non ego*; 'Judaeus Apella believed it, I didn't'). The **Museo Archeologico di Egnathia**, at the edge of the archaeological zone (*open daily 8.30–7.30; T: 080 482 9056*), contains vases, terracottas and Messapian inscriptions discovered in the course of excavations, as well as late antique and early Christian mosaics and a large Messapian chamber tomb of the 4th or 3rd century BC. The site is especially important to archaeologists for the so-called Gnathian ware (characterised by small coloured designs on a black background, and sometimes ribbed; *see box below*) that was made here in the 4th and 3rd centuries BC.

The walled acropolis and the town proper lie respectively on the east and west sides of the road. The town contains a Roman forum paved with large blocks of stone and flanked by remains of a colonnaded portico; at the centre of the square are a well, a tribune and other remains. To the north lies the foundation of a basilica, of uncertain date. Further east are remains of what is believed to be the amphitheatre. The south side of the forum is bordered by shops and houses. Beyond lies a well-preserved stretch of the Via Traiana, which crossed the town at this point. Remains of walls and an arch stand to the east; further south, across the Via Traiana, is a ruined early Christian basilica built with materials from pagan edifices. Also visible are numerous rock-cut tombs and an imposing (7m high) section of the town walls.

GNATHIAN WARE

The style of ancient southern Italian pottery known as Gnathian ware takes its name from the city of Egnathia, though it was produced throughout Apulia for a century after 360 BC. The Messapian settlement of Egnathia, on the southeast coast, had come under strong Greek influence by the 4th century and the origins of Gnathian ware may, in fact, be traceable to *Tarentum* (modern Taranto). Gnathian ware has a dark glazed background with decoration either in colours such as white, yellow or, occasionally, purple, or else in ribbing or a combination of the two. Although the shapes of Gnathian ware are elegant in comparison to other Italic potters' vessels, decoration can be crude. Favourite motifs are representations of wreaths, scrolls of ivy or vines, and ribbons. Female figures or female heads, musical instruments and birds fill up space, and the overall effect can be very fussy. Nevertheless, Gnathian ware had some success in wider markets and examples have been found in France, Spain and along the coast of north Africa as far as Alexandria.   C.F.

The inland road

An alternative to the coast road passes slightly inland, bearing southeast from Monopoli in a straight line through groves of olives and almond trees. Here is **Fasano**, a thriving agricultural town with a Palazzo Comunale dating from 1509, which is developing rapidly as a holiday centre, thanks to its location between the wooded hills of Selva di Fasano (6km west) and the attractive shoreline (7km east). It is known principally for its Zoo-Safari (*open daily 9 or 10–dusk; T: 080 441 4455, www.zoosafari.it*), a large drive-through zoological park with amusements. A *strada panoramica*, which runs along the north rim of the Murge dei Trulli, connects the town with Castellana Grotte.

Just after Montalbano, a dirt track leads left to the Masseria Ottava, a farm near which lies the so-called Dolmen of Cisternino or **Tavole Paladine**, a prehistoric stone monument thought to be a tomb. The straight course of the road ends as you round the northernmost spur of the Murge. The road begins to climb, with views ahead to Ostuni, its white houses silhouetted against the sky.

Ostuni

Ostuni is a town of pre-Roman origin built on three hills. Its centre, composed of steep medieval alleys, is still circled by ramparts. The focus of town life is the triangular Piazza della Libertà, at one end of which stands the exuberant Guglia di Sant'Oronzo (1771). Slightly set back from the square is the little church of the **Spirito Santo** (1637), with its handsome Renaissance portal bearing reliefs of the *Annunciation* and of the *Crowning and Death of the Virgin*. From here Via Vicentini climbs to the old town, passing an 18th-century Carmelite convent and, next door, the Baroque church of Santa Maria Maddalena, with its cupola of coloured majolica.

The **cathedral** stands at the heart of the old quarter. Begun in 1435 and completed some 60 years later, it has an unusual façade of Spanish inspiration, with three rose windows and late Gothic decorative details. The Latin-cross interior was remodelled in the 18th century; in the last chapel on the south can be seen a *Madonna and Child with Saints* by Palma Giovane.

The **Museo di Civiltà Preclassiche della Murgia Meridionale**, in the Convento delle Monacelle at Via Cattedrale 15 (*open Tues–Sat 9–1, Tues–Thur 9–1 & 3.30–7, Sun 10–12.30 & 3.30–7; T: 0831 336 383*), displays the 2,500-year-old skeleton of Delia, a Palaeolithic woman carrying a foetus, found in the cave of Santa Maria di Agnano. Here also are Neolithic, Bronze Age and Iron Age finds as well as an exhibition on ancient Mediterranean agriculture. The 13-hectare archaeological park where the Palaeolithic burial ground was found can be visited by appointment.

Behind the church stands the **bishop's palace**, with its elegant 18th-century loggia. Further on lie the remains of a castle erected in 1198 by Geoffrey, Count of Lecce, and destroyed in 1559. The church of the Annunziata, in the modern town, contains a *Deposition* by Paolo Veronese (stolen in 1975 and recovered in 1977).

PRACTICAL INFORMATION

GETTING AROUND

• **By air:** The towns in this chapter can be reached via any of Puglia's three major airports. AMTAB Bus 16 runs at hourly intervals from 5am–11pm from Piazza Moro, in Bari, to Palese Airport, 8km west of the city, in 35–40 mins. There is also a shuttle (Tempesta) which makes the run in 5–10mins less. SITA buses connect central Brindisi to Casale Airport, 16km north of the city. There is no public transport (other than a taxi service) between Taranto and Grottaglie Airport. More at www.seap-puglia.it. Bari Palese information, T: 080 5800 204, Brindisi Casale information, T: 0831 411 7208, Taranto Grottaglia information, T: 099 562 5204, freephone T: 800 949 944.

• **By road:** Highway robbery is still common in the area, and the Carabinieri discourage visitors from travelling the more isolated country roads.

• **By rail:** The main line from Bari to Taranto touches upon Modugno, Bitetto, Acquaviva delle Fonti, Gioia del Colle, Mottola, Massafra. Intercity trains cover the 115km in c. 65mins, stopping at Gioia del Colle. Slow local trains, stopping at all stations, take just 30mins more. Schedules and fares at www.trenitalia.it. The coastal towns lie on the main Bari–Lecce railway. Fast Eurostar trains make the 150km journey in c. 1hr 40mins, stopping at Monopoli, Fasano, Ostuni and/or Brindisi; slow local trains stop at Mola di Bari, Polignano a Mare, Monopoli, Egnazia, Fasano, Cisternino, Ostuni, San Vito dei Normanni, Brindisi and Squinzano. The Ferrovie del Sud-Est (www.fseonline.it), a private railway, links Bari to Taranto via Rutigliano, Conversano, Castellana Grotte, Putignano, Alberobello, Locorotondo and Martina Franca. Another private line, the Ferrotramviaria SpA (www.ferrovienordbarese.it) runs from Bari to Palese, Bitonto, Ruvo, Corato, Andria and Barletta. Mainline trains connect Bari to Taranto.

INFORMATION OFFICES

Bari Assessorato Regionale al Turismo, Corso Sonnino 177, T: 080 540111, www.pugliaturismo.com; Azienda per la Promozione Turistica, Piazza Moro 33/a, T: 080 524 2361; Ufficio Informazioni e di Accoglienza Turistica, Piazza Moro 32/a, T: 080 524 2244.

Fasano Piazza Ciaia 10; T: 080 441 3086.

Martina Franca Piazza Roma 37, T: 080 4805702.

Ostuni Corso Mazzini 6, T: 0831 301268

Taranto Azienda di Promozione Turistica, Corso Umberto 121, T: 099 453 2397, www.apt.ta.it; Ufficio Informazioni e di Accoglienza Turistica, Corso Umberto 113, T: 099 453 2392.

HOTELS

Alberobello

€€ **Dei Trulli**. A complex of *trulli*, naturally with all modern comforts, in the historic centre of the village. Open all year. Via Cadore 29, T: 080 432 3555, www.hoteldeitrulli.it

Castellana Grotte

€€ **Relais & Le Jardin**. A small (10 rooms), cosy place in the country, with lots of flowers and plants, private balconies, good cuisine. Contrada Scamardella 57, T: 080 496 6330.

Castellaneta Marina

€€ **Golf Hotel**. A quiet, comfortable place with a large, pine-shaded garden. Open May–Oct. T: 099 6439251.

Cisternino

€ **Villa Cenci**. A renovated country manor, with simple rooms (suites in *trulli*) and pool. Open April–Oct. Strada provinciale per Ceglie Massapico, T: 080 444 8208.

Fasano

€€€ **Masseria San Domenico**. ■ Fine old manor house, on an estate with Basilian cave churches and an olive press in a natural cave; spacious rooms with wrought-iron beds; pool, tennis courts. Open April–Dec. Strada Litoranea Provinciale 379 at Savelletri di Fasano, T: 080 482 7769, www.imasseria.com

€€€ **Masseria Torre Coccaro**. ■ Stone floors and high, vaulted ceilings help create a wonderful atmosphere of warmth and coolness together, in the rustic luxury of this 16th-century farmhouse. Contrada Coccaro 8, at Savelletri di Fasano, T: 080 482 9310, www.masseriatorrecoccaro.com

€€ **Borgo San Marco**. Fifteen rooms in a lovely old manor built by the Knights of Malta in the 15th century. Open all year. 33 Contrada Sant'Angelo, T: 080 439 5757, www.borgosanmarco.it

€€ **Masseria Marzalossa**. Lovely 18th-century manor with just 8 rooms. Open March–Oct and 25–31 Dec. Contrada Pezze Vicine 65, T: 080 441

3780, www.marzalossa.it

Gioia del Colle

€ **Svevo**. Modest but comfortable hotel; regional recipes with a creative twist in the well-known restaurant. Via Santerano 319, T: 080 348 2739, www.hotelsvevo.it

Martina Franca

€€ **Relais Villa San Martino**. An elegant country retreat with everything you could possibly desire—including an Arabian hammam. Via Taranto 59, T: 080 485 7719, www. relaisvillasanmartino.com

€ **Dell'Erba**. In a large garden in the historic town centre; comfortable rooms, pool, sauna, gym, riding. Open all year. Via Taranto 1, T: 080 430 1055, www.hoteldellerba.it

Monopoli

€€€ **Il Melograno**. ■ A 16th-century fortified manor surrounded by groves of olive, pomegranate, lemon, orange and prickly pear; beautiful rooms, excellent cuisine, pool, sauna, tennis. Closed Feb. Contrada Torricella 345, T: 080 690 9030, www.melograno.com

Ostuni

€€€ **La Sommità**. An impeccably renovated *relais*, easily the most relaxing place in Ostuni. Via Scipione Petrarolo 7, T: 0831 305925, www.lasommita.it

€€ **Masseria Santa Lucia**. A renovated country manor; spacious rooms with garden patios. Olympic pool, tennis, riding, private beach. Open all year. SS 379, km 23 (Costa Merlata exit), T: 0831 3560, www.masseriasantalucia.it

€€ **Tutosa**. Fine old fortified manor with garden and pool. Open all year. Contrada Tutosa, T: 0831 359046, www.tutosa.it

€ **Masseria Casamassima**. A fine old country manor offering very attractive weekly rates. Road 16, T: 0831 330265, www.masseriacasamassima.it

Polignano a Mare

€€ **Castellinaria**. Immersed in Mediterranean vegetation in a rocky little cove, with sea views from most rooms. Open Dec–Oct. Road 832, at Cala San Giovanni, T: 080 424 0233, www.hotelcastellinaria.it

€€ **Grotta Palazzese**. On the coast, with cosy rooms and a locally famous restaurant in a cave. Open all year. Via Narciso 59, T: 080 424 0677, www.grottapalazzese.it

RESTAURANTS

Alberobello

€€€ **Il Poeta Contadino**. ■
Restaurant famous for its outstanding Puglian cuisine, in the heart of Alberobello. Closed Mon (except July–Sept), Jan and late June–early July. Via Independenza 21, T: 080 432 1917.

€ **La Cantina**. Simple but delicious local fare in the heart of the old town. Closed Tues (except in summer) and late June–early July. Vico Lippolis 9, T: 080 432 3473.

Cisternino

€€ **Osteria Cantone**. Traditional restaurant in an old manor house on the Martina Franca Road. Closed Nov. Contrada Fantese, T: 080 444 6902.

€ **Il Capriccio**. Agreeable restaurant-pizzeria. Closed midday Mon, Wed and Oct–Nov. Via Libertà 71, Contrada Caranna, T: 080 444 2553.

€ **La Botte**. Characteristic trattoria in the old town centre, with summer seating in the piazza. Closed Thur (except in summer) and late Sept–early Oct. Via Santa Lucia 38, T: 080 444 7850.

Fasano

€€€ **Il Fagiano**. Elegant, refined garden restaurant with delicious seasonal dishes. Closed Sun evening and Mon (except in summer), and Jan. Viale Toledo 17, at Selva di Fasano, T: 080 433 1157.

Gravina in Puglia

€ **Osteria di Salvatore Cucco**. Simple *osteria* on the edge of the old town. Closed Sun evening, Mon and mid-Aug. Piazza Pellicciari 4, T: 080 326 1872.

Laterza

€€ **Tenuta dell'Aquila**. Delightful small country restaurant with rooms. Closed Mon and Nov. Via San Falco 1, T: 099 829 6842.

€ **Atelier della Carne**. Two outstanding examples of a traditional local eatery: the *fornello*, or wood oven at the back of butchers' shops where steaks and chops chosen by the client are cooked up and served with utter simplicity. Open evenings only; closed, like the shops, Thur and Sun. Via Roma 51, T: 099 821 8788 and Tamborrino, Via Roma 58, T: 099 821 6192.

Locorotondo

€ **Centro Storico**. Trattoria offering great seasonal dishes. Closed Wed. Via Eroi di Dogali 6, T: 080 431 5473.

Martina Franca

€€ **Al Ritrovo degli Amici**. Restaurant indeed full of 'friends', attracted by good food and wines. Closed Sun evening and Mon (except in summer). Corso Messapia 8, T: 080 483 9249.

€€ **Trattoria delle Ruote**. Trattoria in a *trullo*, with simple *menu du jour*. Closed Mon and one week in Sept. Via Monticello 1, Contrada Primicerio,

T: 080 483 7473.

€€ **Villa Bacco**. Warm, romantic restaurant (with rooms), with good traditional fare. Closed Mon and Jan. Via Madonna del Pozzo 46, T: 080 485 6115.

€ **La Murgetta**. Characteristic restaurant with good local fare. Closed Wed. Strada Statale 172, Contrada Lanzo, T: 080 449 0016.

Mola di Bari

€€ **Van Westerhout**. Innovative interpretations of traditional dishes, *fin-de-siècle* ambience. Closed Sun evening and Tues. Via de Amicis 3–5, T: 080 474 6989.

Monopoli

€ **Osteria Perricci**. Old-fashioned *osteria* in the same family for four generations. Closed Wed, Sept and late Jan–early Feb.Via Orazio Comes 1, T: 080 937 2208.

€ **Il Sagittario**. Restaurant-pizzeria, closed Tues (except in Aug). Contrada San Nicola 42/a, T: 080 690 0059.

Ostuni

€€ **La Taverna**. Good fish restaurant in a renovated farmhouse by the sea just outside town. Closed Wed and Jan. Contrada Rosa Marina, T: 0831 350433.

€€ **Masseria Il Frantoio**. ■ Fine regional fare in a lovely manor house (with rooms) amid olive, citrus and cypress trees, not far from the sea. Closed Sun evening and Nov–Feb. Road 16 km 874, T: 0831 330276.

€€ **Osteria del Tempo Perso**. Characteristic *osteria* in the historic town centre. Closed Mon and late Dec–early Jan. Via Vitale 47, T: 0831 304819.

€€ **Porta Nuova**. Creative cuisine and great views, in the old town centre. Closed Wed. Via G. Petrarolo 38, T: 0831 338983.

Putignano

€€ **Il Cantinone**. Characteristic trattoria with tables among wine vats. Closed Wed and two weeks in July. Via San Lorenzo 1, T: 080 491 3378.

Taranto

€€ **La Fattoria**. Characterful seafood restaurant with good wines and service. Closed Sun and late Aug. Via Abruzzo 7-9, T: 099 737 1161.

€€ **Vecchie Cantine**. Creative fish dishes in a restaurant (with rooms) by the sea. Closed Wed and Sept. Via Girasoli 23, at Lama, T: 099 777 2589.

€ **Da Mimmo**. Simple *osteria* near the Villa Comunale. Closed Wed and late Aug. Via Giovinazzi 18, T: 099 459 3733.

Palo del Colle

€€ **La Stalla del Nonno**. Wine-bar serving hot and cold meals. Open evenings only, closed Sun and Aug. Via XXIV Maggio 26–28; T: 080 629598.

Sammichele di Bari

€ **Cavaliere**. Cordial country restaurant with good service. Closed Sun evening, Tues and Aug. Via de Gasperi 28, T: 080 891 0220.

LOCAL SPECIALITIES

Capurso is known for its handmade textiles and for its ceramics. **Rutigliano** is also good for ceramics, and makes a peculiar kind of terracotta whistle. At **Alberobello** the Caseificio Notarnicola dairy, at Viale Notarnicola 2, has good local cheeses. Pastificio Pmc, at Via Girolamo 34, is a pasta mill selling antique-bronze-tooled pasta, including

orecchiette and other traditional shapes.
Fasano is known for its hand-made
textiles; **Laterza** and **Monopoli** are
famous for their pottery. Good wrought-
iron can be found throughout the
province of Bari.

FESTIVALS & EVENTS

Alberobello
Natale fra I Trulli The Nativity presented
in *tableaux vivants* and with candlelight
processions, late Dec.
Acquaviva delle Fonti
San Vito Procession featuring children
dressed as the saint leading dogs on
leashes, in celebration of the protection
St Vitus gives against hydrophobia, 15
June; *Madonna di Costantinopoli*
Religious and historic feast with procession, pageantry and fireworks, first Tues
in Sept.
Capurso
Madonna del Pozzo To commemorate the
miraculous recovery of a dying priest
(who, at the Virgin's suggestion, drank
the waters of the Spring of Santa
Maria), a float decked with flowers,
lights, and three storeys carrying the
town band, a statue of the Madonna
and a group of Franciscan friars, is
dragged to the hallowed spring, last
Sun in Aug.
Fasano
Maria Santissima del Pozzo Historic re-
evocation of a victory over the Turks,
penultimate weekend in June; *San
Francesco da Paola* The saint's statue is
carried in a boat procession and everyone eats huge amounts of swordfish,
second Sat and Sun in Aug.
Ginosa
Passio Christi In the dramatic setting of

the *gravina* that surrounds the town, the
entire life of Christ is represented in
tableaux vivants accompanied by lights
and music. Much better than the cinema, Weds and Sat before Easter.
Martina Franca
Festival della Valle d'Itria Palazzo Ducale,
July–Aug, T: 080.4805100,
www.festivaldellavalleditria.it
Massafra
Mardi Gras A particularly colourful vari-
ation on the traditional Shrove Tuesday
procession of allegorical floats and
masks.
Monopoli
Madonna della Madia When a 12th-cen-
tury bishop was unable to complete the
new cathedral, the Virgin came to his
assistance, by boat, in the form of a
painted icon, carrying a full cargo of
much-needed roof beams. The event is
re-enacted annually, 14 Aug.
Ostuni
Sagra dei Vecchi Tempi Demonstration of
craft techniques of the past, and sale of
the goods made, 15 Aug; *Cavalcata di
Sant'Oronzo* The customary procession
with the saint's statue is accompanied
here by beautifully appointed horses
and riders, 25–27 Aug.
Putignano
Carnevale The carnival festivities in
Putignano start the day after Christmas,
dedicated to the patron saint, Stephen,
and continue until Shrove Tuesday.
Rutigliano
Sant'Antonio Abate The Feast of St
Anthony Abbot is usually the first day
of Carnival; here it is marked by the
sale of pottery and other clay objects,
notably the imaginatively shaped whistles for which Rutigliano is famous, 17
Jan.

Taranto

Settimana Santa A justly famous Holy Week celebration, with representations of the Passion and Death of Christ and a procession through the city streets, Maundy Thursday–Easter Saturday; *San Cataldo* A silver statue of the 7th-century Irish saint (Cathal or Cathaldus), elected Bishop of Taranto while en route to the Holy Land, is carried in procession by a warship followed by fishing boats and pleasure craft; there are fireworks at the castle and everyone eats *carteddate*, fried pastry made with wine, 10 May; *Stella Maris* A statue of the Virgin is taken to sea while the landlubbers eat free fish and seafood, first Sun in Sept; Giovanni Paisiello Festival Music festival in churches around the city in Nov, T: 099 7303972, www.giovannipaisiellofestival.it

Taranto is also the site of the annual conference of scholars of Magna Graecia.

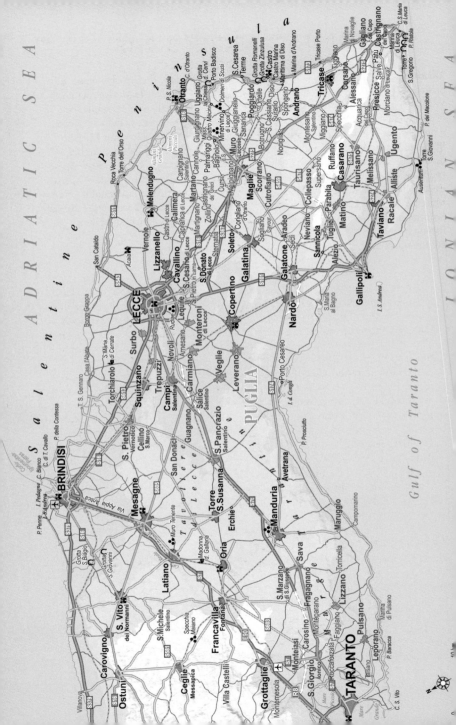

BRINDISI, LECCE & THE
SALENTINE PENINSULA

Brindisi, a provincial capital (pop. 93,000) of modern appearance, has the safest natural harbour on the Adriatic and consequent importance as a trading port with the East. Brindisi, like Bari, is crowded and busy, and though its museums and monuments repay a visit, you are better off staying elsewhere. South of Brindisi the only place of artistic significance is the Romanesque abbey of Santa Maria di Cerrate, near Squinzano (which also houses a small ethnographic museum).

HISTORY OF BRINDISI

Of Messapian origin, the *Bentesion* of the Greeks and the *Brundusium* of the Latins became a Roman city in the 3rd century BC and was used as a naval base in the Second Punic War. In 49 BC Caesar tried unsuccessfully to contain Pompey's ships here on his return from Greece. It was the birthplace of Pacuvius (219–129 BC), painter and dramatic poet, and the goal of the journey described by Horace (*Satire I, 5*). Virgil died here in 19 BC.

The city flourished under Roman rule, was taken by the Saracens in 836, and rose to prosperity again during the Crusades. It was sacked by Louis of Hungary in 1352 and by Louis of Anjou in 1383. Pestilence and the earthquake of 1456 contributed to its decline, and its modern importance dates only from the opening of the Suez Canal in 1869. An important base in both world wars, Brindisi was occupied by Allied troops on 10th September 1943, and on the same day Badoglio's interim government with King Vittorio Emanuele arrived here, having fled before the German advance on Rome.

Today Brindisi derives its wealth largely from agriculture, the processing and packaging of agricultural products, and its chemical industries.

The city centre

The city is built on a peninsula between two landlocked bays, the Seno di Ponente on the northwest and the Seno di Levante on the east. The bays form an inner harbour and are connected with the outer harbour by the Canale Pigonati. The outer harbour is protected by the Pedagne islets and the large island of Sant'Andrea, on which stands the fortress built in 1481 by Ferdinand I of Aragon after the fall of Otranto to the Turks.

Piazza Vittorio Emanuele opens out onto the inner harbour. To the right is the Stazione Marittima; to the left the Lungomare Regina Margherita leads to a marble column, with a remarkable capital, and the base of a second column (ruined in 1528 and later removed to Lecce), which are said to mark the end of the Appian Way. On the opposite bank, to the west of the Canale Pigonati, rises the **Monumento al Marinaio** (1933), by A. Bartoli and L. Brunati, in the form of a rudder, 52m high. This may be reached by ferry and the terrace (lift) commands a fine view of the whole city.

Via Colonne leads away from the harbour and passes beneath the campanile of the cathedral to Piazza del Duomo, the religious centre of the city, comprising the 18th-century **duomo** (begun in the 11th century, rebuilt in 1749) and Seminario, the 14th-century Loggia Balsamo, and the so-called Portico dei Cavalieri Templari. Frederick II married his second wife Yolande in the duomo in 1225. Around the main altar are remains of the original mosaic pavement of 1178, with representations of animals, discovered in 1957 and 1968. The inlaid choir stalls date from the late 16th century; the silver altar frontal, from the 18th century.

Museo Archeologico Provinciale

Open Tues–Sun 9–1, Tues, Thur and Sat 9–1 & 3–6.30; T: 0831 565501.
To the left of the church is the Portico dei Cavalieri Templari, a 15th-century construction with Gothic-style arches that gives access to the museum. It is arranged to form four itineraries devoted to antiquities and collections from Brindisi and its province: statues and inscriptions, prehistoric civilizations and marine archaeology. The main collections are as follows:

Antiquarium: Contains archaeological material from excavations in the city and surrounding territory, notably architectural fragments and capitals; a plaster cast from Trajan's Column in Rome showing the emperor's departure from the harbour at Brindisi during the Dacian campaign; Apulian, Proto-Corinthian, Messapian, and Attic ceramics—including Gnathian ware (*see p. 486*) from the excavations at Valesio, an Attic red-figure *krater* showing a Dionysiac procession and robed figures (5th century BC), an Attic bell *krater* showing Athena with Hercules and Hermes, and an Apulian wine jug with a wedding scene.

Statues and inscriptions: Armoured Roman warrior with a Medusa and a Winged Victory on his cuirass; effigy of Diana (or by another interpretation, *Roma Virtus*); lower part of a seated woman, of Greek workmanship; headless female figure probably representing a Victory or a Muse, in the Hellenistic manner. Several of the inscriptions are in Greek or Hebrew.

Prehistoric collection: Finds from the Palaeolithic to the Bronze Age.

Marine archaeology: A colossal bronze foot from the Secca di Sant'Andrea (4th century AD) and numerous *amphorae* recovered from Roman shipwrecks, as well as a display tracing the discovery of the **Punta del Serrone bronzes**, a find of over 300 sculptures and fragments of sculptures (including two complete statues and seven bronze heads) recovered from the waters just outside Brindisi harbour in 1992. The material is of Hellenistic Greek workmanship, though many of the subjects are Roman.

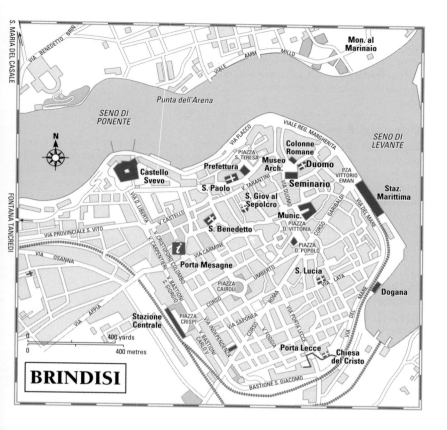

The old centre

The Loggia Balsamo, at the beginning of Via Tarantini, was part of an Angevin palace. Via Tarantini and Via San Giovanni (left) lead to **San Giovanni al Sepolcro**, an 11th-century baptistery of circular plan, erected by the Knights Templar over an early Christian building. The main entrance is decorated with reliefs and fronted by a shallow porch resting on columns (with interesting capitals) carried by lions. The interior follows a horseshoe plan. Eight columns (some antique) support the modern roof, which was built to replace the dome shattered by bombs in the Second World War. An ambulatory runs round the perimeter of the room; on the walls are 13th- and 14th-century frescoes of Christ, the Madonna and Child, and saints. A little southwest is **San Benedetto**, a Romanesque church of 1080, with an elegant cloister.

Overlooking the shore, to the northwest, stands the **Castello Svevo**, built by Frederick II (1227) and enlarged under Ferdinand I of Aragon and Charles V. West of the castle, in the Strada Provinciale San Vito, is the **Fontana Tancredi** (1192), erected by Tancred to celebrate the marriage of his son Roger to Irene of Constantinople. The crusaders are said to have watered their horses at this fountain. To the southeast, along the busy Via Cristoforo Colombo, is the **Porta Mesagne**, a 13th-century Gothic arch in the city rampart, reinforced in the 16th century by Charles V, near which you can see the remains of five tubs, which collected mud brought by the Roman aqueduct.

Other sights of Brindisi

From Piazza Vittorio Emanuele, Corso Garibaldi runs southwest to Piazza del Popolo, the modern centre. From here, Corso Umberto leads to the Stazione Centrale. Just south of Piazza del Popolo is the little church of **Santa Lucia**, preserving traces of its original Romanesque decoration on the south side. Within are fragmentary frescoes from the original building and a fine crypt of 1225. At the southern end of the town, near Porta Lecce, the **Chiesa del Cristo** (1230) has a polychrome façade. Inside is a 13th-century wooden Crucifix and statue of the Madonna.

About 3km north of the city centre (the way is marked, but the roads are too busy to walk comfortably) is **Santa Maria del Casale**, a beautiful Romanesque church (1322) with a polychrome façade and Byzantine frescoes, of which the most complete and impressive is the immense *Last Judgement*, on the entrance wall. Note also the *Madonna with Knights* on the south nave wall, an image clearly connected with Brindisi's importance as a crusader port. The profuse decoration of the apse and transepts is equally fascinating, though less well preserved.

In the Cimitero Comunale are 86 graves of officers and men of the British navy who served with the Adriatic Drifter Fleet (1915–18).

EXCURSIONS FROM BRINDISI

Mesagne and Latiano

Mesagne, a prosperous market town, is the ancient *Messania*. In the old town is the castle, built by Robert Guiscard in 1062, destroyed (together with the town) by Manfred's Saracens in 1254, rebuilt by Manfred himself in 1256 and enlarged and embellished in the 15th and 17th centuries. Originally a heavily bastioned stronghold against pirates, it was transformed into a lordly residence, as the Renaissance loggia that runs along the north and east façades clearly demonstrates. The Palazzo del Municipio, formerly a Celestine convent, houses the **Museo Archeologico Granafei** (*open Mon, Tues, Thur, Fri 8.30–12.30 & 3–7; closed Weds, Sat, Sun and holidays; T: 0831 776065*), which contains Messapian ware of the 7th–2nd centuries BC, Roman inscriptions, and other material of interest, notably a reconstructed Messapian chamber tomb of the 3rd–2nd century BC. The Baroque *Chiesa Madre* has a Gothic crypt with a 16th-century Crucifix and numerous paintings by local artists. On the outskirts of the town lies the little 7th-century church of San Lorenzo, partially rebuilt in the 17th century. Recent restoration has brought some frescoes to light, probably dating from the 15th century.

Latiano has a Palazzo Comunale, originally of the 12th century, rebuilt in 1526 and 1724. At **Muro Tenente** (also called Paretone), to the southeast of the town, are the remains of Messapian walls and tombs identified by some with the *Scamnum* mentioned in the *Tabula Peutingeriana* as lying along the Via Appia between Taranto and Brindisi.

From Latiano a country road to Oria (*see below*) follows more or less the same course as the railway, passing (right) the ruined church of the **Madonna di Gallana**, which contains, in the apse, a large Byzantine fresco of the *Blessing Christ* between two angels, in poor repair.

Francavilla and Grottaglie

At **Francavilla Fontana** are several interesting *palazzi*. The most impressive of these is the Palazzo Imperiali, a castle erected in 1450 by Giovanni Antonio del Balzo Orsini, enlarged in the mid-16th century and rebuilt in 1730 by Michele Imperiali to plans by Ferdinando Sanfelice. Rectangular in plan with crenellated battlements and imposing corner bastions, the building is adorned with a graceful loggia and balcony surmounted by large windows in richly carved surrounds, all of Baroque workmanship. A wide doorway leads to the courtyard, where there are a portico, another loggia, and a 15th- or 16th-century baptismal font. In the Sala del Consiglio, where the town council now meets, 16th- and 17th-century paintings and a fireplace bearing the Imperial arms can be seen. Nearby is the duomo, a sober Baroque edifice with colossal statues of Sts Peter and Paul in the façade and a dome of coloured tiles.

An interesting excursion can be made to the **Specchia Maiano**, north of Francavilla. Leave the town by the road signposted Ceglie Messapica. After c. 8km a country lane diverges left to the Masseria Bottari, a farm; proceed on foot through the field on the right to (c. 500m) the Specchia Maiano, a mysterious dry-work stone edifice of Messapian origin, 20m in diameter and 11m high, made up of six concentric steps of varying heights. Its purpose is unknown.

Grottaglie takes its name from the grottoes in its limestone rocks. The *Chiesa Matrice*, at the centre of the town, was erected in the late 11th or early 12th century. The façade, which dates from 1379, includes a fine Apulian Romanesque portal with octagonal piers on zoömorphic supports. To the right of the façade can be seen the polychrome tile cupola of the Cappella del Rosario. The church of the Carmine, further up the hill, has a beautifully carved *Nativity* of 1530. Behind the massive castle lies the quarter of the celebrated Grottaglie ceramic workers, many of whom still use traditional methods. The countless vases that line the streets and the flat roofs of the houses are a strange sight.

Oria

About 6km southeast of Francavilla Fontana is Oria, on a low ridge in view of the sea on either side. It was the ancient *Hyria*, capital of the Messapians. During the Middle Ages an important Jewish colony lived here, and the Giudecca quarter is still distinguishable. The massive **castle**, built by Frederick II in 1227–33 and enlarged in the

14th century, possibly to plans by Pierre d'Agincourt, stands in an indomitable position on top of the ancient acropolis. It is triangular in plan, the tall enceinte surrounding a spacious garden. The south wall, which faces the town, had three towers: one of these, the four-sided bastion at the southwest corner, was originally the keep of the primitive fortification; the others, built in the Angevin period, are cylindrical in form with rings of corbels that once supported wooden battlements.

The castle, though still a private residence, is open for guided tours (*1 March–15 June 9.30–12.30 & 3.30–6.30; 16 June–15 Sept 9.30–12.30 & 5–8; 16 Sept–31 Oct 9.30–12.30 & 3.30–6.30; winter by appointment; T: 0831 840009; for information, 335 726 1616 for reservations*). Within are a vaulted hall containing a modest collection of antiquities and the rebuilt Norman keep, a tall room with pointed vaults on heavy piers which was once divided, with two floors, as the remains of a fireplace high up on one wall attest, and now contains a collection of arms and armour. A small stairway mounts to the battlements and the Angevin towers, from the tops of which there is a marvellous view of the town and the Tavoliere di Lecce. The much-restored Palazzo del Castellano extends along the northwest wall; certain rooms of the *dimora*, or residence, are shown when not occupied by the family. Across the garden, among the cypresses at the foot of the southeast tower, steps descend to the **Cripta di Santi Crisante e Daria**, an underground chapel dating from the 9th century or earlier. The interior is basilican in form, with three aisles, cruciform piers and four shallow domes (a fifth dome, in the left arm of the transept, was destroyed to make the present entrance). The **Centro di Documentazione Messapica** in the central Palazzo Martini (*open Mon–Sat 8.30–1.30; T: 0831 845703*) has interesting Messapian artefacts and a dig on the premises.

The Museo Civico (*in the Palazzo Comunale; open by appointment; T: 0831 845703*) houses a small collection of Messapian and Graeco-Roman material. The Baroque cathedral, rebuilt after an earthquake of 1743, has a tall, coloured-tile dome of a kind common in this area.

San Vito and Carovigno

San Vito dei Normanni has a 12th-century castle, transformed into a fortified residence in the 15th century. Beyond the town, near its station, lie the Grotta di San Biagio, with paintings by Mastro Danieli (1197), and the Grotta di San Giovanni, also with frescoes.

Carovigno is a large town built on the site of the Messapian *Carbina*. Remains of megalithic walls may be seen to the north and west. The castle, erected in the 14th and 15th centuries as a defence against pirates, was restored in 1906. The almond-shaped bastion at the northeast corner is unusual in Italian military architecture, whereas the triangular ground-plan and tall enceinte are typical of late medieval fortifications. Within are rooms with 19th-century period furniture.

Detail from one of the '*propilei*' flanking the entrance to Piazza del Duomo in Lecce.

LECCE

The chief town of the Salentine peninsula, Lecce (pop. 102,000) is clean and spacious. With its small squares and winding streets, it owes its distinctive charm to the richly decorated Baroque architecture of its churches and houses, which skilfully exploits the properties of local building stone. This *pietra leccese*, a sandstone of warm golden hue, is easy to work when first quarried, but hardens with time to form a surface which stands up remarkably well to erosion. The style to which it gave rise, generally known as *Barocco Leccese*, flourished from the 16th–18th centuries and was applied both to monumental and to private architecture. Of the style's leading exponents, Gabriele Riccardi and Francesco Antonio Zimbalo were most firmly rooted in Renaissance classicism. Giuseppe Zimbalo (Lo Zingarello) was perhaps the most extravagant, whereas Achille Carducci and Giuseppe Cino developed an elegant and (relatively) restrained idiom. Cesare Penna produced much refined sculpture. However, it is perhaps misleading to concentrate on a few 'masters', as in a profound sense this became a popular style, an essential part of the repertory of local artisans. The *Barocco Leccese* remained more a decorative phenomenon than an architectural one, for it never really broke away from the spatial models of 16th-century Rome. Instead, it affirmed itself in the embellishment of traditional architectural forms with imaginative and ingenious sculptural designs. Lecce was the birthplace of the painter Antonio Verrio (c. 1639–1707), who went to England and is known for his work at Hampton Court.

HISTORY OF LECCE

A Messapian settlement, afterwards a Greek town and the Roman *Lupiae*, Lecce is the 10th-century *Licea* and the *Litium* of the Swabian epoch. The ancient city reached its greatest prosperity in the Imperial Roman period, at which time its harbour (today San Cataldo), built by Hadrian, was the most important on the Adriatic after Brindisi. Sacked by Totila in 549, Lecce remained under the Eastern Empire for the next 500 years. During this period it was overshadowed by Otranto, which became Byzantine Italy's busiest port; but it regained its primacy following the Norman conquest and from 1053 to 1463 (the date of its inclusion in the Kingdom of Naples) it was ruled as an independent county.

Later it was known as the Apulian Athens because of its tradition of scholarship, maintained despite the continuous peril of Turkish invasions, from the 15th–18th centuries. Today the city hosts one of Puglia's two universities, the other being in Bari.

In 1647–48 Lecce was the scene of a broadly based anti-Spanish and anti-feudal revolt which, although brutally repressed, continued to smoulder until modern times. In 1734 a second uprising won concessions from the Bourbons that the aristocracy failed to implement; violent social struggles again erupted against the wealthy middle class that had emerged during the period of French domination, without success. Only with the establishment of the Italian Republic, oppression slowly began to ease. The city suffered no damage in the Second World War.

The amphitheatre and the castle

The central Piazza Sant'Oronzo, which is mainly modern in appearance, lies roughly midway between the castle and the cathedral. It is dominated by a Roman column (from Brindisi) bearing a statue of St Orontius, tutelary of the city, appointed Bishop of Lecce by St Paul in AD 57 and martyred during Nero's persecution of AD 66 or 68. The square is partly occupied by the Roman amphitheatre, built in the 1st century BC and excavated in 1938. Only a quarter of the monument is visible. The piers around the outside probably rose in superimposed orders to a height considerably greater than that of the extant fragments; several of their arches are still standing. Only the lower of the two orders of seats remains.

The amphitheatre may be viewed from the walkway that surrounds three sides of it. Within, the elliptical passage that provided access to the lower order of seats, partially hewn out of the rock and partially built in *opus reticulatum*, can be seen to the left or right. Many fragments of the bas-reliefs that decorated the high wall separating the cavea from the arena (depicting wild animals, gladiators, etc), and a few Roman inscriptions, are still visible. More reliefs, in infinitely better condition, can be seen at the Museo Provinciale (*see p. 507 below*). Several tombs dating from the 5th century BC to Roman times were found in the environs.

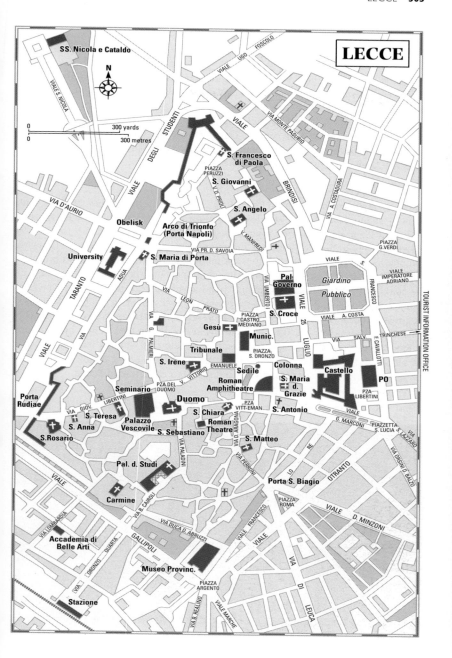

LECCE

SS. Nicola e Cataldo

N

VIALE UGO FOSCOLO

VIALE

VIA MONTE PASUBIO

VIALE S. NICOLA

VIALE DEGLI STUDENTI

VIA A. COSTADURA

0   300 yards
0   300 metres

VIA D'AURIO

S. Francesco di Paola

PIAZZA PERUZZI

S. Giovanni

BRINDISI

S. Angelo

VIA Q. PRIOLI

VIA I. MANFREDI

Obelisk

Arco di Trionfo (Porta Napoli)

PIAZZA G. VERDI

University

VIA PR. D. SAVOIA

S. Maria di Porta

VIALE

VIALE IMPERATORE ADRIANO

TARANTO

VIA ADUA

VIA UMBERTO

Pal. Governo

Giardino Pubblico

VIA FRANCESCO

VIA LEON PRATO

PIAZZA CASTRO MEDIANO

S. Croce

VIALE   A. COSTA

Gesù

VIA G. PALMIERI

Munic.

VIALE 25 LUGLIO

VIA SALV. TRINCHESE

Tribunale

PIAZZA S. ORONZO

F. CAVALLOTTI

S. Irene

EMANUELE

VIA VITTORIO

Sedile

Colonna

Castello

PO

Porta Rudiae

Seminario

Roman Amphitheatre

S. Maria d. Grazie

PZA LIBERTINI

VIA GIOV. LIBERTINI

PZA DEL DUOMO

Duomo

PZA VITT-EMAN.

S. Antonio

VIALE

S. Teresa

S. Chiara

G. MARCONI

PIAZZETTA S. LUCIA

S. ANNA

Palazzo Vescovile

S. Sebastiano

Roman Theatre

VIA D. ARAGONA

VIA PERRONI

S. Matteo

S. LAZZARO

S. Rosario

VIA PALADINI

RE

VIA ORSINI D'BALZO

Pal. d. Studi

Porta S. Biagio

OTRANTO

Carmine

VIA B. CAIROLI

PIAZZA ROMA

VIALE D. MINZONI

VIALE

VIA DUCA D. ABRUZZI

GALLIPOLI

VIALE FRANCESCO

VIALE

VIA DI LEUCA

VIA LOMBARDIA

Accademia di Belle Arti

VIA T. ORONZO QUARTA

Museo Provinc.

PIAZZA ARGENTO

VIA B. REALINO

VIALE MARCHE

Stazione

TOURIST INFORMATION OFFICE

Adjoining the amphitheatre on the west are the **Sedile** (1592), formerly the town hall, and the ex-chapel of St Mark. The lion over the doorway recalls the chapel's restoration by Venetian merchants (1543). Opposite is the Baroque church of Santa Maria delle Grazie, behind which lies the 16th-century castle, the **Castello di Carlo V** (*under restoration at the time of writing*). It consists of two concentric trapezoidal structures separated by a courtyard. The outer fortification, nearly 1km in circumference, was built for Charles V by Gian Giacomo dell'Acaja (*see also p. 512*); the inner structure dates from the 12th century. The grand baronial halls on the first floor make a superb exhibition space. Here and there some ancient features—carved details, sculpted capitals, ceiling bosses—remain.

Santa Croce

A narrow street leads north from Piazza Sant'Oronzo to the impressive church of Santa Croce, the most celebrated of the town's Baroque monuments, dedicated to the saintly hermit Pietro Angeleri, who against his will became Pope Celestine V (*see p. 409*). Begun in 1549 by Gabriele Riccardi, the church was completed in 1679 and bears testimony to the styles of the city's most prominent architects. The façade is built to a general plan by Riccardi, who is only directly responsible for the lower portion, with its columns (note the unusual capitals), blind arcading, and elegant frieze. The elaborate main portal and the two lateral doorways were added in 1606 by Francesco Antonio Zimbalo. The upper portion, which rests on a balcony supported by richly carved mensoles, was executed in 1646 by Cesare Penna to a design by Giuseppe Zimbalo (Lo Zingarello). It centres around an ornate rose window flanked by saints in niches and sculpted columns, and caricature portraits of the architects. The face with the enormous nose (bottom left hand side) is a caricature of Penna.

Detail from the richly carved *Barroco Leccese* façade of Santa Croce.

The **interior**, begun in 1548 by Riccardi and completed after the artist's death by his followers, embodies a conception of spatial elegance reminiscent of Brunelleschi, though with none of Brunelleschi's restraint. Built to a Latin cross plan, it has a nave and aisles separated by columns (note the ornate composite capitals with heads of Apostles, and at the crossing, symbols of the Evangelists), and 14 lateral chapels. The smaller rectangle of the sanctuary has an elegant apse and sculptured portal. Above the crossing, the luminous cupola (1590) and slightly pointed arches bear a rich sculptural decoration that is carried over into the vaults of the transept. In the coffered ceiling of the nave is a 19th-century representation of the Trinity. In the south transept stands the *Altare della Croce*, by Cesare Penna (1637–39), with a small loggetta for the exhibition of relics. The high altar, of coloured marble, was brought from the church of Santi Nicola e Cataldo (*see p. 508 below*). In the chapel on the north side of the sanctuary is the *Altare di San Francesco da Paola* with bas-reliefs of the saint's life by Francesco Antonio Zimbalo (1614–15). The first south chapel has an altarpiece of *St Anthony of Padua* by Oronzo Tiso. Next to it (second south altar) is a *St Michael*, inspired by Guido Reni's famous canvas of that subject in the church of the Cappuccini, Rome. The first north altar shows *St Peter Celestine Renouncing the Pontificate*.

Adjoining the church is the **Palazzo del Governo** (1659–95), initially built as a convent for the Celestines, or 'Franciscan radicals', followers of St Peter Celestine, to a plan attributed to Zimbalo. The courtyard of the palazzo is open, and you can walk through to the clean and pretty public park.

Beyond the gardens are two modest museums run by the Frati Minori (Franciscans), the Pinacoteca d'Arte Francescana (Via Imperatore Adriano 79), with a small collection of paintings, and (around the corner at Via San Michele 4) the Museo Missionario Cinese e di Storia Naturale, with modest collections of Chinese art and crafts, plants, animals, minerals and fossils (*both open Mon–Sat 9–12 or by appointment; T: 0832 455008*).

Piazza del Duomo and vicinity

The enormous, spacious, traffic-free Piazza del Duomo, surrounded on three sides by grand buildings, is the most monumental space in Lecce. The approach to the square is flanked by the so-called '*propilei*', curved entrance piers each topped by a balustrade and three statues. The duomo, founded in 1114 but rebuilt by Giuseppe Zimbalo in 1569–70, has an unusually high campanile (68m), terminating in an octagonal aedicule and two main façades. One of the façades, at the west end of the nave, incorporates statues also by Zimbalo, in a sober Classical design. It fronts onto the smaller square of the elegant Palazzo Vescovile. The other, facing the piazza, is a sumptuous composition containing a statue of St Orontius in a monumental triumphal arch.

The **interior** is a rather ponderous Latin cross with nave and aisles divided by compound piers. The coffered ceiling displays scenes from the life of St Orontius and, in the transept, a *Last Supper*. The first and second south altars were designed by Cesare Penna. Above the altar in the south transept is a painting depicting St Orontius, by

Giovanni Andrea Coppola, perhaps the most prominent painter of the Baroque period in Lecce. The crypt, which dates from 1517, was restored in 1956. The custodian will let you in if it is closed.

The **Palazzo Vescovile**, with a fine loggia, is set back a little from the main square. Constructed in 1420–38, it was rebuilt in 1632 and restored in the 18th century. To the right stands the magnificent **Seminario**, built between 1694 and 1709 to a design by Giuseppe Cino. In the spacious courtyard you can see a richly decorated well, also by Cino.

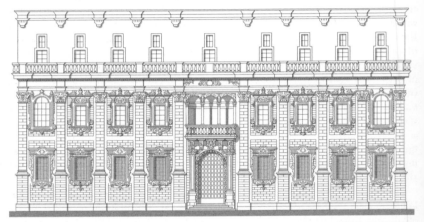

LECCE: SEMINARIO

The southern neighbourhoods

On Piazza Castromediano stands the church of the **Gesù** or Buon Consiglio (1575–79; *open mornings only*). The interior has an enormous, curving high altarpiece by Cino (1699), extraordinarily theatrical in its effect, though the orientation of the church has been altered for worship, and the congregation now faces south. To the right of the high altar is a painting by Giuseppe Verrio (brother of Antonio) of Joseph and his brothers. Via Rubichi leads south from here, passing Via Vittorio Emanuele, a favourite street for the evening *passeggiata*, which leads west past the Theatine church of **Sant'Irene** (completed 1739; *under restoration at the time of writing*), dedicated to Irene of Thessalonica. The façade prominently displays the Lecce coat of arms: a wolf and a holm oak. Further down on the left is Piazza del Duomo, with its fine Baroque buildings (*see above*). Via Augusto Imperatore continues south to the church of **Santa Chiara**, a disputed work by Cino. Its plan is an elongated octagon. Inside it has six altars of elaborate gilded stucco, and a heavy wooden ceiling in poor condition. Above the altars on the four slanted sides of the octagon are grilles through which the Poor Clare nuns attended Mass from their adjoining convent.

A street on the left of the church leads to the small (40m diameter) but well pre-served **Roman theatre**, the only known example of its kind in Puglia. It dates from the Augustan period. Octavian, before he became Augustus Caesar, stayed at Lecce (in 44 BC), on his way back to Rome from Greece following the murder of Julius Caesar.

The extensively restored cavea has twelve rows of seats, although in all likelihood there were initially several more. These are divided into *cunei* by steps that converged upon the orchestra, which was separated from the cavea by a parapet, now replaced by a modern wall. On the performers' side are three rows of broad seats reserved, as was the custom, for the town dignitaries; access to the orchestra was provided by lat-eral passages, one of which is still partially intact. The orchestra floor is particularly well preserved. The *scena* is pierced by numerous holes: some of these may have served for anchoring scenery, but others are more recent. The sculptural decoration of the *proscenium* and the *scena* itself are missing, but excavations of the site have unearthed numerous fragments (mainly Roman copies of well-known Greek origi-nals), now at the Museo Provinciale. There is a small museum attached to the theatre, with its entrance in the pretty Piazzetta Raimondello Orsini (*open Mon–Sun 9–1, Sun by appointment; T: 0832 279196*). To get there, take the street which runs up the other side of the church of Santa Chiara, past the ex-convent of the Poor Clares (the con-struction of which partly destroyed the *scena* of the ancient theatre). Displays include finds from the site and reconstructed rooms with mosaics and frescoes. The lower floor gives an orchestra-level view of the theatre and displays models of the theatre and amphitheatre.

At the beginning of Via Perroni the church of **San Matteo** (1667–1700) has a curvi-linear façade which recalls Borromini's San Carlo alle Quattro Fontane in Rome. The church was designed by Achille Carducci. The elliptical interior has shallow chapels and 12 statues of Apostles on tall plinths. The high altar, an exemplary expression of local workmanship, dates from 1694. Via Perroni leads on past former mansions and through the 18th-century Porta San Biagio to Piazza Roma and the Monumento ai Caduti (1928).

The Museo Provinciale

Viale Francesco Lo Re leads south to the Palazzo Argento and the superbly appointed Museo Provinciale Sigismondo Castromediano (*open Mon–Sat 9–1.30 & 2.30–7.30, Sun 9–1.30; T: 0832 307415*).

First floor

Archaeological collection: The visit begins on the first floor, reached by a spiral ramp. Throughout the installation texts and images cast light on the Palaeolithic, the Neolithic and the Age of Metals in southern Italy, and on Greek and Roman influences in Puglia and the Salentine peninsula. The best displays are at the top of the ramp, and encompass Attic black- and red-figure vases; Apulian ceramics, including a comprehensive collection of Gnathian ware (*see p. 486*) and a fine, extensive collection of Messapian *trozzelle* (vases with high handles on both sides); small bronzes and terracotta statuary from Egnathia and Ruvo; large vases with reliefs, from Canosa; and a singular large basin painted in red, yellow, black and white. There are large bronzes, including hemispherical and conical helmets; bronze belts and belt buckles; cups, bowls, etc, chiefly from Rudiae; small bronzes, including numerous *fibulae*, mirrors, statuettes, etc; terracotta statuettes and architectural ornaments; and a fine group of terracotta children's toys (*tintinnabula*) from Rudiae. Special attention is given to themes related to the daily life of the Messapians—the home, religious beliefs, etc.

Ground floor

Topographical collection: This section contains material dating from the Palaeolithic to the late Roman Imperial period, an eloquent testimony to the cultures that continuously inhabited Puglia over the last 20,000 years. The section begins with finds from Lecce; Rudiae, Cavallino, Roca Vecchio, Vaste, Muro Leccese, Vereto and Ugento follow. The highlight here is the bronze and red-figure Attic pottery from the tomb of a prince, unearthed at Ugento. Here also are statues, reliefs and sculptural fragments found in the Roman theatre and amphitheatre of Lecce.

Porta Rudiae and environs

From Piazza del Duomo Via Libertini continues west past (left) the unfinished church of **Santa Teresa**, built, together with the adjacent Carmelite convent, between 1620 and 1630 to designs by Penna, and completed by Zimbalo. Further on, just inside the city gate, is the Dominican **church of the Rosario** (also known as San Giovanni Battista), Giuseppe Zimbalo's last work, begun in 1691 and completed in 1728. The façade has elements familiar from Santa Croce, and others more reminiscent of Indian architecture. The unusual interior follows the plan of a Greek cross developed around a central, octagonal space. A profusion of sculpture decorates the altars. Across the street stands the former Ospedale Civile (1548), now occupied by the Tobacco Administration. Further on is the 18th-century **Porta Rudiae**, the southwest city gate. Its name recalls the city of *Rudiae* (3km southwest) where Ennius (239–168 BC), the father of Latin poetry, was born. The ruins of Rudiae, which may be reached from Via San Pietro in Lama, are of little interest. They include some Roman streets, the scanty remains of public buildings and ramparts, and numerous tombs.

Santi Nicola e Cataldo

To the north, beyond Porta Napoli (a triumphal arch erected in honour of Charles V in 1548; his coat of arms adorns the outer face) is **Santi Nicola e Cataldo**, the most important Romanesque church of the Salentine and one of the finest Norman monuments in Italy. To get there, go straight ahead to the obelisk, then diagonally right down Viale San Nicola, which leads to the cemetery. The church (*open mornings only*) stands in the cemetery grounds. Founded in 1180 by Tancred, Count of Lecce, its unique character results from a confluence of Byzantine, Arabian and proto-Gothic styles. The Baroque façade, attributed to Giuseppe Cino, incorporates a richly decorated portal (note the heads of women on the architrave and the three orders of freely carved arabesques; the badly damaged fresco in the tympanum dates from the 16th century), and the rose window from the original 12th-century building, together with pilaster strips and statues of saints.

The small, solemnly beautiful **interior** consists of a tall nave, narrow aisles, and a shallow transept, with Saracen arches on compound piers that recall the cathedral of Monreale in Sicily. A marked Burgundian feeling is evident in the nave, particularly in its proportions and in the sense of soaring height they produce. Above the crossing the elliptical dome rises from an unusually high drum. The vaulted roof is also typically northern European. Traces of frescoes can be seen along the walls. In the north aisle is an undistinguished statue of St Nicholas by Gabriele Riccardi; at the end of the south aisle is the 17th-century tomb of Ascanio Grandi, a native poet. The paintings above the lateral altars are by Giovanni Bernardo Lama. The sacristy has a well-preserved 17th-century frescoed ceiling.

A gate to the right of the façade leads to the monumental 16th-century **cloister** (*access also from the sacristy, if open*), at the centre of which stands an elegant Baroque well with spiral columns. To the right is a second, smaller cloister. In the south flank of the church can be seen a fine portal with a fresco of St Nicholas and an inscription regarding the building of the church in the lunette. From the cemetery, on the north side of the building, you can see the blind arcading that runs along the top of the wall, and the singular octagonal cupola, clearly Eastern in derivation.

MANDURIA & ENVIRONS

Manduria is far and away the most interesting place west of Lecce. One of the chief centres of Messapian civilization, it was known even in ancient times for its heroic opposition to the Tarentines, whose mercenary general, Archidamus of Sparta, was killed beneath its walls in a fruitless siege in 338 BC. Now known primarily for its vineyards, it conserves several interesting monuments including Messapian necropoleis and a fine stretch of the ancient walls.

At the centre of the town is the triangular Piazza Garibaldi, dominated on the left by the **Palazzo Imperiali**, built in 1719 over a bastion of the ancient walls, part of which can still be seen. A balcony with an ironwork balustrade runs the length of the façade; inside are an elegant courtyard and two covered staircases. Across the piazza, the town hall occupies the 18th-century Convent of the Carmine. On the upper floor is the **Biblioteca Comunale** (*open Mon–Fri 9–1, Mon and Thur 9–1 & 4.30–6; T: 099 970 2252*), containing an extraordinary collection of first-edition 16th-century medical texts.

The **duomo** (San Gregorio Magno), originally a Romanesque building, was remodelled in Gothic and Renaissance forms. The tripartite façade has a large rose window and three Renaissance portals; the finest, at the centre, incorporates reliefs of the Trinity with angels and the *Annunciation*. On the right side stands the Gothic-Renaissance campanile. The apse, with its two orders of columns, dates from the 16th century. The interior, restored in 1938, has three aisles with rounded arches in the nave and pointed arches and ribbed cross-vaults in the choir. At the beginning of the south aisle is a 16th-century baptismal font with figures of Christ and the Apostles; the twelve statues of saints in the apse date from the 17th century. The two large Baroque chapels, with paintings by local artists, were added in the 18th century. The medieval ghetto, beside the cathedral, survives intact in its original form.

The ancient ruins are crossed by both the road and the railway, and take about one hour to visit. At the heart of the archaeological area, north of the town, is **Pliny's Well**, identified with the *lacus* recorded in the *Natural Histories* (*III, 6*), in which the water maintains a constant level however much is drawn from it. To reach the site, leave Manduria by Via Sant'Antonio; just before the modern church of the Cappuccini, a road on the right leads to the cave (*visit accompanied by a caretaker*) where you can see the famous spring.

Just beyond the Cappuccini lies a well-preserved stretch of the **ancient walls**, the remains of which consist of three more or less concentric circuits surrounded by broad, deep ditches. They suggest that Manduria was for several centuries a strategic bastion against Hellenistic penetration of Messapian territory. The three sets of walls belong to different phases of the city's history. The innermost circuit, which probably dates from the 5th century BC, is c. 2km in circumference and 2m thick. It is made of large, irregular blocks laid lengthwise. The second circuit, attributed to the 4th century BC, is made with carefully cut ashlars placed at right-angles to one another in a typically Greek way, suggesting that its builders adopted Greek architectural methods—presumably from the enemy at *Taras*—while they struggled vehemently to maintain their political independence. The third and most impressive circuit is over 5km in circumference and 5.5m thick. The remains stand in some points at a height of 6–7m. The wall has two distinct faces: one, on the inside, composed of irregular blocks and small stones; the other, on the outside, made of regular blocks laid longitudinally; the middle zone having been filled in with rubble and covered over. It appears to have been erected in the 3rd century BC, perhaps as a defence against Hannibal.

Just north of Pliny's Well is a curious triple gate where converging roads penetrated the outer walls in points a few metres apart, merging in the space between the walls and entering the innermost wall through a single gate. Other gates have been located in the east wall and near the present Via del Fosso. In addition, three of the underground passages that connected the city with the surrounding countryside and were used during sieges (to smuggle in supplies, to send out troops or to evacuate the population) have been found near the Cappuccini and in the wall to the south and east of the church.

The Viale Panoramico, which follows the perimeter of the walls, passes numerous **rock-cut tombs** arranged in groups beside the ancient roads leading out of the town.

These tombs, of which over 2,000 have been identified, have yielded large quantities of Gnathian and other wares of the 3rd century BC, now at the Museo Nazionale in Taranto. Those situated along the north wall also have painted decorations.

Environs of Manduria

At **Avetrana**, southeast of Manduria, the castle was probably built around the end of the 14th century over an earlier fortification. It incorporates a tall rectangular keep surrounded by walls, and on the north a cylindrical bastion with a projecting battlement on Renaissance corbels. Adjoining this structure is a feudal residence of somewhat later date; the large rectangular courtyard, with loggia and portico, is characteristic of 17th-century feudal architecture.

North of Manduria, **Erchie** and **Torre Santa Susanna** both have Basilian cave-churches and 17th- and 18th-century feudal residences.

Campi Salentina and Squinzano

At **Campi Salentina**, a large agricultural centre, the Palazzo Marchesale was built in 1627 over an earlier castle, of which traces are still visible along the east front. The 15th-century church of the Madonna delle Grazie has a dramatic façade (1579) and a richly sculpted portal (1658) by Ambrogio Martinelli.

Four kilometres northeast of Squinzano is the charming abbey of **Santa Maria di Cerrate**, a Romanesque complex of the early 12th century. The simple façade of the abbey church is graced by a richly carved portal and characteristic portico. Within (*open Mon–Fri 9–1 & 2.30–7.30, Sun 9–1*), pointed arches spring from columns with interesting sculptured capitals. A ciborium of 1269 and 13th–16th-century frescoes may also be seen. Housed in a former olive press next to the church is the Museo delle Arti e delle Tradizioni Popolari del Salento (*open daily except Mon 9–1 & 2.30–7.30*), which has an entertaining collection of farm tools and folk objects.

THE SALENTINE PENINSULA

The Salentine Peninsula, devoted largely to the cultivation of vines and olives, also has important tobacco-growing districts. Megalithic remains (dolmens, menhirs, etc) are widespread, though unfortunately somewhat difficult to find; and traces of the Messapian period are visible in cyclopean walls.

The outskirts of Lecce

From Lecce, Road 543 runs through verdant farmland to **San Cataldo**, where there is a popular bathing beach. Near the foreshore are the scanty remains of Porto Adriano, the harbour constructed by Hadrian in AD 130. Many of the large stones from this site were removed in the 19th century to build the breakwater of the modern harbour.

Acaia (on some maps Acaya or Acaja), a small village still largely enclosed by walls, has an interesting castle—a typical Renaissance fortification furnished with an imposing enceinte and large bastions with steep scarps and projecting battlements (only partially visible). Begun in 1506 by Baron Alfonso dell'Acaia and completed in 1535 by his son Gian Giacomo (known for his contributions to the castle of Lecce, the walls of Crotone and Castel Sant'Elmo in Naples), it is perhaps the purest example of Aragonese military architecture in Puglia. The painter Corenzio was born at Acaia, to Greek parents.

Melendugno also has a fine 15th–16th-century castle. At **Roca Vecchia** a grass-covered mound of rubble and a few metres of low walls are all that remain of the *Rocca* built by Walter VI de Brienne, Count of Lecce, in the early 14th century and destroyed by Charles V in 1544. The ruin stands on a rocky ledge overlooking the sea, amid the remains of a Messapian village, which in turn overlies a prehistoric settlement. Here excavations have revealed c. 1,200 metres of megalithic walls with a gate and two square towers, remains of several buildings and cave dwellings cut into the rocky walls of the bay, and numerous graves that have yielded material from the 4th and 3rd centuries BC, now at the Museo Provinciale in Lecce.

The countryside is cultivated all around here, and the fields have good examples of *pagliare*, huts for shelter and the storage of tools, built in a dry-stone technique similar to *trulli* (*see p. 478*), but not whitewashed.

Example of the dry-stone *pagliare*, common in the fields of the Salentine peninsula. The architecture is thought to have affinities with the tholos structures of the ancient Mycenaeans.

OTRANTO

Heading south along the coast from Lecce, you pass the popular bathing beach at Torre dell'Orso, flanked by pinewoods. The road goes through the Alimini lakes district, a growing resort area. A few kilometres further on lies Otranto, a fishing centre and resort situated on a pleasant bay.

HISTORY OF OTRANTO

This was *Hydruntum*, a Greek city and a Roman *municipium*, possibly founded by the Tarentines. It took its name from the stream (the Idro) that runs into the sea here; the townspeople still refer to themselves as *Idruntini*. Located at the mouth of the Adriatic, and separated from the coast of Albania by less than 60 miles of water (now known as the Straits of Otranto), it was one of Republican Rome's leading ports for trade with Greece and Asia Minor, and it is generally thought that the Via Traiana was extended to Otranto to handle this traffic.

Although eclipsed by its rival, Brindisi, in the Imperial age, Hydruntum enjoyed renewed activity under the Byzantines, becoming one of the most important centres of the Eastern Empire in Italy and capital of the region still known as the Terra d'Otranto. Together with Taranto and Bari, it was one of the last Byzantine cities to fall to the Normans, finally surrendering in 1070 to Robert Guiscard. At the time of the Crusades it became an embarkation point for the Orient and a leading centre of trade between Venice, Dalmatia and the Levant. In 1480 a Turkish fleet, allied to the Venetians in the latter's struggle against the Kingdom of Naples, ruthlessly attacked the city and slaughtered its inhabitants. The 800 survivors were promised their lives if they renounced their Christian faith, but none did so; they too were killed on the nearby hill of Minerva, together with their executioner, who confessed himself a Christian after witnessing the unwavering faith of his victims.

Alfonso of Aragon recaptured the city in 1481 and provided it with new and more formidable fortifications, including the castle, featured in Horace Walpole's *Castle of Otranto*. But the town shrank in size and population, its port deserted. The surrounding countryside was abandoned and the marshes, only recently improved, once again bred malaria. Today, Otranto has a modest fishing fleet and is a departure point for the car-ferry to Corfu.

The castle

The castle, at the centre of the town, was built under Alfonso of Aragon between 1485 and 1498 and reinforced by the Spanish in the late 16th century. It is irregular in plan, with cylindrical towers at the corners and a massive spearhead bastion facing the sea. Most of the visible structure (*open Tues–Sun 9–1 & 4–7; T: 0836 801436*) dates from the 16th century; nevertheless, the enceinte shows traces of Roman and medieval masonry, as well as 19th-century restorations. It is certainly not Gothic, and has little to do with Horace Walpole. You enter through the archway on the north side. Within, a narrow entrance hall opens onto the central courtyard; an external staircase climbs to the rooms of the upper floor. Above the main arch are the monumental arms of Charles V.

The cathedral

The street opposite the entrance to the castle descends to the cathedral (Santa Maria Annunziata), founded by the Normans in 1080 and reworked in 1481. In the façade are a fine 15th-century rose window and a Baroque portal of 1764. The basilican interior is divided into a nave and two aisles by 14 marble columns, some antique, from which spring stilted arches. A beautiful **mosaic floor** (1163–65) representing the *Tree of Life*, the *Months* (with the relevant sign of the Zodiac and agricultural or domestic activity), biblical scenes (*Expulsion from the Garden*, *Cain and Abel*, *Noah's Ark* and the *Tower of Babel*), scenes of chivalry (*Alexander the Great* and *King Arthur*) and mythological episodes, occupies the nave and aisles; probes have revealed a Roman mosaic underneath. The roughly made but fascinating Norman work is the largest of its kind. At the end of the south aisle is a rather gruesome chapel with the bones of the inhabitants slain by the Turks, behind wooden doors left open to display them.

Steps in the aisles descend to the **crypt**, with five aisles, semicircular apses, and a vaulted ceiling carried by 42 antique, Byzantine and Romanesque columns with sculptured capitals. On the walls are fresco fragments of various ages and relief panels from a dismantled pluteus.

The church of San Pietro

The north flank of the cathedral leads to Corso Garibaldi, one block before the sea. To the left lie the two main gates to the old town— the Torre Alfonsina (1481), with cylindrical bastions; and the Napoleonic Porta di Terra. To the right is a house where the doorjambs incorporate inscriptions dedicated to Marcus Aurelius and Lucius Verus. Further on, Via San Pietro mounts to the little Byzantine church of San Pietro,

St Peter and his chain, fresco from the Byzantine church of San Pietro.

built in the form of a Greek cross inscribed in a square. It is said to have been the first cathedral of the city. The interior is covered with frescoes of various epochs, some with Greek inscriptions. It has barrel-vaulted ceilings and a cylindrical cupola supported by four squat columns at the crossing. In the walls are indented arches corresponding to the blind arcades of the exterior.

ENVIRONS OF OTRANTO

The interior of the Salentine peninsula possesses several interesting sights. From Otranto, Road 16 runs inland to Maglie, at the centre of the peninsula. Just before reaching the town of Palmariggi turn left. After a few metres turn left again to the **Masseria Quattro Macini**, a farm, near which you can see a group of seven dolmens and standing stones. Five kilometres further south of these lies **Minervino di Lecce**, with a fine Renaissance *chiesa parrocchiale*. Just outside the town, on the road to Uggiano la Chiesa, is the **Dolmen di Scusi** (*pictured overleaf*) the largest and best preserved of these primitive structures. The word dolmen is of Celtic origin, deriving from the Cornish and Breton for table ('*dol*') and stone ('*men*' or '*maen*'). Many similar dolmens occur in Cornwall and Brittany: it is not known if their function was funerary or purely ritual.

Maglie is a manufacturing town containing several Baroque buildings, including the church of the Madonna della Grazia; the *chiesa parrocchiale*, the campanile of which recalls that of the duomo at Lecce; and the monumental Palazzo Capece. The latter houses the Museo Comunale di Paleontologia e Paletnologia (*open daily 9–12 & 6–10, closed Sun morning; T: 0836 485820 or 0836 423198*), which has a collection of fauna from the Pleistocene period and archaeological material from nearby caves (Romanelli, Cardamone).

The coast south of Otranto

Leaving Otranto by the castle, a turning on the left climbs to the hill of Minerva, the name of which may allude to an ancient temple to the goddess. A staircase ascends past the spot where the survivors of the attack of 1480 were executed (*see p. 513 above*); at the top of the steps is the 16th-century church of **San Francesco da Paola**, incorporating the chapel (Santa Maria dei Martiri) erected by Alfonso of Aragon to commemorate the massacre. Two kilometres further south, along the rocky promontory that terminates in the Cape of Otranto, the easternmost point of Italy, lie the ruins (right) of the Basilian abbey of **San Nicola di Casole**, founded in the late Middle Ages, rebuilt in the 12th century and destroyed by the Turks in 1480. In clear weather the view stretches across the Straits of Otranto to Albania, and further south to Corfu.

Beyond the cape the road bears inland and descends, returning to the coast at Porto Badisco, a small hamlet on a rocky cove. Nearby is the **Grotta dei Cervi**, a complex of caves several kilometres long, containing Neolithic paintings of hunting scenes and magic symbols, and rich formations of stalactites. The caves are not open to the public; however, numerous objects (ceramic, bone and flint) found on the site as well as

The Dolmen di Scusi, hidden in an olive grove.

colour photographs of the paintings are scheduled to be housed in an antiquarium. The road climbs and falls along the coast to **Santa Cesarea Terme**, a bathing resort and spa commanding views to the mountains of Albania. Beyond, the coastal road winds past Porto Miggiano, along sheer cliffs covered with prickly pear.

Four kilometres south of Santa Cesarea Terme, a turning on the left descends to a small car park. Ramps and steps lead down the rock wall to the **Grotta Zinzulusa** (*open 10–dusk, guides by appointment; T: 0836 943812*). A long (140m) marine cavern rich in stalagmites and stalactites (*zinzuli* in local dialect), this was occupied in the Upper Palaeolithic period (c. 10,000 BC) and in the Copper Age. It is beloved by zoologists for its peculiar species of small crustacea, which seem to have originated in the eastern Adriatic and suggest that this part of Italy was at one time united to the Balkan peninsula. Nearby, but somewhat difficult of access, is the **Grotta Romanelli**, discovered in 1879 and also inhabited in the Upper Palaeolithic period. The flint implements found here have given their name to a variant of the so-called Gravettian industry. Figures of animals, stylistically similar to groups in France and Spain, have been found engraved on the walls and on loose blocks of stone. Among the other items brought to light here is a stone with schematic drawings in red ochre, considered the oldest painting in Italy. Fossil animal remains discovered in the sediment include warm-climate animals (elephant, hippopotamus and rhinoceros) in the lower levels and cold-climate creatures (goat, northern and steppe birds) in the upper levels. They provide evidence of a variance in the sea level in the Quarternary period, as a result of climate change.

Continuing south, you round a headland to **Castro Marina**, a fishing village and resort with a small, cliff-bound harbour. From here a winding road climbs up to **Castro**, a fortified town with a Romanesque cathedral, perhaps the ancient *Castrum*

Minervae, where Aeneas first approached the Italian shore (*Aeneid III, 521*). The castle, erected in 1572 and fortified in the following century, stands on the site of a Roman fortification later used by the Byzantines and the Normans. The former cathedral retains parts of its 12th-century façade, transept and lateral portals. The north aisle incorporates the remains of a 10th-century Byzantine church. The town offers magnificent views of the sea and the coastline.

At nearby **Andrano** the 13th-century castle was made over into an imposing palazzo by the Caracciolo in the 17th century. Further on is Marina d'Andrano, with its medieval tower. Tricase Porto is a fishing village and resort. **Tricase**, 4km inland, is a large agricultural town with a 14th-century castle rebuilt and extended in the 16th century, and a *Chiesa Matrice* (1770) containing a *Deposition* and an *Immacolata* by Palma Giovane.

Capo Santa Maria di Leuca derives its name from the Greek *leucos*, white. The conspicuous limestone cliff (60m), the *Iapygium* or *Salentinum Promontorium* of the Romans, with a lighthouse, is commonly considered the southernmost point of Puglia—an honour that really belongs to the more modest Punta Ristola, to the west. Marina di Leuca, below the cape, is popular for bathing. The church of Santa Maria Finibus Terrae stands on the site of a Temple of Minerva, close to the point where the Puglian aqueduct ends in an artificial cascade (usually dry).

Boat trips can be made to the several caves on the northwest shore of the cape, beyond Punta Ristola. Among these are the **Grotta del Diavolo**, which has yielded fossil remains of warm-climate animals and Neolithic flint, bone and ceramic objects; the **Grotta della Stalla** and **Grotta Treporte** with their beautiful effects of light and colour, and the **Grotta del Bambino**, also inhabited in prehistoric times. To the east lie the **Grotta Cassafra** and the **Grotta Grande di Ciolo**, both of which present interesting structural and atmospheric effects.

Along the Ionian Sea

The road rounds Punta Ristola and bears northwest, offering good views in all directions. At Torre San Gregorio, a turning on the left leads inland to **Patù** where, opposite the Romanesque church of San Giovanni, you can see the *Centopietre*, a small (7m by 5.5m) rectangular structure of large ashlars with a pitched roof. Some believe the building to be Messapian in origin, while others hold that it was built during the Middle Ages, using stones belonging to earlier buildings.

Continue along the coast, which is distinguished by rocky bays, many dominated by **medieval watch-towers**. These towers can be said to form a continuous monument, an architect's dotted line enclosing the whole of southern Italy. Their purpose was defensive—just as a rampart's is. Like ramparts or fortresses also, they were static arms of defence against a perceived enemy. Fires would be lit on the top of a tower to signal the arrival of hostile ships, and the message would be transmitted up and down the coast, the towers forming a sort of telegraph-before-the-event. Duly warned, the population would be able to hide from the invaders, or muster for the common defence, as the case required. Sometimes the towers hosted small garrisons of troops, though this was more the exception than the rule: in such cases whole villages would grow up around them, offering housing for the soldiers and their families and providing essential support services to the contingent. The towers are particularly thick between Taranto and Gallipoli, where the low coast provided very little natural defence.

Beyond Sant'Antonio, the road is straight and somewhat monotonous, the countryside virtually uninhabited. Near Torre San Giovanni lie the scanty remains of the Roman harbour of *Ausentum*. Just beyond the 16th-century Torre Suda (left), a turning on the right leads inland to Taviano and **Casarano**, birthplace of Pope Boniface IX (reigned 1389–1404). The church of Casaranello (or Santa Maria della Croce) contains the only known early Christian mosaics in Puglia. The ancient building, initially comprising a single nave, was enlarged during the late Middle Ages and remodelled in the 11th, 13th and 17th centuries. The mosaics occupy the vault of the chancel and the cupola; in the former are geometric designs with animals; in the latter, the Cross set against the night sky. Along the nave walls are 13th-century frescoes representing the life of St Catherine and New Testament scenes.

GALLIPOLI & ENVIRONS

Gallipoli, the *Kallipolis* of the Greeks and the *Anxa* of Pliny, is entered by its modern *borgo* on the mainland; the street passes a fountain decorated with antique reliefs, and crosses a bridge of 1603. The old city, its narrow streets tightly packed onto a small island, was the last of the Salentine *Terre* to capitulate to the Normans (1071). Sacked by the Venetians in 1484, it was strong enough to drive off a British naval squadron in 1809. Beyond the bridge is the **castle**, where 34 rebel barons held out for seven months against Charles of Anjou in the 13th century. Rectangular in plan with an imposing enceinte and massive corner bastions, it is fronted by the keyhole-shaped annexe built in 1522 to plans by Francesco di Giorgio Martini, who visited the fortification in 1491–92. The original Byzantine fortress has been incorporated into the polygonal bastion at the southeast corner.

Further west, the Baroque **cathedral** (1630), with an elaborate façade of 1696, is adorned with many paintings by local artists, including a *Madonna and St Orontius* by Giovanni Andrea Coppola, the artist's last work. In the nearby bishop's palace are an *Assunta* by Francesco de Mura and other paintings.

The **Museo Civico** (*Via de Pace 108; open Mon–Sat 9–1 & 4–7; T: 0833 264224*) houses a collection divided into ten sections, encompassing antiquities (largely Messapian sarcophagi and vases), natural history, weapons and clothing, historical and ethnographic relics and curiosities, and prints and paintings of the city.

The Baroque church of **San Francesco** contains wooden carvings of the two Thieves by Vespasiano Genuino, an outstanding achievement of the realistic school of local sculpture. The church of the **Purità** has a richly stuccoed interior and many paintings; the floor is paved with 18th-century majolica tiles depicting baskets of flowers and fruit.

Nardò

Nardò, founded by the Messapians, became a Roman *municipium* under the name of *Neritum*. It retained a decidedly Eastern stamp throughout the Middle Ages, despite repeated efforts to westernise it, and the Greek and Latin rites were practised side by side in its churches until the 15th century. It was taken by the Turks in 1480. Attacked by the Venetians in 1484, it suddenly surrendered after five days of strenuous resistance, an event that has perplexed historians. It participated in the anti-Spanish revolt that shook Lecce and sent repercussions throughout the peninsula, and it adhered enthusiastically to the cause of the Risorgimento.

The triangular Piazza Antonio Salandra, at the centre of the city, is a theatrical piece of town planning that revolves around the exuberant **Guglia dell'Immacolata** (1769). The **Palazzo della Prefettura**, rebuilt in 1772, has an open arcade on the ground floor and a vaulted loggia on the floor above, both with trefoil arches. Above the shop fronts along the other sides of the piazza are ironwork balconies and elegant *logge*, some of which have been wholly or partially walled up. The adjacent piazza takes its name from the church of **San Domenico**, built in the late 16th century but restored, in Baroque form, after 1743. The façade hosts a strange colony of grotesque herms and caryatids.

The former **castle** of the dukes of Conversano, now the town hall, was begun by Giovanni Antonio Acquaviva d'Aragona, who in the early 16th century built the central block (distinguished by its crenellated battlements on unadorned arched corbels) and the mandorla-like corner bastions. The other parts are clearly later additions. Adjoining the medieval town walls is a *largo* containing the curious octagonal aedicule (1603) called the *Osanna*, composed of eight small columns joined by polyfoil arches, surmounted by a segmented stone cupola with eight pinnacles and a sculptured finial.

The **cathedral**, founded by Benedictines in 1090 on the site of a Basilian church, was partially rebuilt after an earthquake of 1230, enlarged in the following century, and modified several times after that, particularly in 1721 by Ferdinando Sanfelice, when additions were made to the façade and interior. The latter was restored in 1900 to an earlier, though not original, form. Within, the nave and aisles are separated by compound piers with engaged columns. The rounded arches on the south side are those of the original building; the pointed arches on the north are part of the 13th-century reconstruction. Above the altars are paintings by local artists and a 13th-century Catalan Crucifix which, according to legend, began to bleed when the Saracens attempted to carry it off. On the walls and piers are frescoes dating from the 13th–15th centuries.

Galatina

Galatina is an important wine-producing centre. It hosted an important Greek colony during the Middle Ages, and the Greek dialect and customs were maintained until the dawn of the modern era. Later, it was incorporated into the county of Soleto. The Franciscan church of Santa Caterina d'Alessandria (*described below*) reflects the wealth and influence of the town's feudal lords, the barons Orsini. Galatina also has a small Museo Civico (Piazza Umberto), with coins and weapons, and a Museo d'Arte Pietro Cavoti (Piazza Alighieri; *both temporarily closed*). The parish church of Santi Pietro e Paolo, though of little interest artistically, once held the cure for tarantism: the miraculous waters of a spring discovered by St Paul, whose journey from the Holy Land to Rome included a stop at Galatina, as locals will tell you.

THE DEVIL MADE ME DO IT

The complex phenomenon of *tarantolati* has given scholars a great deal of material for study and analysis. The best known research was conducted in 1959 by the ethnologist Ernesto de Martino (1908–65), who published his results in *La Terra del Rimorso*.

First of all, it's hard to identify the *taranta*: the chief candidates are *Licosa tarentula* and *Latrodectus guttatus*. The former is a large, aggressive spider whose bite is locally troublesome but has little overall effect; the latter, more modest in appearance and behaviour, has a bite that is inconsequential locally, but causes severe psycho-motorial excitement, headache, diffuse pain, muscular stiffening, kidney failure and sexual dysfunction.

But this doesn't seem to be the essence of *tarantismo* either. In most cases, in fact, the phenomenon occurs in the absence of a physical 'bite'. Clearly, it involves facts and experiences that lie outside the realm of physical pathology.

The process of recovery passes through therapeutic convulsive crises that discharge psycho-emotional tension. It is easy to recognise a pre-Christian legacy behind this 'cure': an integral part of pagan religious piety (particularly the Greek, which was widespread in southern Italy) was maenadism, a form of religious exaltation that was expressed (as tarantism is) in wild, uncontrolled movements. If one gives a demoniacal interpretation to the phenomenon (and an exorcistic slant to its 'cure') the result is clear: the spiritual power of the sacred restores balance and order where evil has wreaked havoc in the individual and in society.

It is interesting to note that the phenomenon of *tarantolati*, recently limited to the Salento and Galatina, was originally common throughout the South. The proof is the well-known Neapolitan popular dance called the *tarantella*, whose frenzied movements are intended to mime the delirium of *tarantolati*.

The church of **Santa Caterina d'Alessandria** was begun by Balzo Orsini in 1384 and completed by his son Giovanni in 1460. It has a façade in the late Apulian Romanesque manner, with three gables lined with arched corbel tables. The central portal (1397) is flanked by slender columns on much-worn lions. It has three bands of intricately carved moulding; those nearest the door show a marked Eastern influence. In the lintel are relief figures of Christ and the Apostles and, above the rounded arches, a Classical pediment, surmounted by a fine rose window. The lateral doorways are placed asymmetrically to the gables above, creating a disturbing sensation of imbalance.

The interior (*apply for admission at the monastery*) is remarkable for its construction and its decorative scheme. Massive walls pierced by wide drop arches separate the nave from the double side aisles. The nave, like the aisleless nave of San Francesco in Assisi, is articulated into bays by clusters of columns and pilasters from which ribbed cross-vaults spring. On the walls and in the vault, numerous frescoes (badly damaged) illustrate the Old and New Testaments and provide insight into the nature of feudal life in Puglia. Superficially resembling the frescoes of Giotto's school at Assisi, they are attributed to central Italian artists working in the early 15th century. Also of interest are the apocryphal account of the life of the Virgin depicted in the south aisle and the episodes from the life of St Catherine of Alexandria in the presbytery. Here, against the north wall, is the tomb of Raimondello del Balzo Orsini, with the deceased depicted supine in a Franciscan habit and again, kneeling, on the sarcophagus. Beyond the sanctuary is the octagonal apsidal chapel constructed by Giovanni Antonio Orsini. The latter's tomb, surmounted by a baldachin with four columns carried by lions, stands against the rear wall.

The treasury contains a silver reliquary shrine and other precious objects, possibly of Puglian workmanship, a portable Byzantine mosaic of the Redeemer set on wood and an icon of the Madonna in a silver-gilt frame.

Soleto

Soleto is interesting for its medieval monuments. A Messapian town, it has been identified with the *Soletum* of Pliny. Like Galatina, it adhered closely to eastern cultural and religious traditions throughout the Middle Ages; the Latin rite was not instituted in its churches until 1598. The parish church of **Santa Maria Assunta**, rebuilt in 1770–83, is flanked by a campanile begun in 1397 by Raimondello Orsini and completed in the early 15th century by Giovanni Antonio Orsini. The structure, which is commonly referred to as the *Guglia di Raimondello*, represents a graceful compromise between Romanesque and Gothic building canons. A similar confluence of styles distinguishes the façade (1347) of the small chapel.

Copertino

Copertino is known for its imposing castle, which stands at the northwest corner of the old town. The overall design was drawn up by Evangelista Menga, who was also the architect of the castles at Mola and Barletta. The fortress is made up of two distinct parts: a Renaissance exterior, rectangular in plan with pointed bastions and a broad moat; and an inner structure of earlier date, which includes the high Angevin keep and the rooms in the north wing, referred to as the Castello Vecchio. The east wall, nearly 120m long, contains an elaborate Renaissance portal surmounted by rosettes and medallions with effigies of illustrious figures. Beyond is a vaulted entrance hall with arrow-loops and offset doorways. The inner court (*open daily 8.30–1.30; T: 0832 931612*) is surrounded by buildings of different epochs; the Renaissance Cappella di San Marco, on the right, has a fine portal and a small rose window. Inside you can see frescoes by a local artist and the sarcophagi of Umberto and Stefano Squardiafico (d. 1562 and 1568 respectively). Adjacent to the chapel is a room with a large fireplace, from which entrance is gained to the vaulted corridor that runs round the north, west and south walls. Steps in the southwest corner of the courtyard mount via a terrace to the monumental apartments of the Castello Vecchio; the Angevin keep is entered through an archway in the southeast corner of the court-yard.

PRACTICAL INFORMATION

GETTING AROUND

• **By air:** The towns in this chapter can be reached via the airport at Brindisi. SITA buses connect central Brindisi to Casale Airport, 16km north of the city, There is no public transport (other than taxi services) between downtown Taranto and Taranto Grottaglie Airport. More at www.seap-puglia.it, the site for all Puglian airports; also, Brindisi Casale information, T: 0831 411 7208, Taranto Grottaglia information, T: 099 562 5204, freephone T: 800 949 944.

• **By rail:** Lecce is the southeastern ter-minus of the Trenitalia (www.trenitalia.it) network. There are Eurostar and Intercity trains from Brindisi and points north, non-stop in 20–25mins. Many towns of the Salentine peninsula (notably Otranto, Maglie, Gallipoli, Casarano, Nardò and Copertino) are served by local trains of the Ferrovie del Sud-Est (www.fseonline.it, T: 800 079 090). The same company operates trains from Martina Franca to Lecce via Cisternino, Ceglie Messapica, Francavilla Fontana and Manduria. A secondary line of the state railways (FS) connects Brindisi and Taranto; trains stop at Mesagne, Oria, Francavilla Fontana and Grottaglie.

INFORMATION OFFICES

Brindisi Azienda di Promozione Turistica, Via Cristoforo Colombo 88, T: 0831 562126; Ufficio Informazioni e di Accoglienza Turistica, Lungomare Regina Margherita, T: 0831 523072
Francavilla Fontana Via Municipio 16, T: 0831 811262.
Lecce Azienda di Promozione Turistica, Via Monte San Michele, T: 0832 314117.; Ufficio Informazioni e di Accoglienza Turistica, Corso Vittorio Emanuele II 43, T: 0832 248092.
Gallipoli Piazza Aldo Moro, T: 0833 262529.
Otranto Piazza Castello, T: 0836 801436.
Santa Cesarea Terme Via Roma 209, T: 0836 944043.

HOTELS

Avetrana
€ **Masseria Bosco**. A delightful old farmhouse lovingly restored to make 12 comfortable rooms and a restaurant serving delicious local delicacies. Via Stazione km 1, T: 099 970 4099; www.masseriabosco.it

Ceglie Messapica
€ **La Fontanina**. Set amid olive and almond groves 9km outside the town, on the Ostuni–Francavilla road; pool, playground, free bikes and a great restaurant. Open all year. Strada Provinciale Ostuni–Francavilla, Contrada Palagogna, T: 0831 380932, www.fontanina.it

Galatina
€ **Hermitage**. Outside the village in a large park, with pleasant rooms, pool, gym, *bocce*. Open all year. Strada Statale 476, km 18; T: 0836 565422.
€€ **Palazzo Baldi**. Eight rooms (and a good restaurant) of refined elegance in a 16th-century patrician residence, once home to the bishop. Corte Baldi 2, T: 0836 568345, www.hotelpalazzobaldi.com

Gallipoli
€€ **Palazzo del Corso**. A romantic little hotel (7 rooms) in a beautifully restored town house with rooftop sauna, whirlpool and aroma therapy baths. Corso Roma 145, T: 264040, www.hotelpalazzodelcorso.it
€€ **Palazzo Mosco**. A second historic property elegantly restored and furnished with charm, under the same management as Palazzo del Corso. Via Micetti 26, T: 0833 266562, www.hotelpalazzodelcorso.it
€ **Relais Corte Palmieri**. The smallest and most intimate of Gallipoli's three historic *hôtels de charme*, in an 18th-century house tucked away in a secluded corner of the old town. Corte Palmieri 3, T: 0833 265318, www.hotelpalazzodelcorso.it

Lecce
€€€ **Patria Palace**. A beautiful reno-vated town house, with good restau-rant, across the square from Santa Croce. Rooms are high quality, spacious and very comfortable, though slightly anodyne. Open all year. Piazzetta Gabriele Riccardi 13, T: 0832 245111, www.patriapalacelecce.it

Marittima di Diso
€€ **Il Convento di Santa Maria di Costantinopoli**. Legend has it that this convent, 30mins south of Otranto, was established by the Madonna di Costantinopoli herself. Purchased by an eminent British couple some years ago and endowed with a fabulous collection of African and Asian art, it is now a delightful small B&B with three rooms and pool. Via Convento, T: 7736 362 328, www.salentonascosto.it/convento.html

Otranto
€€ **Masseria Montelauro**. ■ A splen-didly restored country house, historical-ly authentic on the outside and tasteful-ly modern within, making extensive use of white walls and light-coloured fabrics; rooms with private garden entrance, pool, cooking lessons, horse-riding and walking. Via Uggiano la Chiesa, T: 0836 806203, www.masseriamontelauro.it
€ **Rosa Antico**. On the outskirts of town, in a 16th-century villa with park and orange grove; 10 comfortable rooms, courteous staff. Open all year.

SS 16, T: 0836 801563,
www.hotelrosaantico.it

RESTAURANTS

Brindisi

€€€ **La Lanterna**. Elegant, refined
seafood restaurant in the 15th-century
Palazzo Seripando. Closed Sun and
Aug. Via Giovanni Tarantini 14, T: 0831
564026.

€€ **Penny**. Excellent fish restaurant
(with pizza) near the harbour. Closed
Mon and early Sept. Via San Francesco
1, T: 0831 563013.

€€ **Trattoria Pantagruele**. Restaurant
offering good regional dishes from land
and sea. Closed Sun evening and Mon
in winter, Sat and Sun in July–Aug
(completely closed two weeks in Aug).
Via Salita di Ripalta 1–3, T: 0831 560
605.

€ **Il Cantinone**. Characteristic trattoria.
Closed Tues and mid-Aug. Via de Leo 4,
T: 0831 562122.

Carovigno

€€ **Già Sotto l'Arco**. ■ Unpretentious
but good restaurant. Closed Mon and a
few days in June and Jan. Corso Vittorio
Emanuele 71, T: 0831 996286.

Cavallino

€ **Osteria del Pozzo Vecchio**. *Osteria*
with a strong local following. Open
evenings (lunch also on Sun and holidays), closed Mon and 10 days in Feb.
Via Silvestro 16, T: 0832 611649.

Ceglie Messapica

€ **Cibus**. Warm, family-run trattoria
with commendable local dishes. Closed
Tues and early July. Via Chianche di
Scarano 7, T: 0831 388980.

€€ **Fornello da Ricci**. ■ Delightful
traditional restaurant with garden.

Closed Mon evening, Tues and
Jan–early Feb. Contrada Montevicoli,
T: 0831 377104.

Corigliano d'Otranto

€ **Anichirio**. Simple trattoria. Open
evenings, closed Mon and in July–Aug.
Via Capiterra 5, T: 0836 320839.

Gallipoli

€€ **Bastione**. Romantic restaurant by
the sea, with good fish and wonderful
views. Closed Tues and Nov. Via Riviera
Nazario Sauro 28, T: 0833 263836.

€€ **Capriccio**. Lively trattoria known
for its fresh seafood. Closed Mon
(except in summer). Via Bovio 14,
T: 0833 261545.

€€ **La Puritate**. Restaurant by the
water, in a little square with outside
seating in summer. Closed Wed (except
in summer) and Oct. Via Sant'Elia 18,
T: 0833 264205.

€ **Al Pescatore**. Hotel restaurant
famous for fresh fish. Closed Mon.
Via Zacheo 15, T: 0833 263656.

Lecce

€€ **Borgo Antico**. Traditional Salentine
seafood and broad selection of regional
wines. Closed Mon and late July–early
Aug. Via Bernardini 16, T: 0832
241569.

€€ **Picton**. Characteristic restaurant in
a lovely historic building, serving a
good selection of local dishes. Closed
Mon and late Sept, Jun and Nov.
Via Idomeneo 14, T: 0832 332383.

€ **Cucina Casereccia**. Popular trattoria
near the Villa Comunale. Closed Sun
evening, Mon and early Sept.
Via Costadura 9, T: 0832 245178.

€ **Da Guido & Figli**. Restaurant in a
cool crypt, popular with locals at lunch
time. Via XXV Luglio 14, T: 0832
305868.

Lizzanello (10km southeast of Lecce)
€€ **Fucazzeria da Francesco**. Farm serving traditional local dishes. Open for dinner (lunch by reservation), closed Tues (except in summer). Strada Provinciale per Cavallino, Contrada Caprarica, T: 0832 654481.

Minervino di Lecce
€ **Da Cazzatino**. Good country restaurant. Closed Tues (except in summer) and Oct. Via Manzoni 40, Cocumola, T: 0836 954455.

Nardò
€ **La Barchetta**. Restaurant-pizzeria near the Porto Selvaggio park. Closed Mon (except in summer) and Dec. Via Mastro Gioffreda 5, at Santa Caterina, T: 0833 574124.

€ **Paglialunga**. Fresh fish in a pleasant restaurant by the sea. Closed Mon (except in summer) and Dec. Via Lamarmora 117 at Santa Maria al Bagno, T: 0833 575728.

Otranto
€€ **Da Sergio**. Exquisitely prepared fresh fish, in the historic town centre. Closed Wed (except in summer) and Jan–Feb. Corso Garibaldi 9, T: 0836 801408.

Porto Cesareo (west of Copertino)
€€ **L'Angolo di Beppe**. Creative interpretations of traditional fish recipes. Closed Mon. Via Zanella 22, T: 0833 565333.

San Donato di Lecce (11km south of Lecce)
€ **Da Bruna**. Popular restaurant-pizzeria. Open evenings only, closed Mon and Sept. Via Risorgimento 8, T: 0832 658207.

Sannicola (8km northeast of Gallipoli)
€ **La Casina del Doganiere**. Popular pizzeria. Closed Mon. Via Sferracavalli,

T: 0833 232072.
Taviano
€ **A Casa Tu Martinu**. Traditional *osteria* in an 18th-century town house, with garden seating in summer. Open evenings only, closed Mon and Sept–Oct. Via Corsica 95, T: 0833 913652.

LOCAL SPECIALITIES

Brindisi Pasticceria Esmeralda, at Via de Leo 42, specialises in almond-based recipes. **Francavilla Fontana** is known for its handmade textiles; **Grottaglie** is famous for its pottery. **Lecce** and its province are famous for their handmade wool and cotton rugs, and for their wrought-iron. The entire Salentine is renowned for its papier-mâché, traditionally employed in the making of religious statuettes.

FESTIVALS & EVENTS

Brindisi *Il Cavallo Parato* The bishop accompanies a tabernacle holding the Eucharist, borne by a white horse, through town in a colourful procession recalling an episode of 1250. It seems that St Louis, returning from the Sixth Crusade, was shipwrecked off Brindisi but swam ashore with the Holy Sacrament his ship was carrying and was rescued on the beach by the bishop and carried to safety on the latter's white steed, Corpus Domini (June).

Carovigno *Madonna del Belvedere* At the chapel of the same name, 4km northeast of the town, the Virgin is celebrated by *'nzegne*, tarantella-dancing flag throwers, Tues after Easter and second Sun in Sept.

Copertino *Funerale di Lu Paulinu* Paulinu is the deceased Carnival, borne in effigy through the streets in a hearse, accompanied by *Quaremma* (Lent), his wife, and a procession of clergy and townspeople. On his passage the inhabitants hang out an effigy of an old woman, which remains 'exposed' until Easter. The 'funeral' is celebrated on Ash Wednesday.

Galatina *San Pietro e Paolo* Now simply a religious holiday with festive lights and a solemn procession, this was once the feast of the *tarantolati*, a term broadly applied to anyone with any sort of pathology concerning the brain or central nervous system. Patients were brought here from great distances and treated by drinking from a country spring, later enclosed in the church of Santi Pietro e Paolo. The water's curative powers were a gift, it seems, of St Paul, patron saint of those bitten by poisonous animals. Its presence supposedly makes residents of Galatina immune to poisons, 28–30 June.

Galatone *Sparo del Panno* During Mass on Easter Day explosive charges accompany the unveiling of a statue of the Resurrected Christ, pleasing adults, thrilling children and frightening babies among the faithful.

Lecce National Wine Fair in May–June; *SS Oronzo e Cataldo* (patron saints of the city), 24–26 Aug; Salentine Celebrations, including exhibitions, literary contests, sporting events, etc, in Oct; *Fiera di Santa Lucia* A fascinating fair, beginning on St Lucy's Day, where Nativity figures and crib scenery are sold, accompanied by a *tableau vivant* of the Nativity in the amphitheatre, 13–24 Dec.

Grottaglie *San Ciro* An immense bonfire is lit in the main square, followed by a solemn procession and fireworks—a celebration that has its origins in the observance of the winter solstice, last Sun in Jan; *Giocosa Battaglia* A historic victory over the Turks is the pretext for this week of pageantry and partying, culminating in the presentation of the enemy's colours to the Virgin, 23–30 Aug; *Natale in Gravina* Re-enactment of the Nativity in a lovely natural setting, 24 Dec.

Mesagne *Presepe Vivente* Large, beautiful *tableau vivant* of the Nativity set up on Christmas Day in the former Convento dei Celestini; visited by the Magi on Jan 6.

Oria *Corteo Storico di Federico II e Torneo dei Rioni* Re-enactment of the tournament and festivities that accompanied the wedding of Emperor Frederick II and Yolande of Jerusalem, second Sat and Sun in Aug.

San Vito dei Normanni *Barocco Festival Leonardo Leo* Piazza L. Leo 9, Aug, www.baroccofestival.it

Santa Cesarea Terme *Processione in Mare* Cesarea was a local girl who took refuge in a sea cave to escape her incestuous father, walking on a stormy sea to get there; today her statue is carried by boat, 11 Sept.

PRACTICAL INFORMATION

PLANNING YOUR TRIP

When to go

Southern Italy has one of the pleasantest climates in Europe. Especially on the coast, cloudless skies are the norm and temperatures are mild throughout the year (the average varies between 11°C in winter and 25°C in summer). November and December are the rainiest months, July and August the sunniest. As you move into the mountainous interior, where the temperate influence of the Mediterranean fades, the temperature range becomes considerably greater and precipitation more frequent. Winter in these regions can be quite severe (even snowy), and summer blazing hot. Typical of all seasons is the warm African wind known as the *scirocco*, which can blow for three or four days in a row and often carries fine grains of Sahara sand. Other common winds are the chill northerly *tramontana* and the mild easterly *grecale*. The best months for visiting southern Italy are April (when orange and lemon blossoms fill the air with their sweet scent), May (when the mantle of wild flowers is at its peak), September (when the figs, grapes and prickly pears come in) and October (the month for walnuts, chestnuts and the very first oranges). In July and August, beaches and resorts can be crowded.

Maps

The Touring Club Italiano (TCI, www.touringclub.it) publishes several sets of excellent maps, including *Carta Stradale d'Europa: Italia* on a scale of 1:1,000,000; the *Atlante Stradale Touring* (1:800,000); and the *Carta Stradale d'Italia* (1:200,000). The latter is divided into 15 sheets covering the regions of Italy. These are also published as an atlas (with a comprehensive index) called the *Atlante Stradale d'Italia*, in three volumes. The ones entitled *Centro* and *Sud* cover the southern mainland. These maps are available from TCI offices and at many booksellers.

The Istituto Geografico Militare (www.igmi.org), publishes a map of Italy on a scale of 1:100,000 in 277 sheets and a field survey, partly 1:50,000, partly 1:25,000, which are invaluable for the detailed exploration of the country, especially its more mountainous regions; the coverage is, however, still far from complete at the larger scales and some of the maps are out of date.

Road maps, city maps and custom itineraries (in English) may be found online at www.mappy.com and www.viamichelin.com. Satellite photography at earth.google.com.

Health and insurance

EU citizens have the right to health services in Italy if they have the E111 form (available from post offices). Italy has no medical programme covering US or Canadian citizens, who are advised to take out insurance before travelling. First Aid (*Pronto*

Soccorso) is available at all hospitals, railway stations and airports. For emergencies T: 118 (rescue or ambulance) 113 (State Police) or 112 (*Carabinieri*).

Disabled travellers

All new public buildings are now obliged by law to provide easy access and specially designed facilities for the disabled. Historic buildings are more difficult to convert, and access difficulties still exist. Hotels that cater for the disabled are indicated in tourist board lists. Airports and railway stations provide assistance, and certain trains are equipped to transport wheelchairs. Access to town centres is allowed for cars with disabled drivers or passengers, and special parking places are reserved for them. For further information, contact the tourist board in the city of interest.

ACCOMMODATION

Hotels

A selection of hotels, chosen on the basis of character or location, is given at the end of each chapter. Hotels are classified as expensive (€200 or over), moderate (€100–200), or inexpensive (under €100). It is advisable to book well in advance, especially between May and October; if you cancel the booking with at least 72 hours' notice you can claim back part or all of your deposit. Service charges are included in the rates. By law breakfast is an optional extra, although a lot of hotels will include it in the room price. When booking, always specify if you want breakfast or not. If you are staying in a hotel in a town, it is often more fun to go round the corner to the nearest café. Hotels are now obliged by law (for tax purposes) to issue an official receipt to customers: you can be fined if you leave the premises without one.

Bed and breakfast

B&B accommodation is offered in most areas. Rooms are usually in private homes, and can be booked through a central agency. Contact Caffelletto, Via Procaccini 7, 20154 Milano, T: 02 331 1814, www.caffelletto.it; BedandBreakfast.com, www.bedandbreakfast.com; or Bed & Breakfast in Europe, www.bedandbreakfastineurope.com/italia/en.htm.

Residences

A new type of hotel, called a *residenza*, has been introduced into Italy. Residences are normally in a building, or a group of houses of historic interest, often a castle or a monastery. They may have only a few rooms, and sometimes offer self-catering. They are listed separately in tourist office lists, with their prices.

Farm stays—Agriturismo

The short-term rental of space in villas and farmhouses (*agriturismo*) is an alternative form of accommodation. Terms vary greatly from bed-and-breakfast to self-contained flats. For travellers with their own transport, or for families, this is an excellent (and usually cheap) way of visiting the Italian countryside. Some farms require a minimum stay. Cultural or recreational activities, such as horse-riding, are sometimes also provided. Information is supplied by local tourist offices. The main organisations dealing with *agriturismo* are:

Agriturist, Corso Vittorio Emanuele 101, Rome, T: 06 685 2342, www.agriturist.it.

Terranostra, Via XXIV Maggio 43, Rome, T: 06 468 2370, www.terranostra.it. Terranostra publish an annual list of *agriturismo* accommodation: *Vacanze Natura*.

Turismo Verde, Via Mariano Fortuny 20, Rome, T: 06 324 0111, www.turismoverde.it.

BLUE GUIDES RECOMMENDED

Hotels, restaurants and cafés that are particularly good choices in their category—in terms of location, charm, value for money or the quality of the experience they provide—carry the **Blue Guides Recommended** sign: ■. All establishments highlighted in this way have been selected by our authors, editors or contributors as places they have particularly enjoyed and would be happy to recommend to others. We only recommend establishments that we have visited. To keep our entries up to date, reader feedback is essential: please do not hesitate to email us (www.blueguides.com) with any views, corrections or suggestions.

Camping

Camping is well organised throughout Italy. Campsites are listed in the local information offices' publications. Full details of the sites in Italy are published annually by the **Touring Club Italiano**, (T: 02 8901 1383, www.touringclub.it) in *Campeggi e Villaggi Turistici in Italia*. The **Federazione Italiana Campeggiatori** (T: 055 882 391, www.federcampeggio.it) also publishes an annual guide (*Guida Camping d'Italia*) and maintains an information office and booking service.

Youth hostels

The Associazione Italiana Alberghi per la Gioventù (Italian Youth Hostels Association; T: 06 487 1152, www.ostellionline.org) runs many hostels, which are listed in its free annual guide. A membership card of the AIG or the International Youth Hostel Federation is required for access to Italian Youth Hostels. Details from the Youth Hostels Association, Trevelyan House, Dimple Road, Matlock, Derbyshire, DE4 3YH; T: 0870 770 8868, www.yha.org.uk, and from the National Offices of American Youth Hostels Inc, at Hostelling International-USA, 8401 Colesville Road, Suite 600, Silver Spring, MD 20910; T: 301 495 1240, www.hiayh.org

Religious institutions

Religious institutions sometimes offer simple but comfortable accommodation at very reasonable prices. For listings of convents, monasteries and other religious institutions offering accommodation, contact the Arcivescovado of the city of your choice (for Naples, for instance, the address is: *Archivescovado di Napoli, Napoli, Italia*), or the local tourist information office.

GETTING AROUND

By car

The easiest way to tour southern Italy is by car. Regardless of whether you are driving your own car or a hired vehicle, Italian law requires you to carry a valid driving licence. You must also keep a red triangle in the car (you can hire one from ACI for a minimal charge and return it at the border).

As 80 per cent of goods transported travel by road, lorries pose a constant hazard, and the degree of congestion in even the smallest towns defies imagination.

Certain customs differ radically from those in Britain or America. Pedestrians have the right of way at zebra crossings, although you're taking your life in your hands if you step into the street without looking. Unless otherwise indicated, cars entering a road from the right are given right of way. Trams and trains always have right of way. If an oncoming driver flashes his headlights, it means he is proceeding and not giving you precedence. In towns, Italian drivers frequently change lanes without warning. They also tend to ignore pedestrian crossings.

Roads in Italy

Italy's motorways (*autostrade*; for information, www.autostrade.it) are indicated by green signs or, near the entrance ramps, by large boards of overhead lights. All are toll roads except on the A3 south of Salerno, which is toll free. At the entrance to motorways, the two directions are indicated by the name of the most important town (and not by the nearest town), which can be momentarily confusing. Dual-carriageways are called *superstrade* (also indicated by green signs). Italy has an excellent network of secondary highways (*strade statali, regionali* or *provinciali*, indicated by blue signs marked SS, SR or SP; on maps simply by a number).

Parking

Many cities have taken the wise step of closing their historic centres to traffic (except for residents). Access is allowed to hotels and for the disabled. It is always advisable to leave your car in a supervised car park, though with a bit of effort it is almost always possible to find a place to park free of charge, away from the town centre. However, to do so overnight, or even for brief periods in or around Naples and Bari, is not advisable. Always lock your car when parked, and never leave anything of value inside it.

By rail

Information on rail links is given in individual chapters. The Italian Railways (Trenitalia) run eight categories of trains.

ES (Eurostar), high-speed trains running between major Italian cities.

EC (Eurocity), international express trains running between the main Italian and European cities.

EN (Euronotte), overnight international express trains with sleeping car or couchette service.

IC (Intercity), express trains running between major Italian cities.

E (Espressi), long-distance trains, not as fast as the Intercity trains.

IR (Interregionali), intermediate-distance trains making more stops than the Espressi.

R (Regionali), local trains stopping at all stations.

M (Metropolitani), surface or underground commuter trains.

Booking seats

Seats can be booked in advance, as early as two months ahead and as late as 15mins before departure, from the main cities at the station booking office (usually open daily 7am–10pm), at travel agencies representing Trenitalia, on the Internet (www.trenitalia.it), or by phone (T: 892021). Trenitalia's telephone booking service, called Ticketless, gives you a customer code you must repeat to the train conductor to receive your ticket.

Tickets

Tickets must be bought at the station, from travel agents representing Trenitalia, on the Internet (www.trenitalia.it), or by phone (T: 892021) before starting a journey, otherwise a fairly large supplement has to be paid on the train. Most tickets are valid for 60 days after the date of issue. Some trains charge a special supplement; and on others seats must be booked in advance. It is therefore always necessary to specify which train you are intending to take as well as the destination when buying tickets. You must stamp the date of your journey on the ticket in the meters located on or near the station platforms before you get on the train. There are limitations on travelling short distances on some trains. Children under four travel free and those between four and twelve pay half price. There are also reductions for families, groups, weekend travel, last-minute booking, travel on particular trains, etc.

By bus

Local and long-distance buses between the main towns in southern Italy are not as frequent as they are in the north, and as increasing numbers of residents become independently mobile, the service is diminishing. Except in areas of particular interest to non-residents (such as Sorrento and the Amalfi Coast), most buses now carry school children from the villages to the towns in the early morning, and from the towns to the villages in the afternoon. Buses still serve most towns not reached by rail at least once a day, leaving major cities from a depot usually at or near the railway station.

Information on regional bus services is given in each individual section of this book. Accurate timetables can be obtained from the local tourist boards.

City buses are an excellent means of getting about in most towns, with the notable exception of Naples, where traffic is often paralysed; in this case, the underground railway (Metropolitana) is the swiftest and easiest means of moving across town. Almost everywhere, tickets must be purchased before boarding (at tobacconists, bars, news-stands, information offices and so on) and stamped in a machine on board.

Cycling and walking

Cycling and walking have become more popular in Italy in recent years and more information is available locally. The local offices of the Club Alpino Italiano (CAI) and the Worldwide Fund for Nature (WWF) provide all the necessary information (see individual sections).

Taxis

These are hired from ranks or by telephone; there are no cruising cabs. Before engaging a taxi, it is advisable to make sure it has a meter in working order. Fares vary from city to city but are generally cheaper than London taxis, though considerably more expensive than New York taxis. No tip is expected. Supplements are charged for late-night journeys and for luggage. There is a heavy surcharge when the destination is outside the town limits (ask roughly how much the fare is likely to be).

LANGUAGE

Even a few words of Italian are a great advantage in Italy, where any attempt to speak the language is appreciated. Local dialects vary greatly, but even where dialect is universally used, nearly everybody can speak and understand Italian. Double consonants call for special care as each must be sounded. Consonants are pronounced roughly as in English with the following exceptions:

c and cc	before e and i have the sound of ch in chess.
ch	before e and i has the sound of k.
g and gg	before e and i are always soft, like j in jelly.
gh	always hard, like g in get.
gl	nearly always like lli in million (there are a few exceptions, for example, *negligere*, where it is pronounced as in English).
gn	is like ny in lanyard.
gu and qu	always like gw and kw.
j	like y in you
s	like s in six except when it occurs between two vowels, when it is soft, like the English z or the s in rose.
sc	before e and i is pronounced like sh in ship.

ss	always like the **ss** in dress, with both consonants sounded.
z and **zz**	usually pronounced like **ts**, but occasionally have the sound of **dz** before a long vowel.

Every vowel should be articulated separately in Italian. The stress normally falls on the penultimate syllable; in modern practice an accent sign is usually only written when the stress is on the last syllable, for example, *città*, or to differentiate between two words similarly spelt but with a different meaning: for example, *e* ('and') and *è* ('is').

Customs and etiquette

Attention should be paid to the more formal manners of the Italians. It is customary to open conversation in shops and such places with the courtesy of *buon giorno* ('good day') or *buona sera* ('good evening'). The deprecatory expression *prego* ('don't mention it') is everywhere the obligatory and automatic response to *grazie* ('thank you'). The phrases *per piacere* or *per favore* ('please'), *permesso* ('excuse me'), used when pushing past someone (essential on public transport), *scusi* ('sorry'; also used when something is not heard), should not be forgotten. Shaking hands is an essential part of greeting and leave-taking. In shops and offices a certain amount of self-assertion is taken for granted, as queues are not the general rule and it is incumbent on the inquirer or customer to get him or herself a hearing.

OPENING TIMES

The opening times of museums, sites and monuments have been given in the text, though they often change without warning. National museums and monuments are usually open daily 9am–7pm, plus evening hours in summer. Archaeological sites generally open at 9am and close at dusk. Naturally, as opening times are constantly being altered, care should be taken to allow enough time for variations.

Some museums are closed on the main public holidays: 1st January, Easter, 1st May, 15th August and 25th December. Some smaller museums have suspended regular hours altogether and are now open by appointment only. Their telephone numbers are included in the text, and visits may be booked by calling in advance.

Entrance fees vary according to your age and nationality; British citizens under 18 and over 60 or 65 are entitled to free admission to national museums and monuments because of reciprocal arrangements in Britain, but you need to be able to prove your age. During the *Settimana per i Beni Culturali e Ambientali* (Cultural and Environmental Heritage Week), usually held early in December, entrance to national museums is free for all.

Churches open quite early in the morning (often for 6 o'clock Mass), but are normally closed during the middle of the day (12–3, 4 or 5pm), although cathedrals and some of the large churches may be open without a break during daylight hours.

Smaller churches and oratories are often open only in the early morning, but the key can usually be found by enquiring locally. The sacristan will also show closed chapels and crypts, and a small tip should be given. Some churches now ask that sightseers do not enter during a service, but normally visitors may do so, provided they are silent and do not approach the altar in use. At all times they are expected to cover their legs and arms, and generally dress with decorum. An entrance fee is becoming customary for admission to treasuries, bell-towers, and so on. Many churches have coin-operated lights to illuminate frescoes and altarpieces. In Holy Week most of the pictures are covered and are not shown. Churches are often unaligned. Descriptions in the text always refer to liturgical, not compass north, east, west and south.

Government offices usually work Mon–Sat 8 or 9–1 or 2; businesses Mon–Fri 8.30 or 9–12.30 or 1 & 2.30 or 3–6. Shops generally open Mon–Sat 8.30 or 9–1 and 3.30 or 4–7.30 or 8. Shops selling clothes and other goods are usually closed Mon morning, food shops Wed afternoon, except from mid-June–mid-Sept, when all shops are closed Sat afternoon instead. In resorts during July and August many shops remain open from early morning until late at night.

ADDITIONAL INFORMATION

Banking services

Money can be changed at banks, post offices, travel agencies and some hotels, restaurants and shops, though the rate of exchange can vary considerably. It is easiest to use an ATM machine.

Banks are open Mon–Fri 8.30–1.30 & 2.30–3.30 or 4. The afternoon opening varies from bank to bank, and many banks close early (about 11) the day before a national holiday. Exchange offices are usually open seven days a week at airports and most main railway stations. A limited amount of euros can be obtained from conductors on international trains and at certain stations. For small amounts of money, the difference between hotel and bank rates may be negligible, as banks tend to take a fixed commission.

Crime and personal security

Pickpocketing is a widespread problem in towns all over Italy: it is always advisable not to carry valuables, and to be particularly careful on public transport. Never wear conspicuous jewellery; women should keep their handbags on the side nearer the wall (never on the street side). Crime should be reported at once to the police or the local *carabinieri* office (found in every town and small village). A statement has to be given in order to get a document confirming loss or damage (essential for insurance claims). Interpreters are provided.

Emergency numbers

Police: T: 113 (*Polizia di Stato*) or 112 (*Carabinieri*).
Medical assistance: T: 118.

Electric current

The electrical current in Italy is AC 220 volts/50 cycles. Electrical appliances with a different current need a transformer. Check the voltage with your hotel before using electrical appliances. Appliances manufactured in the UK or America will need an adaptor.

Embassies and consulates

UK	Via Venti Settembre 80/a, Rome, T: 06 4890 3777
US	Via Veneto 121, Rome, T: 06 46741. Open Mon–Fri 8.30–12
Canada	Via Zara 30, Rome, T: 06 4459 8421. Open Mon–Fri 8.30–12.30 & 1.30–4
British Consulate	Via dei Mille 40, Naples, T: 081 401367
US Consulate	Piazza della Repubblica 2, Naples, T: 081 661150

Pharmacies

Pharmacies (*farmacie*) are usually open Mon–Fri 9–1 & 4–7.30 or 8. A few are open also on Sat, Sun and holidays (listed on the door of every pharmacy). In all towns there is also at least one pharmacy open at night (also shown on the door of every pharmacy).

Photography

There are few restrictions on photography in Italy, but permission is necessary to photograph the interiors of churches and museums, and may sometimes be withheld. Care should also be taken before photographing individuals, notably members of the armed forces and the police. Photography is forbidden on railway stations and civil airfields, as well as in frontier zones and near military installations.

Public holidays

The Italian national holidays when offices, shops, and schools are closed are as follows:

1 January	15 August (Assumption)
Easter Sunday and Easter Monday	1 November (All Saints' Day)
25 April (Liberation Day)	8 December (Immaculate Conception)
1 May (Labour Day)	25 December (Christmas Day)
2 June (Republic Day)	26 December (St Stephen)

Each town keeps its patron saint's day as a holiday.

Sales tax rebates

If you're a non-European Union resident, you can claim tax back on purchases made in Italy, provided the total expenditure is more than €150. Ask the vendor for details.

Telephone and postal services

Stamps are sold at tobacco shops (*tabacchi*, marked with a large white 'T') and post offices. *Posta ordinaria* is regular post; *posta prioritaria* receives priority handling, including transport by air mail, and is only slightly more expensive. Correspondence can be addressed to you in Italy c/o the post office by adding '*Fermo Posta*' to the name of the locality.

Phonecards are sold at post offices, tobacconists and some news-stands. For all calls in Italy, local and long-distance, dial the city code (for instance, 081 for Naples), then the telephone number. For international and intercontinental calls, dial 00 plus the country code, then the city code (for numbers in Britain, drop the initial zero), and the telephone number. You can reach an AT&T operator on T: 172 1011, MCI on T: 172 1022, or Sprint on T: 172 1877. For **directory assistance** T: 1244 (numbers in Italy) or 176 (international numbers). You can receive a wake-up call on your phone by dialling 114 and following the prompts (in Italian).

Most car rental agencies can arrange the rental of mobile phones.

Tipping

A service charge of 15 to 18 per cent is added to hotel bills. The service charge is already included when all-inclusive prices are quoted, but it is customary to leave an additional tip in any case. As a guideline and depending on the category of your hotel, a tip of €1–2 is suggested for hotel staff except the conceierge, who may expect a little more (€2–3).

Restaurants add a service charge of approximately 15 per cent to all bills. It is customary, however, to leave a small tip (5–10 per cent) for good service. In cafés and bars, leave 15 per cent if you were served at a table and if a bill does not already include service; and 10–20 euro cents while standing at a counter or bar.

At opera, concerts and the theatre, tip ushers 50 euro cents or more, depending on the price of your seat.

FOOD & DRINK

Restaurants

Italian food is usually good and inexpensive. Generally speaking, the least pretentious *ristorante* (restaurant), *trattoria* (small restaurant) or *osteria* (inn or tavern) provides the best value. A selection of restaurants has been given at the end of each chapter. Prices are given as expensive (€80 or more per head), moderate (€30–80) and inexpensive (under €30). Many places are considerably cheaper at midday. It is always a good idea to reserve.

Restaurants are obliged by law (for tax purposes) to issue a receipt to customers: you can be fined if you leave the premises without one. Prices on the menu do not include a cover charge (shown separately, usually at the bottom of the page), which is added to the bill. The service charge (*servizio*) is now almost always automatically added at the end of the bill; tipping is therefore not strictly necessary, but a few euros are appreciated. Note that many simpler establishments do not offer a written menu.

Bars and cafés

Bars and cafés are open from early morning to late at night and serve numerous varieties of excellent refreshments that are usually taken standing up. As a rule, you must pay the cashier first, then present your receipt to the barman in order to get served. It is customary to leave a small tip for the barman. If you sit at a table the charge is usually higher, and you will be given waiter service (so don't pay first). However, some simple bars have a few tables that can be used with no extra charge, and it is always best to ask, before ordering, whether there is waiter service or not.

Coffee

Italy is considered to have the best coffee in Europe. *Caffè* or *espresso* (black coffee) can be ordered alto or *lungo* (diluted), *corretto* (with a liquor), or *macchiato* (with a dash of hot milk). A *cappuccino* is an espresso with more hot milk than a *caffè macchiato*, and is generally considered a breakfast drink. A glass of hot milk with a dash of coffee in it, called *latte macchiato* is another early-morning favourite. In summer, many drink *caffè freddo* (iced coffee).

Snacks

Gelato (ice cream) is always best from a *gelateria* where it is made on the spot. *Panini* (sandwiches) are made with a variety of cold meats, fish, cheeses, or vegetables, particularly *melanzane* (aubergines) or *zucchine* (courgettes) fried in vegetable oil; vegetarians may also ask for a simple sandwich of *insalata e pomodoro* (lettuce and tomato). *Pizze* (a popular and cheap food throughout Italy), *arancini* (rice croquettes with cheese or meat inside), and other snacks are served in a *pizzeria*, *rosticceria* and *tavola calda*. A *vinaio* often sells wine by the glass and simple food for very reasonable prices. Sandwiches are made up on request at *pizzicherie* and *alimentari* (grocery shops), and *fornai* (bakeries) often sell delicious individual *pizze*, *focaccie* or *schiacciate* (bread with oil and salt) and cakes.

Pasta

Pasta is an essential part of most meals throughout southern Italy. Today, pasta is classified according to its composition and shape. A distinction is drawn between *pasta comune* (spaghetti, rigatoni, lasagne and so on) produced industrially and made of a simple flour and water paste, and *pasta all'uovo* (tortellini, ravioli and so on), made with egg.

Pasta comes in countless forms. An ordinary Italian supermarket usually stocks about 50 different varieties, but some experts estimate that there are more than 600 shapes in all. The differences of shape translate into differences of flavour, even when the pasta is made from the same dough, or by the same manufacturer. The reason for this is that the relation between the surface area and the weight of the pasta varies from one shape to another, causing the sauce to adhere in different ways and to different degrees. Even without a sauce, experts claim to perceive considerable differences in flavour, because the different shapes cook in different ways.

Naples is the classic home of *pastasciutta*, made from a simple flour and water paste rolled into sheets, cut and moulded into the desired shape and then air dried. It is hard and brittle when bought, and when correctly cooked it remains *al dente* (chewy; never soggy), additional moisture being provided by the sauce.

A SHORT HISTORY OF PASTA

Whereas the invention of egg pasta is generally credited to the Chinese, the origin of *pastasciutta* may well be Italian. The Etruscan Tomb of the Reliefs at Cerveteri, near Rome, has stucco decorations representing pasta-making tools: a board and a rolling-pin for rolling out the dough, knives and even a toothed cutting-wheel for making decorative borders. References to lasagne may be found in Cicero and other Roman writers; the name itself is probably derived from the Latin *lagana* or *lasana*, a cooking pot.

By the end of the Middle Ages pasta was known throughout Italy. The 14th-century *Codice del l'Anonimo Toscano*, preserved in the library of Bologna University, contains several serving suggestions; and the poet Boccaccio, in his masterpiece, the *Decameron*, describes an imaginary land of grated parmesan cheese inhabited by people whose only pastime is the making of '*maccheroni e raviuoli*'. Of course, tomato sauce was unheard of until the discovery of America: Boccaccio's contemporaries cooked their macaroni and ravioli in chicken broth and dressed them with fresh butter. An early American appreciator of *pastasciutta* was Thomas Jefferson, who in 1787 brought a spaghetti-making machine from Italy to the United States.

Regional cuisine

The cuisine of southern Italy is as varied as its topography. What follows is a brief summary of the kind of local fare you can expect to find as you explore this culturally and historically diverse region.

Campania

Naples is the historic capital of southern Italy and the region's largest and wealthiest city. It's therefore not surprising that Neapolitan cuisine should be particularly rich and sophisticated, or that Neapolitan recipes should predominate (with slight variations of name and ingredients) in the cuisine of the South as a whole. But the importance of Naples—and its hinterland, Campania—in the culinary field has another origin: the immense variety of fruit, vegetables and grain that grow here. This is the *campania felix* of Roman times, the 'happy land' where everything that is planted, flourishes. It also presents ideal habitats for sheep, cattle and the water buffalo from whose milk *mozzarella di buffala* is made. The combination of wealth, imagination, and excellent raw materials has produced some astounding results.

Antipasti. *Crostini alla napoletana* are among the simplest and tastiest of all crostini. Small, thin slices of bread are covered with mozzarella, chopped anchovies and tomatoes; seasoned with salt and oregano; then lightly toasted in the oven. The *gatto* is fairly common in Neapolitan cooking, although the ingredients often change. It has little to do with the gâteaux of French haute cuisine, notwithstanding its Angevin origins. It is a humble dish, a sort of dumpling made of mashed potatoes, eggs, prosciutto, mozzarella and whatever else happens to be on hand. It is usually served piping hot. *Impepata di cozze* is a simple Neapolitan dish of fresh mussels, poached and dressed with lemon juice, chopped parsley, and olive oil. *Mozzarella in carrozza* (literally 'mozzarella in a carriage') consists of a slice of mozzarella fried between two slices of bread that are dipped in an egg batter, like French toast. *Pagnottine Santa Chiara*, as the name suggests, were invented by the nuns of Santa Chiara. They are savoury cakes made with anchovies, tomatoes, parsley and oregano. *Panzanella alla napoletana* is a favourite salad dish made of crumbled bread, onions, tomatoes, anchovies, basil and garlic (sometimes peppers and green olives are added) all dressed with olive oil. *Peperoni farciti*, stuffed baked peppers, is a peasant dish existing throughout the south in a variety of versions. Three common fillings are olives, capers, parsley, and anchovies; aubergine and tomatoes; macaroni in a savoury sauce. *Taralli col pepe* are rings of crisp bread flavoured with pepper and almonds. Another version uses fennel seeds. *Zucchine a scapece* may be either an antipasto or a side dish. Courgettes are sliced and fried in olive oil, seasoned with vinegar and fresh mint leaves and served cold.

Primi piatti (first courses). *Minestra maritata*, a very old, very typical Neapolitan speciality, is also known as *pignato grasso*. It is a classic winter soup consisting chiefly of beet greens or cabbage boiled with a ham bone and sausages, served hot. *Minestrone napoletano* is similar to all other Italian *minestroni*, with a predominance of yellow courgettes over all the other ingredients. *Zuppa di cardoni*, a rich, tasty dish from the Campanian hinterland, is made of cardoons (an edible thistle) cooked in chicken broth with meat balls, mozzarella, chicken and sausages. *Zuppa alla marinara* is made throughout the south with as many varieties of fish as possible, which are stewed together with clams and mussels in lots of tomato sauce, olive oil, garlic and hot peppers.

Maccheroni cacio e uova is simply macaroni in a cheese and egg sauce, sprinkled with chopped parsley before serving. *Frittata di pasta*, or *pasta fritta*, originally a way of getting good mileage out of leftovers, is now a classic first course in its own right. Vermicelli or macaroni are seasoned with a rich sauce made with meat balls, chopped prosciutto and cheese. The whole concoction, bound together by a few well-beaten eggs, becomes a fragrant and savoury omelette, often considered a complete meal. *Fusilli alla napoletana* are served in a flavoursome sauce made with meat dripping, tomatoes, onions, celery, carrots, ricotta, salami, bacon, garlic and seasoned pecorino cheese. Sometimes spaghetti or macaroni are used instead of fusilli. *Lasagne di Carnevale* is an especially rich dish, popular in Naples at carnival time. Square lasagne are baked in a sauce containing sausages and meat balls, mozzarella, ricotta, and other cheeses and hard-boiled eggs. *Pasta e fagioli all'ischitana*, a speciality of the island of

Ischia, is made with several pasta shapes: spaghetti, tripolini, bucatini and linguine, or whatever leftovers one happens to have on hand. The sauce is made with lots of fresh beans, and is seasoned with hot red peppers. *Pasta alla sorrentina* adds diced scamorza cheese to the tomato sauce, to make it thick and stringy. The pasta thus seasoned is served with lots of grated cheese. *Ragù alla napoletana*, also known as *rrau*, is a delicious sauce for special occasions that is traditionally placed on the stove at dawn and left to simmer slowly all day. It is prepared by melting lard and ham fat in a pan, then adding slices of veal rolled around a filling of grated cheese, garlic, parsley, raisins and pine-nuts. As the sauce cooks, red wine and tomatoes are added. At the end the sauce is used to dress the pasta, while the meat rolls are served as an entrée. *Sartù* is the richest of all Neapolitan dishes. Today only a few Neapolitan restaurants make it regularly, and to taste it at its best you should order it ahead of time. It is a rice pie stuffed with meat balls, sausage, chicken livers, mozzarella, mushrooms, peas, etc. Baked in a mould, it is not only tasty, but also very theatrical.

Timballo di maccheroni, like *sartù*, is a classic dish favoured by the Neapolitan aristocracy. It gradually spread throughout the Kingdom of the Two Sicilies to become one of the most characteristic dishes of southern Italy. It is made with macaroni baked in a pie with a sauce of chicken livers, mushrooms and black truffles. *Spaghetti aglio e olio* is served with a sauce of olive oil, garlic, parsley, and sometimes peperoncini, or hot red peppers; it is best enjoyed after midnight. *Spaghetti alle vongole* is spaghetti in a clam sauce flavoured with onions, tomatoes, cheese and aromatic herbs. Sometimes rice is used instead of spaghetti—*Risotto alle vongole*. *Vermicelli alla carrettiera* (literally 'cart drivers' vermicelli') belongs to a category of pasta (like *spaghetti alla bucaniera* (pirates' spaghetti), and *Maccheroni alla zappatora* (ditch-diggers' macaroni) whose names suggest that their seasoning is so strong that only he-men can be expected to cope with them. In *vermicelli alla carrettiera* a distinctive element is provided by the breadcrumbs that are sprinkled over the pasta instead of parmesan cheese. *Zite ripiene*, a speciality of Caserta, takes the pasta known as *zite* as a basic ingredient, although *conchiglie* or *lumache* (pasta shells) can also be used. The pasta is filled with diced pork, onions, salami or sausage, cheese, spices and eggs, then covered with more cheese and baked. In a Lenten version the filling is made of ricotta, fresh basil and other herbs.

PIZZA

Suffice it to recall here that there is an infinite variety of pizza recipes, all based on bread dough. The secret of a successful pizza is a blazing hot oven. Only violent heat, in fact, is capable of cooking the pizza in such a way that it is soft, yet crunchy at the same time; if the oven is not hot enough, the dough becomes tough as shoe leather. A wood-fired oven is best, although it is possible to produce an acceptable pizza in an electric or gas oven.

Secondi piatti (main courses). *Anguilla in umido* (eel) is a common dish in the Caserta area, where it is still fairly easy to find eels in the irrigation canals. They are cooked in tomato sauce and served on toast. *Anguilla alla griglia* is grilled and basted with a sauce of olive oil, garlic, vinegar and fresh mint leaves. *Baccalà alla napoletana* is a traditional dish of salted cod fillets first floured and fried, then stewed with tomatoes, capers, black olives, raisins, pine-nuts and garlic. *Agnello pasquale* is roast lamb seasoned with rosemary, bay leaf and sage and accompanied by tender new onions and potatoes. Considered a traditional dish at Easter, it also appears year round on the menus of many restaurants. *Braciola alla napoletana* is a rich dish usually reserved for special occasions. An immense slice of beef or pork is covered with chopped provolone, prosciutto, raisins, and eggs; then tightly rolled, tied with string and cooked in tomato sauce. *Cecenielli* literally means little chick-peas, but in a Neapolitan trattoria they are spicy little fish cooked in a flour and water paste, or served on a pizza. *Cervella alla napoletana* is veal or lamb's brain baked with capers, black olives, pepper and breadcrumbs. *Coniglio all'ischitana* In this dish the delicate meat of the rabbit is cut into pieces, browned in olive oil and cooked in white wine, tomato sauce and rosemary. *Costata alla pizzaiola* is a T-bone steak served in a tomato sauce flavoured with garlic and oregano. *Genovese* is the term used by Neapolitans to indicate a particular kind of beef stew-cooked slowly with much onion, olive oil, lard and tomato sauce—that crept into the local culinary tradition through the colony of Genoese merchants who lived in Naples. *Polpo alla luciana* It seems that this manner of stewing octopus—with tomatoes, olive oil, garlic, and hot peppers—was developed by the wives of the fishermen of Santa Lucia. When small octopuses are used, the dish is called *purpetielle affocate*.

Contorni (vegetables). *Carciofi ripieni alla napoletana* is baked artichokes with a delicious filling of meat, mushrooms, onions and tomatoes. *Cianfotta* is a sort of vegetable stew made with potatoes, yellow peppers, onions, tomatoes, aubergines, courgettes and celery. *Insalata di rinforzo*, a traditional Christmas dish, is a hodgepodge of cauliflower, olives, various pickled vegetables, anchovies and capers, mixed together and dressed with olive oil and vinegar. The name comes from the fact that the dish is eaten in more than one day and is continually 'reinforced' with other ingredients, which take the place of the ones eaten the day before. *Melanzane alla partenopea* is an aubergine casserole, like *melanzane alla parmigiana* (which, despite its name, is a Campanian invention). Ingredients are aubergines, caciocavallo and parmesan cheese, tomato sauce and spices. *Peperoni in teglia alla napoletana* are yellow peppers fried in olive oil with capers and anchovies.

Desserts *Coviglie* (*al caffè* or *al cioccolato*) is a traditional Neapolitan dessert much like a mousse. *Pastiera* is a classic that can be found in Campanian *pasticcerie* from November to March. It is a pie filled with fresh ricotta, grains of wheat, rice, or barley boiled in milk, candied fruit, eggs, sugar, spices and other ingredients. Some famous Neapolitan bakers make *pastiera* to order, packing it in such a way that it can stand up to long journeys. *Sfogliatelle* are perhaps the most famous of all Neapolitan breakfast pastries. There are two types, one made with a thin ribbon of crisp dough wound in tight spiral layers (*sfogliatelle ricce*) and the other a simple envelope of soft dough. Both types are filled with fresh ricotta, chopped candied fruit, cinnamon, vanilla, and other ingredients. *Sproccolati*, sun-dried figs filled with fennel seeds and preserved on wooden sticks, are a speciality of Ravello and the Amalfi coast. *Struffoli*, a traditional Christmas dessert, has all the characteristics typical of ancient Greek sweets: it calls for very little sugar, relying for its sweetness on honey, and, to a lesser extent, on candied fruit. It comes in two shapes: the traditional cone and the more modern ring. *Susamelli*, a fusion of the Italian words for sesame and honey, are S-shaped biscuits made with flour, sesame seeds (often substituted with ground almonds), sugar, honey, and candied orange and lemon peel.

Abruzzo and Molise

Easy to defend and hard to conquer, these mountainous regions have resisted foreign influence since Antiquity. Consequently, their culinary traditions are as well-defined as the landscape—though the flavours are less harsh. A place where the cultivation of durum wheat (*grano duro*, over 200,000 tonnes a year) is three and a half times greater than that of soft wheat (*grano tenero*, 60,000 tonnes)—Abruzzo is home to some of Italy's best pasta makers. Molise, in contrast, produces the *peperoncino* with which the pasta of Abruzzo (and other foods in traditional recipes) is seasoned. Molise is also known for its many fine vegetables—particularly Campobasso celery; Bojano, Monteroduni and Montefalconi peppers; and Capracotta lentils, which rival those of Castelluccio in Umbria, as Italy's best. The areas of Abruzzo that don't grow wheat are largely given over to grazing—and produce abundant meat and dairy products. The tradition of *transumanza*—driving herds of sheep from the snowy highlands of central Abruzzo to the Tavoliere di Puglia in the winter, and back again in spring, has all but died out, but its 'ghost' can be seen in thousands of varieties of sausage and salami. The Maiella is known for its snail dishes, and saffron is produced at Piano di Navelli, near l'Aquila, though almost all of what is grown is exported. Sweets are few and simple.

Antipasti. Among the many delicious sausages and salami, the most unusual are undoubtedly *fegato dolce* and *fegato pazzo*. The former is made of liver and offal mixed with honey, citron, orange, candied fruit and pistachios. The latter uses hot red pepper in the place of honey. They're eaten in alternate mouthfuls. In Molise try *prosciutto affumicato*, smoked air-cured ham: the best is from Spinete and Rionero Sannitico. Among seafood starters, *calamaretti all'olio* is a speciality of Pescara: tiny raw calamari are sliced thin and dressed simply with olive oil, vinegar, onion, salt and hot red pepper. Slightly larger *calamaretti* are stuffed with fresh shrimp and slowly simmered in white wine to make *calamaretti agli scampi*.

Primi piatti (first courses). *Brodetto pescarese* is a fish soup made with scorpion fish, dogfish, ray, octopus and lobster seasoned with onion and red pepper. *Fregnacce* are paper-thin crepes rolled around a filling of meatballs, chicken livers, ground chicken breast and and cheese, buttered, dressed with meat sauce and baked in a deep dish. Sweet and sour *pizza rustica* may be an antique (Roman? Samnite?) recipe: sweet short pastry is covered with prosciutto, hardboiled egg yolks, scamorza, fresh and mature pecorino, sliced sausage, bound together by raw egg and seasoned with cinnamon. As a variant the pasta can be cut in smaller triangles to make *panzerotti*. The pie is oven baked, the *panzerotti* are deep fried in olive oil and lard. *Scippelle 'mbusse*, a speciality of Teramo, are crepes made with a simple cheese filling served in chicken broth. Common to both Abruzzo and Molise are *spaghetti alla chitarra*, square-section spaghetti made on a tool resembling a guitar and often dressed with rich meat sauces; and *virtù*, a spring-vegetable soup whose ingredients should be as numerous as the virtues of a good house-wife: seven kinds of meat, vegetables, spices, pasta and, finally, hours on the stove.

Secondi piatti (main courses). Lamb dishes prevail in the mountainous regions of Abruzzo and Molise although *pollo all'abruzzese* (chicken with sweet peppers), and *trota alla brace* (grilled trout) are both typical here. *Agnello cacio e uova* is tender young lamb cut in small pieces and browned in olive oil flavoured with garlic and rosemary, then slowly stewed in water and white wine and finished with a fricassée-like mixture of lightly beaten eggs and grated cheese. *Polpi in purgatorio* is octopus stewed in a pot with olive oil, tomato sauce, garlic, parsley and hot red pepper. *Triglie ripiene* is mullet stuffed with breadcrumbs, garlic and rosemary, and sautéed. A good dish from the interior of Molise is *maiale ai peperoni*, lean pork stewed with sweet peppers, a dash of vinegar, rosemary, and other spices.

Desserts. *Cassata abruzzese* is a pie filled with a delicious nougat-flavoured cream, typical of Sulmona. This town in the Abruzzo highlands is most famous for *confetti di Sulmona*, brightly coloured hard candies arranged to form elaborate compositions, especially flowers. *Mostaccioli* are classic little sweets made from flour, almonds, honey and reduced grape must. Abruzzo is also famous for its *torrone* (nougat), especially L'Aquila's *torrone al cioccolato*, a soft gooey mix of chocolate, hazelnuts, sugar, honey and vanilla; and *torrone di Chieti*, made with dried figs, chocolate, almonds and spices.

Basilicata and Calabria

In sparsely populated Basilicata it's not quantity that abounds, but quality. Recipes have been tested by time: some (like *purea di fave e cicoria*) date as far back as ancient Egypt. An area in which Basilicata excels is cheeses: even the smallest, most remote village is home to a superb local cheese. Most are fresh rather than mature—*mozzarelle*, *burrini*, *provole*, *scamorze* and sweet or spicy ricotta. Equally interesting are Basilicata's sausages and salami. It seems that the art of preserving ground, spiced meat in animal gut was invented here by the Lucani, the region's ancient inhabitants: from these Italic meat-packers the Romans derived the Latin name for sausage, *lucanica*.

Calabria has a fairly uniform culinary tradition, despite the relative isolation in which many towns have stood for centuries. Never a place of abundance, it has late-ly acquired a reputation for excellence—of its citrus fruits (especially bergamot oranges, used for scents and flavourings), its aubergines (reputedly the best in Italy) and its sweet red onions (of which those grown in the area of Tropea are especially valued). In the past the fierce conservatism and abject poverty of the Calabrian farmer put expensive chemical fertilisers out of his reach—which means the region today has become an ideal place to farm organic fruit, vegetables and livestock. Calabrian fishermen, of course, have always gone to sea: much of the exquisite swordfish and tuna for which Italy is famous is fished, processed and packed by *calabresi*.

THE ART & SCIENCE OF TUNA FISHING

'Meat of the poor', tuna was called in southern Italy, because of its abundance and its nutritional value: like anchovies, sardines and mackerel, it is rich in protein and polyunsaturated fats, and its firm flesh is easy to preserve in oil or salt for long periods.

Thunnus thynnus is a powerful swimmer that can weigh up to 400kg and reach a length of two metres. Like all migratory animals, it tends to follow the same route each spring, when it leaves its deep-water home and approaches the coasts to mate. In Italy the tuna arrive by the thousands in April and May, skirting the shores of Puglia, Calabria and Sicily.

Calabresi use the term *mattanza* (derived from Spanish) to designate the capture and slaughter of the fish. The method utilises special traps, called *tonnare*, and has been around for as long as anyone can remember. Sturdy vertical nets are used to intercept entire shoals of fish and convey them toward the so-called death chamber. Here, trapped by the hundreds in a few square metres, they thrash about until they knock each other senseless. The stunned fish float to the surface and are harpooned, their blood splashing over the fishermen and their 'weapons': the scene, unaltered over time, is so bloody that the Greek poet Aeschylus compared it to the slaughter of the Persians at Salamis.

Of the dozens of *tonnare* that once existed in the South, only that on the Sicilian isle of Favignana is still working today, processing 1,000–1,500 tuna each year. The system of nets, or *impianti a mare*, is divided into *tonnare di corso*, situated on the north and west shores to trap inward-bound fish, and *tonnare di ritorno*, on the southwestern coast, along the route followed by outward-bound fish. There is also a series of support structures, the *impianti a terra*, on the shore. Here nets, boats and harpoons are stored, and the tuna is processed and packaged. The fishermen (*tonnaroti*) and drew-master (*rais*) live in humble dwellings around the central courtyard (*bagghiu*) of the processing plant.

The decline of the industry, which began in the period between the two World Wars, has accelerated since the 1960s, for a number of reasons: the competition of Japanese tuna-fishing ships, the intense urbanisation of the coasts, the difficulty of finding specialised labour, and the increasing economic advantages of deep-sea fishing. The Favignana *tonnara* is today almost a symbol, the last vestige of an antique culture in need of study and preservation.

Antipasti. Basilicata doesn't really have a tradition of starters, unless you count the almost limitless variety of salami and cured meats—as the locals certainly do. One of these, *capocollo*, a lightly smoked, air-dried fillet of pork, is popular in Calabria, too. The most popular starter in this region is probably *melanzane sott'olio*, thin aubergine ribbons marinated in salt and vinegar, drained, and packed in oil with hot pepper, garlic and aromatic herbs. *Pomodori sott'olio*, Calabrian style, are little pear-shaped tomatoes, cut in half, sun dried, then packed in oil with garlic, basil, oregano, hot red pepper and other spices.

Primi piatti (first courses). Potenza is famous for its peculiar variety of *ravioli*, filled with ricotta, chopped prosciutto, egg, pepper and parsley, topped with a meat sauce and grated pecorino or baked ricotta. *Sagne chine* is a rich lasagna served on special occasions in Calabria: between the the layers of pasta you'll find meatballs, thick-sliced hardboiled eggs, scamorza and mozzarella, and grated pecorino. *Filei* are thick spaghetti, usually served with a vegetable sauce or sprinkled with breadcrumbs sautéed with olive oil and anchovies, rather than grated cheese. In Calabria, *pitta* means any form of pizza: *pitta chicculiata* is cheeseless, made simply with cubed fresh tomatoes, olive oil and hot red pepper; *pitta maniata* uses two dough disks to envelop a filling of hardboiled eggs, ricotta, provola, salami and the ubiquitous red pepper.

Secondi piatti (main courses). Game dishes are plentiful in the mountains of Basilicata and Calabria, and lamb is present everywhere. In Basilicata *agnello in casseruola* (in dialect, *agnill a la cutturiddi* after the clay caserole dish in which it is prepared) is suckling lamb made with potatoes, onions, bay leaf and olive oil. In *lumache all'origano*, a popular country dish, snails are cooked in a clay pot with tomato sauce, garlic, hot red pepper and oregano. *Murseddu* is one of Catanzaro's most characteristic recipes: tripe and offal are sautéed over a low flame with tomatoes, abundant hot red pepper and aromatic herbs, then spooned into a pitta that has been sliced open to form an envelope or pocket. *Zucca ripiena* is a curious green squash found in both Basilicata and Calabria, filled with ground veal and/or pork, cheese and herbs and cooked in tomato sauce.

Contorni (vegetables). Aubergines are cooked in several different ways: in *agrodolce* (sour wine with chocolate, cinnamon, walnuts and raisins); *al funghetto* (baked with garlic, pepper and oregano); or as *melanzane ripiene* (stuffed and baked). Potatoes, peperoni, aubergines and tomatoes are first cooked separately, then fried up together to make *ciammotta*, Basilicata's signature vegetarian dish. In *mandorlata di peperoni*, bell peppers are cooked in a tomato sauce with chopped almonds. In Calabria you'll find delicious *peperoni ripieni*, peppers stuffed with breadcrumbs, capers and anchovies, first pan-fried then baked with tomato sauce. Matera makes a particularly rich *parmigiana di melanzane*, in which the aubergines are dipped in flour and egg, fried, then baked in a casserole with slices of hardboiled egg, salami, mozzarella and tomato sauce. *Patate in tegame* are Calabrian potatoes *au gratin*, with tomatoes, grated pecorino, olive oil and basil. *Tiella di carciofi* is a casserole of sliced artichokes and potatoes flavoured with garlic, parsley and other herbs.

Desserts. *Panzerotti* in Basilicata are not savoury, as elsewhere, but sweet, stuffed with creamed chick-peas, chocolate, sugar and cinnamon; fried or baked, they are covered with powdered sugar or honey before serving. *Torta di formaggio* is a short-pastry shell filled with ricotta, fresh pecorino, chopped ham, mature pecorino, sliced mozzarella, sugar and egg. *Crucette* are figs stuffed with walnuts, almonds and lemon zest, composed to form a cross, then baked until the sugars caramelise. *Cumpittu*, a soft nougat of honey, sesame seeeds and almonds, is almost certainly a Saracen legacy. On feast days throughout Calabria you'll see stands selling *mostaccioli*, human and animal figures made of flour, honey and cooked wine. The best come from Soriano and Seminara.

Puglia

Puglia is one of the richest, most productive agricultural areas of Italy. Its olive oil is highly appreciated throughout the country and abroad, and its wines are beginning to acquire a reputation as well. But Puglia is also a great place for fresh vegetables: it is the home of *pinzimonio*, the quintessentially Mediterranean bouquet of crudités one simply dips in extra-virgin olive oil and devours with a resounding crunch. Regardless of whether the focus of a dish is fish, meat or vegetables, the highest quality ingredients and the simplest possible preparation are the hallmarks of Puglian cooking. Which is not to say Puglian cuisine is *just* about freshness. Being the easternmost part of the Italian peninsula, Puglia draws heavily on the traditions of Greece, Turkey, Lebanon and North Africa—in stewed or baked vegetable dishes, for example, or honey-rich sweets. Last but not least, Puglians are great bread-makers. Throughout the countryside, and especially on the Murge, families still make their own bread, which they patiently carry to the local baker to be wood-oven baked. Each family has its own 'brand', impressed on the loaf so it can be distinguished from others when it comes out of the oven.

Antipasti. *Cervellata*, a veal and pork sausage flavoured with fennel seeds, a speciality of Martina Franca, and *salsiccia leccese*, in which the same meats are seasoned with lemon zest, cinnamon and cloves, are probably the most delicate and unusual meat starters. *Cozze arracanate*, mussels baked with olive oil, tomatoes, white wine, garlic, oregano and parsley, are among the most delicious seafood starters. *Tarantella* is a 'marriage' of the virtues of land and sea: in this salami, traditionally made in the Taranto area, the 'meat' is spiced tuna.

Primi piatti (first courses). *Panzerotti* are ravioli usually filled with anchovies, capers and strong ricotta cheese (made from ewe's milk). *Capello* is a dome-shaped or conical pie filled with sautéed aubergines and courgettes, sliced (not ground) veal, hardboiled eggs and cheese; it is usually served cold. *Ciceri e tria* is ribbon pasta in a sauce of creamed chick peas, onions and olive oil. *'Ncapriata*, a very old Mediterranean dish (documented in ancient Egypt), is a simple purée of dried broad beans dressed with olive oil and chopped field greens. *Orecchiette* are Puglia's chief contribution to the world of *pastasciutta*: 'little ears' served, usually, with sautéed vegetables (rape, broccoli) or a rich (horse) meat ragout. *Puddica* is a double pizza filled with onions, tomatoes, olives and anchovies, popular in the Salento. The recipe for *zuppa di pesce* (fish soup) varies from town to town: the most delicate is probably made in Gallipoli and features four or five varieties of white fish lightly seasoned with sautéed onion, garlic and parsley.

Secondi piatti (main courses). *Alici arracanate* is just one of the many dishes that feature the large Adriatic anchovies: the fish are filleted and layered in a casserole with breadcrumbs, a mix of garlic, mint and capers, sprinkled with oregano and olive oil, and lightly baked. Elsewhere in Italy a *brasciola* is simply a slice of meat; in *brasciole alla barese* veal is rolled around a filling of ham, parsley and pecorino, then sautéed slowly with tomatoes, olive oil and spices. *Cutturidde* is lamb cooked in a clay casserole with onion, parsley, tomatoes, pecorino, olive oil and water. In *dentice alle olive* this delicate sea-bream (*Dentex dentex*) is oven-roasted with olive oil, a drop of vinegar and a few black olives. In *orata alla griglia* a more robust bream (gilthead, *sparus auratus*) is first marinated in olive oil and lemon juice, then grilled.

Contorni (vegetables). In Puglia grilled vegetables of all kinds, dressed in abundant olive oil (which has a more aggressive flavour than the Ligurian or Tuscan oils) are often served as a main course. *Tiella*, the dialect word for casserole, refers to any vegetable casserole: the most common variety has mushrooms, onions, sliced potatoes, olive oil and spices.

Desserts. *Carteddate*, pinched and twisted ribbons of puff pastry coated with honey, cinnamon and powdered sugar, were once just made around Christmas; now they are available year-round, especially in Bari. *Cauciuni* are unusual little pancakes filled with chocolate, puréed chick-peas, reduced wine, cinnamon and sugar; they can be served hot or cold.

Wine

Most Italian wines take their names from the geographical area in which they are produced, the blend of grapes of which they are made, and the estate on which the grapes were grown. The best come in numbered bottles and are marked DOC (*di origine controllata*). This is Italy's *appellation controlée*, which specifies the maximum yields per vine, geographical boundaries within which grapes must be grown, permitted grape varieties and production techniques. Superior even to DOC is the DOCG (*di origine controllata e garantita*), where the denomination is also guaranteed. At present the only DOCG wines from southern Italy are Fiano d'Avellino, Vermentino di Gallura and Greco di Tufo (white); and Montepulciano d'Abruzzo and Taurasi (red)—though the list is destined to grow. IGT (*indicazione geografica tipica*) normally denotes a *vin de pays*, a wine of theoretically lesser quality than a DOC, though this is not always the case. Draconian DOC rules mean that many excellent wines that do not abide by the book are debarred from DOC categorisation. Simple *vino da tavola* is table wine. It can be excellent, but the quality is not guaranteed.

Campania

The quality of Campanian wines is widely appreciated, even though a relatively small proportion of the region is planted with vineyards.

Possibly the best Campanian wine is **Taurasi**, a dry red (the *riserva* is aged four years) served with fine roasts, and one of the premier wines of southern Italy. It is produced around Taurasi, in Avellino province, and made from the Aglianico grape, with the possible addition of other non-aromatic red grapes (max. 15 per cent).

The same grape is used to make the tasty **Aglianico del Cilento**, a dry red served with roasted and grilled meats; the dry red **Aglianico di Guardia Sanframondi** (or Guardiolo; the *riserva*, aged two years, has a lighter bouquet and smoother flavour), served with roasted and grilled meat; and **Aglianico di Sant'Agata dei Goti**, a robust red rich in tannins, aged at least two years (the *riserva* is aged three), served with roasts and stews.

Aversa Asprinio, a dry, fruity white served with fish or vegetables, or **Aversa Asprinio Spumante**, a dry, sparkling white served as an aperitif or with pastry, are wines from the provinces of Naples and Caserta. The vines are trained to trees—as were the first vines planted in the Mediterranean. Wines from vineyards trained in this fashion bear the terms *alberata* or *vigneti ad alberata* on their labels. The dry white is made from Asprinio and other non-aromatic white grapes, the *spumante* from Asprinio only.

In the province of Avellino the Fiano grape (sometimes mixed with Greco, Coda di Volpe Bianca or Trebbiano Toscano) is used to make **Fiano d'Avellino**, a dry white served with antipasti, fish, and poultry; whereas the Greco and Coda di Volpe Bianca varieties go into the delicious **Greco di Tufo**, a dry, delicate white (sometimes spumante) served with antipasti and fish.

The beautiful, rolling countryside of Guardia Sanframondi, in Benevento province, produces the excellent **Falanghina di Guardia Sanframondi** (or **Guardiolo**, a dry, delicate white served with fish; **Guardia Sanframondi** (or **Guardiolo**) **Bianco**, a delicate, dry white served with vegetables or poultry; **Guardia Sanframondi** (or **Guardiolo**) **Rosato**, a dry rosé served with shellfish and rich fish dishes; **Guardia Sanframondi** (or **Guardiolo**) **Rosso**, a dry red served with roast meat (the *novello* is lighter and served at a lower temperature, the *riserva* is aged two years); and **Guardia Sanframondi** (or **Guardiolo**) **Spumante**, a delicate sparkling white served as an aperitif, with shellfish or with cake.

The wines of Ischia have been highly regarded since the 16th century, when the *Greco* made there was thought to have therapeutic properties. You can't get Ischia Greco these days, but there are some pretty good substitutes: **Ischia Bianco**, a dry white made from Forastera Bianco, Biancolella and other white grapes (the *superiore* is stronger); **Ischia Biancolella** and **Ischia Forastera**, dry, balanced single-varietal whites served with fish and shellfish; **Ischia Rosso**, a dry red; and **Piedirosso** or **Pér e' Palummo**, a dry, medium-bodied, single-varietal red served with pastasciutta and poultry. There is also a **Piedirosso** or **Pér e' Palummo Passito** dessert wine.

The verdant hills around Sant'Agata de' Goti, in Benevento province, produce the excellent **Greco di Sant'Agata dei Goti**, a fresh, fruity white served with poultry; **Piedirosso di Sant'Agata dei Goti**, a robust red, rich in tannins, served with meats; **Sant'Agata dei Goti Rosato**, a delicate rosé served with poultry; and **Sant'Agata dei Goti Rosso**, a dry red served with all meats. The Solpaca district, in the same province, yields the pleasant **Solopaca Bianco**, a dry white served with pastasciutta, risotti, poultry and bolliti, and **Solopaca Rosso**, a dry, intense red served with meats, especially lamb.

The bay-side slopes of Vesuvius produce the very fine **Vesuvio Bianco**, a dry white served with antipasti di mare, zuppe, risotti, fish; **Vesuvio Rosato**, a dry rosé served with antipasti, timballi, fresh cheeses; and **Vesuvio Rosso**, a dry red served with roasts and stews. When these wines have a minimum alcohol content of 12 per cent they are called Lacryma Christi. The dry white **Lacryma Christi del Vesuvio Bianco** is served with fish; **Lacryma Christi del Vesuvio Liquoroso**, a sweet amber wine, with desserts; **Lacryma Christi del Vesuvio Rosato**, a dry rosé with antipasti and poultry; and **Lacryma Christi del Vesuvio Rosso**, a dry red, with meat and poultry.

ORDERING WINE

Red wines are *vini rossi* on the wine list; white wines, *vini bianchi*; rosés, *chiaretti* or *rosati*. Dry wines are *secchi*; sweet wines, *amabili* or *dolci*. *Vino novello* is new wine. *Moscato* and *passito* is wine made from grapes that have been left on the vine or dried before pressing.

When ordering, remember also that many DOC wines come in versions labelled *spumante*, *liquoroso*, *recioto* and *amarone*. *Spumante* is the Italian equivalent of champagne and uses some of the same methods to obtain its foamy (*spumante*) effervescence. It is much bubblier than sparkling whites such as *Prosecco*, which is popular both before meals and as a light dinner wine. *Liquoroso* means 'liqueur-like' and usually refers to dessert wines. The term *recioto* is applied to wines made from grapes that have been dried like raisins; *amarone* is the dry, mellow version of *recioto*.

Many wine critics believe that the 1997 and 1998 vintages are the best of the 20th century for Italian wines. Other good years are 2002 and 2005.

Basilicata and Calabria
The wines from the dry hills and plains of Basilicata and Calabria are excellent and have considerable alcohol levels. They also reflect a very old oenological tradition, dating from before the Greek colonisation.

Basilicata is known for its exquisite **Aglianico del Vulture**, a magnificent red wine that has been cultivated on the volcanic slopes of Monte Vulture since ancient times. One of the few southern Italian wines suited to extended aging, it has an intense ruby-red to garnet colour; a delicate, vinous bouqet that improves with age, and a dry, fresh, balanced, and tannic flavour that becomes velvety over time. Excellent with roasts (it enlivened the table of Emperor Frederick II), all Aglianico del Vulture is aged at least one year; after three years it can be called *vecchio*; the *riserva* is aged five years.

Calabria's most famous wine is certainly **Cirò**, made in the province of Catanzaro, around Cirò, Cirò Marina, Melissa and Crucoli. The white **Cirò Bianco** is made from Greco Bianco grapes, with up to 10 per cent Trebbiano Toscano; it is straw-yellow in colour, with an enticing vinous bouquet and a dry, lively, but balanced flavour. The fabulous red, **Cirò Rosso**, is made from Galioppo grapes, with the possible addition of Trebbiano Toscano and Greco Bianco (max. 5 per cent). The *classico* is grown in a special area in the townships of Cirò and Cirò Marina; the *superiore* is stronger (13.5 per cent, rather than 12.5 per cent) and two years of age qualifies the wine as a *riserva*. There is also a rosé, **Cirò Rosato**, made from the same grapes as the red.

Abruzzo and Molise

Italy's mountainous heart, dominated by the tall peaks of the Gran Sasso and the Majella, has rich rocky soil well suited to the production of fine grapes. Skilled craftsmanship turns the main varieties grown here—Montepulciano, Trebbiano and Sangiovese—into excellent wines.

Controguerra and neighbouring townships in Teramo province produce the delicious **Controguerra Rosso**, a dry, ruby-red, lightly tannic blend of 60 per cent Montepulciano grapes with Merlot and/or Cabernet, with the possible addition of other local red grapes. Served with all meals, it is available also as a *novello* and can be labelled as a *riserva* after twelve months' aging in the cask and six months' fining in the bottle. The Controguerra appellation also includes **Controguerra Bianco**, a dry, somewhat fruity white taken by the *Abruzzesi* as an aperitif or with fish (the *frizzante* is lightly sparkling). **Controguerra Passito Bianco** and **Rosso** are dessert wines made from grapes crushed as late as six months after harvest (the very special *arnoso* has been aged in special casks called *caratelli* for 30 months).

The Montepulciano grape, brought to Abruzzo in the early 19th century, is now grown throughout the region. It goes into the dry red **Montepulciano d'Abruzzo**, served with meat and poultry (the *vecchio* is aged two years); **Cerasuolo d'Abruzzo**, a dry, soft, balanced, dark cherry-red wine served with roast or grilled meats; and **Colline Teramane**, a full, robust but velvety dry purplish-red wine blending 90 per cent Montepulciano grapes with other Sangiovase grapes. **Trebbiano d'Abruzzo**, a dry white served with fish and cheese, is made from Trebbiano d'Abruzzo and/or Trebbiano Toscano grapes.

Grape-growing is gaining momentum in Molise, and there are now two registered appellations, **Biferno** and **Pentro di Isernia**. **Biferno Bianco** is a dry white blend of Terebbiano and Malvasia Bianca grapes, served with poultry and vegetables. **Biferno Rosso** is a delicious blend of Montepulciano, Trebbiano Toscano and Aglianico red grapes, with the possible addition of non-aromatic local red or white varieties, made around Campobasso; it is served with red meat and is also available as a *riserva*. **Biferno Tintilia** is an interesting dry, soft red served with most foods; the *riserva* is aged two years.

Puglia

Puglia is the only region of southern Italy that is not mountainous—which makes viticulture easier. Grape-growing and winemaking are one of the pillars of the region's economy, and Puglia is distinguished for both quantity and the quality of its wines. The tradition has deep roots: the Phoenicians, who practised viticulture as long ago as 2000 BC, introduced new varieties of grapes as well as new techniques of cultivation to the region. The science was so advanced when the Greeks arrived that they called Puglia *Oenotria* ('Wineland').

Aleatico di Puglia is probably the oldest of the Puglian wines. Today it is made from Aleatico grapes, with the addition of small quantities of Negroamaro, Malvasia Nera and Primitivo. It is a strong wine (at least 15 per cent alchohol; the *liquoroso*, made from lightly dried grapes, reaches 18.5 per cent). Aged from five months to three years (*riserva*), it has a full, warm, sweet, balanced flavour best enjoyed with desserts, especially cake and ice cream.

Puglia's most famous white wines are **Locorotondo** and **Martina Franca**. The first is produced in the fairy-tale valleys between Locorotondo, Cisternino and Fasano. Made from Verdeca and Bianco d'Alessano grapes with the possible addition of Fiano, Bombino, and Malvasia Toscana, it is straw-yellow in colour and dry and delicate in flavour. Ideal with fish, it also comes sparkling (*spumante*). The same grapes make up Martina Franca (or Martina). Produced nearby, around Martina Franca, Alberobello, Ceglie, Cisternino and Ostuni, this delicious dry white has enjoyed wide favour since ancient times (also available as a *spumante*).

A similar appellation, Matino, is applied to two wines made in the hills of the Salentine peninsula, mainly from Negroamaro grapes. These are the dry rosé **Matino Rosato**, served with pastasciutta, vegetables, and poultry; and the dry red **Matino Rosso**, served with lamb, roast pork and mature cheeses.

Moscato di Trani, best with cake and ice cream, is an exquisite, naturally sweet amber-coloured dessert wine made from the grapes known locally as Moscato di Trani or Moscato Reale. Famous since ancient times, it has a velvety flavour owed partially to five months' fining; the liquoroso type is aged one year and has a minimum alcohol content of 18 per cent.

The beautiful town of Ostuni, on the coast in Brindisi province, produces the delicious **Ostuni Bianco**, a dry white served with antipasti, pastasciutta, fish, eggs and vegetables; and **Ottavianello**, a delicate dry red made from the local grape of the same name, served with stewed and grilled meats.

West of Barletta are three districts producing excellent dry, full-bodied reds: **Rosso Barletta**, served with meat and game (the vecchio is aged two years); **Rosso Canosa** (or **Canusium**) served with meats, especially lamb (the *riserva* is aged two years); and **Rosso di Cerignola** served with grilled meats (also available as a two-year-old *riserva*).

GLOSSARY OF SPECIAL TERMS

Aedicule (*aedicula*), small niche or opening framed by two side columns and a pediment over the top.

Aedile, Roman official in charge of public water, grain and the organisation of games

Agora, public square or marketplace

Ala (pl. *alae*), literally, 'wing', the lateral part of a building

Ambo (pl. *ambones*), pulpit in a Christian basilica; two pulpits on opposite sides of a church from which the gospel and epistle were read

Amorino (pl. *amorini*) in art, a small, typically winged, baby boy; a putto

Amphora, antique vase, usually of large dimensions, for oil and other liquids

Antefix, ornament placed at the lower corner of the tiled roof of a temple to conceal the space between the tiles and the cornice

Antis, *in antis* describes the portico of a temple where the side-walls are prolonged to end in a pilaster flush with the columns of the portico

Apodyterium, the changing room in an ancient Roman bath

Apulian, of or pertaining to the province of Puglia

Architrave, lowest part of the entablature

Archivolt, moulded architrave carried round an arch

Arcosolium (pl. *arcosolia*), ancient tomb in the shape of a sarcophagus hewn into the rock

Askos (pl. *askoi*), flattish, ancient Greek vessel for oil, with a long spout and single handle

Athenaion, sanctuary dedicated to Athena

Atlantes (or *Telamones*), male figures used as supporting columns

Atrium, forecourt, usually of a Byzantine church or a Classical Roman house

Augustalis, a priest of the imperial cult

Aumbry, recess in a church wall in which sacred vessels are kept, usually near an altar.

Badia, *abbazia*, abbey

Basilica, originally a Roman building used for public administration; in Christian architecture, an aisled church with a clerestory and apse, and no transepts

Basso rilievo, sculpture in low relief: bas-relief in Italian.

Benedizario, a prayer book

Biclinium, a Roman dining bed for two; also, the room where it is located

Bifora, a window divided externally into two equal lights by a column

Biscuit ware, ceramic that has been fired to a solid, firm state, but not vitrified

Black-figure ware, ancient Greek pottery (7th–5th centuries BC) that portrays motifs with a black glaze, with the natural hue of the pot as a background

Borgo, a suburb; street leading away from the centre of a town

Bottega, the studio of an artist; the pupils who worked under his direction

Bradyseism, gradual rising or falling of the earth's surface caused when magma chambers fill or empty over time

Bucchero, Etruscan black terracotta ware

Bucrania, a common form of metope decoration—heads of oxen garlanded with flowers

Calidarium (or Caldarium), room for hot or vapour baths in a Roman bath

Campanile, bell-tower, often detached from the building to which it belongs

Cantoria,singing-gallery in a church

Capital, the topmost element of a column

Capitolium, a temple of Jupiter, Juno and Minerva

Cardo, the main street of a Roman town, at right-angles to the decumanus

Caryatid, female figure used as a supporting column

Catalan, term used in a southern Italian context to describe art (and more particularly architecture) of the Aragonese period, which is in a style typical of that of northwestern Spain

Catapan, in the Byzantine world, the governor of a province

Caupona, in ancient Rome, a tavern

Cavea, the part of an ancient theatre or amphitheatre occupied by the rows of seats and dug into a hillside

Cella, sanctuary of a temple, usually in the centre of the building

Cenobium, monastery where all property is held in common

Chiaroscuro, distribution of light (*chiaro*) and shade (*scuro*), apart from colour in a painting

Ciborium, casket or tabernacle containing the Host

Cipollino, onion-marble; a greyish marble with streaks of white or green

Cippus, sepulchral monument in the form of an altar; a stone marking a grave or boundary

Clerestory, upper part of the nave wall in a church or cathedral, raised higher than the roof-level of the side aisles, and pierced with apertures to allow light into the building

Columbarium (pl. *columbaria*), a building (usually subterranean) with niches to hold urns containing the ashes of the dead

Comitium, polling station in an ancient Roman town

Compluviate, roof in a Roman villa having an aperture to allow rainwater to fall into the pool (impluvium) below

Comunichino, small window or grille through which monks received Communion

Cosmatesque (or *Cosmati*), inlaid marble work using mosaic and coloured glass and stone to decorate pavements, pulpits, choir screens, columns, cloisters, etc.

Cryptoporticus, a semi-underground covered portico used in Roman architecture for the construction of terraces or as a covered market

Cubiculum, bedroom of a Roman house

Cuneus (pl. *cunei*), wedge-shaped block of seats in an ancient theatre

Cyclopean, the term applied to walls of unmortared masonry, older than the Etruscan civilisation, and attributed by the ancients to the giant Cyclopes

Daunii, ancient inhabitants of Puglia, a fraction of the Iapigi (the others being the Mesapii and Peucilli), who came from the Illyrian (east) shore of the Adriatic

Decumanus, the main street of a Roman town running parallel to its longer axis

Decurion, troop commander in the Roman army; or a local official responsible for civil matters and for collecting taxes

Diaeta, in a Roman villa, a room for taking a siesta

Dipteral, temple surrounded by a double peristyle

Diptych, painting or ivory tablet in two sections

Dolium (pl. *dolia*), a very large ceramic jar, like the Greek pithos, used for storage of wine, water, grain, etc. The Villanovans and Etruscans often used dolia for cremation burials. The width of the mouth of the jar ranges from 40cm to 80cm; the overall height anywhere from 1m to 1.5m

Dolmen, a prehistoric monument (possibly a tomb) made up of two or more upright stones supporting a horizontal stone slab

Dromos, long, narrow passage, partly open and partly within a mound, giving access to chamber- or tholos-tombs

Duomo, cathedral

Duumvir, member of a duumvirate, a two-man administrative body in ancient Rome

Engaged columns, columns which partially retreat into the wall

Enneastyle, temple with a portico of nine columns at the end

Entablature, the continuous horizontal section above the capital (consisting of architrave, frieze and cornice) of a Classical building

Entasis, a design technique used to counteract the optical illusion of inner sagging created by the parallel sides of a column. Entasis (meaning 'stretching') involved giving the column a slightly convex curvature with the result that the diameter at the bottom was marginally larger than at the top

Ephebus, Greek youth under training (military or university)

Etruscan, of, relating to, or characteristic of Etruria, an ancient region in central Italy, its inhabitants, or their language

Exedra, semicircular recess in a Byzantine church

Exultet, an illustrated scroll

Ex-voto, tablet or small painting expressing gratitude to a saint; a votive offering

Fauces, the entrance passage of a Roman house (well seen at Herculaneum)

Fictile, moulded of earth, clay, or other soft material

Foliated, decorated with leaf ornament

Forum, open space in a town serving as a market or meeting-place

Frigidarium, room for cold baths in a Roman bath

Fullonica, a dyer's workshop

Fumarola, volcanic spurt of vapour (usually sulphurous) emerging from the ground

Giallo antico, red-veined yellow marble from Numidia

Gnathian ware, type of black pottery from Apulia (*see* p. ???)

Graffiti, design on a wall made with an iron tool on a prepared surface, the design showing in white. Also used loosely to describe scratched designs or words on walls

Grisaille, painting in various tones or grey

Heptastyle, temple with a portico of seven columns at the end

Herm (pl. *hermae*), quadrangular pillar decreasing in girth towards the ground, surmounted by a bust

Heroön, shrine to a deified hero

Hexaform, window or aperture divided into six lights or bays

Hexastyle, temple with a portico of six columns at the end

Historiated, adorned with figurative painting or sculpture, usually comprising a narrative

Hydria, an ancient Greek vessel for water

Hypogeum, subterranean excavation for the internment of the dead (usually Etruscan)

Iconostasis, a screen or partition that divides the public part of a church from that reserved for the clergy

Impluvium, rainwater pool in the atrium of a Roman house

Insula, block of houses in a Roman town

Intarsia, inlay of wood, marble, or metal

Italic, of or pertaining to any of the indigenous peoples of the Italian peninsula

Judas window, small window or flap to allow someone to see without being seen; a peephole

Kore (pl. *korai*), from the Greek word for maiden, term used to describe standing female figures in Archaic art; also a name sometimes given to Persephone

Kouros (pl. *kouroi*), boy; Archaic male figure

Krater, antique mixing-bowl, conical in shape with rounded base

Kylix, wide shallow vase with twin handles and short stem

Lapillus (pl. *lapilli*), tiny fragments of pumice

Lararium, small room or niche in a Roman house used as a type of private chapel or shrine where images of the *lares* or *penates* (household deities) were placed for devotional observances

Largo, an urban space resulting from the intersection of two or more streets or from the widening of a single street

Laura, monastery of the Eastern church

Lekythos, tall, narrow-necked ancient Greek vase with one handle, used for oil

Liberty, name given to the Italian variant of Art Nouveau

Loggia, covered gallery or balcony, usually preceding a large building

Lunette, semicircular space in a vault or above a door or window, often decorated with a painting or relief

Macellum, covered market in an ancient Roman town

Magna Graecia, literally 'Greater Greece', term used to designate the area of southern Italy colonised by the ancient Greeks

Marche, the Italian Marches, the region stretching from the Abruzzo to San Marino, and bordering Umbria and Tuscany

Mater Matuta, the dawn goddess of the Italic peoples

Matroneum, gallery reserved for women in early Christian churches

Menhir, a single upright monolith, usually of prehistoric origin

Mensoles, projecting corbels or brackets supporting a balcony

Mesapii, ancient inhabitants of Puglia, a fraction of the Iapigi (the others being the Daunii and Peucetii), who came from the Illyrian (east) shore of the Adriatic

Metope, carved or painted panel between two triglyphs on the frieze of a Doric temple

Mithraeum, a shrine of Mithras, a Persian sun-god worshipped in imperial Rome

Monoforum, a single-light window, without subdivisions

Narthex, vestibule of a Christian basilica

Naumachia, a mock naval combat for which the arena of an amphitheatre was flooded

Niello, a black substance used in engraved design

Nymphaeum, a sort of summer house in the gardens of baths, palaces, etc., originally a temple of the Nymphs, decorated with statues of those goddesses, and often containing a fountain

Octastyle, a portico with eight columns

Oculus, round aperture, window or recess

Odeon, a concert hall, usually in the shape of a Greek theatre, but roofed

Oecus (pl. *oeci; oikos* in Greek), generic term used to describe a room in an ancient Greek or Roman building

Ogival, term used of Gothic architecture, to describe two arcs meeting in a point

Oinochoe, ancient Greek wine-jug usually of elongated shape for dipping wine out of a krater

Opisthodomos, the back section of an ancient Greek temple, entered from the outside of the building and arranged with two columns in antis on the long walls.

Opus Alexandrinum, mosaic design of black and red geometric figures on a white ground

Opus Incertum masonry of small irregular stones in mortar

Opus Musivum, mosaic decoration with cubes of glass (usually on walls or vaults)

Opus Quadratum, masonry of large rectangular blocks without mortar; in *Opus Etruscum* the blocks are placed alternatively lengthwise and endwise

Opus Reticulatum, masonry arranged in squares or diamonds so that the mortar joints make a network pattern

Opus Sectile, mosaic or paving of thin slabs of coloured marble cut in geometrical shapes

Opus Spicatum, masonry or paving of small bricks arranged in a herringbone pattern

Opus Tessellatum, mosaic formed entirely of square tesserae

Opus Vermiculatum, mosaic with tesserae arranged in lines following the contours of the design

Oscans, a people born of the fusion of the Samnites with the Opici following the elimination of Etruscan power in the second half of the 5th century BC

Paliotto, a vestment, hanging, or covering of any material that covers the front part of a Christian altar

Pantocrator, Christ the Almighty, 'he who rules all'

Pediment, gable above the portico of a classical building

Pelike, ancient Greek jug with a round belly, narrow neck, and two handles

Peribolos, the enclosure or court of a temple, the actual wall or the space enclosed; in early Christian times a church enclosure.

Peripteros, a porch. A peripteral building (temple) is one that is surrounded by a single row of columns on all four sides

Peristyle, court or garden surrounded by a columned portico

Peucetii, ancient inhabitants of Apulia, a fraction of the Iapigi (the others being the Daunii and Mesapii), who came from the Illyrian (east) shore of the Adriatic

Pietà, group of the Virgin and/or saints mourning the dead Christ

Pinacoteca, an art gallery specialising in the exhibition of painting

Pinax (pl. *pinakes*), a plaquette or tablet for inscription or drawing

Piperno, volcanic stone of the Campania region

Piscina, Roman tank; a basin for an officiating priest to wash his hands before Mass

Pithos, large ancient Greek pottery vessel for storing grain

Pleistocene, the earlier part of the Quarternary period (c 1.8 million years ago) or the corresponding system of rocks

Pluteus, a low wall that encloses the space between column bases in a row of columns

Podium, a continuous base or plinth supporting columns, and the lowest row of seats in the cavea of a theatre or amphitheatre

Polyfoil, in Gothic tracery, a term describing the inner decoration of an arch or roundel where the tracery takes the shape of multiple leaf-like 'foils' or lobes

Polyptych, painting or tablet in more than three sections

Predella, small painting or panel, usually in sections, attached below a large altarpiece.

Presepio, literally, crib or manger. A group of statuary of which the central subject is the infant Jesus in the manger

Pronaos, porch in front of the cella of a temple

Propylon (pl. *propylaea*), entrance gate to a sacred enclosure; in plural form when there is more than one door

Proskenion, the area before the stage of a Greek theatre (in Latin, *proscenium*)

Prostyle, building with a colonnade in front of it, typically a temple with a columned porch in front

Prothesis, area connected with the preparation by the deacons of the bread and wine for the Eucharist in a Byzantine church; it can be a recess at the north side of the church, a table or a dedicated chapel.

Prothyrum, Greek: a vestibule or space before a door or gate. Latin: a gate or railing before the door itself

Pseudodipteral, temple with a double peristyle at the front and back, but only a single colonnade along the longer sides

Pulvin, cushion stone between the capital and the impost block

Putto (pl. *putti*) figure of a male child sculpted or painted, usually nude

Quadriga, four-horse chariot

Quaestor, treasury official in ancient Rome

Rhyton, ancient Greek drinking-horn usually ending in the shape of an animal's head

Sacellum, in the ancient Roman world, an unenclosed or roofless shrine

Sacrarium, shrine or niche for religious devotion, typically one in a private home dedicated to the household gods (*lares*)

Samnite, of, relating to, or characteristic of an ancient people, an offshoot of the Sabines, in south-central Italy

Saracenic, type of architecture with elements borrowed from the Arab world, seen in many parts of southern Italy

Scena, the stage building of an ancient Roman theatre

Scoria (pl. *scoriae*), igneous rock, formed of cooled lava

Siculo, of or pertaining to Sicily, as for example Siculo-Norman art

Situla, bucket-type vessel used for Holy water

Skene, the stage building of a Greek theatre (the Latin *scena*)

Skyphos, ancient Greek squat, stemless cup with two opposing, rim-oriented handles. A form particular to Athenian potters

Stamnos, ancient Greek big-bellied vase with two small handles at the sides, closed by a lid

Stele, upright stone bearing a commemorative inscription

Stereobate, platform upon which a temple is built

Stoup, basin containing Holy water, placed at the entrance to a church

Strigil, bronze scraper used in Roman baths and palaestra to remove the oil with which bathers or athletes had anointed themselves

Stylobate, topmost level of the stepped platform on which a temple stood; literally, the solid base on which the columns stand

Sudatorium (pl. *sudatoria*), room for very hot vapour baths (to induce sweat) in a Roman bath

Swabian, of or pertaining to the period of rule by the Hohenstaufen dynasty (1194–1266)

Taberna (pl. *tabernae*), shop in an ancient Roman town

Tablinum, main living and reception room of a Roman house; in later villas, the room where the family archives were kept

Telamones, see *Atlantes*

Temenos, in the ancient Greek world, a sacred enclosure

Tempietto, a small temple

Tepidarium, room for warm baths in a Roman bath

Tessera (pl. *tesserae*), a small cube of marble, glass, brick, used in mosaic work

Tetrastyle, having four columns

Thermae, originally simply baths, later elaborate buildings fitted with libraries, assembly rooms, gymnasia and circuses

Thermopolium, in an ancient Greek town, a bar or tavern serving hot and cold drinks and snacks

Tholos, circular building with a roof constructed by corbelling.

Tondo (pl. *tondi*), round painting or bas-relief

Transenna, open grille or screen, usually of marble, in an early Christian church separating nave and chancel

Travertine, tufa quarried near Tivoli, used as a building material

Trefoil, in Gothic tracery, a term describing the inner decoration of an arch or roundel where the tracery takes the shape of three leaf-like 'foils' or lobes

Triclinium, dining-room and reception-room of a Roman house

Trifora, a window divided into three lights joined by a common architectural motif

Triforium, raised arcaded aisle in a

Gothic church above the nave and below the clerestory

Triglyph, blocks with vertical grooves on either side of a metope on the frieze of a Doric temple

Triptych, painting in three sections

Trullo (pl. *trulli*), rural dwelling of Puglia, built without mortar of local limestone and usually whitewashed, with conical roof formed of flat-pitched spiral courses of the same

stone capped with diverse finials

Tympanum, the triangular face of a pediment within the frame made by the angled and horizontal cornices

Villa, country-house with its garden; also, a Roman farm or estate and, in some southern towns, an urban park

Viridarium (pl. *viridaria*), the garden of an ancient Roman house or villa

Zoöphorus, Classical frieze with animal motifs

ELEMENTS OF AN ANCIENT GREEK TEMPLE

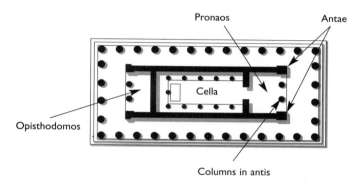

ELEMENTS OF AN ANCIENT ROMAN THEATRE

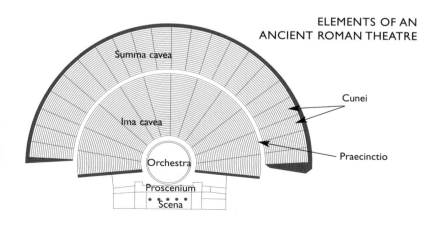

ORDERS OF ARCHITECTURE

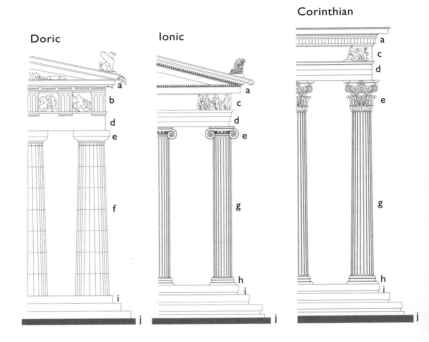

a   Cornice
b   Frieze with triglyphs and metopes
c   Frieze
d   Architrave
(a + b/c + d = Entablature)
e   Capital

f   Shaft (flutes meet in sharp ridges)
g   Shaft (flutes lie between flattened ridges)
h   Base
i   Stylobate
j   Stereobate

RULERS OF NAPLES

Hauteville dynasty

Roger II	d. 1154	Tancred	1189–94
William I	1154–66	William III	1194
William II	1166–89		

Hohenstaufen dynasty

Henry VI	1194–97	Manfred (self-proclaimed regent) d. 1266	
Frederick II	1197–1250	Conradin (heir to the throne)	d. 1268
Conrad (titular king)	d. 1254		

Angevin dynasty

Charles I	1266–85	Ladislas	1386–1414
Charles II	1285–1309	Louis II (supported by	1386–1400
Robert (the Wise)	1309–43	antipope John XXIII)	
Joan I	1343–82	Joan II	1414–1435
Charles III (supported by	1381–86	Louis III (brother of René;	
Pope Urban VI)		nominated to succeed Joan) d. 1434	
Louis I (supported by	1382–84	René (the Good)	1435–1442
antipope Clement VII)			

House of Aragon

Alfonso I (the Magnanimous)	1443–58	Ferdinand II (Ferrandino)	1495–96
Ferdinand I (Ferrante)	1458–94	Frederick	1496–1501
Alfonso II	1494–95		

Viceregal period

Under Spain	1503–1707	Under Austria	1713–34

House of Bourbon

Charles VII (known as	1734–59	Ferdinand IV	1759–1806
Charles III, his title as			
King of Spain after 1759)			

Napoleonic period

Joseph Bonaparte	1806–08	Joachim Murat	1808–15

Kingdom of the Two Sicilies

Ferdinand I (former	1815–25	Ferdinand II	1830–59
Ferdinand IV)		Francis II	1859–60
Francis I	1825–30		

THE ANGEVINS OF NAPLES

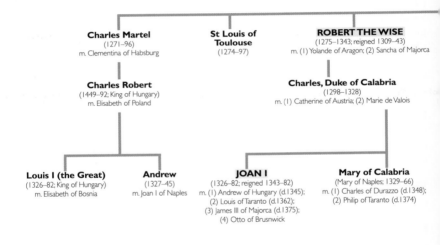

Charles Martel
(1271–96)
m. Clementina of Habsburg

Charles Robert
(1449–92; King of Hungary)
m. Elisabeth of Poland

Louis I (the Great)
(1326–82; King of Hungary)
m. Elisabeth of Bosnia

Andrew
(1327–45)
m. Joan I of Naples

St Louis of Toulouse
(1274–97)

ROBERT THE WISE
(1275–1343; reigned 1309–43)
m. (1) Yolande of Aragon; (2) Sancha of Majorca

Charles, Duke of Calabria
(1298–1328)
m. (1) Catherine of Austria; (2) Marie de Valois

JOAN I
(1326–82; reigned 1343–82)
m. (1) Andrew of Hungary (d.1345);
(2) Louis of Taranto (d.1362);
(3) James III of Majorca (d.1375);
(4) Otto of Brusnwick

Mary of Calabria
(Mary of Naples; 1329–66)
m. (1) Charles of Durazzo (d.1348);
(2) Philip of Taranto (d.1374)

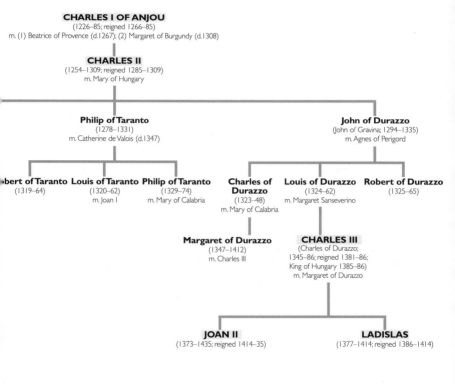

CHARLES I OF ANJOU
(1226–85; reigned 1266–85)
m. (1) Beatrice of Provence (d.1267); (2) Margaret of Burgundy (d.1308)

CHARLES II
(1254–1309; reigned 1285–1309)
m. Mary of Hungary

Philip of Taranto
(1278–1331)
m. Catherine de Valois (d.1347)

John of Durazzo
(John of Gravina; 1294–1335)
m. Agnes of Perigord

Robert of Taranto
(1319–64)

Louis of Taranto
(1320–62)
m. Joan I

Philip of Taranto
(1329–74)
m. Mary of Calabria

Charles of Durazzo
(1323–48)
m. Mary of Calabria

Louis of Durazzo
(1324–62)
m. Margaret Sanseverino

Robert of Durazzo
(1325–65)

Margaret of Durazzo
(1347–1412)
m. Charles III

CHARLES III
(Charles of Durazzo;
1345–86; reigned 1381–86;
King of Hungary 1385–86)
m. Margaret of Durazzo

JOAN II
(1373–1435; reigned 1414–35)

LADISLAS
(1377–1414; reigned 1386–1414)

INDEX

Explanatory or more detailed references (where there are many), or references to places where an artist's work is best represented, are given in bold. Dates are given for all artists, architects and sculptors. Attributions and works of disputed authorship are not indexed. Ancient cities and works of art are given it italics. Numbers in italics are picture references.

A

Abruzzo 369ff
Acaia 511
Acciaroli 279
Acerenza 298
Acquamorta 145
Acquaviva delle Fonte 472
Acquaviva family 476, 477
Acton, Sir Harold 38
Acton, Sir John 24, 40
Aecae, 431
Aemilius Paullus, Lucius 443
Aeneas, *Aeneid* 141, 146, 281, 517
Aesernium 391
Agathocles of Syracuse 327
Agnano Terme 136
Agnone 388, 392
Agrippa 141, 144
Agrippina, mother of Nero 141, 142
Agropoli 279
Ahenobarbus, L. Domitius 400
Ajello, Antonio (16C) 307
Alari Bonacolsi, Pier Jacopo (*see Antico*)
Alaric, Gothic leader 331
Alba Fucens 403–04
Albacini, Carlo (1777–1858) 81
Albanian colonies 293, 324
Alberobello 477–78
Alexander, King of Epirus 310
Alfano, Andrea (1879–1967) 323
Alfedena 392
Alfonso dell'Acaia, Baron 512
Alfonso I of Aragon ('the Magnanimous') 21, 25, 36, 54, 406, 513, 515; (buildings commissioned by) 49, 231
Alfonso II of Aragon 36, 299; (tomb of) 56
Altamura 461–63

Altamura, Francesco Saverio (1826–97) 112, 429
Altomonte 324
Alvino, Enrico (1809–72) 68, 121, 245
Amalfi 16–17, 17, 238, 245–48, *249*
Amalfi Coast 237ff
Amantea 329
Amedeo VI, Count of Savoy 389
Amiternum 416
Ampollino, lake 336
Anacapri (*see Capri*)
Anacletus II, antipope 266
Andersen, Hans Christian 225
Andrano 517
Andrea da Firenze (early 15C) 71
Andrea da Salerno (Andrea Sabatini; 1480–1545) 46, 67, 111, 249, 251, 259, 260, 279, 282
Andrea del Sarto (1486–1530) 99
Andrew of Hungary 36, 58, 153; (tomb of) 70
Andrew, St 247
Andria 441–42
Angeleri, Pietro (*see Celestine V*)
Angevin (*see Anjou*)
Angri 254
Anjou, house of **20–21**, **35–36**, 58, 283, 444
Anselm, St 392, 452
Anthony Abbot, St 240
Antico (Pier Jacopo Alari Bonacolsi; 1460–1528) 104
Antonello da Messina (c.1430–79) 355, *356*
Antonio di Giovanni d'Enrico 413
Anversa degli Abruzzi 399
Aphrodite of Capua 83–84
Aphrodite Sosandra 84

Aprigliano 336
Apulia (ancient) 9, 12, 17, 18, 19, 20, 427
  (*see also* Puglia)
Apulian Romanesque 18, 387, **455**; (Bari)
  455, 456; (Barletta) 440; (Bisceglie) 447;
  (Bitonto) 450; (Matera) 300; (Ruvo)
  449–50; (Trani) 444–47
Aquinas, St Thomas 60
Aragon, house of 21–23, 36 (*see also* Spain)
Archytas, mathematician 480
Arco Felice 146–47
Arcos, duke of 23
Arcucci family 216
Ariano Irpino 265
Aristoxenes, Greek writer 480
Armanino da Modena (13C) 411
Arpi 428, 429
Artemis of Ephesus 82
Ascoli Satriano 14, 429
Asculum 14
Aspromonte 349, 357–59 (battle of) 357,
  358, 359
Assergi 415
Astarita, Giuseppe (17C) 124
Atella 296
Atessa 378
Atrani 249
Atri 371
Aufidena 392
Augustus, emperor 147, 215, 230, 507
Auria, Giovanni Domenico de (16C) 55, 61
Austria, Austrians 23, 24, 25, 41, 42, 357,
  358, 432
Avellino 266–67
Avernus, Lake (Averno) 141
Aversa 153
Avetrana 511
Avezzano 402–03
Avitabili, Antonio (17C–18C) 457

B

Baboccio da Piperno, Jacopo (fl. 1442–50)
  260
Baboccio, Antonio (1351–c.1435) 68
Bacoli 143–44
Badalocchio, Sisto (1585–c.1619) 105
Badia Morronese 399
Badoglio, General Pietro 416, 495
Baedeker, Karl 29

Bagnara Calabra 350
Bagnoli 147
Baia (*Baiae*) 142–43
Balla, Giacomo (1871–1958) 112
Bandinelli, Baccio (1493–1560) 104
Banzi 297
Barba, Gaetano (1730–1806) 287
Barba, Nuzzo (15C–16C) 476
Barbarossa (*see Kheir-ed Din*)
Barbarossa, Emperor Frederick 19
Bari 17, 18, 19, 451–61
Barile 293
Barisano da Trani (late 12C) 250, 444
Barletta 439–41
Baroque towns (Lecce) 501ff; (Martina
  Franca) 479
Barra, Didier (1590–1644) 118
Bartoli, Amerigo (1890–1971) 496
Basil II, emperor 291, 309
Basilicata 291ff
Basilio, sculptor (11C) 457
Bedeschini, Giulio Cesare (17C) 413
Behring, Emil von 215
Belisarius, general 16, 33
Bellini, Giovanni (c.1435–1516) 101, 458
Belvedere Marittimo 320
Benedetto da Maiano (1442–97) 46, 56
Benevento 14, 15, 16, 17, 262–65; (battle
  of) 34, 263
Bentinck, Sir William 41
Berkeley, George 167, 232
Bernardino del Moro (early 16C) 61
Bernardino of Siena, St 406, 410
Bernini, Pietro (1562–1629) 48, 77, 115,
  116, 123, 323
Bertini, Giovanni (14C) 57
Bertini, Pacio (14C) 57
Bertoja (Jacopo Zanguidi; mid-16C) 104
Beuckelaer, Joachim (c.1530–74) 105
Bianchi, Pietro (1694–1740) 75
Biancour, Martin (master gardener; 18C) 157
Bibiena, Giovanni Maria (Giovanni Maria
  Galli da Bibiena; 1625–65) 74
Bidauld, Jean Joseph Xavier (1758–1846)
  106
Bisceglie 447
Bisignano 324
Bitetto 461
Bitonto 450–51

Bizamano, Donato (16C) 458
Boccaccio, Giovanni 21, 35 65
Bohemond, tomb of 442
Bohigas, Oriol (b. 1925) 259
Bojano 391
Boldini, Giovanni (1842–1931) 112
Bomba 378
Bombile, Santuario di 362
Bominaco 405
Bonaparte, Joseph 24, 41
Boniface IX, pope 518
Bonito, Giuseppe (1707–89) 155, 460
Bonocore, Michelangelo (fl. early 18C) 413
Bordone, Paris (1500–71) 458
Borghese, Ippolito (early 17C) 285
Bosco di Monticchio 293
Boscoreale 166
Botticelli, Sandro (Alessandro Filipepi
    1445–1510) 101
Bottiglieri, Matteo (1684–1757) 64
Bourbon 149, 452
Bourbon, house of **23–26**, **38–43**, 281, 370,
    419, 480, 502
Bourdichon, Jean (1457–1521) 116
Bovalino Superiore 362–63
Bovianum 391
Braccio Fortebraccio 406
Bramantino (Bartolomeo Suardi; 1455–1536)
    60
Brancaccio, Salvatore 284
Brancaccio, Salvatore (mid-19C) 284
Brattirò 346
Briatico 344
Brindisi 17, 416, 495–98
Briosco, Andrea (Il Riccio; 1470–1532) 104
Bronze Age, major sites and finds 463, 487
Bronzino (Agnolo di Cosimo Tori; 1503–72)
    103
Brueghel, Pieter the Elder (c.1525–69) 105
Brunati, Luigi (20C) 496
Bruno, St 346, 347, 348
Bruttians, Bruttian 13, 310, 327, 331
Brutus, Marcus Junius 32, 122
Brydone, Patrick 29
Bulwer-Lytton, Edward 194
Buonalbergo 265
Buono, Silvestro (16C) 240
Byzantine, Byzantium 16, 17, 18, 19, 33,
    135, 151, 307, 335, 452, 480, 502, 513;

(art and architecture) 46, 150, 151, 325,
    360, 377, 431, 448, 455, 482, 514, *514*

C
Caccavello, Annibale (c.1515–79) 55, 61
Caccini, Giovan Battista (1556–1613) 115
Caggiano, Antonio 267
Calabria 9, 18, 27, 319ff
Calanna 359
Caldara, Domenico (19C) 429
Calì, Antonio (19C) 75
Calì, Gennaro (1799–1887) 241
Caligula, emperor 142
Calvi Risorta 151
Camigliatello Silano 334
Cammarano, Giuseppe (1766–1850) 75,
    107, 155
Cammarano, Michele (1835–1920) 112
Campanella, Tommaso 359
Campania 10, 15, 135ff
Campi Salentina 511
Campidoglio (Scala) 253
Campigli, Massimo (1895–1971) 460
Campli 418
Campo Imperatore 415, 416
Campobasso 388–89
Campochiaro 391
Camuccini, Vincenzo (1771–1844) 106, 108
Canevari, Antonio (1681–1750) 209
Cannae 14, 443; (battle of) 442, 443; (finds
    from) 441
Canosa di Puglia 442–43, 455
Canova, Antonio (1757–1822) 75, 230
Cantalupo del Sannio 391
Canusium, ancient town 442
Capestrano 374, 404
Capitanata, region 429
Capo Miseno 144
Capo Santa Maria di Leuca 517
Capo Vaticano 348
Capodimonte porcelain 48, 107, 108, 119,
    370
Capraia (*see Tremiti Islands*)
Capri 214–28
    Anacapri 222–25
    Arco Naturale 217
    Baths of Tiberius 214
    Belvedere Cannone 216
    Blue Grotto 224–25

Capri town 215–16
Casa Rossa 223
Certosa di San Giacomo 216, *217*
Damecuta 224
Faraglioni 225
Grotta Bianca 225
Grotta di Matromania 217
Grotta Verde 225
Monte Solaro 224
Palazzo a Mare 214, 215
Punta di Tragara 217
S. Costanzo 215
S. Michele (church) 223, *223*
S. Michele (villa) 222–23
S. Stefano 216
Salto di Tiberio 220
Scala Fenicia 222
Torre di Materita 224
Via Krupp 217
Villa Jovis 216, 220–21
Capua 13, 14, 15, 17, 18, **149–50**, 295
Capurso 471
Caracciolo, Battistello (c.1578–1635) 47, 54, 55, 114, 116, *117*, 124
Caracciolo, Sergianni 71
Carafa family 60, 70, 122, 261, 299, 360; (*see also Paul IV*)
Caramanico Terme 376
Craro, Pietro (15C) 355
Caravaggio (Michelangelo Merisi; 1571–1610) 47, 70, *110*, 111
Cardone, Giovanni Paolo (fl. 1569–86) 411, 413
Carducci, Achille (1644–1712) 501, 507
Carelli, Gabriele (1821–1900) 118
Cargaleiro, Manuel (b. 1927) 245, 254
Cariati 325
Carovigno 500
Carpinone 391
Carracci, Agostino (1557–1602) 105
Carracci, Annibale (1560–1609) 104, 105
Carracci, Ludovico (1555–1619) 105, 464
Carsoli 404
Casal Sabini 463
Casamicciola Terme 232
Casarano 518
Casca Longus, Publius 181
Caserta 25, 154–58, *154*
Caserta Vecchia 158

Cassiodorus 329
Castel del Monte 20, 295, 443
Castel di Sangro 379–80
Castel Fiorentino 430
Castellammare di Stabia 211
Castellana Grotte 477
Castellaneta 472
Castelli 417
Castelli majolica 105, 116, 376
Castro 516
Castrovillari 323
Cataldo, St (*see Cathal*)
Catanzaro 328
Catapanate, Byzantine 17, 452
Cathal, St 482
Catherine of Valois 266
Caulonia 360; (finds from) 355
Cava de' Tirreni 262
Cavaliere, d'Arpino (Giuseppe Cesari; 1568–1640) 113, 115, 409
Cavallini, Pietro (active c.1270–1330) 46, 73
Cave-churches **303–05** 473, 475, 480
Cavour, Camillo 26, 358
Cecita, lake 334
Celano 401–02
Celebrano, Francesco (1729–1814) 62
Celestine V, pope 49, 399, 408, **409**, 434, 504
Celico 334
Cercemaggiore 389
Cerignola 443
Cerio, Ignazio 216
Cerro al Volturno 392
Certosa di San Lorenzo (*see S. Lorenzo*)
Cesura, Pompeo (16C) 413
Cetara 254
Cetraro 321
Challenge of Barletta (*see Disfida*)
Charles I of Anjou 20, 21, 25, 34, 35–36, 126, 263, 296, 404, 428, 430, 444, 518; (buildings commissioned by) 49, 55, 65, 68, 211, 433, 484; (tomb of) 68
Charles II of Anjou 21, 36, 430; (buildings commissioned by) 297, 305, 409, 430
Charles III of Bourbon (Charles VII of Naples) 25, 38, **39**, 74, 75, 98, 100, 119, 154, 197
Charles of Durazzo (Charles III of Naples) 36, 59, 262, 279

Charles V, emperor 22, 37, 49, 108, 283, 346, 398, 512
Charles VIII, King of France 21, 36
Charles, Duke of Calabria 58; (tomb of) 57
Charles Robert, King of Hungary 58
Chelli, Domenico (18C) 74
Chiaiese, Leonardo (fl. mid-18C) 117, 223
Chiarini, Bartolomeo (16C) 124
Chiaromonte 306
Chieti 373–76
Chinard, Phillip (13C) 447
Chiricio, Giorgio de (1888–1978) 460
Cilea, Francesco 349
Cima da Conegliano (Giovanni Battista Cima; ?1459–1507) 299
Cimarosa, Domenico 153
Cino, Giuseppe (1635–1722) 501, 506
Cirella 320
Città Sant'Angelo 371
Civetta, il (*see Herri*)
Civitate 18, 429
Civitella Alfedena 397
Civitella del Tronto 419
Claudius, emperor 45, 400
Clement VII, antipope 36, 59
Cleophrades Painter (6C BC) 96
Clodius Pulcher, Publius 161
Clodt, Baron Peter (1805–67) 73
Clovio, Giulio (1498–1578) 104
Cocceius Auctus, Lucius (1C BC) 121, 137, 141
Cocullo 424
Codazzi, Viviano (c.1603–72) 115
Cola dell'Amatrice (1480–1547) 392, 410, 418
Colantonio, Niccolò Antonio (15C) 46, 109
Colonna, Vittoria 230, 231
Commodus, emperor 215
Conca, Sebastiano (1680–1764) 155
Conforto, Giovanni Giacomo (1569–1630) 77
Conrad of Hohenstaufen 20, 34, 432
Conradin of Hohenstaufen 20, 34, 77, 125, 126, 404; (monument to) 125
Constance de Hauteville 19, 34
Constans II, emperor 430
Conversano 476
Copertino 521–22
Copiae, Roman town 325

Coppola, Giovanni Andrea (1597–1659) 505, 518
Coral fishing 209
Corenzio, Belisario (c.1558–c.1640) 47, 56, 66, 76, 116, 123-124, 430, 512 (tomb of) 123
Corfinio 400
Corfinium 15, 400
Corigliano Calabro 325
Corno Grande 369
Corot, Camille (1796–1875) 350
Corradini, Antonio (1668–1752) 62
Correggio (Antonio Allegri; 1489–1534) 104
Corropoli 369
Corte, Luigi della (19C) 245
Coscile valley 323–24
Cosenza 331–33
Crati valley 324, 330
Crecchio 377
Crispiano 480
Croce, Benedetto 60, 398
Croton 10, 11, 13, 31, 327, 349, 353, 360
Crotone 327
Crusades, First 292
Cumae 10, 13, 31, 145–46
Curia, Francesco (16C–17C) 55
Curius Dentatus, Manius 263

D
D'Annunzio, Gabriele 357, 372
D'Aubigny, le Sieur 149, 349
Daddi, Bernardo (active 1317–50) 101
Dalbono, Edoardo (1841–1915) 118
Dante (Dante Alighieri) 20, 21
Dattoli, Vincenzo (19C) 429
Daunian, Daunians 264, 292, 429, 432, 433, *433*, 441
Del Balzo family 61, 442, 461, 479, 499, 521 (*see also Orsini*)
Delitio, Andrea (active 1430–80) 371, 377, 412
Deserto, convent of 242
Desiderius, Abbot of Monte Cassino 45–46, 151
Diamante 320
Diavolo, Fra' 330
Dickens, Charles 29
Diefenbach, Karl Wilhelm (1851–1913) 216
Dikaearchia (ancient Pozzuoli) 10, 31, 137

Diodorus Siculus 160
Diomedes, hero of Troy 434, 442
Dionisio di Bartolomeo (fl. late 16C) 66
Dionysius I of Syracuse 13, 351, 360
Disfida di Barletta 441
Dolmens 487, 515, *516*
Domenichino (Domenico Zampieri;
  1581–1641) 48, 68, 458
Dominic of Foligno, St 424
Dominici, Antonio de (1734–94) 156
Donatello (Donato de' Bardi; 1386–1466)
  46, 64
Doryphorus 83, 179
Dosio, Giovanni Antonio (1533–c.1610) 66,
  113, 116, 117
Dossi, Dosso (Giovanni Luteri; 1480–1542)
  104
Douglas, Norman 169, 215, 291, 319, 482
Dragut, corsair 216, 229
Dunoy, Alexandre Hyacinthe (1757–1841)
  106

E
Eastern Church 18, 151, 452, 519, 521
Eboli 282
Egnathia 485
Elbeuf, Emmanuel, Prince de 197, 208
Elea (Velia) 279–81
Elia, Alessio de (mid-18C) 285
Ennius, Roman poet 508
Epomeo, Mt 229, 232, 233
Erchie 511
Ercolano (modern town) 209
Etruscan, Etruscans 10, 11, 12, 13, 31, 135,
  145, 152, 169, 277; (architecture and
  remains) 171, 261

F
Fabius Maximus, Quintus (Verrucosus)
  480
Fago del Soldato 334
Falernian (*see Wine*)
Fallascoso 378
Fancelli, Luca (1430–95) 71
Fano Adriano 417
Fanzago, Cosimo (c.1591–1678) 47, 48, **55**,
  56–57, 61, 65, 68, 71, 77, 108, 113, 114,
  118, 120, 122, 347
Fara Filiorum Petri 377

Farnese family **100**, 461
  Alessandro Farnese (*see Paul III*)
  Alessandro, Duke of Parma 94, 100
  Cardinal Alessandro 98, *94*, 100, 103
  Elisabetta Farnese 98, 100
  Ranuccio I 100, 104
Farnese collections (Capodimonte) 98–106;
  (sculptures) 79–83; (*Farnese Bull*) 79–80;
  Farnese Hercules 80
Fasano 486
Fattori, Giovanni (1825–1908) 350
Faun, house of (*see Pompeii*)
Fei, Paolo di Giovanni (d.1411) 69
Ferdinand I of Aragon (Ferrante) 36, 49,
  439; (buildings commissioned by) 323,
  344, 483, 495
Ferdinand II of Aragon (Ferrandino) 36
Ferdinand of Bourbon (Ferdinand IV and I)
  24–25, 38, **39**, 41, 42, 49, 75, 154, 156,
  157, 158, 215, 324, 435, 452
Ferdinand II, King of the Two Sicilies 25–26,
  42, 154
Feriello, Giuseppe (17C) 286
Ferrara, Augusto 225
Fiano d'Avellino (*see Wine*)
Filangieri, Carlo 42
Filangieri, Gaetano 237
Filangieri, Prince Gaetano 124
Finelli, Vitale (fl. early 17C) 61
Fischetti, Fedele (1734–89) 78, 156, 392
Fiumefreddo Bruzio 330
Floridia, duchess of 25, 77, 119
Foggia 428–29
Foix, Odet de (*see Lautrec*)
Fontana, Domenico (1543–1607) 68, 75,
  123, 168, 180, 247; (tomb of) 56
Foresta Umbra 434
Forster, E.M. 252
Fossacesia 380
Francavilla al Mare 372
Francavilla Fontana 499
France, French (medieval) **20–22**, 35, 36,
  37, 149, 150, 349, 428, 441
France, French (Napoleonic) **24**, **40–42**,
  215, 222, 243, 320, 329, 330, 350, 480;
  (*see also Bourbon*)
Franceschi, Girolamo 325
Francesco da Montereale (16C) 412, 413
Francesco da Paola, St 321

Francis I, King of France 22, 108, 398
Francis I, King of the Two Sicilies 25, 42
Francis II, King of the Two Sicilies 26, 43
Francis, St 453
Franks 17
Frederick II, emperor **19–20**, 34, 123, 230, 291, 292, **294**, 296, 331, 332, 369, 398, 400, 406, 428, 430, 439, 452, 453, 461, 471, 496, 526; (buildings commissioned by) 71, 149, 150, 296, 309, 329, 387, 431; (bas-relief of) 451; (portrait bust of) 441
Frentani, Italic people 387
Frosolone 388
Fucino basin 369
Fucino, lake 400
Fuga, Ferdinando (1699–1781) 48, 66, 74, 76
Fusaro, lake 145
Fusco, Agostino (18C–19C) 323

G

Gabriele d'Agnolo (16C) 55
Gaddi, Taddeo (c.1300–66) 101
Gaeta 16, 26, 43
Gagini, Antonello (son of Domenico; 1478–1536) 330, 337, 343, 348
Gagini, Domenico (c.1420–92) 54
Gagliardelli, Giovan Francesco (active early 16C) 376
Gaizo, Giovanni del (18C) 125
Galante, Francesco (1884–1972) 460
Galatina 519
Galizia, Fede (1578–1630) 355
Gallipoli 518
Gallo, Giovanni (early 16C) 284
Gamba, Crescenzo della (active mid–late 18C) 117, 157
Gambarie 359
Garbo, Greta 252
Gardella, Ignazio (1905–99) 233
Gargano peninsula 431–34
Gargano, Monte 17 (*see also Gargano*)
Gargiulo, Domenico (*see Micco Spadaro*)
Garibaldi, Giuseppe 26, **42–43**, 78, 149, 150, 357, **358**, 359, 363
Garvi, Paolo de (early 16C) 371
Gemito, Vincenzo (1852–1929) 112, 118
Gennaro, St (*see Januarius*)

Gentile da Rocca (13C) 412
Gentile, Giovanni 398
Gentileschi, Artemisia (1597–1652) 111
Genuino, Vespasiano (16C) 518
Gerace 362
Gesualdo, Carlo 57, 61
Ghibellines, in southern Italy 20, 430
Giacomo della Porta (?1533–1602) 104, 373
Giambologna (Jean de Boulogne; 1529–1608) 104
Gian Giacomo dell'Acaia (fl. mid-16C) 504, 512
Giaquinto, Corrado (1703–66) 418, 460
Gide, André 252
Gigante, Giacinto (1806–76) 118, 122, 242
Ginosa 472
Gioacchino da Fiore 334, 335, 336
Giocondo, Monna Lisa del 306
Gioffredo, Mario (1718–85) 61, 77
Gioia del Colle 471–72
Gioia Tauro 349
Gioiosa Ionica 360
Giordano, Luca (1632–1705) 48, 61, 64, 66, **67**, 68, 70, 73, 76, 111, 116, 120, 124, 125, 229, 332, 418, *459*, 460; (tomb of) 77
Giordano, Tommaso 98
Giordano, Umberto 429
Giotto (Giotto di Bondone; 1266/67–1337) 46 (school of) *246*, 247, 251
Giovanni da Montorsoli, Fra' (16C) 121
Giovanni da Nola (c.1488–1558) 48, 54, 55, 56, 61, 65, 72, 123
Giovanni da Taranto (13C) 108
Giovanni da Verona, Fra' (c.1457–1525) 56
Giovine, Raffaele (early 19C) 120
Gissing, George 327, 328, 332
Giuliano da Maiano (1432–90) 56, 71
Giulianova 370
Giulio Romano (Giulio Pippi; c.1492–1546) 102
Giusti, Salvatore (fl. early 19C) 107
Gliri, Nicola (fl. late 17C) 460
Gnathian ware 429, 463, **486**, 496, 507
Goethe, Johann Wolfgang von 27, 29, 169
Gonzalo de Córdoba, viceroy 21, 36, 349, 443, 480
Gorky, Maxim 215
Gothic art and architecture 284, 324, 331,

405

Goths 16, 33, 135, 237, 452

Goya, Francisco de (1746–1828) 107

Gran Sasso d'Italia 414

Gravina in Puglia 463–64

Gray, Sir James 39

Greco, El (Domenicos Theotokopoulos; c.1541–1614) 103

Greco, Emilio (1913–95) 411

Greeks in southern Italy, Greek colonies (general) 9–10, **10–13**, 31, 135, 427, 519; (in Basilicata) 291; (Capri) 215; (Croton) 10, 11, 13, 327; (Cumae) 10, 11, 12, 13, 145; (Dikaearchia) 10, 137; (Elea) 279–81; (Heracleia in Lucania) 14, 309–10; (Heracleia/Herculaneum) 197; (Hipponion) 343; (Kallipolis) 518; (Laos) 320; (Locri Epizephyrii) 11, 360–62; (Medma) 349; (Metapontum) 10, 310–12; (Metauron) 349; (Neapolis) 10, 12, 230; (Pithecusae) 10, 12, 230, 233; (Poseidonia) 11, 13, 271; (Rhegion) 10, 351; (Sybaris) 10, 13, 271, 276, 324; (Taras) 10, 12, 14, 309, 480; (Thurii) 13, 309

Gregory IX, pope 19, 20

Gregory VII, pope 259; (tomb of) 260

Gregory XI, pope 59

Gricci, Giuseppe (1700–70) 107, 119

Grimaldi 76

Grimaldi, Francesco (16C–17C) 66, 68

Grimthorpe, Lord 252

Grotta Azzurra (*see Capri, Blue Grotto*)

Grotta Bianca 477

Grotta dei Cervi 515

Grotta del Diavolo 517

Grotta della Pace 141

Grotta di Pertosa 282

Grotta di Putignano 477

Grotta di San Giovanni 500

Grotta di Smeraldo 244

Grotta Romanelli 516

Grotta Zinzulusa 516

Grottaglie 499

Grotte di Castelcivita 278

Grotte di Castellana 477

Grumento Nova 306

Grumentum 306

Guardiagrele 377

Guarino, Francesco (1611–54) 111, 116, 464

Guelphs in southern Italy 20, 21

Guercino (Giovanni Francesco Barbieri; 1591–1666) 350

Guerrisi, Michele (1893–1963) 349

Guglielmelli, Marcello (fl. early 18C) 67

Guglielmo della Porta (1516–77) 80

Guttuso, Renato (1912–87) 350, 429

H

Hackert, Jakob Philipp (1737–1807) 107

Hadrawa, Norbert 216

Hadrian, emperor 142, 502; (arch of) 153

Hamilton, Lady Emma 40, 41

Hamilton, Sir William 39, 41, 166

Hannibal 14, 141, 149, 152, 261, 262, 291, 296, 310, 327, 432, 442, 443, 480 (*see also Punic Wars*)

Hatria 371

Hauteville family 18, 19, 25 (*see also Constance, Robert Guiscard, Roger, William*)

Helena, wife of Manfred 262, 296

Hemingway, Ernest 279

Henry VI of Hohenstaufen, emperor 19, 34, 230, 259

Heracleia (Herculaneum) 197

Heracleia (Lucania) 14, 309–10

Herculaneum 12, 15, 161, 166, **196ff**, *203, 204, 208*; (finds from) 84ff
   House of the Deer 206–07
   House of the Relief of Telephus 207, *208*
   Villa of the Papyri 196; (finds from and copies) 85, 222, 252

Hercules, myths concerning 140

Herodotus 325

Herri met de Bles (Il Civetta; c.1510–50) 105

Hieron of Syracuse 230

Hipponion (ancient Vibo Valentia) 343

Hirpini, Hirpinia 266

Hohenstaufen dynasty 19–20, 34 (*see also Frederick II, Henry VI*)

Honorius II, pope 18

Horace (Q. Horatius Flaccus) 296, 485, 495

Huns 16

Hydruntum (*see Otranto*)

Hyria 499

I

Iapygian, Iapygians 12
Ibsen, Henrik 232, 238
Ilario da Montalbano, Fra' (17C) 307
Illyria, Illyrians 9, 452
Innocent IV, pope 20; (tomb of) 70
Innocent VI, pope 59
Innocent VII, pope 398
Interamnia Praetuttiorum 417, 418
Iron Age, major sites and finds 374, 487
Isabella of England, wife of Frederick II 428, 442
Isaia da Pisa (active 1447–64) 54
Ischia 12, 229–33
Isernia 391
Isis, cult and temples of 92, 95, 180, 264, 265
Isola di Capo Rizzato 328
Isola di Dino 320
Iuvanum 378

J

Jacobello del Fiore (1370–1439) 412, 417
Jacopo della Pila (late 15C) 61, 260
James of the Marches, St 406
James, Bishop of Capua 292
Januarius, St (San Gennaro) 45, 68, 97, 136, 140
Jerace, Francesco (1854–1937) 123
Joan I, queen 21, 36, 55, 57, **58–59**, *58*, 216; (possible portrait of) 297
Joan II, queen 36, 406; (tomb of) 124
Jodice, Mimmo (b. 1934) 112
John of Procida 21
John of Salisbury 335
John Paul II, pope 221
Joli, Antonio (1700–77) 107
Joppolo 348
Julia, daughter of Augustus 434
Julius Caesar, emperor 181, 400, 495
Justinian, emperor 16

K

Kaendler, Johann Joachim (1706–75) 119
Kauffmann, Angelika (1741–1807) 107
Kheir-ed Din, corsair 23, 222, 230
Kopisch, August 225
Krupp, Friedrich 217

L

L'Aquila 406–14
La Fossiata 334
Lacco Ameno 232–33
Lago del Matese 390
Lago di Campotosto 416
Lago di Varano 434
Lagonegro 306
Lagopesole 296
Lama, Giovanni Bernardo (fl. late 17C) 509
Lanciano 377
Lanfranco, Giovanni (1581–1647) 68, 106, 114, 115
Lanino, Bernardino (c.1511–82) 124
Lannoy, Charles de 398
Laos 320; (finds from) 355
Larino 387
Larinum 387
Laterza 472
Latiano 499
Laurana, Francesco (f.1458–1502) 54
Lautrec, Viscount (Odet de Foix) 37, 55, 428
Lawrence, D.H. 252
Lazzari, Dionisio (1617–89) 66, 124
Lazzaroni 37, 41
Le Moine, Guillaume (15C) 76
Lecce 501–09, *501*, *504*, *506*
Lello da Roma (14C) 70
Lenormant, François 286
Leo IX, pope 18, 429
Leonardo da Besozzo (15C) 71, 72
Leonardo da Pistoia 121
Leopardi, Giacomo 121
Levi, Carlo (1902–75) 282, 302, 429
Licosa, island 279
Lippi, Filippino (1457–1504) 101
Locorotondo 479
Locri Epizephyrii, Locrian 11, 327, 349, 353, 354, 360–62; (finds from) 352, 355
Lombards 16, 17, 33, 135, 259, 263, 307, 452; (art, artefacts) 262, 264, 377
Lorenzo di Credi (1439–1537) 101
Loreto Aprutino 371
Lotto, Lorenzo (1480–1556) 101
Louis I, King of Hungary 58, 495
Louis I of Anjou 36, 59, 389, 495
Louis III of Anjou 36, 331, 333
Louis of Taranto 58, 59, 266
Lowe, Sir Hudson 215

Lucania, Lucanian 9, 13, 153, 271, 291, 298, 305, **309–13**, 310, 320
Lucera 19, 429–31
Lucrine, Lake (Lucrino) 140
Lucullus, Lucius Licinius 76, 122, 144
Luini, Bernardino (?1475–1532) 105
Lysias, Athenian orator 325

M
Macchia d'Isernia 391
Madonna dei Miracoli, sanctuary (Abruzzo) 380
Madonna di Gallana 499
Maestro Nicola (early 13C) 451
Magliaccio, Lucia (*see Floridia, duchess of*)
Maglie 515
Magna Graecia **10–13**, 31, 145, 309, 319, 327, 331, 480, 484; (museum of) 351–56
Maida, battle of 329, 350
Maiella, mountains 369, 376, 409
Mainardi, Sebastiano (d.1513) 101
Maiori 254
Malinconico, Nicola (c.1663–1721) 117
Maltese, Giovanni 233
Malvito, Giovanni Tommaso (son of Tommaso; 16C) 46
Malvito, Tommaso (early 16C) 46, 60, 69
Mancinelli, Giuseppe (19C) 75
Mancini, Antonio (1852–1927) 112
Manduria 509–11
Manet, Edouard (1832–83) 350
Manfred of Hohenstaufen **20**, 34, 263, 296, 430, 432, 439, 444, 471, 498
Manfredonia 432–33
Mansi, Nicola 252
Mantegna, Andrea (1431–1506) 101, 102
Manzù, Giacomo (1908–91) 350
Maratea 308, *308*
Marcellus, Roman general 296
Marchesato, region 327
Marco da Firenze (early 15C) 71
Marco da Siena (*see Pino, Marco*)
Marechiaro 122
Margaret of Austria 94, 100, 373, 410
Margaret of Durazzo (tomb of) 260
Margaret of Parma (*see Margaret of Austria*)
Margherita di Savoia 443
Maria Carolina, queen 24, 25, 40, 41, 156, 157

Marina d'Andrano 517
Marina di Praia 244
Marinelli, Domenico (17C–18C) 457
Marius, Caius, general 144
Martin V, pope 406
Martina Franca 479
Martineau, Joseph (18C) 107
Martinelli, Ambrogio (mid-17C) 511
Martini, Francesco di Giorgio (1439–1520) 104, 518
Martini, Simone (c.1284–1344) 46, 109
Martino, Ernesto de 520
Martino, Francesco de (fl. early 18C) 284
Mary of Durazzo, monument to 57
Masaccio (Tommaso di Ser Giovanni di Mone; 1401–28) 99, 101
Masaniello (Tommaso Aniello) 23, 38, 49, 118, 126, 209
Masolino da Panicale (Tommaso Fini; 1383–1440) 101
Massa di Somma 166
Massa Lubrense 242–43
Massafra 473–75, *474*
Masseria fortificata 471
Master of the Beffi Triptych (15C) 412
Master of St John Capistran (15C) 413
Mastro Danieli (late 12C) 500
Mastroberardino, winemaker 188, 267
Mater Matuta, temple of 150
Matera 299–305, *301*
Matese, mountains 390
Matteis, Paolo de (1662–1728) 112, 116, 380
Matthew, St 261
Matthews, Henry 168
Mau, August 173
Maximian, emperor 281
Mazzacurati, Marino (1907–69) 121
Mazzola Bedoli, Girolamo (c.1500–69) 104
Mazzola, Giovanni Battista (fl.1513–50) 321
Mazzoni, Guido (1450–1518) 56
Medma 349; (finds from) 355
Medrano, Giovanni Antonio (1703–?) 73, 98
Megalithic remains 515, *516*
Melendugno 512
Melfi 20, 292–93; (Constitutions of) 292
Melisborgo, Guglielmo (late 19C) 123
Melito di Porto Salvo 363
Menga, Evangelista (16C) 441, 521

Mengs, Anton Raphael (1728–79) 107, 155
Mesagne 498
Mesoraca 337
Messapian, Messapians 12, 476, 485, 498,
    502, 509, 519, 521; (artefacts and finds)
    441, 486, 496, 499, 500, 508, 510, 512,
    518
Meta 238
Metaponto 312
Metapontum 10, 310–12; (finds from) 298
Metauron 349; (finds from) 355
Micco Spadaro (Domenico Gargiulo;
    1612–79) 116, 118, 284
Michael Scotus, astrologer 294
Michelangelo (Michelangelo Buonarroti;
    1475–1564) 80
Michelozzo (Michelozzo di Bartolomeo
    Michelozzi; 1396–1472) 46, 64
Michetti, Francesco Paolo (1851–1929) 112,
    372, 376
Miglionico 299
Miglionico, Andrea (1663–after 1735) 460
Milani, Giacomo (late 18C) 107
Miller, Jacob the Elder (early 17C) 105
Miller, Lady Anne 156, 157
Minervino di Lecce 515
Minervino Murge 443
Minori 253
Minuta (Scala) 253, 253
Mirola, Girolamo (?1530–70) 104
Miseno 144
Misenum, Lake (Miseno) 144
Misenus 144
Modugno 461
Mola di Bari 484
Molfetta 448, 448
Molise 387ff
Moliterno 306
Molpa, ruins of 281
Monna Lisa (*see Giocondo*)
Monopoli 485
Montaguto 265
Montalto 349, 357, 359
Montano d'Arezzo (14C) 266
Monte Cassino 45; (school of) 150, 151
Monte di Procida 145
Monte La Gallinola 391
Monte Nuovo 140
Monte Pollino 321–22

Monte Poro 343, 346
Monte Sannace 471
Monte Sant'Angelo 433
Monte Vulture 293
Montecalvo Irpino 265
Monteroduni 391
Montescaglioso 305
Montevergine 266
Monticchio, lakes 293
Montorio al Vomano 417
Montorsoli, Giovanni Angelo (16C) 345
Morandi, Giorgio (1890–1964) 460
Morano Calabro 323
Morelli, Domenico (1823–1901) 112, 118,
    245, 247, 429
Mormanno 320
Mormanno, Giovanni Francesco (15C) 46,
    55
Moro, Bernardino del (early 16C)
Moryson, Fynes 135, 152
Mosca, Ferdinando (1685–1773) 410
Moscufo 371
Mottola 473
Müller, David (fl. early 17C) 346, 347
Munthe, Axel 215, 222–23, 224
Mura, Francesco de (1696–1782) 71, 76, 78,
    112, 114, 302, 380, 418, 429, 485, 518
Murat, Joachim **24**, **41–42**, 155, 216, 230,
    243, 344, 452
Murge, the 475–80
Muro Tenente 499
Musolino, outlaw 357, 359
Mussolini, Benito 400, 416
Mycenae, culture of 10, 30, 476

N
Naccherino, Michelangelo (1550–1622) 48,
    77, 78, 118, 123, 216, 247
Naples 13, 14, 15, 16, 17, 21, 22, 23,
    25, 26, 27, **29ff**; (history of) 30–44; (art
    and architecture) 45–48
    Ascensione a Chiaia, church of 120
    Borgo Marinaro 76
    Capodimonte 97–112
    Cappella Sansevero 61–63
    Castel Capuano 71
    Castel Nuovo 36, 49, 49, 54
    Castel dell'Ovo 76
    Castel Sant'Elmo 113

Naples contd.
  Catacomb of St Guadiosus 97
  Catacomb of St Januarius/Gennaro 96–97
  Cathedral 68–70
  Conservatorio di Musica 64
  Corso Umberto I 122–23
  Farnese sculptures 79
  Galleria Umberto I 75
  Gesù Nuovo 56, 57
  Gambrinus café 75, 131
  Girolamini, church of 66–67
  Grotta Vecchia 121
  Istituto d'Arte 76
  Ladislas, tomb of 71
  Mergellina 121
  Monte della Misericordia 70–71
  Monteoliveto 55
  Musei di Antropologia, Mineralogia, Zoologia e Paleontologia 123
  Museo Archeologico 78–96
  Museo Civico di Castel Nuovo 54
  Museo delle Carrozze 120
  Museo della Ceramica 119
  Museo di Etnopreistoria 77
  Museo Filangieri 124
  Museo Diego Aragona Pignatelli Cortes 120
  Nisida, island 122
  Nunziatella, church of 76
  Palazzo del Balzo 61
  Palazzo Cuomo 124
  Palazzo d'Angri 78
  Palazzo di Donn'Anna 122
  Palazzo Gravina 55
  Palazzo Maddaloni 77
  Palazzo Reale 75–76
  Palazzo San Giacomo 54
  Palazzo Serra a Cassano 76
  Parco della Rimembranza 122
  Parco Virgiliano 121
  Piazza del Mercato 125
  Piazza del Municipio 54
  Piazza del Plebiscito 73, 75–76
  Piazza Trieste e Trento 75
  Piedigrotta 121
  Pizzofalcone 73–76
  Porta Capuana 71
  Rettifilo 122–23
  Rione Amedeo 120
  S. Agostino alla Zecca 124
  S. Angelo a Nilo 64
  S. Anna dei Lombardi 55
  S. Annunziata 124
  S. Brigida 77
  S. Chiara 57, 59, 60
  S. Croce al Mercato 126
  S. Domenico Maggiore 60
  S. Eligio 126
  S. Ferdinando 77
  S. Francesco da Paola 75
  S. Giacomo degli Spagnoli 54
  S. Giorgio Maggiore 71
  S. Giovanna a Carbonara 71–72
  S. Giovanni Maggiore 123
  S. Gregorio Armeno 64–65
  S. Lorenzo Maggiore 65–66
  S. Maria degli Angeli 76
  S. Maria del Carmine 125
  S. Maria Donnaregina 72–73
  S. Maria Egiziaca 76, 124
  S. Maria Incoronata 55
  S. Maria di Montesanto 78
  S. Maria la Nova 55
  S. Maria del Parto 121
  S. Maria di Piedigrotta 121
  S. Maria in Portico 120
  S. Martino, Certosa di 113–18
  S. Paolo Maggiore 66
  S. Pietro ad Aram 124–25
  S. Pietro a Maiella 64
  S. Pietro Martire 123
  S. Severino e Sossio 123
  S. Spirito 77
  S. Teresa a Chiaia 120
  Santa Lucia quarter 77
  Spaccanapoli 60
  Teatro San Carlo 38, 73–75
  University of Naples 123
  Via Roma 77–78
  Via Monteoliveto 55
  Via S. Gregorio 65
  Via Toledo 37–38, 77
  Villa Floridiana 118–19
  Villa Pignatelli 120
  Virgil's tomb 121
Napoleon Bonaparte 24, 25, 41, 263, 283, 480
Nardò 519
Nardodipace 348

Natali, Giovan Battista (early 18C) 116
National Parks (Abruzzo) 369, 397; (Cilento) 278–79; (Gargano) 431; (Monte Pollino) 321–22; (Vesuvius) 166, 168
Neapolis (ancient Naples) 10, 12, 32, 230
Negroni, Pietro (1503–65) 323
Nelson, Admiral Horatio 40, 41, 230
Neolithic, sites and finds 305, 369, 428, 447, 487, 515, 517
Nero, emperor 32, 45, 140, 142, 210, 502
Netti, Francesco (1834–94) 460
Nicastro 329
Niccolini, Antonio (1772–1850) 75, 98, 106, 108
Niccolò da Foggia (13C) 251
Niccolò di Tommaso (14C–15C) 54
Nicephorus Phocas, emperor 480
Nicholas II, pope 292
Nicholas of Myra, St 452, 456, 468
Nichols, Peter 135
Nicola da Guardiagrele (c.1390–c.1462) 371, 372, 376, **377**, 378, 412, 417
Nicotera 348
Nicotera, Giovanni 281
Nietzsche, Friedrich 238
Nittis, Giuseppe de (1846–84) 112, 441, 460
Nocera Inferiore 262
Nocera Superiore 262
Norman, Normans **17–19**, 34, 149, 259, 292, 335, 346, 369, 429, 432, 439, 441, 444, 452, 455, 463, 513, 518; (art and architecture) 45, 158, 427, 455, 456, 476, 508, 514
Novelli, Pietro (1603–47) 111
Novello da San Lucano 56
Nuceria 169
Nuvolo, Fra' (early 17C) 125

O

Octavian (*see Augustus*)
Oderisius of Benevento (early 12C) 431
Oenotrians 12, 13
Ogliastro Cilento 279
Onofrio d'Alessio (17C) 68
Opi 397
Oplontis 210–11, *210*, *211*
Oppido, Giovanni Donato (17C) 302

Oria 499–500
Orio, Orazio de (early 17C) 114
Orley, Bernaert van (c.1490–1542) 108
Orontius, St 502
Orsaia 279
Orsi Achille de (1845–1929) 118
Orsi, Paolo 327
Orsini family 463, 479, 480, 520, 521
Orsini, Fulvio 94, 95, 98, 99
Ortona 372–73
Ortucchio jaw, the 374
Oscan, Oscans 9, 13, 152, 153, 169, 197, 427; (artefacts) 381
Ostuni 487
Otho II, emperor 359
Otranto 513–15, *514*
Ottaviano 166
Ovid (Publius Ovidius Naso) 398, 399
Ovindoli 402

P

Pacuvius, Roman poet 495
Padula 282
Paduli 265
Paestum 11, 13, 271–78
    Forum 274–76
    Sanctuary of Hera 277
    Temple of Ceres 276, *276*
    Temple of Hera 272–73, *272*
    Temple of Neptune 273–74, *273*
    Tomb of the Diver 3, 278, *278*
Pagliare, stone huts 512, *512*
Painter of Amykos (5C BC) 310
Painter of Edinburgh (early 5C BC) 310
Painter of Policoro (5C–4C BC) 310
Palaeolithic, sites and finds 9, 296, 297, 320, 352, 447, 487, 516
Palagianello 473
Palatine basilicas (Acquaviva delle Fonti) 472; (Altamura) 462–63; (Bari) 456–57; (Barletta) 440
Palinuro 281
Palizzi, Filippo (1818–99) 112, 380, 381, 429
Palma il Giovane (Giacomo Negretti; 1548–1628) 485, 487, 517
Palmi 349
Palmieri, Luigi 168
Palo del Colle 461

Panini, Giovanni Paolo (1691–1765) 106
Paola 321
Papasidero 320, 352
Parisi, Nicola (19C) 429
Parmenides 280
Parmigianino (Francesco Mazzola; 1503–40)
   104
Parthenope (ancient Naples) 10, 32, 31
Parthenopean Republic (first) 23, 38;
   (second) 24, 40, 118, 126, 229, 330, 461,
   480
Passo di Corvo 428
Pasta 537–38
Patire, convent of 325
Patù 517
Paul III, pope (Alessandro Farnese) 79, 80,
   98, 100
Paul IV, pope 373; (birthplace of) 64
Paul, St 137, 502, 520
Pausilypon 147
Pavia, battle of 22, 60, 108, 398
Pedro de Toledo, viceroy of Naples 22, 37,
   143, 327
Pelasgians 427
Pellizza da Volpedo, Giuseppe (1868–1907)
   112
Penna, Cesare (1607–1653) 501, 504, 505,
   508
Penne 371
Penni, Giovanni Francesco (c.1496–c.1536)
   99, 102
Pepe, General Guglielmo 25, 42, 329
Pergolesi, Giovanni Battista 137
Perrinetto da Benevento (15C) 71
Persio, Altobello (mid-16C) 300
Perugino (Pietro Vannucci; 1446–1523) 101
Pescara 371–72
Pescasseroli 397
Pesche 391
Peschici 434
Pescocostanzo 378–79
Peter Celestine, St (*see Celestine V*)
Peter III of Aragon 21, 36
Peter, St 45, 124
Peter Celestine, St (*see Celestine V*)
Petilia Policastro 338
Petrarch 21, 66, 259
Petrini, Francesco (14C) 387
Petronius Arbiter 138, 145

Peucetian, Peucetians 305, 461, 463, 464,
   476
Philip of Anjou 479
Philip of Medma 349
Phlegraean Fields 30, 135ff
Piacentini, Marcello (1881–1960) 351
Piana del Fucino 400
Pianella 371
Piano delle Vigne 349
Piano di Sorrento 237–38
Piano, Renzo (b.1937) 434, 460
Pianosa (see Tremiti Islands)
Picchiatti, Bartolomeo (1571–1643) 61, 124
Pier della Vigna 292, 295
Pierre d'Agincourt (13C–14C) 441, 484
Pierre de Chaulnes (late 13C) 49
Pietra del Pertusillo, lake 306
Pietrabbondante 392
Pietro del Morrone (*see Celestine V*)
Pietro di Martino (mid-15C) 76
Pietro di Stefano (fl. mid-16C) 411
Pindar 145
Pino, Marco (Marco da Siena; ?1520–87) 54,
   55, 111, 458, 483, 485
Pio da Pietralcina, Padre 434
Pisacane, Carlo 281
Pisanello (Antonio Pisano; 1377–1455) 104
Piso, Caius Calpurnius 142
Pithecusae (ancient Ischia) 10, 12, 31, 230,
   233
Pitloo, Anton (1790–1837) 122
Pizzo 343–44
Pliny the Elder 160, 162–65, 186, 211, 267,
   277, 344, 424, 510
Pliny the Younger 144, 161–65
Poerio, Carlo 42, 122
Policastro 279
Policoro 309
Polidoro di Renzo (16C) 377
Polignano a Mare 484
Pompei (modern town) 196
Pompeii 12, 15, 161, 166, 168–96; (finds
   from) 83ff; (painting from) 89–92, 186;
   (wine of) 188
   Amphitheatre 187
   Forum 174–75
   House of Loreius Tibertinus 185
   House of Marcus Lucretius Fronto 190,
   191

Pompeii contd.
House of Menander 182
House of the Faun 193, *193*; (finds from) 87–88
House of the Vettii 192
Temple of Isis 92, 180
Villa of Diomedes 195
Villa of Julia Felix 187
Villa of the Mysteries 195–96
Pontecagnano 261
Pontone (Scala) 253, *253*
Pontormo (Jacopo Carucci; 1494–1556) 103
Popoli 404
Poppaea Sabina, wife of Nero 210
Portici 166, 209
Poseidonia (Paestum) 13, 31, 271
Posillipo 121–22
Posillipo School 118, 122, 242, 370, 460
Positano 243–44
Potenza 298
Pozzuoli 137–40
Praetuttii, ancient people 370, 417
Praia a Mare 320
Presti, Fra' Bonaventura (mid-17C) 113
Preti, Mattia (1613–99) 61, 64, 66, 124, 302, 332, **336–37**, *337*, 355, 412, 414
Prignano Cilento 279
Primario, Gagliardo (fl. early 14C) 73
Procida 229
Puglia 427ff
Puglian aqueduct 296, 427, 517
Pulo, il 463
Punic Wars 14, 306 (*see also Hannibal*)
Punta del Serrone bronzes 496
Punta della Campanella 243
Punta Licosa 279
Puteoli 12, 121 (*see also Pozzuoli*)
Pyrrhus, King of Epirus 14, 263, 291, 309, 480
Pythagoras 310, 327

Q
Quaglia, Pier Paolo (late 19C) 123
Quartararo, Riccardo (1443–1506) 56
Queirolo, Francesco (1704–62) 62

R
Raimondi, Guglielmo (19C) 245
Ramage, Craufurd Tait 9

Ramsay, Allan (1713–84) 230
Raphael (Raffaello Sanzio; 1483–1520) 98, 99, 101
Rapolla 293; (sarcophagus of) 292
Ravello 250–52, *251*
Reggio Calabria 351–57
Rende 330
Reni, Guido (1575–1642) 67, 106, 115
Rhegion (Reggio Calabria) 10, 351; (finds from) 355
Riace Bronzes 352, 353, 354
Ribera, Jusepe (José de Ribera; 1591–1652) **47–48**, 56, 68, 111, 113–14, *114*, 115, 116, 124, 414, *414*
Riccardi, Gabriele (mid-16C) 501, 504, 509
Riccio, il (*see Briosco*)
Richard Coeur-de-Lion 440
Rionero in Vulture 293
Rionero Sannitico 392
Ripacandida 293
Ripe 419
Ripoli culture 369
Rivello 307
Rivisondoli 378
Robbia, Andrea della (1435–1525) 410
Robbia, della (family; 15C–16C) 124
Robert of Anjou ('the Wise', King of Naples) 21, 36; (tomb of) 57
Robert Guiscard (Robert de Hauteville) **18**, 260, 261, 292, 331, 348, 429, 439, 452, 455, 513; (buildings commissioned by) 299, 335; (supposed tomb of) 297
Roberto d'Oderisio (14C) 46, 55, 109
Roca Vecchia 512
Rocca Imperiale 309
Roccaraso 378
Roccatagliata, Niccolò (16C–17C) 104
Roccella Ionica 360
Rodi Garganico 434
Roger I (Hauteville) 18, 262, 266, 331, 347
Roger II (Hauteville) 18, 245
Roger of Melfi (12C) 442
Rome, Romans (general) 10, 11, 13, **14–16**, 16, **31–33**, 32, 135, 137, 152, 169, 215, 230, 238, 250, 259, 271, 291, 296, 306, 309, 331, 351, 360, 390, 513
Roman sites and remains 136, 242, 253, 381, 507; (Bacoli) 144; (Baiae) 142–43; (Benevento) 15, 264, 265; (Capri)

220–21, 224; (Capua) 152–53;
(Herculaneum) 196ff; (Oplontis) 210–11;
(Paestum) 274; (Pompeii) 168ff;
(Pozzuoli) 138–40; (Stabiae) 211–12;
(Velia) 280; (Venosa) 297
Romanesque art and architecture 298, 431,
482, 511 (*see also Apulian Romanesque*)
Romolo di Antonio da Settignano (early
16C) 60
Romualdo, sculptor (11C) 442
Romulado di Bari (13C) 447
Rondone, Alessandro (16C–17C) 113
Rosa, Carlo (?–1678) 461
Rosa, Francesco de (1600–54) 111, 116
Rosa, Slavatore (1615–73) 47, 302
Rosarno 349
Rossano 325
Rossellino, Antonio (Antonio Gambarelli;
c.1427–79) 46, 56
Rossetti, Dante Gabriel 380
Rosso Fiorentino (Giambattista de' Rosso
1494–1541) 103
Rubi, vases from 449
Rudiae, ruins of 508
Ruffo, Cardinal Fabrizio 24, 40, 330, 461
Rufolo family 250, 251
Ruskin, John 167, 210
Ruther, Karl (17C) 408, 413
Rutigliano 476
Ruvo di Puglia 449, *449*

S
S. Angelo in Formis 46, 150, 151
S. Caterina (near Conversano) 477
S. Croce (Lecce) 504–05
S. Donato, Santuario 293
S. Francesco da Paola (Otranto) 515
S. Ippolito, abbey of 293
S. Leonardo (Gargano) 431
S. Lorenzo, Certosa of 282–87
S. Lucia (Matera) 303
S. Lucia, chapel of (Massafra) 475
S. Maria di Anglona 307
S. Maria d'Arabona 376
S. Maria Assunta (Bominaco) 405
S. Maria del Bosco 348
S. Maria di Cerrate, abbey of 511
S. Maria di Collemaggio 408, *408*, 409
S. Maria Finibus Terrae 517

S. Maria d'Idris (Matera) 303
S. Maria dell'Isola 476
S. Maria dei Polsi, sanctuary of 359
S. Maria della Roccella 329
S. Maria di Siponto 432
S. Martino, hermitage of 336
S. Nicola di Casole, abbey 515
S. Pellegrino (Bominaco) 405, *405*
S. Pietro ad Oratorium 405
S. Vincenzo, Badia di 392
S. Vito, abbey of 484
Sabelli, ancient people 13
Sabines 11, 416
Saepinum, ruins of 389–90
Saint-Non, Abbé de (Jean-Claude Richard)
285
Sala Consilina 282
Salentine Peninsula 511–22
Salerno 17, 151, 259–60, *260*
Sallust 410, 416
Salvati, Salvato (fl. mid-16C) 411
Salviati, Francesco (1510–63) 99, 103
Sambatello 359
Sammartino, Giuseppe (1720–93) 48, 61,
62–63, *63*, 114, 156
Sammichele di Bari 471
Samnites 11, 13, 31, 32, 135, 137, 145,
152, 169, 197, 291, 387, 388, 390, 391;
(art, architecture and remains) 171, 198,
203, 261, 264, 389, 391, 392; (Samnite
Wars) 31
San Cataldo 511
San Clemente in Casauria 376
San Demetrio Corone 324
San Domino (*see Tremiti Islands*)
San Ferdinando di Puglia 443
San Fili 330
San Giovanni in Fiore 335
San Giovanni Rotondo 434
San Giuseppe 166
San Leucio 158
San Lucido 330
San Marco di Castellabate 279
San Nicola (*see Tremiti Islands*)
San Nicola Arcella 320
San Pietro 337
San Prisco 153
San Sebastiano (Abruzzo) 397
San Sebastiano (al Vesuvio) 166

San Severo 429
San Vito dei Normanni 500
San Vittorino 416
Sanfelice, Ferdinando (1675–1748) 47, 48, 76, 98, 499, 519
Sangro, Raimondo di 61, 62–63
Sannazzaro d'Alessandro (early 16C) 300
Sano di Pietro (1406–81) 412
Sanseverino family 56, 123, 282-283, 285, 299
Sant'Agata sui Due Golfi 242
Sant'Eufemia Lamezia 329
Santa Caterina (Scala) 253
Santa Cesarea Terme 516
Santa Domenica 348
Santa Maria Capua Vetere 152–53
Santa Maria Maggiore 262
Santa Severina 335
Santacroce, Girolamo da (1480–1556) 48, 55, 56, 472
Santafede, Fabrizio (1560–c.1634) 55, 68, 71, 78, 111, 389, 414, 430
Santo Stefano in Aspromonte 359
Sanvitale, Barbara Sanseverino 104
Sapri 281
Saracen, Saracens 17, 18, 19, 34, 142, 144, 145, 152, 215, 230, 243, 271, 299, 331, 336, 341, 350, 359, 387, 389, 430, 451, 452, 461, 463, 464, 471, 479, 480, 495, 498
Saracenic art and architecture 45, 217, 245, 247, 250, 251, 253, 259, 431
Sassi, the (Matera) 303–05, 304
Scala 250, 252–53
Scalea 320
Scanno 400
Scarlatti, Alessandro 64, 78
Schedoni, Bartolomeo (1578–1615) 106
Schiavi di Abruzzo 392
Scilla 350
Scipio Africanus 14, 146
Scrivà, Pier Luigi (16C) 113, 411
Scupula, Giovanni Maria (early 16C) 458
Scurcola Marsicana 404
Scylla 350
Sebastiani, Antonio (early 18C) 106
Sebastiano del Piombo (Sebastiano Luciani; c.1485–157) 102
Seminara 349

Senape, Antonio (1788–1850) 118
Senise 306
Sepino 389
Serafini, Paolo de', da Modena (late 14C) 440
Sergius of Naples 34
Serra San Bruno 346–48
Serracapriola 429
Sersale 337
Servile War, third 153
Sforza family 263, 452
Sforza, Attendolo 406
Sforza, Francesco 336
Sharp, Samuel 74
Shelley, Percy Bysshe 160, 167, 274
Sibari 324
Sibyl of Cumae 145, 146
Sicilian Vespers 21, 25
Sicily 10, 14, 16, 17, 18, 19, 20, 21, 25, 26, 358; (*see also Two Sicilies*)
Siculians 360
Sidicini, ancient people 150
Signorelli, Luca (?1440–1523) 101
Signorini, Telemaco (1835–1901) 460
Sila, La 333–38
Silvestro dall'Aquila (15C) 409, 410, 412, 414
Simeon of Syria (11C) 247
Simeone da Ragusa (13C) 441
Simone da Firenze (early 16C) 306
Simonetta, Cecco 335
Simonetta, Giovanni 335
Sinni valley 306
Sipontum 432
Sirens, myths concerning 31, 279
Siris 13, 301
Sironi, Mario (1885–1961) 460
Social War 15, 31, 135, 169, 369, 391
Sodoma, Il (Giovanni Antonio Bazzi; 1477–1549) 111
Solario, Andrea (c.1465–1524) 124
Soleto 521
Solfatara di Pozzuoli 137
Solimena, Francesco (1657–1747) 48, 54, 56, 60, 66, 68, 112, 114, 123, 125, **126**, 223, 302, 414, 463; (birthplace of) 262
Sons, Jan (1553–?1611) 104
Sorianello 346
Soriano Calabro 346

Sorrento 16, 238–42, *239*
Spain, Spanish 21, **22–23**, **36–38**, 349, 419, 441, 483, 502, 513, 519
Spartacus 15, 152, **153**, 160, 310
Specchia Maiano 499
Specchie, grave monuments 463
Spezzano Albanese 324
Spezzano della Sila 334
Squillace 329
Stabiae 161, 211
Stanzione, Massimo (?1585–?1656) 56, 66, 67, 76, 77, 114, 115, 116, 123, 302
Statius, Publius Papinius 166, 242
Stefano da Putignano (16C) 458, 484
Stefano di Trani (13C) 447
Steinbeck, John 244
Stendhal 29
Stephen II, Duke of Naples 33
Stephen, Leslie 135
Stigliano 306
Stilo 359–60
Stomer, Matthias (c.1600–50) 458
Strabo 12, 160, 277
Succivo 153
Sulla, Lucius Cornelius 15, 169, 194, 211
Sulmona 369, 398–99
Swabian, Swabians 362; (architecture) 211, 431, 499 (*see also Frederick II, buildings*)
Swinburne, Henry 37
Sybaris, Sybarites 10, 13, 31, 271, 276, 310, 320, 324, 327

T
Tagliacozzi Canale, Nicola (mid-18C) 114, 117
Tagliacozzo 404; (battle of) 34, 404
Tagliolini, Filippo (1745–1809) 98, 107, 119
Tancred, King of Sicily (Tancred de Hauteville) 19, 498, 509
Tange, Kenzo (1913–2005) 30
Tantino, Giovanni da Ariano Irpino 302
Tanucci, Bernardo 23, 24, 39
Tarantism 482, 520
Taranto 17, 31, 480–84, *483*
Taras/Tarentum 10, 12, 14, 310, 476, 480
Tarqinius Superbus, Etruscan king 145
Tasso, Torquato 55, 238, 240, 241, 242
Taurasi (*see Wine*)
Taurianum 349–50

Taverna 336–37
Tavole Paladine (Puglia) 487
Tavole Palatine (Metapontum) 311
Tavoliere della Puglia 427
Teano 150
Teanum Apulum 429
Teggiano 282
Telesio, Bernardino 331
Teramo 417–18
Terentius Varro, Gaius 443
Termoli 387
Terra di Bari 439–61
Terranova 324
Terzigno 166
Theodore of Antioch 294
Thomas Aquinas, St 259
Thomas of Celano 401
Thorvaldsen, Bertel (1770–1844) 108, 125
Thurii 13, 325
Tiberius, emperor 144, 215, 220
Tino da Camaino (c.1285–1338) 46, 57, 61, 73
Tintoretto (Jacopo Robusti; 1519–94) 458
Tiso, Oronzo (1729–1800) 460, 505
Titian (Tiziano Vecellio; c.1485–1576) 98, *99*, 103, *103*, 111
Toma, Gioacchino (1836–91) 112
Tomb of the Diver (*see Paestum*)
Torre Annunziata 210
Torre del Greco 166, 209
Torre Galli 344, 346
Torre Santa Susanna 511
Torregaveta 144
Tortelli, Benvenuto (mid-16C) 124
Tosti, Francesco Paolo 373
Totila, Gothic leader 33, 502
Trajan, arch of (Benevento) 15, 264
Tramontano, Count 302
Trani 444–47, *445*, *446*
Tremiti Islands 434–35 (Capraia) 435; (Pianosa) 435; (San Domino) 434; (San Nicola) 435
Tricarico 299
Tricase 517
Trinita di Cava, La, abbey of 262
Trinita, La, abbey of 297
Troia 431
Troisi, Massimo 229
Tropea 344–45

Trulli 478
Tuna, tuna-fishing 544
Turks, Turkish 23, 216, 324, 363, 513, 514, 515, 519
Tursi 307
Two Sicilies, kingdom of 25, 36
Tyrannicides 80–81

U

Ugento, finds from 508
Urban IV, pope 34
Urban VI, pope 36, 59, 262, 279
Urban VIII, pope 336

V

Vaccaro, Andrea (1604–70) 61, 76, 111, 116, 124, 387, *413*, 414, 458
Vaccaro, Domenico Antonio (1678–1745) 47, 48, 54, 60, 112, 114, 118, 123, 267, 302, 380
Vaccaro, Lorenzo (father of Domenico Antonio; 1655–1706) 114
Vaglio Basilicata 298
Valente, Pietro (early 19C) 120
Valentino, Rudolph (Rodolfo Guglielmi) 472
Valeriano, Giuseppe (1542–96) 56
Vallo della Lucania 279
Vallo di Diano 282
Vanni, Andrea (1332–1414) 109
Vanni, Lippo (14C) 109
Vanvitelli, Carlo (son of Luigi; 1739–1821) 78, 124, 145
Vanvitelli, Luigi (1700–73) 48, 61, 78, 124, 154, 156, 157, 262, 264
Vasari, Giorgio (1511–74) 56, 99, 111
Vasto 380–81
Vedius Pollio, Publius 122, 147
Velia 279–81
Venafro 392
Venosa 296–97
Ventaroli 151
Venusia 296, 297
Venusti, Marcello (1512–79) 102
Vernet, Claude Joseph (1714–89) 107
Veronese (Paolo Caliari; 1528–88) 458, 485, 487
Verrio, Antonio (1639–1707) 501
Verrio, Giuseppe (brother of Antonio; 1636–1708) 506

Vervloet, Frans (1795–1872) 118
Vesuvius, Mt 15, 24, 153, 160–68, 169, 224
Vettii, house of (*see Pompeii*)
Via Appia 14, 153, 472, 494
Vibo Valentia 343
Viceroys of Naples 22, 23, 36, 38, 73
Vico Equense 237
Vieste 434
Vietri sul Mare 254
Vigée-Lebrun, Elisabeth-Louise (1755–1842) 108
Villa Cimbrone (*see Ravello*)
Villa Meo-Evoli 485
Villa of Poppaea (*see Oplontis*)
Villa of the Mysteries (*see Pompeii*)
Villa of the Papyri (*see Herculaneum*)
Villa Rufolo (*see Ravello*)
Villa San Michele (*see Capri*)
Villavallelonga 397
Vinaccia, Giovanni Domenico (late 17C) 66, 284
Vinchiaturo 389
Virgil (Publius Vergilius Maro) 33, 495
Visconti, Luchino 233
Vitruvius (Marcus Vitruvius Pollio; 1C BC) 160, 186, 199
Vittoria, Alessandro (1525–1608) 104
Vittorio Emanuele II, king 26, 42, 98, 150, 358
Vittorio Emanuele III, king 377, 416
Vivarini, Alvise (1445/6–1503/4) 441, 476
Vivarini, Antonio (c.1415–84) 458
Vivarini, Bartolomeo (c.1432–c.99) 300, 323, 458, 484
Volaire, Pierre Jacques (?1727–1802) 107
Volturno, battle of 43, 149
Vouet, Simon (1590–1649) 111, 116

W

Wagner, Richard 238, 251
Waldensians 321
Walpole, Horace 513
Walton, Sir William 233
War cemeteries (Bari) 461; (Brindisi) 498; (Caserta) 158; (Moro River) 373; (Salerno) 262; (Sangro River) 380
Warrior of Capestrano 374, *375*
Western Church 18, 151, 519
William de Hauteville, King of Sicily ('the

Bad') 19, 452, 453
Wilson, Edmund 369, 410
Wine (general) 547–51; (Falernian) 267;
    (Fiano d'Avellino) 267, 547; (Pompeian)
    188; (Taurasi) 267, 547
Witz, Konrad (c.1400–?44) 105
World War One 27, 377, 480, 498
World War Two 27, 154, 259, 264, 283,
    351, 416, 428, 480, 495
Wouthers, Petrus (17C) 460

X
Xenophanes, philosopher 280

Y
Yolande of Jerusalem, wife of Frederick II
    442, 496, 526

Z
Zacharias, pope 335
Zaganelli, Francesco (1484–1532) 101
Zagarise 337
Zancani Montuoro, Paola 277
Zanguidi, Jacopo (*see Bertoja*)
Zanotti Bianco, Umberto 277
Zeno, philosopher 280
Zeuxis (5C BC) 309
Zimbalo, Francesco Antonio (b.1567) 501,
    504, 505
Zimbalo, Giuseppe (Lo Zingarello; nephew
    of Francesco Antonio; 1620–1710) 501,
    504, 505, 508
Zocchi, Cesare (1851–1922) 410

Contributors to this volume

Nigel McGilchrist (N.McG.) is an art historian who has lived in the Mediterranean—Italy, Greece and Turkey—for over twenty-five years, working for a period for the Italian Ministry of Arts and then for six years as Director of the Anglo-Italian Institute in Rome. He has taught at the University of Rome, for the University of Massachusetts, and was for seven years Dean of European Studies for a consortium of American universities. He lectures widely in art and archaeology at museums and institutions in Europe and the United States, and lives near Orvieto.

Charles Freeman (C.F.) is a freelance academic historian with a long-standing interest in Italy and the Mediterranean. His *Egypt, Greece and Rome, Civilizations of the Ancient Mediterranean* (second edition, Oxford University Press, 2004) is widely used as an introductory textbook to the ancient world. His most recent book, *The Horses of St.Mark's* (Little Brown, 2004), is a study of the famous horses through their history in Constantinople and Venice. He leads study tours of Italy for the Historical Association and has recently been elected a Fellow of the Royal Society of Arts.

Alexandra Massini (A.M.) is an art historian educated at the Courtauld Institute of Art, London. She was born in Rome, where she now lives teaching art history courses for Italy-based US Universities such as Rutgers and Vanderbilt. In the past she has worked for Sotheby's, the Thyssen Museum in Madrid and a number of cultural associations in Italy and Europe, as well as working as a freelance writer and organising art exhibits and cultural events.

Lord Michael Pratt is a freelance author and researcher, who has published books on the history of the Ionian Islands, and *Nelson's Duchy*, a study of the Sicilian Duchy of Bronte which was given to Nelson. He has also written *Great Country Houses of Central Europe*, which was translated into four languages. It is a study of the great country houses of Poland, the Czech Republic and Hungary, and is currrently being translated into those three languages. He divides his time between England and Italy.

contd. from p. 6

Editor-in-chief: Annabel Barber
Assistant editor: Judy Tither
Editorial assistant: Sophie Livall
Editorial board: Charles Freeman, Nigel McGilchrist

With special thanks to Joseph Kling, for his text on Campanian wine; Nigel McGilchrist, for the entry on the Museo Archeologico in Naples; and to Richard Robinson and Deidre McMullin.

Layout and design: Anikó Kuzmich
Maps: Dimap Bt and Imre Bába
Floor plans: Imre Bába

Photography
Photo editor: Róbert Szabó Benke

Cover images
Top: Olive grove near Lecce (photo: Enzo Cositore)
Bottom: Titian: *Danaë* (Capodimonte Museum, Naples. Courtesy of the Fototeca della Soprintendenza Speciale per il Polo Museale Napoletano)
Spine: Fourteenth-century *Madonna and Child* from Amalfi (photo: Annabel Barber)
Title page: Detail from the Tomb of the Diver, Paestum (Alinari Archives, Florence)

Other photographs by Phil Robinson: pp. 260, 272, 273, 276, 301, 304, 308, 445, 446, 448, 474, 478, 483, 512; Róbert Szabó Benke: pp. 28, 49, 57, 72, 82, 88–89, 125, 203, 204, 208; Annabel Barber: pp. 58, 223, 239, 246, 249, 253, 501, 504, 514, 516; Judy Tither: pp. 174, 193, 210, 211; Theodora Elliott: pp. 217, 251; Enzo Cositore: pp. 378–79; Alinari Archives, Florence: pp. 3, 191, 278; Roger-Viollet/Alinari: p. 63; Archivio Seat/Archivio Alinari: pp. 375, 405, 433. Other images courtesy of the Fototeca della Soprintendenza Speciale per il Polo Museale Napoletano: pp. 99, 103, 110, 114, 117 (last two ©Luciano Pedicini, Archivio dell'Arte); Soprintendenza per il Patrimonio Storico Artistico e Etnoantropologico della Basilicata: p. 303, no. 38 del 06/07/2006 del Ministero per i Beni e le Attività Culturali; Museo Nazionale Archeologico di Reggio Calabria: pp. 352, 353, 356; The National Archaeological Museum of Naples/Soprintendenza per i Beni Archeologici delle Province di Napoli e Caserta: p. 96; Pinacoteca Provinciale di Bari: p. 459; Ministero per i Beni e le Attività Culturali—Soprintendenza per il Patrimonio Storico, Artistico e Etnoantropologico per l'Abruzzo di L'Aquila—Archivio fotografico: pp. 413, 414.

Printed in Hungary by Dürer Nyomda Kft, Gyula

ISBN 978-1-905131-18-1